Strategic Facilities Planning

Strategic Facilities Planning

Capital Budgeting and Debt Administration

Alan Walter Steiss

LEXINGTON BOOKS

A Division of
ROWMAN & LITTLEFIELD PUBLISHERS, INC.
Lanham • Boulder • New York • Toronto • Oxford

LEXINGTON BOOKS

A division of Rowman & Littlefield Publishers, Inc.
A wholly owned subsidiary of The Rowman & Littlefield Publishing Group, Inc.
4501 Forbes Boulevard, Suite 200
Lanham, MD 20706

PO Box 317
Oxford
OX2 9RU, UK

British Library Cataloguing in Publication Information Available

Library of Congress Cataloging-in-Publication Data

Steiss, Alan Walter, 1937–
Strategic facilities planning : Capital budgeting and debt administration / Alan Walter Steiss.
p. cm.
Includes index.
ISBN 0-7391-0841-7 (alk. paper) — ISBN 0-7391-1116-7 (pbk. : alk. paper)
1. Budget—Handbooks, manuals, etc. I. Title.

B3317.S95 2005
193—dc22 2005001171

Printed in the United States of America

The paper used in this publication meets the minimum requirements of American National Standard for Information Sciences—Permanence of Paper for Printed Library Materials, ANSI/NISO Z39.48–1992.

Contents

Chapter 1

GOVERNMENT RESPONSIBILITIES FOR STRATEGIC FACILITIES

Two fundamental government responsibilities stem from the broad objective to "promote the general health, safety, morals, and public welfare." First, the actions of individuals must be regulated to ensure that they will not be detrimental to the general populous. And second, public services and facilities must be provided for the mutual benefit of all or a majority of citizens. The imposition of regulations and controls in the public interest is as old as history itself. Of more recent origins, the provision of public services and facilities has become widely accepted as a basic responsibility of government. Segments of the public might complain when taxes are increased to provide new schools or to expand public welfare programs. It is generally acknowledged, however, that significant economies can be derived from such government activities—economies that could not be achieved if each citizen was required to provide for these facilities and services on an individual basis.

As applied in this presentation, *strategic facilities* refer to relatively large-size, fixed capital assets, having a relatively long life, funded by expenditures of a nonrecurring nature, and designed to provide new or expanded government capacity for the delivery of public services. The availability of such facilities can have a profound effect on the form and functioning of a community. They represent very large investments of public resources, usually exert their effects over many decades, and are not easy to modify once these facilities are built. Therefore, a systematic planning effort is vital in making decisions about the construction and financing of strategic facilities.

Strategic Facilities Planning

Strategic facilities planning has its origins in the private sector as corporate entities seek to develop a more comprehensive approach to capital budgeting, space planning, operational assessments, and modernization or deferred maintenance techniques. The primary objective is to address high priority areas of financial exposure represented by physical facilities and the operating systems that support them. Organizations adopting this approach are interested in creating more cost-effective and long-term solutions to their facility needs. Major expenses—and major mistakes—in the design and construction of facilities can be avoided by adopting the fundamental steps of strategic planning to ensure that all of the right questions are asked. As the value of a more strategic approach to the planning of major facilities is demonstrated and documented, these procedures are being adopted by other organizations in the private and public sectors, either as part of a broader strategic planning process or as freestanding applications.

Strategic Planning Defined

The concept of strategic planning has evolved over the past three decades in response to the need for a more dynamic planning process. What is sought is a planning process that permits the efficacy of strategic decisions to be continually tested against the realities of current conditions and, in turn, to be corrected and refined as necessary—in short a process that links long-term organizational strategy with day-to-day operational events.

Strategic planning is designed to (1) clarify an organization's goals and objectives, (2) determine policies for the acquisition and distribution of organizational resources, and (3) establish a basis for translating policies and decisions into specific action commitments. Strategic planners identify the long-range needs of an organization, explore the ramifications and implications of policies and programs designed to meet these needs, and formulate strategies to maximize the positive aspects and minimize the negative aspects of the foreseeable future. Strategic planning focuses on the need to make the critical decisions that will ensure an organization's ability to successfully respond to an environment that is dynamic and changing (often in unpredictable ways). This emphasis stands in contrast to other long-range planning approaches which assume that current knowledge about future conditions is sufficiently reliable to ensure the validity of the plan over the duration of its implementation. The primary output of strategic planning should be a series of guidelines within which more detailed plans and programs can be designed and implemented. The basic components and tools of strategic planning will be discussed in further detail in Chapter 2.

A Strategy-Driven Approach to Facilities Planning

Organizations frequently take a cost-driven approach to address their facility needs. Although this approach might be quickly implemented and cost-effective, it nevertheless is lacking in vision and often fails to address the actual delivery of goods and services. And it has only a moderate, long-term impact on improving the overall performance of the organization as a whole.

In contrast, tangible goals and planned targets are established through a strategy-driven approach to the analysis of an organization's facility needs. While requiring a more deliberate time frame, this strategy-driven approach is designed to deliver a clear vision for the future, achieve employee support, strengthen the organization's competitive position, and enhance its overall performance.

Strategic facilities planning involves an interdisciplinary team of planners, architects, administrators, real estate experts, social scientists, and data managers dedicated to delivering customized sets of applicable processes and methods. When successfully undertaken, strategic facilities planning results in integrated, comprehensive, transparent processes that position an organization to better develop, produce, and deliver its products and services.

The need to identify and analyze an organization's facility requirements begins long before consideration is given to the actual construction phase. Effective strategic facilities planning aligns the strategic objectives of an organization with its physical needs, thus working to ensure that facilities provide essential support to the organization's mission. These plans must be flexible documents, appropriate and applicable to both immediate and long-term objectives. Overlapping needs and potential shared capacities should be addressed in a process that, by definition, is proactive. An effective strategic facilities plan includes data and recommendations to guide organizations through the financing of new construction and renovations, site and facility selection, acquisitions, contractual real estate decisions, relocations, consolidations, downsizing, and mergers.

Facilities planning recognizes that every strategic decision has a direct impact on an organization's capital assets and needs. The mission of the strategic facilities plan, therefore, is to develop an adaptable approach based upon the specific and unique considerations of the individual organization. Planners begin to develop the plan by understanding the needs of the organization's business processes and operations, building on whatever internal analyses have already been completed or are ongoing. The short-, mid-, and long-term goals of the organization must be defined, the range of their products and services must be clearly identified, and the limitations and opportunities confronting the organization must be examined. A situation assessment (sometimes referred to as a SWOT analysis) might be undertaken to compile current information about the organization's strengths and weaknesses and performance information highlighting critical external issues (opportunities and threats) that face the organization and should be addressed in the strategic plan.

The plan is entirely dependent upon a comprehensive understanding of these specific needs. And, conversely, the evaluation of current facilities and the planning, design, and implementation of new facilities is dependent on these requirements. Strategic facilities plans provide a combination and range of services as required by the organization to maximize the value of its physical assets. The team considers such factors as the current position of the organization and its capital asset base, its overall direction and the projects currently underway, how the mission of the organization might change, and how these changes might affect the organization's capital needs.

Using this approach, the planners apply gathered data, modeling tools, and scenario alternatives to study the capital assets that the organization currently holds. These data often includes lease and ownership information, building assessments, square footages, space utilization standards, and location characteristics. Strategic facility planning can serve as a mechanism to analyze and improve current facility operations. The focus is on a proactive approach that incorporates best practices, benchmarking, and forward-thinking applications in a continuous improvement environment. This analysis might be undertaken as part of a broader process reengineering initiative, or it might be conducted as a freestanding exercise.

Following these steps, the various goals and objectives of each unit in the organization must be explored and integrated into the facility plan portfolio. Based on overall goals, future space and capital needs are defined, starting with anticipated services, expected staffing changes, and potential new technologies. These needs are then used to predict future personnel requirements, demographics, space utilization, maintenance, and capital and operating costs.

Once a clear definition of the organization's situation has been established, the planners and designers can begin to consider how to balance current facility requirements with overall long-term needs and issues. These needs and issues might include workforce demographics, operating processes, organizational structure, community and government relationships and requirements, market position, and capacity rates and volumes. All of these forces combine to define the individual elements of the strategic facilities plan.

The final product of this process is not an inflexible document but an insight into how different decisions will affect the organization's work processes, cash flow, debt load, and return on investment. The plan should be a living document that makes concise recommendations for implementing the plan's results within a realistic time frame. Two examples of strategic facilities planning initiatives are outlined in Appendices A and B at the end of this chapter.

Strategic Facilities Planning and Capital Budgeting

Strategic facilities planning must be integrated with an organization's capital budgeting process, resulting in savings in terms of costs and time and the attainment of more functional and effective facilities. A *capital budget* identifies the capital expenditures to be incurred to meet long-term needs for public improvements (strategic facilities) and the means of financing these commitments for the current fiscal period. A capital budget often is supported by a *capital improvements program* (CIP), which documents improvement priorities over a longer time period (usually five to six years). An even longer time horizon (fifteen to twenty years) might also be developed to provide an analysis of the fiscal resources available to support long-term debt commitments. The questions asked as part of this integrated process ensure that the organization clearly defines the scope of its capital projects and their fit with the mission and strategic goals and objectives.

The planning process must be undertaken in a manner that incorporates all that is important and significant to the organization. Some of these factors are respect for the existing organizational culture and image, impact on work processes and activities, existing operations and conditions, future influences, preferred locations, staffing and design criteria, growth strategy, and future plans. The final product must be consistent with the organization's overall mission and strategies.

Change is the only constant in today's organizational environment. New operational models are emerging, the balance of power is invariably shifting toward customers/clientele, and the pace of operations is accelerating exponentially. Amidst this turbulence, organizations need strategies for the development of their capital assets that will help them simultaneously manage their growth and provide for the present. By aligning an organization's capital assets with its long-term mission, strategic facilities planning can help maximize agility, increase return on investment, and ultimately help position the organization to better deliver its products and services to meet the needs of its clientele.

Components of Strategic Facilities Planning in the Public Sector

Strategic facilities in the public sector involve capital expenditures of a nonrecurring nature, designed to provide new or expanded government capacity for the delivery of public services. Planning can assist public officials in the development of long-range strategies by:

- Analyzing community needs, demographic characteristics, and economic conditions;
- Forecasting future revenue and expenditure requirements;
- Evaluating the costs and benefits of alternative investments; and
- Assessing various fiscal policies and methods of financing strategic facilities.

The primary objective is to guide the provision of major public facilities of large-size, fixed nature, and/or having a relatively long life within the limits of available public resources. Thus, providing strategic facilities in the most effective and efficient manner must involve planning, programming, financing, and debt administration (see Figure 1-1). The objective of this initial chapter is to examine each of these component phases briefly to provide a framework for the more detailed discussions in the chapters that follow.

The Planning Phase

Long-range planning of strategic facilities has lagged significantly behind other development in the field of financial management. As governments began to assume greater responsibilities for the provision of public services and facilities, only the most evident needs were addressed. And these needs often were dealt with in somewhat haphazard fashion. Many state and local governments made no provision for the overall supervision of public expenditures through a comprehensive budgetary process. Urban development during the first half of the twentieth century was characterized by the uncoordinated construction of public works. If any financial resources remained after the most obvious obligations were met, other capital projects might be initiated.

Strategic facilities planning provides a means of assuring that capital projects will be carried out in accordance with a well thought-out and defensible system of priorities reflecting both public needs and the government's ability to pay. It promotes coordination among the various departments and agencies of government and thereby helps to circumvent overlapping or conflicting programs. It protects against undue influence by pressure groups, representing special interest that might attempt to force the adoption of "pet projects" at the expense of more urgent or more meritorious improvements.

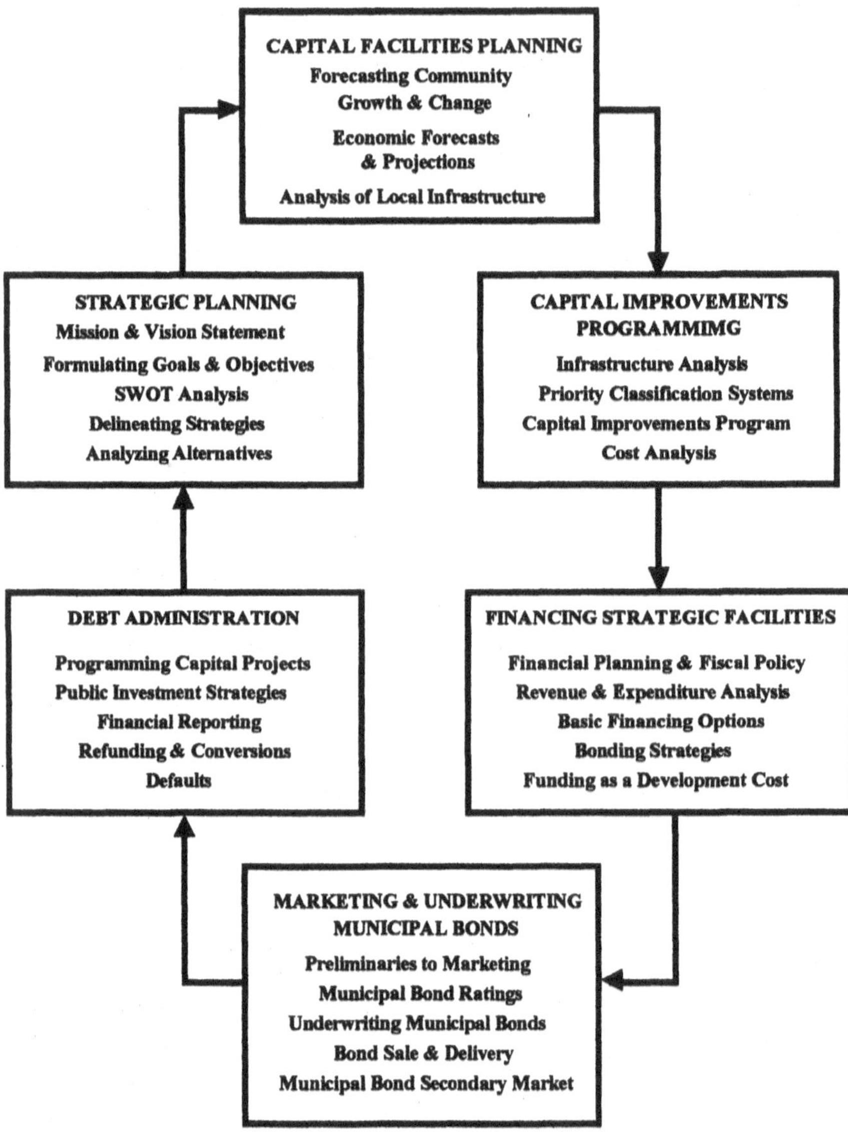

Figure 1-1 Components of Strategic Facilities Planning

Through strategic facilities planning, bond issues or other revenue-producing measures can be foreseen and action taken before the need becomes so critical as to require emergency financing measures. Advanced planning extends the period of time available for the proper technical design of facilities and provides justification for the advance acquisition of properties needed for improvements, thereby taking advantage of lower market values. Such planning also permits a continual, systematic appraisal of personnel and equipment needs, resulting in a number of operational economies.

Strategic facilities planning should be built upon a continuous assessment of community/client preferences, an identification of goals and objectives, demographic estimates and economic forecasts, and projections of development expectations. Data on future community needs must be sufficiently reliable to justify decisions that involve relatively large, long-term commitments of financial resources. The following elements should be included in this planning framework:

- *External factors.* Demographic shifts, changes in economic activities, social trends, scientific and technological change, emerging land use patterns, and so forth that might influence the service programs of the community or nonprofit organization.
- *Total service demands.* Assumptions, standards, and criteria used to quantify and project facility and service needs must be clearly identified and tested against available trend analyses.
- *Service delivery responsibilities.* Present and future roles of various levels of government, as well as private enterprise, in the provision of facilities and services must be examined. Such an evaluation might include recommendations regarding the elimination of overlapping responsibilities through coordination or realignment.

Forecasting Community Growth and Change

The demand for public improvements is a function of growth. However, emphasis on meeting growth demands does not imply a "self-fulfilling prophecy." In crisis situations, local governments might be panicked into uneconomical investments and overdevelopment. Strategic facilities planning can help avert these service crises, thereby contributing to more realistic patterns of growth.

To anticipate the types of improvements required, the population to be served should be delineated to the fullest extent possible. An aging population, for example, will require specialized health facilities and housing. Young adults just starting families will require schools, day-care centers, and recreational facilities. Income levels, household size, and other demographic and economic characteristics provide vital information as to public facility needs and service expectations.

Demographic projections often are based on an *age-cohort survival model*, which analyzes the population by narrow age categories (cohorts) according to vital statistics on births, deaths, and net migration patterns (inflows or outflows of population). Further breakdowns can also be made by race, sex, income, and so forth. These forecasts are not merely linear projections of past conditions. It is important to understand the current demographic composition of the community in order to identify any unique characteristics that might influence the structure of the population in the future. For example, the transient student population of a college town is influenced by factors other than the typical demographic components and cannot be "aged" in the cohort structure with the resident population.

The basic mathematics of the age-cohort survival model are fairly simple. Five-year cohorts are "stepped up" through each iteration (see Table 1-1), and the results of this "aging" of cohorts are then modified by adjustments for births, deaths, and net migration. Making appropriate assumptions about birth rates, death rates, and migration is not an easy task, however. Many projections turn out to be inaccurate or unrealistic in terms of actual demographic data. Procedures for developing population projections appropriate to the planning and programming of strategic facilities will be examined in some detail in Chapter 3.

Mistakes in projecting population can be quite costly. The baby boom that began in the late 1940s and lasted until the early 1960s produced huge increases in public school enrollments. In the 1960s and early 1970s, many localities assumed that this trend would continue into the foreseeable future and made substantial investments in new school buildings. Enrollments peaked a few years into the 1970s, however, and then started downward. Today, many school districts are still paying off the bonds on school buildings that have significantly declining enrollments. Many communities are willing to dispose of existing school buildings at a fraction of their cost to buyers who are willing to convert them to other uses, such as for retailing, offices, or housing. At the same time, shifts in residential areas, coupled with new architectural concepts for the design of public schools, have placed additional demands on communities regarding the provision of appropriate educational facilities.

Economic Forecasts and Projections

Assumptions concerning population growth or decline should be based, in part, on economic activities. Therefore, economic forecasts are an important factor in the preparation of demographic projections. A locality experiencing rapid economic growth, for example, will likely experience a wave of worker in-migration. Forecasts must be made of age and socio-economic characteristics of these new groups to ensure adequate provision of basic public facilities and related services.

Economic projections and forecasts, in turn, must be translated into capital improvement needs. The attraction of young workers and their families to an area experiencing economic growth will likely result in increased demands on the educational system. The momentum of economic activities will be adversely affected if these demands are not addressed.

Future economic conditions also determine the financial capacity of a community to pay for new strategic facilities. Economic indicators—including data on employment, cost of living, disposable income, building activity, and bank

Table 1-1
Age-Cohort Survival Model
City of Rurbana

Age Cohorts Base Year	Population Base Year	Survival Rates*	Age Cohorts Plus 5 Year	Surviving Population Plus 5 Years
			Under 5	6,656**
Under 5	6,047	0.99173	5-9	5,997
5-9	6,782	0.99780	10-14	6,767
10-14	6,705	0.99777	15-19	6,691
15-19	7,543	0.99537	20-24	7,508
20-24	9,689	0.99382	25-29	9,629
25-29	6,398	0.99299	30-34	6,353
30-34	4,608	0.99136	35-39	4,568
35-39	4,124	0.98795	40-44	4,074
40-44	4,233	0.98127	45-49	4,153
45-49	4,081	0.97099	50-54	3,962
50-54	3,564	0.95468	55-59	3,402
55-59	3,239	0.93271	60-64	3,021
60-64	2,939	0.89949	65-69	2,643
65-69	2,400	0.85451	70-74	2,051
70-74	1,776	0.78990	75-79	1,403
75-79	1,272	0.69571	80-84	885
80-84	757	0.54790	85-89	415
85-89	371	0.37028	90-94	137
90-94	108	0.17810	95-99	19
95-99	20	0.08608	100+	2
100+	3			
Totals	76,660			80,336

*Application of actuarial tables on the probability of dying to actual mortality data.
**Children under age 5 born to females of child-bearing age.

deposits—can be used to analyze trends and to suggest the future revenue capacity of the community.

Economic base studies divide the local economy into two broad categories:

1. *Basic or export industries*—those industries producing goods and services (and capital) for distribution to markets outside a defined local economic area; and
2. *Nonbasic or service industries*—those producing goods and services that are consumed within the local economic area (see Figure 1-2).

Thus, a distinction must be made between economic activities that bring new money into the community (basic industries) and those that simply result in the re-circulation of money (service industries). An underlying assumption of this approach is that expansion of basic activities usually results in growth of service activities and, thus, growth in the total economy. Forecasts of economic growth are based on multipliers that relate local activities to exports.

As suggested in Figure 1-2, employment data of some industries or firms must be apportioned between the basic and nonbasic sectors. Once these data have been sorted, ratios can be calculated to reflect current conditions in the local economy. Various assumptions can be tested using these ratios to determine the impact of increases or decreases in employment in the basic sector.

Assume, for example, that the current basic to nonbasic ratio is 1 to 1.5 (each job in a basic industry generates 1.5 jobs in the service sector). A new economic activity that adds 100 jobs to the basic sector will increase total employment by 250 jobs. If 35% of the total population is in the labor force, the ratio of basic employment to total population will be approximately 1 to 7.

Economic base multipliers and location quotients can be generated for various measurements, including (1) employment data, (2) payrolls, (3) value added, (4) value of production, (5) physical production, and (6) dollar income and expenditure accounts.[1] Each of these measures has shortcomings, and therefore all feasible techniques should be used in any economic base study. The capacity to predict future conditions can be further extended and refined by adding other measures and indexes.

Employment growth generally fosters population growth because job opportunities attract new residents. However, the process works the other way as well. Population growth creates employment in retailing, wholesaling, personal services, and related activities. In fact, the relationship goes still further because pools of labor and capital that have been built up to serve a local population, in time, might foster the growth of manufacturing and other activities that are not directly related to servicing the local population. The role of economic analysis in strategic facilities planning will be discussed in further detail in Chapter 3.

The Local Infrastructure

Land use studies are a part of planning for strategic facilities. It is not possible, for example, to plan for sewer construction without having definite ideas about what areas of the community need to be provided with sewers. Land use studies also are very important for identifying land suitable for various types of strategic facilities and for estimating the cost of such public improvements—the cost of

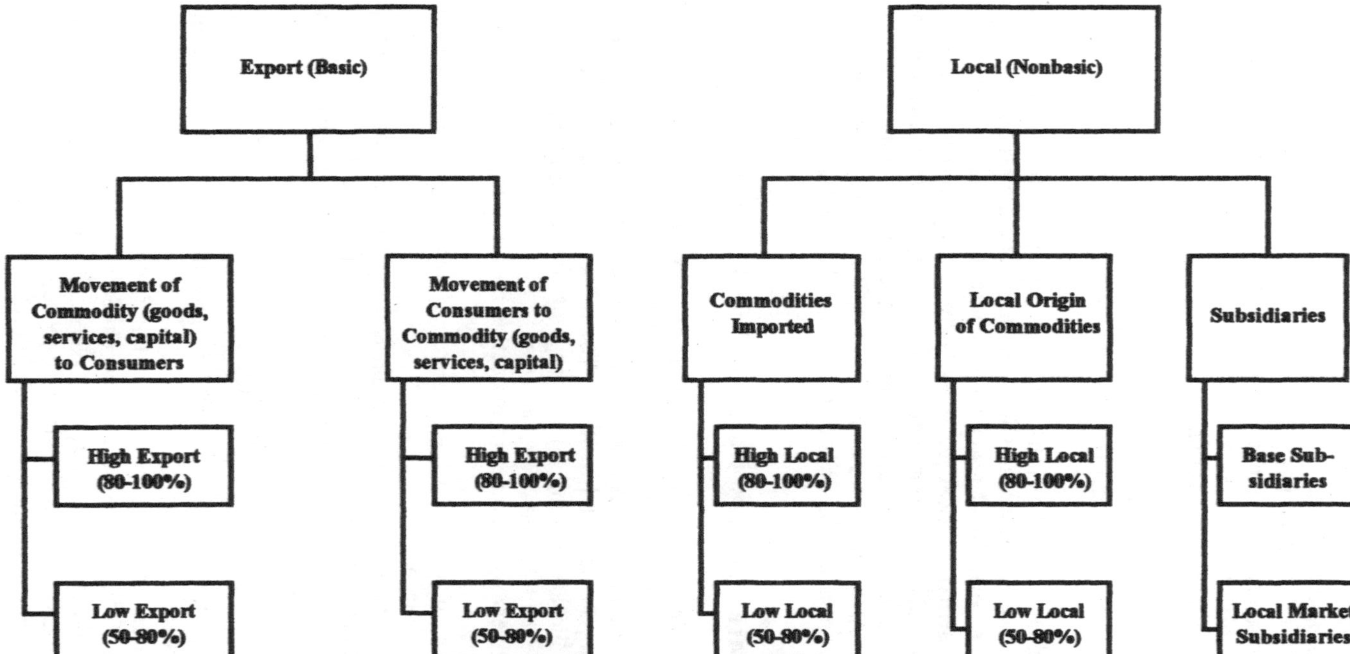

Figure 1-2 Urban Economic Structure

sewers, roads, and other facilities can be greatly influenced by topography, subsoil conditions, and the like.

The results of the land use studies must be consistent with the economic and population forecasts. If a land use study does not indicate the availability of enough developable area to accommodate projected population and employment increases, serious thought should be given to scaling down those projections.

Programming Strategic Facilities

The deterioration of the urban infrastructure is a very serious problem of national scope. Recognition of the magnitude of the infrastructure problem unfortunately comes at a time when fiscal resources are constrained at all government levels. During recent period of fiscal pressures, many local governments have deferred maintenance spending as a "temporary measure" to ease their financial burdens. Such spending deferrals, however, have only multiplied future repair needs and investment requirements. As a consequence, public officials and administrators have had to confront a number of difficult, complex, and often politically sensitive decisions.

Infrastructure Problem from the Local Viewpoint

The programming of strategic facilities should be based on a system of priorities which, in turn, should be linked to the goals and objectives set forth in a strategic facilities plan. Procedures must also be developed for the continuous evaluation of existing services and facilities. The process by which limited financial resources are allocated among a wide range of competing public improvements should include the following key elements:

- A basic inventory and a set of indicators for assessing the condition of the infrastructure systems of the community.
- Determination of current conditions and range of potential infrastructure improvement needs.
- Analyses of the maintenance, repair, and replacement options for different improvement proposals (including the "do-nothing" option).
- Analyses of risks and uncertainties associated with various investment options, culminating in a ranking of investment proposals.
- Evaluation of available financing options.
- Programming, budgeting, and scheduling of specific improvement projects.

The basic components involved in the programming of strategic facilities are further delineated in Chapter 4.

Difficult questions must be faced in the context of the local political environment. Therefore, local officials need solid information and sound analytic procedures to address these issues effectively. The need is especially critical, as local governments must allocate increasingly constrained resources to competing long-term investment alternatives. Such information and analysis are essential to assure that funds are being spent on the "right" proposals.

The development and maintenance of a geographic information system (GIS) provides spatial data regarding the location, condition, and capacity of strategic facilities. The data storage/handling capacity of the computer makes it possible to maintain relatively large data sets on the current inventory of strategic facilities. The application of current GIS technology makes it possible to carry out various types of calculations and estimates that otherwise would be too laborious and time-consuming to contemplate.

Modeling and simulation techniques have been used effectively in various aspects of strategic facilities planning. Computer-assisted models can provide general direction to management decisions in the initial iterations and more detailed specifications in subsequent cycles of project planning, scheduling, and control.

Priority Classification Systems

Each proposed project should be measured and evaluated against the total capital expenditure needs of government through a sound system of priorities. Approaches to the assignment of priorities include (1) those that stress intangible values, and (2) those that undertake to quantify various criteria to develop a numerical scoring system. A six-way breakdown of priorities under an intangible approach is shown in Table 1-2, along with criteria for assigning capital projects to each of these categories. An examination of these suggested criteria reveals several areas in which more measurable indices could be developed. Hatry, Millar, and Evans have proposed eleven criteria for the evaluation of capital project requests, as summarized in Table 1-3.

A number of governments have assigned numerical weights to each criterion and use multipliers to calculate an overall summary score for each proposal. The criteria usually are a mixture of economic, political, social impact, and distribtional considerations. The criterion judged to be most important or most significant is given the highest score (frequently based on units of ten or some multiple of ten). All other criteria are then ranked in relation to this score. The resulting summary scores are then used to rank the proposals. Thus, for example, "protection of life and maintenance of public health" might be ranked as the most important criterion and given a score of 100. "Conservation of resources" might be judged to be nearly as important and given a score of ninety. On the other hand, "aesthetic and cultural values" might be ranked relatively low, scoring only twenty points. Procedures for evaluating and ranking capital project requests will be detailed in Chapter 4.

It should be evident that any effort to develop such an objective approach must be based, to a large degree, on subjective judgments. Ranking procedures are not intended to make decisions on improvement proposals "automatic." They are not a substitute for judgment and consideration of the political environment. Rather, they provide more substantive information—in effect, making explicit issues and trade-offs that are always present but often hidden. At the same time, it must be recognized that in government, "the actual choice and establishment of final priorities are still accompanied by the political process of compromise, a give-and-take between all groups concerned."[2]

Table 1-2
General Criteria for
Strategic Facilities Priority System

Category	General Criteria
1. **Urgent**	Projects that cannot reasonably be postponed; projects that would remedy conditions dangerous to public health, welfare, or safety; projects required to maintain a critically needed program; projects needed to meet an emergency situation.
2. **Essential**	Projects required to complete or make fully usable a major public improvement; projects required to maintain minimum standards as part of a ongoing program; desirable self liquidating projects; projects for which external funds for over 65% of costs are available for a limited period.
3. **Necessary**	Projects that should be carried out within a few years to meet clearly demonstrated anticipated needs; projects to replace unsatisfactory or obsolete facilities; remodeling projects for continued use of facilities.
4. **Desirable**	Adequately planned projects needed for the expansion of current programs; projects designed to initiate new programs considered appropriate for a progressive community; projects for the conversion of existing facilities to other uses.
5. **Acceptable**	Adequately planned projects useful for ideal operations but which can be postponed without detriment to present operations if budget reductions are necessary.
6. **Deferrable**	Projects recommended for postponement or elimination from immediate consideration in the current strategic facilities plan; projects that are questionable in terms of overall needs, adequate planning, or proper timing.

Adopted from: Alan Walter Steiss, *Local Government Finance: Capital Facilities Planning and Debt Administration* (Lexington, Mass.: Lexington Books, 1978), 38.

Capital Improvements Program

A *capital improvements program* (CIP) usually spans a five- to six-year period to reflect the more immediate, detailed portions of the long-range strategic facilities plan. Projects should be arrayed in the CIP according to their priority ranking.

Responsibility for preparing the CIP is shared by a number of groups and individuals within government: the chief executive, the legislative body (e.g., city council), the finance agency, the planning agency, and various operating departments. Each plays an important role in the decision-making process. As Coughlin has observed: "Each group attempts to look at the program as a whole and make decisions about its parts. But, because of its particular function and position, each group sees the problems with a slightly different emphasis."[3]

Operating departments are primarily concerned with their efficiency and are likely to view the entire capital improvements program in terms of its impact on their own project requests. As a consequence, these departments will tend to overemphasize the importance of their own requests in assigning priorities.

As the "watch-dog" of expenditures, the position of the finance agency is somewhat counter to that of the operating departments. This agency must be concerned primarily with maximizing the returns from individual projects, while achieving economies in the total program. Each proposed project must be examined critically to evaluate the potential "needs" that it is designed to serve. Emphasis often is given to the short-run implications of the strategic facilities plan.

The planning agency, in turn, must have a greater concern for the long-range implications and the functional relationship among projects as they fit together to further the objectives of the strategic facilities plan. In order to explore some of the more subtle ramifications of the individual project requests, the planning agency frequently must develop projections beyond the immediate needs embodies in the "justifications" submitted by the operating department.

The final decisions regarding capital expenditures must rest with the chief executive and the governing body. As the elected representatives of the people, these officials must share a primary concern for the broader interests and the welfare of their constituents. However, their particular functions and positions dictate that they emphasize different aspects of the capital improvements program. The chief executive must assume a position that places primary emphasis on middle-range objectives, falling somewhere on the continuum between the short-range perspective of the finance agency and the longer-range viewpoint of the planning agency. The chief executive must also pay particular attention to the political consequences of capital expenditure decisions. The governing body must also take cognizance of the political implications of decisions, but it tends to gravitate toward more immediate objectives of the CIP, placing particular emphasis on the cost factors involved.

The drawbacks to this approach, in terms of the time required to carry out the process and the compromises that often are necessary, should be obvious. As one student of government has put it: "Rome wasn't built in a day—but it would have taken a heck of a lot longer if the construction proposals had to go through our modern form of democratic government." To circumvent the delays

Table 1-3
Suggested Evaluation Criteria

Fiscal impacts. Explicit consideration should be given to initial costs of development and subsequent costs of operation, maintenance, and repair. Revenues might be generated or reduced. Increases or decreases in energy requirements should be included as part of cost impact. Estimates should be made of any potential cost liabilities.

Health and safety effects. Project justifications should include assessment of health- and safety-related effects, such as anticipated reduction in traffic accidents, elimination of health hazards, long-term effects of asbestos in public buildings.

Economic effects. Information on the economic effects should included the likely impact of the project on (1) property values, (2) the tax base, (3) employment opportunities, (4) personal income, (5) business income, and (6) the stabilization or revitalization of declining neighborhoods.

Quality of life and service. Both beneficial and adverse effects on the quality of life should be considered. Estimates should be provided as to the duration and severity of service disruptions and the number of persons likely to be affected.

Distributional effects. Estimates of the number of persons likely to be affected should be broken down by age groups, economic status, neighborhoods or districts, residential or commercial areas, handicapped persons, and so forth.

Project feasibility. Projects should be evaluated for special problems that might arise including legal issues, compatibility and compliance with the strategic facilities plan, impact on prior investments, and degree of public support for or opposition.

Implications of project deferral. Impact of deferring the project should be examined in terms of each of the previous criteria. What will be the added costs? What and who will be disbenefited, and how? What are the trends in the bond market?

Risk and uncertainty. Consequences of substantial risks and uncertainties should be included in the overall project evaluation.

Interjurisdictional relations. Special coordinating activities might be required if a proposed project has significant adverse or beneficial effects on other jurisdictions.

Advantages accruing from other proposals. Relationship between projects should be identified, particularly if the initiation of one project will affect the costs or benefits of another project.

Adapted from Harry P. Hatry, Annie P. Millar, and James H. Evans. "Guide to Setting Priorities for Capital Investments," *Guides to Managing Urban Capital*, Volume 5 (Washington, D.C.: The Urban Institute Press, 1984), 9.

that arise from this approach, the strategic facilities plan and capital improvements program must be developed with a spirit of close coordination and cooperation among the various groups involved.

Even after legislative action has been taken in adopting the CIP, funds must still be made available. Therefore, another opportunity for review occurs at the time appropriations are made, or in the case of an issuance of general obligation bonds, at the time the referendum is placed before the voters. Of course, even after appropriations are made, changes and adjustments are still possible prior to construction or acquisition. If the original project requests are based upon a sound planning foundation, however, the need for such changes should be minimal.

A strategic facilities plan has a far better chance of success if it has political support from the outset. The requirement that a bond issue be approved through a public referendum provides an opportunity to build public backing for the entire strategic facilities plan. Unfortunately, local governments have not been particularly successful in promoting bond referenda. The local business community, which requires adequate infrastructure support to be cost competitive, seldom has been enlisted as an effective partner in generating public support for the plan.

Analysis of Costs

Effective strategic facilities planning requires analytical techniques that can accommodate the *risk* and *uncertainty* associated with future decisions regarding the commitment of scarce public resources. Future costs are influenced by (1) scope and quality of the services to be delivered; (2) volume of activity required to deliver these services; (3) methods, facilities, and organizational structure required to perform the program activities; (4) qualities and types of labor, materials, equipment, and other cost elements required by these programs; (5) price levels of the various cost elements. These cost elements are examined further in Chapter 5.

Monetary costs include research and development costs, investment costs, and the costs of operations, maintenance, and replacement. It also is important to consider the marginal or incremental costs of increasing the size or scope of a capital project. Some costs are fixed—they are the same regardless of the size or duration of the project. As a project increases in size or scope, these costs are distributed over a larger number of service units. Other costs are variable—they might change significantly as the scope of the project is increased. It also is appropriate to look beyond these monetary costs to what economists call opportunity costs, associated costs, and social costs.

Discounted cash flow techniques examine future negative and positive cash flows (costs and benefits) required to produce the desired returns from particular investments. Cost-benefit analysis requires that estimates of both the direct and indirect costs and the tangible and intangible benefits be translated into a common measure, usually (but not necessarily) a monetary unit. The cost-benefit approach, first outlined by Otto Eckstein, involves an identification of (1) an objective function, (2) constraints, (3) externalities, (4) time dimensions, and

(5) risk and uncertainty. Benefits that accrue in the present usually are worth more to their recipients than benefits anticipated some time in the future. Resources invested today cost more than those invested in the future, since one option would be to invest the same funds at some rate of return that would increase their value.

Under cost-effectiveness analysis, the preferred alternative either (1) produces a desired level of performance at the minimum cost or (2) achieves the maximum level of performance possible for a given level of cost. Although costs can ordinarily be expressed in monetary terms, non-monetary indexes—measures of effectiveness—are usually applied to represent levels of achievement. Three supporting analyses are required under the cost-effectiveness approach:

1. Cost-goal studies are concerned with the identification of feasible levels of achievement.
2. Cost-effectiveness comparisons assist in the identification of the most effective program alternative.
3. Cost-constraint assessments determine the cost of employing less than the most optimal program.

Cost-benefit and cost-effectiveness analysis can be applied at two pivotal points: (1) in the planning stage, based on anticipated costs and benefits, and (2) after a project has been implemented to assess whether the magnitude of net outcomes justify the costs incurred. Further specifics regarding the application of cost-benefit and cost-effectiveness analyses in planning and programming strategic facilities are provided in Chapter 5.

Methods of Financing

A strategic facilities plan will not solve all of the fiscal problems of local government. It may or may not result in a reduction of taxes or public debt. Planning assists in providing suitable responses to public needs, of appropriate quality, when and where they are required. The results are more expeditious and wise expenditures of public funds, whereby each dollar spent yields a more effective return in terms of desired public improvements.

Financial Planning and Fiscal Policy

The demand for public services and facilities increases and changes as a function of growth and the social and economic characteristics of the community. However, local revenues have tended to increase at a slower rate, creating an ever-widening fiscal gap for many localities. The inelasticity of local revenues is attributable, in part, to the tax structure, which forces local governments to rely heavily on local property taxes. Such taxes have proven to be relatively unresponsive in meeting increasing demands for public services and facilities.

Other taxes have also not been very productive at the local level. Unilateral taxation of income, sales, or business by local governments often results in shrinkage of the local tax base. If one municipality introduces such taxes, economic activities tend to locate beyond the taxing jurisdiction (for example, major shopping facilities located just outside the taxing jurisdiction of cities).

The manufacturing, transportation, and agriculture sectors of the economy have evidenced massive increases in productivity. Increases in public sector productivity, however, have been much less significant. Government services tend to be labor intensive and not readily amenable to the substitution of capital for labor. Instruction in the public schools, for example, is delivered in roughly the same way as it was 100 years ago—one teacher in front of a class of twenty to thirty pupils. As a consequence, the relative cost of public services has risen more rapidly compared to many other goods and services.

As the expenses of local government have risen, taxpayer resistance has also increased—the most notable example being manifest in Proposition 13, passed in California in 1978. Comparable tax limitations, although not as severe, were subsequently passed in a number of other states.

Thus, it is not difficult to understand the fiscal bind in which many local governments find themselves. Taxpayers demand good schools, adequate police and fire protection, and other public services. At the same time, however, they often resist any increases in local taxes to pay for these services.

Most intergovernmental aid is from the state rather than the federal government. Much of the state funds received by local governments in the past, however, have been really "pass-through" money from federal sources. As federal transfers to the states have diminished, state support for the responsibilities of local governments has also declined. For all of the above reasons, careful estimating of revenues and planning of expenditures is an important part of the strategic facilities planning process. The fundamentals of local revenue sources—property taxes, income and sales taxes, other miscellaneous revenues, and intergovernmental transfers—are discussed in Chapter 6.

Revenue and Expenditure Analyses

A sound revenue policy must be based on a thorough assessment of the need for public service and strategic facilities. Estimates should include an analysis of the revenues to be collected if existing fiscal policies are maintained. New revenue sources or shifts in yields from current sources under alternative policies must also be analyzed.

Sources of revenue should be disaggregated into appropriate categories and projected over a number of years. Demographic and economic forecasts are important in estimating the size of the tax base in the future. The impact of inflation must also be considered in estimating the magnitude of revenue sources such as sales and property taxes. The availability of intergovernmental aid also must be estimated. Considerable uncertainty is involved in such analyses, and the likelihood of any municipality accurately projecting its revenues over the next decade is quite small. Nevertheless, there is no good alternative to the use of such projections.

Expenditure data should also be separated into major categories. Data from past fiscal years assist in determining appropriate multipliers for each expenditure category. For example, past data might be examined to project the cost per pupil of primary school education. Population projections for the community provide enrollment estimates in future years. This analysis yields a first approximation of the real costs. Future costs might then be adjusted for projected inflation to yield the actual dollar costs. Note that one uncertainty (projected cost per pupil) is being multiplied by a second uncertainty (number of pupils) and then by a third uncertainty (changes in the value of the dollar). Therefore, the results of such analyses are necessarily only very rough approximations. Procedures for analyzing revenues and expenditures are outlined in Chapter 6.

Three Basic Financing Options

A sound fiscal policy seeks to develop an appropriate mix among three basic methods of financing strategic facilities: (1) from current tax revenues; (2) by building a reserve fund; and (3) through the issuance of municipal bonds or other forms of borrowing. Few local governments have the capability to finance vital public facilities strictly from current revenues, either on a "pay-as-you-go" basis or by setting aside funds to build a capital reserve. Therefore, the power to borrow is one of the most important assets of government. These basic methods for financing capital projects are discussed in further detail in Chapter 6.

Supporting capital improvements from current revenues (on a "pay-as-you-go" basis) is less costly than borrowing because it avoids the added cost of interest payments. It might be argued, however, that most public projects provide services over many years and, therefore, should be paid for by people according to their use or benefit—that is, should be financed on a "pay-as-you-use" basis.

Financing capital projects through a *reserve fund* (sometimes called a *capital reserve*) involves setting aside a portion of current revenues to be invested each year in order to accumulate sufficient funds to initiate a project at some future date. The amount (N) that must be placed annually at compound interest (r) for a term of n years to create a reserve fund (S) can be calculated by means of the following formula:

$$N = S \frac{r}{(1 + r)^n - 1}$$

To develop a reserve fund of $2 million at the end of ten years, for example, would require an annual investment of $151,736 compounded at 6%.

Local governments often borrow to finance major public facilities on the assumption that future economic and population growth will make the debt service payments (principal and interest) more feasible. Jurisdictions also might borrow on the assumption that, as inflation erodes the real value of the dollar, the actual burden of debt declines, making repayment easier. Future events may or may not prove these assumptions correct.

In general, long-term borrowing is appropriate under the following conditions:

- To finance capital projects that will not require replacement for many years, such as a city hall, auditorium, major health facility, or sewage disposal plant.
- To initial projects that can be financed by service charges to pay off the bond commitments.
- To meet urgent needs for public health and safety purposes or other emergency reasons.
- Where special assessment bonds are the only feasible means of financing improvements in the absence of subdivision regulations or other controls.
- Where intergovernmental revenues are available on a continuous basis to guarantee the security of the bonds.
- For financing capital projects in newly annexed areas or areas of rapid expansion where the demands on local tax resources are comparatively large and unforeseen.

Bonding Strategies

A *bond* is a promissory note ensuring that the lender will receive periodic payments of interest (at some predetermined rate) and at maturity (the due date), repayment of the original sum (principal) invested. Although referred to as municipal bonds, this broad investment category includes bonds issued by any political subdivision—cities, counties, school districts, or special purpose districts—public agency, authority, or commission, or by a state, territory, or possession of the United States. In addition to their tax-exempt status, municipal bonds possess three significant features:

1. *Security* of municipal bonds is generally considered second only to that of federal government bonds.
2. *High marketability*, assuring that investors can always sell municipal bonds if they wish to do so.
3. *Diversity,* enabling investors to obtain municipal bonds in geographic areas and at maturities of their preference.

Various categories of municipal bonds are identified in Table 1-4. The debt service costs of two basic types of bonds—a straight serial bond and an annuity serial bond—are shown in Table 1-5, with interest calculated over ten years at 6%. As this comparison illustrates, the total debt service cost of the straight serial bonds is less than that of the annuity serial bonds, given comparable interest rates. Advantages and disadvantages of each of the basic bond categories will be further discussed in Chapter 7.

Innovative Fiduciary and Fiscal Instruments

Faced with reduced profit margins in the late 1970s, many institutional investors that traditionally supported the municipal bond market curtailed their bond buying. Tax-exempt bond yields were forced to unprecedented highs, and as a

Table 1-4
Categories of Municipal Bonds

Municipal bonds can be classified according to the source of security.

General obligation bonds are backed by the "full faith, credit, and taxing power" of the issuing locality and are the most secure of the municipal issues, since the issuing authority has the power to levy taxes at a level necessary to meet debt service requirements.
Special tax or ***special assessment bonds*** are payable only from the proceeds derives from a special tax (such as highway bonds payable from a gasoline tax) or from a special assessment levies against those who benefit from the facilities constructed (e.g., special assessments for curbs and gutters in residential areas).
Revenue bonds are obligations issued to finance a revenue-producing enterprise—such as the construction of a toll road or bridge, parking structure, sewage treatment plant, and other facility with a predictable revenue generating capacities. Both the principal and interest of such bonds are paid exclusively from the earnings of the enterprise.

Municipal bonds can be classified according to method of redemption.

Term bonds become due in a lump sum at the end of the term of the loan; all bonds in the issue reach maturity and must be paid off at the same time. The lump-sum principal payment is met by making annual payments to a *sinking fund.*
Serial bonds are retired by annual installments directly from tax revenues, or in the case of revenue bonds, from earned income. Serial bonds have simpler retirement requirements and offer greater flexibility in marketing and in arranging the debt structure of the jurisdiction or public organization.

- With annuity serials, the debt service payment is approximately the same each year (as with a home mortgage). The portion of the annual payment devoted to interest is higher in the early years of the issue but declines as payments toward principal are made (as the outstanding principal is retired).
- Straight serial bonds require annual payments of principal of approximately equal amounts. Interest payments are large in the early years and decline gradually as the bonds approach maturity.

Table 1-5
Debt Service Charges on $1 Million for Ten Years

Straight Serial Bonds
(6% on declining principal)

Year	Outstanding Principal	Principal Payment	Interest Payment	Total Debt Service
1st	1,000,000	100,000	60,000	160,000
2nd	900,000	100,000	54,000	154,000
3rd	800,000	100,000	48,000	148,000
4th	700,000	100,000	42,000	142,000
5th	600,000	100,000	36,000	136,000
6th	500,000	100,000	30,000	130,000
7th	400,000	100,000	24,000	124,000
8th	300,000	100,000	18,000	118,000
9th	200,000	100,000	12,000	112,000
10th	100,000	100,000	6,000	106,000
Total		$1,000,000	$330,000	$1,330,000

Annuity Serial Bonds
(6% on outstanding principal)

Year	Outstanding Principal	Principal Payment	Interest Payment	Total Debt Service
1st	1,000,000	75,868	60,000	135,868
2nd	924,132	80,420	55,448	135,868
3rd	843,712	85,420	50,623	135,868
4th	758,467	90,360	45,508	135,868
5th	668,107	95,782	40,086	135,868
6th	572,325	101,528	34,340	135,868
7th	470,797	107,620	28,248	135,868
8th	363,177	114,070	21,791	135,868
9th	249,100	120,922	14,946	135,868
10th	128,178	128,178	7,690	135,868
Total		$1,000,000	$358,680	$1,358,680

consequence, a number of innovative fiduciary and fiscal instruments were devised. The characteristics of these investment instruments are discussed in further detail in Chapter 7.

Zero coupon bonds, for example, take advantage of federal tax laws that entitle bondholders to forego tax-free income over the life of their investment in order to receive tax-exempt capital gains when the bonds reach maturity. The result is a sort of tax-free income, accrued annually from the time the bonds are first issued. Zero coupon bonds sell at substantial discounts from the face value of $1,000 because they pay no interest. By paying the full face value upon maturity, however, they offer capital gains that might be as much as twenty times the original investment, depending on the length of time until the issue matures.

The interest rates on *stepped coupon bonds*, in general, start at lower levels and progressively increase to higher levels as the time to maturity increases. All bonds in the issue are sold at the full face value. The substantial increase in coupon payments each year is intended to provide a hedge against inflation and thus make the bonds more marketable.

Compound interest bonds return to the investor at maturity the principal plus interest compounded at a specified rate. Unlike zero coupon bonds, which sell at a discount, these bonds sell at face value. However, an investor in a compound interest bond still pays less for the bond than it will be worth at maturity. An investor knows exactly what the total return will be—the rate of return is guaranteed for ten to twenty years.

The interest paid by the issuer on a *flexible interest bond* changes over the life of the bond based on some interest index printed on the bond itself. The interest index most often used is the average weekly rate of Treasury bills or bonds issued during the preceding interest period.

A *tender option bond* offers the investor the option of submitting the bond for redemption before it reaches maturity (in order to take advantage of other investment options). Investors usually might "tender their option" to redeem a bond five years after the date of issue or on any anniversary date thereafter. In return for this option, the investor accepts a slightly lower interest rate.

These more innovative investment instruments stem from the willingness of government officials to deal with the uncertainty of future markets for financing strategic facilities. Careful application of these new financing techniques might provide capital resources that otherwise would be unavailable to localities. More conventional approaches to the financing of strategic facilities should not be abandoned, however, unless officials are satisfied that sufficient benefits will accrue compared to the risks.

Funding Strategic Facilities as a Development Cost

In the past, the private sector often was involved in designing, constructing, and financing major capital improvements, such as water systems, roads, or mass transit systems. This practice has largely been abandoned in recent years. However, developers of new subdivisions and some commercial or industrial projects might be required to pay the infrastructure costs created by their developments.

This shift to private sector financing has been most pronounced in high-growth states and especially those faced with strict limitations on the issuance of bonds or increases in taxes. The recent trend has been to require private developers to finance more of the "off-site" capital costs that can be shown to be "reasonably related" to the public capital costs attributable to development.

An equity charge to new subscribers to fund expanded sewer and water services to meet increased demands, for example, has been upheld by the courts provided that a linkage between the expansion and the requirements of new development can be demonstrated. This charge relieved older subscribers from having to pay the cost of major system expansions.

Impact fee systems have been approved in some localities, covering the additional costs for roads, parks, and schools generated by new development. The developers are charged according to the anticipated use of the expanded capacity of public improvements generated by new subdivisions. Developers know from the outset how much they will have to pay for a given type and scale of project. The locality achieves the necessary expansion of strategic facilities without having to finance these improvements from local tax revenues.

Revenue Bonds and Lease-Purchase Financing

During the past thirty years, revenue bonds have increased as a percentage of the volume new bond issues from 48% in 1975 to the present level of about 65%. Other mechanisms for financing strategic facilities and equipment have also emerged in the past thirty years, including lease-purchase agreements, tax-exempt leveraged lease (or TELL) financing, certificates of participation (COPs), and private activity bonds. The focus of Chapter 8 is on the legal and financial requirements that distinguish these mechanisms from more traditional approaches to funding capital projects.

Revenue bonds are issued when it is clear that only the users of a strategic facility should pay for that facility. Revenue bonds are not ordinarily subject to the debt limitations imposed on local governments. While revenue bonds constitute an obligation of the issuing jurisdiction, the obligation extends only to the payment of the bonds from a special source of revenue. In general, the types of projects suitable for revenue bond financing include:

- Projects that can be readily operated on a service charge or user-fee basis.
- Projects for which experience, either under public or private operation, has demonstrated the potentialities for self-support.
- Projects that can produce sufficient revenue without jeopardizing other important economic or social objectives of the community.

Revenue bonds can play an important role in the long-range planning of strategic facilities. It must be clearly established, however, that revenues generated by the proposed project are sufficient to (1) cover the cost of operations, maintenance, and debt service; (2) provide a comfortable margin of working capital; and (3) create a reserve fund for emergencies and to cover possible declines in income. In short, revenue bonding must be approached with the principles of sound management and debt administration firmly in mind.

Lease-purchase agreements have been used to finance the acquisition of equipment, such as computers and motor vehicles, for over thirty-five years. More recently, long-term projects, such as the acquisition of real property, have also been financed using lease-purchase agreements. Under this approach, a government might use a nonprofit corporation or a governmental entity as a lessor to finance the acquisition of an asset. This arrangement is commonly used to finance the construction of schools, prisons, and public recreational facilities. The lessor serves as a channel to the financial markets for the lessee. The government that seeks to acquire the property agrees to make lease payments to the lessor. The lessor, in turn, issues revenue bonds, which are secured by the flow of lease payments. Tax-exempt leveraged lease (TELL) financing further extends this approach by involving the private sector as the lessor of the facility. An appropriate financing authority issues the revenue bonds and provides loan funds to the private entity to secure the purchase of the publicly leased facility.

In the past, the typical municipal bond was a general obligation bond, backed by the full-faith and credit of the issuing jurisdiction, sold by competitive bid, underwritten by a bank, and sold to a bank or other traditional financial institution. In today's bond market, however, the typical municipal bond is a revenue bond, sold through negotiation, underwritten by a bond syndicate or municipal bond dealer, and sold to individual investors and bond mutual funds.

Marketing and Underwriting Municipal Bonds

The successful marketing of a bond issue depends on the confluence of many factors, including forces in the marketplace that are beyond the control of local governments. Following accepted marketing procedures, however, can go a long way to reducing the uncertainties that confront municipal officials in this important undertaking. Chapter 9 is devoted to a discussion of the procedures for marketing and underwriting municipal bonds.

Preliminaries to Marketing

Municipal bond issues are regulated by constitutional provisions, general statutes, special acts, and local charters that vary from state to state and are not always conveniently codified. Therefore, expert legal advice is important to ensure compliance with all applicable requirements. An attorney whose legal opinions satisfy the market where the bonds are to be sold must approve each issue. Bond ordinances or resolutions should set forth the nature and limits of the security to be offered. Some form of popular referendum is required in most states for the authorization of general obligation bonds.

At least two weeks in advance of the date set for opening bids, the official notice of sale should be published in *The Daily Bond Buyer* and perhaps in regional bond publications. Adequate publicity through the notice of sale gives prospective bidders the opportunity to form their bidding accounts.

The publication of all essential facts concerning the financial condition of the jurisdiction proposing to issue bond is as important as any other factor in the successful marketing of municipal bond. The brief statistical form, approved by the Investment Bankers Association and the Government Finance Officers Association, should be sent to the investment bankers and other institutions interested in the jurisdiction's securities.

Municipal Bond Ratings

Municipal bonds are rated only in terms of credit risk and not in terms of their investment merits. Bond ratings reflect two basic risk factors: (1) the possible dilution of the quality of the bonds by an inordinate increase in debt, and (2) the potential for impairment of the jurisdiction's ability to meet principal and interest payments under depressed economic conditions. Rating analysts evaluate a wide range of information concerning economic, debt, financial, and governmental considerations to determine a bond rating. This information is supplied by the jurisdiction and/or derived independently by the analyst.

Three nationally recognized rating organizations—Standard and Poor's Corporation; Moody's Investors Service, Inc.; and Fitch Investor's Service—rate a wide variety of bonds: tax-supported, revenue or enterprise supported, lease-rental, hospital revenue, mortgage-backed housing, higher education revenue, student loan revenue, and refunded bonds. These rating services use symbols, arranged in order from bonds with the least credit risk to those with the greatest risk. The opinions of the rating services might differ on specific issues. Most issues are rated only by one service.

State and local governments insure their bond offerings to obtain the highest ratings possible and, thereby, lower their borrowing costs. Bond insurance guarantees that the interest and principal on the insured bonds will be paid if the issuer of the bonds fails to make these payments for whatever reason. Investors are attracted to insured bonds because their investments are more secure. In addition, insured bonds have greater liquidity and price protection than uninsured bonds.

Underwriting Municipal Bonds

The funds required to finance strategic facilities are provided by large investment syndicates—temporary alliance of underwriters formed to purchase bonds from the issuer. Underwriters, in turn, sell the bonds to individual investors at a price higher than the purchase price paid to the issuing jurisdiction. In some cases, however, the bonds can only be sold at a price lower than the purchase price and, therefore, the underwriters take a loss in the transaction.

The public sale begins with the publication of an official notice of sale that delineates the proposed purpose, size, maturities, and structure of the anticipated issue, along with instructions for submitting bids. Local governments in most states are required to sell general obligation bonds by competitive bidding, usually through submission of sealed bids. The sale of revenue bonds might be negotiated, however. It often is advantageous to have an underwriter participate from the outset in setting up a revenue bond.

The investment syndicate seeks to balance two objectives: (1) high enough yields on the bonds to attract investors and (2) low enough cost to the issuer to win the bid. Competitive bids are awarded to the syndicate that offers to buy the issue at the lowest interest cost to the issuer. Several calculations must be made in order to determine a *net interest cost*—the bid that the underwriters will make on the bonds—and the *production* of the bonds at the posted prices—the anticipated return to the underwriters from the sale of the bonds.

Underwriters usually do not charge a commission when they sell municipal bonds. They act as principals rather than as agents. Their profit is the *spread*—the difference between the price the underwriter pays the issuer for the bonds and the price the underwriter receives from the resale of those bonds to investors. The spread is based primarily on the size of the issuance and market conditions at the time of the sale.

Outside dealers might buy bonds from the syndicate for their customer. The non-member's profit is known as the dealer's or selling concession and is taken out of the underwriter's profit or takedown.

Bond Delivery and Sale

The bonds should be delivered at the earliest practical date after the sale (no later than thirty days). However, before the bonds are delivered, information required to establish a *bond register* should be recorded. The interest due on each date of maturity and the principal payments or payments into a sinking fund should be calculated. With such records, a complete schedule of debt service requirements can be readily prepared for the current budget and for all outstanding debt obligations.

The bonds are then distributed to the members of the syndicate, who fill their orders and send the payments to the senior manager. Once the manager has received all the payments, the profits are distributed among the members of the syndicate.

Municipal Bond Secondary Market

Bonds might be offered to the investing public for a second time—hence the term *secondary market*. The secondary market provides individual and institutional investors the opportunity to buy and sell municipal bonds prior to their maturity dates. The secondary market for municipal bonds is not a formal market—there are no public listings of sale offerings and no regular trading hours. Municipal bonds are most often traded in *over-the-counter markets*, in which any individual might establish an account or might arrange for a recognized dealer to act as an agent. The volume of transactions in the secondary market exceeds that of the new issue market at an estimated annual ratio of twenty to one.

Secondary trading is very competitive, with spreads ranging from 1/4 of a point ($2.50 per bond) to two points ($20.00) in the case of obscure issues or odd lots. The average dealer's spread is $10.00 per $1,000 bond.

Municipal Bond Investors

Four categories of investors purchase municipal bonds: (1) property and casualty insurance companies, (2) commercial banks, (3) mutual funds, and (4) individual investors. The market shares of these investors have shifted over the past few decades, due to economic events and changing federal legislation. Commercial banks dominated the municipal bond market in the 1960s and 1970s. However, mutual funds and individual investors superseded banks in the 1980s.

The Tax Reform Act of 1986 eliminated many long-standing loopholes, leaving municipal bonds as the last significant remaining tax shelter. Other provisions of the Act made municipal bonds less attractive to banks and insurance companies. By 1994, 38.9% of all municipal bonds were held by mutual funds, bank personal trusts, and money market funds; individual investors held 35.5%; property and casualty insurance companies held 12%; and commercial banks held only 8.2%.[4]

Debt Administration

The greater diversity of bond offerings currently available to local governments has resulted in increased complexity and responsibility for the administration of public debt. Debt administration involves the management of the resources required for the acquisition or construction of a strategic facility and the servicing of the debt obligations that might result from the issuance of bonds to finance these improvements.

Use of Network Analysis to Program Capital Projects

If a capital project is to be successfully implemented, three elements must be coordinated into a project plan and operations schedule:

1. Operations: the things that must be done (activities or jobs), each with a sequential relation to other operations and each requiring resources for some time period.
2. Resources: the things utilized in a project, normally reduced to a common standard of cost, but including personnel, equipment, materials, and time.
3. Constraints: conditions imposed by outside factors, such as budgetary limits, completion deadlines, availability of resources, inputs from other units, and so forth.

Project planning should provide a blueprint for project implementation and should include (1) an identification of project tasks and activities, (2) specifications of performance requirement and functional plans related to organizational responsibilities, and (3) development of cost estimates and budgets. An operations schedule details the order or sequence in which the project activities must be carried out. This schedule must reflect the total resource capacity assigned to the project and should take into account the availability of resources, the sequence of activities or jobs, the resource requirements, and possible starting times for each activity. An effort must also be made to level the use of resources to avoid dramatic shifts in resource requirements (particularly personnel).

Network analysis provides a mechanism for identifying and displaying the tasks and activities required to successfully carrying out a project. It also offers a basis for determining the order (sequence and/or priority) in which these activities should be undertaken and the means for establishing the critical linkages among tasks/activities. Procedures and techniques of network analysis are outlined in Chapter 10, with particular application to strategic facility projects.

Program Evaluation and Review Technique (PERT)—the more sophisticated approach to network analysis—is designed to deal with large-scale projects characterized by (1) unclear objectives, (2) multiple or overlapping management responsibilities, (3) relatively high levels of uncertainty as to time and cost requirements, and (4) complex problems of logistics. The *Critical Path Method* (CPM) has been described as a "back-of-an-envelope" or "in-the-field" approach. CPM is *job*- or *activity*-oriented and is applicable to well-defined projects, under a single management, with relatively clear objectives and limited levels of uncertainty.

PERT and CPM facilitate the selection of a "best route" to be followed to reach project objective. Potential delays and obstacles to the successful implementation of the project plan are also identified. PERT and CPM are excellent tools of communication—interrelationships of all activities in a project are shown graphically and the assignment of responsibilities for project supervision and management is clearly indicated. In developing a schedule, the critical path is determined not so much by the duration of the various activities, but by the segment of resources that can be assigned to complete each activity.

Project management is best served by a real-time control system that responds to situations according to their degree of urgency. Deviations from the predicted schedule should be used to revise the project plan, adjust resource allocations, and recalculate the overall time required to implement the balance of the project. In the final analysis, the procedures adopted for the planning, scheduling, and control of a strategic facility project are still tools that are only as good as the managers who use them.

Public Investment Strategies in Debt Administration

Local governments often are able to meet current obligations and, at the same time, have some uncommitted cash left over to invest. An investment portfolio that is well managed can be an important source of additional revenue that does not involve tax increases or assumption of additional debt. Investment strategies appropriate to the administration of long-term debt are detailed in Chapter 11.

Principal factors to be considered in selecting an investment are (1) safety/risk, (2) price stability, (3) liquidity/marketability, (4) maturity, and (5) yield. In general, securities with little risk, high liquidity, and short maturity also have low yields. For an investment to provide a high yield, one or more of the other criteria must be compromised.

The majority of states allow local governments to invest in a variety of securities (see Table 1-6). Federal obligations, such as T-bills and federal agency securities, are practically riskless, since the full faith and credit of the federal government back them. Other securities carry varying degrees of risk and, therefore, must offer higher interest rates. In many states, however, local governments are prohibited from investing in banker's acceptances and commercial paper that generally earn higher rates of return.

Derivatives—one of the most complicated securities yet invented—have received considerable coverage in the media in recent years, largely stemming from the fiscal crises that some local governments must face as a result of the these investments. Derivatives were devised in the mid-1980s to help large corporations guard against sudden shifts in global financial markets. The value of these securities is based on, or derived from, an underlying asset, such as Treasury bonds, corporate stocks and bonds, foreign currencies, or commodity contracts. In the early 1990s, investment brokers found a new market for these complex securities—local finance officers with little formal education in finance but millions of dollars in taxpayers' funds to invest. Since derivatives offer above-average returns when short-term interest rates are low, many localities responded to the aggressive sales tactics of brokers and invested in securities—in some cases, with disastrous consequences.

Tracking the Funds for Capital Improvements

A *capital project fund* records proceeds derived from the issuance of bonds or other long-term obligations, from intergovernmental grants, or as transfers from other funds. Revenue from bond sales or transfers from state or federal grants often are received before these resources are needed to acquire the capital asset. These funds should be invested and the interest earned should be transferred to the *debt service fund* to partially offset the amount needed from the general fund for the first interest payment. Debt service funds account for (1) the accumulation of resources to pay the principal and interest on long-term debt and (2) the investment and expenditure of those resources. The principal and interest on serial bonds are serviced annually, and, therefore, no resources are accumulated on which interest can be earned. However, funds to service the principal on term bonds, zero coupon bonds, and compound interest bonds can be invested since these resources are not needed until the debt matures.

A *sinking fund* is used to spread the cost of repayment over the duration of the bond issue. The management of a sinking fund is a complex task, however, and should not be undertaken without adequately trained personnel and proper safeguards to protect the integrity of the funds. Local governments in most states are restricted as to the types of sinking fund investments that can be made—usually being limited to federal, state, and municipal bonds. An annual independent audit should be made of all sinking fund transactions. Procedures for the administration of capital project funds, debt service funds, and sinking funds are outlined in Chapter 12.

Table 1-6
Investment Instruments Used by Local Governments

U.S. Treasury bills (T-bills) are the most important money market instrument available for local government investment; they represent an obligation of the federal government to pay a fixed sum of money after a specified period of time from date of issue.
Federal agency securities are issued by government-sponsored, privately-owned agencies that established to implement federal policies and include Federal Farm Credit bonds, Federal Home Loan Bank bonds and discount notes, and Federal National Mortgage Association bonds.
Certificates of deposit (CDs) are receipts for funds that have been deposited in a commercial bank for an agreed upon period of time.
Repurchase agreements are contracts between two parties whereby one party sells an instrument (such as a T-bill) to the other and agrees to buy it back at a later date (often the next day) at a specified higher price.
Banker's acceptances, usually created in conjunction with foreign trade transactions, are time drafts negotiated by commercial banks to finance the shipment or storage of goods.
Commercial paper includes promissory notes of finance corporations or industrial firms that offer higher yields than T-bills.

Accurate debt records—including auditable ledgers as to the identity, purpose, and amount of debt commitment associated with capital projects—are vital to short-term and long-term fiscal operations. All fixed assets purchased, constructed, or obtained by contract are recorded at cost in the *general fixed assets account group*. The *long-term debt account group* is used to maintain records of long-term liabilities, such as serial bonds, long-term notes, and long-term commitments arising from lease or purchase agreements.

Financial Reporting

Accurate and complete reporting of public debt obligations develops confidence on the part of investors and the general public as to the fiscal management of a jurisdiction or public organization. Annual financial reports should include all outstanding debt by type of issue (general obligation, special assessment, or revenue bonds) and should provide a computation of the jurisdiction's legal borrowing status.

Prompt payment of all principal and interest requirement is the most direct evidence of sound debt administration. A *bond and interest register* and the ledgers for bonded debt and interest form a ready basis for the development of a payment calendar. The funds for principal and interest payments must be allotted in a timely manner to provide the cash when it is needed. A sufficient fund balance must be carried over from the previous fiscal year and/or provision must be made to generate adequate funds early in the new fiscal year.

The final step in servicing a municipal debt involves the recording and canceling of coupons and bonds that have been paid. Many commercial banks and trust companies that serve as paying agents for municipal bonds include all phases of recording and cancellation as part of their services.

Refunding and Conversions

Refunding involves the issuance of new bonds to retire outstanding bonds that carry higher interest rates. The process involved in refunding or converting bonds is described in Chapter 12. Five elements need to be considered in refunding: (1) the timing of the sale, (2) the maturity schedule of the refunding bonds, (3) the time of settlement on the new bonds, (4) the refunding costs, and (5) the redemption provisions for the refunding bonds. Refunding generally involves the exercise of a call provision included in the original issue to permit the bonds to be refunded at lower rates, if the market changes or the locality's credit rating improves.

The refunding of the outstanding debt might also be appropriate in order to eliminate or modify restrictive covenants. Refunding mature or maturing bonds should be avoided if at all possible, however, and if necessary, should be undertaken with great discretion. A municipality might find it necessary to refund outstanding debts to avoid default or serious disruption of fiscal operations. Such emergencies should be anticipated and the necessary steps taken with sufficient lead-time to resolve the problem in an orderly and businesslike manner.

Defaults

Defaults are likely to result in a sharp decline in the credit standing of the municipality, skepticism among lenders, and major difficulties in negotiating favorable interest rates on future bond issues. Defaults fall into three general classifications:

1. Minor or temporary defaults involve failure to meet the maturity payment of a single security or temporary postponement of interest payments as a result of unanticipated revenue declines, the shutting off of normal lines of bank credit, and/or a temporary inability to market refunded bonds.
2. A second, more serious class of defaults involves municipalities that have encountered such fiscal problems as peak debt service in a period of low-paying capacity, serious breakdowns in the local economic base, and/or abnormally high tax delinquency.
3. The most serious defaults involve situations in which the jurisdiction is confronted by abnormally high debt, severely curtailed revenues, and significant accumulation of operating deficits, with little or no prospect for correction except through a comprehensive refunding plan.

Faced with default, a local jurisdiction should take the initiative in preparing and implementing a refunding plan to demonstrate good faith and competence and to gain the necessary cooperation from investors. Attempting to cover up the fiscal status of the local government merely exacerbates uncertainty, increases expenses, and ultimately might result in the municipality being placed in receivership.

The refunding plan must provide (1) mechanisms to release current accounts from all accumulated deficiencies and (2) financing procedures that will maintain balanced operations. Most states have adopted legislative measures to circumvent the financial catastrophe that were faced by many governments during the Great Depression. The ultimate responsibility, however, still rests with local officials to adopt debt administrative procedures that will protect their community from "mortgaging its future." Procedures for dealing with potential or actual defaults are discussed in Chapter 12.

Summary and Conclusions

The planning of strategic facilities involves a unified series of steps to carry out the policy aims of government. The interrelated character of all expenditures, whether for new or existing capital outlays, must be recognized in this process, and their joint evaluation must be carried out in arriving at expenditure decisions. As a management tool, strategic facilities planning provides a coordinative mechanism for all phases of capital construction—estimation, submission, approval, execution, and post audit.

Capital budgeting is a political process. While any budget contains some automatic decision, the important fact is that most decisions relating to capital investments are policy decisions. Economic and other criteria are employed in the strategic facilities planning process, but they are defined within and conditioned by the broader political context. Ultimately, the efficiency and effectiveness of the strategic facilities plan is measured by the results of executive and legislative action.

Notes

1. Richard D. Andrews, "Mechanics of the Urban Economic Base," *Land Economics* (November 1953): 344-349; "Urban Economics: An Appraisal of Progress," *Land Economics* (August 1961): 223-225; "Economic Planning for Small Areas: An Analytical System," *Land Economics* (May 1963): 145-155; "Economic Planning for Small Areas: The Planning Process," *Land Economics* (August 1963): 253-264.
2. William B. Rogers, "Fiscal Planning and Capital Budgeting," *Planning 1954* (Chicago, Ill.: American Society of Planning Officials, 1954), 96.
3. Robert E. Coughlin, "The Capital Programming Problem," *Journal of the American Institute of Planners* 26 (February 1970): 39.
4. Penelope Lemov, "After the Fiscal Quake," *Governing* 8, no. 5, (February 1995): 34.

Appendix A
Strategic Facilities Planning: A Private Sector Case Study

A specific example of an effective strategic can be found in the work undertaken for one of the Big Three American automakers. This company, burdened with a rigid and largely unresponsive hierarchical structure, used a strategic facilities plan to spark change throughout the company. The operational goals, as identify by management, were to optimize workflow, especially within particular product development groups, to increase creative teamwork throughout the organization, to achieve the highest possible return-on-net-assets (RONA), and to implement common processes and systems to foster maximum efficiency and response to changing conditions.

The project team partnered with the client's strategic facilities planning team to establish an ongoing process directed at reaching these goals. Work of the team included:

- A situation analysis designed to identify available base data on current space use and building conditions, facilities costs and related financial accounting and planning processes, and facilities planning and management systems, procedures, and staff organization.
- Identification of key influences on the corporation's business, such as product times to market, brand identity, employee satisfaction, return-on-net-assets, and how facilities link with these business issues.
- Long-range strategic visioning, including evaluation of alternative location scenarios based on business needs, regional demographics, costs, identity, labor, community, and other drivers.
- Development of common definitions and metrics for space measurement and creation of a graphic and numeric database of information comprised of existing space use by type and business unit.
- Calculation of actual space used by function and space utilization efficiency.
- Strategic oversight of development of new workplace standards.
- Site framework master planning for several sites in several cities.

Based on these recommendations, the company divested its holdings in certain capital assets, while choosing to invest more heavily in others. Perhaps the greatest advantage of the process was that the company was able to consolidate various and diverse work groups in greater concentrations. This consolidation facilitated communication and interaction among the different groups and greatly reduced the "fiefdom" mentality that had existed in the far-flung and inflexible facilities arrangement.

The plan resulted in smarter engineering and a more streamlined corporation. The plan also helped the company with such bottom-line factors as managing structural costs, eliminating facilities redundancies, and creating facility adjacencies.

Work continues toward aligning the company's facilities strategies with its facilities planning. Perhaps most significant to the client are the benefits incurred from bringing together their diverse business units to discuss strategic facilities issues and macro-programs. These sessions have become a forum for interchange of business planning ideas to move the company's future vision forward.

Strategic facilities planning accelerates response time, improves coordination of major expenditures, coordinates short-term activities with long-term goals, saves money through efficient use of resources, avoids crisis decision making, and is a tool for visualizing the future and moving the organization to its strategic goals.

Appendix B
Strategic Facilities Planning at UNC-Charlotte

The University of North Carolina at Charlotte faces tremendous challenges and opportunities over the next five years. The University has embarked on the largest Capital Construction Program in its history. It is anticipated that academic square footage will double between 2002 and 2007. The student population will increase from 18,000 students to over 25,000 in five years. Further, the University recently achieved research-intensive status and seeks to attain research-extensive status within eight years. As a result, the purpose of many of the facilities on campus will change from teaching to research. Changes in facilities maintenance and operation must follow this change in focus. In addition to all of this growth and change, the University must deal with constrained budgets, expanding and diversified personnel requirements, and rapid growth of the metropolitan area surrounding the campus.

A Strategic Plan was developed by the Facilities Management Department in an attempt to address the challenges and opportunities of the next five years. This Plan identifies the University's mission, vision, values, and goals. The Plan also details objectives, strategies, and action plans that will lead to achievement of the vision and goals. The Plan was developed in a series of leadership meetings, planning sessions, and employee discussions between March and September 2001. It is intended to support the University vision and goals, the Business Affairs Division Plan 2002-2007, and the Academic Plan 2002-2007. These Plans form the University's road map to an exciting future.

As part of the Plan, the Department of Facilities Management has committed to excelling at three key business drivers:

1. Teamwork
   - Internal and
   - External
2. Customer Service
   - Quality products and services
   - Delivered on time and under budget
   - In the right quantity
   - Communicated in a consistent way
3. Continuous Improvement
   - Streamline processes
   - Exploit Technology
   - Optimize resources

Chapter 2

STRATEGIC PLANNING

Strategic planning has been a vital ingredient in the corporate decision-making process for over forty years. As King and Cleland explain, strategic planning in the private sector:

> involves the development of objectives and the linking of these objectives with the resources which will be employed to attain them. Since these objectives and resource deployments have impact in the future, strategic planning is inherently future oriented. Strategic planning, therefore, deals primarily with the contrivance of organizational efforts directed to the development of organizational purpose, direction, and future generation of products and services and the design of implementation policies by which the goals and the objectives of the organization can be accomplished.[1]

The term *strategic* is applied to these planning activities to denote linkages with the goal-setting process, the formulation of more immediate objectives to move the organization toward its goals, and the selection of specific actions (or strategies) required in the allocation of organizational resources to assist in achieving these objectives. The term also was adopted to distinguish the scope of this process from the forecasting and other piecemeal efforts undertaken in industry, business, and government in the name of "planning."

Origins of Strategic Planning

Many organizations that undertake long-range planning place considerable emphasis on the extrapolation of expected developments into the future. Management then compares these forecasts of future performance with what may be considered desirable according to some set of goals and objectives for the organization. The discrepancy between desirable goals and objectives and expected performance is commonly called the *planning gap*. Forecasting is only one of the ingredients in the planning process, however. Forecasts involve educated guesses about the future. A major purpose of planning is to support strategic decision-making with the formulation of alternative courses of action that will have long-term, desirable consequences.[2]

From One-Shot Optimization to a Strategic Planning Process

Many traditional planning efforts, in both the public and private sectors, have tended to be "one-shot optimizations," drawn together periodically, often under conditions of stress. Once the "best plans" were laid, little attempt was made to test their continued efficacy against the realities of current conditions.

It has been said that: "Few plans survive contact with the enemy." And indeed, rarely are policies and programs executed exactly as initially conceived. Random events, environmental disturbances, competitive tactics, and unforeseen circumstances conspire to thwart the implementation of plans, policies, and programs. Static plans, fixed targets, and repetitive programs are of relatively little value in a dynamic society.

What is required is a planning framework within which strategic decisions can be subjected to continuous testing, correction, and refinement. Through such an approach, alternative courses of action can be identified and analyzed, and a desirable range can be established within which choices can and should be made. The concept of strategic planning, as it has evolved over the past forty years, offers an important response to this need for a more dynamic planning process. Bryson defines strategic planning as "a disciplined effort to produce fundamental decisions and actions that shape and guide what an organization is, what it does, and why it does it. To deliver the best results, strategic planning requires broad yet effective information gathering, development and exploration of strategic alternatives, and an emphasis on future implications of present decisions."[3]

A Planning Hierarchy

An important component in the development of strategic planning is the recognition of a planning hierarchy in which the respective planning responsibilities at various levels within an organization are more clearly articulated. In applications in the private sector, Robert Anthony describes this hierarchy as consisting of (1) strategic planning, (2) management planning, and (3) operational control.[4] Management planning is a pivotal ingredient in this approach, involving (1) the programming of approved goals into specific projects, programs, and activities; (2) the design of organizational units to carry out approved programs; (3) the staffing of those units; and (4) the procurement of the necessary revenues to support the approved programs.[5]

In the absence of a strategic planning framework, however, management planning can become disjointed and counterproductive. At the same time, without the consistent follow-through of management planning (programming and budgeting), strategic planning may be little more than a set of good intentions with little hope of realization. Thus, the linkages among the basic components of the planning hierarchy are as important as the components themselves.

A Strategic Planning Model

Strategic planning involves an examination of alternative courses of action and the impacts and consequences that are likely to result from their implementation. Explicit provision should be made for dealing with the uncertainties of probabilistic futures. The art of management is to reduce uncertainty and to bring risk within the bounds of tolerance. In this context, strategic planning can play an important role by assisting in organizing goals and objectives and in developing feasible action plans to achieve them. In so doing, major priorities can be ordered, the impacts of resource decisions can be assessed, and activities and functions of the organization can be integrated into a more cohesive whole.

Basic Components of the Model

The strategic planning model advocated in this application consists of five basic components:

1. Basic research and analysis to determine systems readiness
    a. Collect basic data, prepare inventories, and conduct needs assessments
    b. Identify issues, problems, or choices critical to the future well being of the organization
    c. Clarify roles and responsibilities, identify constituencies or client groups to be served and engage key stakeholders in the process
    d. Develop an organizational profile and collect and analyze environmental information
2. Statements of mission, vision, goals, and objectives
    a. Formulate the mission of the organization
    b. Delineate significant structural change required to realize the mission statement
    c. Define the desired state of the system (vision statement)
    d. Identify strategic objectives to achieve the desired state
    e. Develop an objectives matrix
    f. Redefine the desired state of the system in light of more detailed objectives
3. SWOT Analysis/Situational Assessment
    a. Conduct internal and external environmental analyses
    b. Diagnose macro level trends and related considerations and conduct micro level technical and applied studies, including facilities analyses and specific needs assessments
    c. Delineate a planning horizon
4. Formulate strategies and analyze program alternatives
    a. Identify strategies for organizational development
    b. Prepare strategies that address how to develop, manage, and deliver programs
    c. Develop strategies that focus on administrative and support needs and their impacts on the organization's efficiency and effectiveness
    d. Delineate and analyze program alternatives to achieve desired strategies
5. Policy alternatives and resource recommendations
    a. Translate goals and objectives into general policies
    b. Formulate explicit policy sets
    c. Delineate effectiveness and efficiency measures
    d. Establish decision guidelines for the allocation of financial resources

Linkages among these basic components are shown in Figure 2-1.

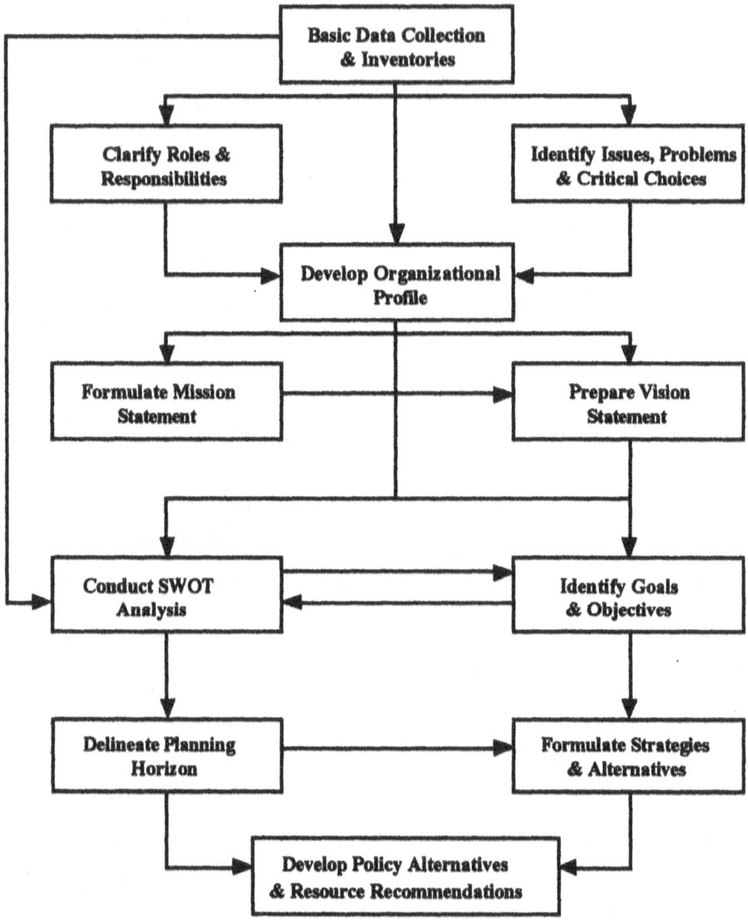

Figure 2-1 Schematic Diagram of the Strategic Planning Process

This model of strategic planning assumes that a concentration of systemic data can provide the basis for theoretical constructs—preliminary goals and objectives—as to the desired future state of the organization or community. The emphasis is on an orderly evolution from a broad mission statement, to statements of more specific goals and objectives consistent with the organization's mission, to more explicit policies and implementing decisions. This emphasis seeks to establish or to reinforce linkages that are missing in other planning approaches. The absence of consistency from the general to the specific is one of the major shortcomings of more traditional planning efforts.

The process for formulating goals and objectives also serves as a vehicle for avoiding the tendency to posit future plans merely on the basis of an extrapolation of existing conditions. Policies—factual premises representing what can be done—can be tested against goals—value premises representing what should be done. Statements of goals and objectives play a vital role in the day-to-day process of decision making. The application of this approach can go a long way toward circumventing the inherent danger of sacrificing the basic merits of the strategic plan to technical or politically expedient considerations. When compromises must be made—as they always will—decisions can be more clearly based on the optimal or normative conditions outlined in the statements of goals and objectives.

Systems Readiness

While many proponents of planning may suggest that "a little planning never hurt," many organizations initiate major planning efforts before they are ready to take on such a significant commitment. The subsequent results are almost always less than satisfactory. Therefore, a number of important issues must first be addressed in assessing the organization's readiness to undertake strategic planning:

- The leadership of the organization must have an active and involved commitment throughout the strategic planning process.
- Major crises that might interfere with long-range thinking should be resolved before beginning the planning process.
- Management should have a clear understanding of the purpose of planning and what it can and cannot accomplish, as well as a general consensus about expectations.
- Sufficient resources must be commitment to adequately assess current programs and the organization's ability to meet current and future client needs
- The organization's leaders must be willing to question the status quo and to look for new approaches to perform and evaluate current and future processes for "doing business."

If these elements cannot be accommodated satisfactorily at the outset of the process, the organization should rethink its overall commitment to strategic planning. "Too little planning" can result in false expectations and recommendations that fall far short of meeting the organization's needs and/or fulfilling its true potential. "Too much planning" can consume excessive time and resources and can fail to produce results that justify such commitments. "Enough planning" is when the organization's leadership understands the process and has achieved a consensus about a clear organizational direction.

Five tasks must be carried out to pave the way for strategic planning:

1. Identify five to ten significant issues, fundamental problems, or choices critical to the future well being of the organization that should be addressed during the planning process.
2. Clarify roles (who does what in the process) and engage key stakeholders in the process.
3. Create a planning committee (five to seven individuals) to spearhead the process; the committee should involve both "visionaries" and "actionaries."
4. Develop an organizational profile and collect and analyze environmental information.
5. Identify the information that must be collected to help make sound decisions, including historical financial information, projected cash flows, and budgets.

Mission and Vision Statements

It is important for an organization to articulate its overall mission in terms of what it is, what it is doing, and where it is going. A mission statement typically describes an organization in terms of its:

- *Purpose*: Why the organization exists and what it seeks to accomplish.
- *Business*: The main methods or activities the organization undertakes to fulfill this purpose.
- *Values*: Principles or beliefs that guide the members of an organization as they pursue the organization's purpose.

The stated mission of the American Red Cross, for example, "is to improve the quality of human life, to enhance self-reliance and concern for others, and to help people avoid, prepare for, and cope with emergencies."[6] The mission statement of the Internal Revenue Service is to "Provide America's taxpayers top quality service by helping them understand and meet their tax responsibilities and by applying the tax law with integrity and fairness to all."[7]

In defining purpose, it is essential that the focus be on outcome and results rather than on methods. For example, the purpose of a mental health counseling agency would not be simply "to provide counseling services"—that describes a method rather than an intended result. Rather, the purpose of the agency might be "to improve the quality of life" for its clients. Purpose statements usually identify the problem(s) or condition(s) that the organization will address and the change in the status of these problems/conditions that the organization hopes to bring about through its efforts.

Group discussions (through retreats, focus groups, and similar gatherings) of the elements and nuances of an organization's mission is important. However, one or two individuals should be assigned the follow-up task of writing the mission statement.

A vision statement should present a guiding image of what success will look like, formulated in terms of an organization's anticipated contribution to the broader society. A vision statement is more encompassing than a mission statement in that it seeks to provide an image of success that will motivate people within the organization to work together. A vision statement should be appropriate to the organization's mission, realistic and credible, yet ambitious, well articulate and easily understood, and responsive to change. It should be consistent with the organization's values and should challenge and inspire the group to achieve its mission.

Many organizations combine their mission and vision into a single statement. However, often the mission statement focuses primarily on the organization's responses to current issues, problems, and challenges. Under such circumstances, a vision statement might be appropriate to provide some stretch, to inspire its members to strive for a higher level of attainment, and to trigger the necessary changes the organization's structure and processes to bring about the longer term improvements and broader contributions to society.

Formulating Goals and Objectives

In strategic planning, tentative sets of goals and objectives are formulated and then tested in the context of specific horizon alternatives, allowing new factors to emerge and be considered. In short, a deductive approach replaces the more traditional inductive techniques of planning. This deductive approach should increase the awareness of the participants with respect to the changes that might be taking place within the organization. However, it also should allow these participants to react to these changes in accordance with their own values, norms, and expectations.

Most organizations operate, explicitly or implicitly, with a hierarchy of goals and objectives.[8] At the top of the hierarchy are the relatively durable goals—statements of desired results or outputs drawn from the broad purpose of the organization. These goals delineate the reason for an organization's existence, often framed in rather broad, immeasurable, and abstract terms as a mission statement. In turn, they must be translated into more specific objectives to give guidance to personnel at all levels within the organization. These objectives provide the critical bridge between the broad goals of an organization and specific action commitments.

Herbert Simon has described the relationship among goals and objectives as a means-ends chain, wherein lower level objectives (or processes) are intended to delineate the means for achieving higher level goals (or purposes). A process is at a low level in the hierarchy of means and ends, while a purpose is a collection of activities, the orienting value or aim of which is at a high level in the means-end hierarchy.[9]

The same goal might give rise to quite different objectives—either because different groups or individuals from different perspectives frame them or because they are deliberately varied in order to stimulate a dialogue from which mutual understanding and clarification might emerge or be enhanced. By the same token, different objectives (or sets of objectives) might lead to the same goal but with varying costs and benefits. The action programs associated with each objective might involve different capital and operating costs. Approximations of these costs and benefits might assist in the discussions among various groups and the public in general in the further clarification of goals.

Strategic objectives define the expected change in conditions, welfare, or behavior as a consequence of the initiation of some project, program, or activity. Strategic objectives specify what the organization proposes to do and *why* it proposes to do so. The tendency, however, is to focus on the *how*. Thus, an appropriate strategic objective of a municipal fire department might be: "Reduce current response time to all fire and emergency vehicle calls by 25% during the next two years." A statement: "Build, equip, and staff a third fire station during the next two years" tells how the strategic objective might be accomplished and should be reserved for the next level in the delineation of specific program actions.

Management objectives should describe specific program actions in terms of *how* and *where* specific resources (project budgets) will be used. Management objectives identify the commitments required to translate a strategic objective into specific activities. Management objectives often reflect staffing requirements or other resource commitments required to achieve a single key result. Such objectives usually are internal to the organization and are often associated with and identified through such techniques as management by objectives (MBO). Management objectives should be precise, measurable, and time bound. This degree of specificity is not easily achieved. The tendency often is to state objectives that simply describe current activities. In order to avoid this pitfall, objectives should be expressed in words of change—for example, to develop, to increase, to reduce, to eliminate, to prevent, to maintain, and so forth.

Management objectives, in turn, should be related to performance measures and measures of effectiveness. These measures can be used to identify the service units, constituents, and/or products associated with the activities of the organization. They provide mechanisms to determine the success (or lack thereof) of a project or program in achieving agreed-upon strategic objectives.

Operational objectives most often are associated with the implementation and control of specific tasks and the assignment of specific resources to achieve strategic and management objectives. Whereas the principal focus of strategic objectives is effectiveness, the keynote of operational objectives most often is efficiency. Operational objectives frequently reflect explicit performance measures that can be adopted by the organization to monitor its activities.

An operational objective often represents the best current statement of the most appropriate way to get the job done. Operational objectives should provide a basis for action. The primary purpose should be the detailed identification of activities and techniques that should be carried out in the implementation of a project or program. Operational objectives might involve the determination of specific resource requirements (personnel, equipment, materials, capital expenditures) and their appropriate order of commitment (project schedules) to ensure that specific tasks are carried out efficiently. Operational objectives often include references to relatively short-term completion dates (e.g., one to two years).

An Iterative Process

While the delineation of objectives may be initiated sequentially, more often they are identified through a series of iterations (Figure 2-2). Strategic objectives, for example, may be further clarified through the establishment of appropriate management objectives and related programs and subprograms of an organization. This clarification, in turn, might assist in determining which activities should be placed within each subprogram. It may not be possible, however, to formulate precise statements of strategic and management objectives until operational objectives and their related activity schedules have been examined in some detail. The establishment of such schedules, in turn, might require careful examination of alternative strategies and associated measures of efficiency and effectiveness. Thus the process must be viewed from the top-down in terms of strategic objectives and from the bottom-up in terms of the organizational activities designed to carry out these objectives.

One of the advantages with this hierarchy is that, if someone begins by describing a management objective, the question can be raised as to the appropriate strategic objective to which it relates. Why is the organization making resource commitments to a particular project or set of activities? In what way will this commitment further the overall strategic objectives of the organization?

This approach can also be applied in the other direction. Those persons that are charged with the implementation of an agreed-upon strategic objective could begin to explore appropriate management and operational objectives in their respective areas of responsibility. As is usually the case, each strategic objective must be supported by several management objectives, and each management objective is likely to be tied to several operational objectives.

Objectives Matrix

Explicit recognition is given in the strategic planning model to the fact that value inputs (personal biases) are likely to occur at critical points, namely, in connection with the formulation of more explicit objectives. This tendency can never be completely eliminated. Therefore, statements of objectives must be formulated within a concise framework that provides an opportunity to clearly identify conflicting positions, that is, statements of existing or potential value conflicts. An objectives matrix, as outlined in Figure 2-3, provides a basis for the identification of such conflict situations.

Conflicts can emerge on several different levels. The first dimension of potential conflict is between the overall objectives of the organization and those of individuals or groups within the organization or served by the organization. A second level of possible conflict arises from territorial considerations (that is, the prerogatives of various units within the organization or community). A third level of conflict emerges with regards to explicit issues and the various viewpoints that can be brought to bear on their resolution.

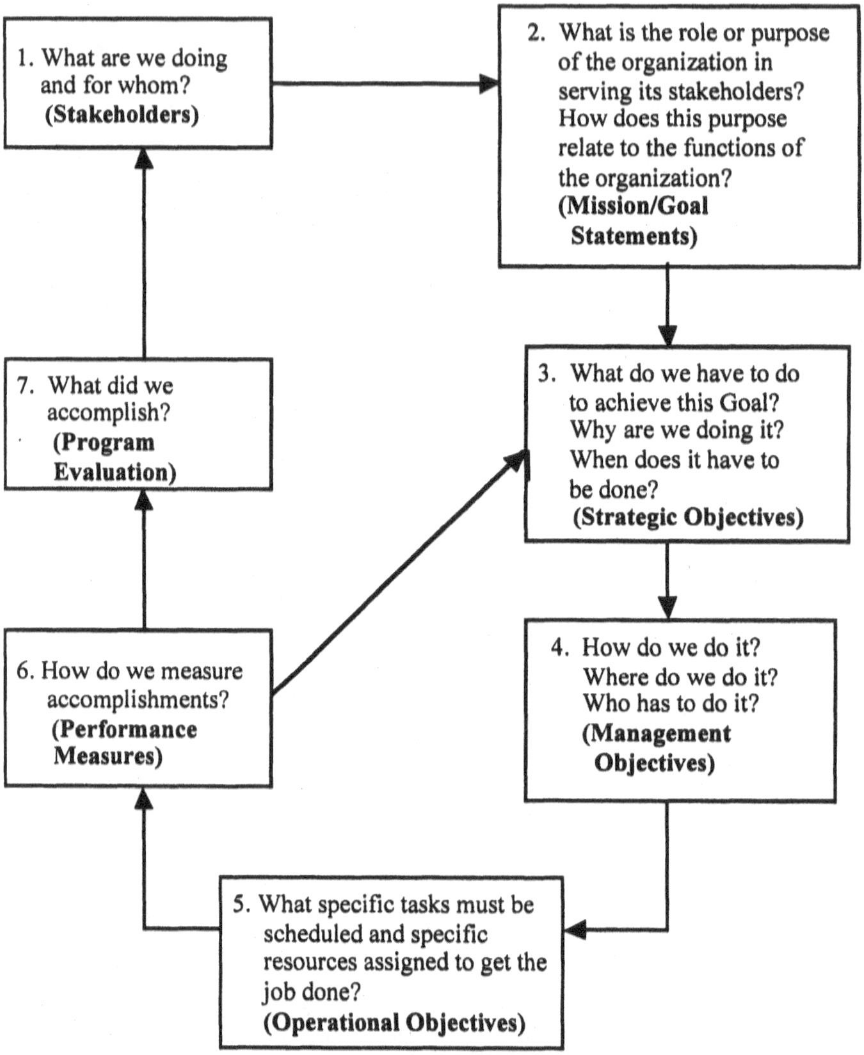

Figure 2-2
Iterative Process for Setting Objectives

	Organizations			Individuals		
	Territorial Prerogatives			Territorial Prerogatives		
	Unit A	Unit B	Unit n	Unit n	Unit B	Unit A
Viewpoint/ Issue 1						
Viewpoint/ Issue 2						
Viewpoint/ Issue 3						
Viewpoint/ Issue n						

Figure 2-3
Illustrative Format for Objectives Matrix

The objective matrix is built through a series of iterations, involving a broad cross-section of participants. First, an objective statement is posited for each identified issue area. These objectives are then categorized according to the three conflict levels. At the end of the first round, a number of cells in the matrix should be filled in and others will likely remain empty. The next iteration should focus on filling in the empty cells by identifying objectives that parallel (that complement or are in conflict with) those previously identified in the particular dimensions. This round might reveal additional issue areas, which produces yet another cycle. The end product of this phase of the analysis should be a fully articulated matrix, with each cell containing one or more objectives. Finally, those objectives should be identified that (1) are clearly in conflict with one another, (2) evidence potential conflict or consensus, or (3) are mutually reinforcing.

The purpose of this analysis within the strategic planning process is to more clearly identify both the potential conflicts and the areas of agreement and congruence. The objectives matrix merely provides a convenient scorecard for recording these points, so as to avoid the tendency to assume that objectives are mutually exclusive.

This approach has been successfully applied in small focus groups through the use of a modified Delphi technique and on a broader basis using a series of questionnaires and public meetings. The matrix can reveal different levels of understanding regarding the broader goals of the organization. Respondent conflict can be expected and must be analyzed. The general premise underlying this matrix approach is that information regarding conflicts among participants will be valuable in identifying levels of comprehension with respect to complex organizational issues. That is, it is better to know about these existing and potential conflicts at the outset than to get part way into a course of action and have it rapidly deteriorate when the conflicts surface.

SWOT Analysis

Many organizations first become involved in strategic planning by conducting an assessment of the challenges that confront them and their possible responses to these conditions. A SWOT analysis (sometimes referred to as a situation assessment) is a relatively easy-to-use technique for getting a quick overview of an organization's strategic situation. Such an assessment involves the compilation of current information about the organization's strengthens and weaknesses and performance information highlighting critical external issues (opportunities and threats) that face the organization and should be addressed in a strategic plan.

A key component of a SWOT analysis is an evaluation of the effectiveness and efficiency of the organization's current programs and processes, which should include:

- Process evaluations based on quantitative data (records review, descriptive statistics, performance evaluations) and qualitative data (what people say about the organization's programs).
- Assessments of program impacts on clients in terms of:
  Inputs: Resources required to operate the programs
  Throughputs: Processes through which the programs are operated
  Outputs: Immediate, observable results of the programs
  Outcomes: How the programs affect the client's life
  Impacts: Long-term benefits to clients and/or the broader society

Techniques of cost-benefit analysis may be applied in evaluating the inputs and outputs of an organization's programs. However, it might be difficult to apply cost-benefit techniques to many of the programs and projects of public and nonprofit organizations. It any case, the results of such analyses should not be used as the sole criterion, but might provide a helpful tool when it comes to making difficult choices about the use of scarce resources. Management techniques for examining throughputs—such as process reengineering, benchmarking, and quality improvement—can be applied as part of this basic assessment.

A SWOT analysis should include:

- Internal and external stakeholders' perceptions about the organization, collected through brainstorming sessions, focus groups, in-person or telephone interviews, and questionnaires.

- External trends that influence the organization, categorized into political, economic, social, technological, demographic, and legal forces, and including such circumstances as changing client needs, increased competition, changing governmental regulations, and so forth.

Senior management must respond to the following questions from their own point of view and from the point of view of the people with whom they deal:

11. Strengths: What are your organization's advantages? What does it do well? It is important to be realistic, but not to be overly modest.
12. Weaknesses: What could be improved? What is currently being done ineffectively and inefficiently? What should be avoided? Weaknesses should be considered from both an internal and an external perspective. It is best to be realistic now and to face any unpleasant truths as soon as possible.
13. Opportunities: Where are the good chances for change or improvement? What are the interesting trends? Useful opportunities can come from changes in: (a) technology and markets on both a broad and narrow scale; (b) government policy; (c) social patterns, population profiles, lifestyle changes, and so forth.
14. Threats: What obstacles does the organization face? What is the competition doing? Are the required specifications for its mission, products, or services changing? Is changing technology threatening the market position of the organization? Does the organization have bad debt or cash flow problems?

Carrying out a SWOT analysis will often be illuminating—both in terms of pointing out what needs to be done and in putting current problems into perspective.

A simple matrix can be used to record the strengths and weaknesses and the opportunities and threats confronting the organization. The intersecting cells of the matrix (Figure 2-4) provide a vehicle for identifying and recording initial strategies that may be adopted in response to the SWOT analysis. For example, if an organization has recently upgraded its information technology to include e-commerce capabilities (strength), it may be well positioned to take advantage of opportunities to accelerate financial and other transactions using the Internet.

Current strategies—patterns of operation and allocation of resources—should be analyzed to determine if they remain effective and should be continued in the future. Additional research might be needed to identify new opportunities that can be pursued (e.g., new products or services, new target markets, etc.), which may include an identification of start-up costs, competitor analyses, long-term financial projections, and break-even analyses. The products of a SWOT analysis include a database of quality information and a list of critical issues—the most important issues with which the organization needs to deal.

Delineating a Planning Horizon

A planning horizon is the farthest point that can be anticipated based on an interpretation of what is known about existing conditions and emerging trends. As with the natural horizon, the planning horizon continues to recede as the body of information on which it is based is enlarged and clarified. As a consequence,

	STRENGTHS List strengths	**WEAKNESSES** List weaknesses
OPPORTUNITIES List opportunities	Use strengths to take advantage of opportunities	Overcome weaknesses by taking advantage of opportunities
THREATS List threats	Use strengths to avoid threats	Minimize weaknesses and avoid threats

Figure 2-4
SWOT Matrix

adjustments in long-range goals and objectives are both necessary and possible. Therefore, the horizon concept provides a more dynamic approach to strategic planning.

The planning horizon of any organization or community can be determined through the application of both objectives (measurable) and subjective criteria. The service capacity of the organization, for example, might represent one such criterion. Optimal staff-client ratios may provide another criterion. In both of these examples, the criteria are closely ties to the availability of resources. And the criteria must be adjusted as resource availability changes. Some horizon criteria are products of the level of technology available at any given time. Other criteria are established on a somewhat more subjective basis, which might be altered (and should be re-evaluated) from time to time as changes occur in the demographics of the community or in the organization's client profiles.

A strategic plan formulated on the horizon concept yields a series of policy alternatives to guide future activities toward some desired state. The horizon concept offers the basis for a thesis rather than merely a synthesis—the more traditional cumulative approach to planning. This thesis emerges from a series of hypotheses or what-if studies, whereby various mixes of programs to serve the needs of the community (or constituent groups within the community) are explored within the overall parameters of the planning horizon.

Each alternative has different implications for the distribution and management of strategic facilities and related resource requirements. A number of combinations and permutations are possible based on a relatively well defined set of pure alternatives. From these hypotheses, the mix that best fits the mission statement can be identified and set forth as the thesis of what should be (that is, the desired future state of the community or organization). Strategies, programs, and policies can then be developed to implement this chosen alternative.

Formulating Strategies and Analyzing Alternatives

Strategies focus on the approaches to be taken to achieve the general and specific results sought by the goals and objectives that have been delineated. Ideally, a set of goals and objectives is agreed upon and then the critical issues that need to be addressed in order to achieve those goals and objectives are identified. It may not possible, however, to reach broad consensus on goals and objectives, in which case it may be necessary to move directly from a review of the mission, mandate, and SWOT analyses to the identification of strategic issues.[10]

Hierarchy of Strategies

Strategies typically are a blend of deliberate and purposeful actions and as-needed reactions to unanticipated developments and external pressures. Since strategies are the *means* for achieving objectives, it follows that three different categories or levels of strategies can be identified:

1. Organizational strategies reflect strategic objectives and outline planned avenues for organizational development (e.g., develop new program initiatives, collaborations, mergers, acquisitions, etc.).
2. Programmatic strategies are designed to implement management objectives and address how to develop, manage, and deliver programs (e.g., implement prenatal health care services for disadvantaged expectant mothers).
3. Functional strategies focus on administrative and support needs and their impacts on the organization's efficiency and effectiveness (e.g., install a financial system based on an accrual method of accounting).

Strategies involve a blend of rational, scientific initiatives, and intuitive, educated best guesses. An effort should be made to identify ways to synthesize opportunities and strengths. Making lists of critical issues and then brainstorming how organizational strengths or other skills can be applied to address these critical issues often can result in the identification of viable strategies. It is important to ask several key questions during this evaluation. Does the proposed strategy address the critical issue? Is it aligned with the organization's mission?

Is this approach financially viable? Frequently at this stage, additional information will be required and/or the conclusions reached during the SWOT analysis might need to be reevaluated.

Strategy making is a dynamic process. Rarely are strategies so well conceived and durable that they can avoid periodic reevaluation, refinement, and recasting as needed. Even the best-laid strategic plans must be adapted to shifting conditions, changing constituent needs and preferences, and emerging opportunities and challenges. The maneuvering of competing organizations, experience of what is and is not working, and fresh thinking about how to improve the organization's performance should be incorporated into an evolving strategic plan. Frequent fine tuning and tweaking of strategies is quite normal. Strategies are formed over a period of time and then reformed as changes begin to mount. Key elements of an organization's strategies often emerge in bits and pieces as a blend of holdover approaches, fresh actions and reactions, and potential approaches still in the planning stage.

Quantum changes in strategies are needed occasionally, especially in crisis situations (where many adjustments often must be made quickly to produce a substantially new strategy almost overnight). However, such major changes cannot be made too often without creating undue confusion and disrupting ongoing performance. When strategies change so rapidly and fundamentally that the plan must undergo major overhauls every few months, managers are almost certainly guilty of poor strategic analysis, erratic decision making, and weak "strategizing."[11] Well-crafted strategies normally have a life of at least several years, requiring only minor adjustments to keep them in tune with changing circumstances.

Analyzing Program Alternatives

Program alternatives provide the fundamental building blocks for strategic planning. A program alternative can be defined as a group of interdependent, closely related activities or services that contribute to a common objective or set of objectives. Each alternative should bring together all costs associated with its execution—a time-span of expenditures that often extends beyond the current fiscal period.

A set of activities, cutting across several agencies or departments, focusing on problems of juvenile delinquency can constitute a program. The establishment of a trauma unit in a hospital emergency room is an example of a program. The internal auditing process within the controller's office might be defined as a program. A university research center concentrating on the environmental sciences might be treated as a program or might have a number of programs associated with its research mission.

Formulating program alternatives is perhaps the most critical part of the strategic planning process. Some program alternatives may focus on issues that are relevant to the organization as a whole. The majority of these alternatives, however, relate to management (programmatic or budgetary) concerns and operational or tactical activities. An effort should be made to specify the key results to be accomplished within a specific time period. While program alternatives should be realistic and attainable, they should also present a challenge to improve conditions consistent with existing policies, practices, and procedures. A program alternative must also be consistent with the resources available (or anticipated) and should assign responsibility and accountability, even in joint efforts.

Most public programs extend beyond the period of the annual budget. Therefore decisions regarding the allocation of resources can have significant implications well beyond the fiscal year under consideration. The extended time horizon of strategic planning makes explicit provision for this characteristic of public resource commitment by shifting the focus of decision from the traditional one-year cycle to a longer time frame. Multi-year program plans should be developed as inputs to each year's budget deliberations. These multi-year statements must be more than linear extrapolations of the current commitments and must reflect the complex shift in demands from increasing or decreasing constituent groups.

Emphasis on program alternatives involves a shift in focus from traditional groupings of activities, based on organizational lines of responsibilities, to programs and subprograms directed toward the achievement of explicitly identified public objectives. A shift is also evident in the approach to resource allocation (budgeting). The traditional line-item/object of expenditure budget focuses on inputs, such as expenditures for personnel, material and supplies, travel, and equipment. The programmatic approach tends to emphasize the outputs of particular efforts that might involve more than one public agency or organizational unit.

Explicit Policy Sets

Various policies are adopted to support efforts to implement strategies and achieve stated objectives. Policies clarify what can and cannot be done in pursuit of an organization's objectives. They guide decision making and facilitate solutions to repetitive or recurring problems. Policies provide a basis for management control, promote consistency and coordination across organizational units, and reduce the amount of time managers must spend making decisions. They outline an organization's expectations of its employees. They set boundaries, constraints, and limits on the kind of administrative action that can be taken to reward and sanction behavior. Policies clarify what work is to be done and by whom. They promote the delegation of decision making to appropriate managerial levels where various problems usually arise.

In the context of strategic planning, policy statements are intended to cover the range of actions required from the identification of goals and objectives to the point at which those goals and objectives are attained. Therefore, the formulation of policy embraces various points on a continuum of means, ranging from long-range, general, and educational objectives to more immediate, specific, and action-oriented programs. The number of points along this continuum, of course, will vary from situation to situation.

Five categories of policy might be suggested, ranging from norms and values on the one hand to relatively specific procedural guidelines on the other.

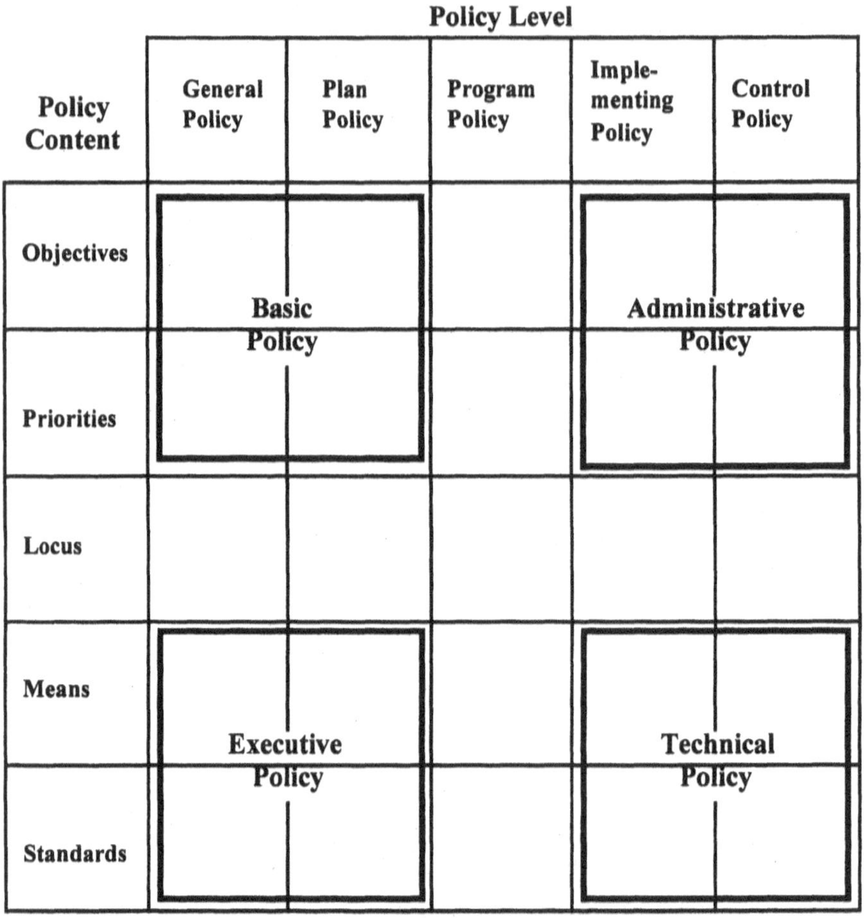

Figure 2-5 Multiple-Policy Matrix

General policies anchor one end of the continuum and control policies anchor the other. Between these extremes are arrayed strategic policies, program policies, and implementation policies (see Figure 2-5).

The other dimension of this policy matrix is defined by (1) what is to be accomplished (objectives), (2) when it is to be accomplished (priorities), (3) where it is to be accomplished (locus), (4) how it is to be accomplished (means), and (5) standards for the evaluation of accomplishments. These five factors help to define the content of policy statements.

As shown in Figure 2-5, four quadrants in the policy matrix require the attention of various participants in the policy-making process. Basic policy is primarily of a strategic nature and focuses on objectives and priorities. Executive policy is required to establish operational means and standards within the framework of the strategic plan. The objectives and priorities of implementation and control are part of the realm of administrative policy, whereas the means and standards of implementation and control, in most instances, are technical in nature. Each of these quadrants suggests a particular realm of responsibility for the formulation of policy and, furthermore, delimits the focus and emphasis appropriate to each of these realms. The notion of explicit policy sets, therefore, underlines the importance of maintaining these parameters to ensure that one policy quadrant does not encroach unduly on the responsibilities of another quadrant.

The area formed by the demarcation between these four quadrants also is important to define. The vertical plane represents the trade-offs that must be made between executive and administrative policy, while the horizontal plane represents the overlap between strategic, managerial, and operational considerations. It is in these areas that conflicts between policies are most likely to occur.

Effectiveness measures must be formulated and applied to monitor the achievement of goals and objectives. Effectiveness measures involve a scoring technique for determining the status of an organization at certain points in time. They are indicators that measure both direct and indirect impacts of specific resource allocations in the pursuit of certain goals and objectives.

Effectiveness measures can be defined by (1) establishing current levels and types of performance in the organization in discrete categories, (2) estimating the current impacts of resources on this performance, and then (3) defining the desired levels and types of performance. The development of positive statements of performance provides a base from which change can be defined and evaluated.

Performance must be defined in output-oriented terms based on a vocabulary of understandable policy and program variables. Policy and program variables, in turn, must identify administrative and executive policies and those patterns of performance to be affected. An important assumption in the development of effectiveness measures is that they can be derived or inferred from current conditions (but are not limited to those conditions). Current operations and their effects must be continually monitored (through the basic data collection component of the strategic planning model). This continuous evaluation is probably the most effective means available for initiating a strategic planning and decision-making system within an existing organizational structure.

Strategic Plan Implementation

Webster's Dictionary suggests that "to implement" means "to provide for the accomplishment or carrying into effect of a purpose." In the context of strategic planning, implementation is the process by which an organization moves from the formulation of a strategic plan into the operations necessary to achieve the specific objectives identified within the plan.

The Written Plan

The first step in the implementation of a strategic plan is to put it down on paper—to draft a final planning document and submit it for review by key decision makers. The following sections are commonly included in a strategic plan:

1. Introduction or cover letter by the chief executive officer, giving a "stamp of approval" to the plan.
2. Executive summary to provide the reader with an understanding as to what the organization aims to accomplish and what are most important components of the strategic plan.
3. *Organization profile and history* to provide a context for the strategic plan.
4. *Critical issues* to make explicit the strategic thinking and assumptions behind the plan.
5. *Mission and vision statements*, which should be capable of standing alone without any introductory text.
6. *Strategic objectives* that specify what the organization proposes to do and why and the organizational strategies that outline proposed avenues for organizational development.
7. *Management objectives* that describe specific program actions in terms of how and where specific resources (project budgets) will be used and the programmatic strategies that address how to develop, manage, and deliver programs and projects.
8. *Operational objectives* associated with the implementation and control of specific tasks and the assignment of specific resources and the *functional strategies* that focus on administrative and support needs and their impacts on the organization's efficiency and effectiveness
9. *Appendices* to include any additional documentation that will enhance the readers' understanding of the plan.

Senior staff should be consulted to determine whether subsequent detailed action plans can be developed for accomplishing the goals and objectives proposed by the strategic plan. Three important attributes of a good annual operating plan are:

1. An appropriate level of detail—enough to guide the work but not so much that it becomes overwhelming, confusing, or unnecessarily constrains creativity;
2. A format that allows for periodic reports on progress toward specific goals and objectives; and
3. A structure that coincides with the strategic plan—goal statements for both levels should be the same, while objective statements may differ with greater specificity evident in the operating plan.

The strategic plan should answer key questions about priorities and directions in sufficient detail to serve as a guide for action plans. Real and potential conflicts should be identified, because such conflicts, if left unresolved, will inevitably undermine the potency of the strategic plan.

Implementation Feasibility Analysis

A strategic plan is successfully implemented if the actual operations correspond reasonably well to the planned operations and the actual outcomes correspond to the planned or anticipated outcomes. Organizations often are more accustomed to measuring activity levels in terms of inputs (dollars spent) rather than the outputs produced (objectives achieved). The same dollars spent on different objectives (or on alternative approaches to the same objective) might yield greatly varied results. Systematic analysis of program outputs is a cornerstone of more effective management. To undertake such analyses, explicit program measures (performance measures and measures of effectiveness) must be identified and quantified.

Two basic approaches to program analysis are:

1. Fixed cost approach, where the objective is to maximize benefits for an established level of costs or predetermined budget allocation; and
2. Fixed benefits approach, where the objective is to determine the minimum level of expenditure necessary to achieve some agreed-upon level of benefits.

The first approach often characterizes cost-benefit analyses. The second is frequently followed in cost-effectiveness analysis.

Under the cost-benefit approach, an alternative is selected based on its marginal benefit/cost ratio—for an alternative to be chosen, the increase in benefits must be greater than the increase in costs. Cost-benefit analysis assumes that both costs and benefits are capable of being expressed in the same monetary units. Cost-effectiveness measures, on the other hand, help to determine the alternative that provides the most effectiveness for the least cost.

Many of the activities of government and nonprofit organizations cannot be sufficiently quantified for successful application of the techniques of cost-benefit analysis. As a consequence, rough surrogates often are developed to approximate the monetary measures of costs and benefits. It is important to recognize, however, that many decisions regarding the delivery of public services cannot be predicated solely on a positive cost-benefit ratio (in which the measurable benefits exceed the costs). It might be necessary to commit public resources to the resolution of critical problems where the benefits are long-term, intangible, and/or not measurable in specific monetary terms.

Ideally, an analysis of the feasibility of implementing a new program or policy should be performed prior to making the final selection, since an alternative that is highly cost-effective might be very difficult to implement. All too often, however, policy makers assume that if they can design it, someone else can implement and manage it. Many public policies are adopted with little thought to the particular actions that will be necessary to implement them and scant attention to the specifics of program management.

This reliance on bureaucratic discretion merely shifts the responsibility for authentic policy making to the administrative apparatus. A major factor in making a choice from among the available alternatives is likely to be the relative difficulty of managing a program or project. Therefore, the implementation of broad public policy often takes the path of least resistance, rather than the most appropriate course to an effective solution.

Even if an implementation feasibility analysis is not performed until after the decision on a specific program has been made, useful knowledge can be gained which, in turn, will likely increase the probability of successful implementation. Planning must be an iterative process, involving continuous refinement and modification as dictated by changing circumstances in program delivery. The probability that revisions will be required increases significantly as the time-span of the decisions increase.

An analysis of implementation feasibility can be costly in terms of both financial and other resources. Therefore, the need for such an assessment should be determined base on an examination of each alternative on two dimensions:

1. The degree of consensus among the individuals and groups involved in or affected by the program and
2. The magnitude of change that each program represents when measured against existing policies.

The degree of consensus should be based on an evaluation of the attitudes of at least five groups:

1. The target group—those who will benefit from the project or program and/or will be required to adapt to new patterns of action.
2. Political leadership, consisting of elected officials in legislative and executive positions, party leaders, and influential political actors.
3. Administrative and operating bureaucracies directly charged with policy execution and program management.
4. Elites in active constituencies—organized publics, interest groups, and community leaders.
5. Individuals and professional organizations that serve as oversight groups, such as consultants, internal analysts, policy research contractors, and program evaluators.

Incremental policy changes, in which new programs depart only slightly from present programs, require the least change. New programs designed to foster sweeping developmental and social changes require much higher degrees of change and therefore are more difficult to implement.

Performance Measures

Evaluation has been a watchword in both the private and public sectors for over four decades. Despite considerable fanfare, however, systematic evaluation of public programs and policies remains more a promise than a practice. Public goals and objectives often are nebulous and ill defined. Consequently, the measurement of program results is often even more elusive. As Wholey has pointed out, "From the point of view of decision-makers, evaluation is a dangerous weapon. They don't want evaluation if it will yield the 'wrong' answers about programs in which they are interested."[12] Thus, in spite of the emphasis placed in strategic planning on evaluation, its application has largely been limited to postmortems of abandoned or drastically altered programs or has focused on isolated components of larger program issues.

Once policies and programs are implemented, measurement techniques should be applied to help in the determination of needed improvements and modifications. Program analysis tends to be prospective; program evaluation focuses on the actual performance of ongoing or recently completed activities. Program analysis and program evaluation represent an iterative cycle—analysis precedes program commitments and evaluation assesses the impacts and effectiveness of these decisions and commitments.

Performance measures should be formulated and applied to determine the level of achievement associated with agreed-upon goals and objectives. These measures involve a scoring technique for assessing the status of an organization at certain points. Performance must be defined in output-oriented terms, derived or inferred from current conditions. Secondary measures of effectiveness—surrogates—often must be used to test alternative approaches and to evaluate costs.

Continuous Process, Not a Panacea

Strategic planning must be a continuous process performed in annual cycles and coupled with direct involvement of key management personnel. The cyclical nature of this process offers an opportunity to introduce the various components in a series of refinements rather than on a whole-cloth basis. Formalization of the process is at the very root of successful strategic planning, however.

The Information Requirements of Strategic Planning

The strategic planning process can be characterized by a concern with the processes by which goals and objectives are formulated and policy decisions are made. It provides an extended time horizon on which to base decisions and emphasizes a more comprehensive program structure. Formal mechanisms are applied for ongoing evaluations in terms of agreed-upon objectives, involving the application of quantitative techniques of analysis. Each of these elements has special information needs.

An underlying assumption is that more rational decisions will be made if management is provided with well-organized, factual information at key points in its deliberations. Any decision, of course, is based on both fact and value. The principal contribution of the strategic planning approach is the strengthening of the factual basis for decision through the development of information management and program evaluation systems.

Such information systems, however, are highly dependent upon the storage and retrieval capacity of modern data-processing hardware and software. These systems, in turn, are vulnerable to the problems of GIGO (garbage in—garbage out) that confront the use of computers in decision making. Various standardized reporting formats and turnaround documents might be required in an effort to increase the consistency, reliability, and validity of information. Turnaround documents are periodic reports that provide data inputs to the information system and information back to the originating agency. Unfortunately, as more attention is devoted to the form of the reports and less to the content, there is the increased danger of the "medium becoming the message."

Completing the Forward Pass

Bear Bryant, the legendary football coach, once said that whenever you throw a forward pass, four things can happen, and three of them are bad. Unfortunately, the same thing can be said about attempts to implement a strategic plan. There are four possible consequences, three of which are relatively undesirable. First, a relatively poor plan can be developed; that is, the theory on which the plan is based is not very good and/or the analysis is not very sound. Even if this plan is successfully implemented, it is likely to end in failure. Such a plan will not meet the needs of the community or organization, since it is not an accurate reflection of these needs. The problem here is not in the implementation stage but in the planning stage.

Second, a relatively poor strategic plan that is poorly implemented will surely end in failure. And third, a plan that is poorly implemented is not likely to be successful in achieving the objectives envisioned in the original planning effort.

The final possible consequence is the desirable one—a good strategic plan is formulated (that is, one based on a reasonable theoretical basis, a comprehensive identification of objectives, and a sound analysis of the feasibility of implementation), and this plan is successfully implemented. The end result, therefore, is a successful program or project. The pivotal component in this formula for success is the careful and complete delineation of objectives.

As Dale McConkey has observed:

> Even the most technically perfect strategic plan will serve little purpose if it is not implemented. Many organizations tend to spend an inordinate amount of time, money, and effort on developing the strategic plan, treating the means and circumstances under which it will be implemented as after-thoughts! Change comes through implementation and evaluation, not through the plan. A technically imperfect plan that is implemented well will achieve more than the perfect plan that never gets off the paper on which it is typed.[13]

This overview of the rudiments of strategic planning runs the risk of generating an impression that the process is simple and relatively easy to implement. This is not the case, however. Communities and organizations that have adopted this approach are well aware that it is not a panacea. Strategic planning will not immediately resolve all problems confronting an organization or community. Nor is its implementation easy to administer. A firm commitment by those who will be involved to see the process through is essential to be successful.

Notes

1. William R. King and David I. Cleland, *Strategic Planning and Policy* (New York: Van Nostrand Reinhold, 1978), 6.
2. For a further discussion of the origins of strategic planning in private and public applications, see Alan Walter Steiss, *Strategic Management for Public and Nonprofit Organizations* (New York: Marcel Dekker, Inc., 2003), Chapter 3.
3. John M. Bryson, *Strategic Planning for Public and Nonprofit Organizations* (San Francisco, Calif.: Jossey-Bass Publishers, 1995), 4-5.
4. Robert N. Anthony and Glenn W. Welsch, *Fundamentals of Management Accounting* (Homewood, Ill.: Richard D. Irwin, 1974), 303.
5. Alan Walter Steiss, *Public Budgeting and Management* (Lexington, Mass.: Lexington Books, 1972), 148.
6. www.redcross.org
7. www.irs.gov
8. For a further discussion of this hierarchy, see Max D. Richards, *Organizational Goal Structures* (St. Paul, MN: West Publishing, 1978), 1-35
9. Herbert A. Simon, "The Proverbs of Administration," reprinted in Jay M. Shafritz and Albert C. Hyde, eds., *Classics of Public Administration* (Chicago: Dorsey Press, 1987), 171.
10. John Bryson [*Strategic Planning for Public and Nonprofit Organizations* (San Francisco, Calif: Jossey-Bass Publishers, 1995), 111] suggests that this approach might be necessary if there is no agreement on goals or the agreement is too abstract to be useful; if developing a consensually based vision would be difficult; if no hierarchical authority can impose goals on other stakeholders; or if the development of goals or visions seems unwise because of the turbulence that the organization is undergoing.
11. Arthur A. Thompson Jr. and A. J. Strickland III, *Strategic Management: Concepts & Cases* (Boston, Mass.: Irwin/McGraw-Hill, 1996), 9.
12. Joseph S. Wholey, "What Can We Actually Get from Program Evaluation?" *Policy Science* 3 no. 3 (1972): 362.
13. Dale McConkey, "Planning in a Changing Environment," *Business Horizons* (September-October 1988): 66.

Chapter 3

FORECASTING COMMUNITY GROWTH AND CHANGE

Establishing goals and objectives for public service programs and determining standards of service for carrying out these programs are essential elements in strategic facilities planning. Service standards often are delimited in measurable, quantitative terms. Standards for public open space, for example, can be expressed in terms of the number of acres per given unit of population and/or in terms of optimum times or distances required for residents to travel to enjoy various forms of recreational experiences. Health-care standards often can be expressed in terms of hospital beds and/or medical personnel per thousand population, educational facilities in terms of classroom-pupil ratios, library facilities in terms of client capacity and time-distance factors, and so forth. While some standards are more difficult to quantify, those that can be measured provide an important means of assessing existing public facilities and programs in light of desired objectives and population or client groups to be served.

Population Estimates and Projections

To translate standards of service into future strategic facility needs, it is necessary to have well-founded estimates of future population, including demographic and geographic distribution. Projective computations were introduced in the field of demography only a few decades ago. As Roland Pressat, a noted French demographer, has observed, until very recently these projects (frequently known as "conditional forecasts") have had no predictive pretensions,

> . . . they simply illustrate the effect on a population (on its total or its age and sex composition) of the operation of certain fertility and mortality conditions, chosen for specific purposes—whether they be hypotheses whose realization is doubtful or hypotheses singled out because they represent extreme situations between which the real situations seem certain to take place.[1]

In short, demographers (and planners using the techniques of demography) have applied the concept of a range of projections in lieu of more definitive estimates of future population characteristics for a given study area. Unfortunately, such future population parameters often are extrapolated from current data with insufficient detail to be of very much utility to the planning of strategic facilities. The statement that the population of city X in 2010 will be between 150,000 and 175,000 does not provide an adequate basis for the development of strategic facilities commitments.

Definitions

For purposes of strategic facilities planning, it is necessary to develop fairly detailed estimates and projections of population by age-cohorts. Such detail is particularly applicable to the identification of public facility needs associated with certain age groups (such as school facilities, health-care facilities, housing for the elderly, and recreational needs).

The concepts of population estimates and population projections often are confused even though the distinction between the two is relatively simple and straightforward. Both concepts involve the generation of a number that is intended to indicate the size of the population of a given geographic area at a specific point in time. Both techniques make use of a basic demographic equation

$$P2 = P1 + B - D + I - O$$

which indicates that the population at any given point in time (P2) is a function of the population at a previous point in time (P1) plus the amount of natural increase (births minus deaths) and the net migration (in-migration minus out-migration) during the interim.

Population estimates refer to the size of the current population in the area. Estimates are calculated in lieu of an actual census count and are used to update population data gathered during the last census. Population estimates generally are based on direct components of population change, such as the actual number of births and deaths occurring between the date of the previous population count and the date of the estimate. In the absence of direct data, a population estimate might be based on symptomatic indicators of the components of population change, such as changes in school enrollments or the number of motor vehicles being registered

Population projections refer to the size of the population at some point in the future. Population projections indicate what changes might occur, given assumptions inherent in the projection method and data. Since projepopula, they cannot be based on actual data that comprise the components of population change. Rather, they must be based on an extension of either current or expected population trends into the future. Analysts typically develop more than one set of projections, each set embodying a different set of assumptions. Projections might represent minimum, maximum, and midpoint growth rates, but all projections should be plausible.

A *population forecast* involves the application of expected population trends to a base population. In the case of a population forecast, there is an implied expectation that the forecasted population will closely approximate the value of the population at some future date. A population forecast is judgmental; it is the set of projections deemed most likely to occur.

Projections do not necessarily lead to forecasts. Agencies often prepare sets of projections ranging from slow to rapid growth so that users might select the forecasts that most closely approximate their needs. Using projections that are on the high or low side can provide a margin of safety in projecting future public services requirements, facility needs, or property tax revenue.

Alternative projections might be based on the same method, differing only in their designated growth rates, birth rates, population densities, and so forth. Or they might be the result of different methods. All projection methods have weaknesses and strengths. Some analysts attempt to mitigate the weak points by averaging together projections obtained by two or more different methods to produce a set of most likely projections.

Components of Population Change

Population change involves three separate components: births, deaths, and migration. Component models consider the separate effects of each of these factors and require more comprehensive and detailed data than usually are available to local planners. Models that use the net effects of the three components are called *noncomponent models*. Most models that project population below the state scale are usually of the noncomponent variety because of data limitations.

Noncomponent models might be based on past patterns of net population growth, or they might relate net growth to some indicator information, such as increases in the supply of housing or changes in the economic base of the community. Symptomatic data often are useful in these models because there is a reasonable correlation between population size and various other events, such as tax returns, voter registration, school enrollments, telephone installations, utility meter connections, occupancy permits issued, and motor vehicle licenses. However, noncomponent models lack detailed age-sex breakdowns that are useful in planning for different housing types, schools, recreational facilities, and other community services. Overall, it is desirable, although not always possible, to consider the three components of population change separately and to combine, not average, their effects. This approach is particularly important for mid- and long-range projection periods because the forces that influence births, deaths, and migration might not be correlated.

Births and deaths are referred to as vital statistics. The numerical difference between births and deaths is called natural increase (or decrease). Death rates in urban industrial nations at peace tend to be fairly stable over time and space. Therefore, age-specific mortality rates for the nation as a whole often are applied to local area population projections.

A crude death rate is a gross statistic that indicates the number of deaths per year for each 1,000 people in a given geographic area. No detail is provided as to age and sex distribution. The crude death rate is based on vital statistics that usually are readily available on an annual basis and is easy to calculate. The formula for the crude death rate is as follows:

$$\text{CDR} = \frac{\text{number of deaths in the year}}{\text{midyear population}} \times 1{,}000$$

If the total population in a given area is 625,000 and the number of death annually is 6,000, then the crude death rate would be (6,000/625,000) x 1,000 = 9.6. Similar calculations could be made for males and females in the population or for whites and nonwhites.

A crude birth rate indicates the number of births each year per 1,000 population, but provides no information as to the age or sex distribution. As with the crude death rate, the numerator (number of births) is based on data gathered from vital statistics registration information, while the denominator consists of a midyear population estimate. If 13,000 births are recorded in a given year in an area with a total population of 625,000, the crude birth rate would be (13,000/625,000) x 1,000 = 20.8.

The general fertility rate is the ratio of births to women of childbearing age (defined as fifteen to forty-four years of age). Unlike the crude birth rate, the general fertility rate is calculated using the population that is most likely to give birth. Thus, the general fertility rate overcomes one of the disadvantages associated with the crude birth rate by taking into account the gender structure of the population.

The age specific fertility rate is an extension of the general fertility rate that provides an even greater level of specification by calculating fertility rates for each five-year age cohort of women, beginning with the fifteen to nineteen age group through the forty to forty-four age group. By using a more narrowly defined age group in its calculations, the age specific fertility rate provides better controls over the bias that might be introduced by the variations in fertility levels over the span of the reproductive ages.

Birth rates and fertility rates change fairly slowly and are subject to regional, racial, and ethnic differences. Birth rates used in population projections often are determined empirically for the area under analysis. It is important, however, to allocate births to the city of residence of the mother. Otherwise, the births assigned to the city's hospitals will not materialize as school children, leading to erroneous conclusions, suggesting an out migration of children.

Migration is the most difficult component to estimate or project at the local level. Migration is subject to relatively rapid fluctuations and is influenced by the size, shape, location, and economic base of the locality. A large county or city will have a lower proportion of migrants than will a small one, since many moves cover a relatively short distance. A narrow geographic entity will experience more migration across its boundaries than will a broad one. A city located close to state boundaries might be impacted by migration more than one that is centrally located, particularly if there is a twin city on the other side of the state line. The population of a region can be divided into "stayers" and "chronic migrants." Middle management executives are an example of this latter group. Chronic migrants account for about half of the moves in any given economic area, and these moves appear to be relatively insensitive to local employment conditions. On the other hand, the location of a major new economic activity might have a very significant impact on the current and future population of an area.

In the absence of official data on migration, it is necessary to examine other types of data that might serve as an indicator of migration. These are called symptomatic indicators since they might be symptoms of migration just as certain physical conditions might be symptomatic of a particular disease. The major source of symptomatic data on migration come from those things that one might do when first moving to a new location. For example, most states require new residents to obtain a valid driver's license within thirty to ninety days after moving into the state. Many jurisdictions require new residents to obtain a local automobile registration after moving into the area. The issuance of new telephone numbers to residential customers is another indicator. Property tax data might also serve as a means of tracking migration. None of these indicators provide a perfect data source for migration, however. They are all subject to intervening variables that must be taken into account.

The intercensal component method of estimating migration makes use of what demographers refer to as the population balancing equation. This equation represents the difference in population at two points in time as a function of birth minus deaths plus in-migration minus out-migration. The intercensal component method rewrites the basic population equation as follows:

$$I - O = P2 - P1 - B + D$$

Assume that the population of a given area in 1990 was 65,257 and the population of the area in 2000 was 72,487, for an increase of 7,230. If the number of births recorded in the ten year period was 10,115 and the number of death recorded in this decade was 5,810, then the net migration can be determined, as follows:

$$\text{Net Migration} = 72{,}487 - 65{,}257 - 10{,}115 + 5{,}810 = 2{,}925$$

It might be desirable to calculate a migration ratio based on the resulting estimate of net migration. The migration ratio would be determined by dividing net migration by birth minus deaths and multiply the results by 1,000. Using the previous assumptions, the migration ratio would be 2,925 divided by (10,115 - 5,810) x 1,000 = 679.4.

The reverse survival rate method is a more flexible approach to estimating migration in that it might be used to produce net migration estimates by age, race, and sex groups as contrasted to the total net migration estimate resulting from the intercensal component method. Estimates of net migration are produced by applying ten-year survival rates to the number of individuals recorded in a particular age cohort in the earlier census. The results are used to predict the number of members in that cohort who should have survived to the current census. Survival rates are derived from actuarial tables (or "life tables"). The difference between the actual number of individuals in the cohort that has been "aged" by ten years and the estimated number based on the survival rate is assumed to be the estimated migration.

For example, if in 1990 there were 14,000 individuals in the twenty to twenty-four age cohort and the ten-year survival rate was 0.983073, the expectation would be that in 2000 approximately 98.3% of these individuals (or 13,763) would have survived to be in the thirty to thirty-four age cohort. If the census count for the thirty to thirty-four cohort in 2000 showed 14,300 people, then the difference of 537 is assumed to be the result of in-migration over out-migration. The application of this information to making population projections will be discussed in greater detail in the case study included in this chapter.

Types of Models

Approaches for making population projections fall into four general categories: (1) ratio allocation methods, (2) mathematical extrapolation methods, (3) econometric methods, and (4) cohort component methods. Ratio allocation methods are used to allocate an existing population projection for a state or region among the subareas that comprise the larger area. Mathematical extrapolation methods involve the application of a selected growth rate into the future. Econometric methods project population as part of an overall forecast of economic conditions in an area and usually generate a population projection by linking future population levels to expected future employment. Cohort component methods project population by examining separately the three major components of population change: births, deaths, and net migration. Cohort component methods generally result in projections with the highest level of detail by age, race, and sex of any projection method.

The choice of a projection method is best made by considering its relative accuracy, the type and quality of data available, and the scale of the analysis. The geographic level of the projection, the length of the projection period, the purpose of the projection, and the budget and time frame implications of the projection must also be considered. The simpler methods have a wider range of application and might be used to produce population projections at almost any geographic level. Econometric and cohort component models have more extensive data demands and might be less appropriate for smaller geographic areas. A classification of well-known projection and estimation methods and the circumstances under which they are most appropriately used is provided in Table 3-1.

A trend extrapolation model is a fairly simplistic model that applies the historical growth pattern to project the future growth pattern. Nearly all projection methods, to some extent, extrapolate past or present trends into the future. A trend extrapolation model deals with the net effects of births, deaths, and migration rather than with the individual components of population change. After past population growth data are plotted (either the actual numbers or the rates of growth), a curve is fitted to the data plot and is extended into the future. Past growth might show a linear, exponential, or logistic curve over the historic period (see Figure 3-1). Linear and nonlinear regression formulas also can be used. The prime disadvantage of trend extrapolation methods is the lack of detail regarding the components of population. Future growth rates also become dependent upon the depth of the historical period analyzed. If the past twenty-five years are examined, for example, the projections might be influenced by a rapid period of growth in the 1980s. However, projections might be considerably different if only the past ten years are used in the analysis.

In comparative forecasting, the past growth pattern of a locality is examined in conjunction with growth patterns of older, larger, civil divisions. The assumption behind this method is that the locality's growth pattern will match that of communities that are more advanced in their stage of growth. Comparative forecasting might be useful for making short-term projections, but it is not

Table 3-1
Comparison of Population & Estimation Methods

Type of Model	Estimation or Projection	Types of Data Used: Historical Counts	Vital Statistics	Other Indices
NONCOMPONENT:				
Trend extrapolation	Both	X		X
Comparative forecast	Projection	X		
Ratio trend	Both	X		
Density ceiling	Projection	X		
Ratio correlation	Estimation	X		X
Housing unit	Both	X		X
Market force	Projection	X	X	X
GKM	Projection	X	X	X
COMPONENT				
Residual	Estimation		X	
Vital rates	Both		X	
Cohort-survival	Both		X	
Cohort-component	Both		X	
Composite	Both	X	X	X

Type of Model	Period S = Short M = Middle L = Long	Scale L = Local S = State N = Nation	Complexity S = Simple M = Moderate C = Complex
NONCOMPONENT:			
Trend extrapolation	S	L	S-M
Comparative forecast	S	L	S
Ratio trend	S-M-L	L-S	S
Density ceiling	M-L	L	M-C
Ratio correlation	S	L	M-C
Housing unit	S-M	L	M-C
Market force	S-M-L	L-S-N	M-C
GKM	S-M-L	L-S	M-C
COMPONENT			
Residual	S	L-S-N	S
Vital rates	S	L-S	M
Cohort-survival	S-M-L	L-S-N	M-C
Cohort-component	S-M-L	L-S-N	M-C
Composite	S-M-L	L-S	M-C

Adapted from Michael R. Greenberg, et al., *Local Population and Employment Projection Techniques* (New Brunswick, N.J.: The Center for Urban Policy Research, 1978).

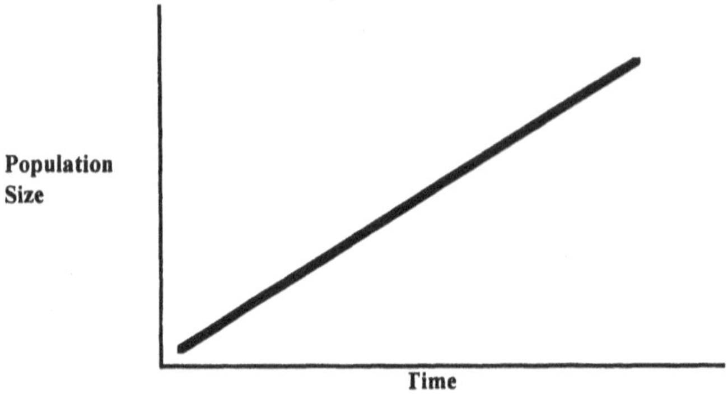

Linear Projection

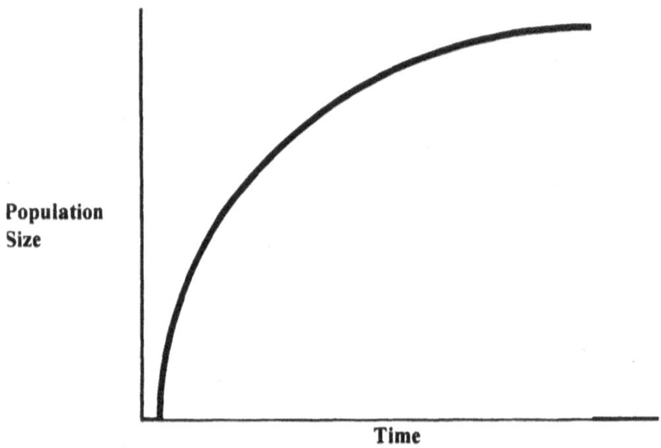

Exponential Projection

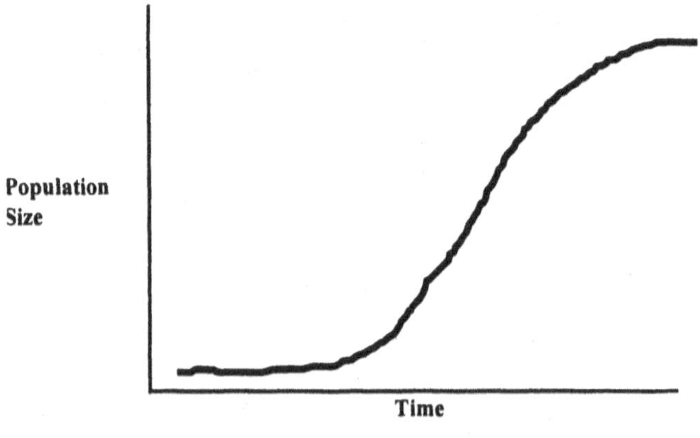

Logistic Curve Projection

Figure 3-1 Trend Extrapolation Model

appropriate as an estimating method. There might be no reason to assume that factors currently affecting the components of population will produce the same patterns of net growth that are exhibited by the older minor civil divisions.

The ratio trend or step-down technique assumes that the relationship of a locality to some larger geographic entity—the county or state—will prevail in the future. For example, if a city accounted for 25% of the county's population in 2000, it might be assumed that it will account for 25% of the county's projected population in 2010 and 2020. Or, if the city's share of the county's population has been growing over the years, it might be assumed that its share will continue to increase according to the same pattern in the future. This method presupposes that projections at the larger scale represent greater degrees of reliability and component detail that are not possible to achieve at the small scale of analysis. As with the two previous techniques, this method is flawed in that historic trends might not hold in the future. The length of the historical period used for determining the ratios also will influence future growth rates. Sometimes there is no simple, clear-cut, historic relationship between a city and the surrounding county or region.

Density ceiling models employ capacity constraints. Such models are built on the premise that the population will either stabilize or decline when a given density is reached. The density model might use linear, exponential, or logistic curves to express population density growth rates. Maximum population levels typically are determined through zoning and land use patterns that affect population density. The advantage of density ceiling models is that they provide useful means of constraining the levels of population projection. They also provide empirical detail regarding probable concentrations and distributions of population. These models also provide a basis for testing the consequences of various changes in zoning configurations. The obvious disadvantage of the density model is the accuracy in the selection of maximum densities. These methods are subject to the same flaws as methods that extrapolate net population growth.

The ratio correlation method is a technique for estimating rather than a projection technique. It is similar to the ratio trend method except that population is treated as a function of some other variables—employment, number of housing units, motor vehicles registrations, or other symptomatic data. Multiple regression might be used to determine the historic relationship of the population to the selected independent variables. Current shares or logarithms of past shares might also be used to express the relationship among the variables. An advantage of this method is that it uses indicators of actual population to determine growth rates. It also can provide details on the spatial or occupational distribution of the population.

The housing unit method is a technique used for both projection and estimation purposes. A family-size multiplier is used to establish a relationship between the number of dwelling units and the population. Dwelling units can be estimated by examining utility or telephone connections, building permit data, vacancy rates, construction data, home interviews, and other local records or by conducting land use surveys. Net changes in dwelling units are presumed to indicate net changes in population. For example, if the family-size multiplier were 3.5, the addition of 500 occupied dwelling units over some period of time would yield an increase in population of 1,750.

Market force methods are generally more complex causal models. This broad classification includes the following techniques: holding capacity, deterministic regression models, multiplier studies, and mathematical programming. Linear regression might be used to formulate equations that will relate population distribution to such factors as vacant land, accessibility to work, land values, the presence of minority group populations, and other important variables. Employment forecasts drawn from an economic base study, income and product accounts, or input-output techniques might be converted to population forecasts by the use of multipliers. The future distribution of population might be projected based on procedures designed to improve economic conditions. For example, an objective—such as minimizing travel time to work—might be sought, subject to equations representing constraints on supply and demand for developable land, availability of services, and other factors.[2] These models are more applicable at the state and regional scales because more information about causal relationships is available than at the scale of local government.

The Greenberg-Kruckeberg-Mautner (GKM) model seeks information at different scales of analysis. It combines historical extrapolation, ratio trend, and density ceiling alternatives at the local scale. These projections are then constrained by federal-state-county population projections developed by component and market force techniques. The model gives the user the option of five separate sub-models to project local population. It is quite useful when state projections are to be distributed to various minor civil divisions within its boundaries.

Component Models

The residual method is used for making population estimates. It begins with a known population, usually based on the last census. Records of births and deaths are examined, and the population adjusted accordingly to produce an estimate of current population. The difference between this anticipated population and the actual population is assumed to be the result of net migration. This method is relatively simple and does not require age-sex breakdowns of the population.

The vital rates method is a ratio technique that relates total population to births and deaths. Ratios are developed between births and deaths at the state and local level using historical records. Birth and death rates for the local unit are then determined by substituting into the ratio the known state rates for the estimated period and solving for the local rates. The rates are used to develop estimated populations based on births and deaths. The estimates are then averaged to reduce errors involved in each of the projections. This method is both an estimating and a projection technique. It assumes that a change in the rate of vital statistics signals a change in population size. A drawback of this method is the assumption that the relationship between the vital statistics and population remains constant. The difficulty of developing accurate ratios between total population and births and deaths is another problem with this approach. Rapid migration will also affects the age structure and will impact the vital statistics, producing inaccurate estimates.

The cohort-survival model is the most basic method for providing details as to the age-sex distribution. However, this model does not account for the migration component. The future population is projected on the basis of growth due to natural increase. The current population is disaggregated into male and female age cohorts. Each cohort spans a five-year period. Age-specific death rates (or survival rates) are developed and applied to each cohort. Each cohort group is then "aged forward" toward the final projection year, with mortality applied to the survivors at five-year intervals. Age-specific fertility rates also are applied to female cohorts between the ages of fifteen and forty-four to determine the number of children born during each five-year period. These births are added to the bottom of the pyramid and aged forward accordingly.

The advantage of this technique is the detail provided in projecting future demand for age-specific needs, such as schools, jobs, or services for the elderly. It is a fairly accurate forecasting technique when migration is either known or negligible. Various methods of estimating and projecting migration can be added to the basic model. The result is known as a cohort-component method.

The Bureau of the Census has developed various cohort-component methods. Under Method I, school enrollment data are applied to estimate the migration component. Net migration is assumed to be the difference between the growth rate of school-age cohorts at the national level and the growth rate in the locality that is under study. Under Method II, the migration component is assumed to be the difference between the anticipated school-age population, based on natural increase, and the actual population of school age. The grade progression method is a variation of Method II in which school enrollment is broken down by grades. Cohort component models are effective in creating alternative projections because of the relative simplicity of varying assumptions (e.g., high fertility rate might be used with low migration, or vice versa).

The shortcoming of these census methods is the tendency to underestimate young married couples, elderly, and single migrants. Other migration estimates can be made by extrapolating migration trends from past decades (e.g., by using a residual method) or by applying a ratio-correlation method that relates migration to symptomatic data, such as number of dwelling units.

The composite model applies different techniques to different segments of the total population. Like the component method, it uses age-specific information on births and deaths. Instead of analyzing the three components of change, however, the population is projected for different age groups using different methods and then summed for a total population figure. The composite model takes advantage of the fact that different methods are better focused for estimating the population of different groups.

The Final Choice of Methods

No population indicator can be considered the best measure in all situations. The choice for a particular application involves consideration of several factors, including the desired level of accuracy, ease of calculation, desired detail in estimates or projections, and the availability of data. In the final analysis, the choice of the methods employed will almost always involve a trade-off of some sort. The chief determining factors in the selection process usually include the level of accuracy, data availability, and the composition of the final product. The requirements of strategic facilities planning often dictate a level of detail that has greater specificity than the level of available data. As a result, carefully constructed assumptions are required to bridge the data deficiencies.

Case Study: Population Estimates

This case study is designed to illustrate the cohort-survival model for population estimates and projections. All projection techniques require the adoption of a number of assumptions, and therefore they are only as accurate and valid as are these assumptions. The calculations and associated assumptions become particularly problematic in intercensual years when the analysis moves further away from a sound database. Nevertheless, the strategic facilities planner has little choice but to make the best use of the data and techniques available.

Population Estimate for the City of Rurbana

Knowledge about current demographic conditions provides a critical starting point on which to build the assumptions that will influence population estimates and projections. Of particular importance is an understanding of the social characteristics of the population (e.g., average household size, average income, racial and ethnic mix, median years of education, and so forth).

An understanding of the community's current economic base and trends evident in the local economy also provides important inputs to the development of assumptions for population estimates. Employment and occupational characteristics as well as the economic base structure of the area should be used as indicators of possible shifts in factors that influence future demographic characteristics. For example, demographers are predicting a continual decline nationally in fertility rates, reflecting the widespread use of birth control devices, later family formation practices, increased involvement of women in the labor force, and the overall conditions of the economy. The extent to which these factors might be present in a given local economy might influence the assumptions applicable to population estimates and projections.

Woodley Blueridge, a senior planner in the Department of Planning and Budget, was assigned responsibility for the development of current intercensual population estimates for the City of Rurbana. These estimates, in turn, will provide a basis for future population projections in conjunction with the city's strategic facilities plan.

Rurbana is an emerging metropolitan center with a fairly diverse economic base that includes light manufacturing and fabrication, regional retailing and wholesaling, and professional services. It also serves as a regional center for various insurance companies. A major state university is located in Rurbana, with current enrollment of 23,500 students, approximately 10,000 of whom live off campus in the community. Rurbana's population is largely middle to upper-middle income families, whose heads of households work in the white-collar industries or are associated with the state university.

Rurbana is located beyond the immediate influence of other metropolitan centers and serves as a regional trade center for the surrounding rural areas. Most suburban residential areas have been annexed to the city as they emerged, although there are some scattered residential areas in the surrounding rural county. In short, Rurbana is a freestanding metropolitan center.

Mr. Blueridge began his assignment by gathering available information about the population of Rurbana from the most recent Census (completed five years previously). As shown in Table 3-2, Rurbana experienced considerable growth in the intercensual period for which comparative data were available. During these ten years, the city's population increased by 30.35%, rising from 76,660 to 99,925. This compares to a 17.2% increase in the state's population during this same period.

Transient Resident Student Population

In examining the data in Table 3-3, Blueridge noted that the ten to fourteen age cohort showed an increase of 38.66%, the fifteen to nineteen cohort increased by 38.97%, while the twenty to twenty-four cohort recorded a phenomenal 91.02% increase. Blueridge reasoned that the overall increase in the enrollment at the university, coupled with the growth of the local economy, which afforded job opportunities for younger members of the labor force, accounted for the significant increase in the fifteen to twenty-nine age group. As a consequence of the decision not to construct any additional dormitories, the number of university students living off-campus in Rurbana increased over the ten years between censuses from approximately 6,250 to 10,000.

The transient resident student population (TRSP) in the critical age cohorts from fifteen to twenty-nine must be analyzed separately from the resident population. The TRSP represents university students who were living off campus in Rurbana and were counted in the most recent Census. The TRSP does not include students who commute from outside of Rurbana. The vast majority of the TRSP does not "move" with the respective cohorts, but it is continually replaced as new students enroll in the university. Increases in the TRSP occur at rates different from the natural growth of the resident population.

The TRSP at Minus Ten Years was approximately 6,250 (these data were derived from the enrollment records of Thomas Jefferson University). The TRSP in the Base Year totaled 10,000. The distribution of the TRSP was as follows:

Age Cohort	Minus Ten Years	Base Year
15-19	1,250	1,875
20-24	3,125	5,375
25-29	1,875	2,750

Table 3-2
Age-Sex Cohorts: City of Rurbana

	Base Year			Ten Years Previously		
Cohorts	Totals	Males	Females	Totals	Males	Females
All Ages	99,925	49,911	50,014	76,660	39,076	37,584
Under 5	7,565	3,815	3,750	6,047	3,048	2,999
5 to 9	8,475	4,345	4,130	6,782	3,474	3,308
10 to 14	8,385	4,292	4,093	6,706	3,431	3,275
15 to 19	9,425	5,052	4,373	7,543	4,842	2,701
20 to 24	12,810	7,260	5,550	9,689	5,528	4,161
25 to 29	9,700	4,895	4,805	6,398	3,235	3,163
30 to 34	7,477	3,731	3,746	4,608	2,290	2,318
35 to 39	5,155	2,480	2,675	4,124	1,984	2,140
40 to 44	5,291	2,656	2,635	4,233	2,125	2,108
45 to 49	5,092	2,480	2,612	4,081	1,987	2,094
50 to 54	4,455	2,111	2,344	3,564	1,689	1,875
55 to 59	4,045	1,890	2,155	3,239	1,515	1,724
60 to 64	3,670	1,620	2,050	2,939	1,299	1,640
65 to 69	3,000	1,286	1,714	2,400	1,029	1,371
70 to 74	2,221	918	1,303	1,776	734	1,042
75 to 79	1,591	603	988	1,272	482	790
80 to 84	946	295	651	757	236	521
85 & over	622	182	440	502	148	354
Under 18	28,956	14,760	14,196	23,165	11,808	11,357
65 & over	8,380	3,284	5,096	6,707	2,629	4,078
Median Age	26.7	24.1	28.2	26.2	23.3	28.7

Table 3-3
Net and Percentage Change in Age Cohorts
(Residual Method)

Cohorts	Net Change	Net Change in Surviving Cohort*	Percentage Change
Under 5	1,518	–	--
5 to 9	1,693	–	--
10 to 14	1,679	2,338	38.66%
15 to 19	1,882	2,643	38.97%
20 to 24	3,121	6,104	91.02%
25 to 29	3,302	2,157	28.60%
30 to 34	2,869	-2,212	-22.83%
35 to 39	1,031	-1,243	-19.43%
40 to 44	1,058	683	14.82%
45 to 49	1,011	968	23.47%
50 to 54	891	222	5.24%
55 to 59	806	-36	- 0.88%
60 to 64	731	106	2.97%
65 to 69	600	-239	- 7.38%
70 to 74	445	-718	-24.43%
75 to 79	319	-809	-33.71%
80 TO 84	189	-830	-46.73%
85 & over	120	-650	-51.10%
Totals	23,265	8,484	36.47%

*Number of persons in a given age-cohort minus the number of persons in a ten-year younger cohort ten years previously.

When the TRSP is removed from the population base at Minus Ten Years and from the most recent census, the overall ten-year increase in population is 27.72% [(99,925-10,000)/(76,660–6,250)]. This increase is still significant when compared to statewide trends and suggests that the economy of Rurbana was growing during this period and attracting new residents.

The Components of Demography

Blueridge determined that the crude birth rate for Rurbana is 18 per 1,000 and the crude death rate is 8 per 1,000. On this basis, he calculated that the population of Rurbana might be expected to grow through natural increase from the adjusted census level of 89,925 to an estimated level of 94,447 five years later, as illustrated in Table 3-4.

Table 3-4
Population Growth Through Natural Increase

Year	Total Population	Death Rate 8/1,000	Birth Rate 18/1,000
0	89,925	719	1,606
1	90,812	726	1,622
2	91,708	734	1,637
3	92,612	741	1,654
4	93,525	748	1,670
5	94,447		
Difference	4,522	3,668	8,190

Blueridge assumed that if the growth rate of the previous ten-year census period continued through the past five years, the current population would be approximately 101,627. He arrived at this figure by taking the square root of the percentage increase in population over the previous ten-year census period (i.e., the square root of 1.2772, which equals 1.13013), which he then multiplied times 89,925 = 101,627. Taking the square root provides an estimate of the effective rate of increase for the five-year period. The tenth root would provide an annual effective rate of increase. Since the figure of 27.72% represents an accumulative rate of growth over a ten-year period, it is not possible to determine an annual rate of increase by merely taking 1/10 of this figure.

Blueridge considered the difference between these two estimates—101,627 minus 94,447 = 7,180—to be the consequence of in-migration. This increase represents 61% of the total estimated growth, which is approximately the same portion of the overall increase in population accounted for by net migration during the ten years of the previous census period.

Construction of an Abridged Life Table

Crude birth and death rates provide some notion as to the overall growth that a given locality is experiencing. However, they do not reveal whether the rate of growth is really high or low in light of potentials for births and deaths. Since the crude rates are computed on the basis of the total population, to provide such an estimate, the crude rates must be refined by adjusting for a more accurate base that includes those components which are correlated with specific mortality and fertility rates.

There is no conventional procedure for determining a specific mortality rate. The problem is usually solved by the application of a standardized rate, through the use of so-called "life tables." These tables are compiled by actuaries and demographers to represent the life expectancy for different age groups in a given population (broken down on a regional basis by sex and by other relevant characteristics). Thus, a life table provides a means of treating age-specific mortality rates of a population in such a way as to show what the mortality experience of a cohort would be throughout its collective lifetime (assuming age-specific mortalities remain unchanged). The construction of the life table merely consists of reducing a given cohort by age-specific mortalities until the last individual member disappears.[3]

After examining several standardized life tables, Blueridge concluded that it would be more appropriate to construct a specific life table for Rurbana. The following component information is required to construct such a table:

1. Age interval and interval size
2. Population in base year
3. Number of deaths in base year
4. Mortality rate, which is equal to number of deaths divided by population in the base year.
5. Probability of dying
6. Survival rate which, is equal to 1.0 minus the probability of dying.
7. Number of a hypothetical population, usually set at 100,000, entering each interval
8. Number dying in each interval, which is equal to number of individual entering each interval times the probability of dying for that interval.
9. Number of years lived in each interval—i.e., (8) divided by (4)
10. Number of years lived in each interval and all succeeding intervals—the summation of data in column 9
11. Life expectancy at age x, which is equal to (10) divided by (7).

An application of these data requirements for the City of Rurbana is illustrated in Table 3-5. To understand the calculation procedures that Blueridge applied, follow the population of 7,550 in the fifteen to nineteen age cohort. From the local vital statistics maintained by the Health Department, Blueridge determined that nine persons died in this age cohort during the Base Year. Therefore, the mortality rate is approximately 0.0011921. According to actuary tables, the probability of dying for this age cohort (given this mortality rate) is 0.00576.

The reason that the probability of dying is not the same as the mortality rate is that the mortality rate is based on an observed population within which all living persons of a particular age group are counted. The life-table population, however, is a cohort analysis. Thus, the deaths between age five and nine, for example, will reduce the life-table base at each year. To apply the mortality rate to the entire number entering the age group, therefore, would understate the actual number of deaths in the cohort and, thus, reduce the probability of dying. This factor is true for all ages except zero to one, where the morality rate overstates the probability of dying because of the skewed character of the age distribution of deaths. Actuary tables were developed to provide the corrections of mortality rates necessary to determine more accurate probabilities of dying values. Over the years, these tables have become an accepted standard for demographic analysis.

Table 3-5 Construction of an Abridged Life Table for the City of Rurbana

(1) Age Interval	(2) Base-Year Population without TSRP	(3) Number of Deaths in Base-Year	(4) Mortality Rate (3/2)	(5) Probability of Dying (Actuary Tables)	(6) Survival Rate (1-(5))	(7) Hypothetical Number Entering Each Interval	(8) Number Dying in Each Interval (7 x 5)	(9) Number of Years Lived in Each Interv. (8)/(4)	(10) Number of Years Lived in Interval & All Succeeding Intervals	(11) Life Expectancy at Age X (10)/(7)
Under 1	1,430	26	0.0181818	0.01801	0.98199	100,000	1801	99,055	7,081,458	70.81
1-4	6,135	5	0.0008150	0.00322	0.99678	98,199	316	310,383	6,982,403	71.10
5-9	8,475	3	0.0003540	0.00188	0.99812	97,883	184	519,856	6,672,020	68.16
10-14	8,385	3	0.0003578	0.00187	0.99813	97,699	183	510,637	6,152,164	62.97
15-19	7,550	9	0.0011921	0.00576	0.99424	97,516	562	471,280	5,641,527	57.85
20-24	7,435	12	0.0016140	0.00799	0.99201	96,954	775	480,029	5,170,247	53.33
25-29	6,950	10	0.0014388	0.00706	0.99294	96,180	679	471,790	4,690,218	48.77
30-34	7,477	12	0.0016049	0.00802	0.99198	95,501	766	477,229	4,218,428	44.17
35-39	5,155	12	0.0023278	0.01119	0.98881	94,735	1060	455,394	3,741,198	39.49
40-44	5,291	18	0.0034020	0.01689	0.98311	93,675	1582	465,069	3,285,805	35.08
45-49	5,092	27	0.0053024	0.02664	0.97336	92,093	2453	462,683	2,820,736	30.63
50-54	4,455	37	0.0083053	0.04049	0.95951	89,639	3629	437,010	2,358,053	26.31
55-59	4,045	52	0.0128554	0.06207	0.93793	86,010	5339	415,283	1,921,043	22.34
60-64	3,670	68	0.0185286	0.08886	0.91114	80,671	7168	386,884	1,505,760	18.67
65-69	3,000	83	0.0276667	0.12893	0.87107	73,503	9477	342,531	1,118,875	15.22
70-74	2,221	88	0.0396218	0.18052	0.81948	64,026	11558	291,707	776,344	12.13
75-79	1,591	99	0.0622250	0.27039	0.72961	52,468	14187	227,992	484,637	9.24
80-84	946	90	0.0951374	0.38521	0.61479	38,281	14746	155,000	256,645	6.70
85-89	461	89	0.1930586	0.62972	0.37028	23,535	14820	76,766	101,645	4.32
90-94	133	44	0.3308271	0.82190	0.17810	8,714	7162	21,650	24,878	2.85
95-99	24	11	0.4583333	0.91392	0.08608	1,552	1418	3,095	3,228	2.08
Over 100	4	4	1.0000000	1.00000	--	134	134	134	134	

Survival rates are of particular importance to the subsequent estimates that Blueridge made. By applying the survival rate to each cohort, the population in that cohort in the base year can be "stepped up" to the next appropriate cohort(s). For example, the 7,550 persons in the fifteen to nineteen age cohort in the Base Year have a survival rate of 0.99424 (i.e., 1.000000 minus 0.00576). Therefore, 7,507 might be expected to survive to the twenty to twenty-four age cohort. If this cohort maintains the survival rate of 0.99201, then 7,447 might be expected to survive to the twenty-five to twenty-nine age cohort, and so forth.

For the purposes of his analysis, Blueridge could have concluded his calculations at this point. However, he continued the procedures to complete the abridged life table. Applying the appropriate survival rates, it might be seen that of the 100,000 hypothetical people entering the population, 97,516 "survived" to age fifteen to nineteen. By applying the probability of dying factor (0.00576) to this surviving population, it is expected that 562 will die while in this cohort. The number of years lived in each interval for the fifteen to nineteen cohort is 562 divided by 0.011921 (i.e., the mortality rate) or 471,280. After calculating a similar figure for each successive cohort, these data are summed. As shown in Table 3-4, the cumulative sum to the fifteen to nineteen age cohort is 5,641,527. Dividing this number by the number of people entering the fifteen to nineteen cohort (i.e., 97,516) produces a Life Expectancy for the cohort of 57.85 years.

Life tables tend to provide conservative estimates of life expectancy, since mortality is exaggerated by under-numeration and the assumption that mortality will remain constant is not warranted. Actually, mortality in most age categories decreases during the lifetime of a cohort.

Blueridge made an initial five-year population estimate without migration, as shown in Table 3-6. In this estimate, he used the survival rates calculated in the construction of the life table to "step-up" the various five-year cohorts. He then applied fertility rates (number of children under five years of age per 1,000 women) to estimate the number of children born in this five-year period. In calculating the number of females in the various childbearing age groups five years beyond the base population point, Blueridge assumed that the ratio of males to females in the respective age cohorts would remain constant. The surviving population without new births is 86,588, or 3.71% lower than the Base Year population without the transient resident student population. However, the 7,063 new children estimated to be born in the five-year period would result in a population increase of 4.14%.

Migration (Cohort-Component Method)

The problem of securing an accurate measure of internal migration is very complex and has not yet been systematized in the way that the measures of fertility and mortality have been. Therefore, this phase of demographic analysis will tax the ingenuity of the researcher who undertakes its study. Several points should be remembered, however.

1. Migration is generally a function of economic conditions—a growing economy will attract in-migrants; a static or declining economy will produce out-migrants.
2. Mobility is not equal in all age cohorts—higher rates of migration (both in and out) generally occur in the early years of economic productivity (i.e., the twenty to twenty-nine age cohorts).
3. Young children seldom migrate by themselves—their patterns of migration are a function of their parents.
4. Communities that have retirement potentials might experience an unusual in-migration at the sixty-five-plus age groups.

Blueridge reasoned that a crude migration rate could be calculated for a given community by determining over a ten-year period the expected population without migration and comparing these statistics with the actual population at the end of that period. Any differences, plus or minus, can be assumed to be a result of migration. And if the socioeconomic consequences that produced these differences can be assumed to hold for the next time period, these crude rates can be applied in making estimates and projections.

Pursuing this approach, Blueridge developed the population analysis summarized in Table 3-7. The age cohorts from ten years prior were "survived" to the base year data over the census period. It was necessary for Blueridge to do two sets of calculations since the survival rates were for five-year periods. These calculations revealed that of the initial 70,410 persons (76,660 minus 6,250 transient resident student population), 64,780 "survived" the ten years between censuses or conversely, 5,630 died.

As shown in Table 3-7, Blueridge computed a percentage change through migration for each cohort from ten to fourteen through eighty to eighty-four in the Base Year. The significant in-migration in the twenty-five to twenty-nine, thirty to thirty-four, and thirty-five to thirty-nine age cohorts is not too surprising since these are years of high career mobility. What is somewhat surprising is that there was not a greater increase through migration in the older age groups (over sixty-five), since Rurbana has many qualities to make it an attractive community for retirement (except for the relatively high property values).

It might be argued that this approach to the formulation of net migration factors is built upon a number of major assumptions that require careful examination. These assumptions appear to be defensible, however. It is assumed that the survival rates computed for the Base Year can be applied in calculating the surviving population from ten years previously. Since survival rates in most urban areas, such as Rurbana, are improving with time, this assumption tends to understate the impact of migration. The elimination of children under ten years of age also tends to underestimate the impact of migration. In short, any errors introduced by this approach are in the same direction and are on the conservative side.

The final data set Blueridge required for his initial population estimates was the fertility ratio of women in Rurbana in the Base Year and the number of children under age five per 1,000 women. These estimates are shown in Table 3-8.

Table 3-6 Population Estimate (without Migration): City of Rurbana

Age Cohorts Base Year	Population Base Year without TRSP	Survival Rates	Age Cohorts Plus 5 Years	Surviving Population Plus 5 Years	Child-Bearing Females Percent Base Year	Number Plus 5 Years	Fertility Rate	Children Under 5
			Under 5	7,063				
Under 5	7,565	0.99398	5-9	7,519				
5-9	8,475	0.99812	10-14	8,459				
10-14	8,385	0.99813	15-19	8,369	48.81%	4,085	235	960
15-19	7,550	0.99424	20-24	7,507	46.40%	3,483	305	1,062
20-24	7,435	0.99201	25-29	7,376	43.33%	3,196	565	1,806
25-29	6,950	0.99294	30-34	6,901	49.54%	3,419	605	2,068
30-34	7,477	0.99198	35-39	7,417	50.10%	3,716	200	743
35-39	5,155	0.98881	40-44	5,097	51.89%	2,645	160	423
40-44	5,291	0.98311	45-49	5,202				
45-49	5,092	0.97336	50-54	4,956				
50-54	4,455	0.95951	55-59	4,275				
55-59	4,045	0.93793	60-64	3,794				
60-64	3,670	0.91114	65-69	3,344				
65-69	3,000	0.87107	70-74	2,613				
70-74	2,221	0.81948	75-79	1,820				
75-79	1,591	0.72961	80-84	1,161				
80-84	946	0.61479	85-89	582				
85-89	461	0.37028	90-94	171				
90-94	133	0.17810	95-99	24				
95-99	24	0.08608	100 +	2				
100 +	4							
Totals	89,925			93,651		20,544		7,063

Table 3-7 Population Analysis: Base Year and Minus Ten Years with TRSP

Age Cohorts Minus 10 Years	Population Minus 10 Years	Cohort Survival Rates	Surviving Population Minus 5 Years	Cohort Survival Rates	Surviving Population Base Year	Age Cohorts Base Year	Population Base Year	Net Migration	Percent Change through Migration	5-year Migration Multiplier
						Under 5	7,565			
						5-9	8,475			
Under 5	6,047	0.99398	6011	0.99812	5999	10-14	8,385	2386	39.4522%	18.09%
5 to 9	6,782	0.99812	6769	0.99813	6757	15-19	7,550	793	11.6987%	5.69%
						TRSP	1875			
10 to 14	6,706	0.99813	6693	0.99424	6655	20-24	7,435	780	11.6328%	5.66%
						TRSP	5375			
15 to 19	6,293	0.99424	6257	0.99201	6207	25-29	6,950	743	11.8106%	5.74%
TRSP	1250					TRSP	2750			
20 to 24	6,564	0.99201	6512	0.99294	6466	30-34	7,477	1011	15.4086%	7.43%
TRSP	3125									
25 to 29	4,523	0.99294	4491	0.99198	4455	35-39	5,155	700	15.4754%	7.46%
TRSP	1875									
30 to 34	4,608	0.99198	4571	0.98881	4520	40-44	5,291	771	16.7341%	8.04%
35 to 39	4,124	0.98881	4078	0.98311	4009	45-49	5,092	1083	26.2615%	12.37%
40 to 44	4,233	0.98311	4162	0.97336	4051	50-54	4,455	404	9.5525%	4.67%
45 to 49	4,081	0.97336	3972	0.95951	3811	55-59	4,045	234	5.7230%	2.82%
50 to 54	3,564	0.95951	3420	0.93793	3207	60-64	3,670	463	12.9789%	6.29%
55 to 59	3,239	0.93793	3038	0.91114	2768	65-69	3,000	232	7.1626%	3.52%
60 to 64	2,939	0.91114	2678	0.87107	2333	70-74	2,221	-112	-3.7968%	-1.92%
65 to 69	2,400	0.87107	2091	0.81948	1713	75-79	1,591	-122	-5.0908%	-2.58%
70 to 74	1,776	0.81948	1455	0.72961	1062	80-84	946	-116	-6.5243%	-3.32%
75 to 79	1,272	0.72961	928	0.61479	571	85-89	622	51	4.0437%	2.00%
80 to 84	757	0.61479	465	0.31540	147	90-94		-147	-19.3905%	-10.22%
Over 85	502	0.31540	158	0.31540	50	Over 95		-50	-9.9477%	-5.10%
Totals	76660		67749		64780		99925	9105		

Population Estimate

To formulate an estimate of the current population that included migration, Blueridge calculate a surviving population for each age cohort in the Base Year population. Blueridge then determined net migration by applying the square root of the Percent Change through Migration data (from Table 3-6) to the equivalent Base Year cohort. This number was then added to the surviving population to provide an estimated population for each cohort five years later. Net migration for the Under 5 cohort was based on the assumption that children will be brought into this cohort in the same ratio as children under the age of five in the total population.

Application of these procedures resulted in the population estimates shown in Table 3-7. These data suggest an estimated population for Rurbana of 99,936, excluding the estimated 12,000 transient resident student population. The estimated resident population of 99,936 represents an increase of 10,011 over the resident population in the Base Year. Net migration (5,572) accounts for 55.7% of the growth, while natural increase (7,776 births minus 3,337 deaths = 4,439) accounts for 44.3% of the growth in population (excluding TRSP). The TRSP grew by 20% during the five-year period (from 10,000 in the base year to 12,000 in the current estimate).

The twenty-five to twenty-nine, thirty to thirty-four, and thirty-five to thirty-nine age cohorts account for the most significant population increases through in-migration. These multipliers are in keeping with the expectation that job opportunities within Rurbana's economy would attract younger workers.

The approach used by Woodley Blueridge in formulating a population estimate for a period five years after the last Census can be applied to develop population projections for a six-year capital improvements program. These projections should provide important detail as to the age composition and, consequently, the particular public service and facility needs of this future population.

The Role of Economic Analysis

As Klosterman has observed: "Information about an area's future population is incomplete without a parallel understanding of the local economy that largely shapes its future."[4] If the local economy is strong, population growth usually is brisk due, in large measure, to net migration attracted by employment opportunities. In times of economic trouble, an area often will experience a loss of population—a direct result of a stagnant economy.

Urban Economics

Economists see the urban structure from two basic perspectives. First, they might pursue a descriptive approach that views the city as a matrix of locations for firms—a necessary translation of a national economy into spatial terms. Second, urban economists see the city itself as an economic unit—as a kind of

Table 3.8 Population Estimates with Migration: City of Rurbana

Age Cohorts Base Year	Population Base Year	Surviving Population	Percent Change-Migration	Net Migration	Age Cohorts Plus 5 Years	Estimated Population	Child-Bearing Females Percent Base Year	Number Plus 5 Years	Fertility Rate	Children Under 5
					Under 5	7,776				
Under 5	7,565	7,519	18.09%	1,369	5-9	8,888				
5-9	8,475	8,459	5.69%	482	10-14	8,941				
10-14	8,385	8,369	5.66%	475	15-19	8,844	48.73%	4,310	235	1,013
TRSP						2,250				
15-19	7,550	7,507	5.74%	433	20-24	7,940	48.81%	3,875	305	1,182
TRSP	1,875					6,450				
20-24	7,435	7,376	7.43%	552	25-29	7,928	46.40%	3,679	565	2,078
TRSP	5,375					3,300				
25-29	6,950	6,901	7.46%	518	30-34	7,419	49.54%	3,676	605	2,224
TRSP	2,750									
30-34	7,477	7,417	8.04%	601	35-39	8,018	50.10%	4,017	200	803
35-39	5,155	5,097	12.37%	638	40-44	5,735	51.89%	2,976	160	476
40-44	5,291	5,202	4.67%	247	45-49	5,449				
45-49	5,092	4,956	2.82%	144	50-54	5,100				
50-54	4,455	4,275	6.29%	280	55-59	4,555				
55-59	4,045	3,794	3.52%	142	60-64	3,936				
60-64	3,670	3,344	-1.92%	-70	65-69	3,273				
65-69	3,000	2,613	-2.58%	-77	70-74	2,536				
70-74	2,221	1,820	-3.32%	-74	75-79	1,746				
75-79	1,591	1,161	2.00%	32	80-84	1,193				
80-84	946	582	-10.22%	-97	85-89	485				
85-89	461	171	-5.10%	-24	90-94	147				
90-94	133	24	0.00%	0	95-99	24				
95-99	24	2	0.00%	0	100 +	2				
100 +	4	0								
Totals	99,925	86,588		5,572		111,936		22,532		7,776

mega-firm, based upon relations between buyers and sellers, contractors and subcontractors (with the household as the smallest firm), all involved in a giant export-import business. The city is a center of production, trade, and distribution. In this view, even local government can be equated to a firm.

The economic city is a complex system that, among other things, provides interaction for the production and consumption of goods. Buyers and sellers meet at all levels; goods are assembled and distributed; labor and materials are brought together for manufacture. Communication and transportation channels are developed and utilized; power is produced and supplied. Financial mechanisms are concentrated in urban areas to assemble and allocate—through monetary processes—the capital goods used in production. These mechanisms also supply the medium of exchange. Space for economic functions is sorted out to the various users—itself a productive activity. Government services are also a major factor of production, since they supply critical human wants and needs—security, control, and regulation. Thus, it must be recognized that the economic system is composed of a number of subsystems, each of which must be identified and studied in order to understand more fully the total economic system and its interaction with other dimensions of the urban environment.

The subsystems of the economic city depend upon a division of labor among firms, involving competition and cooperation within the framework of the marketplace, with certain advantages and disadvantages accruing. These factors, in turn, can be analyzed in terms of location theory, multiplier effects, economies of scale, and marginal economies of operations. The city is "in business," and its economic position might be estimated in terms of a "balance of trade."

Figures 3-2 and 3-3 illustrate the complex economic factors involved in the location of any economic activity. In dealing in a causative manner with major shifts in the structure of the economy, an analyst might consider:

- Shifts in demand away from products with relatively high cost of materials toward highly finished and complex products with minor material costs (supply factor)
- Shifts in transportation structure (in terms of rates) against the cost of materials and finished goods (supply factor)
- Introduction of labor saving technologies at various stages of processing (supply factor)
- Shifts in the price structure for new materials, finished goods, or labor (demand factor)
- Increased competition and substitution of products by consumers (demand factor)
- Increased affluence and a rising demand for more differentiation in products that are manufactured most effectively in close proximity to the mass market (demand factor)

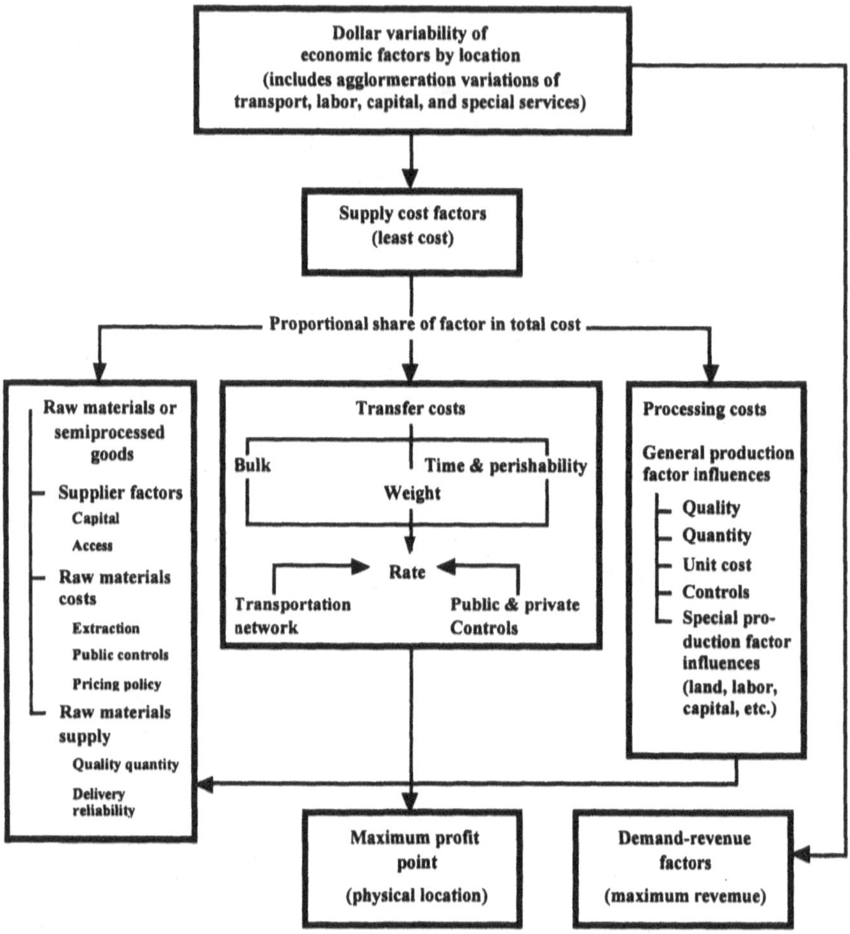

Figure 3-2 The Supply Side of an Urban Economy

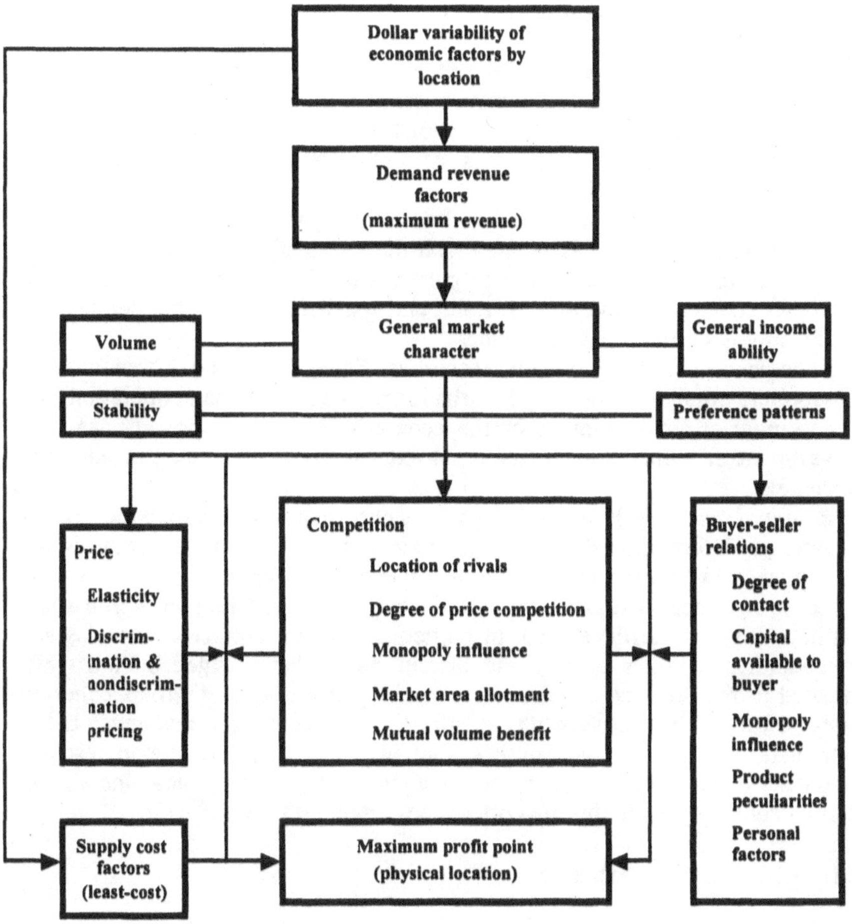

Figure 3-3 The Demand Side of an Urban Economy

Several core areas of study might be identified within the field of urban economics, including studies of:

1. *Structure and growth of the urban economy.* The city is viewed in its role as a component of the national economy—an element in a national system of cities. Problems of urban growth and decline are included under this study area.
2. *Intrametropolitan organization and change.* The focus is on the spatial dimensions of the urban economy, in terms of the organization of economic activities, their relations to the form of the city, and the allocation of economic resources. Land use patterns, urban housing, and urban transportation are specific topics of interest.
3. *Urban public services and welfare.* Primary concern is with the urban public economy. Problems associated with the efficient allocation of public resources and the interaction of the public and private sectors are addressed. Topics covered include federal, state, and local finance and the demand for and supply of urban public services.
4. *Economics and urban human resources.* Focal topics are households as suppliers of labor services in the urban market and the urban population as a consumer of final products of the economy. Migration, poverty, and investment of human capital (including education) are examined in an urban context.
5. *Regional accounts.* Primary focus of this core area is the systematic organization of information flows for economic analysis. The urban region is the relevant unit for the application of urban economic analysis.

These core areas of urban economics have grown at different rates, and some are still relatively underdeveloped. In particular, human resource economics and the economics of urban poverty and discrimination have lagged behind when compared to the other core areas, reflecting in part the lack of group cohesion among researchers concerned with specific topics under these headings. Labor economists, consumption economists, human ecologists, and human resource economists have rather diverse points of view, so that communications among potential contributions to this area of concern often has been difficult.

Economic Impact Studies

Economic impact studies examine the phenomena of dollar inputs entering a regional economic structure, the process by which dollars circulate throughout the system, the process of dollars leaving the system as regional output, and the total wealth generated and its distribution (see Figure 3-4). Economic inputs create (1) economic impacts (employment, taxes, etc.); (2) political impacts (public revenues, service demands, etc.); and (3) physical impacts (spatial expansion-contraction, social diseconomies, pollution, etc.). The function of economic impact depends on whom one asks. Idealistically, its function should be socioeconomic welfare. If it does not attain the function of economic welfare, the process of substantial economic impact is sometimes called exploitation. Traditionally, economic impact has always been associated with the functional concept of progress.

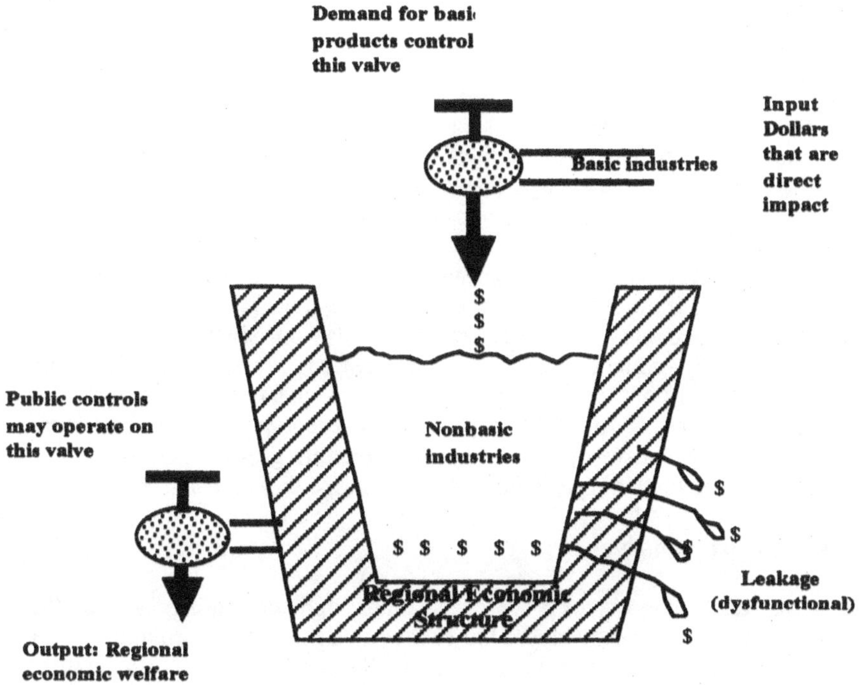

Figure 3-4
The Basic-Nonbasic Wash Bucket Principle

Thompson discusses economic impact in terms of stages of urban growth.[5] In the first stage—the stage of export specialization—one firm or several firms from the same industrial category dominate the local economy. Secondary economic activities are highly dependent upon the economic well-being of the principal industry. As the economic system is broadened and new industries, customers, and/or local suppliers are added, the region moves to the second stage of export complex. Critical linkages exist between basic industries and their suppliers and customers. The stage of economic maturity is reached when new "homegrown" or "own-use" productive activities replace imports. In this third stage, the service sector has reached puberty. In the fourth stage, the localized economy has become a regional metropolis, connecting and controlling neighboring cities in its hinterland. In this stage, the export of service becomes a major economic function. Thompson defines a fifth stage beyond the regional metropolis, which he labels the stage of technical-professional virtuosity. In this stage, the economic system has achieved national eminence in some specialized economic function.

Thompson notes that economic growth might hesitate and stagnate between any of these stages if the momentum at the end of a stage is not strong enough to carry the local economy to the next stage. He also introduces the concept of the "urban ratchet"—when the urban economy reaches a size in which certain functions are "locked-in" (due to capital investment, markets, and so forth), it will not slip backward. While it is not possible to accept any of these classifications as the complete answer to the impact of economic growth, they serve as a necessary first step in gaining a fuller understanding of these phenomena.

Input-Output Analysis

Input-output analysis provides a somewhat more sophisticated approach to the study of economic impact, wherein the economic structure of a community or region is defined and measured in terms of an inter-industry system or matrix. Input-output theory has existed since 1877, when Leon Walras first conceived the basic model in the context of general equilibrium theory. It was not until 1931, however, that the method was first applied to the urban economy in the work of Wassily W. Leontief.[6] Unlike other forms of complex urban systems analysis, the theoretical framework for input-output analysis existed long before computer technology made practical the extensive inversions of mathematical matrices. Widespread application of this approach in an urban context has been hampered, however, by data deficiencies and the lack of adequate models.

Input-output (IO) analysis seeks to model the interrelationships of production and distribution in the economy through a system of simultaneous equations that can be solved for the total input and output requirements of any particular set of economic activities. As applied to a regional or urban economy, IO analysis provides a complete structural description of the transactions taking place and the linkages from each intermediate flow among sectors of the economy. Responses to demands arising from outside the region are also identified. Thus, input-output theory postulates that any given line of economic activity bears a measurable relationship to every other economic activity in the region.

These relationships, in turn, can be set forth in a series of equations (that can be readily solved by computers). The regional or urban economy is subdivided into appropriate sectors of individual industries (for example, food processing, shoe manufacturing, banking, and so forth) or groups of similar industries (for example, agriculture, finance, wholesaling, retail trade, etc.). Interindustry relationships can then be expressed in terms of what Leontief called a huge revenue expenditure accounting system or transaction table.

The sectors of the economic system might be arrayed in a double-entry transaction table (see Table 3-9). Each sector is included on the column side of the table as a purchaser of goods and services from other sectors. And each sector appears on the row side as a supplier of products to other sectors. Thus, the revenue side of the ledger sheet shows how the output of every industry is distributed to other industries (sectors) in the economy. The expenditure side records for each industry the distribution of inputs per unit of output from all other industries. The entries in the transaction table often are expressed as coefficients, derived by dividing each input in a given column by the total of all inputs in that column (see Table 3-10).

The economic sectors shown in the transaction table might be classified as internal (within the regional economy) or external (outside the regional economy). Obviously, the greatest detailed breakdown is with those sectors internal to the region. While some models disaggregate external sectors in some detail, often only one "rest-of-the-world" (ROW) sector accounts for all external sectors. In Table 3-9, the so-called "other demand sector" includes government purchases and investments through private capital formation.

Each column in Table 3-9 reflects the purchases (inputs) of the industry sector identified in the column heading from the industries listed at the left of the table. Payments to employees, holders of capital, and government entities are included in the first two rows of the Final Payments section and represent the "value added" by the industry in question. Purchases from industries outside the region are identified as "imports," shown in the last row of the final payments section. These imports might be either goods not produced in the region or goods that are produced in insufficient quantities to meet local needs. The sum of the entries in each column represents the total purchases by the industry in question. Profits, losses, depreciation, taxes, and so forth are recorded in the table as final payments. Therefore, the total purchases and payments must equal total sales—inputs must equal outputs.

The basic quadrants of an input-output table are shown in Figure 3-5. Consumer behavior—consumption patterns of households and other local final users of goods and services such as governments and private investors—is identified in Quadrant I. Another important component of Quadrant I is the export column. This column shows sales to other industries and consumers outside the regional economy. These sales are regarded as final, since these goods and services would not normally reappear in the region in the same form.

Production relationships in the economy are depicted in Quadrant II. This quadrant shows the ways in which raw materials and intermediate goods combine to produce output for sale to other industries and to ultimate consumers. This quadrant is the most important component of the table, as it is the

Table 3-9
Hypothetical Input-Output Matrix

SELLING INDUSTRY / BUYING INDUSTRY		Extraction (1)	Construction (2)	Manufacturing (3)	Trade (4)	Service (5)	Total Industry Demand (6)	Household Expendtures (7)	Other Local Payments (8)	Exports (9)	Total Final Demand (10)	Total Demand (11)
Extraction	(1)	46	8	150	1.5	18	223.5	24.5	22	149	195.5	419
Construction	(2)	3.5	0	11	3.5	73.5	91.5	0	450.5	88	538.5	630
Manufacturing	(3)	35.5	103.5	347.5	27.5	89	603	319	283	2336	2938	3541
Trade	(4)	13	56	130	18	64.5	281.5	641	40	242.5	923.5	1205
Services	(5)	25.5	55	215.5	139.5	497.5	933	1066	131	707	1904	2837
Total Local Inputs	(6)	123.5	222.5	854	190	742.5	2132.5	2050.5	926.5	3522.5	6499.5	8632
Households	(7)	149	166.5	924	596	1151	2986.5	25	631	0	656	3642.5
Other Payments	(8)	65.25	47.75	406	341	600.5	1460.5	-947.5	-236	-274.5	0	1460.5
Imports	(9)	81.25	193.25	1357	78	343	2052.5	944.5	264	-3248.5	-2040	12.5
Total Final Payments	(10)	295.5	407.5	2687	1015	2094.5	6499.5	969.5	895	-3248.5	-1384	5115.5
Total Inputs	(11)	419	630	3541	1205	2837	8632	3020	1821.5	274	5115.5	13747.5

Table 3-10
Hypothetical Input-Output Matrix
Showing Coefficients

SELLING INDUSTRY / BUYING INDUSTRY		Extraction (1)	Construction (2)	Manufacturing (3)	Trade (4)	Service (5)	Total Industry Demand (6)	Household Expendtures (7)	Other Local Payments (8)	Exports (9)	Total Final Demand (10)	Total Demand (11)
Extraction	(1)	0.110	0.013	0.042	0.001	0.006	0.026	0.008	0.012	0.544	0.038	0.030
Construction	(2)	0.008	0.000	0.003	0.003	0.026	0.011	0.000	0.247	0.321	0.105	0.046
Manufacturing	(3)	0.085	0.164	0.098	0.023	0.031	0.070	0.106	0.155	8.526	0.574	0.258
Trade	(4)	0.031	0.089	0.037	0.015	0.023	0.033	0.212	0.022	0.885	0.181	0.088
Services	(5)	0.061	0.087	0.061	0.116	0.175	0.108	0.353	0.072	2.580	0.372	0.206
Total Local Inputs	(6)	0.295	0.353	0.241	0.158	0.262	0.247	0.679	0.509	12.856	1.271	0.628
Households	(7)	0.356	0.264	0.261	0.495	0.406	0.346	0.008	0.346	0.000	0.128	0.265
Other Payments	(8)	0.156	0.076	0.115	0.283	0.212	0.169	(0.314)	(0.129)	(1.001)	0.000	0.106
Imports	(9)	0.194	0.307	0.383	0.065	0.121	0.238	0.313	0.145	-11.856	-0.399	0.001
Total Final Payments	(10)	0.705	0.647	0.759	0.842	0.738	0.753	0.321	0.491	-11.856	-0.271	0.372
Total Inputs	(11)	1.000	1.000	1.000	1.000	1.000	1.000	1.000	1.000	1.000	1.000	1.000

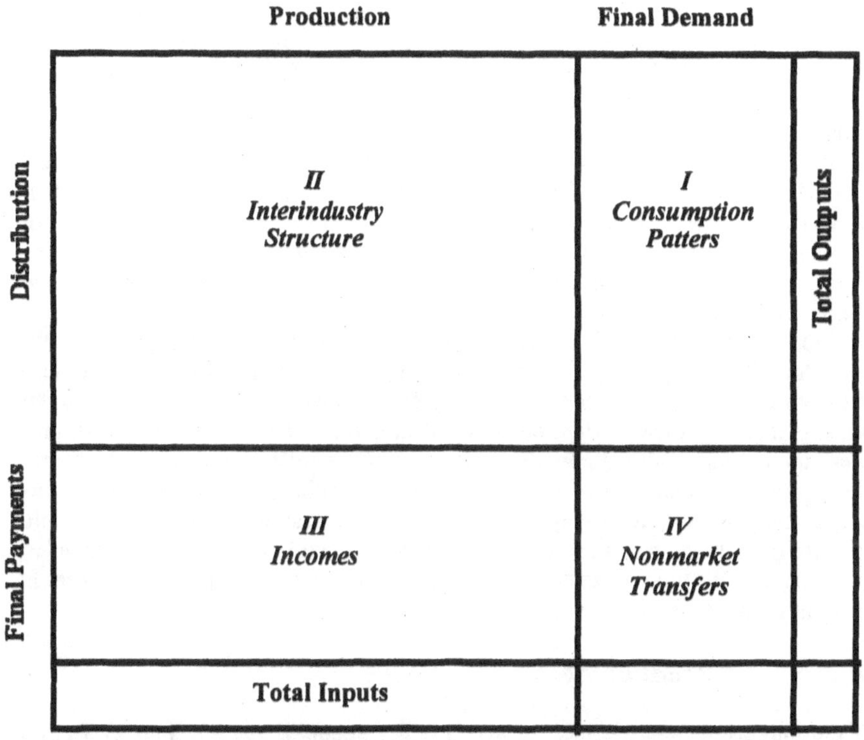

Figure 3-5
Transaction Table as a Representation of the Economy

basis for the input-output model. As many as 500 industries might be included in this quadrant.

Incomes of primary units of the economy are shown in Quadrant III, including the incomes of households, the depreciation and retained earnings of industries, and the taxes paid to various levels of government. These payments are also called value added. These incomes frequently are recorded as one value-added row, since they are hard to identify individually. Quadrant III also includes payments to industries outside the economy for materials and intermediate goods that are imported into the region. These payments to resource owners and to outsiders are called "final payments" since they leave the industrial system of the region.

Quadrant IV identifies primarily nonmarket transfers between sectors of the economy and might properly be labeled the "social transfers" quadrant. This quadrant includes gifts, savings, and taxes of households, surpluses and deficits of governments and their payments to households, and intergovernmental transfers. Quadrant IV also typically includes purchases by final demand sectors from industries outside the region.

IO analysis is well suited to comparative studies, statistical analyses, and certain forms of dynamic problem solving. It can provide a precise snapshot of the intricacies of a regional economy, illustrating the specific indirect impacts of economic activities, so that dollars can be traced throughout the system. By holding the economic structure constant, the effects of changes in income flow (inputs) can be tested.

Input-output analysis is relatively expensive and difficult to conduct, however. As a consequence, it often is accepted as a precise and flawless tool—which it is not. Since it is complex, impressive, and has intellectual status, biased arguments might be couched in esoteric terms to accomplish predetermined goals. There is potential for errors in the collection of data. Improper sector groupings can mask important economic welfare considerations. Input-output analysis is a relatively static approach. It assumes that the economic structure (supply channels and production costs) remains constant over extended time periods. Without frequent (and costly) revisions, it quickly can become dated in a rapidly changing economy.

Income and Product Accounts

As the name implies, the income and product accounts approach to economic analysis involves a system of double-entry bookkeeping (similar to that used in input-output analysis). Unlike IO analysis, however, income and product accounts are established on the basis of asset changes without tracing interchanges in physical inventories. Therefore, a more inclusive view of all forms of income-producing activities can be obtained under this approach.

Until recently, income and product accounts have been viewed primarily as tools for the study of the national economy. Over the past seventy-five years, the Gross National Product (GNP)—now known as the Gross Domestic Product—and other income statistics have become familiar indicators of the well being of the national economy. Annual analyses of economic growth and economic projections have been developed on the basis of these indicators.

Application of these concepts at the regional or urban level, however, poses some very different problems. In national accounts, closure in the economic system can be achieved by introduction of a "rest-of-the-world" (ROW) account. At the regional or urban scale, this approach has several pitfalls because boundaries must be established arbitrarily and might cut across important ties with other regions.

In a system of income and product accounts, the economy is seen as a mechanism for the production of goods and services for final disposition as export sales, private investment in industry and business, government purchases, and household consumption. The first three areas of final demand might be viewed as originating outside of the local economy and are independent of total income. The fourth element—household consumption—is internal and dependent on total income. Since the total income is the sum of external and internal income, a basic relationship can be established between current and future levels of consumption.

An example of an income and product accounts is shown in Table 3-11. Six accounts are outlined in the table. The household income and household transfer rows show the receipts side of the household account. The total of these two rows represents personal income. The household expenditure column details the payment side. The investment account is shown in the capital residual row (retained earnings, depreciation, savings) and the investment column. Local, state, and federal government accounts are shown in their respective rows and columns. And the rest-of-the-world account is shown in the row labeled "purchases from nonlocal industry" and in the column "net exports."

A gross regional product (GRP) can be measured in terms of the expenditures of final consumers—households, investors, governments, and private units outside of the regional economy. In Table 3-11, the GRP is $5,114.8 million, as shown in the "total final demand" for the purchases of goods and services. Household expenditures (personal consumption) accounted for 59% of the GRP, while private investment accounted for 10.7% of the GRP. Both of these percentages are below the national averages, where approximately 65% of the GDP is accounted for by personal consumption and 15.2% of the GDP is generated by private investments. Government expenditures represent 24.8% of the GRP, which is higher than the 19% that government expenditures contribute to the GDP.

A regional multiplier (*K*) can be applied to determine the impact of shifts in either local economic activity or total income, where *Y* is the value added in the local market and *T* is total income (100%).

$$K = \frac{1}{1 - Y/T}.$$

For example, if an external economic activity accounts for 60% of total income and the local market contributes 40%, the regional multiplier is 1.67. In other words, assuming that the multiplier value remains constant, for every $1 million of additional value added for export, there will be approximately $670,000 of additional local economic activity. Or, if an increase of $100,000 is experience in the local income level, eventually total income will increase by $167,000.

While these figures are based on the assumption that the multiplier remains constant, this need not be the case. The multiplier might be modified in making projections if new lines of activity are introduced into a region or other events lead to changes in its relative competitive advantages in relation to other regions. The use of regional multipliers in economic forecasting requires the preparation of projections that are presumed to be in balance with anticipated economic growth in all regions.

Table 3-11
Income and Product Accounts

Account Receiving/Making Payment	Sales to Processing Sectors	Household Expend-itures	Private Invest-ments	Expenditures of Governments			Net Exports	Total Final Demand	Total Receipts
				Local	State	Federal			
Purchases from Local Processors	2,131.8	2,049.8	350.1	115.2	108.1	352.7	3,522.8	6,498.8	8,630.6
Purchases from Nonlocal Industry	2,039.8	944.5	200.5	34.7	29.0		-3,248.5	-2,039.8	0.0
Total Purchases from Industry	4,171.6	2,994.3	550.6	149.9	137.0	352.7	274.4	4,459.0	8,630.6
Household Income	2,970.7	24.9		197.7	93.2	340.1		655.9	3,626.5
Total Purchases of Goods and Services	7,142.3	3,019.2	550.6	347.6	230.2	692.8	274.4	5,114.8	12,257.1
Household Transfers	15.3			12.8	47.7	264.3		324.8	340.0
Capital Residual	754.8	217.9					-422.1	-204.2	550.6
Local Government Income	120.1	94.5			111.5	11.8	28.1	245.9	366.0
State Government Income	214.7	85.5		5.5		102.2	-13.8	179.4	394.1
Federal Government Income	383.5	549.5			4.8		133.4	687.6	1,071.1
External Transfers									
Total Outlays	8,630.6	3,966.5	550.6	366.0	394.1	1,071.1	0.0	6,348.3	14,978.8

Ratio-Stepdown Methods

So-called ratio-stepdown or approximation methods offer a somewhat less complex and less costly approach to urban economic analysis. Under this approach, comparative analyses are developed as to an urban region's share in the national productive activity. Standard measures are used such as value added by manufacturing, retail and wholesale sales, and receipts from services. Comparisons are expressed as a percentage of the larger economic region or nation. By making such comparisons over time, it is possible to determine if the relative position of the region under study is improving, remaining constant, or deteriorating. The apportionment technique—a variation on the ratio-stepdown method—introduces an element of control by making parallel analyses of all subareas of the larger region and balancing the results with the total before proceeding to the actual stepdown.

Ratio-stepdown methods reflect the combined effects of interindustry and interregional flows and indicate where gross changes are occurring over time. However, since these methods cannot trace flows between industries within and among regions, they do not provide a direct measure of linkage. Rather, these approaches provide only a crude cross-sectional view of the gross effects that commodity flows have as they influence total transactions.

Econometric Models

Efforts have been made on an experimental basis to apply the techniques of econometrics to the analysis of urban and regional economic systems. Econometrics consists of the application of modern statistical techniques and procedures to theoretical mathematical models. These models, however, suffer from the limitations of mathematical models in general and the fact that statistical methods frequently are based on assumptions that do not hold strictly for the specific data under analysis.

Econometric models are derived from certain basic economic axioms or assumptions; for example, the "law of supply and demand" and the "theory of the market." Economists assume that consumers maximize their utility, while the prices of all commodities and services and the consumers' income are given independently of their actions. From this assumption, certain properties can be derived with regard to individual demand functions for all commodities and services. Econometricians attempt to quantify and "formulafy" these relationships into statistically testable models. While these models seem to hold considerable potential, to date, their application to urban economic systems has been relatively limited. The complexity of the formula involved has prevented wider testing.

Economic Base Studies

Regional economic approaches—input-output analysis, regional accounts systems, and econometric models—have been used infrequently in the study of the urban economy as a consequence of the complexities of their analytical procedures and major data obstacles. In contrast, economic base studies employ less complicated analytical procedures and are designed to utilized standard data that are reported on a regular basis. Economic base studies have received widespread application and have been a standard technique of analysis for the urban planner for nearly eighty years.

The underlying foundation of economic base studies has been stated by Thompson as follows: Cities survive by selling products or services to the "outside world," thereby gaining the wherewithal with which to pay for indispensable imports, i.e., goods and services not produced in the local economy. By extension, cities rise and fall with the growth and decline of their export industries.[7]

Economic base studies divide the urban economy into two broad categories:

1. *Basic or export industries*—those industries producing goods and services (and capital) for distribution to markets outside a defined local economic area; and
2. *Nonbasic or service industries*—those producing goods and services that are consumed within the local economic area (see Figure 3-6).

Thus, a distinction is made between those economic activities that bring new money into the community (basic industries) and those that simply result in the recirculation of money (service industries). The underlying assumption is that expansion of basic activities usually results in growth of service activities and thus, growth in the total economy.

Economic base theory builds on the premise that a local economy has greater strength and resiliency when its principal economic activities are not closely tied to local markets. It is assumed that a local economy can better insulate itself from economic downturns by developing economic activities that rely largely on external markets. These external markets have a greater likelihood of remaining strong even if the local economy experiences problems. In contrast, a local economy wholly dependent upon local factors will likely experience significant difficulty in responding to downturns in the economy.

Some theorists draw parallels between the economic base approach and international trade theory. Economic base studies focus attention on "export balances," which become a measure of the strength of the urban economy much in the same manner that export balances have an important influence on the position of the national economy. As with international trade theory, rising export balances have positive implications, while declining balances, if allowed to continue, have negative repercussions. In economic base theory, fluctuations in the level of a community's exporting base are a prime cause of changes in urban economic activity. Consequently, forecasts of economic growth are based on multipliers that relate local economic activities to exports.

Richard Andrews has made perhaps the most exhaustive analysis of the economic base concept. He has suggested that a "purely" basic or nonbasic industry is something of a rarity.[8] For the most part, industries serve a mixture of export and local markets and might be more basic or more nonbasic but seldom exclusively so.

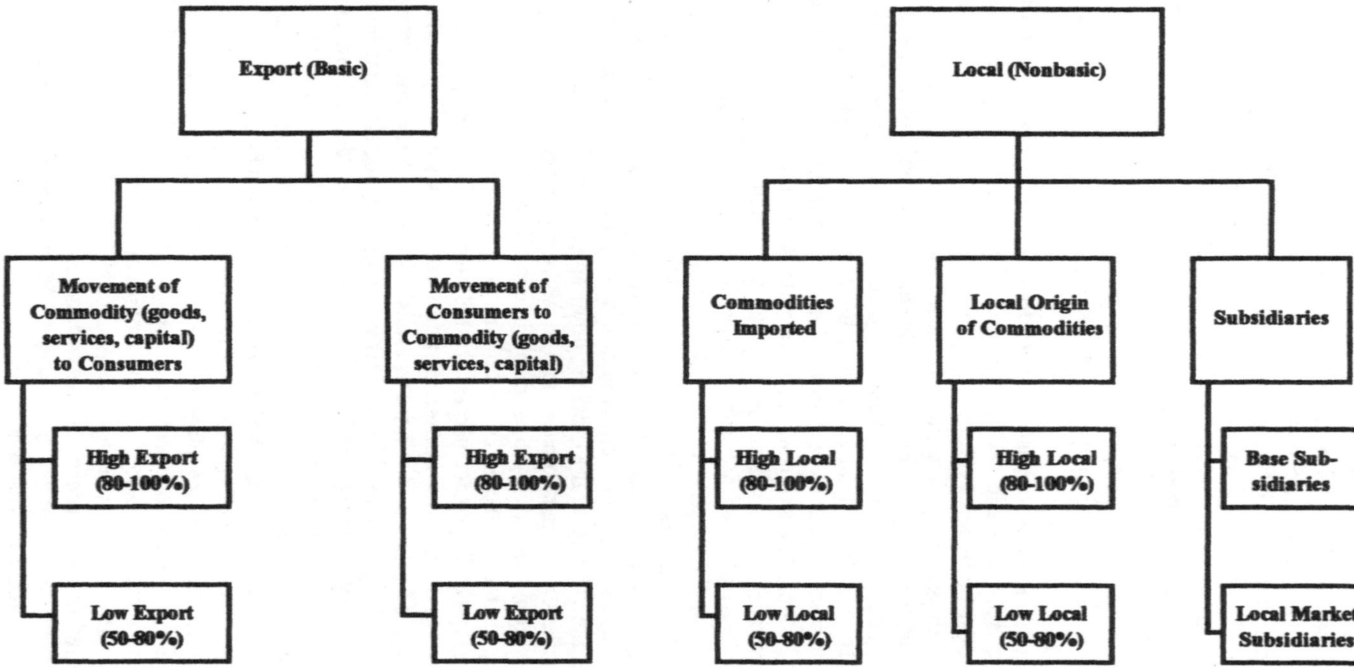

Figure 3-6 Urban Economic Structure

As suggested in Figure 3-6, employment data of some industries or firms must be apportioned between the basic and nonbasic sectors. Andrews suggests that a distinction be made between those firms in which 80% to 100% of their sales is either export-oriented or locally oriented (high export or high local) and those in which 50% to 80% of their sales has such identifiable orientations. He also subdivides class 3 firms (which he called "subsidiaries") into 3A (base subsidiaries) and 3B (local market subsidiaries). Examples of base subsidiaries would include advertising, mailing services, machine parts, package manufacturing, and so forth. Local market subsidiaries might be represented by accounting and legal services, delivery companies, industrial laundry services, canteen suppliers, and so forth.

Where the boundaries of the base area are drawn can influence the determination of what activities are basic and what activities are service or local-oriented. Using the political boundaries might result in too narrow a definition, thereby distorting the analysis. Expanding the boundaries too far might result in an encroachment on the base area of other economic centers. Several criteria have been developed and tested to determine the best technique for delineation. N.B.S. Gras advanced the following guidelines for delineating the boundaries: (1) shifts in transportation systems; (2) service areas of daily newspapers and other advertising media; (3) dependence of outlying financial institutions for clearances and reserves; (4) provision of auxiliary services to hinterland firms; (5) extent to which local facilities are used for storage, shipping, and marketing by firms in the "hinterland;" and (6) "service area" for cultural facilities, institutions of learning, and recreational facilities. William J. Reilly developed an empirical approach through an examination of some 132 American cities. His Law of Retail Gravitation states that: "two cities attract retail trade from any intermediate city or town in the vicinity of the breaking point approximately in direct proportion to the population of the two cities and in inverse proportions to the square of the distances from these two cities to the intermediate town," distance being measured along the most direct improved highway.[9]

More recently developed techniques for delineating the retail trade area include consumer surveys, using household interviews on a sampling basis, and sampling surveys of retail and service establishments to determine "customer draw." Parking surveys also are used whereby automobile license plate numbers recorded in the central business district or regional shopping centers are checked for home addresses against license registration records. Whatever approach or combination of approaches is used, the final results usually are translated into jurisdictional boundaries so that standard sources of data can be used.

The experimental work of Homer Hoyt provided the foundation for the contemporary economic base model. Hoyt observed that when employment is used as a measure, a ratio occurs between basic and nonbasic activities. While Hoyt suggested that this ratio was about 1 to 1, empirical studies have shown that it varies over a relatively narrow range—from 1 to 0.5 to 1 to 2 (with the basic activity computed as the constant). Some writers have interpreted these ratios to mean that for every worker in the basic sector of the economy, a given number of jobs are created in the service sector.

The base multiplier can be calculated by the following ratio:

$$\text{Base Multiplier} = \frac{\text{Total Employment in Year i}}{\text{Basic Employment in Year i}}$$

Various assumptions can be tested, using these ratios, to determine the impact of increases or decreases in employment in the basic sector. Assume, for example, that the current basic to nonbasic ratio is 1 to 1.8 (i.e., each job in a basic industry generates 1.8 jobs in the service sector). In that case, a new economic activity that adds 100 jobs to the basic sector will increase total employment by 280 jobs. If 35% of the total population is in the labor force, the ratio of basic employment to total population will be approximately 1 to 8.

These multipliers have been used in making population projections as well as projections of employment and economic activities (assuming a constant or predictably changing ratio). Unfortunately, these values do not necessarily remain constant for long periods of time; that is, the ratios can exhibit significant shifts, depending upon changes in the economy of the urban area and national economic conditions.

Employment data are also used to calculate location quotients, sometimes called coefficients of localization or specialization. If a given community is highly specialized in the production of a particular commodity relative to the region or nation, the product might be presumed to be an export item. Therefore, solving the following equation for X determines the number of workers that would be employed in industry A if the community produced just enough of that industry's product to supply its own needs.[10]

$$\frac{X}{\text{total local employment}} = \frac{\text{national employment in industry A}}{\text{total national employment}}$$

If actual employment is in excess of X, then industry A might be assumed to be export oriented; if actual employment is below X, then products of this industry are assumed to be imported.

The use of location quotients provides a relatively inexpensive way of measuring exports for a given community. However, the results obtained depend on the level of Standard Industrial Classifications (SIC) applied.[11] No variation might be noted until four-digit SIC codes (or lower) are used. Another criticisms of location quotients is the possibility that a community might be more productive than the national average in terms of output per employee (and therefore would have a lower employment ratio in a given industry). It might also be argued that residents in one community might have significantly different tastes than those in other communities.

Economic base multipliers and location quotients can be generated for various units of measurement, including: (1) employment data, (2) payrolls, (3) value added, (4) value of production, (5) physical production, and (6) dollar income and expenditure accounts. However, each of these measures has shortcomings, and therefore all feasible measuring techniques should be used in any economic base study.[12] The capacity of the analysis to predict future conditions can be further extended and refined by adding other measures and indexes.

Using employment as the measure of economic activity encounters problems of seasonal and part-time workers. Output per worker (productivity) might increase without parallel increases in employment. Rise in productivity might be associated with an increase in the rate and total wage assigned to the individual jobs. While payrolls provide a more significant indicator of economic activity and opportunity than the mere number of jobs, these data are open to highly significant price change adjustments. Payrolls might provide a clue to the standard of living to be expected in a community if these data can be obtained in terms of annual remuneration distributions.

Physical production, value added, and value of production have advantages for analysis within particular sectors of the economy. However, these measures do not apply to all sectors and therefore have limited application. Further, value added and value of production might be clouded by complex price movements and might encounter problems associated with intangible inputs and value products (e.g., educational institutions). Dollar income and expenditures accounts in combination with employment data would provide the most comprehensive measure of economic activity. However, the complexity and difficulty of tracing monetary transactions, coupled with data reporting problems, limit the application of these measures. As a consequence, the two primary measures of economic base studies have been employment and payroll data.

Employment growth generally fosters population growth because job opportunities attract new residents. But the process also works the other way. Population growth creates employment in retailing, wholesaling, personal services, and related activities. In fact, the relationship goes still further because pools of labor and capital that are built up to serve a local population, in time, may foster the growth of manufacturing and other activities that are not directly related to servicing the local population.

Much of the present-day appeal of economic base studies stems from their seemingly simplistic application. However, this simplicity can also lead to fallacious and contradictory results. As Ralph Pfouts has pointed out, the panacea of basic industries has led communities into an economic development policy not unlike the doctrine of mercantilism.[13] Studies have shown that an appreciable proportion of basic industry is necessary for urban growth and development. However, it does not follow that this alone is sufficient for growth and development. Pfouts has suggested that the service component might be more important as an indicator of growth potential than the basic component. Therefore, he proposes a community income analysis as a substitute approach for economic base studies.

Hans Blumenfeld has also identified a number of misconceptions and contradictions in the economic base concept.[14] He notes that the applicability of the economic base approach tends to decrease with increasing size of the urban center and tends to increase with increasing specialization and division of labor between centers. Therefore, large metropolitan centers survive and grow because the existence of highly developed and diverse business and consumer services enable such centers to attract new basic industries for those that might decline. Blumenfeld concluded that the nonbasic activities of such centers are the permanent and constant element—the truly basic sector of their economy. He proposed the substitution of studies that would consider the potential vulnerability of local economic activities to outside competition and the potential capacity of local economic activities to expand into outside markets. These studies would be coupled with "balance of payment" studies that would consider all types of payments, giving equal weight to both imports and exports.

William Schaffer has suggested that economic-base models suffer from old age.[15] So many analysts have built these models with varying levels of quality, and they have been criticized so often that little remains except the concept. The criticisms of economic base studies include the following:

- Short run nature of the analysis.
- Lack of spatial considerations.
- Simple adaptations of national models.
- Data used in these models are normally available for administrative units (counties) that might be poorly defined as economic regions.
- Capacity constraints are ignored.
- Perfect elasticity of supply is assumed for inputs.
- The study area is pitted against the rest of the world, showing no interdependence between regions.
- Multipliers vary with size of region. As a region grows, it becomes more diversified, importing less and so increasing local consumption and the multiplier. Larger regions tend to influence neighbors more and therefore enjoy larger feedback effects.
- Use of an employment multiplier to analyze income changes assumes that employment and per capita income are perfectly correlated. This might be the case in a simple economy with perfectly elastic supplies of labor. However, the world is not simple.
- Exports are assumed to be the sole determinant of economic growth. Many other determinants of growth have been overlooked or ignored because of early attempts to formulate multipliers and the ease with which simple multipliers could be constructed.

Although castigated for decades, the economic base model has survived as a very succinct expression of the power of demand in regional income determination. A recent review by Andrew J. Krikelas provides perhaps the clearest and most complete statement of the current status of the economic base model.[16]

Economic Dominants Analysis

One of the most conspicuous flaws in existing systems of urban economic analysis is that they are not dynamic or continuous. As a consequence of methodological limitations and cost factors, most of these approaches are applied on a one-time basis. More dynamic techniques, such as systems of accounts and industrial complex analysis, suffer from data limitations that make their application very difficult.

Given these limitations, Andrews has proposed an approach that provides an in-depth analysis of selected industry groups rather than broad or universal enterprise coverage. Andrews has labeled this approach economic dominants analysis.[17] He has suggested that the appropriate objectives in the study of urban economics are the determination of optimum size and character of the economic system and the attainment of maximum operating efficiency of the dominant parts of the system as measured by means of carefully conceived goals. Dominants might be export or local in their market orientation. As industry groups, they claim an arbitrary minimum proportion of total area employment—3%, 4%, or 5%, depending on the local economic structure (and cost constraints of conducting the study).

In-depth analysis is based on the hypothesis that the character of the total urban or regional economy can be understood and roughly predicted by means of a continuing study of those industries or economic activities that dominate an urban area in terms of employment and other strategic factors. Empirically, it is often found that employment dominance is an adequate guide to a more complete picture of overall economic dominance. Therefore, other determinants, such as payroll and productivity, can be shifted to later stages and used as weighting factors in the determination of relative importance of dominants in the formulation of development policy.

Under this approach, selected economic dominants (industry groups) are subjected to:

- Macro-analysis—involving national-, regional-, and state-level analyses of dominant industry group economic trend characteristics;
- Micro-analysis—detailed economic examination of a sample of local firms within each dominant industry groups; and
- Integration of macro and micro findings to determine the nature and degree of deviation between the performance of firms at the local level and trends of the same industry groups at the national, regional, and state levels.

A principal objective of the macro-analysis is to provide a more complete understanding of the nature and functioning of the broad industry group of which a local dominant industry is a small part. This analysis also seeks to establish a scale of performance. Trends at state, regional, and national levels are identified against which the performance characteristics and trends of a local dominant industry group can be measured. A basic assumption is that the pattern of conformities and divergences resulting from comparisons of macro with micro data will provide substantial clues to the prognosis of local area activity.

The objectives of the micro-analysis are to:

- Establish an analytical bond between local industry groups and their broad-scale counterparts identified under macro-analysis.
- Identify single problem and problem patterns of dominant industry groups at the local level not revealed by the macro-analysis.
- Extend data coverage beyond the macro-analysis in order to objectify local problem situations more clearly and thereby to provide the detail necessary for positive economic planning.

The product of this analytical procedure is an understanding of the individual strengths, weaknesses, locational peculiarities, tendencies, and general growth potential of each of the dominant industry groups that make up the local economy.

A macro-mirco synthesis involves an across-the-board integration of selected industry group data. It is accomplished by means of the following two steps: (1) formal analytical identification of primary linkage relationships among export and ancillary (local) dominants industry groups at the local level; and (2) summation of the individual dominants on an employment basis for the current year. With the macro-micro synthesis complete, it is a relatively simple matter to show the significant relationship between the total employment of the dominants and each of several economic indicators for the current year.

Subdominant industry groups also might be identified—industry groups with employment shares just below the minimum level of dominants but still of significant size. Subdominants are not subjected to first-round macro-analysis and micro-analysis. They are included in the system because they represent an underlying "seedbed" of established economic activity that is vital to development planning.

This approach, like the others discussed, has its shortcomings. Andrews identified the following weaknesses in his approach: (1) the balance of the economy must be inferred from trends evident in the dominants—problem of generalizing from less than the total universe; and (2) the inability to determine whether the share of the total economy represented by dominant industry groups is adequate.[18] The analytical approach does not deal with a random sample, which is inherent in the concept of dominance. The analysis must be on a continuing basis to be used effectively. Given these limitations, however, the economic dominants approach holds a good deal of promise. It is relatively simple to undertake, and it lends itself to the more dynamic objectives of a continuous study. Furthermore, in-depth surveys of local industry groups can provide a good deal of spin-off information that cannot be obtained from abstract statistical analyses.

Summary

The urban economy has been studied primarily in terms of three conceptual systems—input-output analysis, income and product accounts analysis, and economic base studies. It should be apparent that there are a number of similarities in these three conceptual approaches. By shifting emphasis, changing units of measurement, or expanding or reducing the number of sectors included, one approach becomes more like the other two. As data sources become more extensive and more refined, and as the data handling capacity of computers receives wider utilization, it is likely that the "rough edges" of these three models will be smoothed away so that they nearly fit as a single system of analysis. When this is accomplished, the integration of broader theoretical concerns of urban economics will be possible.

Notes

1. Roland Pressat, *Demographic Analysis: Methods, Results, Applications*, translated by Judah Matras (Chicago: Aldine-Atherton, 1972).
2. For a further examination of these methods, see John W. Dickey and Alan W. Steiss, "Programming Models in the Systemic Planning Process, *Urban and Regional Ground Transportation: Surveys and Readings*, edited by James J. Murray (Durham, N.C.: Planning-Transport Associates, Inc., 1973).
3. For a further discussion regarding the construction of an abridged life table, see Chin Long Chiang, *The Life Table and Its Applications* (Malabar, Fla: Robert E. Krieger Publishing Company, 1984), Chapter 7.
4. Richard E. Klosterman, *Community and Analysis Planning Techniques* (Savage, Md.: Rowman and Littlefield Publishers, Inc., 1990), 113.
5. Wilbur Thompson, *A Preface to Urban Economics* (Washington, D.C.: Resources for the Future, 1963).
6. Wassily W. Leontief, *The Structure of the American Economy, 1919-1939* (Oxford: Oxford University Press, 1951), 11.
7. Thompson, *op. cit.*, chapter 1.
8. Richard D. Andrews, "Mechanics of the Urban Economic Base," *Land Economics* (November 1953): 344-349; "Urban Economics: An Appraisal of Progress," *Land Economics* (August 1961): 223-225; "Economic Planning for Small Areas: An Analytical System," *Land Economics* (May 1963): 145-155; "Economic Planning for Small Areas: The Planning Process," *Land Economics* (August 1963): 253-264.
9. William J. Reilly, *The Law of Retail Gravitation* (New York: G.P. Putnam Sons, 1931), 9.
10. Charles M. Tiebout, *The Community Economic Base Study* (New York: Committee for Economic Development, 1962), 47.
11. Most economic data used in economic base studies are taken from the U.S. Census Bureau's *County Business Patterns*. These data are collected annually and provide employment and payroll information for counties and cities throughout the United States. A Standard Industrial Classification (SIC) was developed to organize these employment and payroll data.
12. Andrews, "Economic Planning for Small Areas: The Planning Process," *Land Economics* (August 1963): 253-264.
13. Ralph W. Pfouts, "An Empirical Testing of the Economic Base Theory," *Journal of the American Institute of Planners* (Spring 1957).
14. Hans Blumenfeld, "The Economic Base of the Metropolis," *Journal of the American Institute of Planners* (Fall 1955).
15. William A. Schaffer, *Regional Impact Models* (Morgantown, W.Va.: Regional Research Institute, West Virginia University, 1999).
16. Andrew C. Krikelas, "Why Regions Grow: A Review of Research on the Economic Base Model," *Economic Review of the Federal Reserve Bank of Atlanta* (1992): 16-29.
17. Andrews, "Economic Planning for Small Areas: An Analytical System," *Land Economics* (May 1963): 143-155.
18. *Ibid.*, 151.

Chapter 4

PROGRAMMING STRATEGIC FACILITIES

Current practices for allocating limited public resources to meet strategic facility needs are lacking in several dimensions. Critical decisions often are based on inadequate data or on traditional engineering standards. While such standards are helpful, they simply are not sufficiently comprehensive to provide the information required to evaluate the trade-off options among competing strategic facility proposals. Highly subjective assessments often are used with little systematic information on infrastructure conditions, proposal impacts, financing alternatives, or the analysis of repair and replacement options. Local discussions concerning the selection of priorities among competing projects often are intensely political debates. All too often, in the absence of sound data and analysis, the "squeaky wheel" approach to decision making prevails.

Improving Local Practices

Some efforts have been mounted in recent years to improve capital budgeting procedures in local governments. These efforts have focused primarily on discussions of the organization of the process, administrative practices, and overall financial issues. Sound analytical procedures for the selection of strategic facility proposals, for the most part, have not been adequately addressed. Five tasks—described in the following sections—cover specific elements involved in the programming of strategic facilities. In these tasks, a major concern must be to balance the desirability of more sophisticated analytical tools with the technical limitations and political considerations of local government.

Geographic Information Systems

The need for corrective action should be based on an assessment of major components of the local infrastructure—monitored over time and compared to benchmark data where possible. Analysis of repair and replacement alternatives can be undertaken when information on the current condition of the infrastructure is combined with cost accounting data on maintenance expenditures. Priorities among proposed improvement projects can be more readily determined once the conditions of individual segments of the infrastructure are clearly identified.

Application of the techniques of geographic information systems (GIS) can be of considerable assistance in maintaining an inventory of infrastructure conditions. GIS is computer-based technology capable of assembling, storing, manipulating, and displaying geographically referenced information (that is, data identified according to their locations). Different types or layers of information are combined depending on the purpose of the analysis. GIS technology can be used to map the location of existing public improvements, to find the best location for a new strategic facility, to analyze environmental damage resulting from natural or man-made events, to detect a pattern of similar crimes in a city, and so on. Once the relevant data are loaded into the GIS, periodic updates and analyses can be accomplished with relative ease.

The primary requirement for GIS-compatible data is that the locations for the relevant variables are known. Location may be annotated by x, y, and z coordinates of longitude, latitude, and elevation, or by such criteria as ZIP codes, street addresses, or highway mile markers. Existing digital information, which may not be in map form, can also be converted into forms that a GIS can recognize and use. For example, census data can be converted to map-like form, serving as layers of thematic information in a GIS. Likewise, digital satellite images can be analyzed to produce a map-like layer of digital information about vegetative covers.

GIS software provides the functions and tools needed to store, analyze, and display geographic information. Key components of GIS software are:

- Tools for entering and manipulating geographic information such as addresses or political boundaries
- A database management system (DBMS)
- Tools to create digital maps that can be analyzed, queried for more information, or printed for presentation
- An easy-to-use graphical user interface (GUI)

Over the past few years, a whole industry has emerged, focusing on the collection and packaging of data useful to GIS applications—from creating basic street maps to integrating census data to finding optimal business locations. As a result, both the cost and time required to implement GIS applications have been greatly reduced. GIS can use data from a wide range of proprietary and standard map and graphics, file formats, images, computer-aided design (CAD) files, spreadsheets, relational databases, and many more sources. These data may be acquired free of charge or may be fee-based. Data can come from commercial, nonprofit, educational, and governmental sources, other GIS software users, as well as the public organization developing the GIS. Primary sources of GIS data are shown in Table 4-1.

Data capture—putting the information into the system—is the most time-consuming component of GIS work. Data that are not already in digital form can be captured through the use of various techniques. Maps can be hand-traced with a computer mouse to collect the coordinates of map features. It is also necessary to specify the identities of the objects on the map as well as their spatial relationships. Electronic scanning devices can be used to convert map lines and points to digits. Editing of information that is automatically captured can be difficult, however. Electronic scanners record blemishes on a map just as faithfully as they record the map features. A fleck of dirt, for example, might connect two lines that should not be connected. Extraneous data must be edited from digital data files.

Table 4-1
Primary Sources of GIS Data

- ***TIGER*** (Topologically Integrated Geographic Encoding and Referencing): A digital database developed at the Census Bureau to support its mapping needs for the Decennial Census. Topological structure of the database defines the location and relationship of streets, rivers, railroads, and other features to each other and to the numerous geographic entities for which the Census Bureau tabulates data from its censuses and sample surveys.
- ***Census Watch***: Provides immediate access to the most recent information on Census-related data resources, redistricting, online GIS mapping, education and training, as well as news and articles.
- ***Geospatial Data Clearinghouse***: More than 100 spatial data servers from different organizations can be searched through a single interface created by the U.S. Federal Geographic Data Committee.
- ***Geospatial One-Stop***: Part of the new Office of Management and Budget E-Government initiative to improve the effectiveness, efficiency, and customer service throughout the federal government. Implementation will provide: (1) standards and models for geospatial data content; (2) an interactive index to geospatial data holdings at the federal and non-federal levels; and (3) an online access point to geospatial data.
- ***Geography Network***: A collaborative, multi-participant system for publishing, sharing, and using digital geographic information on the Internet. Many types of geographic content can be accessed, including dynamic maps, downloadable data, and more advanced Web services. Managed and maintained by the Environmental Systems Research Institute, Inc.
- ***Urban and Regional Information Systems Association*** (URISA): A nonprofit association of professionals using information technology to solve problems in planning, public works, the environment, emergency services, utilities and throughout state, regional, and local governments. URISA is dedicated to advancing the effective application of information technology in decision making and the use and integration of spatial information technology to improve the quality of life in urban and regional environments.
- ***GISPortal***: One of the top Web sites for Geographic Information System industry, providing information on over 1,000 sites.
- ***GeoCommunity Data Depot***: Offers free data from all over the world or users can pay a fee for a custom-cut CD.
- ***GIS Jump Station***: Many of the sites listed offer data either for download or for sale.

GIS makes it possible to link or integrate information that is difficult to associate through any other means. Thus, GIS can use combinations of mapped variables to build and analyze new variables. Using water company billing information and GIS technology, for example, it is possible to simulate the discharge of materials from the septic systems of a neighborhood that is upstream from a wetland. The bills show how much water is used at each address. The amount of water a customer uses will roughly predict the amount of material that will be discharged into the septic systems, so that areas of heavy septic discharge can be located using GIS.

Making maps with GIS is much more flexible than traditional manual or automated cartography approaches. Cartographic databases that are GIS-based can be both continuous and scale free. Map products can then be centered on any location, at any scale, and show selected information that has been symbolized effectively to highlight specific characteristics. As long as the data are available, a map can be created anytime to any scale for any purpose.

Map information in GIS must be manipulated so that it registers or fits with information gathered from other maps. Digital data may have to undergo projection conversions to integrate them into GIS before they can be analyzed. A projection is a mathematical means of transferring information from the three-dimensional curved surface of the earth to a two-dimensional medium—paper or a computer screen. Different projections are used for different types of maps because each projection method is particularly appropriate to certain uses. Since much of the information in GIS comes from existing maps, GIS use the processing power of the computer to transform digital information gathered from various sources with different projections to a common projection.

Image data from a satellite can be interpreted by a computer to produce a land use map that can be "read into" GIS in raster format—data files consist of rows of uniform cells coded according to data values. Raster data files can be manipulated quickly by the computer. However, these files are often less detailed and may be less visually appealing than vector data files, which can approximate the appearance of more traditional hand-drafted maps. Vector digital data have been captured as points, lines (a series of point coordinates), or areas (shapes bounded by lines). The property boundaries for a housing subdivision are an example of data typically held in a vector file.

GIS can restructure data into different formats. For example, a satellite image map can be converted into a vector structure by generating lines around all cells with the same classification, while determining the cell spatial relationships, such as adjacency or inclusion. Thus GIS can be used to analyze land use information in conjunction with property ownership information. Some other common applications of GIS technology are outlined in Table 4-2.

One of the main benefits of developing GIS is improved management of an organization and its resources. Data sets can be linked together by common locational data, such as addresses. Such linkages, in turn, can assist departments and agencies in sharing their data. By creating a shared database, one department can benefit from the work of another—data can be collected once, entered into GIS, and used many times.

Table 4-2
Applications of Geographic Information Systems

Data modeling: GIS can be used to depict two- and three-dimensional characteristics of the earth's surface, subsurface, and atmosphere from a limited number of point measurements.
Information retrieval: GIS can "point" at a location, object, or area on a screen and retrieve recorded information about it from off-screen files.
***Topological modeling*:** GIS can recognize and analyze the spatial relationships among mapped phenomena to determine conditions of adjacency (what is next to what), proximity (how close something is to something else), and containment (what is enclosed by what).
***Networks*:** GIS can simulate the route of materials along a linear network. It is possible to assign values, such as direction and speed, to the digital stream and to "move" objects through the network system.
***Overlay*:** Using a series of maps that depict various types of data, GIS can produce a new map layer or overlay that ranks or orders data according to some predetermined criteria.
***Data output*:** GIS can produce graphics on screen or on paper that convey the results of analysis to decision makers. Wall maps and other graphics can be generated, allowing the viewer to visualize and thereby understand the results of analyses or simulations of potential events.
***Mapmaking*:** Researchers are working to incorporate the experience of traditional cartographers into GIS technology for automated production of maps.
***Site selection*:** Information can be combined and manipulated in GIS to address planning and natural resource issues. GIS can be used to locate a potential site for new facilities that meet predetermined criteria. Particularly useful when several physical factors must be considered and integrated over a large area.
***Emergency response planning*:** GIS can be used to combine road network and earth science information to analyze the effect of natural disasters on the response time of fire and rescue squads.
***Simulating environmental effects*:** Existing digital data can be combined and displayed using a function that creates perspective drawings. Map types can be combined and displayed in realistic three-dimensional perspective views that convey information more effectively than traditional, two-dimensional maps.
***Graphic display techniques*:** Graphic display techniques in GIS make relationships among map elements visible, heightening one's ability to extract and analyze information.

There is a vast difference between seeing data in a table of rows and columns and seeing it presented in the form of a map. The difference is not simply aesthetic—it is conceptual. The way data are presented can have a profound effect on the connections made and the conclusions drawn from these data. GIS provides the layout and drawing tools that help present facts with clear, compelling documents.

Users no longer have to be specialists to work with GIS, and they can be located anywhere. In the past, the high-bandwidth requirements of image-intensive geo-spatial files necessitated that users be relatively close to a server. However, GIS can now be applied in a distributed environment and even with remote users through Web servers and the Internet. David Sonnen, an analyst with IDC Research, predicts that: "Within three years, GIS technology will be largely invisible. It'll just be part of the infrastructure, and IS [information systems] will be handling geographic information just like integers and floating point queries within a buffer."[1]

Location-based services are among the more important emerging applications within GIS. Wireless applications of GIS range from on-board navigation systems in vehicles to business uses such as petroleum prospecting and exploration. All wireless carriers are required by the E911 mandate of the FCC to be able to locate the majority of their 911 callers by the end of 2002 and to locate all callers by December 2005.

Through a function known as visualization, GIS technology can be used to produce images—not just maps, but also drawings, animations, and other cartographic products. These images allow researchers to view their subjects in ways that literally never have been seen before. The images often are equally helpful in conveying the technical concepts of GIS subjects to non-scientists.

Advances in GIS and supporting technologies have led to the development of decision support systems that facilitate the strategic planning process. Several decision support systems available on the market today do not require a high degree of GIS expertise. These GIS-based support systems facilitate the formulation and testing of alternative development scenarios and the determination of their likely impact on future land use patterns and associated population and employment trends. As a consequence, public officials able to make better informed strategic decisions. The ultimate objective is to bring together all potential players to work collaboratively on a common vision for the community.

According to a recent survey of 1,156 local governments, conducted by Public Technology Inc. on behalf of the U.S. Department of the Interior, 97% of the governments with populations of at least 100,000 and 88% of those with populations between 50,000 and 100,000 use GIS technology.[2] Of the smaller jurisdictions with less than 50,000 population, 56% also use some GIS applications. The survey report indicates that GIS applications have become significant resources in a number of local government functions, including public works, financial management, public safety, and economic development. Examples of these applications are summarized in Table 4-3. The report suggests that the federal government should take the lead in promoting GIS by sponsoring outreach programs and training for local officials, volunteer programs to assist in project work, and Internet access to GIS tools and resources. State and local governments should also promote "best practices," provide education, and conduct surveys regarding GIS applications.

The old adage "better information leads to better decisions" is true for GIS. GIS provides a comprehensive tool to query, analyze, and map data in support

Table 4-3
Local Government Applications of GIS Technology

Application	Percent of Respondents
View aerial photography	77%
Support property tax management and taxation services	70%
Provide public access information	57%
Capital improvements programming, design, and construction	41%
Permitting services, emergency preparedness, and response activities	38%
Computer-aided response activities	33%
Support crime tracking and investigative activities	28%

of the decision-making process. Many disciplines can benefit from GIS techniques. An active GIS market has resulted in lower costs and continual improvements in the hardware and software components of GIS. These developments, in turn, will result in a much wider application of the technology throughout government, business, and industry

Current Infrastructure Conditions

Appropriate condition measures and assessment procedures should be identified for each of the basic infrastructure components: streets, bridges, water and sewer networks, transit vehicles, and so forth. Three categories of indicators should be considered:

1. Engineering-type assessments such as measures of water pipe capacity loss, bridge condition ratings, etc.;
2. Performance measures such as number of sewer line stoppages, frequency of bus breakdowns, service calls for water line repairs, etc.; and
3. Service impact indicators such as numbers of citizen complaints and losses arising from system failures (e.g., water main breaks, basement-flooding incidents from sewer back-ups).

Appropriate indicators should be drawn from a variety of sources, including engineering practices and federal and state rating schemes. A small group of indicators should be selected for each infrastructure component. These indicators should offer valid measures of current conditions and ensure that reliable information can be obtained over time. The selection will be facilitated by seeking the advice of professional groups and by examining the experience of other local governments that have implemented such assessment procedures. Efforts should be made to identify assessment procedures that are reliable (e.g., that minimize dependence on judgments that may differ among surveyors) and yet, at the same time, are practical (e.g., that minimize extensive data gathering or use of expensive equipment in the assessment process). The selected indicators and assessment techniques must be tested under appropriate conditions for representative projects in each infrastructure area.

Standardized definitions should be prepared for each indicator. Where possible, benchmarks should be established for the selected performance measures, such as system failures and breakdown rates. For example, information on frequency of bus road calls may be limited to include only road calls attributable to mechanical failures, rather than more minor maintenance repairs. This information, in conjunction with rules of thumb developed by practitioners, should provide measures of the mean and range of performance levels against which the performance of the local infrastructure can be compared and evaluated.

Special attention should be given to procedures of collecting data for condition assessments that might result in cost savings. In some cases, new procedures will be warranted. In others, existing information can be utilized. Often the computerization of data will be required. Cost options should be identified for all approaches to data collection.

The product of this task should be a description of appropriate condition indicators and procedures for obtaining information on a regular (e.g., semi-annual or annual) basis. Estimates should be made of the data collection costs and of the reliability and validity of the collection procedures.

Replacement Analysis

In practice, condition indicators will point out problems in the infrastructure, suggest the current extent of these problems, and indicate likely candidate projects for improvements. This type of analysis, however, will not indicate whether a strategic facility should be repaired or replaced. Nor will it identify the associated costs and service level impacts of choosing either option.

The purpose of replacement analysis is to assess the trade-offs among four options: (1) replace the facility or equipment; (2) rehabilitate or undertake a major overhaul; (3) continue to provide current maintenance with emergency repairs as required; or (4) cut back maintenance spending and defer repairs. The fourth option may be the least expensive in the short run, but usually it is the most costly in the long term.

Replacement analysis provides information on the likely costs, impacts on service levels, and risks of the choices involved. Typical issues include:

- Should certain streets be resurfaced or seal-coated now or should spending be deferred at the risk of more costly reconstruction in the future?
- Should a deteriorated bridge deck continue to be repaired, receive extensive rehabilitation, or be entirely replaced?
- Should a program of sewer line repairs be continued, pipes replaced, or existing infiltration and inflow into sewers be accepted, with consequent backups and basement flooding incidents?
- Should a break in the city's water supply system be repaired or should the main be replaced?
- Should buses that are breaking down considerably more frequently than the industry standard continue to receive regular maintenance and repair, be given major overhauls, or be replaced?

Each of these questions involves specific technical considerations and special factors. However, the appropriate type of analysis is quite similar.

Depreciation curves should be developed where possible for different components of the infrastructure. Such curves show the rate of deterioration as a function of such factors as age, original construction material, climate, intensity of use, and the like. Unfortunately, while some general guidelines concerning useful service durations do exist, these typically do not relate to individual segments of the local infrastructure.

Procedures must be formulated for replacement analysis that seems feasible and appropriate for local governments. The technical literature from the related fields of engineering economy, capital budgeting in the private sector, and cost-benefit and cost-effectiveness analysis should be examined. Much of the work in these fields has focused on the choices available to private enterprise. Applications in the private sector have the simplifying advantage that the outputs of investments, as well as the costs, can be expressed adequately in dollar terms.

In the public sector, nonmonetary impacts—such as water quality, transportation delays, number of sewer stoppages and backups, and the like—must also be considered. Infrastructure maintenance issues can be discussed in these circumstances primarily in terms of dollars. Even in these cases, however, it will generally be necessary to undertake a brief analysis to ascertain that service-level impacts do not reduced an otherwise economically preferable option.

Equipment replacement models use methods of operations research generally aimed at minimizing future net costs by estimating the time for replacement. Optimal replacement occurs when operating and maintenance costs (plus loss of resale value) exceed the cost (annualized) of replacement plus the operating and maintenance cost of the new equipment. In short, the cost of maintaining the existing equipment for another year is compared to the cost of purchasing new equipment and operating it for the same period.

The technical literature and existing efforts related to replacement analysis by local, state, and federal governments should be examined. For example, the Environmental Protection Agency requires analyses of the economic trade-offs between sewer rehabilitation and treatment plant expansion as part of the grant application process. There is a scattering of related studies by local governments.

In addition to the basic principles of economic analysis, detailed procedures should be developed to include cost estimations, application of discount rates to provide the basis for more thorough cost-benefit analysis, and an examination of the distributional effects. Major sources of information regarding the estimation of costs include maintenance records, engineering estimates, and bids. However, local governments often have difficulty in using such information to project the costs of various alternatives. Procedures for the explicit consideration of full costs (i.e., operating and maintenance costs, as well as investment costs) should be developed when feasible. The use of statistical cost analysis techniques should be explored to make better estimates of future costs.

Cost-benefit and cost-effectiveness analysis techniques should be applied if the scope of the proposed project warrants this depth of analysis. Cost-benefit techniques have been successfully applied in the examination of transportation alternatives and in the assessment of water resource projects. To date, however, problems of how to meaningfully impute dollar values to service-level impacts and how to handle distributional effects have limited the utility of cost-benefit analysis at the local level. In cost-benefit analysis, nonmonetary products are translated into monetary terms by imputing dollar values to outputs (such as reduced travel time, lives or injuries avoided, the value of recreation time, etc.). In cost-effectiveness analysis, outputs are expressed in different units, with the results presented in the form of trade-offs rather than cost-benefit ratios.

Discounting is important in considering the time stream of costs and benefits. Discount rates that are appropriate for local analyses, however, often are unclear. These measures, if stated in monetary terms, often represent dollar imputations rather than actual dollar outlays. These considerations—applicable to replacement analysis and to the construction of new strategic facilities—will be discussed in further detail in Chapter 5. Suffice it to say at this point that several issues must be resolved in applying the techniques of cost-benefit and cost-effectiveness analysis at the local level.

Procedures should be developed to examine the distributional effects of investment choices within a locality. Distributional consequences are of considerable concern to public officials and, of course, to the public. The numbers of citizens affected, as well as their location and demographic, economic, and social characteristics, should be considered. Condition indicators often can be disaggregated by neighborhoods or districts within the jurisdiction to gain a better understanding of the distributional effects of various proposed improvements. The installation and maintenance of a geographic information system can facilitate this more detailed analysis.

Consideration of Risk and Uncertainty

Risk and uncertainty are key elements in choosing among alternative investments for public improvements. The following procedures should be considered in making such choices:

- Sensitivity analysis assesses the relative magnitude of changes in costs and output indicators if key elements in the analysis have different values than those considered most likely.
- Contingency analysis permits the construction of alternative future scenarios (e.g., a substantial buildup in traffic on a road segment or bridge) and an examination of the effects of each scenario for maintenance or replacement options.
- Probabilities can be applied to uncertain events so that an "expected value" and a distribution of likely total costs and outcomes can be generated for each alternative.
- Uncertainty factors can be included in the discount rate to reduce net benefits computed in future years.

Sensitivity analysis is designed to measure (often quite crudely) the possible effects that variations in uncertain decision elements (for example, costs) may have on the alternatives under analysis. In most investment decisions, a few key parameters exhibit considerable uncertainty. The analyst must determine a set of

Table 4-4
Illustration of Sensitivity Analysis

Cost Levels	Alternative A	Alternative B	Alternative C
Expected values of certain costs	$ 90,000	$ 80,000	$100,000
Optimistic expected values of uncertain costs	$ 10,000	$ 30,000	$ 20,000
Expected values of all costs	$100,000	$110,000	$120,000
Rankings	1	2	3
Pessimistic expected values	$110,000	$115,000	$ 90,000
Expected values of all costs	$200,000	$195,000	$190,000
Rankings	3	2	1
Most likely expected values	$ 60,000	$ 40,000	$ 20,000
Expected values of all costs	$150,000	$120,000	$170,000
Rankings	2	1	3

Composite Expected Values

Alt. A = [.50(150,000) + .30(200,000) + .20(100,000)] = $155,000
Alt. B = [.50(120,000) + .30(195,000) + .20(110,000)] = $140,500
Alt. C = [.50(170,000) + .30(190,000) + .20(120,000)] = $166,000

expected values for these parameters (as well as other parameters). Recognizing that these expected values may be, at best, "guesstimations," several values (optimistic, pessimistic, and most likely) may be used in an attempt to ascertain how sensitive the results might be to variations in the uncertain parameters.

Table 4-4 illustrates how sensitivity analysis can be used to determine the variations in rankings among several alternatives, based on unanticipated costs. First, expected values are set for all costs that are certain (those components for which some reliable basis exists for establishing an estimated cost). Three values are then determined for the uncertain costs. The optimistic cost represents an assessment of cost based on the assumption that everything will go right with the project—that all of the uncertainty is resolved favorably. The pessimistic cost represents the opposite assumption. The most likely cost figure falls somewhere between these two extremes.

Two points concerning uncertainty are illustrated in Table 4-4. First, the range of uncertainty may vary from alternative to alternative (for alternative A, the uncertain range is $10,000 to $110,000; for alternative B, $30,000 to $115,000; and for alternative C, $20,000 to $90,000). Second, uncertain costs may not always be the critical factor in determining the "best" alternative. For example, although uncertain costs for alternative C vary over the narrowest range, this alternative still ranks third except under conditions of high—or pessimistic—uncertain costs.

Probability theory also can be applied in connection with sensitivity analysis. Assume, for example, that the probability of the most likely costs being realized is 50%; the most pessimistic costs, 30%; and the most optimistic costs, 20%. The composite expected values for all costs are shown at the bottom of Table 4-4. Given these assumptions, alternative B is the preferred alternative.

Contingency analysis is designed to examine the effects on alternative choices when a relevant change is postulated in the evaluation criteria. This approach can also be used to determine the effects of a major change in the general decision environment or "ground rules" within which the problem situation exists. In short, contingency analysis is a "with and without" approach. In the field of public health, for example, alternative approaches to environmental health might be evaluated with and without a major new code enforcement program. In a more local context, a public service organization might evaluate various sites for the location of its headquarters under existing conditions of client distribution and access routes. Additional evaluations might then be made, assuming different client distributions and other route configurations.

A fortiori analysis (from the Latin, meaning "with stronger reason") is a method of deliberately "stacking the deck" in favor of one alternative to determine how it might stand up in comparison to other approaches. Suppose that, prior to analysis, alternative C is strongly favored by the governing board. In performing the analysis on C in comparison to the other feasible alternatives, a deliberate choice is made to resolve any major uncertainties in favor of C. The analyst would then determine how each of the other alternatives compared under these circumstances. If some alternative other than C looks good (that is, if C does not emerge "with stronger reason" as the best alternative), there may be a very valid case for dismissing the initial intuitive judgment that favored C. This type of analysis can be carried out in a series of trials, with each alternative, in turn, being favored in terms of the major uncertainties.

These three techniques for dealing with uncertainty may be useful not only in a direct analytical sense, but they may also contribute indirectly to the resolution of problem situations. Through sensitivity and contingency analyses, for example, it may be possible to gain a better understanding of the critical uncertainties of a given problem. With this knowledge, a new alternative might be formulated that would provide a reasonably good hedge against a range of more significant uncertainties. While this often is difficult to do, when it can be accomplished, it may offer one of the best ways to offset the uncertainties of a problem situation.

Qualitative statements should be made about the relative amount of uncertainty and risk involved in each alternative. Individuals knowledgeable about the operations under study should be called upon to make judgments as to the uncertainty of various elements in the analysis. The magnitudes of uncertainty, in turn, are used to estimate the effect of the uncertainties on the major evaluation criteria (the cost and service level effects). The latter information indicates the risk involved in making any particular choice. Risk analysis involves modeling situations to provide estimates of the probability of major consequences of certain governmental actions.

It is important to assess how these various approaches can be applied to the problems of maintaining the local infrastructure. More sophisticated and resource-demanding techniques will likely be applicable only to major investment decisions. Procedures should be developed for making more explicit the trade-offs in local investment decisions.

Consideration of Financing Options

Financing constraints play a major role in decisions regarding capital outlays in most jurisdictions. In considering financing options in each infrastructure area:

- Sources of capital funds should be clearly delineated.
- Availability of specific matching grants to help subsidize any further capital expenditures should be identified.
- Steps that could be taken to finance further capital outlays should be outlined.
- Ramifications of pursuing these options should be assessed in terms of their relative costs and service level impacts (e.g., state funded projects frequently require higher construction standards, and thus higher costs, than locally funded projects).

General procedures for financing alternatives must be integrated into the initial assessment of strategic facility projects. Limited efforts have been made at the local level to integrate financial option analysis into individual project selection, however.

The availability of federal and state aid programs, for example, influences both the feasibility and net cost of local improvement projects. Federal grants may provide a significant boost to local capital spending, but they also can affect local objectives, particularly for infrastructure repair and rehabilitation. Historically, federal programs for strategic facility projects have been biased toward new construction.

Understandably, local governments seek to leverage their resources. However, providing the local match for projects eligible for state or federal support can divert funds from vital maintenance-related investments that receive no external assistance. For example, local governments may find their efforts to repair and rehabilitate local sewer systems frustrated by the realities of federal funding. Although eligible for federal grants, in practice these projects are far down the federal and state priority lists. Thus, local governments frequently are faced with the option of constructing a new interceptor sewer that may require a maximum of 25% local funds or funding sewer line replacement projects that typically require 100% local financing.

Strategic facilities can be financed in a number of ways—on a pay-as-you-go basis, from reserve funds, or through short- or long-term borrowing. These financing methods must be evaluated in terms of the fiscal policies of the community and in light of the particular strategic facility needs. Methods for financing strategic facilities are discussed in further detail in Chapters 6 and 7.

Cataloging Proposed Projects

The cataloging of the proposed strategic facility projects together with pertinent explanatory data for each project serves as an important step in the programming process. The capital budget is formed from this catalog of projects that are, at least, compatible with the strategic facilities plan and, at best, are explicitly called for by the plan.

Procedures for preparing this catalog are relatively straightforward. The chief administrator or coordinating staff agency sends out forms and instructions annually, soliciting project requests from each department or agency to guide in the preparation of a capital improvements program (CIP). The instructions should indicate briefly the purpose and use to which the requested information will be put, the date on which the information should be complete, and to whom it should be submitted. The procedures to be followed in providing information relative to plans and estimates for projects should also be delineated. It may be pointed out, for example, that while the long-range strategic facilities plan contains numerous recommendations for capital improvements, other projects may be required to keep pace with the needs of the community or to replace worn out or obsolete equipment or facilities.

Each agency is required to complete several standard forms in compiling its project list. If the requested projects are not included in the strategic facilities plan (or comprehensive plan), the agency's list should be accompanied by a recommendation that the plan be modified or enlarged to include such indicated improvements. In filling out these forms, the agencies should be cognizant that the cost and priority estimates include only those projects for public improvements that have a relatively long life expectancy. Ordinary repairs and maintenance usually are not recorded as a capital project.

Form A (see Table 4-5) provides an overall summary of the anticipated projects to be undertaken within the operating responsibilities of a given department or agency. This form is used to record all construction projects and the related equipment requirements, including the purchase of land, major repairs or alterations of existing buildings, and grading and development of land. The distribution of financing should be indicated over the programming period (five to six years), the recommended method of financing should be identified, and additional operating expenditures arising from the proposed improvement should be delineated. Each project should be given a priority assignment, listing the major criteria considered by the submitting agency for each project in order of their relative importance. Only those projects required during the next six years should be entered on Form A. The column "prior" should show any sums of money that have been made available previously in support of the project. The column "later" should show the estimated amount needed for project completion after the current six-year program period, as appropriate.

Table 4-5

Estimate for Six-year Capital Improvements Program (Form A)

Recommended Financing

GR General revenues
SC Service charges
UT Utility revenue
GOB General obligation bonds

FA Federal aid
SA State aid
SR Specific reserves
WC Working Capital

City of

Summary sheet of

Date submitted

Status of Plans

0 No plans needed
1 First request
2 Preliminary estimate received
3 Surveys completed
4 Work on plans scheduled
5 Sketch plans in preparation
6 Sketch plans completed
7 Detailed plans in' preparation
8 Detailed plans & specifications

Proposed Priority	Project Number	Name & Location of Project	Finance Method	Total Estimated Cost	Year in Which Expenditure is Required								Additional Operating Costs	Status of Plans	Remarks (Benefits) and References to Overall Capital Facilities Plan
					2003-2004	2004-2005	2005-2006	2006-2007	2007-2008	2008-2009	Prior	Later			

It is important to fill in the column showing "additional operating costs" whenever such items are involved in a project. These costs constitute a continuing annual expense that may result in a serious fiscal burden for the jurisdiction and, therefore, must be considered carefully. Any anticipated operating income should also be entered for similar consideration. If a project will involve savings or expenses, these estimates should be so indicated under "remarks."

Form B (see Table 4-6) is used to record the more detailed information as to costs and the supporting justification for each project entered on Form A. Form B includes the purpose of the project, its location and physical description, estimated total costs, expenditures requested during the programming period, effects on the operating budget, additional capital expenditures needed to make the project fully usable, suggested method of financing, and so forth. The justification for each project should be spelled out in the sections pertaining to purpose and need. This justification should include the reasons or benefits of the particular services to be rendered, the character of the area, the number of people, and the value of property served. Any drawings, plans, pictures, or other supporting documentation concerning the project request may accompany this second form. The relationship to any other project within the department or a project of another department should be stated. Specific facilities or utilities (i.e., sewage, water, power, roads, sidewalks, etc.) that need to be coordinated with the project should also be described on Form B. Other agencies or organizations that are concerned or associated with the project should be identified.

A third form, which sometimes is combined with Form A, is concerned with a review and updating of previously requested projects. This third form serves as a "progress report" for projects that are currently in the capital improvements program. For projects that have been deferred from early programs, this form serves notice of their deferred status and provides an opportunity for a reevaluation of such project needs.

As one capital budgeting official put it, in the initial years of a strategic facilities planning process, the listing of projects according to an agency's own estimates of need and priority are likely to range from "a poor man's shopping list" to a "letter to Santa Claus." After a relatively short period, however, experience has shown that the priority estimates of individual agencies become more realistic and provide a useful means to assist the planners and programmers in the compilation of overall priority schedules.

The principal function of these forms is to provide a uniform and standardized method of indicating the justification for projects to be included in the capital improvements program. The justification should not only include a statement concerning the importance of the individual project requests but also an indication of how the project relates to overall goals and objectives, as well as the more specific service program of the agency and the interrelation among the various projects.

Ranking Capital Project Requests

In all likelihood, for any given budget period, the overall cost of the proposed projects will exceed the available financial resources. Therefore, decisions regard-

Table 4-6
Individual Project Estimate for
Six-year Capital Improvements Program (Form B)

Program Period

City of ____________________ **Project number** ________

1. Department **2. Division**

3. Description of Project
(a) Name, physical description, location
(b) Purpose ____________________
(c) Shown on map attached
( ) yes ( ) no

4. Need for project (use separate sheet if necessary) ____________________

5. In capital facilities or comprehensive plan? Reference

6. Estimated cost
A. Planning (totals a, b, c) __________
(a) Architect fees
(b) Engineering __________
(c) Inspections
B. Land __________
C. Construction
(a) Labor __________
(b) Nonlabor
D. Misc. Equipment __________
E. Furnishings
F. Other __________

Total estimated cost __________
Prior funding

7. Relation to other projects __________

8. Future burden
(a) Annual cost __________
(b) New staff
(c) Future expenditure for equipment

9. Income from project (estimated annual, direct and indirect) __________

10. Construction period __________

11. Status of plans and specifications __________

12. Proposed method of construction (contract or in-house)

13. Project expenditures by years
2004-2005
2005-2006 __________
2006-2007
2007-2008 __________
2008-2009
2009-2010 __________

Endorsement (to be completed by department head)

14. Priority rating ______
15. Year recommended for construction ______
16. Method of financing ____________________

ing project requests should be based on measurable and defendable criteria that establish priorities among needs. Information derived from the previous tasks—infrastructure condition assessments, repair and replacement cost options, service impacts, risk considerations, and financing alternatives—can provide a basis for priority ratings. Such procedures should seek to combine criteria to provide an overall summary score, without losing the backup information on individual criterion for each proposal. Economic costs and benefits often can be quantified in such priority systems. With few exceptions, however, social benefits and costs have yet to reach this level of quantification. Various "political factors" seldom are included among such criteria but are brought to bear on the final rankings.

Systems for assigning priorities can be divided into two approaches: (1) those that stress intangible values and (2) those that seek to quantify various criteria to develop a numerical scoring system. Each of these approaches has its merits and its shortcomings, and, to the extent possible, elements from each should be incorporated into a sound priority classification system.

Under an intangible approach, preference is given to those projects that contribute to "the protection of life, health, and public safety." A second important consideration assigns priority to projects designed to meet current deficiencies in existing facilities, based on some standard of service. While deficiency criteria often are expressed in rather general terms, it may be possible to establish some quantifiable measures based on these general statements. These criteria can then be applied to determine the essential level of service and the harm arising from a deficiency of service. It often is difficult, however, to develop measures that are comparable across functions lines (e.g., parks versus schools, health facilities versus sewer improvements).

Priority consideration also might be given to projects designed to conserve or maintain some existing properties, investment, or resources, or those that demonstrate some substantial economic or social benefit to the community. Established facilities may depend on new projects to realize their full potential, and therefore, such projects also might be given a high priority, as would projects that are self-supporting or self-liquidating. Special consideration may also be given to projects for which substantial state or federal subsidies are available. Finally, special consideration would be given to emergency situations.

A six-way breakdown of priorities is shown in Table 4-7, along with criteria for assigning capital projects to each of these categories. An examination of the suggested criteria will reveal several areas in which more measurable indices could be developed.

In recent years, a number of local governments have begun to identify a set of ranking criteria against which each proposed capital project is rated. Numerical weights are assigned to each criterion and used as multipliers to calculate an overall summary score for each proposal. The resulting summary scores are then used to rank the proposals. The criteria usually are a mixture of economic, political, social impact, and distributional considerations. Criteria sometimes overlap and might include process criteria (such as "conformance with the comprehensive plan") as well as outcome criteria.

Table 4-7
General Criteria for Strategic facilities Priority System

Category	General Criteria
1. **Urgent**	Projects that cannot reasonably be postponed; projects that would remedy conditions dangerous to public health, welfare, or safety; projects required to maintain a critically needed program; projects needed to meet an emergency situation.
2. **Essential**	Projects required to complete or make fully usable a major public improvement; projects required to maintain minimum standards as part of a ongoing program; desirable self liquidating projects; projects for which external funds for over 65% of costs are available for a limited period.
3. **Necessary**	Projects that should be carried out within a few years to meet clearly demonstrated anticipated needs; projects to replace unsatisfactory or obsolete facilities; remodeling projects for continued use of facilities.
4. **Desirable**	Adequately planned projects needed for the expansion of current programs; projects designed to initiate new programs considered appropriate for a progressive community; projects for the conversion of existing facilities to other uses.
5. **Acceptable**	Adequately planned projects useful for ideal operations but which can be postponed without detriment to present operations if budget reductions are necessary.
6. **Deferrable**	Projects recommended for postponement or elimination from immediate consideration in the current strategic facilities plan; projects that are questionable in terms of overall needs, adequate planning, or proper timing.

Adopted from Alan Walter Steiss, *Local Government Finance: Capital Facilities Planning and Debt Administration* (Lexington, Mass.: Lexington Books, 1978), 38.

Under a *numerical priority system*, the criterion judged to be most important or most significant is given the highest score (frequently based on units of ten or some multiple of ten). All other factors are then ranked in relation to this score. Thus, "protection of life and maintenance of public health" may be ranked most important criterion and assigned a score of 100. "Conservation of resources" may be judged to be nearly as important and thereby given a score of ninety. On the other hand, "aesthetic and cultural values" may be ranked relatively low, scoring only twenty points. These categories often are further divided into a number of subcategories and scores are accumulated for any given period. It should be evident that any effort to develop such an "objective" approach must be based, to a large degree, on subjective judgments.

While priority systems should have some degree of flexibility, they must be stable enough to offer substantial justification for the scheduling of projects and the allocation of funds within the capital improvements program. The priority system—whether developed on a more subjective, intangible basis or on a numerical system—must be tailored to the particular goals and objectives of the individual jurisdiction. One locality may be interested primarily in furthering industrial growth and development. Another may have tourism and the development of the recreational industry as a basic objective. A third may place primary emphasis on the preservation of a well-maintained residential atmosphere. In the final analysis, the planners and administrators must exercise their best professional judgment in working with the various operating agencies in assigning priorities. At the same time, it must be recognized that in government, "the actual choice and establishment of final priorities are still accompanied by the political process of compromise, a give-and-take between all groups concerned."[3]

Ranking procedures are not intended to make decision making on capital improvement proposals "automatic." They are not a substitute for judgment and consideration of the political environment. Rather, they provide more substantive information—in effect, making more explicit those issues and trade-offs that are always present but often hidden.

Evaluation Criteria

Hatry, Millar, and Evans have suggested eleven criteria for the evaluation of proposed capital improvements (see Table 4-8).[4] Most cities require a written description or justification of each project as part of the departmental submissions. Often these statements are so general, however, that the process of comparing and selecting among competing projects becomes very subjective. For these evaluation criteria to be useful, information should be submitted on each of the relevant factors.

Fiscal Impacts

In addition to data on the expected costs of each proposed project, information should be provided on operating and maintenance (O&M) costs. Often projects are intended to reduce future O&M costs, particularly those involving the rehabilitation of existing facilities. Estimates of such reductions might be an important factor in justifying those projects. Explicit consideration of initial development costs (site acquisition and preparation, construction, and purchase of

Table 4-8
Suggested Evaluation Criteria

Fiscal impacts:	Development costs and operation, maintenance, and repair costs should be considered. Potential cost liabilities of undertaking (or not undertaking) a project should be estimated.
Economic effects:	Estimates should be made of likely impacts on property values, the tax base, employment opportunities, personal and business income, and the revitalization of declining neighborhoods.
Health and safety effects:	An assessment should be made of health- and safety-related effects.
Quality of life:	Beneficial and adverse effects on the quality of life should be considered.
Quality of service:	Estimates should be made of the duration and severity of service disruptions and the number of persons likely to be affected.
Distributional effects:	Estimates of the number of persons likely to be affected should be broken down by age groups, economic status, neighborhoods or districts, handicapped persons, etc.
Project feasibility:	Special problems should be evaluated, including legal issues, compliance with the strategic facilities plan, impact on prior investments, and degree of public support or opposition.
Implications of project deferral:	Impact of deferring a project should be examined in terms of the previous criteria.
Risk and uncertainty:	Consequences of risks and uncertainties, when substantial, should be include in the overall project evaluation.
Interjurisdictional relations:	Special coordinating activities may be required if proposed project has significant adverse or beneficial effects on other jurisdictions or agencies that serve the area.
Advantages accruing from other proposals:	Relationship among projects should be identified, particularly if one project will affect the costs or benefits of another project.

Adapted from Harry P. Hatry, Annie P. Millar, and James H. Evans, "Guide to Setting Priorities for Capital Investments," *Guides to Managing Urban Capital*, Volume 5 (Washington, D.C.: Urban Institute Press, 1984), 9.

equipment) and subsequent costs of operation, maintenance, and repair of the facility is sometimes referred to as life-cycle costing. Requirements for life-cycle costing will be discussed further in Chapter 5.

Other fiscal impact considerations include:

- *Changes in revenue.* Capital projects may result in a reduction in revenues (for example, when private land is taken off the tax roll for a capital project site) or may generate new revenues (for example, when charges are levied for public services).
- *Impact on energy requirements.* Estimated changes (increases or decreases) in energy requirements should be included as part of the O&M cost impact of a project.
- *Legal liability.* Estimates should be made of any potential cost liabilities of undertaking (or not undertaking) a capital project, such as for flood damage resulting from the diversion of a natural stream.

Economic, Health, and Safety Effects

Information on the economic effects of proposed projects should included the likely impact of the project on (1) property values, (2) the tax base, (3) employment opportunities, (4) personal income, (5) business income, and (6) the stabilization or revitalization of declining neighborhoods. These impacts may be more evident in capital projects proposed in response to community growth and expansion. However, projects aimed at maintaining or upgrading the existing infrastructure may also have significant economic effects.

Project justifications should include an assessment of health and safety-related effects, such as anticipated reduction in traffic accidents, elimination of health hazards arising from sewer problems or poor water quality, or long-term health hazard effects of asbestos in public buildings. Data should be provided on the estimated number of persons affected and the severity of the effect. These data should indicate anticipated improvements in such conditions if the proposed project is implemented

Quality of Life and Service and Distrbutional Effects

Consideration should be given to both beneficial and adverse effects on the quality of life—environmental, aesthetic, and social factors. Although proposed projects may not generate major health problems, the potential for noise, air, or water pollution should be taken into account in evaluating items to be included in the capital improvements program. Increased travel times and other inconveniences to the public should also be evaluated. Some projects may involve lengthy disruptions of service and inconvenience to users during construction. Repair or reconstruction of bridges, streets, or water and sewer lines may involve rerouting of traffic, temporary interruptions of service, or even relocation of households. Estimates should be provided as to the duration and severity of such disruptions and the number of persons likely to be affected.

Capital projects vary with respect to the number of citizens affected, and inevitably, projects affect various sectors of the community differently. Depending on the particular type of project, estimates should be provided as to the number of persons likely to be affected. Where appropriate, these data should be broken down by age groups, economic status, neighborhoods or districts, residential or commercial areas, handicapped persons, and so forth.

Project Feasibility and Implications of Project Deferral

Projects should be evaluated for any special problems that may arise in implementation (for example, the need for permits or other authorization), including legal issues. The compatibility and compliance of the project with the strategic facilities plan should be assessed. If the project is a continuation of previous improvements, the impact on prior investments should be identified. The degree of public support for or opposition to the project should be evaluated, and any special interest groups involved should be identified. Efforts should be made to determine the time required to obtain federal or state approvals, the time required to ensure the necessary citizen support, and lead times for architectural and engineering plans, construction bidding, and material acquisition. The availability of staff resources required to carry out the proposed project also should be explored.

The impact of deferring the project should be examined in terms of each of the previous criteria. Deferring projects is especially tempting for public officials when the locality is financially hard-pressed in the current fiscal year. Before the decision to defer is made, however, local officials should obtain an estimate of the possible effects of such a decision, such as higher future costs and the extent of inconvenience or harm to the citizens of the community. Who will be affected and how will they be disbenefited? Is intergovernmental assistance more or less likely to be available in the future? What are the trends in the bond market—are interest rates on long-term municipal bonds increasing or decreasing?

Other Evaluation Criteria

All capital projects involve some risk and uncertainty. Uncertainty can arise, for example, from cost estimates (especially in projects involving new technologies or procedures) and in the quality of service (because of uncertainties about the durability and reliability of new materials). There are always risks in the bond market. When such risks and uncertainties are substantial, the consequences should be included in the overall project evaluation.

Special coordinating activities may be required if a proposed project has significant adverse or beneficial effects on other jurisdictions or agencies that serve the same area. Examples include water supply projects where the source (reservoir or aquifer) is outside the municipality or a landfill project in one jurisdiction that may handle solid waste disposal for other jurisdictions.

The relationship between capital projects should be identified, particularly if the initiation of one project will affect the costs or benefits of another project. An obvious example is improvements to water supply mains that can be under taken at lower cost if coordinated with street improvements in the same area. If two or more projects can be undertaken together at a lower cost than if done separately, the combined effort may rate a higher priority.

Capital Improvements Program

When all proposed projects have been analyzed, a composite capital improvements program (CIP) should be prepared for review and adoption by the chief executive and governing body. A capital improvements program represents the more immediate and more detailed portions of the long-range strategic facilities plan and usually spans a five- to six-year period. Local governments have found with experience that six years is a convenient period for the detail programming of capital expenditures, permitting sufficient lead time for the design and other preliminary work required by such projects. Projects included in the CIP should be arrayed according to their priority ranking.

CIP Report

The capital improvements program should be made available in report form to civic groups and interested citizens in addition to being distributed to the operating departments. The report should cover three main topics:

1. Explanation of the various considerations and policies brought to bear on the development of priorities—legal requirements, magnitude of projected capital needs, the fiscal resources of the jurisdiction, and so forth.
2. A listing of the major projects now under construction or for which funds have been appropriated.
3. A detailed description of the capital improvements program, with a listing of projects by agency and by priority to be included in the capital budget and to be undertaken in the following five years. The *capital budget* identifies the capital expenditures to be incurred in the next fiscal year and the means of financing these commitments.

The detailed description of each project should include a brief statement as to its general purpose and reason for its inclusion in the CIP. Capital costs, operating costs, the source of funds, the method of financing, and the financing schedule should be set forth in the report for each project.

In many jurisdictions, the capital budget is prepared, reviewed, and adopted concurrent with the annual operating budget. In some localities, however, the capital budget is subject to legislative review and adoption on a fiscal cycle different from that of the operating budget. In either case, public hearings generally are required before the capital budget is adopted. These hearings permit citizens to express their sentiments on the proposed budget and should be widely publicized. A summary of the tentative budget should be published, together with a notice of the time and place of the hearing. Although relatively few citizens attend unless they are irate over some aspect of the budget, public officials should be prepared for surprises. The turnout may be much larger than anticipated, and officials must be prepared to answer any and all questions.

Following the public hearings, the capital budget should again be discussed in executive session in an effort to reach consensus. The governing body may approve the budget by resolution, or it may adopt a separate appropriation ordinance that lists specific amounts for specific projects and agencies. An appropriation ordinance provides a more effective benchmark for budget administration and post-auditing.

After a capital budget has been adopted, another opportunity for review occurs at the time appropriations are made or, in the case of an issuance of general obligation bonds, at the time the bond referendum is placed before the voters. Of course, even after appropriations are made, changes and adjustments are still possible prior to construction or acquisition. If the original project requests are based upon a sound planning foundation, however, the need for such changes should be minimal.

Capital Costs and Debt Burden

To be most effective, the programming of strategic facilities should undertake to level off annual costs and to avoid erratic fluctuations. Annual costs, when measured against tax resources and available subsidies, determine the tax burden generated by the capital improvements program.

The definition of debt is key to calculating the debt burden of a jurisdiction. *Direct net debt* is defined as gross debt of a jurisdiction less all revenue bonds, other self-supporting debt, and cash flow notes. *Overall net debt* is the sum of direct net debt and the jurisdiction's proportionate share of the debt of other overlapping government units (for example, the county, school district, and special purpose district). The overall net debt represents the total burden imposed on a given property tax base by the local jurisdictions empower to incur debt.

Per capita debt is a measure of the proportionate amount of debt borne by each resident, determined by dividing the amount of outstanding debt (either direct net debt or overall net debt) by the population of the jurisdictions. Some jurisdictions establish the annual debt limit on this basis. If the growth of long-term debt is proportionate to the increased demands of a growing resident population, then debt ratios will not change significantly. When long-term debt increases faster than the rate of population growth, however, debt levels may reach or exceed the jurisdiction's ability to pay.

The debt to property value ratio measures the burden of debt on a locality's *ad valorem* (property) tax base. This ratio provides an indication of the burden that the existing debt places upon all property owners within the jurisdiction. The property tax base serves as a proxy for local wealth and, therefore, to some degree, reflects the capacity to provide public services.

Most states have established a limit on the dollar amount of debt that local governments can incur. This *debt limit* typically is expressed in terms of a percentage of taxable property values within the jurisdiction—usually 2% to 4% of current assessed value. For example, if the assessed value of property in a given locality is $3.5 billion and the debt limit is based on 2% of the assessed value, the locality can have no more than $70 million in outstanding debt at any point in time. The presumption is that with further development, the assessed value of property will increase and, therefore, the debt limit will increase sufficient to accommodate the additional borrowing necessary to finance the new strategic facilities required to meet the needs of the growing population.

Failure on the part of the state to adjust borrowing limits to a realistic basis, however, may result in various forms of circumvention. Localities might create debt authorities—special districts established in order to avoid either tax or debt limits—or might develop various types of subsidiary debt.

Each of these ratios presumes that the bonded debt burden is distributed equitably among the population and across the total real property wealth of the community. When the tax burden is not borne equally by all of the major taxpaying segments of the community, however, the capacity of the jurisdiction to afford additional debt may be adversely affected. This situation occurs when a significant portion of the property tax base falls on nonresidential taxpayers, such as business and industry or rental properties.

The overall bonded debt burden is determined by the total capital costs, together with the schedule and financing methods. When the tax or debt burden becomes too great for public resources, it may be necessary to reduce the level of improvements scheduled until their costs fit to these resources.

Standards of service must also have a degree of "built-in" flexibility. To be meaningful, they must represent actual performance or benefits. As new operational techniques are introduced or as new demands arise, it is important that such standards be flexible enough to permit adjustments to meet changing conditions.

Trends in Capital Outlays of Local Governments

According to the *2002 Census of Governments*, there are 87,849 units of local governments in the United States, the distribution of which is shown in Table 4-9. The numbers of county and municipal governments have remained fairly stable over the past forty years (municipal governments increased by only 8% during this period). However, striking changes are evident during this period in the numbers of school districts and special purpose districts. The number of school districts decreased by 61% between 1962 and 2002, largely through district consolidations. During this same period, the number of special purpose districts increased by 93%, as localities created special authorities, in part to circumvent state-imposed limits on general debt obligations.

Local governments expended nearly $130 billion in capital outlays in fiscal year (FY) 1999, an increase of 164% over the capital outlay expenditures in FY 1985. During this same fifteen-year period, total direct expenditures by local governments increased by 140%, from $386.8 billion in FY 1985 to $928.7 billion in FY 1999 (see Table 4-10). Capital outlays accounted for 14% of all direct expenditures by local governments in FY 1999. Education, at $42.1 billion, accounted for the largest functional category of capital outlays (32.4%) in FY 1999. Capital outlays in support of education increased by 380.5% from FY 1985 to FY 1999.

Table 4-9
Distribution of Local Government Units: 1962 to 2002

Type of Government	1962	1972	1982	1992	2002
County	3,043	3,044	3,041	3,043	3,034
Municipal	18,000	18,517	19,076	19,279	19,431
Town and township	17,142	16,991	16,734	16,656	16,506
School district	34,678	15,761	14,851	14,422	13,522
Special district	18,323	23,885	28,078	31,555	35,356
Totals	91,186	78,198	81,780	84,955	87,849

Source: U.S. Census Bureau, *2002 Census of Governments, Governmental Units in 2002*, series GC02-1(P).

Capital outlays by local governments in support of air and water transportation facilities increased by 260.5% in this fifteen-year period. These expenditures, for the most part, were made by special district authorities created to finance the development of local airports and terminal facilities.

In FY 1985, public utilities accounted for the largest category of capital outlay expenditures (23.6%). However, over the past fifteen years, local expenditures in support of utilities increased by only 62%, and in 1999 accounted for 14.5% of total capital outlays.

In FY 1999, local governments had $858.8 billion in debt outstanding, as shown in Table 4-10. Historically, the long-term debt of local governments was in the form of general obligation bonds, guaranteed by the full faith and credit of the issuing jurisdictions. By FY 1999, however, only 42% of the debt outstanding was guaranteed by full faith and credit. With the emergence of special purpose districts and authorities, an increasing portion of local government debt is being issued as revenue bonds (56% in FY 1999).

Educational facilities accounted for a significant component (20%) of the long-term debt obligations of local governments in FY 1999. To a large extent, debt obligations for education are in the form of general obligations bonds issued by county or municipal governments on behalf of schools districts. Public utilities accounted for 21% of the debt outstanding in FY 1999; the majority of these debt obligations are in the form of revenue bonds issued by special authorities. The public debt in support of private purposes is a relatively recent trend in local government finance. This category of debt will be discussed in further detail in Chapter 7.

Table 4-10

Local Government Capital Outlays

In Millions of Dollars

Function	1985	1990	1994	1995	1996	1997	1998	1999
Education	8,766	18,744	20,418	25,667	29,858	33,162	37,362	42,124
Utilities	11,610	13,996	16,056	16,801	16,149	17,746	17,599	18,827
Highways	6,073	9,017	9,508	10,874	11,255	12,235	13,059	13,920
Sewerage	5,738	8,023	7,215	8,040	8,413	9,116	8,422	9,091
Air & Water Transportation	2,038	3,817	5,966	4,323	4,399	5,538	5,612	7,346
Parks & Recreation	1,845	3,276	3,228	3,435	4,163	4,639	4,861	5,463
Hosuing & Community Development	3,179	3,878	3,872	4,340	4,441	5,265	5,342	5,413
Health & Hospitals	1,671	2,316	2,782	2,481	2,790	2,811	3,418	3,423
Natural Resources	660	952	647	935	998	983	1,007	1,010
Other	7,660	13,559	14,913	16,715	17,518	20,320	20,748	23,356
Totals	49,241	77,578	84,606	93,611	99,984	111,814	117,430	129,974
Direct Expenditures	386,753	575,404	710,366	751,438	786,120	827,648	874,664	928,671
Percent of Direct Expenditures	12.73%	13.48%	11.91%	12.46%	12.72%	13.51%	13.43%	14.00%

Source: U.S. Census Bureau, *1980-90 Historial Statistics on Governmental Finances and Employment;* and *Government Finances, Series GF,* No. 5, annual.

Table 4-11
Local Government Debt Outstanding: 1999
In Millions of Dollars

	Dollars	Percent of Total
Debt Outstanding	858,767	100.00%
Short-term debt	15,177	1.77%
Long-term debt	843,590	98.23%
Full faith & credit	359,543	41.87%
Nonguaranteed	484,047	56.37%
Long-term debt by purpose	843,590	100.00%
Education	169,104	20.05%
Utilities	178,279	21.13%
Public debt for private purposes	137,179	16.26%
Other	359,028	42.56%

Table 4-12
Local Government Public Works Expenditures
In Millions of Dollars

Function	1990	1995	1998	1999
Highways	26,314	30,216	35,243	36,776
Air & water transportation	9,971	9,320	11,604	13,892
Sewerage	21,688	22,121	24,515	25,852
Solid waste management	11,525	13,331	14,130	14,110
Water supply	24,433	27,863	31,897	33,924
Mass transit	17,222	20,904	21,889	22,433
Totals	111,153	123,756	139,277	146,986

Summary and Conclusions

The programming of capital improvements involves five major tasks:

1. Evaluation of current infrastructure conditions
2. Analysis of replacement options
3. Consideration of risk and uncertainty associated with various improvement proposals
4. Examination of financing options
5. Ranking capital project requests

A major concern in carrying out these tasks must be to balance the application of advanced analytical tools with the political considerations and technical limitations of the local government environment.

Most jurisdictions require a justification of each project as part of the departmental submissions. The process of comparing and selecting among competing projects often becomes very subjective, however, because these statements are so general.

A capital improvements program (CIP) represents the more immediate and more detailed portions of the long-range strategic facilities plan. The CIP should be prepared for review by and adoption by the chief executive and legislative body. Projects included in the CIP should be arrayed according to their priority ranking. Capital and operating costs, source of funds, method of financing, and financing schedule should be provided for each project. The capital budget identifies the capital expenditures to be incurred in the next fiscal year and the means of financing these commitments.

The total capital costs, together with the schedule and financing methods, determine the overall debt burden. When the tax or debt burden becomes too great, it may be necessary to reduce the level of improvements scheduled until their costs fit to the available public resources.

From FY 1985 to FY 1999, capital outlays by local governments increased at a faster rate than total direct expenditures. The significant increase (380.5%) in capital outlays in support of education during this period contributed to this differential. Educational facilities accounted for 17.8% of capital outlays in FY 1985; by FY 1999, this share increased to 32.4%. Educational facilities accounted for 20% of the long-term debt obligations of local governments in FY 1999.

Notes

1. David Sonnen, as cited in Daintry Duffy, "GIS Goes Worldwide," *Emerging Technology—CIO Magazine* (August 1, 2002): 12.
2. Dibya Sarkar, "Local Governments Use GIS," *Federal Computer Week* (December 11, 2003): 2.
3. William B. Rogers, "Fiscal Planning and Capital Budgeting," *Planning 1954* (Chicago, Ill.: American Society of Planning Officials, 1954): 96.
4. Harry P. Hatry, Annie P. Millar, and James H. Evans, "Guide to Setting Priorities for Capital Investments," *Guides to Managing Urban Capital*, Volume 5 (Washington, D.C.: The Urban Institute Press, 1984).

Chapter 5

COST ANALYSIS AND LONG-TERM RESOURCE COMMITMENTS

As noted in Chapter 4, if the scope of the proposed strategic facilities project warrants, cost-benefit and cost-effectiveness analysis techniques should be applied to determine the most appropriate use of limited public resources. Under cost-benefit analysis, estimates must be made of both direct and indirect costs and tangible and intangible benefits of a project. Costs and benefits are then translated into a common measure, usually (but not necessarily) a monetary unit. In cost-effectiveness analysis, benefits (outputs) are expressed in terms of levels of achievement—usually represented by measures of effectiveness or other nonmonetary indices—with the results presented in the form of tradeoffs rather than cost-benefit ratios.

Dimensions of Cost

Accounting data connote precision, and precision often is assumed to have its own virtue. It is important to recognize, however, that the numbers provided in financial statements and balance sheets are condensed from many detailed accounting records and reports. Therefore, any further analyses of costs based on these data must be undertaken with full awareness of the abstractions that have already been made. While accounting data reflect the financial dimensions of an organization, other important factors that might impinge on the overall viability of a proposed strategic facility and must also be considered.

Monetary Costs and Economic Costs

No decision is free of cost, whether or not the decision leads to the actual commitment of financial resources to a capital project. Choices among alternative strategies for the accomplishment of the goals and objectives of any organization are likely to involve many costs. The tendency, however, is to consider costs strictly in terms of dollar inputs—the financial resources required to support personnel, equipment, materials, and so forth. Future costs that cannot be easily measured in dollar terms all-too-often are dismissed as non-cost consideration. Such costs, however, might have important implications beyond their measurable monetary value.

The monetary costs associated with a strategic facility are those commonly reflected in financial accounts. They include research and development costs, investment costs, and the costs of operations, maintenance, and replacement (see Figure 5-1). Often it might be appropriate to look beyond these monetary costs to what economists call opportunity costs, associated costs, and social costs.

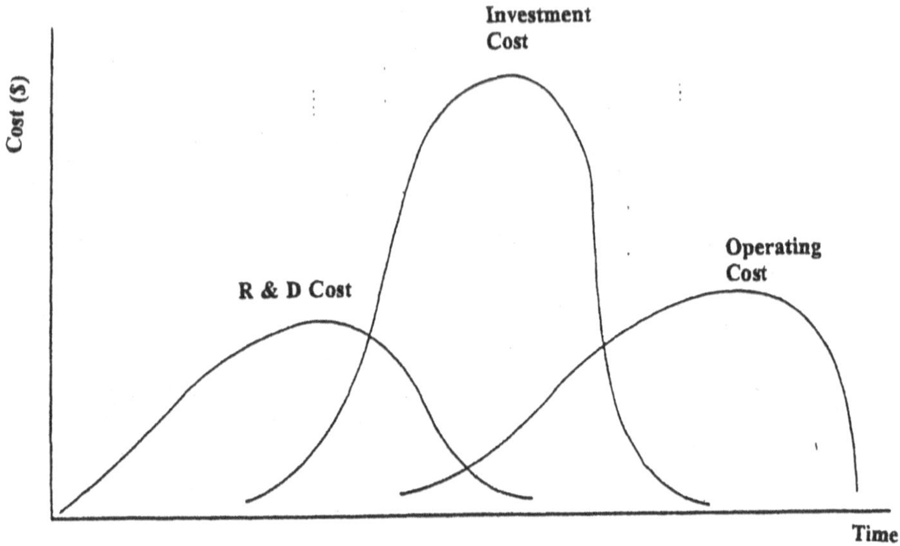

Figure 5-1 Life Cycle Costs Plotted Against Time

Research and development (R&D) involve "front-end" costs that might or might not figure into the actual expenses of a given capital project. R&D costs incurred explicitly in support of a given strategic facility should be included as a project expense. However, general R&D costs that eventually benefit more than one project or program must be considered as *sunk costs* and should not be included in the direct cost estimate for a specific project or program. Funds invested in research efforts to improve the safety of limited access highways, for example, represent a sunk cost as related to any specific highway project. The expenditure of funds in support of research leading to the design of a new bridge to be constructed on Interstate 95, on the other hand, should be include as a project cost in connection with improvements to I-95.

Investment costs are expenses incurred to obtain future benefits. Such investments might be classified as sunk costs or actual project outlays, depending on their timing. Consider the decision to build a public health clinic on land that was purchased some years earlier for some other public purpose. The additional investment cost required to prepare the site for the clinic should be considered as a project outlay. However, the previous investment for the land purchase is a sunk cost. Expenditures involved in the construction of the clinic, of course, would be considered to be a project cost.

Sunk costs can become an *inheritable asset* if previous investments can be used to the particular advantage of one alternative over another. The decision to utilize a prior investment should not be based solely on its inheritable asset potential, however. For example, if the location of a health clinic on a previously purchased site would be an inferior alternative in view of identified client needs, this decision would simply result in "throwing good money after bad."

Investment costs vary primarily with the size of a particular project, but not with its duration. *Recurring costs*, on the other hand, involve operating and maintenance costs that vary with both the size and duration of the project. Such recurring costs include salaries and wages, employee benefits, maintenance and repair of equipment, miscellaneous materials and supplies, transfer payments, insurance, and direct overhead costs. These recurring, or operating costs, do not add to the stock of capital. Rather, they are incurred to maintain the value of the existing capital stock.

In preparing cost estimates, it is important that recurring costs be considered over the life of the project and not just in the initial fiscal period. Operating costs often increase gradually as a new project comes on line and the potential client base expands. These costs often reach a peak prior to a decision to terminate the project when repair and maintenance costs are relatively high. Operating costs "zero out" when the project is terminated. At this point, however, there might be some "terminal value" to the initial investment (for example, when a facility can be used for some other public purpose or sold to the private sector).

As these distinctions suggest, some project costs are *fixed*, that is, they are the same regardless of the size or duration of the project. Other costs are *variable*; that is, they might change significantly as the scope of the project is increased. Some uncertainty might exist regarding these costs, particularly if the project has a relatively long duration. It is important, therefore, to consider the marginal (or incremental) costs of increasing the size or scope of a project.

Suppose, for example, that the decision is whether to build one or two public health clinics. It might be possible to get quantity discounts on materials and equipment that would reduce the cost of a second clinic. As a result, suppose the cost of building one clinic is $2,300,000, and the cost of building two clinics is $4,000,000. The average cost of each clinic would be $2,000,000; however, the marginal cost of the second clinic would be only $1,700,000.

If resources are committed to one project or program, the opportunity has been preempted to use these resources elsewhere. The concept of *opportunity costs* can be illustrated by returning to the health clinic example. Having determined the monetary cost of the proposed facility, it might be appropriate to describe some of the alternative uses of these resources. For example, for what other purpose might the land be used? For what other purposes might the required staff salaries be expended? If bonds are to be issued, what other uses might be made of the funds required for interest and principal payments?

An attempt should be made to estimate the value of these alternative uses if they are deemed to be sufficiently important. This evaluation would consider the benefits that must be given up if the decision is made to go ahead with the proposed clinic. Keep in mind that a basic purpose of cost analysis is to estimate the value of alternatives forgone. Opportunity costs might be extremely important in making decisions among alternative project strategies.

Associated costs are "any costs involved in utilizing project services in the process of converting them into a form suitable for use or sale at the stage benefits are evaluated."[1] The beneficiaries of public programs and services often incur associated costs. The associated costs that must be borne by users of public recreational facilities, for example, include the incremental costs of travel, food, lodging, and so forth. If access to a recreational facility is improved, so that the users' travel costs are reduced, then these savings in associated costs might be considered as benefits arising from the improved access.

Social costs can be defined as the subsidies that would have to be paid to compensate persons adversely affected by a project or program for their suffering or "disbenefits." Such compensation rarely is made (except perhaps when affected individuals enter into litigation and are awarded damages). Thus, social costs represent an analytical concept.

In making a cost analysis, social costs can be handled in one of two ways.[2] These costs might be treated as "external" and subtracted from the perceived value of the project to obtain a net social value. Alternatively, they might be treated as opportunity costs, by examining the potential benefits to those individuals who are likely to be affected if the project funds were spent for some other public purpose. For example, the location of a sewage treatment facility might result in reduced property values in adjacent residential areas. These losses might be treated as "negative benefits" and subtracted from the overall benefits of the project to the larger community. Alternatively, the benefits that would accrue to these property owners from an alternative use of project funds (for example, development of a park site) might be calculated. The project with the larger yield would represent the better use of these resources.

Social costs often carry significant emotional overtones and, therefore, might be difficult to evaluate. Unfortunately, if social costs are included in a cost analysis, they are seldom treated fairly. Such cost considerations are either underplayed by proponents of a project or overplayed by its opponents. Nevertheless, such an evaluation might be a very important factor in the decision to invest organizational resources in a project or program.

Factors Influencing Future Costs

Developing cost estimates for capital construction is generally a fairly straightforward process. An initial consideration involves the distribution of effort between outside contractors and in-house staff. The scope of major capital projects often requires the involvement of considerable outside contractors, since local jurisdictions usually do not maintain the pool of skilled labor necessary to undertake such efforts. However, in-house personnel might undertake some components of a project (e.g., preliminary site preparation, installation of utilities, landscape of the competed project).

The jurisdiction might elect to solicit preliminary bids from outside contractors based on engineering specifications and architectural drawings. Cost estimates might also be prepared by staff based on similar projects in other localities to provide a basis for comparison with solicited bids. Provision should be made in these capital cost estimates for the impact of inflation, since in all likelihood the construction will be carried out over several years. It might also be appropriate to take into consideration the method of financing (e.g., from current revenues or through the issuance of bonds).

As noted in Chapter 4, it is important to include an estimate of future operating costs in determining the cost of a capital project. Operating costs constitute a continuing annual expense that might result in a serious fiscal burden for the jurisdiction and, therefore, must be considered carefully. The following factors should be considered in estimating the operating costs associated with a strategic facilities project:

1. Scope and quality of the services or products to be delivered by the project.
2. Volume of activity required to deliver these services or products.
3. Methods, facilities, and organizational structure required to perform these activities.
4. Qualities and types of labor, materials, equipment, and other cost elements required by these programs.
5. Price levels of the various cost elements.

These cost factors should be considered: (1) in the development of the project design; (2) in the preparation of a capital budget request; and (3) after commitments have been authorized, as the project enters the implementation phase.

Personnel costs (labor) are the most critical element for most organizational operations. Therefore, performance measures are useful to financial managers. Such measures often are expressed in terms of personnel hours required to carry out particular activities or programs (workload measures). Unit cost standards might be established for activities that are of a type and importance to justify the application of cost accounting procedures. For nonroutine (nonrecurrent) activities, however, workload and unit cost measures might not adequately represent the cost elements involved. In such cases, management might have to rely on more subjective measures to provide an adequate basis for cost estimates.

Current records of personnel activities might provide sufficiently accurate and reliable data to determine current workloads (units of production or workload measures) and to provide a basis for estimating future levels of activities. In some cases, however, it might be necessary to undertake more extensive analyses of the nature and scope of the activities involved. Further refinements are possible where cost accounting procedures have been adopted.

Having established the volume of work required to carry out the anticipated activities, it might be appropriate to examine alternative methods and organizational approaches to determine if greater efficiency and effectiveness can be attained. Work methods should be analyzed to establish an appropriate mix of personnel, equipment, supplies, and other operating requirements to do the job with the least effort and at the least cost. Particular attention should be given to possible increases in productivity through simplified procedures and the use of labor-saving equipment.

Personnel costs are subject to management control in two important areas: salary rates and job classifications. Periodic reviews should be made to determine that each employee has the proper work assignment in view of his or her pay rate. All too often, skilled employees with higher pay classifications are assigned tasks that lower-rated persons should perform. Eliminating positions at the lower end of the pay scale might result in serious false economies if higher-paid personnel eventually have to do the work previously assigned to these positions.

Changes in salary plans should be made only after a thorough study of such factors as trends in the cost of living, rates paid by comparable organizations, and employee benefits, including sick leave, vacations, extra holidays, and the security of time in service. Improved employee benefits can often provide a bigger payoff to employees than increases in salaries and wages, which are likely to be subject to a larger "tax bite." Sound personnel and compensation policies will yield economic benefits in the long run.

Prices for materials, supplies, and equipment can be controlled to some extent by scheduling purchases to take advantage of the lowest price consistent with necessary quality. Trends in the prices of frequently used commodities should be continuously analyzed, and appropriate inventories should be maintained for those items subject to price fluctuations. At the same time, the cost of maintaining inventory (space requirements, shelf life, anticipated price changes, and so forth) also must be considered.

Traditional Methods for Analyzing Direct and Indirect Costs

In undertaking a cost analysis, it is also important to distinguish between direct and indirect costs. A *direct cost* represents a cost incurred for a specific purpose that is uniquely associated with that purpose. Direct cost components involved in any project, program, or process include (1) labor or personal services (salaries, wages, and related employee benefits); (2) contractual services (services purchased from outside sources); (3) materials and supplies (consumables); and (4) equipment expenses (sometimes categorized as fixed asset expenses). In analyzing the overall operations of a day care center, for example, the salary of the center's manager would be considered a direct cost. However, the center might be divided into several units, according to different age groups of children, with a portion of the manager's salary allocated to each unit. Then the manager's salary would be considered an indirect cost of each unit. An *indirect cost* is generally considered to be any cost associated with more than one activity or program that cannot be traced directly to any of the individual activities. In the public sector, the terms *indirect cost* and *overhead* often are used interchangeably.

Most accounting systems currently in use record and distribute costs by one of the following methods:

- Organizational units or elements
- Budgetary accounts
- Traditional cost accounting procedures, with indirect cost allocated on some formula basis

Each of these approaches has advantages and disadvantages, and each has met the needs of both private and public organizations in the past. Yet, each method fails to meet the full informational requirements for cost management.

Under an organization-based accounting system, the identifiable direct costs are distributed to the various elements of the traditional bureaucratic structure—departments, bureaus, agencies, and so forth. Indirect costs are usually recorded and paid from a central repository with no attempt to further subdivide or distribute these costs to organizational units. In many organizations, only direct salary costs are distributed to the organizational elements. This approach is inadequate for making important decisions regarding variations in the output of the organization. Costs are not applied to the ultimate output, activities, projects, or process flows of the organization.

Budgetary accounts track costs in a manner very similar to that of the organizational unit approach. Historically, public organizations have been most concerned with ensuring that total expenditures do not exceed the allocated budgetary resources. Consequently, accounting systems became a safeguard mechanism to capture commitments, undelivered orders, and expenditures. Cost data are normally divided by organizational units in order to track the execution of the budget. The major objective is to ensure the full use the resources assigned to each unit rather than to enhance productivity or to reduce expenses. Any attempt to conserve resources, in fact, might lead to a reduction in future budget allocations.[3] As with organizational accounting systems, no provision is made to relate cost to output or, in most cases, to even define output.

Cost accounting procedures were originally developed to help industries estimate the full costs of manufacturing goods, including the variable costs (labor and raw materials) involved in production as well as the fixed cost (overhead or indirect costs). This accounting method was sufficiently accurate for managerial budgeting and planning in a fundamental business environment. Traditional costing models use direct cost factors (e.g., labor hours, machine hours, material dollars) as surrogates to allocate overhead or indirect costs to the various products.

If total direct costs of a firm were $800,000 and the associated indirect cost was $400,000, then the indirect cost rate would be 50%; that is, for every dollar of direct cost, the firm also spent $.50 on indirect cost items. If one of the products of the firm was widgets, and the direct costs associated with producing widgets were $40,000, then the indirect cost allocation would be $20,000, and the total cost would be $60,000. The cost per unit of production is determined by the sum of the total costs divided by the number of units produced or processed. For example, if the firm produced 20,000 widgets at a total cost (direct and indirect) of $60,000, the unit cost of production would be $3.00. In order to make a profit, the firm would have to sell each widget at a price in excess of $3.00.

These cost allocation factors tend to vary proportionately with the volume of goods produced or services provided. Costs become more difficult to assign, however, as the range of goods and service provided increased. This difficulty is due, in part, to an increasingly complex production environment that has resulted in added layers of indirect or overhead costs that cannot be precisely allocated.

With the recent advent of activity-based accounting procedures, it has been determined that the traditional cost accounting methodology can create a significant difference in output cost because of the manner in which indirect or overhead costs are allocated to output. This difference in distribution can skew the ultimate price of the output, leading to poor management decisions.

Process-Oriented Approach

Robin Cooper and Robert Kaplan of the Harvard Business School suggest that the traditional approach to cost accounting is flawed because certain cost behavior is a function of the activities carried on in supporting departments and should not be driven by volume-related allocation factors.[4] Activities describe what an organization does. The primary function of an activity is to convert resources (e.g., labor, material, and technology) into outputs (e.g., products and services).

The activity-based costing (ABC) model, which Cooper and Kaplan developed, reconfigures how organizations manage costs by attaching costs to activities—the processes or procedures that cause work to be performed in an organization (see Table 5-1). Cost management and cost control can then focus on the areas that generate cost rather than on where the costs are reported. In this way, the total cost of all traceable activities is based on how much of each activity is consumed by the product or service, regardless of organizational or functional boundaries. A fundamental premise of ABC is that managers can learn how to identify and eliminate waste by focusing on the root cause of a cost rather than merely addressing the symptoms.

The major difference between activity-based costing and traditional cost accounting is that ABC is a process-oriented accounting method, based on the recognition that labor-intensive processes might represent the single largest contributor to the increasing cost of doing business. Activity-based costing recognizes that, while common processes or activities might be performed within each functional area, the traditional prorating method does not truly account for the usage variance in process costs that might exist in different units.

A commercial production line, for example, might consume more direct labor, material, and even space than the facilities required for a small, high-precision, manufacturing process undertaken for the NASA space shuttle program. However, the administrative overhead required to support the space shuttle contract is likely to be extraordinarily high, inflated by the additional (indirect) labor needed to perform such activities as the nonroutine handling of the small parts procurements, more stringent acceptance testing, and NASA contract reporting requirements. In this environment, provision can be made under ABC for a surrogate form of direct costing by accounting for the significant variance in indirect costs and proportionately allocating those costs to the end-item products that consume them.

A further example to demonstrate that the traditional method of applying overhead directly to the output can misstate the true cost of production is provided in Table 5-2. Even though this example has been simplified for demonstration purposes, it nonetheless is an accurate representation of how the activity-based methodology more fairly distributes costs with fewer arbitrary allocations normally associated with traditional cost accounting procedures. Activity-based costing gives a more accurate picture of output costs by tracing overhead cost through the activities that are actually used to produce the output rather than by a straight allocation method.

Table 5-1
The ABC Glossary

Activity

- *Total cost of activity*: Total amount of direct and overhead charges associated with or allocated to a single activity.
- *Cost driver*: A measurable factor that represents the amount of performance and creates or affects the costs within a single defined activity, i.e. the number of iterations, amount of effort, etc.
- *Elapsed time*: Total amount of time, including the amount of time delay created while awaiting processing, consumed to complete the activity or an iteration of the cost driver.
- *Cycle time*: The amount of time to complete one cycle or iteration of the cost driver without including delay or wait times.

Process

- *Total cost of the process*: Total cost of all the activities in a process determined by the amount of the cost driver for each activity in relation to the output of the process
- *Cost of a single iteration*: Total cost of a single incident or cost driver allocation for each activity in a process flow which might be equal to the total cost when a single iteration occurs at each activity in the flow.

Output

- *Cost of the output*: Total cost of the activity model allocated by the applied activity drivers to the output of the activity model.

Identification of Change Opportunities

- *Significant cost consumption*: Activities identified that have an evidently larger consumption of inputs and mechanisms or the value of the output is less than the value of the inputs.
- *Significant time use*: Activities identified that have evidently larger time periods or use of time or large, non-value, delay periods.

Evaluation of Change Alternatives

- *Cost comparison*: Analysis of the allocated costs from the activity model to two or more alternative process methods.
- *Time comparison*: Analysis of the total time or cycle times of two or more alternative process methods.

Table 5-2
Comparative Costing Example: Production Site JKL

Site JKL produces two products: Output A and Output B. The average production, JKL costs, and market price are as follows:

	Average Production	JKL Cost	Market Price
Output A:	200 units	$110	$125
Output B:	800 units	$ 20	$ 18

Managerial Analysis: Output A is very competitive and is carrying the operation. Output B is costing too much and should be eliminated from production.

Before making a final decision, a request was made to provide more analysis using the new activity-based costing methodology as a comparison to the current traditional system. The following information was gathered:

Direct Costs
Output A: $100 per unit
Output B: $ 10 per unit
Overhead Costs in Purchasing Department
Annual workload: 10,000 purchase orders
Annual cost: $10,000
Purchase orders required per unit of Output A: 30
Purchase orders required per unit of Output B: 5

Cost Distribution Table

Traditional Cost Accounting
Total Output / Total Overhead = Amount per Unit of Output
1,000 / $10,000 = $10

Activity-Based Accounting
Activity Cost / Activity Workload = Amount per Unit of Activity
$10,000 / 10,000 = $1

Activity Units x Amount per Unit			= Total Output Cost per Unit of Output
Output A:	30 x	$1	= $30
Output B:	5 x	$1	= $ 5

Total Cost per Unit Output

Traditional Cost

	Direct Cost	+	Overhead	=	Total Cost
Output A:	$100	+	$10	=	$100
Output B:	$ 10	+	$10	=	$ 20

Activity-Based Cost

	Direct Cost	+	Overhead	=	Total Cost
Output A:	$100	+	$30	=	$130
Output B:	$ 10	+	$ 5	=	$ 15

Activity-Based Analysis: When costs are traced to the amount of the activity actually used, Output A is actually more expensive than originally thought and, furthermore, is not competitive in the market. Output B is competitive and should be retained.

Management of JKL decided to ignore the new analysis and implement the decision to eliminate Output B.

Results of the Decision: With Output B eliminated along with all associated costs, the output price for A immediately reverted to the remaining costs. Purchasing was unable to eliminate the costs and the price for Output A rose to $130 per unit. This new price made Output A impossible to sell.

Direct Material	+ Overhead	= Total Cost	/ Production	= Price
$20,000	+ $6,000	= $26,000	/ 200	= $130

Alternative Decision: If JKL's management had made its decision based on the ABC analysis, then Output A would have been eliminated. Had this decision been implemented then the following results would have occurred:

Direct Material	+ Overhead	= Total Cost	/ Production	= Price
$8,000	+ $4,000	= $12,000	/ 800	= $ 15

The elimination of Output A had no effect on the organization since the remaining costs were those associated with Output B and Output B always was competitive within the market.

Although manufacturing firms might gain the greatest benefit from ABC in the area of overhead cost allocation, the approach offers benefits to service industries in the tracking of both direct and indirect costs. The process orientation makes ABC valuable and applicable to all types of organizations, including government, nonprofit organizations, and colleges and universities.[5]

The ABC approach is likely to produce a more accurate representation of indirect costs attributable to final cost objectives than using surrogate measures, such as direct labor hours or direct material dollars, as a means for allocating costs to products. However, the ABC method is more complex and requires additional time and effort to determine the attribution of indirect costs. In many situations, it is uncertain whether markedly different results are obtained by using the ABC method instead of more traditional approaches. ABC can only be fully implemented in organizations that have a clear understanding of the body of activities that are commonly performed in all functional areas. If the costing system is used to determine fees or prices or to measure performance of selected activity centers or indirect cost pools, then the more complex ABC methodology might be appropriate.

Cost-Benefit Analysis

It has been suggested that: "One can view cost-benefit analysis as anything from an infallible means of reaching the new Utopia to a waste of resources in attempting to measure the unmeasurable."[6] Many of the criticisms of cost-benefit analysis are equally applicable to other analytical techniques. Since systematic analysis is difficult, costly, and troublesome, all too often, the assertion is made that more intuitive approaches should be applied. This is not a valid argument, however, for abandoning efforts to improve techniques for cost analysis.

Benefit Investment Analysis

The principal objective of long-term investments in the private sector is to maximize profits. Industries frequently average as much as 50% of their total resources in long-term investments. Much of this commitment, of course, is involved in the development of an appropriate cash flow (annual profit margin) and in routine replacement.

New concepts and tools were introduced in the private investment decision process in the mid-1950s, when it became evident that intuitive modes, developed in an era of relative easy profits through rapid industrial expansion, were no longer applicable. These new discounted cash flow techniques apply the principles of compound interest in a way that takes into account the differences in the worth of money over time. The input data used by each method focuses on the future negative and positive cash flows (costs and benefits) required to produce the desired returns on the particular investment.

In applying these methods, the present value of future streams of both costs and benefits must be determined by multiplying each stream by an appropriate discount factor, which can be expressed as:

$$1 \div (1 + i)^n$$

where i is the relevant interest rate per year and n is the number of periods into the future that the benefits and costs will accrue. If, as is the usual case, i is positive, the farther in the future that an event is expected to occur, the smaller is its present value. High discount rates mean that the present is valued considerably over the future; that is, there is a significantly higher regard for present benefits than for future benefits and/or a willingness to trade some larger amount of future benefits for smaller current benefits.

Of the various discounted cash flow methods used in investment decisions, two techniques are particularly relevant to cost analysis in the public sector. The *net present value* method gives the algebraic difference in the present worth of both outward cash flows and inward flows of income or benefits. In some cases, an investment might have a terminal value (T) at the end of the analysis period. Annual expenses (K) for the administration, operation, and maintenance of the project and the annual income (R) from sales revenues, receipts, or their equivalent must also be discounted to present values to be included in the analysis.

Thus, the formula for calculating net present value can be expressed as follows:

$$NPV = -I + T \div (1 + i)^n - K\,[(1 + i)^n - 1] \div i(1 + i)^n + R\,[(1 + i)^n - 1] \div i(1 + i)^n$$

where I represents the initial investment, the present worth of the terminal value is calculated by multiplying T times the appropriate discount factor, and K and R are multiplied by the present worth factor of a uniform series.

The *equivalent uniform annual net return* (EUANR) combines all costs and all expenses into one single annual sum that is equivalent to all disbursements uniformly distributed over the analysis period. This method also includes an income or benefit factor. The solution to the formula indicates the amount by which the equivalent uniform annual income (or benefits) exceeds (or is less than) the equivalent uniform annual cost. The EUANR formula can be represented as follows:

$$EUANR = -I\,[i(1 + i)^n] \div [(1 + i)^n - 1] + T\,[i \div [(1 + i)^n - 1] - K + R$$

where the initial investment (I) is multiplied times a capital recovery factor, the terminal value (T) is multiplied by a sinking fund factor, with K and R representing uniform annual expenses and uniform annual income respectively. R includes return on investment (depreciation and net profit).

To illustrate the application of these two methods of discounted cash flow analysis, assume that management is confronted with two alternative investment decisions, as shown in Table 5-3. Alternative A has an initial investment cost of $1.1 million and annual costs of $629,200. At the end of the fifteen-year period of analysis, it is estimated that alternative A will have a terminal value of $600,000. Alternative B has an initial investment cost of $2 million and annual

Table 5-3
Cash Flow Data for Analysis of Alternatives

Cash Flow Items	Alternative A	Alternative B
I = Initial investment	$1,100,000	$2,000,000
T = Terminal value	$ 600,000	$1,000,000
A = Annual administrative cost	$ 100,000	$ 90,000
J = Annual operations cost	$ 280,000	$ 295,500
M = Annual maintenance cost	$ 120,000	$ 100,000
K = Total of A, J, & M	$ 500,000	$ 485,500
R = Annual income	$ 629,200	$ 700,000
i = Rate of interest per annum	8%	8%
n = Analysis period	15 years	15 years

Capital recovery factor = 0.1168395
Present worth factor = 0.3152417
Present worth of a series = 8.5594798
Sinking fund factor = 0.0368295

EUANR/ Alt. A = -$1,100,000(0.1168295) + $600,000(0.0368295) + $129,200
= -$128,512 + $22,098 + $129,200
= $22,786

EUANR/ Alt. B = -$2,000,000(0.1168295) + $1,000,000(0.0368295) + $214,500
= -$233,659 + $36,830 + $214,500
= $17,671

NPV/ Alt. A = -$1,100,000 + $600,000(0.3152417) + $129,200(8.5594798)
= -$1,100,000 + $189,145 + $1,105,885
= $195,030

NPV/ Alt. B = -$2,000,000 + $1,000,000(0.3152417) + 214,500(8.5594798)
= -$2,000,000 + $315,242+ $1,836,008
= $151,250

costs of $700,000. At the end of the fifteen years, the estimated terminal value of alternative B is $1 million.

Applying the formula for the equivalent uniform annual net return method, it can be shown that alternative A has an EUANR of $22,786, whereas alternative B has an EUANR of $17,671. Therefore, all other things being equal, alternative A is the better investment. Similarly, alternative A has a net present value of $195,030, whereas alternative B has a net present value of $151,250. It should be noted that the EUANR for any project can be converted to the NPV by multiplying the EUANR by the present worth factor for a uniform series (which in the above example is 8.5594798).

These two techniques of investment analysis have counterparts in the cost analysis of public investments. The net present value method is similar in concept to the net benefits criterion, while the equivalent uniform annual net return method has its counterpart in the annual net benefits approach.

Basic Components of Cost-Benefit Analysis

The crux of cost-benefit analysis lies in a statement of the problem. As Anatol Rapoport has observed: "The success with which any problem is solved depends to a great extent on the clarity with which it is stated. In fact, the solution of the problem is, in a sense, a clarification (or concretization) of the objectives."[7] Vague problem statements lead to vague methods, where success is doubtful or, at best, erratic. The more a given situation can be clarified, the better the classification of the problem or issue, and the greater the promise of a successful solution.

The formulation of the cost-benefit approach was first outlined by Otto Eckstein. Under this analytical approach, the resource allocation problem is clarified through the identification of: (1) an objective function, (2) constraints, (3) externalities, (4) risk and uncertainty, and (5) time dimensions.[8]

Selecting an *objective function* involves the identification and quantification, in dollar terms to the extent possible, of the benefits and costs associated with each alternative course of action. Benefits are the net outcomes, both tangible and intangible, of a project. Specification of benefits sometimes might be relatively straightforward, as in many technical and industrial projects. For many public projects, however, benefits often are diffuse, intangible, and difficult to define and measure. Costs are somewhat easier to identify. They are the direct and indirect inputs—the resources required to carry out the project or program. The evaluation of opportunity costs—the value of foregone opportunities—might be complex, however, even for projects for which extensive impact data are available.

Constraints are the "rules of the game"—that is, the limits within which a solution must be sought. Solutions that are otherwise optimal frequently must be discarded because they do not conform to these imposed rules. Constraints often are incorporated into mathematical models as parameters or boundary conditions.

Projects might have external or spillover effects—side effects or unintended consequences that might be beneficial or detrimental. These *externalities* often are difficult to identify and measure, therefore they frequently are excluded from the analysis initially in order to make the problem statement more manageable. The long-range effects of these phenomena must ultimately be considered, however, usually after the objective function and model have been tested and the range of feasible alternatives has been narrowed.

Costs and benefits occurring at different points in time must be made commensurable—that is, translated into a common unit of measurement. It is not sufficient merely to add the estimated benefits and subtract the estimated costs. The impact of deferred benefits and future costs must be taken into account. In so doing, the analyst encounters the problems of risk and uncertainty.

In developing a cost-benefit analysis, it is important to recognize that dollar values are not equal over time. Benefits that accrue in the present usually are worth more to their recipients than benefits anticipated some time in the future. Similarly, resources invested today cost more than those invested in the future, since one option would be to invest the same funds at some rate of return that would increase their value. Therefore, the equivalent present value of future streams of both costs and benefits must be determined by multiplying each stream by an appropriate discount factor.

The choice of the discount rate might make the difference between acceptance and rejection of a project. Unfortunately, no simple guidelines are available for determining an appropriate discount rate for public investments. Two common bases for discounting can be used, however, reflecting both local conditions and the marketplace for investments. The cost of borrowing the capital necessary to finance a strategic facility project provides one basis for determining an appropriate discount rate. The rate of return that could be realized if an equivalent amount were invested for the same period of time offers another basis. Thus, if borrowing the necessary capital at 6% could finance a project, or if an investment of equivalent funds could be expected to yield 7%, either of these percentages might be used to discount future costs and benefits.

Although the choice of a particular discount rate might be difficult to justify, the procedures for discounting are quite simple. Once an appropriate rate has been chosen, a table of discount factors can be consulted to determine the appropriate figure to apply to each year in the stream of costs and benefits. As the data in Table 5-4 illustrate, however, the selection of the discount rate can significantly affect the final decision.

A comprehensive cost-benefit analysis of a capital project requires that estimates be made of both the direct and indirect costs and the tangible and intangible benefits. Costs and benefits are discounted to their present values and must be translated into a common measure, usually (but not necessarily) a monetary unit. Costs and benefits are then compared by computing: (1) a benefit/cost ratio (discounted benefits divided by discounted costs), (2) net benefits (discounted benefits minus discounted costs), or (3) some other value (such as an internal rate of return) that summarizes the results of the analysis. Given adequate estimates, cost-benefit analyses offer relatively straightforward assessments of economic efficiency, providing information on which to base decisions regarding the effective allocation of available resources among economically desirable alternatives.

Table 5-4
Discounting $100,000 Annually Over Ten Years

Year	Discount Factor @ 8 Percent	Value	Discount Factor @ 10 Percent	Value
1	0.925926	92,593	0.909090	90,909
2	0.857339	85,734	0.826446	82,645
3	0.793832	79,383	0.751315	75,132
4	0.735030	73,503	0.683013	68,301
5	0.680583	68,058	0.620920	62,092
6	0.630170	63,017	0.564472	56,447
7	0.583490	58,349	0.513156	51,316
8	0.540269	54,027	0.466505	46,651
9	0.500249	50,025	0.424095	42,410
10	0.463193	46,319	0.385541	38,554
Total		$671,008		$614,455

Criteria for Analysis

Once an objective function has been identified, the next step in the analysis is to select an indicator of "success"—that is, an index that will yield a higher value for more desirable alternatives. Conceptually, such an indicator involves the maximization of something. Businesses, for example, seek to maximize profits. Public officials are presumed to seek maximum benefits for their constituencies. An inability to quantify overall benefits, however, has led to the identification of cost minimization as the objective function in many cost-benefit analyses.

It is frequently suggested that the goal of cost-benefit analysis should be to maximize benefits and minimize costs. In reality, however, both cannot be accomplished simultaneously. Costs can be minimized by spending nothing and by doing nothing, but, in that case, no benefits result. Benefits derived from a particular project or program can be maximized by committing organizational resources until marginal benefits are zero. However, such action might require far more resources than are available. Therefore, some composite criterion is needed. Three obvious choices are:

- Maximize benefits for given costs.
- Minimize costs while achieving a fixed level of benefits.
- Maximize net benefits (benefits minus costs).

The first cost-benefit criterion to be used in the quantitative evaluation of alternatives was the *benefit/cost ratio*, introduced by the Flood Control Act of 1936. A benefit/cost ratio is defined as the present value of benefits divided by the present value of costs (or average annual benefits over average annual costs). Thus, for example, if the discounted stream of benefits over the expected duration of a project or program equals $1,600,000, and the discounted stream of costs equals $1,200,000, the benefit/cost ratio is 1.33.

A variation on the basic benefit/cost ratio emphasizes the return on invested capital by segregating the cost of operations and subtracting them from both sides of the ratio. In the previous example, assume that the present value of operational costs represents $400,000 of the total stream of costs. Subtracting operational costs from both total benefits and total costs results in the following net benefit/cost ratio:

$$\frac{\$1{,}600{,}000 - \$400{,}000}{\$1{,}200{,}000 - \$400{,}000} = \frac{\$1{,}200{,}000}{\$\ 800{,}000} = 1.50$$

The net benefit/cost ratio becomes larger as operational costs account for an increasingly larger proportion of total costs. If, for example, the net operational costs were $600,000, the net benefit/cost ratio would be 1.67.

Net benefit/cost ratios might be preferable in the private sector, where capital might be a greater constraint than operational expenses, especially when taxes are considered. A number of economists, however, argue for the use of gross benefit/cost ratios in public sector applications. Their contention is that legislative bodies should consider the cost of operations as well as capital costs and should give agencies credit for savings on operational costs by permitting them to spend more on capital costs.

Net benefits is the criterion recommended, if not used, most frequently in contemporary cost-benefit analysis. Net benefits measure difference, whereas benefit/cost calculations produce a ratio. The results of these two techniques are not always interchangeable. The fact that the net benefits of alternative A are greater than those of alternative B does not imply that the benefit/cost ratio of A is greater than that of B. Suppose, for example, that the benefits of alternative A have a present value of $600,000 and that the costs have a present value of $200,000. The net benefits of this alternative would be $600,000 minus $200,000 = $400,000, and the benefit/cost ratio would be $600,000 divided by $200,000, or 3.0. If the present value of benefits of alternative B was $400,000, and the present value of costs was $80,000, alternative B would have lower net benefits ($400,000 - $80,000 = $320,000), but a higher benefit/cost ratio ($400,000/$80,000 = 5.0). In addition to knowing the benefit/cost ratio for a given project, it is also necessary to know the size of the project.

The size of the project is important in another respect. Suppose that two projects each offer net benefits of $10,000. One involves a present value of benefits of $2 million and a present value of costs of $1.99 million. The other project has a present value of benefits of $100,000 and a present value of costs of $90,000. Now suppose that something goes wrong, so that the calculations of costs and benefits are off by 10%. The first project might have a negative benefit of as much as $200,000, whereas the second would do no worse than break even.

Cost-Benefit Analysis: An Example

An underlying assumption in benefit investment analysis (BIA) is that cost and benefits will remain relatively constant over the life of the project. This assumption permits the application of the capital recovery factor, present worth factor, present worth of a series factor, and the sinking fund factor in calculating the net present value and the equivalent uniform annual net return.

In reality, however, costs and benefits seldom remain constant. Costs might increase due to inflation or increases in the numbers of units of service provided. Benefits might accrue more slowly at the outset of a project and then increase as additional "customers" are reached. In short, both costs and benefits are likely to be moving targets during the course of the analysis. For this reason, a year-by-year discounting of costs and benefits, as shown in Table 5-5, often is preferred over a benefit investment analysis.

The data in Table 5-5 is drawn from the cash flow data presented in Table 5-3. The initial investments required by each of the alternatives are expressed in terms of the annual debt service payments to support the fifteen-year annuity serial bonds, issued at 6% interest for $1,100,000 and $2,000,000 respectively. Annuity serial bonds have uniform annual debt service payments, and therefore the discounted costs diminish over the fifteen-year period of analysis. The administrative costs associated with each alternative are assumed to increase at an annual rate of 6%. The operation and maintenance (O&M) costs for alternative A is also projected to increase at 6%, while the O&M costs for alternative B is projected to increase at an annual rate of 5%.

Benefits for both alternatives are projected to increase at an annual rate of 4%, while the terminal values ($600,000 for alternative A and $1,000,000 for alternative B) become a benefit in the fifteenth year of the analysis (and must be discounted accordingly). The discount rate applied to costs and benefits is 8%, as stated in Table 5-3. A range of other assumptions could be made about the annual rates of increases (or decreases) in the costs and benefits of these two alternatives. However, these fairly limited assumptions serve to illustrate why a more detailed cost-benefit analysis is necessary.

Using the benefit investment analysis approach, alternative A—with a NPV of $195,830 and an EUANR of $22,786—appears to be the preferred alternative over B—with a NPV of $151,250 and an EUANR of $17,671. However, as shown in Table 5-5, when the prospect of increases in costs and benefits are considered, alternative B has the higher NPV ($473,592) and benefit/cost ratio (1.0639) than alternative A (with a NPV of -$93,348 and a benefit/cost ratio of 0.9868). Factors contributing to the higher NPV for alternative B include the differential rate of increase in operation and maintenance costs and the spreading of the initial investment over the fifteen-year project.

Limitations of Cost-Benefit Analysis

Cost-benefit techniques do not solve all problems relating to the allocation of scarce organizational resources. Cost-benefit analyses provide only limited assistance in establishing priorities among various goals and objectives. Such

Table 5-5
Comparison of Cost-Benefit Analyses

Alternative A

Year	Debt Service Costs	O&M Costs @6%	Admin. Costs @6%	Discounted Costs	Discount Factor	Benefits	Discounted Benefits
1	113,259	400,000	100,000	567,832	0.925926	629,200	582,593
2	113,259	424,000	106,000	551,491	0.857339	654,368	561,015
3	113,259	449,440	112,360	535,884	0.793832	680,543	540,237
4	113,259	476,406	119,102	520,965	0.735030	707,764	520,228
5	113,259	504,991	126,248	506,692	0.680583	736,075	500,960
6	113,259	535,290	133,823	493,027	0.630170	765,518	482,406
7	113,259	567,408	141,852	479,932	0.583490	796,139	464,539
8	113,259	601,452	150,363	467,373	0.540269	827,984	447,334
9	113,259	637,539	159,385	455,318	0.500249	861,104	430,766
10	113,259	675,792	168,948	443,739	0.463193	895,548	414,812
11	113,259	716,339	179,085	432,607	0.428883	931,370	399,449
12	113,259	759,319	189,830	421,897	0.397114	968,624	384,654
13	113,259	804,879	201,220	411,585	0.367698	1,007,369	370,408
14	113,259	853,171	213,293	401,650	0.340461	1,047,664	356,689
15	113,259	904,362	226,090	392,070	0.315242	1,089,571	343,478
Totals	$1,698,885	$9,310,388	$2,327,597	$7,082,061		$12,598,841	$6,799,568
Terminal Value							$189,145
NPV					-$93,348		
B/C					0.9868		

Alternative B

Year	Debt Service Costs	O&M Costs @5%	Admin. Costs @6%	Discounted Costs	Discount Factor	Benefits @4%	Discounted Benefits
1	205,926	395,500	90,000	640,209	0.925926	700,000	648,148
2	205,926	415,275	95,400	614,370	0.857339	728,000	624,143
3	205,926	436,039	101,124	589,888	0.793832	757,120	601,026
4	205,926	457,841	107,191	566,677	0.735030	787,405	578,766
5	205,926	480,733	113,623	544,658	0.680583	818,901	557,330
6	205,926	504,769	120,440	523,756	0.630170	851,657	536,688
7	205,926	530,008	127,667	503,903	0.583490	885,723	516,811
8	205,926	556,508	135,327	485,032	0.540269	921,152	497,670
9	205,926	584,334	143,446	467,085	0.500249	957,998	479,238
10	205,926	613,550	152,053	450,006	0.463193	996,318	461,488
11	205,926	644,228	161,176	433,742	0.428883	1,036,171	444,396
12	205,926	676,439	170,847	418,245	0.397114	1,077,618	427,937
13	205,926	710,261	181,098	403,469	0.367698	1,120,723	412,087
14	205,926	745,774	191,964	389,373	0.340461	1,165,551	396,825
15	205,926	783,063	203,481	375,916	0.315242	1,212,174	382,128
Totals	$3,088,890	$8,534,322	$2,094,837	$7,406,331		$14,016,511	$7,564,681
Terminal Value							$315,242
NPV					$473,592		
B/C					1.0639		

analyses are of limited usefulness in evaluating projects of relatively broad scope or in comparing projects with widely differing objectives.

The basic purpose of cost-benefit analysis is not simply to maximize the ratio of benefits to costs. At times, the "equalization" of benefit/cost ratios might serve as a necessary condition for achieving a desired goal. When a benefit/cost ratio is less than one (i.e., when the discounted costs are greater than the discounted benefits), the basic objective might to determine ways to reduce costs or increase benefits to achieve "unity." More often, however, other factors must be considered in selecting an appropriate or "best" decision. These factors include: (1) the time stream of costs and benefits and the time preference for present as opposed to future consumption of goods or services; (2) limitations imposed by revenue (budgetary) constraints; and (3) the question of whether project objectives can be specified in sufficient detail to permit a fuller identification of direct and indirect costs and benefits.

It is virtually impossible to eliminate the need for subjective judgment in the process of making decisions for any organization. Nonetheless, a more systematic approach to the comparison of costs and benefits—including consideration of time preference and of the marginal productivity of capital investments—can contribute significantly to providing a more rational basis for such decisions. This is particularly true when compared with the uncoordinated, haphazard, and intuitive nature of many more traditional approaches.

Cost-Effectiveness Analysis

Cost-effectiveness analysis provides a basis for selecting among competing projects or programs when resources are limited. Techniques of cost-effectiveness analysis originated in the late 1960s and early 1970s. Initially these techniques were used in situations where benefits could not be measured in units commensurable with costs. In these early applications, a level of output or effectiveness was usually taken as a given. Several alternative methods of achieving this level of effectiveness were then examined in order to identify the alternative that had the lowest costs. These initial studies revealed many important aspects of decision making with respect to the allocation of scarce resources.

Output Orientation

In contemporary applications of cost-effectiveness analysis, the emphasis is on the use of measures of effectiveness (MOEs) to monitor progress toward achieving agreed-upon objectives. The extended time horizon of cost-effectiveness analysis leads to a fuller recognition of the need for life-cycle costing—that is, analysis of costs over the estimated duration of the project or program.

Henry Levin and Patrick McEwan use various examples from studies and articles, ranging from education to public health, to introduce the principles and techniques of cost-effectiveness analysis.[9] They take into account both the costs and the effects of selecting alternatives and suggest methods of minimizing the costs of research. They provide expanded coverage of the concept of cost effectiveness from types of technique to use, to how to interpret the data, and how to relate input data to outcome measures. A comprehensive bibliography of sources on cost analysis is also included.

The effectiveness of a project or program is measured by the extent to which, if implemented, some desired objective will be achieved. Since an objective usually can be achieved in more than one way, the analytical task is to determine the most effective approach from among several alternatives. The preferred alternative either (1) produces a desired level of performance at the minimum cost or (2) achieves the maximum level of performance possible for a given level of cost. Although costs can ordinarily be expressed in monetary terms, nonmonetary indexes or measures of effectiveness usually represent levels of achievement. Such indices measure the direct and indirect effects of resource allocations.

Cost-effectiveness analysis can be viewed as an application of the economic concept of marginal analysis. The analysis must always move from some base that represents existing capabilities and existing resource commitments. The objective is to determine what additional resources are required to achieve some specified additional performance capability. Thus, the focus is on incremental costs.

Measures of effectiveness involve a basic scoring technique for determining the increments of output achieved relative to the investment of additional increments of cost. Measures of effectiveness are often expressed in relative terms—for example, percentage increase in some measure of educational attainment, percentage reduction in the incidence of a disease, or percentage reduction in unemployment. These measures facilitate comparisons and the rank ordering of alternatives in terms of the costs involved in achieving identified goals and objectives. However, since benefits are not converted to the same common denominator, the merit of any single project cannot be ascertained. Nor is it possible to compare which of two or more projects with different objectives will produce the better returns on investment. It is only possible to compare the relative efficacy of alternatives with the same or similar goals and objectives.

Applications in the Field of Medicine

Weinstein and Stason introduced health clinicians and medical practitioners to cost-effectiveness analysis in 1977, suggesting that: "If these approaches were to become widely understood and accepted by the key decision makers in the health-care sector, including the physician, important health benefits or cost savings might be realized."[10] While this hope has yet to be fully realized, cost-effectiveness analysis has since become a significant feature in medical literature.[11]

In the field of medicine, cost-effectiveness analysis often is used as a technique for comparing the relative value of various clinical strategies. In its most common form, a new strategy is compared with current practice (e.g., the low-cost alternative) in calculating a cost-effectiveness ratio. The result might be considered as the price of the additional outcome to be purchased by switching from current practice to the new strategy. If the price is low enough, the new strategy is considered to be cost-effective—meaning that the new strategy is a good value. Being cost-effective does not mean that the strategy saves money. And just because a strategy saves money does not mean that it is cost-effective. The very notion of cost-effective requires a value judgment—what one analyst might think is a good price for an additional outcome, another might not.

Consider two strategies intended to lengthen life of patients with heart disease. One strategy is relatively simple and cheap (e.g., aspirin and beta-blockers); the other is more complex, more expensive, and more effective (e.g., medication plus cardiac catheterization, angioplasty, stents, and bypass). For simplicity, it might be assumed that doing nothing has no cost and no effectiveness.

Since cost-effectiveness analysis is about marginal (also called incremental) costs and benefits, the marginal cost of the simple strategy is the difference between the cost of that strategy and the cost of doing nothing. The marginal cost for the more complex strategy is the difference between the cost of the complex strategy and the cost of the simple strategy (not the cost of doing nothing). The calculation is similar for effectiveness. The final outcome measure for the analysis is the C/E ratio—the ratio of marginal cost to marginal effectiveness (see Table 5-6).

Types of Analyses

A comprehensive approach to cost-effectiveness analysis requires three supporting analyses:

1. *Cost-output studies* are concerned with the identification of feasible levels of achievement.
2. *Cost-effectiveness comparisons* assist in the identification of the most effective alternative.
3. *Cost-constraint assessments* determine the cost of employing less than the most optimal project or program.

The objective of a cost-output study is to identify for each alternative the relationship that approximates the sensitivity of costs (inputs) to changes in the level of goal achievement (outputs). Costs might change in direct proportion to the level of achievement; that is, each additional increment of input (cost) might produce an equivalent increase in output (level of achievement). However, if output increases more rapidly than costs, then the alternative is operating at a level of increasing return. This condition is represented by a positively sloped curve that rises at an accelerating rate, as illustrated by the initial segment of cost curve B in Figure 5-2. If costs increase more rapidly than output, the alternative is operating in an area of diminishing returns (as in the upper segment of cost curve B).

Cost-effectiveness analysis requires a model that can relate incremental costs to increments in achievement. For some types of problems, practical models can be developed with relative ease. For other problems, cost curves can be approximated from historical data. As the input-output relationships associated

Table 5-6
Cost-Effectiveness Ratios

Strategy:	Do Nothing	Simple	Complex
Cost	$0	$5,000	$60,000
Marginal cost	--	$5,000	$55,000
Effectiveness	0 years	3 years	8 years
Marginal effectiveness	--	3 years	5 years
C/E Ratio	--	$1,667/year	$11,000/year

with various alternatives are better understood, the construction of cost curves and effectiveness scales should become increasingly more sophisticated.

Assuming that the costs associated with different achievement levels can be determined for each alternative, the problem remains—how to choose among these alternatives. In principle, the rule of choice should be to select the alternative that yields the greatest excess of positive effects (attainment of objectives) over negative impacts (resources used, costs, and negative spillover effects). In practice, however, this ideal criterion is seldom applied, as there is no practical way to subtract dollars spent from the nonmonetary measures of effectiveness

The best approach, therefore, might be a cost-effectiveness comparison of program alternatives, as illustrated in Figure 5-2. Alternative A achieves the first level of output (O1) at a relatively modest level of cost (C1A). Nearly twice the amount of resources (C1B) would be required to achieve the same level of effectiveness using alternative B. Both alternatives achieve the second level of output (O2) at the same level of cost (C2). Alternative B requires a lower level of resources (C3B) to achieve the third level of output (O3). And only alternative B achieves the fourth level of output (O4), since the program cost curve of alternative A is not projected to reach this level of effectiveness.

Which of these two program alternatives is more desirable? To answer that question, it is necessary to define the optimum envelope formed by these two cost curves. If resources in excess of C2 are available, then alternative B is clearly the better choice. However, if available resources are less than C2, alternative A provides greater effectiveness for the dollars expended.

In general, it might not be possible to choose between two alternatives simply on the basis of cost-effectiveness unless one alternative dominates at all levels of goal achievement. Usually, either a desired level of performance must be specified and then costs minimized for that effectiveness level, or a cost limit must be specified and achievement maximized for that level of resource allocation.

In practice, however, organizations might chose to implement an alternative that is not the most effective one technically available. Among the more obvious reasons for this decision are legal constraints, technical capacity, employee rights, union rules, and community attitudes. The purpose of a cost-constraint assessment is to examine the impact of these factors by comparing the cost of

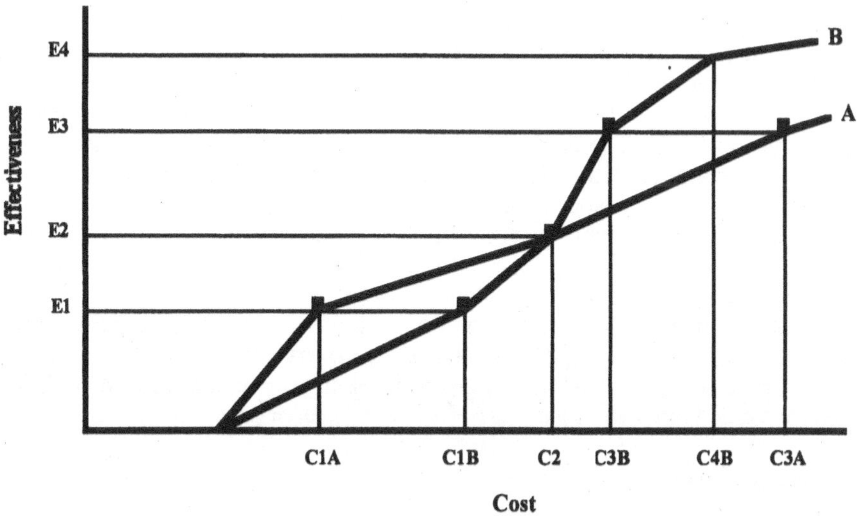

Figure 5-2 Cost-Effectiveness Analysis in Graphic Form

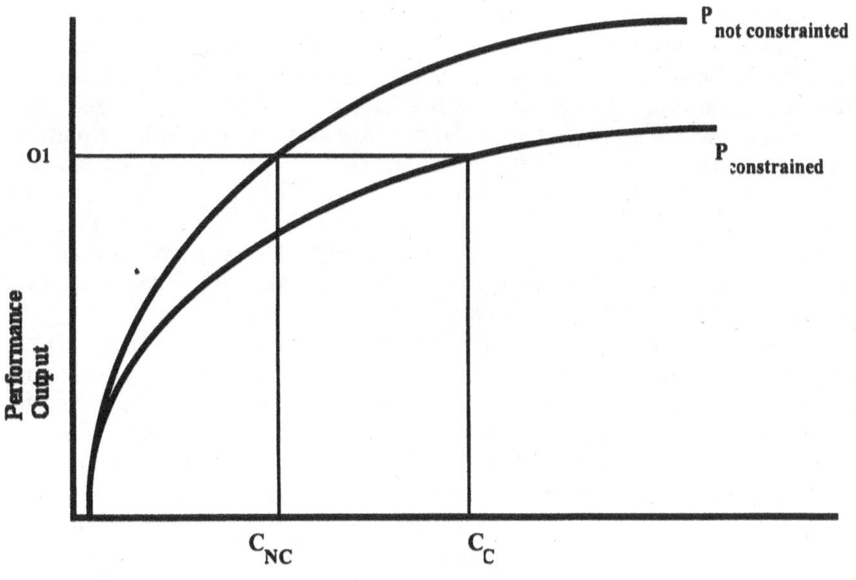

Figure 5-3 Cost-Constraint Analysis in Graphic Form

the project or program that might be adopted if no constraints were present with the cost of the constrained alternative.

This analysis, shown graphically in Figure 5-3, starts with the expressed goal O1 and two programs (*P constrained* and *P not-constrained*). *P not-constrained* represents the most effective alternative as determined by cost-effectiveness analysis. The constrained alternative, however, might be the only project or program available. The cost of the constraints to the agency is the difference between the cost of *P constrained* and *P not-constrained*.

Once this cost differential has been identified, decisions can be made as to the feasibility of eliminating the constraints. This assessment gives decision makers a basis upon which to estimate how much might be saved by relaxing a given constraint. By the same token, the cost of the constraint suggests the amount of resources that might be committed to overcoming it. In some cases, however, maintaining a constraint might be more important for social or political reasons than implementing a more effective project or program.

Optimum Envelope

Significant shifts in the configuration of cost curves frequently occur in the formulation of alternatives as additional levels of effectiveness are sought. Thus, alternative A might provide the most desirable C/E ratio at one level of effectiveness (and cost), whereas at a higher level of effectiveness (and cost), some other alternative might provide the more desirable ratio.

The following case study illustrates this situation. Assume that it has been determined that some 3,000 workers in a given state become unemployed each year due to technical obsolescence. Jobs for which they have been trained and are skilled are eliminated through the mechanization of industrial processes. The state seeks to establish an effective program to retrain all or a significant portion of these workers to new skills through an intensive one-year course. To provide this training, it is necessary to develop regional training centers, build new facilities, hire new instructional personnel, and so forth. It is expected that the program will operate over a ten-year period. Through this program, it is anticipated that the workers will be employable at desirable skill levels ten years earlier than if they had to attain these skills on their own.

Two alternatives are identified to meet these objectives. Alternative A is an equipment-intensive approach, involving extensive use of programmed learning techniques, videotape libraries to upgrade basic skills, the use of computers to achieve self-paced learning, and so forth. This alternative only requires five instructors per training center and has a trainee-instructor ratio of sixty to one. Alternative B is a teacher-oriented approach, involving team-teaching techniques. It requires twenty instructors per training center and has a ten to one trainee-instructor ratio. The trainee capacity at training centers for alternative A is 300 and for alternative B, 200. The costs for each alternative are summarized in Table 5-7.

It is now possible to examine how program costs and effectiveness (benefits) are related in the tests for preferredness. Since decision makers do not know

Table 5-7
Alternative Program Costs

Item of Cost	Program A	Program B
Development costs	$13,000,000	$1,000,000
Investment per training center	$ 1,500,000	$ 500,000
Operating costs per year per center	$ 1,750,000	$ 3,000,000

Table 5-8
Total Costs over Ten Years
(in thousands)

Program A					
Centers	0	3	6	8	10
Trainees	0	900	1,800	2,400	3,000
R&D	$13,000	$13,000	$13,000	$13,000	$13,000
Investment	–	$ 4,500	$ 9,000	$12,000	$15,000
Operations	–	$ 5,250	$10,500	$14,000	$17,500
Totals	$13,000	$22,750	$32,500	$39,000	$45,500
C/E Ratios	–	$25,278/ worker	$18,056/ worker	$16,250/ worker	$15,167/ worker

Program B					
Centers	0	5	9	12	15
Trainees	0	1,000	1,800	2,400	3,000
R&D	$ 1,000	$ 1,000	$ 1,000	$ 1,000	$ 1,000
Investment	–	$ 2,500	$ 4,500	$ 6,000	$ 7,500
Operations	–	$15,000	$27,000	$36,000	$45,000
Totals	$ 1,000	$18,500	$32,500	$43,000	$53,500
C/E Ratios	–	$18,500/ worker	$18,056/ worker	$17,917/ worker	$17,833/ worker

the level of training that can be supported given limited resources, it is necessary to develop a schedule of costs and benefits over the full range of workers to be trained each year (i.e., 0 to 3,000). Alternative A would require ten training centers for 3,000 trainees and alternative B would require fifteen centers. The development, investment, and ten years of operating costs are summarized in Table 5-8 for various levels of coverage.

Based on these data, it is possible to identify the best alternative given either a fixed budget or a specified level of benefits. Program B is preferred for all budgets under $32.5 million because it would have a greater trainee capacity. For all trainee loads less than 1,800, Program B is preferred because it will cost less than Program A. For budgets above $32.5 million or trainee loads above 1,800, Program A is preferred. For example, at a budget of $22.75 million, Program B could accommodate 1,000 trainees each year for $18.5 million for a C/E ratio of $18,500 per worker. At this same funding level, Program A has an annual capacity of 900 trainees and a C/E ratio of $25,278 per worker. However, if the objective is to handle an annual training load of 2,400 workers, then Program A would cost $39 million at a C/E ratio of $16,250 per worker, whereas Program B would cost $43 million with a C/E ratio of $17,917 per worker. This brief example illustrates how fixed costs (i.e., R&D costs), investment costs (per center), and variable costs (operating costs) can impact the overall cost configuration in different ways.[12]

Cost-Effectiveness Analysis: Project Complementarity

Many situations require the analysis of program alternatives that represent widely disparate approaches to achieve a common objective. Often these alternatives are difficult to compare on the basis of total costs and overall effectiveness because of dissimilarities in cost components, impacted population, and so forth.

Four projects have been proposed to increase family incomes in an economically depressed rural region; $4 million have been made available to be allocated among these proposed projects. The projected capital and annual operating costs for each of these projects are shown in Table 5-9.

An analysis of the potential effectiveness of these four alternatives indicates that the public recreational facility would employ approximately 470 workers at wages 20% higher than the current annual family income of $12,000. The job-training project has the potential of increasing incomes of approximately 920 workers by 25%. The agribusiness improvement project has the potential of increasing the incomes of approximately 480 workers by 35%. The industrial park project would employ approximately 850 workers at wages 40% higher than the current annual family incomes.

Cursory review of these four alternatives might lead to the conclusion that the industrial park alternative is the most desirable project since it is projected to result in a 40% increase in the income levels of some 850 workers. However, if these four alternatives were evaluated on the basis of their cost-effectiveness ratios, the job-training program, with a C/E ratio of 1.278, would be ranked first. The job-training project also has the highest C/E ratio for capital costs

Table 5-9
Cost-Effectiveness Analysis: Project Complemnentarity

Project Alternatives	Recreation Facility	Job Training	Agri-Business	Industrial Park
Cost per project	$1,400,000	$2,160,000	$1,760,000	$3,400,000
Capital costs	$1,000,000	$ 960,000	$1,200,000	$2,000,000
Operating costs	$ 400,000	$1,200,000	$ 560,000	$1,400,000
Projected increase	20%	25%	35%	40%
Workers affected	470	920	480	850
Project effectiveness	$1,128,000	$2,760,000	$2,016,000	$4,080,000
C/E ratio	0.806	1.278	1.145	1.200
C/E ratio for capital costs	1.128	2.765	1.680	2.040
C/E ratio for operating costs	2.820	2.300	3.600	2.914

(2.875), but the lowest C/E ratio for operating costs (2.300). The industrial park project ranks second in terms of its C/E ratio (1.200), the agribusiness project ranks third, and the recreational facility is a poor fourth (its C/E ratio is below one). The job-training project utilizes only $2,160,000 of the funds available, whereas the industrial park project utilizes $3,400,000 of the allocated monies.

It would be feasible to initiate the job-training project and either the agribusiness project or the recreational project and still stay within the budgetary constraint of $4 million. The job training and recreational projects have a combined effectiveness of $3,888,000 at a cost of $3,560,000, for a C/E ratio of 1.092. The job-training project in combination with the agribusiness project would produce an overall effectiveness of $4,776,000 at a cost of $3,920,000, for a C/E ratio of 1.218. These two projects in combination would affect some 1,400 workers, increasing their average income by 28.4%.

An important contribution of cost-effectiveness analysis lies in the determination of most effective alternatives under project interdependence—that is, when the effectiveness of one project can be increased by the initiation of some other related project. Interdependence among projects focused on achieving a common goal is known as project complementarity. For example, the development of an industrial park and the initiation of a job-training project, taken separately, each had a relatively high cost-effectiveness ratio. It is conceivable that these two alternatives, taken together, would have a cost-effectiveness impact even greater than that evidenced by their independent C/E ratios. Thus, if two or more complementary projects are under consideration for inclusion in a single program package, the effectiveness measure for each alternative should be set aside in favor of an effectiveness measure for the alternatives taken in combination.

Suppose that the job-training project was designed specifically to complement the agribusiness improvement project, such that the combined package would generate projected total effects of $5,180,000 or approximately $400,000 more than the two projects evaluated separately. Since the package would cost $3,920,000, the resulting C/E ratio would be 1.321, higher than any of the other ratios taken separately. The combination of a job-training project and the development of an industrial park is outside the budgetary constraint of $4 million (costing $5.56 million to initiate). However, it would be useful to examine these two alternatives in combination as a final step in the evaluation. Suppose that this package also increased the level of effectiveness by $400,000 (from $6,840,000 to $7,240,000), given the total cost of $5,560,000, the resulting C/E ratio of 1.302 would still be below the ratio of the job-training/agribusiness package. Assuming that there was no budgetary constraint, the increase in effectiveness of the job-training/industrial park package would have to be $505,000 to be competitive with the job-training/agribusiness package (i.e., $6,840,000 plus $505,000 = $7,345,000 divided by $5,560,000 = 1.321).

One further package alternative might be explored. Suppose that the development of the industrial park includes provision for some job training, whereas the job-training project assumed the need for some expenses in job placement. If the combination of these two alternatives produced as small as a 1.5% reduction in the project costs, then the resulting cost-effectiveness ratio would be 1.322, making this package competitive with the job-training/agribusiness package (assuming no budgetary constraint).

The combined package of job-training/industrial park development is approximately 39% over the budget limit of $4 million. It might be possible to develop a smaller package that would bring the combine alternatives into the range of the budgetary constraint while reducing the overall effectiveness by 25% or less. If this could be accomplished, then the C/E ratio would be $5,430,000 divided by $4,000,000 = 1.358, making the modified package the most desirable alternative.

The point of this discussion is to illustrate the further analyses that are possible and should be carried out in the cost-effectiveness approach. The application of analytical techniques such as sensitivity analysis and contingency analysis can play an important role in these further explorations of the complementary relations among proposed projects.

Limitations of Cost-Effectiveness Analysis

Cost-effectiveness analysis serves to discipline an organization. Systematic use of cost-effectiveness analysis forces an organization to think much harder about what it is doing and to consider alternative ways of achieving its agreed-upon goals and objectives. The actual process of reviewing outputs and results and trying to compare them with the costs, in many cases, might be more important than the actual numbers arrived at through the cost-effectiveness analysis.

Cost-effectiveness analysis cannot give an unambiguous answer to whether a project is worth undertaking, however. No easy rule of thumb is available, such as, "If the internal rate of return is over 10%, proceed with the project."

Cost-effectiveness analysis can only give relative answers: "If there are two approaches A and B to reach a specific objective, and if A is less costly than B, then choose A."

The lack of a single monetary measuring rod for benefits/results means that alternatives aimed at reaching the same objective must be identical in qualitative as well as quantitative terms. If not, it is like comparing apples and oranges. If, for example, alternative literacy programs produce functionally literate adults at the same unit cost but the reading scores are substantially better with one of the approaches, there is no clear-cut answer as to which is the better alternative.

A third problem is that the benefits or results of certain projects or programs might be extremely difficult to measure because they are intangible. This is particularly true for activities aimed at shaping policy, particularly if the change in policy is not of the organization's own making, but only indirect and involving the need to convince another organization to change its policy.

A fourth general problem with cost-effectiveness analysis is common to any attempt to estimate the impact of a particular project, program, or activity. Activities under analysis rarely happen in isolation. Other factors might have strong positive or negative impacts on the objective(s). In the field of public health, for example, it is well known that the medical status of a population depends on a whole range of social, educational, and environmental factors—besides the purely medical factors. If several of these factors change at the same time, it is difficult to assess the effect of each one, particularly if the joint effect is greater than the effect of each one in isolation.

Risk and Uncertainty

Programming capital projects often involves future events that are inevitably characterized by uncertainty. It is important to recognize such uncertainty and to explicitly deal with it from the outset. An assessment should be made of uncertainty and risk based on available estimates of the costs and benefits of alternative approaches. A risk is taken no matter what the decision. Even the decision to do nothing involves the risk of lost opportunity. An effective manager, whether in the public or private sector, must be aware of how opportunity, innovation, and risk are interrelated and must be willing to take risks appropriate to his or her level of responsibility.

Uncertainty, Risk, and Probability Functions

One manager's uncertainty might be another's acceptable risk. What one manager might interpret as an uncertain situation to be avoided, another might see as an opportunity, albeit involving some risk. Although the two terms often are mistakenly used interchangeably, the distinction between uncertainty and risk is important.

In planning strategic facilities, risk and uncertainty must be confronted from two primary sources: (1) statistical uncertainty and (2) uncertainty about the state of the real world in the future. The first type of uncertainty is usually less troublesome to handle. It arises from chance elements in the real world and would exist even if the second type of uncertainty were zero. Monte Carlo and related probability techniques can be used to deal with statistical uncertainty when it is encountered.[13]

Establishing a probability function can bring problems within more manageable bounds by reducing uncertainty to some level of risk that might be tolerable, depending on the risk threshold of the manager or organization. Probabilities can be established either *a posteriori* (by induction or empirical measurement) or *a priori* (by deduction or statistical inference).

The second type of uncertainty—uncertainty about the future state of the real world—is more troublesome for strategic facilities planning. In such cases, the use of sophisticated statistical techniques might be little more than expensive window dressing. When the environment is uncertain, an expected value approach often must be applied. Expected value is determined by multiplying the value products across all possible outcomes. In mathematical terms, expected value (EV) can be expressed as:

$$EV = P1\$1 + P2\$2 + \ldots Pn\$n$$

where P stands for probability, $ stands for the value of an outcome, and

$$P1 + P2 + \ldots Pn = 1$$

The concept of expected value was introduced in Chapter 4 in connection with the application of sensitivity analysis to determine the variations in rankings among several alternatives based on uncertain costs. Three cost estimates—optimistic, pessimistic, and most likely—were made for the uncertain cost components of three alternatives (see Table 4-4). The initial sensitivity analysis was inconclusive—a different "best alternative" was identified for each of the cost estimates. However, when the expected values were determined, based on the probability of each of the cost estimates occurring, alternative B, with an EV of $140,500, appeared to be the preferred course of action, as shown in the following calculations:

$$\text{Alternative A} = [.50(150{,}000) + .30(200{,}000) + .20(100{,}000)] = \$155{,}000$$
$$\text{Alternative B} = [.50(120{,}000) + .30(195{,}000) + .20(110{,}000)] = \$140{,}500$$
$$\text{Alternative C} = [.50(170{,}000) + .30(190{,}000) + .20(120{,}000)] = \$166{,}000$$

Uncertainty, Risk, and Expected Utility

The assumption that people actually behave rationally in the manner suggested by the mathematical notion of expected value often is contradicted by observable behavior in risky situation. People are willing to buy insurance, for example, even though they know that the insurance company makes a profit. People are willing to buy lottery tickets even though the chances of winning are minimal. Consideration of the problem of insurance and the so-called "St. Petersburg paradox" led Daniel Bernoulli, an eighteenth-century mathematician, to propose that these apparent contradictions could be resolved by assuming that people act so as to maximize their expected utility, rather than expected value. Thus, people buy insurance because the consequences against which they are insured are significant in view of the costs. People are willing to invest small amounts of money in lottery tickets, even though the probability outcome is highly uncertain, because the payoff is so high relative to their expected utility.

Extensive research has been performed in the area of risk and uncertainty because the behavior of decision makers often appears to be contrary to commonly accepted axioms of rational behavior. Although no exact probabilities might exist for the success or failure of a particular event, Kassouf has observed that an individual with "clear-cut, consistent preferences over a specified set of strategies . . . will act as if he has assigned probabilities to various outcomes."[14] The values for the probabilities will be unique for each individual and not unlike the values of utility that might be assigned to an individual through a study of his or her social preferences. The obverse of social preferences, of course, is risk aversion, a subject on which opinions vary.[15]

As most economists will now admit, utility theory alone cannot resolve the disputes over social preference and aversion to risk. There are numerous situations in which managers will have to obtain a more careful reading of the various utility functions or preferences of their clientele and the organization as a whole. As Stokey and Zeckhauser explain, strategic choice under uncertainty is a threefold process:[16]

1. Alternatives must be assessed to determine what probabilities and payoffs are implied for individual members of the organization and its clientele.
2. Attitudes toward risk of these individuals must be evaluated to determine the certainty equivalents of these probabilities and payoffs.
3. Having estimated the equivalent benefits that each alternative offers to different members of the organization and its clientele, the decision maker must select the preferred outcome.

Although this process might sound simple, it often is very complex in application. Some basic tools have been developed to aid in unraveling these complexities.[17] These techniques can be brought into play, however, only after a fairly good understanding of organizational and clientele preferences has been attained. Once the groundwork for approximating utility has been laid, the public manager will be better prepared to address uncertainties in a more systematic fashion.

A basic objective is to reduce uncertainty by bringing to light information that will clarify relationships among elements in the decision process. This reduction of uncertainty might cause the risk associated with a particular choice: (1) to remain unchanged, (2) to decrease (as in the case where a reduction in uncertainty permits the assessment of more definitive probabilities), or even (3) to increase (as happens when the additional information reveals risk factors that previously were unknown). Thus, although risk and uncertainty are interrelated, they must be treated independently in many situations.

Computer-Assisted Cost Analysis

In recent years, computer-based methods have become a significant tool for cost analysis. Interactive software allows the nonprogrammer to use the computer to test the assumptions on which an analysis is based, to consider the risk associated with different alternatives, and to explore a range of possible decision scenarios. Computer-assisted methods provide a basis for the continuous fine-tuning of a plan so as to anticipate things to come and adjust to unanticipated events that might arise as a capital project is implemented.

In early approaches to interactive planning, a fixed structure was used to provide the capacity to pose "what if" questions about certain input variables. Simultaneous equations were used to forecast the organization's performance based on various scenarios. Obviously the results of such analyses are only as valid as the projections made by the planners. However, examining different scenarios increases management's awareness of potential problems and its preparedness to deal with them when they occur.

Individuals lacking experience in computer programming often were unable to use these early models, however. They needed to learn a new, unfamiliar computer language that was difficult to communicate. The inflexibility associated with procedural languages frequently forced the user to make input statements in a sequence that was different from the structure of the actual problem. Software packages designed to eliminate these problems are now available. Such software is, in the jargon, "user-friendly." Menus and submenus are written in English and allow users with very little programming experience to select the analytical steps appropriate to their needs. These packaged programs use a nonprocedural approach in which no correct or predetermined sequence of statements is required to describe the problem. Thus, they offer a great deal of flexibility in terms of both model design and subsequent modifications that might be necessary.

Modern interactive packages provide a number of important options in addition to generating reports for various "what if" questions. Models applicable to particular conditions confronting an organization can be developed and used to: (1) project the costs and benefits associated with various alternatives, (2) analyze cash flow requirements, (3) optimize leverage, and (4) compare lease versus purchase options for different depreciation schedules. Models can often be consolidated or combined so that managers in different functional areas of the organization can use the same planning package (and assumptions) to design models to meet their particular needs. By combining these models, it might be possible to attain an overall "meta-model" for the whole organization.

Goal-seeking procedures can also be applied in such models. Certain targets (goals) are set by management, and the computer works back from these targets to determine the conditions that will have to prevail to achieve the specified goals. Goals can be viewed as constraints to problem solving, and in some in stances, it might be necessary to relax some of the constraints (lower the targets) in order to arrive at a feasible solution. Many computer-based systems also have the capacity to introduce and analyze risk and uncertainty.

Available software packages make it possible to perform sensitivity analyses to determine how an optimal solution might change if some of the key variables in the model should change. Models often respond to key assumptions, while the majority of variables might have little effect on the results. Thus, management has a means of selecting those variables that require a more detailed analysis. This selection is the first step in performing risk analysis.

Summary

In the allocation of limited fiscal resources to strategic facilities, it might be assumed that most organizations consider both the payoffs and the pitfalls associated with various project requirements. These assessments, however, are often haphazard and uncoordinated, with little systematic effort to quantify benefits or to include all costs appropriate to the particular alternatives under consideration.

Factors influencing future costs must be examined as part of the programming of strategic facilities. Monetary costs—research and development costs, investment costs, and the costs of operations, maintenance, and replacement—are commonly reflected in financial accounts. In strategic facilities planning, it often is necessary to look beyond these monetary costs to opportunity costs, associated costs, and social costs. A thorough analysis must also distinguish among (1) fixed and variable costs, (2) recurring costs, and (3) marginal or incremental costs. These costs should be examined over the life of the project under analysis. The need to adopt an extended time dimension in such cost assessments has led to the development of cost-benefit analysis.

Cost-benefit and cost-effectiveness analysis can be applied at two pivotal points in the evaluation of resource commitments. In the planning stage, cost-benefit analyses are based on anticipated costs and benefits. Such analyses are not necessarily empirically based. After a project has been implemented and shown to have a significant impact, cost-benefit and cost-effectiveness analyses can be used to assess whether the costs of the project are justified by the magnitude of net outcomes. Such after-the-fact analyses should be based on detailed studies of available empirical data.

Cost-benefit and cost-effectiveness models need not be adopted whole cloth. A number of subroutines might be introduced into ongoing cost analysis procedures. Decision inputs can be developed to include considerations of time preference and marginal productivity of capital investment. The techniques of cost-curve analysis can be applied to a variety of decision situations. The examination of expenditures in terms of objectives and the evaluation of total benefits for alternative expenditures can be important derivatives of these analytical techniques. The extended time horizon adopted in these methods leads to a fuller recognition of the need for life-cycle costing and benefits analysis. The importance of incremental costing, sunk costs, and inheritable assets also is underlined by this extended perspective. Cost-output and cost-constraint analyses add other important dimensions to the information available to the decision maker. As the complexity of the resource allocation problem becomes more evident, other subroutines might be adopted, depending on the availability of data and the capabilities of the analyst.

Uncertainty can be reduced and risk can be brought within tolerable limits through the generation of management information that clarifies critical relationships among elements in the decision process. Various methods have been formulated for converting uncertainty to risk—including the use of objective and subjective probabilities and the techniques of sensitivity analysis, contingency analysis, and a fortiori analysis. Applying the concept of expected utility provides more in-depth insights into the critical dimensions of strategic decisions.

Interactive computer software has become a significant analytical tool for strategic facilities planning, making possible the application of on-line, real-time decision support systems. Traditional methods of cost analysis use hindsight to determine why things went wrong. Computer-assisted methods provide a basis on which to anticipate (and accommodate) change before its full impact occurs. Most computer-based systems can also be used to analyze risk and uncertainty.

Notes

1. U.S. Congress, House Subcommittee on Evaluation Standards, Report to the Interagency Committee on Water Resources, *Proposed Practices for Economic Analysis of River Basin Projects* (Washington, D.C.: U.S. Government Printing Office, May 1958), 9.
2. For a further discussion, see Ronald H. Coase, "The Problem of Social Cost," *Journal of Law and Economics* 3 (October 1960): 1-44.
3. Under this approach, specific budget allocations often are limited as to their fiscal year carry-over. Unspent allocations may revert to the general treasury at the end of the fiscal year. Year-end reversion of funds is often cited as a major shortcoming of traditional budgeting procedures. Units have no incentive to conserve resources and, in fact, this approach promotes year-end spending. In attempting to "zero out" budget allocations as the end of the fiscal year approaches, units must exercise caution to ensure that the purchases made will withstand the test of a post-audit—that is, that the unit is eligible to incur such items of expenditure.
4. Robin Cooper and Robert Kaplan, "Activity-Based Costing," *Journal of Cost Management* (Summer 1988).
5. For a further discussion regarding the possible applications of activity-based costing in the public sector, see Alan Walter Steiss, *Strategic Management for Public and Nonprofit Organizations* (New York: Marcel Dekker, Inc., 2003), Chapter 7.
6. A.R. Prest and R. Turvey, "Cost Benefit Analysis: A Survey," *The Economic Journal* (1965): 583.
7. Anatol Rapoport, "What Is Information?" *ETC: A Review of General Semantics* 10 (Summer 1953): 252.

8. Otto Eckstein, *Water Resource Development* (Cambridge, Mass: Harvard University Press, 1958).
9. Henry M. Levin and Patrick J. McEwan, *Cost-Effectiveness Analysis*, 2nd edition (Thousand Oaks, Calif: Sage Publications, 2000).
10. M.C. Weinstein and W.B. Stason, "Foundations of Cost-Effectiveness Analysis for Health and Medical Practice," *New England Journal of Medicine* (1977): 716-721.
11. For a listing of relevant articles, see American College of Physicians, "Primer on Cost-Effectiveness Analysis," *Effective Clinical Practice* (September/October 2000): 253-255.
12. For a further discussion of potential applications of cost-effectiveness analysis in the public sector, see Alan Walter Steiss, *Local Government Finance* (Lexington, Mass.: Lexington Books-D.C. Heath and Company, 1975), 240-259.
13. For a discussion of Monte Carlo techniques, see E.S. Quade, *Analysis for Public Decisions* (New York: American Elsevier, 1975).
14. Sheen Kassouf, *Normative Decision-Making* (Englewood Cliffs, N.J.: Prentice-Hall, 1970), 46
15. For a broader discussion, see Jack Hirshleifer and David L. Shapiro, "The Treatment of Risk and Uncertainty," in Robert H. Haveman and Julius Margolis, eds., *Public Expenditures and Policy Analysis*, 2nd ed. (Chicago, Ill.: Rand McNally, 1977), 180-203.
16. Edith Stokey and Richard Zeckhauser, *A Primer for Policy Analysis* (New York: Norton, 1978), 252.
17. Howard Raiffa, *Decision Analysis* (Reading, Mass.: Addison-Wesley, 1968). For an introductory discussion of Markov chains, see Stokey and Zeckhauser, *A Primer for Policy Analysis*, Chapter. 7.

Chapter 6

METHODS OF FINANCING STRATEGIC FACILITIES

There is a growing body of evidence that the deterioration of the urban infrastructure in the United States is a serious problem of national scope. Articles in the popular press, research sponsored by various federal agencies, and congressional hearings have contributed to increased national concern regarding the status of highways, streets, bridges, water and sewer systems, health and educational facilities, and so forth in our cities and towns. What was once viewed as a "big city problem" is now recognized as a much more widespread concern. Unfortunately, recognition of the seriousness and magnitude of the problems of the urban infrastructure comes at a time when public resources are constrained, especially among state and local governments. During the recent period of fiscal stress, many local governments have deferred maintenance spending as a "temporary measure" to ease their financial burdens. Such spending deferrals, however, have only multiplied future repair needs and investment requirements. Therefore, public officials and administrators have had to confront a number of difficult, complex, and often politically sensitive decisions regarding the financing of strategic facilities.

Financing Options

The options for financing strategic facilities are similar to those available to any individual or family: (a) pay cash out of current earnings, (b) save money for future acquisitions, or (c) borrow on anticipated earning power. A sound, long-range fiscal policy will seek to develop an appropriate mix among these three methods of financing strategic facilities.

Pay-As-You-Go Financing

Supporting strategic facilities on a "pay-as-you-go" basis from current revenues encourages government to "live within its income." Premature commitment of funds is minimized and credit is conserved for times of emergency when ample credit may be vital. Pay-as-you-go financing avoids the added cost of interest payments and therefore is less costly than borrowing.

On the other hand, the pay-as-you-go approach may result in an undue burden being placed on present taxpayers to finance some future need from which they may not fully benefit. Achieving user-benefit equity—an important objective—may require that the construction of strategic facilities be financed in a manner that will spread the burden over the life of the improvements. Thus, it may be argued that projects providing public services over many years should be paid for by people according to their use or benefit—that is, should be financed on a "pay-as-you-use" basis.

Excessive commitment to pay-as-you-go may prevent a locality from undertaking the construction of essential strategic facilities because such projects are deemed too costly to be carried out using only annual operating funds. In point of fact, few governments today have the capability to finance strategic facilities strictly on a "pay-as-you-go" basis.

Reserve Funds

Financing strategic facilities through a reserve fund (sometimes called a capital reserve) can be thought of as the opposite of borrowing in that the timetable is reversed. A portion of current revenue is invested each year in order to accumulate sufficient funds to initiate some project in the future. The amount (S) of a reserve fund that is generated by a fixed investment (N) placed annually at compound interest (r) for a term of n years can be expressed by the following formula:

$$S = N \frac{[(1+r)^n] - 1}{r}$$

Thus, an investment of $20,000 (N) each year for ten years (n) at 5% interest (r) will yield a reserve fund (S) of $251,558.

Conversely, the amount (N) that must be placed annually at compound interest (r) for a term of n years to create a reserve fund (S) can be calculated by means of the following formula:

$$N = S \times \frac{r}{[(1+r)^n] - 1}.$$

Should the objective be to develop a reserve fund (S) of $2 million at the end of ten years (n), an investment of $159,009 per year (N) would be required if the rate of return on the investment (r) were 5%. Simple computational routines using these basic formulas can test various assumptions as to appropriate investment periods under different interest rates.

To illustrate this point, assume that a municipality is considering a major addition to its community health center. Construction costs are estimated to be $1,000,000 (in current dollars), with an additional $100,000 for site preparation and $300,000 for equipment. Site preparation and construction costs are increasing at a rate of 8% a year, and the cost of equipment is estimated to be increasing at 12% a year. Four different financing approaches that the municipality might consider are outlined in Table 6-1. Given the cost assumptions, the fourth alternative is the "least cost" approach in terms of the municipality's investment. Achieving the least cost, however, is not necessarily the only consideration, for there are pros and cons to any financing strategy.

Table 6-1
Cost Analysis of Funding Alternatives

<u>Alternatives</u>

1. Fund the project from current revenues over a four-year period, with site preparation in year 1, construction in years 2 and 3, and equipment acquisition in year 4.
2. Fund site preparation out of current revenues and issue straight serial bonds for the $1,300,000 in construction costs and equipment.
3. Build a capital reserve fund over four years until the adjusted project costs of $1,807,161 have been accumulated, at which time the project can be constructed.
4. Establish a capital reserve fund with annual payments made from this fund to cover the project schedule outlined under alternative 1.

<u>Cost Analysis</u>

Alternative 1

Site Preparation: Year 1	=	$100,000
Construction: Year 2 = ($500,000 x 1.08)	=	$540,000
Construction: Year 3 = ($500,000 x 1.1664)	=	$583,200
Equipment: Year 4 = ($300,000 x 1.4049)	=	$421,478
Total Cost		$1,644,678

Alternative 2

Site Preparation	$ 100,000
Principal & Interest on 5-Year Straight Serial Bond @ 6%	$1,495,000
Total Cost	$1,595,000

Alternative 3

Site Preparation and Construction = ($1,100,000 x 1.2597)	=	$1,385,683
Equipment = ($300,000 x 1.4049)	=	$ 421,478
Total Cost		$1,807,161
Annual Payments to Reserve Fund @ 5% = $ 419,283 x 4	=	$1,677,132

Alternative 4

Year	Carry Forward	Payment to Reserve	Cost	Reserve Balance
1		$391,590(1.05) = $411,170	$100,000	$311,170
2	$311,170 +	$391,590(1.05) = $722,340	$540,000	$182,340
3	$182,340 +	$391,590(1.05) = $593,509	$583,200	$ 10,308
4	$ 10,308 +	$391,590(1.05) = $421,478	$421,478	$ 0
Total Cost		= $391,590 x 4 =		$1,566,360

Borrowing

Like all governmental powers, the capacity to borrow must be used with critical regard for its justifiable purposes and with a clear understanding of its safe and reasonable limits. A sound borrowing policy seeks to conserve rather than exhaust credit. The ability to borrow when necessary on the most favorable market terms is an objective that applies to governments just as it does in business and industry.

Local governments often borrow to finance major facilities on the assumption that future economic and population growth will make the debt service payments (principal and interest) more feasible. Future events may or may not prove this assumption correct.

Jurisdictions also may borrow on the assumption that inflation will make repayment easier. As inflation erodes the real value of the dollar, the actual burden of a given dollar of debt declines. A municipality that issued thirty-year bonds in 1970 was paying debt service in 2000 with dollars worth perhaps one-third their initial value. However, unless one's crystal ball is unfailingly accurate, relying on inflation to lift the burden of debt can be a high-risk strategy.

States often impose borrowing limits on local governments. These limits typically are cast in terms of dollars of outstanding debt as a percentage of the jurisdiction's real property tax base. Beyond any state imposed limits on borrowing, municipalities are restrained by the fact that this year's borrowing must be paid back from revenues in subsequent years. When the debt service burden of a municipality becomes overly large in comparison to its the tax base, the bond rating of the municipality may be lowered and the cost of borrowing may increase. Companies that rate municipal bonds (and thereby influence the interest rate that must be offered to place such bonds) emphasize the importance of "good fiscal stewardship" in this regard.

Funds borrowed by government have maturities ranging from a few days to several decades. For purposes of discussion, it is possible to divide government borrowing practices into three categories: (1) short-term loans with maturities of a year or less, (2) intermediate loans with maturities over one year but not more than five years, and (3) long-term loans with maturities of over five years. While the latter category is most commonly associated with long-range financing of strategic facilities, each may have a role in the financial planning of a municipality, county, or public authority.

Short-term borrowing is most frequently used to smooth out irregularities between expenditure and income flows and to temporarily finance operations during periods when tax receipts and other revenue sources fall short of expectations. Such borrowing takes various forms—bills, certificates, or notes sold to banks or other investors, bank loans, warrants paid out in lieu of cash, and unpaid bills and claims.

Municipal notes are short-term, interest-bearing securities used to help manage cash flow or to assist in financing a capital project. Bond Anticipation Notes (BANs) are issued on a short-term basis to provide more immediate financing of projects that eventually will be financed through long-term bonds. An authorized bond issue might be postponed to avoid poor market conditions.

Or the objective might be to combine several projects into one larger bond issue, and BANs may be issued while the larger issue is being prepared. Notes may also be issued to finance municipal operations in anticipation of future tax receipts (TANs), future revenues (RANs), with the expectation of receiving grants from the state or federal government (GANs), or to fund construction of housing projects (construction loan notes or CLNs). Companies, such as Standard and Poor's and Moody's, that provide ratings for long-term securities also rate municipal notes in terms of their credit risk.

Intermediate borrowing has limited but definite uses. Cities operating largely on a pay-as-you-go basis may resort to loans of intermediate maturities when exceptional expenditures cannot be met from current revenues. The outstanding debt of many municipalities is primarily in the form of callable bonds—bonds that may be called in and the principal paid in full after a specified period. Over time, it may be possible to convert a portion of such debt to a lower rate of interest by floating a new intermediate loan.

In general, long-term borrowing is appropriate (1) where the project is of a type that will not require replacement for many years, such as a city hall, auditorium, major health facility, or sewage disposal plant; (2) where the project can be financed by service charges to pay off the bond commitments; or (3) where needs are urgent for public health and safety purposes or other emergency reasons. Long-term borrowing might also be appropriate where special assessment bonds are the only feasible means of financing improvements in the absence of subdivision regulations or other controls. Borrowing might also be necessary where intergovernmental revenues are available on a continuous basis to guarantee the security of the bonds. Long-term borrowing might be used to finance projects in newly annexed areas or areas of rapid expansion where the demands on local tax resources are comparatively large and unforeseen. Bond strategies appropriate to long-term borrowing will be discussed in detail in Chapter 7.

Use of Property Taxes to Finance Strategic Facilities

More political controversy, public press, and research are generated each year concerning the property tax than any other source of local government revenue. The property tax is under considerable criticism, especially as the mainstay of local support for public education. The stubborn fact, however, is that this form of taxation has demonstrated the capacity to withstand severe and protracted attacks and continues to be the most important single source of local government revenues in the United States. In addition, the valuation of property subject to taxation continues to be the primary basis upon which the debt limits of local governments are established.

Property Taxes

The full faith, credit, and taxing power of the local government support the majority of general obligation bond issues. The debt service payments on these bonds are funded from local property tax revenue. The traditional justification for the use of the property tax to finance strategic facilities has been that the ownership of property constitutes a fair index of wealth. Therefore, it is appropriate to require contributions in support of public facilities and related services in proportion to this accepted measure of wealth. However, property taxes are applied to gross and not net wealth, and some types of wealth are excluded. Property taxes are not based on the value derived from current transactions (as is the usual case for income and sales taxes), but they require value-estimation procedures (i.e., property assessments). These procedures are considered a primary weakness of local property taxation.

The term *property tax* is ordinarily used to describe a group of taxes that are levied on the value of different kinds of property determined by the individual states to be subject to taxation. Property taxes are usually levied on an *ad valorem* basis—that is, according or in proportion to the value of the property subject to taxation.

Local property taxes usually take two forms:

1. Real property tax is levied on the assessed valuation of taxable land and improvements, thereupon. Real property is classified according to use.
2. Personal property tax has been applied at one time or another to the assessed value of tangible and intangible personal property.

Taxable tangible personal property may include furniture and household equipment, automotive equipment, boats, farm animals, and inventories. Taxable intangible personal property may include stocks, bonds, and other assets representing a property right that is not tangible in character.

For decades, the valuation of both real property and personal property relied largely on the periodic reporting by the owners of the property subject to taxation. Personal reporting is still the primary method by which personal property is taxed, ordinarily because the tax assessor has few alternate sources of information—or, if assessors have access to this information (e.g., from federal tax data on personal income), they may be reluctant to use these sources.

The objective of the assessment process is to assure that all properties subject to the tax rate appear on the tax roll, with a proper notation as to the taxable status of each property. The assessment process should determine property values that are internally consistent in order that taxpayers can be subject to the same effective millage rate and thereby bear their equitable share of the tax load.

The amount of revenue generated from property taxes is a function of two variables: the tax or millage rate and the ratio of assessed value to true market value. *True market value* represents the price at which a willing buyer and a willing seller would reach agreement on the sale of a property. The net assessed value is often set at some percentage of true market value. As a general rule, applying 100% of true market value helps to increase equity among taxpayers. When assessed values are only a small percentage of market value, the coefficient of dispersion (a measure of the difference from uniformity) tends to be high. Conversely, the coefficient of dispersion tends to be low when the ratio of assessed to market value is high (e.g. approaching 100%). However, if a reasonable degree of internal consistence is achieved, it matters little in terms of tax equity whether the assessment process is based on 50%, 70%, or 100% of the true market value.

Millage rates usually are expressed in terms of dollars per $1,000 (or $100) of net assessed value. If the millage rate were $20 per $1,000, the tax on a property with an assessed value of $150,000 would be $3,000 ($150,000/$1,000 x $20). If the millage rate in an adjacent community is $15 per $1,000, it cannot be assumed that the tax yield on an equivalent property would be only $2,250. To draw comparisons between jurisdictions, it is necessary to know the ratio of assessed value to true market value. In the example, assume that the property assessed at $150,000 has a true market value of $250,000. Therefore, the assessment ratio is 60% (i.e., the assessed value at $150,000 is 60% of the true market value). If the assessment ratio in the second jurisdiction is 75%, then the assessed value of a parcel with a true market value of $250,000 would be $187,500, and the tax yield from a $15 per $1,000 millage rate would be $2,812.50.

Some states require localities to establish separate millage rates for general government expenditures and for expenditures in support of public education. Many localities also have identified separate millage rates for capital expenditures. These separate millage rates provide taxpayers with further information as to how the jurisdiction proposes to distribute the revenues generated from property taxes.

General approaches to property assessment are outlined in Table 6-2. The comparative sales approach is most often applied to residential property when there is a sufficient number of reliable sales transactions. The income approach is appropriately used for properties bought and sold largely on the basis of income production. The cost approach is especially applicable for special or unique properties that are seldom exchanged in the real estate market and generate no income.

The frequency with which property assessments are conducted will also impact the revenue yield from property taxes. An *annual assessment* updates the values for all real property each year. While computer-based information systems make annual assessments possible, a complete physical inspection each year of the total inventory of real property within a jurisdiction would be a major undertaking and is unlikely. If annual assessments are required (or desired), weighted values are often applied to physical characteristics identified in previous inspections, with changing market conditions accommodated on a neighborhood basis.

Mass cyclical assessment are an alternative to annual assessments, whereby all properties in the taxing jurisdiction are assessed in a particular year and the determined values do not change until the next scheduled assessment, except for new construction, demolition, or change in use. States prescribe mass cyclical assessments at intervals ranging from two years (e.g., Iowa) to ten years (e.g., Connecticut).

Between these two extremes is the procedure whereby a specific component of the real property inventory in a jurisdiction is reassessed each year. For example, if a three-year cycle were applied, one-third of the properties would be

Table 6-2
Appraisal Techniques Used to Estimate the Value of Real Property

1. ***Comparative sales*** or ***market data approach***: The value of a given property is estimated by comparing it to similar properties that have recently been sold. Since a number of actual transactions are required to achieve meaningful comparisons, this approach is relatively ineffective for unique, one-of-a-kind properties.
2. ***Income approach***: Future returns to be derived from a given property (e.g., office building, apartment building, commercial facility) are converted into their present value equivalent in order to estimate the amount that a knowledgeable investor would be willing to pay for the future income stream.
3. ***Cost approach***: Value is estimated by adding the depreciated cost of improvements on a property to the estimated land value. Either the comparative sales or the income capitalization approach is usually used to estimate land values. The cost of improvements may be estimated by determining (a) the cost of constructing a replica of the building at current prices for materials, labor, workmanship, construction standards, etc.; or (b) the current cost of replacing the building with a structure having equivalent utility.

assessed each year. All properties would be subject to reassessment over the three-year period.

The property tax rate (millage) typically is set as part of the annual budget process. A determination must first be made as to (a) how much the jurisdiction will likely have to spend in the coming fiscal year and (b) how much revenue will likely be generated from nonproperty tax sources and intergovernmental transfers. Assume that budget requirements for the coming fiscal year are estimated to be $230 million. Based on revenue trends over the past five years, it is estimated that $72 million will be generated from various nonproperty sources. It is further estimated that $90 million will be granted through intergovernmental transfers from state and federal sources. The balance of $68 million would have to come from property tax revenue. If the assessed value of taxable property in the jurisdiction is $4,250,000,000 and the tax rate is based on 100% of the assessed value, then a millage rate of $16 per $1,000 would be sufficient to generate $68 million (i.e., $16 times $4,250,000,000/1,000 = $68,000,000).

Many local governments operate under legal restraints as to the annual adjustments that can be made in the property tax rate. In those circumstances, the general ratio of assessed valuation to market value becomes important as it provides a second variable in determining the yield from property taxes. In the previous example, assume that the current ratio of assessed value to market value is 75%. The tax base for the jurisdiction would then be $3,187,500,000 (i.e., 75% of $4,250,000,000). In order to generate $68 million from property taxes, the millage rate would have to be $21.33 per $1,000. However, assume that the current millage rate is $19.10 per $1,000 and that the city council is limited to no more than a 5% increase over the current rate. If the ratio of assessed value to market value were to be increased from 75% to 80%, the tax base would be $3,400,000,000, and a millage rate of $20 per $1,000 would yield $68,000,000. The $20 per $1,000 millage rate would be within the 5% increase limit.

The ratio of assessed value to market value also has a bearing on the *debt limit* of a jurisdiction. Debt limits typically are expressed in terms of a percentage of taxable property values—usually 2% to 4% of assessed value. Failure to adjust borrowing limits to a realistic basis may result in various circumventions, including the creation of debt authorities—special districts established in order to avoid either tax or debt limits—or the development of various types of subsidiary debt.

Advantages and Disadvantages of Property Taxes

The property tax has proven to be very durable in spite of the predictions by experts of its demise. It remains the mainstay of local government revenues. According to the most recently available data from the Census Bureau, property taxes accounted for 72.3% of all general tax revenues of local governments. The structure of the property tax can be adapted to the preferences of different groups in society. For example, local officials can target tax relief to deserving groups or can shift the tax burden to segments of the community with greater ability to pay. Local property taxes can also be structured as an incentive to attract business investments. The principal advantages claimed for the property tax are:

- *Local autonomy*. Property taxes have enabled local governments to maintain relative autonomy from state and federal control, thereby countering the tendency toward the centralization of power at higher levels of government.
- *Degree of stability*. Especially in periods of economic adversity, the property tax continues to be a consistently high producer of income—with lesser amounts of downward adjustments than would be the case for income, sales, or gross receipts taxes.
- *Benefit principle*. The property tax provides a manner in which contributions can be required of the owners and/or occupants of property in some degree proportionate to the benefits (services) being rendered, e.g., police protection, fire protection, refuse collection and disposal.
- *Index of wealth*. Ownership of property is an index of a person's wealth and, therefore, property taxes fall more heavily upon wealthy families with large holdings than upon lower income families who own or occupy only small amounts of taxable property
- *Equity of coverage*. Absentee property owners who benefit from local services are required to pay their "fair share."
- *Ease of administration*. Property taxation is difficult to evade, which facilitates collection by local governments.
- *Social objectives*. Property tax has a valuable social effect in that the owners of properties that are not productive or of marginal value are encouraged to develop the properties or to sell them to others. Thus, a man and wife or a

widow who occupies a house suitable for a large family may be encouraged to vacate the house that can serve a broader social purpose through occupancy by a large family.

In spite of its longevity, the property tax is unpopular with many taxpayers because it represents a tax on unrealized gains—a tax on wealth rather than on income.[1] The property tax is particularly onerous for those who are "property rich" but "cash poor," such as elderly residents living on a fixed income. Among the other disadvantages frequently cited are:

- The tax is regressive—it tends to absorb (in the case of residential property) a greater proportion of the income of low-income families than higher income families.
- The increasing list of exemptions tends to accentuate the inequities inherent in the tax.
- The yield is not as flexible as some other kinds of taxation. In periods of inflation, assessments fail to rise in relation to actual changes in value.
- The problems of administration are substantial. Concerns about inequitable appraisals and reappraisal give rise to taxpayer anxieties. Where efforts are made to perform the assessment function on a current and more equitable basis, administration tends to become rather expensive in relation to yield.
- The tax tends to discourage improvements. The process of making improvements, or even of careful current maintenance, tends to increase property values, and these increased values, in turn, require higher tax payments.
- The lump sum payment requirements (annual or semiannual) are a burden on some residents.
- Differences between adjacent taxing districts result in unnatural competition both for the location of new residential developments and for the location, or relocation, of economic activities necessary to sustain the entire economic/social community.

Suggested improvements in property assessment practices include: (1) a workable assessment law that achieves more efficient administration; (2) larger assessment districts; (3) a competent, professionally trained staff with a well-structured internal organization, adequate pay, protection against dismissal for doing a good job; and (4) adequate financial support. State supervision is frequently cited as a necessity in achieving substantive equity between taxpayers both within a taxing district and also between taxing districts.

Land Value Taxation

More than a century ago, Henry George advocated the taxation of land value in the name of social equity. Contemporary economists have advocated land value taxation as an efficiency-enhancing policy that favors economic development. One approach of such a tax reform would be to permit local governments to adopt split-rate property taxation. Under this approach, a municipality could lower the tax rate on buildings and other improvements, while raising the tax rate on land values in order to maintain the desired level of public services. The

Commonwealth of Pennsylvania has had this form of property taxation since 1913. Some fifteen cities in the Commonwealth have adopted two-rate property taxation, with the cities of Pittsburgh and Scranton pioneering this effort at tax reform. Current research suggests that taxing land values more heavily than building and improvement values could foster urban revitalization and at the same time, help to protect undeveloped land.[2] Oats and Schwab have suggested that lowering the tax rate on building values relative to land values helped to spur downtown commercial construction in Pittsburgh during the 1980s, despite the sharp decline of the city's steel industry.[3]

However, unless distributional impacts are explicitly taken into account in the design of such property tax reform, George's concern for social equity is unlikely to be served. Industrial and commercial properties frequently have a higher ratio of building value to land value than is the case with residential properties. Therefore, raising the tax rate on land values in order to pay for a rate reduction on property improvements could have a regressive impact on the distribution of property tax payments. Owners of office buildings and other commercial and industrial properties are likely to enjoy lower tax bills while many homeowners might find increased tax bills after implementation of a split-rate taxation approach.

Local Non-property Taxes

Tax levies on non-property items provide another source of local revenue that may be dedicated, in part, to finance strategic facilities. Non-property tax revenues often are dedicated to specific public improvements—for example, a portion of the admission or user fees for access to public recreation sites may be earmarked for improvements for these facilities.

Significant reliance on non-property taxes by local government is a relatively recent phenomenon, having its genesis in the 1930s when property owners often were confronted with property taxes well beyond their capacity to pay—resulting in the sale of property to cover delinquent taxes. In some ways, the shift to non-property taxes accompanied a basic shift from a rural to an urban economy. In a rural-agricultural society, the ownership of property was long understood to be a major indicator of wealth and, therefore, of an ability to pay taxes. Today, evidence of ability-to-pay is represented to a much greater degree by money income than by title to real property. Some non-property items are more difficult to evaluate and equitably assess for tax purposes, however, making this alternative more costly for local governments to administer.

Gross Receipts Taxes

Gross receipts taxes imposed on businesses and occupations are measured by the gross income of the enterprise. Many municipalities use this method to tax the privilege of engaging in business. In some cases, all or a portion of the revenue generated from this tax is earmarked for improvements that benefit commercial enterprises (e.g., improved parking, upgraded street lighting in the business district, etc.). In some localities, gross receipts taxes have replaced former flat-rate business licenses; in others, it has been the product of new, permissive tax legislation.

In a few instances, this tax is a broad-based, general business tax. More often, it is imposed only on certain kinds of businesses. For example, localities in Pennsylvania impose a mercantile tax on wholesale and retail businesses. Usually, gross receipts tax rates are low and often uniform for businesses within the same class. When levied at uniform rates on all kinds of enterprises, the gross receipts tax bears no relationship to the profitability of the entity being taxed. The tax is on gross receipts and, therefore, it impacts low-profit businesses relatively harder than those with a high profit margin.

General Retail Sales Tax

Local sales taxes, like their state counterparts, are primarily taxes on retail sales of tangible personal property. The theory is that what a consumer spends is a good measure of his or her taxpaying ability. This construct has obvious limitations. The retail sales tax is harshly regressive unless food for off-premises consumption is exempt. Exemptions to local sales taxes are dictated by various considerations and, thus, follow no uniform pattern. In some instances, there are exemptions for food or food and drugs in order to lighten the burden on lower income individuals. This practice complicates administration and may substantially reduce yield. However, it goes far toward eliminating the regressive nature of the sales tax and gives more flexibility for using higher rates. One or more specific services, such as public utilities, may also be included in the tax base.

Not all localities may be authorized by the state to levy a local retail sales tax. In some states, cities over a certain size may be authorized to levy a separate local sales tax, while smaller cities and counties do not have this prerogative. Local sales taxes imposed in one jurisdiction and not in others in the same local trade area tend to disturb intercommunity economic relations. Some retail outlets will likely choose to locate (or relocate) beyond the taxing jurisdiction.

Localities may petition to have the local sales tax levied as a supplement to the state sales tax. This add-on approach mitigates the need for a separate (and somewhat costly) collection and enforcement program, including audits of the records of local merchants (who constitute the taxpayers).

Numerous municipalities levy selective sales or excise taxes on specific commodities or services in lieu of applying a general retail sales tax (see Table 6-3). Some jurisdictions use both the general sales tax and special excise taxes.

Gross receipts, retail sales, and selective sales taxes, taken together, account for only 5.4% of the total revenue of local governments, according to the most recent data available from the Census Bureau (see Table 6-4). However, this tax category accounts for 20.8% of the total revenue collected by state governments, some portion of which is then shared with local governments through revenue sharing or grant-in-aid or programs.

Table 6-3
Selective Sales Taxes

Business license taxes: Often discriminatory and bear little relation to benefits received or the ability to pay. These taxes should receive systematic and frequent revisions to avoid equity problems.
Public utility taxes: Good revenue producers, without requiring heavy administrative expense. Legal and political basis for a utility tax is that the levy is imposed for the privilege of exercising a franchise. The tax is almost always passed on to the consumer, however.
Admission and amusement taxes: Well suited for local use; relatively easy to administer; tax so-called nonessential expenditures; and obtain revenue from nonresidents using local facilities. They are, to some extent, benefit taxes—recouping some of the expense of such special services as police, fire protection, traffic regulation, and inspection. These taxes are a minor source of local revenue, however.
Motor fuel taxes: Local levy was prevalent in the 1920s and 1930s. Today only a few counties and municipalities are involved in locally administered fuel taxes. The preference is to share in the state collected tax on a formula basis—usually based on the amount collected within the county or municipality.

Localities often will earmark all or a major portion of the revenue derived from a local sales tax to support strategic facilities, especially educational facilities. As in the case of the separate property tax millage rate, this approach increases visibility as to the justification/purpose of the tax levy.

Income Taxes

Individual and corporate income taxes are a major source of state revenues, accounting for 40.7% of the general tax revenues collected in FY 1998-1999. Local jurisdictions in sixteen states have also been authorized to levy income taxes on individuals, and six states have authorized the levy of local corporate income taxes. About 3,500 local governments levy local income taxes (for the most part on employee payrolls). However, only 900 of these localities are outside of the Commonwealth of Pennsylvania. At the local level, income taxes account for only 6.2% of the general tax revenues.

In their broadest application, income taxes apply to (1) the gross income from salaries and wages of residents earned both within and outside the city and (2) the gross income from salaries and wages of nonresidents earned within the city. In some cases, income taxes may also be applied to (1) the net profits of professions and unincorporated businesses of residents from activities wherever conducted, (2) the net profits of professions and unincorporated businesses of nonresidents from activities conducted within the city, and (3) the net profits of corporations from activities conducted within the city. The local incomes tax on salaries and wages generally provides no personal exemptions or deductions.

Tax credits are sometimes specified in the case of overlapping jurisdictions or nonresidents, however.

Licenses, Permits, and Service Charges

Most local governments have broad responsibilities in the supervision of various kinds of business and other activity within the community. In most situations, a fee is charged in conjunction with the issuance of a license or permit. For example, local building codes regulate construction. Part of the enforcement consists of the examination of plans for compliance with local codes and issuance of building permits, along with varying degrees of inspection to see that the construction is in accordance with the approved plans. In like manner, licenses are issued for food vendors and permits are required for parades, circuses, and a host of other activities.

Service charges generally bear a direct relation to the cost of providing the service, thus freeing tax revenue for other applications. As defined by the Bureau of the Census, service charges are amounts received from the public for performance of specific services benefiting the person charged and from sales of commodities and services—except by city utilities. They include fees, assessments, and other disbursements for current services, rents and sales derived from commodities or services furnished incident to the performance of particular functions, and the gross income of commercial activities, such as parking lots and school lunch programs.

Miscellaneous General Revenue

Motor vehicle licenses are widely used as a source of local revenues. Some localities require such licenses of nonresidents as well as residents. Often these revenues are dedicated to the maintenance of local streets or other transportation-related improvements. In many states, motor vehicles are taxed as personal property in addition to being licensed for operation.

Special assessments are imposed on real property. These assessments differ from property taxes, however, in that they are related to a specific benefit, need not be uniform throughout the jurisdiction, and generally allow no exemptions. They are compulsory, however, and require formal assessment. Special assessments frequently are levied to support bonds issued to finance the construction of public facilities and improvements that benefit specific properties, such as sidewalks, curbs and gutters, improved fire protection systems, the paving and maintenance of streets, and sewer and water extensions.

Investment revenue consists of earnings on deposits and securities, other than the earnings of insurance trust funds or employee retirement systems. Local governments accumulate cash balances for a number of reasons and often are able to meet current obligations and, at the same time, have some cash left over to invest in interest yielding securities. Such investments offer a source of additional revenue without increasing taxation, using funds which otherwise are temporarily unproductive. In some cases, the interest earned on short-term investments is earmarked in support of capital improvement programs (see Chapter 11 for a more detailed discussion of short-term investment strategies).

The sale of property involves receipts from the sale of real property and improvements thereon. Receipts from the disposition of commodities, equipment, and other personal property, and from the sale of securities are excluded from this revenue category, however. In some cases, revenues received from the sale of public property are reinvested in new strategic facilities. The use of tax-exempt leveraged lease (TELL) financing as a method of providing strategic facilities is discussed in further detail in Chapter 8.

While no one of these sources is very large, charges and miscellaneous revenues taken together account for over 38% of all general revenue received by local governments. These sources of local revenue increased by over 200% in the past ten years, outpacing the growth in all other sources of general revenue.

Utility Revenues

Many local jurisdictions own and operate public utilities, either under the direct auspices of the local government or through special authorities. Revenues derived from these public utilities, for the most part, are dedicated to the maintenance, operations, and long-term development of the utility systems. Many of these publicly owned utilities are authorized to issue revenue bonds to finance strategic facilities, the bonds being secured by the revenues generated by the utility's operations. In some cases, modest surpluses may develop that can be used for other general purposes. More often, however, these publicly operated utilities may require "back stopping" or "bail outs" from general revenues to cover emergency situations or to expand capacity to meet substantial growth in the community.

Revenue from publicly owned utilities accounted for 8.14% of all local revenues collected in FY 1998-1999 (see Table 6-4). Electric power supply systems accounted for 49% of this total, while water supply systems accounted for 37.3%. The balance of the revenue was generated by transit systems (8.1%) and gas supply systems (5.5%).

Intergovernmental Revenues

Intergovernmental revenues can be categorized as to source and function. The reporting system of the Census Bureau does not provide data as to the amount of state aid to local governments which, in fact, is flow-through federal funds conveyed to the state and then passed on to local governments. Therefore, the fact that state intergovernmental transfers often are eight to ten times that of the federal government is somewhat misleading. As shown in Table 6-4, the Census Bureau attributed to state governments over 90% of all intergovernmental transfers made to local governments in FY 1998-1999. However, state governments received 20.7% of its total revenue through intergovernmental transfers from the federal government.

Table 6-4
State and Local Government Revenue: FY 1998-1999
(in millions)

	State & Local Government	Percent of Total	State Government	Percent of Total	Local Government	Percent of Total
General Revenue	**1,167,646**	65.08%	**655,984**	56.90%	**511,662**	53.73%
Taxes	815,341	45.45%	499,943	43.37%	315,398	33.12%
Property	239,672	13.36%	11,654	1.01%	228,017	23.94%
Sales & Gross Receipts	290,993	16.22%	239,367	20.76%	51,626	5.42%
General Sales	200,627	11.18%	164,378	14.26%	36,249	3.81%
Selective Sales	90,366	5.04%	74,989	6.50%	15,377	1.61%
Individual Income	189,309	10.55%	172,764	14.99%	16,545	1.74%
Corporate Income	33,922	1.89%	30,766	2.67%	3,157	0.33%
Motor Vehicle Licenses	15,342	0.86%	14,083	1.22%	1,259	0.13%
Other	46,103	2.57%	31,309	2.72%	14,795	1.55%
Charges and Miscellaneous	352,305	19.64%	156,040	13.53%	196,264	20.61%
Utility Revenue	**81,880**	4.56%	**4,356**	0.38%	**77,524**	8.14%
Water Supply	29,039	1.62%	122	0.01%	28,917	3.04%
Electric Power	40,890	2.28%	2,823	0.24%	38,067	4.00%
Gas Supply	4,244	0.24%	7	0.00%	4,236	0.44%
Transit	7,708	0.43%	1,404	0.12%	6,304	0.66%
Insurance Trust Revenue	**273,968**	15.27%	**238,838**	20.72%	**35,130**	3.69%
Intergovernment Transfers	**270,628**	15.08%	**253,692**	22.01%	**328,015**	34.44%
From Federal Government	270,628	15.08%	238,941	20.73%	31,687	3.33%
From State Government		0.00%	0	0.00%	296,328	31.12%
From Local Government		0.00%	14,751	1.28%	0	0.00%
TOTAL REVENUE	**1,794,122**	100.00%	**1,152,870**	100.00%	**952,330**	100.00%

Grant-in-Aid Programs

Intergovernmental revenues may be given in the form of grants-in-aid or shared revenues. The function of grants-in-aid is two-fold: (1) to assist disadvantaged municipalities in the provision of needed public services and facilities in an attempt to achieve stabilization, equalization, and support of such governments; and (2) to provide impetus for the expansion of particular programs and activities. Grants-in-aid usually are provided for specific purposes (e.g., in support of public health, welfare, and education). The receiving government often is required to meet a set of minimum standards established by the granting government. Such categorical grants often seek to encourage local government units to shift expenditures to particular functions or to provide certain public services and facilities in a manner and at a level consistent with state and national interests.

When distributed on the basis of need, state aid should consider relative economic capacity, local tax effort, legal restrictions on taxing ability, and fixed service costs. This basis of distribution, however, can perpetuate inefficient units of local government. Nonetheless, the state should accept some measure of responsibility because: (1) the state uses local units as vehicles of administration; and (2) the state sets minimum standards and procedures with regard to selected functions or activities. The state also sets legal limits on local borrowing and taxation options. Alternatives to direct state assistance through grants-in-aid include: (1) state assumption of performance of services, thus obviating the need for local financing; and (2) increased state technical assistance in areas such as investment and marketing.

Direct federal aid to local governments began in the 1930s with welfare relief programs. Such aid was extended to low-income housing construction and payments in lieu of taxes. During World War II, federal aid centered on public works and related services and on government-financed housing projects. Two important post-war aid programs were the Federal Highway Act of 1944 and the Federal Aid Airport Act of 1949. In 1960, forty-six federal aid programs directed to local governments were underway. By 1970, Congress was dangling almost 500 large and small conditional aid carrots before state and local goverments, collectively worth about $25 billion a year. However, with the passage of 1972 federal budget, the emphasis shifted away from the categorical grants to revenue sharing.

Shared Revenues

General revenue sharing was adopted by the federal government to apportion part of federal revenues to local governments with few, if any, restrictions as to project or purpose. Such shared revenues were designed to grow as the personal income tax base of the federal government increased. In 1974, Congress enacted special revenue sharing legislation in the field of urban renewal, model cities, and certain other programs. A major component of these programs involved major capital improvements to the urban infrastructure. These special revenue sharing initiatives marked the beginning of a return to the array of categorical grants by the federal government to state and local governments.

In February 1981, President Reagan proposed the elimination of most direct federal support for local government, with other federal programs folded into block grants or receiving severe cuts in funding levels. Although Congress made a number of changes in the format of the block grants and provided somewhat more transitional funding than Reagan proposed, most of the President's proposals with were enacted. Except for some support for urban transportation planning, area-wide aging funds, and some transition funding from HUD, EPA, and DHHS, the federal government, in effect, withdrew its financial support from local governments that had taken over thirty years to build. Federal revenue sharing programs were finally abolished in 1986.

Federal aid to state and local governments shrank significantly during the Reagan and Bush administrations, both as a percentage of the gross domestic product and as a percentage of state and local government expenditures. The recession of 1990-1991 pushed many state and local governments to near crisis conditions. In 1992, for example, the state of California confronted a budget deficit in the range of $12 billion, resulting in significant cutbacks in services, layoffs of public employees, and reductions in formula-funded programs for local governments. The Clinton administration evidenced little interest in across-the-board increases in aid to state and local governments. While the current Bush administration has provided some state and local support for homeland security programs, the traditional responsibilities of local government that received federal funds in the past have largely been ignored. In all likelihood, most local governments will continue to operate under considerable fiscal pressures for some time to come.

Shared taxes represent a proportional allocation to localities of a tax collected or imposed by a higher level of government, usually the state but, in some cases, a regional taxing authority. Except for motor fuel taxes, which usually are dedicated to road improvements, generally no requirements are specified. As a consequence, shared taxes may be used for any public purpose. The sources of these shared taxes may include state sales taxes (usually allocated based on the location of the retail activities), state income taxes (which may be allocated by the locus of economic activities or by residence of the income earners), or even state property taxes.

A mismatch still exists among governmental levels in the financial responsibility for provision of public services and facilities. This imbalance is caused by (a) the widespread practice of forcing the local property tax to serve as the primary underwriter of both local general government and the local school system, and (b) the heavy burden that welfare expenditures have placed on state and local governments. With the major exception of public education, formulas for the distribution of state aid generally fail to recognize significant variations in the fiscal capacity of local jurisdictions to support public services. Few if any states have grant-in-aid programs that constitute a true "system."

State Aid for Education

The responsibility for primary and secondary education in the United States has traditionally been at the local level—either vested with independent school districts or, in larger cities, with the municipal government. This approach has permitted local decision making and control. However, state governments have the ultimate responsibility for the provision of public education, as spelled out in state constitutional provisions.

State aid programs for education have expanded significantly in the past two decades in an effort to reconcile this apparent contradiction between the mandated uniformity and consistency at the state level and the freedom of local choice. While the state share of funding for education varies widely (from under 8% in New Hampshire to over 90% in Hawaii), the national average places state funding on a par with local support (each contributing approximately 47%, with the balance of 6% coming from federal sources). Local revenues in support of education are almost exclusively from property taxes. State funds come from sales and income taxes, with state lotteries, in some cases, playing an increasing role.

Efforts to achieve an appropriate balance between state responsibility and local control have resulted in a complex state aid formula, the elements of which often are subject to change as legislators seek to establish hybrids that meet diverse requirements and expectations. The result, in large measure, is systems of state aid with which no one is fully satisfied.

Three general approaches have been developed to distribute state aid for education:

1. *Flat grants.* In a few states, general and categorical grants are provided to every school district at the same dollar amount per pupil, with no distinction made between high- and low-affluent districts.
2. *Target tax rates.* In about three-fourths of the states, state aid per pupil equals the difference between a base-level of local support (the minimum acceptable amount of local funding as determined by the state) and the per pupil revenue that would be collected from a statewide target tax rate applied to the district tax base. The school district usually is required to spend at least the base-level amount to receive the state aid.
3. *Percentage equalizing.* Various state formula have been further developed to ensure that all districts will raise the same level of funding per pupil from a given tax rate. The district tax rate is applied to the actual tax base of the district and to a state-established guaranteed tax base. The state aid provides the difference between these two levies. Other factors may be included in the state formula, such as adjustments for difference in operating costs, special education service requirements, capital construction initiatives, and so forth.

Under a "base-level" approach, a determination is made by the state as to the minimum acceptable amount to be provided from local sources in support of primary and secondary education. The state then sets a statewide tax rate target and determines how much revenue would be collected if this statewide tax were to be applied to the tax base of each school district. Seldom is a statewide tax for education actually levied, however. The funds to support state aid for education usually comes from a number of sources.

State aid is then provided in terms of the difference between the base level of local support and the level of revenue that would be derived from the statewide target tax rate. For example, assume that the statewide target tax rate is $16.25 per $1,000 of assessed value and the base-level support is set at $7.50 per $1,000 of assessed value. For every local tax dollar spent in support of education, the jurisdiction would receive $1.167 in matching state aid (up to the per pupil threshold). The $1.167 is calculated by subtracting the local share ($7.50) from the state target ($16.25) and dividing the result ($8.75) by the local share (i.e., $8.75/$7.50 = $1.167).

The base-level support and the state target level can also be expressed on a per pupil basis. For example, in FY 2002, per pupil expenditures for elementary and secondary schools in the Commonwealth of Virginia were $7,452. If this level were to be set as the state target, then the base level might be set at $3,500 per pupil. To receive the state aid, this base-level support would have to be provided from local sources. Under this formula, for every local tax dollar spent in support of education, the state would provide $1.13 (i.e., $7,452 minus $3,500 = $3,952 divided by $3,500 = $1.13).

Local Expenditures and Revenues

State and local government expenditures have been increasing at phenomenal rates over the past four decades, often outstripping the overall growth of the national economy as measured by the Gross Domestic Product (GDP). Since 1960, state and local government expenditures financed from all sources have increased at a compound rate of 9.1% per year, while the GDP rose at an annual average rate of 7.7%. The annual growth rate of state and local government spending slowed in the 1990s, averaging 6.1% per year. However, this annual increase still exceeded the 4.7% annual average growth rate of the GDP.

Elasticity of Local Expenditures and Revenues

The relationship between changes in local government expenditures and the Gross Domestic Product can be examined by a useful measure suggested by James Heilbrun.[4] This index, which Heilbrun calls the "elasticity of local spending," is defined by the following ratio:

$$\text{ELS} = \frac{\text{Percentage Change in Local Government Expenditures}}{\text{Percentage Change in GDP}}$$

When local government expenditures are increasing at a faster rate than the GDP, the value of ELS will be greater than one. Between 1960 and 1990, the ELS for all local governments had a value of 1.17 (i.e., 9.73% divided by 8.29%). The ELS in the 1990s was 1.29 (6.1% divided by 4.7%).

Heilbrun also suggests that by dividing the percentage change in local tax revenues by the percentage change in GDP, it is possible to define the elasticity of local revenue sources. If the value of the elasticity of local revenue sources is equal to the value of the elasticity of local spending, and if all expenditures are paid out of local sources, then local government could finance the growth of expenditures year-by-year with no increase in tax rates. The growth of the GDP would induce just enough expansion in the local tax base to provide the revenues needed to pay for growing expenditures. However, since the end of World War II, the elasticity of local revenues has been far below that of local spending, thus contributing to the persistent financial problems encountered by most local governments.

Estimates of the elasticity of property taxes throughout the United States vary from a low of 0.8 to a high of 1.3, with the majority of such estimates placing the value in the range between 0.8 and 1.0. On a national basis, the general sales tax collected by local governments is estimated to have an elasticity of between 1.0 and 1.27, with the majority of estimates falling at 1.0. In other words, the growth of revenues from the general sales taxes closely parallels the growth of the GDP. The elasticity of other sources of general revenue (such as taxes on particular commodities and miscellaneous fees and charges) tends to be well below 1.0. When these components are added together, it appears that the elasticity for the aggregate of local taxes and charges, at best, is about 1.0 and perhaps somewhat lower. With an expenditure elasticity of about 1.29 and a revenue elasticity of 1.0 or less, it should be clear why local governments are under continual pressure to raise tax rates or to adopt new revenue sources if they are to finance anticipated increases in local expenditures.

These discrepancies in the elasticity of local expenditures and revenues have an important bearing on the capacity of local governments to finance strategic facilities. A community's ability to accumulate capital reserves or to borrow to finance long-term capital investments is conditioned, in large measure, by its overall financial solvency. Any strategic facilities plan must be formulated within the financial capacity of government to pay for its needs and desires. A community that cannot meet its short-term expenditure demands from existing (and projected) sources of revenue will have great difficulty in securing willing investors for its long-term bonds. Under such circumstances, investors are likely to demand higher interest rates to offset the risk. To propose strategic facilities that the government cannot afford, or to propose improvements without a clear notion of how they will be paid for, is to invite unrealistic programs that, from the beginning, are destined to prove unsuccessful.

Estimating Local Revenues

The first step in a revenue analysis is to determine any modifications in existing policies that will be required to finance the desired service programs and related capital expenditures. An analysis of available revenues under existing fiscal policies provides a basis for determining the most effective means by which revenues and expenditures can be brought into equilibrium, i.e., by increasing the former or reducing the latter.

Sources of revenue for a given jurisdiction should be examined at least at the level of detail shown in Table 6-4. Each source should be tabulated over a sufficiently long period to establish valid trend lines that take into account both boom and recession periods. Each revenue source may require a different formula in order to forecast a reliable budget figure. It is also necessary to develop and project appropriate indices against which various sources of revenue can be matched in order to make future estimations. Some revenue sources may produce essentially the same yield from year to year, while other revenues may fluctuate significantly and cannot be relied upon to produce the same amount from one period to the next. Some sources are dependent upon the fiscal policies of other levels of government (e.g., federal and state aid programs). Other sources are directly or indirectly related to the level of service and capital expenditures provided by government.

For each revenue source, the yield must be estimated by determining how frequently the item subject to tax (or charge) will occur. No source of revenue should be estimated solely on collections of the previous year. Some revenue sources are more stable than others. However, a high level of stability should not lull the administrator into the pitfall of routine estimating.

The second step is to explore the ramifications of alternative fiscal policies. This examination should include an analysis of (1) ways by which the revenue derived from existing sources might be increased or might decreased; (2) the availability and/or feasibility of new sources of revenue; and (3) the effect of varying borrowing policies on available resources. This analysis must be a continuous process, particularly in light of the ever-increasing demands being placed on local governments for services and facilities.

The analyses of revenues available under existing fiscal policies and of alternative methods of financing must be brought together to focus on recommendations regarding future fiscal policies. This comparison should provide the chief executive and governing body with the basis for a clear, explicit series of policy statements to guide the planning and programming of strategic facilities as well as the determination of appropriate operating expenditures.

The following points illustrate the items that should be covered in statements of fiscal policy.

1. The total amount of funds to be expended annually in order to achieve and maintain desirable levels of public services.
2. Policies with regards to new revenue sources.
3. The role that state and federal assistance will play in supporting public services and facilities.
4. The relationship between the operating budget and the capital budget.
5. Fiscal policies that are applicable to the current debt outstanding.
6. The ratio to be applied among the various methods of financing strategic facilities (i.e., what portion will be available from annual revenues and how much must be financed through borrowing or other methods of financing).
7. The types and maturities of bonds to be issued to finance strategic facilities.

8. The relationship between public improvements that are self-supporting and those that are tax-supported and the terms and conditions under which self-liquidating facilities are feasible.

Every effort should be made to level off and reduce the outstanding debt of government at the earliest possible date. Capital expenditures must be carefully scheduled to ensure a reasonable outstanding debt structure in relation to the general level of the economy, the sources of revenue available, and the overall ability to pay for these improvements. Bond issues should have a limited life to minimize the debt service charges.

It may be suggested from experience that at least 20% of strategic facilities should be financed from current revenues. While this level will vary from area to area and from year to year, as a matter of fiscal policy, an effort should be made to establish a clearly defined range within which these adjustments can be made. According to recognized finance principles, annual debt service charges payable from general revenues should not exceed 25% of the total funds available.

Estimating Local Expenditures

A similar "divide-and-conquer" approach should be applied in estimating local expenditures. Each particular class of expenditure should be projected on the basis of various explicit assumptions regarding the supply and demand associated with a particular public service. Three set of variables should be considered:

1. *Service variables*: projections of the way in which the level of service or manner in which services are provided will change, given some assumed change in the demand for services by the population.
2. *Demographic variables*: including projections of the size, age, and racial composition of the population.
3. *Salary variables*: projections of the levels or rates of increase for public employees in various salary and wage classes.

Specific statements concerning these major variables should be associated with each expenditure estimate. Local government officials who have the best access to pertinent facts should supply these statements. Different assumptions should be tested in instances where a high degree of confidence cannot be attached to a particular projection (due to uncertainty).

Explicit statements concerning service levels permit the testing of the impact of decisions to expand or contract particular public services over some defined period. Separate information inputs should be provided for each year for which projections are to be made. Unlike simple extrapolation techniques, this approach yields estimates and projections that are more independent (that is, are not unduly influenced by past trends). This approach can deal with a wide range of assumptions simultaneously—some services can be expanded, some contracted, others held at their present level. The capacity to test different alternatives is not readily available in the more traditional techniques.

Separate estimates of future expenditures should be provided at the level of detail shown in Table 6-5. For complex categories of expenditures, further subdivisions may be made so that separate activities and responsibilities within departments can be examined in some detail. One of the advantages of inde-

Table 6-5
State and Local Government Expenditures: FY 1998-1999

(in millions)

	State & Local Government	Percent of Total	State Government	Percent of Total	Local Governments	Percent of Total
Direct General Expenditures	**1,398,533**	86.41%	**584,542**	84.66%	**813,991**	87.71%
Education	483,259	29.86%	126,185	18.28%	357,075	38.47%
Libraries	6,841	0.42%	316	0.05%	6,525	0.70%
Public Welfare	215,190	13.30%	182,238	26.39%	32,952	3.55%
Health	47,628	2.94%	24,857	3.60%	22,771	2.45%
Hospitals	71,733	4.43%	29,535	4.28%	42,199	4.55%
Streets & Highways	93,018	5.75%	56,242	8.15%	36,776	3.96%
Parking Facilities	1,014	0.06%	0	0.00%	1,014	0.11%
Airports	12,632	0.78%	1,013	0.15%	11,619	1.25%
Other Transportation	3,498	0.22%	970	0.14%	2,529	0.27%
Police Protection	53,367	3.30%	7,810	1.13%	45,557	4.91%
Fire Protection	21,262	1.31%	0	0.00%	21,262	2.29%
Correction	45,598	2.82%	30,770	4.46%	14,828	1.60%
Environment	18,232	1.13%	13,601	1.97%	4,631	0.50%
Sewerage	26,980	1.67%	1,128	0.16%	25,852	2.79%
Solid Waste Management	16,067	0.99%	1,958	0.28%	14,110	1.52%
Community Development	25,234	1.56%	2,385	0.35%	22,848	2.46%
Parks & Recreation	23,417	1.45%	3,843	0.56%	19,574	2.11%
General Administration	49,106	3.03%	17,185	2.49%	31,921	3.44%
Financial Administration	27,593	1.70%	15,372	2.23%	12,221	1.32%
Other General Expenditures	89,570	5.53%	41,348	5.99%	48,221	5.20%
Interest on General Debt	67,294	4.16%	27,785	4.02%	39,508	4.26%
Utilities	**104,851**	6.48%	**8,779**	1.27%	**96,072**	10.35%
Water Supply System	34,089	2.11%	164	0.02%	33,924	3.66%
Electric Power System	38,132	2.36%	2,521	0.37%	35,611	3.84%
Transit System	28,522	1.76%	6,089	0.88%	22,433	2.42%
Gas Supply System	4,108	0.25%	4	0.00%	4,103	0.44%
Insurance Trust Expenditures	**115,172**	7.12%	**97,144**	14.07%	**18,028**	1.94%
Total Direct Expenditures	**1,618,556**	100.00%	**690,465**	100.00%	**928,091**	100.00%
Capital Outlays	**176,610**	100.00%	**68,509**	100.00%	**129,974**	100.00%
Education	54,418	30.81%	12,294	17.94%	42,124	32.41%
Streets & Highways	51,906	29.39%	37,986	55.45%	13,920	10.71%
Hospitals	4,116	2.33%	1,394	2.03%	2,722	2.09%
Corrections	3,807	2.16%	2,515	3.67%	1,292	0.99%
Environment	3,359	1.90%	2,349	3.43%	1,010	0.78%
Parks & Recreation	6,486	3.67%	1,023	1.49%	5,463	4.20%
Sewerage	9,718	5.50%	1,128	1.65%	9,091	6.99%
Solid Waste Management	1,366	0.77%	171	0.25%	1,195	0.92%
Utilities	21,861	12.38%	3,034	4.43%	18,827	14.49%
Other Capital Expenditures	19,573	11.08%	6,615	9.66%	34,330	26.41%
Debt Outstanding	**1,369,253**	100.00%	**510,486**	100.00%	**858,767**	100.00%
Short-Term	17,844	1.30%	2,667	0.52%	15,177	1.77%
Long-Term	1,351,408	98.70%	507,819	99.48%	843,590	98.23%
Full Faith & Credit	488,868	35.70%	129,326	25.33%	359,543	41.87%
Nonguaranteed	862,540	62.99%	378,493	74.14%	484,047	56.37%
Debt by Purpose	**1,351,408**	100.00%	**507,819**	100.00%	**843,590**	100.00%
Education	245,272	18.15%	76,168	15.00%	169,104	20.05%
Utilities	194,930	14.42%	16,652	3.28%	178,279	21.13%
Public Debt for Private Purposes	351,072	25.98%	213,893	42.12%	137,179	16.26%
Other	560,134	41.45%	201,107	39.60%	359,028	42.56%

pendent projections is that additional categories can be readily added when and where they are deemed appropriate. Since major activities are projected using separate equations, it should be possible to depict interrelationships between activities within the same category and to examine the implications of various expenditure patterns arising from different program mixes.[5]

Estimates of future expenditures should be built on two basic sets of factors: (1) estimates of expenses arising from personnel, and (2) those expenses linked to nonpersonnel related factors. Projections should be made for each category of expenditure regarding the total number of employees and their distribution among various skill and wage levels.

With these data as a base, both the number of employees in a particular wage or salary class and the average annual salary or wage and staff benefit costs for that class should be projected and summed to produce total personnel expenditures. Personnel projections are related both to the demographic characteristics of the population (which can be used as a measure of the demand for public services) and to policy decisions (or policy alternatives) as to the level and quality of services provided.

A personnel schedule for the Investigation Division of the City of Rurbana Police Department is shown as Table 6-6. A 5% cost-of-living increase is applied to the salaries budgeted for existing personnel for the current fiscal year. Newly requested positions (a sergeant, an inspector, two detectives, a property clerk, a lab technician, and a secretary) are budgeted at the entrance level of the monthly salary range appropriate to each of these positions. Overtime payments are budgeted at 10% of the total salary request. Employee benefits are calculated as a percentage of the total salary request plus the overtime allowance. Retirement and pension benefits represent 11% of these costs, while social security (FICA) contributions are 6.85% of these costs. Group insurance contributions are 2% of salary and overtime costs. The cost to the City of Rurbana for medical and hospital insurance will increase from 14.3% for the current fiscal year to 15% for the next fiscal year.

Nonpersonnel items consist of contractual services, materials and supplies, travel costs, utilities, equipment, and debt service charges. These items should be estimated using linear regression equations that express the functional relationships between nonpersonnel expenditures and personnel expenditures (or, alternatively, total number of personnel). Some nonpersonnel items are closely related to staffing levels (for example, office equipment, supplied, travel costs). Pricing considerations more directly influence other nonpersonnel items.

Calculations should be made regarding debt service requirements. Information regarding the amount of debt outstanding, plans for new capital expenditures, and expectations concerning future interest rates should be applied to derive forecasts of the principal and interest payments on public debt. Policy variables should be used to examine the mix of techniques available for the financing of long-term capital expenditures.

Table 6-6
Personnel Schedule for Investigation Division
City of Rurbania Police Department

Position Title	Current Authorized Personnel	Requested Personnel	Monthly Salary Range	Current Budget	Next Fiscal Year
Lieutenant	1	1	3,200-3,800	42,000	44,100
Laboratory Supervisor	1	1	3,000-3,600	40,800	42,840
Sergeant	2	3	2,800-3,400	74,400	111,720
Inspector	3	4	2,700-3,300	111,600	149,580
Detective	15	17	2,500-3,100	522,000	608,100
Photographer	1	1	2,300-2,900	32,400	34,020
Property Clerk	1	2	2,200-2,800	27,600	55,380
Laboratory Technician	2	3	2,100-2,700	52,800	80,640
Photographer Technician	1	1	1,900-2,500	24,000	25,200
Secretary	2	3	1,700-2,300	46,800	69,540
Clerk-Stenographer	4	4	1,600-2,200	96,000	100,800
Subtotal: Salaries	33	40		$1,070,400	$1,321,920
Overtime Payments				$107,040	$132,190
Employee Benefits					
1610 Retirement & Pension Benefits				129,520	159,952
1620 Social Security Contributions				80,655	99,608
1640 Group Insurance				23,550	29,082
1650 Medical/Hospital Insurance				168,375	207,938
Subtotal: Employee Benefits				$402,100	$496,580
Total				1,579,540	$1,950,690

Summary

The demand for public services and facilities changes as a function of growth and the social and economic characteristics of the community. Governmental responsibilities have expanded in recent years—in ensuring quality education, in the provision of social services, in dealing with environmental matters, and in many other areas. This expansion has come about in some areas because of citizens demanding more and improved public services and facilities. In other instances, the pressure for an expanded local role has come largely from mandates and requirements imposed by state and federal government.

Growth and stabilization of the economy are concerns of local governments in terms of maintaining an adequate tax base, an adequate level of public service, an appropriate level of capital investment, and reasonable stability of public revenue. These concerns often have resulted in a "scramble for rateables," that is, efforts to attract economic activities (industry and commercial developments), the tax revenues from which exceed the cost of providing essential public services and facilities.

Financial management is complicated at the local level by the complexity of economic interrelationships produced by over 87,800 units of local government, often with functional and geographic overlapping responsibilities. This multiplicity of jurisdictions and balkanization of responsibilities makes it very difficult to achieve appropriate economies of scale in the delivery of public services and facilities.

Efforts to develop regional approaches to the provision of public facilities represent an important response to this problem. Regional airports, consolidated school districts, park and recreational systems, solid water disposal facilities, and sewer and water supply systems that serve multiple jurisdictions are examples of efforts to find solutions to public needs at an appropriate scale to achieve greater economy, efficiency, and effectiveness in operations.

However, not all public goods can or should be provided on a regional or statewide basis. Concepts of "grass roots democracy" and "home rule" are vital components of the philosophy of local government in this country. As a consequence, local governments remain the primary provider of public facilities and services that citizens access on a daily basis—streets, sewer and water supply systems, primary and secondary education systems, parks and recreational facilities, and so forth.

Financial analysis and planning provide the foundation for effective financial management. An analysis must be made of the various sources of revenue available under current fiscal policies. In particular, an examination must be made of the revenue sources under the direct control of the local jurisdiction. Alternative fiscal policies and methods of financing should be explored to include an analysis of adjustments in the tax rate (millage) and other fee schedules and the current debt structure. Fiscal policies should be formulated in light of these analyses to deal with revenues, operating expenditures, capital improvement, debt commitments, and the complex relationships among these fiscal components.

Notes

1. Robert L. Bland, *A Revenue Guide for Local Government* (Albuquerque, N.M.: American Classical College Press, 1989), 34.
2. Richard W. England, "Perspective: A New England Approach to Preserving Open Space," *Regional Review*, Federal Reserve Bank of Boston 12, no. 1 (2002): 2-5.
3. Wallace E. Oats and Robert M. Schwab, "The Impact of Urban Land Taxation: The Pittsburgh Experience," *National Tax Journal* 50, no. 1 (1997): 1-21.
4. James Heilbrun, *Urban Economics and Public Policy* (New York: St. Martin's Press, 1974), 324-330.
5. For a further explanation of how this approach might be applied, see Claudia DeVita Scott, *Forecasting Local Government Spending* (Washington D.C.: The Urban Institute, 1972).

Chapter 7

FINANCING STRATEGIC FACILITIES THROUGH LONG-TERM BORROWING

The power to borrow is one of the most important assets of local government. Few governments today have the capability to finance strategic facilities strictly on a "pay-as-you-go" basis. Excessive commitment to pay-as-you-go financing might prevent a locality from doing things that really need to be done because the capital projects are too costly to be carried out using only annual tax revenues.

Bonding Strategies

A bond is a promissory note ensuring that the lender will receive periodic payments of interest (at some predetermined rate) and at maturity (the due date) will be repaid the original sum (principal) invested. Thus, a ten-year term bond for $2 million with a 7% interest rate will pay the bondholders $140,000 in interest each year (usually in semiannual installments) and at the end of ten years, the $2 million will be repaid. Although referred to as "municipal bonds," this broad investment category includes bonds issued by any political subdivision (cities, counties, school districts), special purpose districts (public agency, authority, or commission), or by a state, territory, or possession of the United States.

Basic Characteristics of Municipal Bonds

The *price* of a municipal bond is usually quoted as a percentage of its face value (sometimes referred to as the "clean price"). The face value is the amount the bond issuer pays the bondholder at maturity. Most municipal bonds are issued with face values of $1,000 or $5,000.[1] Municipal bonds may be sold at a discount or at a premium. The quoted price of a bond selling at a 5% discount, for example, would be 95 (i.e., 95% of $1,000 or $950). The quoted price of a bond selling at a 3% premium would be 103 (i.e., 103% of $1,000 or $1,030).

When new municipal bonds are issued at a discount, the discount is considered to constitute part of the compensation that the issuer has contracted to pay for the use of the money loaned. Therefore, the discount is equivalent to interest for federal tax purposes. However, when a bond is purchased at a discount and then sold or redeemed for a price in excess of the purchase price, only the interest is exempt from federal tax. The additional yield when realized is taxable as a capital gain. Thus, if a bond with a 3.25% interest rate, maturing in ten years, were purchased initially for $1,000 and then resold for $958.60, the semiannual interest payments of $16.25 would be exempt from federal income tax. However, when the second bondholder redeems the bond for $1,000 at the maturity date, the appreciation of $41.40 would be considered to be a capital gain for federal income tax purposes.

The actual payment exchanged between two parties might be different from the quoted price. Bonds purchased between interest payments, for example, accrue interest that is proportional to the interest period. Therefore, the buyer must pay the seller the quoted price plus any accrued interest. This sum is known as the *invoice price* of the bond. For example, a bond issued on July 1 with a 6% coupon rate that is purchased on October 1 at par or face value would cost the buyer $1,000 plus $15 for the accrued interest (i.e., 6% x $1,000 x 3/12),

The *coupon rate* is the annual rate of interest on the face value of the bond that the issuer agrees to pay the bondholder until maturity. The term "coupon" comes from the manner by which the interest on bonds historically was redeemed. A series of coupons were attached to the bond certificate, one coupon for each interest payment stipulated in the bond's indenture. At each coupon payment date, the bondholder would clip the appropriate coupon and present it for payment. Today, most municipal bonds are offered in registered form and do not require the actual presentation of coupons for interest payments.

In 1983, Congress required municipal bonds be in registered or book-entry form for the interest income to be exempt from federal income taxes. Registered bonds do not have certificates. Instead, a depository—a brokerage house, bank, or other financial institution—keeps records of ownership for its members. All new issues of municipal bonds (with minor exceptions) are assigned a CUSIP number, which provides a unique identification of the security.[2] Transferring the ownership of a bond is accomplished by changing the records on the books of the depository and its members to reflect the transaction.

Interest earned on municipal bonds is exempt from federal taxation and usually from state taxes in the state in which the bond is issued. Forty-one states, however, do levy taxes on interest earned on municipal debt issued in other states. Tax-exempt municipal bonds generally carry lower interest rates than taxable corporate bonds. A municipal bond with a 6% yield will provide an investor in the 33% federal tax bracket the same annual return as a taxable corporate bond with a yield of 8.96%. The equivalent yield is determined by dividing the tax-free yield by 1 minus the investor's tax bracket (see Table 7-1).

This tax exemption is, in effect, a federal subsidy that reduces borrowing (debt service) costs for local governments. In April 1988, the Supreme Court overruled a major 1895 precedent, by holding that the Constitution does not protect state and local governments against federal taxation of the interest received by holders of their bonds. This ruling upheld a relatively minor tax provision passed by Congress in 1982. However, the chairmen of the Senate and House tax-writing committees immediately went on record that the decision was not expected to prompt Congress to impose any new federal taxes on municipal bonds.

In addition to their tax-exempt status, municipal bonds possess three significant features:

1. The *security* of municipal bonds is generally considered second only to that of federal government bonds.

Table 7-1
Taxable-Equivalent Yields

Tax Exempt	Tax Brackets					
Yield	10%	15%	25%	28%	33%	35%
2%	2.22%	2.35%	2.67%	2.78%	2.99%	3.08%
3%	3.33%	3.53%	4.00%	4.17%	4.48%	4.62%
4%	4.44%	4.71%	5.33%	5.56%	5.97%	6.15%
5%	5.56%	5.88%	6.67%	6.94%	7.46%	7.69%
6%	6.67%	7.06%	8.00%	8.33%	8.96%	9.23%
7%	7.78%	8.24%	9.33%	9.72%	10.45%	10.77%
8%	8.89%	9.41%	10.67%	11.11%	11.94%	12.31%
9%	10.00%	10.59%	12.00%	12.50%	13.43%	13.85%
10%	11.11%	11.76%	13.33%	13.89%	14.93%	15.38%

2. Municipal bonds have high *marketability*, assuring that investors can always sell them if they wish to do so.
3. The *diversity* of municipal bonds enables investors to obtain bonds in geographic areas and at maturities of their preference.

Periods of slower economic growth and lower short-term interest rates help to boost the value of tax-exempt bonds, as does the uncertainty of declining stock market returns.

Types of Bonds

General obligation bonds are backed by the full faith, credit, and taxing power of the issuing jurisdiction. For many investors, general obligation (GO) bonds are seen as the most secure of the municipal issues, since the issuing authority has the power (and obligation) to levy taxes at a level necessary to meet debt service requirements. The levy of taxes has practical limits, however. For local jurisdictions, the most common taxing power is on property. Income, sales, and other taxes usually secure state-issued general obligation bonds. In effect, the security of general obligation bonds is based upon the economic resources of taxpayers in the issuing jurisdiction.[3]

Double-barreled bonds are tax exempt bonds that are backed by a pledge of two or more sources. These bonds are quite likely general obligation bonds that are additionally backed by a second source of revenue, which usually increases their safety. GO bonds issued by a local government on behalf of a public sewer and water commission that are also backed by revenue generated by the public utility are examples of double-barreled bonds.

Special tax bonds are payable only from the proceeds derives from a special tax (such as highway bonds payable from a gasoline tax). *Special assessment bonds* are payable from levies against those who directly benefit from the capital improvements (e.g., special assessments for curbs and gutters in certain residential areas). Special assessments place a major share of the financing burden on those individuals or properties receiving the greatest benefits from the improvements. The rising cost of special assessment bonds in recent years has resulted in a majority being secured additionally by a pledge of full faith and credit, making them general obligation bonds. Sometimes referred to as *limited tax bonds*, these general obligation bonds often are secured by a specified maximum tax rate within the taxing power of the issuing authority

A *revenue bond* is an obligation issued to finance a capital project of a revenue-producing enterprise—such as the construction of a sewage treatment plant, parking structure, toll road or bridge, or other facility that has fairly predictable revenue generating capacities. Both the principal and interest of such bonds are paid exclusively from the earnings of the enterprise. As a general rule, such issues do not have any claim on the general credit or taxing power of the governmental unit that issues them. A system of sinking funds and operating controls typically is established to assure investors that the financial affairs of the project will be maintained in good order and all commitments will be honored. These provisions will be discussed in further detail in Chapter 8.

Revenue bond financing is best suited to projects that (1) can operate on a service charge or user-fee basis; (2) have the potential to be self-supporting, previously demonstrated under public or private operation; and (3) can produce sufficient revenue without jeopardizing other important economic or social objectives of the community. Problems of social equity might arise when traditionally tax-supported functions are placed on a service charge basis. Facilities supported by service charges also frequently produce benefits to individuals who do not pay for them—for example, enhanced land values that might accrue to speculative holders of unimproved real estate.

Many local capital improvements can only be financed through the issuance of tax-supported general obligation bonds to provide full project funding or the local match. However, faced with increasing rehabilitation needs, spiraling construction costs, and limited bonding authority, many cities might need to consider alternative arrangements for financing capital projects traditionally funded through general obligation bonds. For example, local governments are exploring increased use of revenue bond financing for projects with identifiable revenues that can be pledged to debt repayment.

Local governments have a number of possibilities for combining and substituting funding sources. The use of revenue bonds to finance capital construction in one area—such as a water system—might free up general obligation bonds for financing other portions of the infrastructure—such as streets—where service pricing is not feasible. Restricted funds might be used to free up block grants for other capital purposes. These financing alternatives should be made explicit in the initial evaluation and ranking of capital investment projects.

Industrial development bonds are issued by an Industrial Development Agency that has been created by a jurisdiction to develop industrial or commercial property for the benefit of private users. Funds raised from this type of bond issue are used to pay for the construction of a new facility, which is then leased to a corporate guarantor. The safety of an industrial revenue bond depends on the credit worthiness of the corporate guarantor.

Housing revenue bonds are issued by both state and local governments. These bonds are secured by mortgage repayments on single family homes.

Added protections come from federal subsidies for low-income families, FHA insurance, VA guarantees, and private mortgage insurance.

Method of Redemption

Municipal bonds can also be classified into two general types according to the method of redemption. *Term bonds* become due in a lump sum at the end of the term of the loan. All of the bonds in the issue reach maturity and must be paid off at the same time. *Serial bonds* are retired by annual installments directly from tax revenues, or in the case of revenue bonds, from earned income. Serial bonds have simpler retirement requirements and offer greater flexibility in marketing and in arranging the debt structure of the jurisdiction or public organization.

The lump-sum principal payment on term bonds is met by making annual payments to a *sinking fund*. These annual payments, when invested at compound interest, should produce the amount of principal due at maturity. Frequent actuarial computations are required to determine the adequacy of sinking funds to meet principal payments at maturity. Some states do not permit the issuance of bonds for which the principal is funded solely through a sinking fund. With proper investment safeguards, however, term bonds do offer some advantages. Term bonds might serve to finance public utilities and other enterprises that do not have established earning records. Debt service obligations are lower during the initial years of operations since principal payments are not required.

There are two types of serial bonds: annuity serials and straight serials. With annuity serials, debt service payments can be structured to be approximately the same each year (similar to a home mortgage). The portion of the annual payment devoted to interest is higher in the early years of the issue since the interest rate is applied against the outstanding principal. As the portion of the annual payment devoted to principal payment increases, the amount of interest decreases. The payment schedule for an annuity serial bond with interest calculated at 6% on the outstanding principal for the life of the loan is shown in Table 7-2.

Straight serial bonds require annual payments of principal of approximately equal amounts. Interest payments are larger in the early years and decline gradually as the bonds approach maturity. A payment schedule for straight serial bonds, with interest calculated over ten years at 6% on a declining principal, is also shown in Table 7-2. Note that the total debt service cost of the straight serial bond issue is less than that of the annuity serial because the principal on the straight serial bonds is paid down more quickly.

Callable bonds are issued with the provision that they can be paid off—called in for payment—prior to their maturity date. Virtually all bonds are now issued with a "date of first call" provision, after which the issuer can choose to retire the bonds before the stated maturity date. In general, the date of first call for municipal bonds is five to ten years after the date of issue. The call provision normally is exercised with appropriate notice only on interest payment dates. Callable bonds can afford greater flexibility in the jurisdiction's debt

Table 7-2
Debt Service Charges on $1 Million for Ten Years

Straight Serial Bonds
(6% on declining principal)

Year	Outstanding Principal	Principal Payment	Interest Payment	Total Debt Service
1st	1,000,000	100,000	60,000	160,000
2nd	900,000	100,000	54,000	154,000
3rd	800,000	100,000	48,000	148,000
4th	700,000	100,000	42,000	142,000
5th	600,000	100,000	36,000	136,000
6th	500,000	100,000	30,000	130,000
7th	400,000	100,000	24,000	124,000
8th	300,000	100,000	18,000	118,000
9th	200,000	100,000	12,000	112,000
10th	100,000	100,000	6,000	106,000
Total		$1,000,000	$330,000	$1,330,000

Annuity Serial Bonds
(6% on outstanding principal)

Year	Outstanding Principal	Principal Payment	Interest Payment	Total Debt Service
1st	1,000,000	75,868	60,000	135,868
2nd	924,132	80,420	55,448	135,868
3rd	843,712	85,420	50,623	135,868
4th	758,467	90,360	45,508	135,868
5th	668,107	95,782	40,086	135,868
6th	572,325	101,528	34,340	135,868
7th	470,797	107,620	28,248	135,868
8th	363,177	114,070	21,791	135,868
9th	249,100	120,922	14,946	135,868
10th	128,178	128,178	7,690	135,868
Total		$1,000,000	$358,680	$1,358,680

structure. Bonds might be recalled and refunded at more favorable terms if (1) the market or the jurisdiction's credit rating improves, (2) the initial retirement schedule proves too rapid, or (3) a period of declining revenue is encountered. The callable feature can be used to avoid overly rigid fiscal responsibilities, while at the same time permitting more rapid retirement if the project's revenue capacity expands. Terms of the call will dictate whether the issuer must pay a premium to investors. A premium for callable bonds might erode any resulting savings from refunding. For example, a 1% premium on a 7% callable bond

Table 7-3
Total Debt Service Costs for
Annuity Serial Bonds under
Different Maturities and Interest Rates
(Face Value = $1 Million)

Rank	Maturity	Interest Rate (r)	(1 + r)^n	Total Debt Service
1	10 years	5.5%	1.70814	$1,326,678
2	10 years	6.0%	1.79085	$1,358,680
3	10 years	6.5%	1.87714	$1,391,047
4	10 years	7.0%	1.96715	$1,423,775
5	10 years	7.5%	2.06103	$1,456,859
6	10 years	8.0%	2.15893	$1,490,295
7	15 years	5.5%	2.23248	$1,494,384
8	10 years	8.5%	2.26098	$1,524,077
9	15 years	6.0%	2.39656	$1,544,442
10	10 years	9.0%	2.36736	$1,558,201
11	10 years	9.5%	2.47823	$1,592,662
12	15 years	6.5%	2.57184	$1,595,292
13	10 years	10.0%	2.59374	$1,627,454
14	15 years	7.0%	2.75903	$1,646,919
15	20 years	5.5%	2.91776	$1,673,587
16	15 years	7.5%	2.95888	$1,699,309
17	20 years	6.0%	3.20714	$1,743,691
18	15 years	8.0%	3.17217	$1,752,443

would eliminate the net savings if the bonds were refunded at 6%. Procedures for refunding outstanding bond issues will be discussed in further detail in Chapter 12.

Comparison of Bond Strategies

Simple computational routines can be used to assess the impact of different bonding strategies—that is, different maturity periods and interest rates. Table 7-3, for example, shows the total debt service for a $1 million annuity serial bond issue with various interest rates and terms of maturity.

Such computations can provide considerable assistance in determining the appropriate method of financing a given project or series of projects. How much could be saved, for example, by investing in a sewer expansion project now, rather than delaying the project for three years? Assume that the current project cost is $5 million. An annuity serial bond issued for twenty years at 6% interest (shown as Alternative A in Table 7-4) would cost $435,923 annually in debt service, or more than $8.7 million over twenty years. If construction costs were to increase by 8% per year, three years hence the project would cost $6,298,560. A twenty-year annuity serial bond would have to be available at 3.318% to break even when compared to the current option at 6%.

Table 7-4
Comparison of Costs and Benefits of Two Financing Alternatives

	Debt Service	Costs	Discounted	Costs	Discount			Discounted	Benefits
Year	Alternative A	Alternative B	Alternative A	Alternative B	Factor @6%	Alternative A	Alternative B	Alternative A	Alternative B
1	435,923	436,000	411,248	411,321	0.94340			0	0
2	435,923	436,000	387,970	388,038	0.89000	300,000		266,999	0
3	435,923	436,000	366,009	366,074	0.83962	400,000		335,848	0
4	435,923	491,122	345,292	389,015	0.79209	500,000		396,047	0
5	435,923	491,122	325,747	366,995	0.74726	600,000	300,000	448,355	224,177
6	435,923	491,122	307,309	346,222	0.70496	600,000	400,000	422,976	281,984
7	435,923	491,122	289,914	326,624	0.66506	600,000	500,000	399,034	332,529
8	435,923	491,122	273,503	308,136	0.62741	600,000	600,000	376,447	376,447
9	435,923	491,122	258,022	290,694	0.59190	600,000	600,000	355,139	355,139
10	435,923	491,122	243,417	274,240	0.55839	600,000	600,000	335,037	335,037
11	435,923	491,122	229,639	258,717	0.52679	600,000	600,000	316,073	316,073
12	435,923	491,122	216,640	244,073	0.49697	600,000	600,000	298,182	298,182
13	435,923	491,122	204,378	230,257	0.46884	600,000	600,000	281,303	281,303
14	435,923	491,122	192,809	217,224	0.44230	600,000	600,000	265,381	265,381
15	435,923	491,122	181,895	204,928	0.41727	600,000	600,000	250,359	250,359
16	435,923	491,122	171,599	193,328	0.39365	600,000	600,000	236,188	236,188
17	435,923	491,122	161,886	182,385	0.37136	600,000	600,000	222,819	222,819
18	435,923	491,122	152,723	172,062	0.35034	600,000	600,000	210,206	210,206
19	435,923		144,078		0.33051	600,000	600,000	198,308	198,308
20	435,923		135,923		0.31180	600,000	600,000	187,083	187,083
Totals	$8,718,460	$8,674,830	$5,000,000	$5,170,331		$10,800,000	$9,000,000	$5,801,783	$4,371,214

Benefit/Cost Ratio

Alternative A $\frac{\$5,801,783}{\$5,000,000} = 1.03407$ Alternative B $\frac{\$4,371,214}{\$5,170,331} = 0.75343$

As an alternative, if the municipality could invest $436,000 annually in a capital reserve at 8% interest (compounded semiannually), a reserve fund of $1,528,665 would accumulate in three years. This reserve could be applied to the project cost of $6,298,560, leaving $4,769,895 to be financed through borrowing (Alternative B). An annuity serial bond for this amount, at 6% for fifteen years, would cost approximately $491,122 in annual debt service, or $7,366,824 over fifteen years. When combined with the annual contributions to the capital reserve fund ($436,000 x 3 = $1,308,000), the total cost of this alternative would be $8,674,824.

To complete this decision scenario, it is necessary to consider the benefits that might accrue from expanding the sewer system three years earlier. Such a comparison is provided in Table 7-4. It is assumed that benefits will begin to accrue one year after the system expansion is initiated, totaling $300,000 in year 2, $400,000 in year 3, $500,000 in year 4, and $600,000 each year thereafter. Benefits for Alternative B would begin in year 5—that is, one year after the deferred project is initiated—and would total $300,000 in year 5, $400,000 in year 6, $500,000 in year 7, and $600,000 each year thereafter. For purposes of this illustration, these benefits might be assumed to represent the net income from the project—that is, the funds remaining after operating and maintenance costs have been met.

As the calculations show, Alternative A has a benefit/cost ratio of 1.03407 and net benefits of $801,783. Alternative B has a benefit/cost ratio of 0.75343 and negative net benefits of $799,117. Alternative B is not a good investment. The municipality would be better off initiating the project now rather than deferring it for three years. By programming basic computational routines to accept various parameters, public officials can assess a wider range of alternatives that might not otherwise be readily apparent.

Bond Options for a Prenatal Health Care Clinic

The following case study is designed to further illustrate the decision process involved in selecting a bond strategy from among the available options. The Jefferson County Council has authorized the construction of a new prenatal health-care clinic as part of the overall services of the Health Department. The cost for construction and acquisition of capital equipment is estimated to be $2.6 million. The County Council has further authorized a ten-year bond issue to finance these costs.

Four alternative bond strategies are proposed by the financial consultant hired by the County to assist in the placement of this bond:

1. A ten-year annuity serial bond with a 5.25% interest rate.
2. A ten-year straight serial bond with a 5.5% interest rate.
3. A ten-year term bond with a 5% interest rate and a sinking fund estimated to accrue at 4.5% interest.
4. A ten-year stepped coupon bond with an average coupon rate of 5.01%.

Which of these alternatives is the preferred bond strategy for Jefferson County?

The annual debt service for the ten-year annuity serial bond can be determined by applying the following formula:

$$\text{Annual Debt Service} = \text{Principal x } \frac{(r)(1 + r)^n}{(1 + r)^n - 1}$$

$$\text{Annual Debt Service} = \$2,600,000 \text{ x } \frac{(.0525)(1.0525)^{10}}{(1.0525)^{10} - 1}$$

$$\text{Annual Debt Service} = \$340,812$$

Therefore, for the total debt service for the ten-year annuity serial bond would be $3,408,120. The payment schedule, assuming semiannual interest payments and annual payments of principal, is shown in Table 7-5.

The total debt service for the ten-year straight serial bond can be determined by applying the following formula:

$$\text{Total Debt Service} = \text{Principal} + [(N + 1)/2 \text{ x r x Principal}]$$
$$\text{Total Debt Service} = \$2,600,000 + [11/2 \text{ x } .055 \text{ x } \$2,600,000]$$
$$\text{Total Debt Service} = \$3,386,500$$

The first year debt service on the straight serial bond would be $403,000, again assuming semiannual interest payments and annual payments of principal. Each year, annual payments would "step down" by $14,300, as shown in Table 7-6.

The annual interest payments on the ten-year term bond at 5% would be $130,000. The amount that would have to be invested annually in the sinking fund to ensure an accrual of $2.6 million at the end of ten years can be determined by applying the following formula:

$$\text{Annual Sinking Fund Payment} = \text{Principal x (r)} \div (1 + r)^n - 1$$
$$\text{Annual Payment} = \$2,600,000 \text{ x } (.045) \div (1.045)^{10} - 1$$
$$\text{Annual Payment} = \$2,600,000 \text{ x } 0.08137846$$
$$\text{Annual Sinking Fund Payment} = \$211,585$$

The annual interest and sinking fund payments total $341,585. The total debt service over the ten-year period would be $3,415,850, as shown in Table 7-7.

The payment schedule for the stepped coupon bond issue is more complex than the other options, as shown in Table 7-8. Interest must be paid on the outstanding principal associated with each step in the coupon rate. For example, the interest for year 8 is equal to the interest on $420,000 at 6% plus $380,000 at 5.5% plus $330,000 at 5%. The average coupon rate for this stepped coupon bond is 4.9%. The total debt service would be $3,416,130.

The question remains: Which of these alternatives is the preferred bond strategy for Jefferson County? If the County can afford the initial debt service payment of $430,000, then the straight serial bond would be the preferred option, since the total debt service is $21,620 less than the annuity serial bond and $29,350 less than the term bond. The term bond and the annuity serial bond have approximately the same annual costs. If the County believes that it might

Table 7-5
Annuity Serial Bond

Year	Outstanding Principal	Principal	Rate	Interest	Fiscal Total
1	$2,600,000	$204,312	5.25%	$136,500	$340,812
2	$2,395,688	$215,038	5.25%	$125,774	$340,812
3	$2,180,650	$226,328	5.25%	$114,484	$340,812
4	$1,954,322	$238,210	5.25%	$102,602	$340,812
5	$1,716,112	$250,716	5.25%	$90,096	$340,812
6	$1,465,396	$263,879	5.25%	$76,933	$340,812
7	$1,201,517	$277,732	5.25%	$63,080	$340,812
8	$923,785	$292,313	5.25%	$48,499	$340,812
9	$631,472	$307,660	5.25%	$33,152	$340,812
10	$323,812	$323,812	5.25%	$17,000	$340,812
Totals		$2,600,000		$808,120	$3,408,120

Table 7-6
Straight Serial Bond

Year	Outstanding Principal	Principal	Rate	Interest	Fiscal Total
1	$2,600,000	$260,000	5.50%	$143,000	$403,000
2	$2,340,000	$260,000	5.50%	$128,700	$388,700
3	$2,080,000	$260,000	5.50%	$114,400	$374,400
4	$1,820,000	$260,000	5.50%	$100,100	$360,100
5	$1,560,000	$260,000	5.50%	$85,800	$345,800
6	$1,300,000	$260,000	5.50%	$71,500	$331,500
7	$1,040,000	$260,000	5.50%	$57,200	$317,200
8	$780,000	$260,000	5.50%	$42,900	$302,900
9	$520,000	$260,000	5.50%	$28,600	$288,600
10	$260,000	$260,000	5.50%	$14,300	$274,300
Totals		$2,600,000		$786,500	$3,386,500

Table 7-7
Term Bond

Year	Outstanding Principal	Sinking Fund	Rate	Interest	Period Total	Sinking Fund
1	$2,600,000	$211,585	5.00%	$130,000	$341,585	$211,585
2	$2,600,000	$211,585	5.00%	$130,000	$341,585	$432,691
3	$2,600,000	$211,585	5.00%	$130,000	$341,585	$663,747
4	$2,600,000	$211,585	5.00%	$130,000	$341,585	$905,201
5	$2,600,000	$211,585	5.00%	$130,000	$341,585	$1,157,520
6	$2,600,000	$211,585	5.00%	$130,000	$341,585	$1,421,194
7	$2,600,000	$211,585	5.00%	$130,000	$341,585	$1,696,732
8	$2,600,000	$211,585	5.00%	$130,000	$341,585	$1,984,670
9	$2,600,000	$211,585	5.00%	$130,000	$341,585	$2,285,565
10	$2,600,000	$211,585	5.00%	$130,000	$341,585	$2,600,000
Totals		$2,115,850		$1,300,000	$3,415,850	$2,600,000

Table 7-8
Stepped Coupon Bond Issue

Year	Outstanding Principal	Principal	Rate	Interest	Period Total
1	$2,600,000	$140,000	3.00%	$119,980	$259,980
2	$2,460,000	$160,000	3.25%	$115,780	$275,780
3	$2,300,000	$180,000	3.50%	$110,580	$290,580
4	$2,120,000	$200,000	3.75%	$104,280	$304,280
5	$1,920,000	$230,000	4.00%	$96,780	$326,780
6	$1,690,000	$260,000	4.30%	$87,580	$347,580
7	$1,430,000	$300,000	4.60%	$76,400	$376,400
8	$1,130,000	$330,000	5.00%	$43,900	$373,900
9	$800,000	$380,000	5.50%	$35,650	$415,650
10	$420,000	$420,000	6.00%	$25,200	$445,200
Totals		$2,600,000		$816,130	$3,416,130
Average Coupon Rate			4.90%		

Table 7-9
Stepped Coupon Bond Issue

Year	Outstanding Principal	Principal	Coupon Rate	Interest	Fiscal Total
1	$2,600,000	$420,000	3.00%	$103,440	$523,440
2	$2,180,000	$380,000	3.25%	$90,840	$470,840
3	$1,800,000	$330,000	3.50%	$78,490	$408,490
4	$1,470,000	$300,000	3.75%	$66,940	$366,940
5	$1,170,000	$260,000	4.00%	$55,690	$315,690
6	$910,000	$230,000	4.30%	$45,290	$275,290
7	$680,000	$200,000	4.60%	$35,400	$235,400
8	$480,000	$180,000	5.00%	$26,200	$206,200
9	$300,000	$160,000	5.50%	$17,200	$177,200
10	$140,000	$140,000	6.00%	$8,400	$148,400
Totals		$2,600,000		$527,890	$3,127,890
Average Coupon Rate			4.92%		

be able to achieve a better rate of return on the sinking fund than 4.5% in future years, then the term bond would be the preferred alternative between these two options. Finally, the stepped coupon bond, while it is the most costly of the four options, does have the advantage of considerably lower annual payments in the initial years.

If it were possible to schedule more bonds to mature in early years, the interest costs for the stepped coupon bond issue could be lower. For example, the repayment schedule for the principal on the $2.6 million bond issue shown in Table 7-8 might be reversed, so that the initial payment were for $420,000, the second year payment for $380,000, and so forth. In so doing, the Jefferson County Council could save $258,610 in interest costs over the straight serial bond issue. The average coupon rate would be 4.92% (see Table 7-9).

Innovative Fiduciary and Fiscal Instruments

Large institutional investors, such as fire and casualty insurance companies, have traditionally supported the municipal bond market. However, faced with reduced profit margins in the late 1970s, many of these institutional investors curtailed their municipal bond buying. Bond issuers were forced to make yields more attractive to prospective buyers, resulting in significant increases in interest costs. Investors were unwilling to lock into fixed returns, feeling uncertain about inflation, tax liabilities, and yield curves. State and local government still needed to borrow, however, and investors still needed to earn returns. As a consequence, a number of new fiduciary and fiscal instruments were devised to meet these respective needs.

Zero Coupon Bonds

Zero coupon bonds (also called "zeros") were introduced into the tax-exempt bond market in the late 1970s and quickly became a hot item in public finance. Individual bond buyers especially favor "zeros" as a form of original investment discount bonds. Zero coupon bonds may be issued as either general obligation bonds or as revenue bonds.

Zero coupon bonds sell at substantial discounts from the customary face or par value of $1,000, because they pay no interest. By paying par upon maturity, however, they offer capital gains that might be as much as twenty times the original investment, depending on the length of the issue and the equivalent rate of return on the original investment. For example, single-family mortgage revenue bonds, issued in 1982 by the Virginia Housing Development Authority, priced at $250 per $1,000 maturity amount, for an annualized yield of 11.83% at maturity in 1994. The 1982 Virginia issue also included bonds priced at $100, providing an annualized yield of 12.45% at maturity in 2001, as well as some priced at $20, which will yield an annualized 12.58% in 2014.

Federal tax laws entitle bondholders who forego tax-free income over the life of their investment to receive tax-exempt capital gains upon maturity. For example, fifteen-year zero coupon bonds, purchased for $250 and held to maturity, will provide a tax-free capital gain of $750. According to the IRS, this capital gain is equivalent to $50 in tax-exempt income each year ($750 divided by 15). The earnings are the equivalent of a 10.4% compound interest on the original investment.

Zero coupon bonds might be attractive to investors who are interested in investing for a future need, such as college tuition for their children or retirement. Since the interest on a zero coupon bond, in essence, is automatically reinvested in the bond, this type of bond might appeal to investors who expect future interest rates to decline or want the convenience of not having to deal with how to reinvest their returns. Local governments that issue zero coupon bonds are able to delay interest payments until their final maturity.

From the municipality standpoint, issuing zero coupon bonds means that a much larger face value (value at maturity) must be issued. For example, as shown in Table 7-10, if the objective were to obtain $10 million from ten-year zero coupon bonds sold at $558 per $1,000 face value, the municipality would have to issue bonds that at maturity would be worth $17,921,147 (i.e., $10 million divided by $558 x $1,000). Debt limits usually apply to the par value of bonds, and therefore zero coupon bonds usually use the same level of debt capacity as a non-zero coupon bond for the same amount. However, "zeros" result in less proceeds from the bonds because they are sold at a discount.

Since all interest on zero coupon bonds is paid at maturity, the issuer must have substantial funds available for what is effectively a balloon payment. Annual payments usually are invested through a sinking fund that is designed to accumulate a sum sufficient to cover the principal payment at maturity. As shown in Table 7-10, annual payments of $1,458,402, invested in a sinking fund earning 4.5%, would yield the $17,921,147 required to retire the ten-year zero coupon bonds. Thus, the $10 million borrowed initially cost the jurisdiction $14,584,018 in payments to the sinking fund.

Brokerage firms have purchased traditional coupon-bearing, long-term issues and have stripped the coupons from the bonds. Each component is then sold separately. In effect, the bond becomes a zero coupon bond, with the guarantees of the issuing public agency. Without coupons, the value of what is called the *corpus* is significantly reduced. For example, a 14% corpus, maturing in the year 2011, could have been bought in the early 1980s for about $40 per $1,000 bond face amount, providing a compounded annual yield to maturity of 11.5%. In other words, over thirty years, each $40 invested would increase about twenty-five times to maturity in the year 2011.

Stepped Coupon Bonds

In traditional serial bonds, each maturity has a single coupon rate payable over the life of the bond. *Stepped coupon bonds*, on the other hand, use a serial maturity schedule, with coupon rates that usually start at lower levels and progressively increase to higher levels, even though all the bonds in the issue are usually sold at par (see Table 7-11). Stepped coupon bonds are particularly applicable to the financing of projects that require interest payments to be made from project revenue. At the outset, when project revenue might be more limited, the coupon rates can be lower than in later years when the revenue stream is more substantial.

The substantial increase in coupon payments each year is intended to provide the investors with a hedge against inflation and thus make the bonds more marketable. The assumption is that, as the purchasing power of paper money goes down each year, stepped coupons give bondholders more paper money to keep pace with inflation.

A stepped coupon issue can be structured to be competitive with other types of bond strategies in spite of this "hedge-against-inflation" feature. For example, the ten-year stepped coupon bond shown in Table 7-11 has an average coupon rate of 6.06% and would cost the issuing jurisdiction $13,779,750 in interest and principal payments. This total debt service compares favorably with the $13,839,934 required in Table 7-10 to fund the ten-year zero coupon bond issue.

Compound Interest Bonds

The interest component of a *compound interest bond* (also called capital appreciation bond, accumulator, or municipal multiplier bond) is held by the issuer and compounded at a stated rate. At the maturity of the bonds, the investor

Table 7-10
Zero Coupon Bond Issue for $10 Million

Year	Annual Rate of Increase @6%	Sinking Fund @ 4.5% Annual Payment	Sinking Fund @ 4.5% Accumulative Value
1	$591	$1,458,402	$1,458,402
2	$627	$1,458,402	$2,982,432
3	$665	$1,458,402	$4,575,044
4	$704	$1,458,402	$6,239,322
5	$747	$1,458,402	$7,978,494
6	$792	$1,458,402	$9,795,928
7	$839	$1,458,402	$11,695,147
8	$889	$1,458,402	$13,679,831
9	$943	$1,458,402	$15,753,825
10	$1,000	$1,458,400	$17,921,147
Totals		$14,584,018	

Discount Price of Bond =	1,000/((1.06)^10)-1 =	$558
Amount of Bonds Issued =	$10 Million/558 * 1,000 =	$17,921,147
Sinking Fund Payment =	P*(r)/((1 + r)^n) - 1 =	$1,458,402

Table 7-11
Stepped Coupon Bond Issue for $10 Million

Year	Principal	Coupon Rate	Interest	Fiscal Total
1	$540,000	2.50%	$524,150	$1,064,150
2	$615,000	3.00%	$510,650	$1,125,650
3	$690,000	3.50%	$492,200	$1,182,200
4	$780,000	4.00%	$468,050	$1,248,050
5	$885,000	4.50%	$436,850	$1,321,850
6	$1,000,000	5.00%	$397,025	$1,397,025
7	$1,155,000	5.50%	$347,025	$1,502,025
8	$1,265,000	6.00%	$283,500	$1,548,500
9	$1,460,000	6.50%	$207,600	$1,667,600
10	$1,610,000	7.00%	$112,700	$1,722,700
Totals	$10,000,000		$3,779,750	$13,779,750

Average Coupon Rate 6.06%

receives a lump sum, consisting of both the principal and interest. Although purchased at face value, an investor in compound interest bonds pays much less for the bond than it would be worth at maturity. For example, a ten-year bond with a face value of $1,000, earning at a compound interest rate of 6%, would be worth $1,790.85 at maturity. Earning at a compound interest rate of 6.5%, the bond would be worth $1,877.14 at maturity.

The main advantage of compound interest bonds is that an investor knows exactly what the total return on his or her investment will be. With a traditional coupon bond, the bondholder must reinvest the semiannual interest payments at the then-prevailing rate. Thus, the overall return is uncertain. Compound interest bonds guarantee the current rate of return for the duration of the issue—as much as fifteen to twenty years. This type of bond combines the investment multiplying power of compound interest with the income-sheltering feature of traditional tax-exempt bonds.

As with zero coupon bonds, the interest on a compound interest bond is reinvested in the bond, making this type of bond particularly appealing to investors who expect future interest rates to decline. However, if interest rates are expected to increase, investors might be reluctant to invest in compound interest bonds or zero interest bonds.

For an issuer, the greatest advantage to compound interest bonds relative to zero coupon bonds is a legal one. Debt limits usually apply to the par value of bonds. Compound interest bonds and zero coupon bonds with the same par value will utilize the same debt capacity. However, zero coupon bonds are sold at a discount, and therefore the compound interest bonds of the same par value will result in more bond proceeds. Thus, issuers who are approaching a debt limit might find compound interest bonds to be more desirable than zero coupon bonds. However, since all interest is paid at maturity, the issuer must have substantial funds available for what is effectively a balloon payment.

The annual payments to a sinking fund (earning 4.5%) for compound interest bonds with an annual rate increase of 6% are shown in Table 7-12. Note that these annual payments are $1,031 lower than the annual payments to the sinking fund required to service the zero coupon bonds under the same assumptions (see Table 7-10).

Payments to a sinking fund must be structured to earn a sufficient sum to cover the appreciated capital, that is, the accumulated interest and principal costs. At some point during the duration of the bond, the issuing jurisdiction might begin to make interest payments to the bondholders. The total annual payments are much higher, however, because interest must now be paid on the interest that has accumulated as additional capital (principal). It has been estimated that a compound interest bond can cost the municipality 3.5 times as much in annual sinking fund payments when compared to a more conventional term bond where only the principal payments are deferred and paid in a lump sum when the bonds mature (see Table 7-13). However, since annual interest payments must be made on the outstanding principal of a term bond, the total debt service costs of a compound interest bond generally is 10% to 15% higher than a comparable term bond.

Table 7-12
Compound Interest Bond Issue for $10 Million

Year	Annual Rate of Increase @6%	Sinking Fund @ 4.5% Annual Payment	Sinking Fund @ 4.5% Accumulative Value
1	$10,600,000	$1,457,371	$1,457,371
2	$11,236,000	$1,457,371	$2,980,324
3	$11,910,160	$1,457,371	$4,571,809
4	$12,624,770	$1,457,371	$6,234,912
5	$13,382,256	$1,457,371	$7,972,854
6	$14,185,191	$1,457,371	$9,789,003
7	$15,036,303	$1,457,371	$11,686,879
8	$15,938,481	$1,457,371	$13,670,160
9	$16,894,790	$1,457,371	$15,742,688
10	$17,908,478	$1,457,371	$17,908,480
Totals		$14,573,710	

The often-stated justification for the use of compound interest bonds is that the cost impact of the capital project is deferred until more direct beneficiaries of the facility can participate in the payment of these costs (e.g., through increased tax revenues). The impact of the additional interest costs (the interest on the appreciated capital) can be partially absorbed *if* the investments in the sinking fund are carefully managed. Failure to structure an appropriate sinking fund in connection with a compound interest bond, however, can create a floating debt of significant proportions.

Tender Option Bonds

A *tender option bond,* also known as a *put bond,* offers the investor the option of submitting the bond for redemption before maturity. Under this bond format, investors might "tender their option" to redeem a bond, usually five years after the date of issue or on any anniversary date thereafter. Thus, the investor can withdraw from a longer-term commitment in order to take advantage of a new investment opportunity that provides a higher yield. In return for this option, the investor usually accepts a lower yield. The issuer pays a lower rate of interest (usually about one percentage point less than for conventional bonds of the same maturity), and consequently, the cost to the jurisdiction is lower. However, a tender option bond typically returns more to the investor (about 0.75%) than conventional bonds that mature on the first prescribed put date (e.g. five

Table 7-13
Comparison of Capital Appreciation Bond and Conventional Term Bond 15-Year Maturity @ 6.5% with Sinking Fund @ 4.5%

	Capital Appreciation Bond				**Conventional Term Bond**		
	Accrued		*Sinking*				*Sinking*
Year	*Principal*	*Interest*	*Fund*	*Year*	*Principal*	*Interest*	*Fund*
1	1,000,000	65,000	112,320	1	1,000,000	65,000	31,876
2	1,065,000	69,225	229,695	2		65,000	65,187
3	1,134,225	73,725	352,351	3		65,000	99,996
4	1,207,950	78,517	480,527	4		65,000	136,372
5	1,286,466	83,620	614,471	5		65,000	174,385
6	1,370,087	89,056	754,443	6		65,000	214,109
7	1,459,142	94,844	900,713	7		65,000	255,620
8	1,553,987	101,009	1,053,565	8		65,000	298,999
9	1,654,996	107,575	1,213,296	9		65,000	344,330
10	1,762,570	114,567	1,380,214	10		65,000	391,701
11	1,877,137	122,014	1,554,644	11		65,000	441,203
12	1,999,151	129,945	1,736,923	12		65,000	492,934
13	2,129,096	138,391	1,927,405	13		65,000	546,992
14	2,267,487	147,387	2,126,459	14		65,000	603,483
15	2,414,874	156,967	2,334,470	15		65,000	662,516
16	2,571,841	167,170	2,551,841	16		65,000	724,205
17	2,739,011	178,036	2,778,994	17		65,000	788,670
18	2,917,046	189,608	3,016,369	18		65,000	856,037
19	3,106,654	201,933	3,264,426	19		65,000	926,434
20	3,308,587	215,058	3,523,645	20		65,000	1,000,000

	Capital Appreciation Bond		Conventional Term Bond
Capital Appreciation	$3,523,645		
Total Interest	$2,523,645	Total Interest	$1,300,000
Annual Payments to Sinking Fund	$112,320		$31,876
Ratio of Annual Sinking Payments of CAB to Term Bond			3.52
Total Costs	$2,246,404		$1,937,523

years into the bond duration). In other words, a tender option bond with a fifteen-year maturity and a five-year put date might carry a 4.75% interest rate, compared to a 5.75% rate for a conventional bond with a fifteen-year maturity. A conventional bond with a five-year maturity, in turn, is likely to carry an interest rate of 4% under similar investment circumstances.

Tender option bonds might also be issued with a simultaneous call date, on which the issuer can call in and pay off the bonds. Thus, the issuer and the bondholder have equal rights to cash in the bonds when market conditions and interest rates are favorable from their perspective. If interest rates go down, the issuing government will probably call in a put bond. Conversely, if interest rates go up, the bondholder can "tender the option" to be paid at face value by the issuer.

A variation on the tender option bond approach has been used primarily in conjunction with mortgage revenue bonds used to finance low-income housing. Instead of offering a "put" option, the issuer is required to call in the bonds for early payment at face value as sufficient funds become available. Thus, for example, a bondholder might have purchased such bonds with the expectation of holding them for eight years. But, as rental income from the housing units reaches predetermined thresholds, the authority is required to call in some portion of the outstanding bonds. The bonds are redeemed by lottery: the individual bondholder does not know when or if his or her bond will be called in for redemption. When all the bonds to be called from this fund are lumped together, the maturity is referred to as a *supersinker*.

Floating Rate Bonds

The idea of issuing tax-exempt bonds with a floating interest rate has been adapted from the Eurocurrency market. As the name implies, the interest paid by the issuer (yield) on a *floating rate bond* changes over the life of the bond based on some index printed on the bond itself. This approach provides stability to both the issuer and the bondholder throughout the life of the bonds, particularly during times of interest rate volatility. This feature stands in contrast to traditional fixed-rate bonds on which the interest rate remains constant while the market value of the bonds might change when interest rates rise or fall.

The interest index most often used is the average weekly rate of Treasury bills or bonds issued during the preceding interest period. For example, the floating rate for a short-term bond might be pegged at 67% of the average weekly T-bill quote, while the rate for a longer term issue might be set at 75% of the average weekly quote on thirty-year Treasury bonds (see Table 7-14).

An additional feature of floating rate bonds is a swing limit—a pre-established range within which the interest (cost to the public agency) might vary. Bonds issued in the late 1980s, for example, had floating interest rate limits of 7% minimum to a maximum of 12.5% over the life of the bonds.

As with other municipal bonds, the maturities of floating rate bonds vary. Such bonds usually have call and/or put features that specify the earliest dates at which bondholders can get their investment back at par. Some recent floating rate bonds have been structured so that they can be redeemed at the end of a

Table 7-14
Floating Rate Bond Issue for $10 Million

Date	Interest Index*	Interest Rate Rate @ 75%	Interest	Principal Payment	Annual Debt Service
12/1/05	8.25%	6.19%	$309,375		
6/1/06	8.20%	6.15%	$307,500	$1,000,000	$1,616,875
12/1/06	7.85%	5.89%	$264,938		
6/1/07	7.75%	5.81%	$261,563	$1,000,000	$1,526,500
12/1/07	8.00%	6.00%	$240,000		
6/1/08	8.20%	6.15%	$246,000	$1,000,000	$1,486,000
12/1/08	8.25%	6.19%	$216,563		
6/1/09	8.20%	6.15%	$215,250	$1,000,000	$1,431,813
12/1/09	8.15%	6.11%	$183,375		
6/1/10	7.98%	5.99%	$179,550	$1,000,000	$1,362,925
12/1/10	7.78%	5.84%	$145,875		
6/1/11	7.90%	5.93%	$148,125	$1,000,000	$1,294,000
12/1/11	8.10%	6.08%	$121,500		
6/1/12	8.12%	6.09%	$121,800	$1,000,000	$1,243,300
12/1/12	7.86%	5.90%	$88,425		
6/1/13	7.76%	5.82%	$87,300	$1,000,000	$1,175,725
12/1/13	7.65%	5.74%	$57,375		
6/1/14	7.90%	5.93%	$59,250	$1,000,000	$1,116,625
12/1/14	8.00%	6.00%	$30,000		
6/1/15	8.10%	6.08%	$30,375	$1,000,000	$1,060,375
Totals			$3,314,138	$10,000,000	$13,314,138
Average Interest Rate		6.00%			

* The interest index has been constructed to yield an average interest rate comparable to the stepped coupon, zero coupon, and compound interest bond issues. In actual application, the interest index may be several percentage points lower than shown in this example.

given calendar period. Floating rate certificates issued by the State of Washington, for example, pay interest each month. Bondholders might elect on the fifteenth day of each month in which the interest payments are due either (1) to accept a new interest payment date at the same rate as the previous month, or (2) to tender the bonds for purchase by the state at par. Although they are basically bonds, floating rate bonds with short demand features are often called notes or *certificates of indebtedness*.

Since floating bonds have less risk of principal erosion, interest costs generally are lower than on long-term, conventional bonds. The savings in interest costs to the issuer can be very substantial. The difference between a traditional bond and a flexible floating rate bond is often as much as 3 to 3.5 percentage points.

Variable Rate Demand Bonds

Variable rate debt first gained popularity during the 1970s as short-term, variable rate demand notes. However, long-term, *variable rate demand bonds* also have become popular in the last few years. As with floating rate bonds, the rate of interest is reset periodically based on a specified index. A wider variety of indices are used in connection with variable rate bonds, however. The demand feature allows investors to require the issuer or a specified third party to purchase these bonds at specified times, such as when the interest rates are reset.

The most common variable rate bond is the *lower floater* in which the interest rate is adjusted weekly relative to a specified index designed to reflect the current market.[4] When the interest rate is adjusted, bondholders often can require redemption of lower floater bonds after giving seven-days notice. Other debt structures allow different timetables for redeeming the bonds; these vary from monthly to multiyear demand obligations. A put option that can be exercised in fewer than thirty days is called a continuing put.

The structure of long-term, variable rate demand debt involves a rather complicated credit system. The bond issuer usually enters into an agreement with a credit facility—typically a commercial bank. The bank provides a letter of credit to the issuing jurisdiction. Should bondholders exercise the put option and redeem the bonds before maturity, the issuing jurisdiction enlists the services of a remarketing agent. The remarketing agent usually has the flexibility to reset the interest rate within a range of the index in order to allow the bonds to trade at par. An effort is then made to remarket the bonds. If some bonds remain unsold, the remaining cash needs are met by the agreement between the issuing jurisdiction and the credit facility, which either purchases the unsold bonds or makes a loan to the issuer. The issuing jurisdiction must pay the fees associated with the remarketing agent and the credit agreement. If the credit facility is required to provide cash, the issuing jurisdiction also will incur interest on the funds, which typically is tied to the bank prime rate or higher.[5]

Bond rating companies use a two-part bond rating approach for variable rate demand bonds. The first component of the rating, referred to as the credit rating, focuses on the creditworthiness of the issuer to meet debt service requirements over the life of the bonds. The second component, the liquidity rating, reflects the ability of the issuer to make timely payments under the demand feature. The latter is usually based on the rating of the bank that supplies the letter of credit.

Caps, Floors, and Collars

Issuers of variable rate demand bonds face the possibility that interest rates might increase substantially in the future. A system of *caps*, *floors*, and *collars* has been developed to help municipal bond issuers avoid widely fluctuating interest rates on their variable rate debt. Caps, floors, and collars are derivative products through which bond issuers can maintain their interest rate payments within set boundaries.[6]

Under an *interest rate cap* (also called a ceiling), a bond issuer enters into a contract with a counterparty that agrees to pay the issuer if a specified interest rate index rises above a certain percentage rate, known as the cap or strike rate. In exchange, the counterparty receives a one-time premium from the bond issuer. The amount of the premium depends on the bond maturity date and on the size of the contract (bond principal) upon which the interests amounts are determined. The more distant the maturity date, the larger the principal, and the lower the strike level, the larger the up-front fee. If the floating interest rate remains below the strike rate for the duration of the contract, the cap purchaser receives no payments. In effect, the bond issuer is buying an insurance policy to protect against high interest rate payments on its variable rate bonds.[7]

Under a particular cap agreement, for instance, the bond issuer might buy a cap with a strike rate of 4%. If the applicable tax-exempt bond index, such as the Public Securities Association (PSA) index, stays below 4%, the issuer receives no payments. However, if the index rises to 4.25% during the term of the agreement, the issuer would receive from the counterparty funds equivalent to the 0.25% in interest payments.

In calculating the cost-effectiveness of purchasing a cap, the bond issuer must compare the required up-front fee to the expected present value payments to be received under the cap. A risk adverse issuer, however, might value the security of a known limit on debt payments enough to warrant a purchase of a cap even though its premium might exceed expected payments under the cap.[8]

A *floor* is the mirror image of a ceiling. With a floor contract, the bond issuer receives an up-front fee from a counterparty. If the interest rate index falls below the floor or strike level, the bond issuer makes payments to the counterparty. Under the terms of a particular floor agreement, for example, if an issuer sold a floor with a strike price of 4% and the J.J. Kenny Index dropped to 3.5%, the issuer would pay the counterparty an amount based on the 0.5% difference. Similar to a cap agreement, if the floating index rate does not fall below the strike level, the bond issuer pays nothing.[9]

In entering into a floor agreement, the up-front premium that the bond issuer receives must be compared with the payments that must be made if the floating interest rate falls below the strike level. The issuer might bet that the premium can be retained without making any payments. A counterparty buys a floor if it predicts that interest rates will fall, and it can recoup on the contract.[10]

A *collar* is the simultaneous purchase of a cap and sale of a floor by the bond issuer. Under this contract, the government entity trades any benefits from a potential fall in the interest rate index for protection against excessive interest rates. Under a collar agreement, the issuer defines a specific range for its interest rate payments, eliminating some of the uncertainty associated with issuing variable rate debt. The closer the cap and floor strike rates are set, the more the bonds will resemble fixed rate obligations.

The collar costs the issuer less than a cap, but it still sets a limit on future debt service payments. An issuer might elect to enter into the floor provision of the collar with the goal of offsetting the cost of the cap part of the agreement. The cap and floor levels of the collar agreement can even be determined so that they perfectly offset each other.

The main advantage of caps and collars is the protection they offer against rising interest rates. They can provide an issuer the stability associated with fixed rate debt, while allowing the issuer to take advantage of the lower interest rates often associated with variable rate debt.

Four types of risk are associated with caps, floors, and collars:

1. Under these agreements, the issuer is exposed to the credit risk of the counterparty—it might default on payments owed. This kind of risk, of course, only materializes when the contract is "in-the-money," that is, when the interest rate index rises above the strike level.
2. Rollover risk occurs when the term of the bond does not coincide with the term of the derivative agreement. Rollover risk refers to the possibility that the issuer will be unable to enter into a satisfactory new contract when the original one expires.
3. Basis risk takes place when the interest index tied to the derivative contract does not exactly match the interest rate on the underlying variable rate bonds. This risk sometimes develops when the issuer's credit rating is downgraded.
4. Market risk refers to the possibility that the issuer's remarketing agent will not be able to locate a buyer for variable rate bonds. If the bond issuer has contracted for a cap or a collar to hedge variable rate risk, the issuer will be "over-hedged" if the bonds do not remain outstanding.[11]

In addition, the issuer and counterparty might incur risk if the assumptions or predictions they make about interest rate levels or the steepness of the yield curve prove wrong. Caps and collars become more valuable under times of interest rate volatility—the measure of the amount of change expected in the future. Also, caps become more valuable as the yield curve steepens.[12]

A 1994 survey by the Government Finance Officers Association indicates that only approximately 6% of the issuers of municipal bonds had used derivative products in connection with bond sales, with more than one-third of those issuers being from California and Florida. About 17% of these derivative users had entered into caps, floors, or collars, with 5.5 years as the average term of contract. In discussing the reasons for entering into derivative agreements, the users cited lower borrowing costs, the need to lock-in current interest rates, the decrease in interest rate risk, and the reduction of debt service uncertainty.[13]

Detachable Warrant Bonds

A warrant gives the bondholder the right, at some future date, to purchase more of the same securities to which the warrant is attached, at the same price and rate of return as the original bonds. In exchange for that right, the issuer pays a lower rate of interest (about one-half of a percentage point less) than offered on otherwise comparable securities. The marketability of such bonds depends on the opinion of prospective buyers as to expected fluctuations in interest rates. Buyers of detachable warrant bonds anticipate that interest rates will decline, and they will be able to purchase additional bonds at the prior interest rate. If interest rates rise, however, the savings to the issuer become real because of the initial lower interest cost.

The Municipal Assistance Corporation of the City of New York issued the first public tax-exempt detachable warrant bonds in 1982. These bonds gave the holders warrants that could be exercised for two years. The expectation was that, even if interest rates declined during the two-year period, the savings from the lower interest payments over the life of the bond issue would amount to about \$11 million. Since interest rates held relatively constant during this period, the actual long-term savings were even greater.

Inflation Protection Securities

Every investment represents a balancing of acceptable risk and potential awards. While the interest rate for most securities is guaranteed, a rise in inflation means that the interest dollars earned will not buy as much as the investor had anticipated.

Treasury inflation protection securities (TIPS)—issued for the first time in January 1997—trade one kind of risk for another. The tradeoff for buyers of these securities is that they accept a lower stated rate of return in exchange for a guarantee that their buying power will not be diminished by inflation alone. As with other notes and bonds, when an inflation-indexed note or bond is purchased, the buyer receives interest payments every six months and a payment of principal when the security matures. The difference is that, unlike the situation with other notes and bonds, the interest and redemption payments for TIPS are tied to inflation.

The value of the principal of these securities is adjusted based on the Consumer Price Index.[14] At maturity, the security is redeemed at its inflation-adjusted principal amount or its par value (the amount paid to buy the security), whichever is greater. In the unlikely event of deflation, built-in safeguards ensure that the final payment will not be less than what the buyer paid for the security in the first place.

The fixed rate of interest of TIPS is applied to the inflation-adjusted principal. If inflation occurs throughout the life of the security, every interest payment will be greater than the previous one. On the other hand, in the rather unusual event of deflation, interest payments will decrease. Specifically, each interest payment is calculated by multiplying the inflation-indexed principal (regardless of whether it is greater or less than the par value) by one-half the interest rate determined at auction.

The Treasury auctions ten-year inflation-indexed notes in July, October, and January. Like other Treasury notes and bonds, TIPS are exempt from state and local taxes, but they are subject to federal income tax. In any year when the principal of the security grows, the gain is considered reportable income for that year even though the inflation-adjusted principal will not be received until the security matures.

Assume, for example, that the interest rate established by the auction is 3.75%. The semiannual interest payment on a $1,000 security would be $18.75. If, at the time of the first payment, the principal has been adjusted by 2% to reflect the impact of inflation, then the interest payment would be $19.13. Another 2% adjustment in the second six months would yield a second interest payment of $19.51. Assuming that the 2% semiannual adjustment in the principal continued through the ten-year period, the interest earned on this security would total $464.69, and the security at maturity would have a redemption value of $1,485.95 (see Table 7-15).

Since the adjustment for inflation in the principal is subject to capital gains, an investor could face adverse tax consequences should inflation surge. The break-even inflation rate for a taxpayer in the 28% bracket is 8.5%. In the example, the $485.95 increase in the face value of the security would be subject to capital gains, and at 28%, the tax would be $136.07. Therefore, the total return on this investment would be $464.69 in interest plus $485.95 in principal minus $136.07 in taxes for a total of $814.57. To earn the same return on a traditional ten-year security, the investor would have to obtain an interest rate of 8.146%.

Funding Strategic Facilities as a Development Cost

The difficulties of obtaining public funds for capital projects have prompted many localities to look to the private sector for help. It was once common to rely on the private sector to design, construct, and finance major capital improvements, such as water systems, roads, or mass transit systems. While this practice was largely abandoned several decades ago, in more recent years, developers of new subdivisions and some commercial or industrial projects have again been required to pay all or a portion of the infrastructure costs created by their developments.

This shift to private sector financing has been most pronounced in high-growth states, and especially those faced with strict limitations on public bonding or tax rate increases. It has been estimated, for example, that private developers financed more than half of all state and local capital projects in California in the 1980s and 1990s, either by direct installation of strategic facilities or by the payment of fees in lieu of facility dedication. The recent trend has been to require private developers to finance more and more of the off-site capital costs. Although each state has its own body of court rulings on these requirements, the courts generally have upheld off-site dedications that can be shown to be reasonably related to the public capital costs attributable to development.

Table 7-15
Increases in Principal and Interest on an Inflation Protection Security

Semi Annual Interest Payments	Principal	Interest Rate	Interest Payment
1	$1020.00	3.75%	$19.13
2	$1040.40	3.75%	$19.51
3	$1,061.21	3.75%	$19.90
4	$1,082.43	3.75%	$20.30
5	$1,104.08	3.75%	$20.70
6	$1,126.16	3.75%	$21.12
7	$1,148.69	3.75%	$21.54
8	$1,171.66	3.75%	$21.97
9	$1,195.09	3.75%	$22.41
10	$1,218.99	3.75%	$22.86
11	$1,243.37	3.75%	$23.31
12	$1,268.24	3.75%	$23.78
13	$1,293.61	3.75%	$24.26
14	$1,319.48	3.75%	$24.74
15	$1,345.87	3.75%	$25.24
16	$1,372.79	3.75%	$25.74
17	$1,400.24	3.75%	$26.25
18	$1,428.25	3.75%	$26.78
19	$1,456.81	3.75%	$27.32
20	$1,485.95	3.75%	$27.86
Total Interest			$464.69

An early test case occurred in 1981, when the Suburban Sanitary Commission, which provides sewer and water services in northern Virginia, established a system expansion offset charge (SEOC). The SEOC was defined as an equity charge on new residential and commercial subscribers to fund new or expanded capital projects required to meet the increased service demands. The SEOC was designed to exempt older system subscribers from having to pay the cost of these new facilities. The SEOC was a lump sum, nondeferrable fee in addition to water and sewer service connection charges. The fee differential was set at three times the fee paid by existing residents to finance new or expanded capital projects. The legality of the SEOC was challenged. The court decision held in favor of the Commission as long the linkage between the expansion and the requirements of new development could be clearly demonstrated.

Developers are required to contribute to infrastructure costs under the Adequate Public Facilities Ordinance in Montgomery County, Maryland. Each developer, for example, is assessed a proportional share of the cost of providing the additional capacity required to accommodate the trips generated by households and commercial activities in that developer's subdivision during the morning peak traffic hours. Other localities in Maryland have adopted or are considering the adoption of similar APF ordinances.

The State of Texas requires developers outside areas currently serviced by sewer and water systems to establish a Municipal Utility District. The developer is responsible for installing all the facilities necessary to provide these services. Once the system is built, the developer might operate it, sell it to the residents, or find another form of private management.

Cash proffer systems have been adopted by a number of counties and some cities where the demand for facilities and services from residential growth have outpaced tax revenues. A cash proffer is a fee paid by developers in conjunction with rezoning requests. In Hanover County, Virginia, for example, the average gap between the cost of services and the amount of taxes to be derived from new development is calculated and projected twenty years into the future. The projection coincides with the financing of capital improvements through the issuance of twenty-year bonds. This figure is adjusted each fiscal year. In 2003, when developers submitted a rezoning request, they were required to proffer a payment of $7,866 per single-family residence proposed for development, whether a house, townhouse, or apartment. The cash proffer is then distributed to support major capital costs—49% going to support capital costs associated with county schools, 34% to support roads, 8.5% to support fire and rescue squads, 5% to support parks and recreation, and 3.5% to support libraries.

In Elk Grove, California, several *benefit assessments* have been adopted that are applicable to new residential development. An assessment of $150 is levied to benefit the police department, while a $125 assessment is to support road maintenance. Other annual assessments are made for street lighting and landscaping. Unlike cash proffers, which are one-time fees, the city plans to levy these assessments in perpetuity.

Broward County, Florida, implemented one of the more innovative and sophisticated impact fee systems, covering additional road, park, and school costs generated by new development. Under this approach, fees are adjusted annually to the GDP price deflator for the previous twelve months and are deposited in a non-lapsing trust fund. Revenues for parks are set at a level equal to the assessed value of that which would otherwise be dedicated or are calculated according to the type of residential unit in a development. School fees are determined in a similar fashion based on provisions in the county code for impacts generated by specific types of housing units and the number of bedrooms they contain. A computerized model is used to determine the proportional share of road capacity that the developer must finance. Each subdivision development is charged according to its share of use of expanded or extended network segments.

Notwithstanding early legal challenges, the system in Broward County appears to be working fairly effectively. Developers benefit by knowing beforehand how much they will have to pay for a given type and scale of project, and the county achieves the necessary strategic facilities with a minimum processing time and negotiations and without having to finance them.

The Brookings Institution has recently published a comprehensive report on the use of impact fees to finance capital improvements that traditionally have been financed from property taxes.[15] The report addresses the controversy regarding impact fees through a comprehensive review of the academic literature concerning the economic effects of impact fees. An analysis of the relationship between impact fees and job creation is presented, based on data collected for the period from 1993 to 1999, for the sixty-seven counties of Florida. The key findings of the report are summarized in Table 7-16.

Opponents assert that impact fees stifle investment by serving as a de facto tax on capital and thereby driving economic development and job growth to other jurisdictions that do not impose such fees. Supporters argue that impact fees represent an investment in the community, spurring economic growth through more timely provision of new capital improvements and the facilitation of access to buildable land. The Brookings report shows that impact fees provide a practical and valuable contribution to the financing of local infrastructure needs. By assisting in the funding of capital improvements, uncertainty and risk for developers is reduced, the predictability in the development process is improved, and indirectly, local employment is promoted. The report concludes that: "Faced with the growing demand for investment and the public resistance to tax increases, localities in growing regions that institute impact fees might become more prosperous in the long run than communities in such regions that do not have them."[16]

A Note of Caution

For over eighty years, the municipal bond market was focused on three basic bond types—term bonds, annuity serial bonds, and straight serial bonds. Bonds issued during this period, whether general obligation bonds, revenue bonds, or special assessment bonds, followed one of these three basic formats in terms of the method of redemption.

In the dynamic and uncertain period of the 1980s, however, state and local governments had to develop financing programs that are more responsive to the overall financial conditions and fiscal policies than these traditional general obligation and revenue bonds. The federal tax reform bill, passed in August 1986, had a number of effects on the future supply of tax-exempt financing. The act eliminated significant tax breaks to banks, among the biggest buyers of municipal bonds prior to the enactment of this act. The impact of the 1986 tax changes are still being felt today, as the market has continued to shift from institutional buyers to retail customers with smaller pocketbooks. Restrictions on the types of projects that can be financed by tax-exempt bonds, along with statewide caps on the volume of new issues, resulted in a reduction in municipal bond issues.

Table 7-16
Summary of Findings
Study of Impact Fees and Economic Data

- Property tax revenues increasingly fail to cover the full costs of strategic facility needs. Political resistance to increases in property taxes compromises the more conventional methods for financing capital improvements required to accommodate new development.
- Impact fees offer a more efficient means of financing capital projects than general taxes and ensure benefits to those who pay them. While impact fees do not cover the full price of capital improvements, they do provide a more direct economic linkage between those paying for these improvements and those receiving benefits.
- Impact fees increase the supply of buildable land by providing local government with additional resources to construct roads, extend sewer and water facilities, and improve drainage so as to open new land parcels for development.
- Impact fees have complex effects on housing prices. Impact fees tend to lower raw land prices, as predicted by conventional economic theory. However, the amount of the fee reflecting the value of infrastructure improvements is recovered in the sales price. In addition, the sales price often reflects an increase greater than the impact fee due to the perception that public facilities will be provided at a desired level and quality as a consequence of these fees.
- Impact fees do not slow job growth. Such fees tend to provide assurances that necessary public improvements will be provided and, thereby, help to stimulate economic development rather than detract from it.

Adapted from Arthur C. Nelson and Mitch Moody, *Paying for Prosperity: Impact Fees and Job Growth* (Washington, D.C.: The Brookings Institution, June 2003).

The reduction in the supply of new issues, in turn, has tended to increase the relative value of municipal bonds, particularly in states that have historically low municipal debt.

The second important effect of the tax bill was the lowering of the maximum federal tax bracket from 50% to 33%. Municipal bonds continue to be attractive relative to taxable alternatives for the vast majority of investors whose marginal tax rates are at the higher end of the federal tax schedule. At the same time, since federal tax brackets have been lowered, the state portion of an individual's total effective tax bracket becomes larger. As a consequence, the exemption from state taxes offered by municipal bonds to residents of the state of issue becomes more important.

New financing techniques are not a panacea for meeting the needs of local government for expanded strategic facilities. More conventional approaches should not be abandoned unless officials are satisfied that sufficient benefits will accrue compared to the risks. The development of more innovative approaches stems from the willingness and ability of state and local governments to accept and deal with the uncertainty of future markets for financing strategic facilities. Practical concerns are also part of the equation, including the political acceptability of such approaches, the ability of government to structure and manage these creative financing mechanisms and, of course, the laws that govern capital financing. Interest payments are still the cost that governments must pay for the use of other people's money. Careful application of new financing techniques, however, might uncover some real opportunities to provide capital resources that otherwise would be unavailable.

Notes

1. Large institutional investors, securities depositories, and other bondholders with significant amounts of securities often keep their holdings as large denomination registered security known as a jumbo certificate.
2. CUSIP numbers are named for the Committee for Uniform Securities Identification Procedure, which was established to deal with the securities transfer problems that developed during the late 1960s. These numbers are assigned by the CUSIP Service Bureau (which is part of Standard and Poor's) under contract with the American Bankers Association. The first six numbers or letters of the CUSIP number identify the issuer of the security. The next two numbers or letters identify the particular security of the issuer. The last number is a check digit, used for processing purposes to help ensure the accuracy of the first eight digits.
3. If the real estate taxes on a given property are not paid, the property can be sold at auction. Bondholders have a superior claim on the proceeds from such sales above mortgages, mechanical liens, and other encumbrances.
4. William Dawson, "Variable Rate Demand Notes," in *The Handbook of Municipal Bonds and Public Finance*, eds. Robert Lamb, James Leighland, and Stephen Rappaport (New York: New York Institute of Finance, 1993), 531-535.
5. John E. Peterson, "Debt Markets and Instruments," in *Local Government Finance: Concepts and Practices*, eds. John E. Peterson and Dennis R. Strachota (Chicago: Government Finance Officers Association, 1991), 308
6. Derivative securities will be discussed in further detail in Chapter 11.
7. Bruce McDougall, "Derivatives De-Mystified," *Canadian Banker* 101, no. 2 (March 1994): 28.
8. Kathryn Engebretson and Gary Gray, "An Introduction to Municipal Derivative Products," *Government Finance Review* (February 1993): 22-23.
9. *Ibid.*, 23.
10. J.P. Morgan and Co., "Municipal Swaps," in *The Handbook of Municipal Bonds and Public Finance*, eds. Robert Lamb, James Leighland, and Stephen Rappaport (New York: New York Institute of Finance, 1993), 440-441.
11. Engebretson and Gray, *op. cit.*, 444-445.
12. Aaron Pressman, "Quick Study: Interest Rate Caps, Floors, and Collars Help Buyers Hedge, Bet on Rate Moves," *The Bond Buyer* (December 1, 1993), 6.

13. Aaron Pressman, "Derivatives Study Queries GFOA Members," *The Bond Buyer* (June 6, 1994), 10-A.
14. Inflation will be measured by the Consumer Price Index for urban areas (CPI-U), without any adjustment for recurring seasonal variations. The CPI-U is published monthly by the Bureau of Labor Statistics and is a measure of the average change in consumer prices over time for a fixed market basket of goods and services, including food, clothing, shelter, fuels, transportation, charges for doctors' and dentists' services, and drugs.
15. Arthur C. Nelson and Mitch Moody, *Paying for Prosperity: Impact Fees and Job Growth* (Washington, D.C.: The Brookings Institution, June 2003).
16. *Ibid*, Executive Summary.

Chapter 8

REVENUE BONDS AND LEASE-PURCHASE FINANCING

The marketplace for municipal bonds has undergone significant changes in the past twenty-five years. The volume of new bond issues has increased enormously, from just over $30 billion in 1975 to in excess of $300 billion by the end of the millennium. During this period, revenue bonds increased as a percentage of the volume of new issues from 48% in 1975 to a peak of 76% in 1985 to the present level of about 65%. Other mechanisms for financing strategic facilities and equipment have also emerged in the past twenty-five years, including lease-purchase agreements, tax-exempt leveraged lease (or TELL) financing, certificates of participation (COPs), and private activity bonds. The focus of this chapter is on the legal and financial requirements that distinguish these mechanisms from the more traditional approaches to funding strategic facilities.

Revenue Bonds

Two principal reasons for issuing revenue bonds, rather than general obligation bonds, are:

1. Revenue bonds are based on the concept that only the users of a strategic facility financed by the sale of bonds should pay for that facility.
2. Revenue bonds are not ordinarily subject to the statutory or constitutional debt limitations imposed on local governments.

While revenue bonds constitute an obligation of the issuing jurisdiction, the obligation extends only to the payment of the bonds from a designated source of revenue.

Historical Background

Revenue bonds were used in England over 235 years ago to finance toll bridges, turnpikes, and canals. The first revenue bond law in the United States was not enacted until 1897, when provision was made in the state of Washington for the issuance of $350,000 in bonds by the city of Spokane, secured solely by a pledge of revenue of its waterworks systems. Spokane adopted this then-novel borrowing mechanism for the same reason that influenced subsequent expansion of its use—state restrictions on the general borrowing and taxing powers of municipalities that limit the use of general obligation bonds.

The concept of a commission or authority (i.e., a municipal corporation formed for the purpose of constructing and operating certain facilities that might or might not be confined within a given municipality) became a part of the revenue bonding process in this country from its earliest applications. Special water districts, with the right to sell revenue bonds but without the power to levy taxes, were established in the state of Maine in 1899.

The creation of the Port of New York Authority in 1921 directed widespread attention to the possibilities of revenue bonds as a method of borrowing. The depression of the early thirties, however, was most instrumental in the significant expansion of the use of revenue bonds to provide needed capital funds to hard-pressed municipalities. During this period, the federal government sought to promote local public works, particularly those projects of a self-liquidating nature, through grants and loans to shore up the declining general borrowing power of state and local governments.

Following World War II, revenue bonds came to represent at least a third and at times as much as 45% of all tax-exempt bonds issued in a given year. By the mid-1950s, almost all states had some sort of enabling legislation authorizing the use of revenue bonds. An estimated $9.5 billion in revenue bonds were outstanding. The list of varied and diverse projects financed by revenue bonds included: water, sewer, electric, and gas systems; bridges, tunnels, turnpikes, parkways, and expressways; dock and harbor facilities; airports, parking facilities, and mass transit; stadiums, arenas, and auditoriums; hospitals, sanitariums, and college dormitories; public housing projects; swimming pools, golf courses, and other public recreation facilities; hydroelectric power projects; and even municipal cemeteries.

Appropriate Uses of Revenue Bonds

Capital projects financed through the use of revenue bonds often enables the issuing jurisdiction to bypass its debt limits and the requirement for voter authorization. In addition, it often is possible to finance construction without raising taxes, even though in some cases the bonds issued by the authority established to administer the project carry a contingent guarantee from the local government that benefits from the capital project.

Revenue bonds should not be issued merely to evade sound and reasonable debt limits or to pursue speculative projects. When a jurisdiction has an adequate borrowing capacity at its disposal, the primary consideration should be which type of bonds can be issued at the lowest debt service cost. In general, the types of projects suitable for revenue bond financing include:

1. Projects that can be readily operated on a service charge or user-fee basis.
2. Projects for which experience, either under public or private operation, has demonstrated the potentialities for self-support.
3. Projects that can produce sufficient revenue without jeopardizing other important economic or social objectives of the community.

Revenue bond financing and the use of special districts or authorities have raised a number of fundamental questions. Widespread use of special districts has severely inhibited the creation of multipurpose agencies and metro-governments that might be more effective in the solution of complex urban service delivery problems. Economists argue that special districts and authorities, through their revenue bonding powers, have distorted the municipal bond market by offering the investor a higher yield than general obligation bonds can provide.

Problems of equity might arise when traditionally tax-supported functions are placed on a service charge basis. Facilities supported by service charges also frequently produce benefits to individuals who do not pay for them—for example, enhanced land values that might accrue to the speculative holder of unimproved real estate. Limited mechanisms, such as tax roll-back provisions, have been devised to tap such increases in the value of undeveloped properties when they are sold for development at a higher use.

Revenue Bond Laws

The authority to issue revenue bonds is generally established through state enabling legislation. These laws identify the governmental units authorized to borrow by issuing revenue bonds and the types of projects to which the enabling legislation applies. They provide a general grant of power to acquire, construct, improve, or extend the particular capital improvements, to issue revenue bonds, and to pledge revenues to the payment of these bonds. The issuing body is required to establish sufficient charges or rates to operate and maintain the project and to meet the principal and interest requirements of the bond issues. Guarantees must be provided to ensure that the revenue bonds have all the qualities of negotiable instruments under the appropriate laws of the state. Enabling legislation usually includes provisions governing the procedures for the authorization and sale of revenue bonds (including regulations relating to public referenda) and provisions designed to secure the successful operation of the capital project.

Revenue bonds should be planned as to their terms, conditions, and safeguards with two objectives in mind: to suit the nature of the project and to attract investors. Principles to be observed in planning bonds can be outlined as follows:

1. Bonds should be scheduled for retirement well within the useful life of the project; that is, the rate of amortization of the bonds should at least equal an appropriate rate of depreciation on the facility.
2. The retirement of bonds should be distributed in such a way as to allow a comfortable margin of revenue coverage for debt service without the need to charge abnormal rates or fees.
3. The maturity schedule should be established to reflect the anticipated income pattern of the project. The amount of combined annual interest and amortization should follow an even or possible slightly rising trend in order to coincide with the prospective pattern of revenues.
4. The first payment on principal should be deferred until the operations of the facility have become well established.
5. Assurances must be evident to the investor from the outset (through granting of reasonable covenants) that (a) the project will receive businesslike management, (b) bond funds will be properly expended, and (c) construction will be carefully inspected.

6. Safeguards also must be provided to ensure that (a) the plant and equipment will be properly maintained after the project is operational, (b) the rate structure or fee schedule is designed to keep the project self-supporting, and (c) adequate working capital and reserves will be maintained.

Revenue bonds can be issued as any of the bond options discussed in the previous chapter—serial maturities, term bonds, zero coupon bonds, stepped coupon bonds, or serial and balloon maturities. In most cases, revenue bonds are callable prior to maturity through the utilization of surplus funds or a mandatory sinking fund. This callable provision might apply to all or a portion of the outstanding bonds. Serial maturities usually are called in inverse numerical order, while in most instances, term bonds are called by lot.

In a number of states, revenue bond issues can be established through negotiated sales. Therefore, financial advisors can be drawn from the special expertise and experience of bond underwriters or from associated financial consulting organizations. Avoiding the use of qualified fiscal and legal advisors is a false economy and will usually result in higher interest costs many times over the fee for expert advice.

On the whole, revenue bonds have had a good credit rating. Defaults that have occurred can be traced to mistakes in planning and management, such as:

1. Failure to adhere to appropriate state enabling legislation,
2. Underestimating operating costs or overestimating anticipated revenues,
3. Excessive expenditures for property acquisition,
4. Failure to segregate and safeguard project revenues in accordance with the covenants of the bond ordinance or resolution,
5. Insufficient care in engineering studies, and
6. Failure to allow sufficient time for the completion of the project before bond payments begin to come due.

Sources of Revenue

Sources of revenue in support of revenue bonds can be classified in five general categories:

1. User charges are one of the oldest and most common sources of revenue. In financing utility systems (e.g., sewer and water systems), many localities issue bonds payable solely from such revenues. When a municipality guarantees debt service payment in the event these revenues are insufficient, the bonds are sometimes referred to as a "double barreled" security.
2. Tolls and fees collected and the marginal income of *concessions* (e.g., automobile service facilities and restaurants along turnpikes, space lessees and parking lots at airports, etc.) are often used to finance bonds to construct turnpikes and other transportation facilities.
3. Special taxes derived from an additional levy on such items as tobacco, alcoholic beverages, and other goods and services considered semi-luxuries might be dedicated to support the debt service of revenue bonds.
4. Under a lease-back arrangement, bonds are usually issued by an authority to finance construction of a given facility, which is then leased to the state, school district, or city at a rental level calculated to be sufficient to pay

interest and retire the indebtedness. Funds for the rental payments are obtained by the lessee from various sources, including legislative appropriations, special taxes, and direct taxes.

5. Industrial revenue bonds have been issued by local governments (mostly in the South) since 1936 to finance the construction of factories or other business facilities. These facilities are then leased to private business. Industrial revenue bonds also are issued to purchase factories or other facilities from private businesses that are then leased back to the sellers.

The use of public credit to "buy" the location of new businesses in a community has been strongly opposed by many financial organizations, including the Investment Bankers Association. However, legislatures in a growing number of states have authorized this type of debt as a means of enticing new industry. To obtain tax-exempt status, these so-called private activity bonds must meet the test of qualification outlined in federal tax law. These requirements are outlined in a subsequent section of this chapter.

In their haste to find a lessee of the property, public officials might not take the necessary precautions to investigate the financial stability of the enterprise or to safeguard the investment by insisting that the lease extend over the life of the bonds. As a consequence, the community or state runs the risk of having a contingent liability become an actual one. Or the jurisdiction might become saddled with debt for special facilities for which another lessee cannot be found.

In some instances, a group of citizens might form a nonprofit corporation. This nonprofit entity issues corporate bonds, constructs or otherwise acquires the project, leases the project to a private firm (or possibly to the local government if the intent is to circumvent existing debt limitations), and pays the bond debt service from the rentals received under the lease. If the IRS determines that the corporation is truly nonprofit, then the interest on the bonds might be free from federal income taxation.

Covenants on Revenue Bonds

Certain covenants are spelled out in all bond resolutions or trust indentures for the protection of the investors. Among other things, these covenants establish appropriate and clearly defined fiscal policies that, in turn, are protected against political tampering. It has been said, "covenants that protect the bondholder have equal protection to the bond issuer." Failure to incorporate the following provisions into the basic bond instruments generally result in higher interest rates.

1. *Rate covenant* pledges the issuing body to fix rates, with revisions when necessary, that are sufficient to meet operation and maintenance charges, as well as annual debt service requirements, and to provide for certain reserves. Rates must be maintained sufficient to provide some minimum margin of safety over the costs and charges incurred in the previous fiscal period. For example, for toll facilities, the covenant often calls for rates to be set at approximately 120% of the foregoing charges.

2. *Maintenance and insurance covenant* requires that the properties be maintained in good repair and working condition at all times. Insurance must be carried on the facility corresponding in amount and in kind to the coverage normally carried under a similar private enterprise.
3. *Records and financial reports* must be kept and provided for audit annually by independent certified public accountants. Revenues must be deposited in a special fund and kept separate from all other funds of the jurisdiction.
4. *Consulting engineers* must be placed on a retainer, when certain types of projects are undertaken, to perform certain "watchdog" duties over the operations of the facility. This practice is common with sewer and water systems and toll roads (at the state level).
5. *Nondiscrimination covenant* guarantees that neither preferential treatment nor discrimination shall be applied to any groups in the matter of payment of rates for services. This covenant ensures that charges will be equitable to all users.

Distribution of Revenues

The order in which revenues generated by self-supporting projects shall be applied—sometimes referred to as the "flow of funds"—is usually set forth in the bond resolution or trust indenture as a series of covenants. In most cases, a basic fund, known as the *reserve fund*, is established, into which all receipts and income derived from the operation of the project are deposited. Moneys in the reserve fund are then distributed each month by the trustee or other handler of funds in the order described below.

The first claim on the reserve fund usually is a prorated amount to meet the cost of *operation and maintenance*, as set forth in the annual budget. Without proper O&M funds, a facility might experience severe loss of income. Therefore, revenue bonds most commonly are payable from net revenues, that is, gross receipts less operating and maintenance costs.

The *bond service account* constitutes an amount that, with other such monthly payments, will be sufficient to pay the next semiannual interest payment as well as the principal of the next bonds that are maturing. In the case of term bonds, a mandatory sinking fund is usually required in lieu of principal payments on serial bonds.

Payments into a *debt service reserve fund* are usually accumulated and maintained as a back up to meet debt service requirements. In the case of serial bonds, this fund is gradually built up to equal one-year's maximum principal and interest requirements. In the case of term bonds, the requirement usually is two years' interest.

A *renewal and replacement fund*, sometimes called a replacement reserve, is established to replace equipment or provide necessary repairs beyond normal maintenance. Funds are paid into this account in an amount recommended by the consulting engineer and might be cumulative.

Payments are made into a *reserve maintenance fund* to meet unusual or extraordinary maintenance charges that have not been budgeted. Some jurisdictions combine the reserve maintenance and renewal and replacement funds. In other cases, an effort is made to establish a *working capital fund* equivalent to about one-tenth of a year's gross revenues to cover such unforeseen contingencies.

Moneys remaining in the reserve fund after the foregoing distributions are made can be placed in a *surplus fund*, to be divided into various categories such as the following:

1. Redemption account used to retire bonds in advance of maturity.
2. Payment in lieu of taxes when an authority purchases a going operation that has been a corporate unit. Payments might be made in lieu of taxes either by legislative requirement or to create good will.
3. Other lawful payments including improvements and extensions of the facility, support of other bond interest, and so forth.

Issuance of Additional Bonds

When a strategic facility is being constructed, it is not always possible to foresee what the future might hold. It might be necessary to increase the size of the facility or to make other improvements that will require additional financing. Therefore, sufficient leeway should be provided in the indenture or resolution to permit the issuance of additional bonds.

If bonds of equal rank are permitted, safeguards must be set up to protect against the undue dilution of the security of the original bonds. There are two basic types of trust indentures:

- *Closed-end indentures*, which do not permit the issuance of parity bonds other than those necessary to complete the project where initial financing proves insufficient; and
- *Open-end indentures*, which permit the issuance of additional bonds but provides a formula prescribing the conditions to be met.

In the first case, additional bonds must be junior in lien to the then-outstanding bonds. The debt service requirements of the initial issue have first claim on the funds in the bond service account. As a consequence, the new issue often carries higher interest charges.

Special Assessment Bonds

Special assessments generate tax revenue for a particular improvement or purpose that benefits specific property owners or neighborhoods. Special assessments often are prorated for each property owner, based on the benefits that each owner will receive from the improvement. The key element of the special tax assessment is its specificity. Moreover, unlike typical general taxes, the property owners themselves often initiate special assessments.

Special assessments begin with a proposal for improvement, detailing the requested improvement project and the property parcels that will be affected by the special assessment. The proposal is submitted to the specific agency, department, or authority responsible for special assessments. The governing authority must post a public notice, notifying the general public that a proposal has been filed. This public notice typically indicates a hearing date, during which the responsible government authority will receive input about and discussion regarding the proposal. Many areas require notices to be sent directly to the property owners who will be affected by the proposed improvements. In addition, a sign might be posted at the site of the proposed improvements, informing the public of the proposal and scheduled hearing. Property owners affected by the improvements might argue against it during the hearing, especially if the proposal was initiated by the government without the consent of the property owners.

If the proposal is approved, the local government must enact a local ordinance authorizing the proposed improvement and its special assessment. Most local governments look more favorably on improvements and projects that will contribute to the community without any new taxes being levied on the general public.

The total cost of the project must be divided between the property owners who will benefit from it. The allocation of the cost is typically done on either an equal division or as a pro-ratio, based on the size of the affected properties. An equal division or fractional basis allocates the cost somewhat evenly between the affected properties. For example, forty homes line either side of a street. The owners initiate a proposal for new sidewalks and streetlights. The total cost for these proposed improvements is calculated at $120,000. The owners will share the cost equally, so each property owner will receive a special assessment for $3,000 on his or her upcoming tax bill.

The proportional or cost-per-size basis takes into account the size of the parcels that will benefit from the improvement. For example, the same forty homes as above initiate the same proposal. However, twenty of the properties are actually double-sized lots, with twice the width of the standard lots in the area. The other twenty have standard lot sizes. On a prorated or cost-per-size basis, the owners of the double-sized parcels should pay twice as much the owners of the regular-sized parcels. The owners of the double-sized parcels in this instance would be assessed $4,000 each, while the owners of the regular-sized parcels would be assessed only $2,000 each. The special assessments do not have to be paid in one lump sum; typically they are paid in installments over a number of years.

General (ad valorem) liens have automatic lien rights on the affected properties. Special assessments require the approval of the local court to place a lien on the affected real estate parcels. The process for obtaining such a lien is called both "petition and approval" and "confirming the assessment role." The local court reviews the proposal for assessment, and detractors are once again given an opportunity to file opposing statements. The court's approval establishes the lien on the properties. Finally, when the proposed improvement or project is finished, the local governing authority receives a "special assessment warrant" to issue and collect the tax bills for the special assessment.

Special assessment bonds often are issued to finance such localized improvements. These bonds are considered a special form of revenue bonds since the debt service is payable only from the proceeds derived from a special assessment levied against those individuals or properties that benefit from the improvements. In some cases, however, the property owners who must pay the assessments have had little or no say in the issuance of the bonds for which they must meet the debt service commitments.

The Mello-Roos bonds in the State of California illustrate this situation. After the passage of the property tax cutting Proposition 13 in June 1978, funding for local infrastructure improvements dried up. The State legislature adopted special legislation (Government Code Section 53311, et seq.) that permitted the creation of Community Facilities Districts (CFDs) to finance, through special taxes, certain designated public services and capital projects by levying special taxes. Local governments were empowered to cooperate with developers to achieve more flexible funding options to finance schools, streets, sewer and water facilities, parks and recreational areas, and other specific improvements primarily in new residential areas.

Billions of dollars of bonds were issued to finance these improvements. The homeowners served by these facilities, in turn, were obligated to pay off the bonds through annual assessments added to their property tax bills. The taxes are continuing liens and are levied against all property owners within the designated service area.

Until the residential development has been completed and all of the property has been transferred to individual owners, however, the burden of the assessment must be shared by the developer and the homeowners who have moved into the area. When the California real estate market experienced slow downs in the early 1990s, some developers where forced to file for bankruptcy, prompting banks or other investors to begin foreclosure proceedings on the development. The bank then assumed financial responsibility for the special assessment bonds. In many cases, bond payments were delinquent, and the banks either had to assume this additional obligation or use any reserves in the bond offering to pay off the bondholders.

In 1994, nearly 5% of all Mello-Roos bond issues were reported as experiencing some degree of financial difficulty primarily due to significant delinquencies. The value of the bonds in trouble was nearly $300 million. Examples include:

- An $8.1 million bond issue by the County of Los Angeles in 1988 for a Mello-Roos district in which nearly 22% of the bond payments were delinquent by local real estate developers.
- A $7.4 million Mello-Roos district in the northwest area of the City of San Bernardino that experienced a 77% delinquency rate.
- A 211-acre housing and commercial project in the City of Oxnard on which the developer stopped payment on the bonds in 1991 and the bonds went into default in October 1993.

Several changes in the Mello-Roos enabling legislation were adopted in 1993 in an effort to prevent abuses and to reduce risks to municipalities and homeowners in the event of default caused by bankrupt developers. Tighter rules for policing the bonds were adopted. City and county agencies are now required to limit fee increases to homeowners in the event of default. Developers are required to do a better job of disclosing to homebuyers that they will be living in a Mello-Roos district and how much in special district taxes they will be required to pay.

The annual Mello-Roos levy is collected though the county property tax bill. Lot size or square footage of the home determines the amount of the levy. It is not an ad valorum tax, such as the basic property tax. The basic tax rate (as mandated under Proposition 13) is limited to no more than 1% of the assessed market value of the home. Often, school bonds can add another quarter percent. A community in which a Communities Facilities District has been created under Mello-Roos legislation might levy an additional $850 per year on standard lots and $1,200 per year on oversized or premium lots. On a home assessed for $100,000, the additional $850 in would translate to 0.085% on top of the base tax and school bonds, resulting in a combined tax rate of almost 2.1%. However, if the value of a home in the same CFD is higher, the combined rate drops (assuming that the property is not subject to a premium on lot or home size). For example, a home assessed for $175,000 is still subject to the base tax of 1% and the school bonds of a quarter percent. But the same $850 Mello-Roos represents 0.486% of this property's assessed value, resulting in a combined blended tax rate of only 1.736%.

Many special assessment bonds are financed through a uniform annual fixed levy similar to the approach used in Mello-Roos districts. In some cases, however, the improvement is deemed to benefit some properties to a greater extent than others, and the assessment is made on some sort of sliding scale. The installation or upgrading of a system of fire hydrants, for example, might result in lower homeowner insurance costs to those properties in closer proximity to the hydrants. Therefore, individual assessments might be determined by the property's distance from the fire hydrant system.

Private Activity Bonds

A private activity bond is a municipal bond used either entirely or partially for private purposes. To qualify as a private activity, tax-exempt bond, the debt must fit into one of the seven categories outlined in Table 8-1, must meet volume cap requirements, and must satisfy several other requirements detailed in section 147 of the federal tax statutes.

IRS Regulations

Under Title 26, section 141 of the Internal Revenue Code, as amended by the Tax Reform Act of 1986, municipal bonds are classified as private activity bonds if:

- More than 10% of the proceeds from such bonds are used in support of private business activities (the business or use test), *and*
- More than 10% of the bond principal or interest is secured by payments from private business or individuals (the security interest test).

Only those private activity bonds issued for purposes expressly specified in tax law can be tax-exempt.

Table 8-1
Categorical Definitions for Private Activity Bonds

Exempt facility bonds used to finance certain types of facilities, including:

- government-owned airports, docks, and wharves;
- mass commuting facilities;
- facilities for the furnishing of water, sewage treatment, or solid waste disposal;
- qualified residential rental projects;
- facilities for local furnishing of electric energy or gas;
- local district heating or cooling facilities;
- qualified hazardous waste facilities; and
- high-speed, intercity rail facilities.

Qualified mortgage bonds used to finance multifamily housing and single-family housing.

Qualified veterans mortgage bonds used to assist veterans in financing housing.

Qualified student loan bonds used to finance student loan programs.

Qualified 501(c)(3) bonds used to finance facilities for nonprofit corporations.

Qualified small issue bonds, also called an Industrial Development Bond (IDB), used for manufacturing facilities with capital less than $10 million looking three years back or three years forward.

Qualified redevelopment bonds issued for use in areas that the government designates as distressed areas or enterprise zones.

Bonds issued to finance property owned by an organization that is exempt under section 501(c)(3) are tax-exempt provided that:

- No more than 5% of the bond's net proceeds are used in private trade or business; and
- No more than 5% of the bond's net proceeds are secured by facilities used in a private trade or business or by the income generated from such facilities.

Tax-exempt bonds issued on behalf of 501(c)(3) nonprofit organizations are primarily to finance the construction or rehabilitation of housing projects. The main advantage of 501(c)(3) bonds is the lower interest cost generally realized as compared to that obtainable through private commercial financing. Another advantage is that 501(c)(3) bonds are not included under the volume cap placed on private activity bonds.

The IRS rules provide comprehensive guidance regarding the application of the private use and private security tests, with detailed instructions and examples. Private use might result from ownership or leasing of financed property, a loan of proceeds, or other actual or beneficial use of financed property under a management or incentive payment contract, output contract, or other arrangement. The private business use of allocated proceeds is determined according to the annual use of the facility beginning with the issue date or the date the facility was placed into service. The proposed rules cover determination of average private use, including allocations for various patterns of use.

In addition to meeting the private use test, bondholders must not be substantial users of the facility. Qualification also depends on the average maturity of the bond issue being not longer than 120% of the economic life of the facility. A limit of 25% of a tax-exempt, private-activity bond issue might be used to purchase land for nonfarming purposes. The tax code places a similar set of restrictions and exceptions on the acquisition of existing property.

Characteristics and Limitations of Private Activity Bonds

Tax-exempt bonds offer private entities lower interest rates than they would otherwise be able to obtain. A government can use private activity bonds to give economic incentives to targeted activities or geographic areas. Some economists believe that the incentive given by tax-exempt status through private activity bonds creates positive economic effects beyond the individual project or program that is being financed.

The purpose of private activity bonds must be specifically defined and must be used according to the limitations of the state and federal statutes. The numerous and strict limitations on private activity bonds make them inflexible. Changes in their purpose might make them subject to state and federal taxes.

Substantial limitations on the use of private activity bonds were included in the 1986 Tax Reform Act. A unified volume cap was enacted which restricts the amount of private activity debt issued within a state during any calendar year. The volume cap was set at $50 per capita or $150 million, whichever is greater. The cap was put in place for all private activity bonds except for veterans mortgage bonds, qualified 501(c)(3) bonds, exempt facilities bonds for airports, docks, and wharves, and 75% of high-speed intercity rail facilities. Volume caps often result in significant competition for private activity bonds. In 1994, for example, the State of Texas had a volume cap of $902 million in private activity bonds. In that year, Texas had to turn down $863 million in requests for private activity bonds that would have been in excess of the volume cap.

The states lobbied Congress for substantial increases in the volume cap. Under the Omnibus Appropriations Act of 1998, the caps were increased to the greater of $55 per capita or $165 million beginning in fiscal year 2003. The cap was then to increase each fiscal year by $5 per capita or $15 million until fiscal year 2007, when it would reach a maximum level of $75 per capita or $225 million, whichever is greater. On December 21, 2000, President Clinton signed into law an acceleration of the increase in the volume cap. Under the new law, each state's private-activity bond cap rose in two stages to the greater of $75 per capita or $225 million by 2002. Beginning in 2003, the cap is to be indexed to inflation.

The Internal Revenue Code provides for each state to devise an allocation formula or process for allocating the state's ceiling. This provision has given each state the ability to allocate this limited resource in a manner consistent with the needs of the state. In most cases, the volume of tax-exempt private activity bonds is restricted by aggregate annual limits imposed by the IRS Code on bonds issued within each state.

Special Purpose Tax Credit Bonds

A number of proposals have been introduced in Congress to establish various special purpose tax credit bond programs. Under such programs, instead of receiving interest payments from the issuer, an eligible bondholder is allowed annual federal income tax credits while the bond is outstanding. These credits compensate the bondholder for lending money to the issuer and function as payments of interest on the bond.

Currently, only the Qualified Zone Academy Bonds (QZABs) has been enacted. These bonds were authorized by the Taxpayer Relief Act of 1997 to be issued by state and local governments to benefit public schools located in enterprise communities or empowerment zones or those schools where at least 35% of students are eligible for school lunch assistance. Eligible investors include banks, insurance companies, and corporations actively engaged in the business of lending money. Individual investors—a potentially strong source of demand for tax-preferred investments—are excluded as QZAB investors. Recently proposed changes to the program, however, would open the market for QZABs to other investors, including individuals.

Congress authorized only $400 million of QZAB issuance per year for four years, only a small portion of which has actually been used. This $1.6 billion amount is allocated among all the states, so any one state receives a relatively small allocation. The annual cap is allocated among the states in proportion to their respective populations with income below the poverty line. Unused authority to issue QZABs might be carried forward to subsequent years.

The small size and short term of the program results in several problems.[1] First, it is difficult for bond issuers, attorneys, underwriters, investors, and others associated with municipal bond transactions to commit resources to develop the necessary expertise on a new and unknown financing vehicle when very little issuance will be permitted to take place. Second, the small issuance volume has resulted in no significant secondary market for QZABs. A lack of market liquidity discourages investors and raises costs for issuers.

Market participants point to a number of other features of the QZAB program that limit its attractiveness to issuers and broker-dealers. These include concerns over issuer borrowing costs, liquidity, and the complexity of the program compared to more traditional debt issuance. There are also concerns that the QZAB credit rate, as currently set, is generally lower than that required to avoid discount and interest cost to the issuing government. The credit rate is set too infrequently to respond to market conditions.

Recent proposals for changes in the QZAB program recommend that credit accrual dates be set quarterly, timed to match quarterly estimated tax payment dates. This adjustment would help minimize a mismatch in timing between when a tax credit accrues and when a cash flow is generated for an investor. In addition it has been suggested that future tax credit bond proposals should not limit how long the tax credits can be carried forward. Other recommendations for change include:

- The ability to strip the tax credit from the underlying debt instrument and market the tax credit separately. This change would permit the debt portions of tax-credit bonds to be sold to tax-exempt investors such as pension funds.
- Exemption for issuers from the requirement to rebate arbitrage earnings to the federal government, as is the case with other tax-exempt bonds. Arbitrage restrictions applied to traditional municipal bonds have resulted in uneconomic incentives and have imposed significant compliance costs on states.

Lease-Purchase Financing

Lease-purchase financing has become popular among state and local governments. In 1980, lease-secured debt totaled less than $1 billion. By the end of the 1980s, however, that figure had grown to between $7 and $8 billion.[2] Over the last ten years, lease purchases have been widely used to finance the acquisition of equipment, such as computers and motor vehicles. And more recently, lease-purchase agreements to finance more costly, long-term projects, such as the acquisition of real property, are on the rise.

Lease-Purchase Agreements

Lease-purchase financing can take the form of a lease-purchase agreement, a lease with option to purchase, a conditional sale agreement, or an installment sale agreement. Certain elements are common to the agreement (by whatever name):

- A government unit acquires an asset by making a series of lease payments that are considered installments toward the purchase of the asset.
- The agreement is carefully drafted not to create a debt.
- Installment payments are usually characterized as rent.
- Installment payments include a specified interest component.
- Title to the asset might be transferred to the government unit either at the beginning or at the end of the lease term.

Standard provisions that are found in most lease-purchase agreements are shown in Table 8-2.

A lease-purchase arrangement differs from a "true" lease. A "true" lease, by its terms, does not contemplate that the lessee will eventually own the property—when the lease expires, the lessor retains ownership of the property. Under a lease-purchase agreement, the lessee acquires full ownership of the property covered by the lease by making all of the lease payments over the full term of the lease and, in some instances, by paying an additional, but nominal, option purchase price for the property.

Table 8-2
Standard Provisions of Lease-Purchase Agreements

A lease-purchase agreement is a contractual arrangement setting forth the terms and conditions governing the transaction, including:

- Introductory provisions
- Representations and covenants of the lessee
- Lease term and payment schedule
- Provisions for termination in the event of non-appropriation
- Responsibilities of lessee
- Consequences if the leased property is damaged, destructed, or condemned
- Warranties and disclaimer of warranties
- Assignment provisions
- Title and security interest
- Option to purchase the property
- Default and remedies

Lease-purchase agreements will require the lessee to furnish certain additional documents, which typically include the following:

- A certified copy of the resolution adopted by the governing body of the lessee authorizing the transaction.
- Evidence of insurance covering the leased property as required by the terms of the lease/purchase agreement.
- An opinion of the lessee's counsel regarding the transaction, including an opinion as to due authorization, execution, and delivery of the agreement by lessee; the legal, valid, and binding nature of the agreement and its enforceability against lessee; and an opinion regarding the tax-exempt status of the interest component of the rent payments.

The main players in a lease-purchase agreement are (1) the lessee—a government unit; (2) the lessor—a private firm, vendor, or another governmental entity; and (3) investors. After arranging an agreement, the lessor often will assign the rights to the lease payments to a number of investors.

The most important benefit of lease-purchase agreements is the flexibility that they offer. Lease purchases can be entered into much more quickly than bonds, often within sixty to ninety days of initial authorization.[3] Expedited issuance can save money by avoiding inflation in acquisition or construction costs. In addition, lease-purchase financing allows the government to avoid some of the substantial referendum costs associated with general obligation bond financing. Lease purchases enable a government both to avoid committing a large share of operating revenues to the cash purchase of an asset and to preserve its general obligation debt capacity.

Lease purchases allow governments to acquire expensive equipment that costs too much to fund from one fiscal year's budget but is too small or has too short of a useful life to finance with bonds or other long-term debt.[4] Lease purchase can thus be a powerful and flexible financing tool for state and local governments.

If not properly structured, however, a lease-purchase arrangement can create an unconstitutional debt. A lease-purchase contract does not create a debt if the parties lawfully and reasonably contemplate that the obligation will be satisfied out of current revenues or out of some fund currently within the immediate control of the governing body. Under the laws of some states, a lease-purchase agreement with a term of more than one year does not obligate public moneys in a future year. Therefore, such an agreement does not constitute indebtedness if the governmental unit has the option to terminate the lease at the end of each fiscal year if funds are not appropriated.

The *non-appropriation clause* is a key characteristic of a lease-purchase agreement, which distinguishes it from general obligation tax-exempt debt. This clause states that if the lessee government fails to make the specified lease payments, the agreement is terminated. As a result of the non-appropriation clause, a lease-purchase agreement represents a weaker pledge toward repayment than general obligation debt.

The provisions in the lease purchase agreement regarding non-appropriations must be carefully scrutinized to ensure that the local government is not required to pursue funding before it can terminate the agreement. In *City-County Solid Waste Control Board*, *supra*, a Texas court held that such a provision created an unconstitutional debt and held that the lease was void. If the lease purchase agreement is voided because it is found to create an unauthorized debt, the governmental entity might still be subject to liability under an alternate theory for the value of the benefit received. The jurisdiction's credit rating might also be impaired.

The risk of non-appropriation frequently prompts parties in a lease-purchase agreement to insist that several provisions be included to strengthen the commitment of the lessee toward repayment.

- Non-substitution clause: In the event of non-appropriation, the lessee cannot acquire or use, for some specified period of time, property similar to that described in the agreement.
- Essential purpose statement: Maintains that the asset serves a vital public function, thus implying that the government will likely make the necessary appropriation.
- "Best effort" clause: Requires the government lessee to make its "best effort" to get the legislature to appropriate funds. In 1992, however, the Texas Supreme Court left standing a ruling that "good faith effort" clauses, which require a public entity to seek annual appropriation of lease payments, establish unconstitutional debt.[5]
- Security of interest provision: Ensures that if the lessee terminates the agreement, the lessor has the right to take possession of the leased property. In some states, municipalities are not permitted to grant such a security interest in municipal property.[6]
- Lease-purchase agreements related to the construction of a facility: A lessee might be required to maintain insurance against the risk of construction

delay or failure of completion. Lessees might also need to maintain reserve funds to protect investors against the threat of non-appropriation.

The representations and covenants that lessees are required to make by the terms of the agreement typically address, in part, the validity and enforceability of the lease-purchase arrangement. In most cases, a resolution will be passed that authorizes a lease-purchase arrangement with a particular party prior to the government receiving a copy of the lease-purchase agreement. If the agreement requires certain representations of lessee, it might be necessary for the public body to pass additional resolutions in order to satisfy the requirements of the lease. This could delay the transaction. Some of the standard representations in a lease/purchase agreement are:

- The lessee has full power and authority to enter into the lease-purchase agreement.
- The governing body of lessee has duly authorized specific individual officers or officials to execute and deliver the lease-purchase agreement on behalf of the governing body.
- All competitive bidding requirements have been met.
- The leased property is essential to the governmental functions of lessee.
- Monies have been budgeted for the current fiscal year for the rental payments to become due during the current fiscal year.

Certain other provisions of the agreement might be unacceptable to the governmental body and/or unenforceable. The agreement should be carefully reviewed, and the lessor should be asked to remove or revise any objectionable provisions.

Lease-purchase financing is generally more expensive than general obligation bond financing. As a consequence of the risk of non-appropriation, lease purchase bonds typically bear an interest rate of 10 to 100 basis points higher than general obligation bonds.[7] A major equipment purchase that might be funded with a five-year general obligation bond at 7% interest might require annual interest payments of 7.5% to 8% (50 to 100 base points higher) if financed under a lease-purchase agreement. In addition, a lease purchase might involve additional issuance costs, such as payments to insure against the risk of construction delay and failure of completion.

Master Lease-Purchase Program

A master lease-purchase program consolidates individual lease purchases into a single lease-purchase program in order to achieve lower interest rates, tighter controls, and lower administrative costs. Typically, a centralized governmental unit (e.g., purchasing department) issues tax-exempt debt to finance the purchase of various assets—such as vehicles, equipment, or computers—on behalf of other departments. The centralized unit then enters into a standardized lease-purchase contract with each of the other departments. The lease-purchase payments received from these departments are used to repay the debt.

Significantly lower interest rates often can be obtained through a master lease-purchase program than would be available through individual vendor-financed lease purchases. The centralization and standardization of the lease-purchase contracts also can result in lower administrative costs and tighter controls over lease purchases. Centralizing financing procedures reduces the likelihood of vendor leases being entered into without the proper authorization. Some states and local governments, however, have encountered unwillingness by agencies to participate in a master lease-purchase program because of a perception that such programs reduce their purchasing flexibility and autonomy.

Master lease-purchase programs often are financed through the issuance of commercial paper—short-term, unsecured promissory notes, usually backed by a line of credit with a bank. Periodically the commercial paper might be converted into a fixed rate bond with a five- to seven-year maturity. The use of commercial paper allows the local government to issue additional debt on an as needed basis without incurring large incremental issuance costs.

Certificates of Participation

Certificates of participation, commonly referred to as COPs, are widely used as a mechanism for financing of lease-purchases. COPs were pioneered in California as a way of getting around Proposition 13 and other debt limits. In a tax-exempt lease purchase financed through COPs, individual investors purchase fractional interests in a particular lease. Certificates are generally issued in $5,000 denominations and can receive investment ratings from a rating agency. Each certificate signifies that the investor owns a proportional interest in the lease payments to be made by the governmental entity. However, a buyer of a COP does not have the security and protection provided by a bond. If the issuer does not make the annual appropriation, in all likelihood the holder of the COP will not be paid.

In a typical transaction, a bank acts as the broker between the lessor (a private firm) and the lessee (the public authority or government). The lessor assigns the lease and lease payments, along with its rights and obligations, to the bank as trustee. The bank, in turn, issues certificates of participation through a competitive or negotiated sale to underwriters. The tax-exempt status is passed through to owners of the COPs who receive the distribution of the interest component of the lease.[8]

Certificates of participation can be traded in the secondary market, making them more marketable. Therefore, issuers are able to obtain a lower interest rate on COPs than on other types of lease-purchase financing. The relatively small denominations of the COPs spread the risk associated with lease-purchase transactions and facilitate an active secondary market.[9]

Tax-Exempt Leveraged Lease Financing

In today's investment market, tax-exempt leveraged lease (or TELL) financing is often more versatile and cost-effective than conventional borrowing. In TELL financing, local jurisdictions generate capital funds by selling public facilities. The sale is financed through tax-exempt revenue bonds. Once the buildings have been sold, the jurisdiction leases back the facility at subsidized rates, thus "leveraging" the private investment. The results are sharply reduced financing costs, a new pool of unrestricted funds for capital projects, and greater financial flexibility for borrowers. TELL financing can greatly reduce the cost of borrowing on capital projects of $5 million or more.

The main participants in TELL financing are a public jurisdiction, a limited partnership, a financing authority, and the bondholders (see Figure 8-1). Any government unit or public agency that is authorized to issue special purpose revenue bonds or industrial development bonds might take advantage of leveraged lease financing. The jurisdiction offers to sell a public facility to a private investor (usually operating as a special purpose limited partnership). The private investor buys the facility by making a down payment and, over a five-year period, contributing equity equal to 25% to 30% of the sales price. The jurisdiction then leases back the building on a long-term basis for continued use. The infusion of equity by the investor reduces rents significantly during the first five years.

The balance of the sales price is financed by tax-exempt revenue bonds issued on behalf of the partnership and loaned by a qualified financing authority (such as an industrial development authority). Underwriters arrange the tax-exempt bond financing and structure the sale and leaseback transaction to meet the requirements of the bond market, the private investors, and the government. The lease serves as collateral for the loan, which, in turn, secures the bond issue. The proceeds of the sale then finance the intended capital project.

Assume, for example, that a municipality wants to upgrade and add to public parking facilities in the downtown area. The municipality currently owns an office building in the area that houses several local government agencies. The municipality sells the office building to a private company for $10 million. The company provides an initial down payment of $1 million and guarantees additional equity payments of $2.5 million over the next five years. An appropriate financing authority issues a revenue bond for $9 million and uses the proceeds to provide a loan to the private company to fund the balance of the purchase price. The municipality leases back the office building from the private company. The lease is structured to provide the funds required by the private company to show a net profit after it has covered its loan payment obligations to the financing authority. The financing authority, in turn, applies the loan payments to meet the annual debt service requirements on the revenue bonds. The municipality uses the $10 million received from the sale of the office building to undertake the improvements to the downtown parking facilities.

In purchasing the existing facility, the private investors obtain the tax benefits associated with ownership. The subsidized base payments during the initial five years are a reflection of the value of these benefits. Lease payments represent the cost of financing to the governmental unit. In reducing the magnitude of the lease payments, TELL successfully reduces the effective borrowing cost below the issuer's current tax-exempt rate.

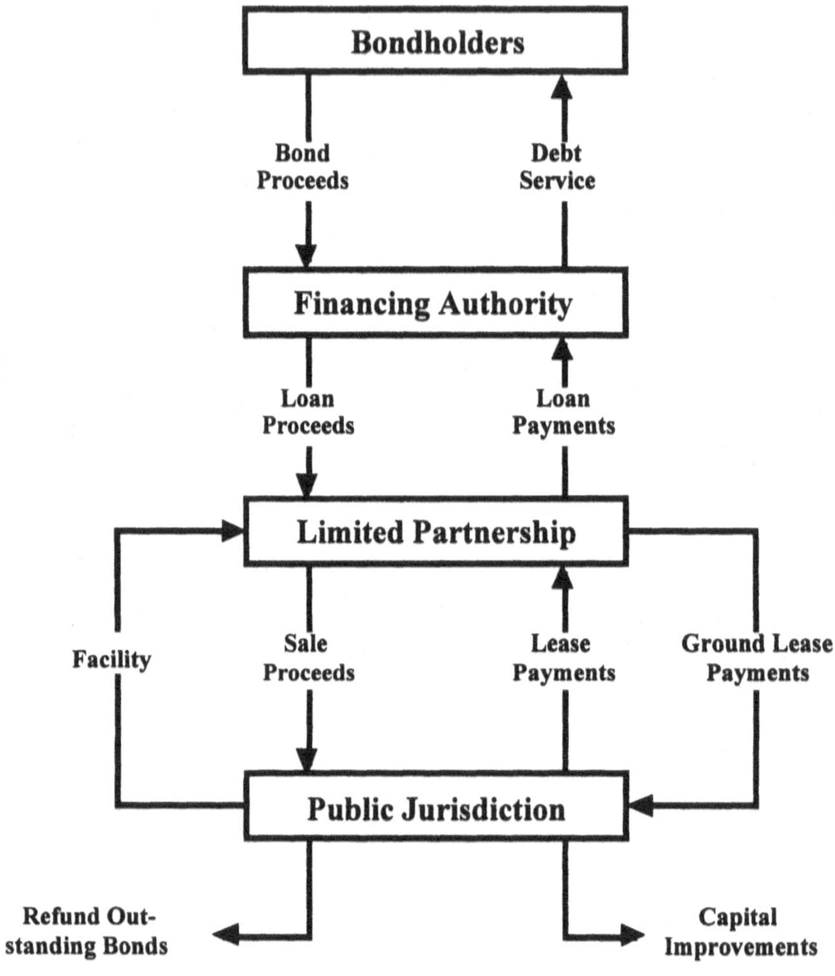

Figure 8-1
Structure for Tax-Exempt Leveraged Lease Financing

Although investors own the building, the lease is carefully written to provide the government with maximum flexibility and control over the use and final disposition of the building. Typically, a jurisdiction leases back the building for a period of thirty years on a net-net basis; that is, the jurisdiction assumes the basic operating and maintenance costs. In so doing, the jurisdiction retains control over the day-to-day management and operations of the facility. In addition, the lease usually provides the government with several renewal options and with rights to repurchase the facility. As a further protection, the public agency often retains ownership of the land, leasing it to the investors for an extended period (e.g., forty to fifty years). At the end of the land lease, the land and improvements automatically revert to the government.

Under TELL financing, the repurchase price cannot be negotiated in advance of the sale. However, lease provisions can shield the jurisdiction from inflated real estate values at the time of repurchase. These safeguards include the land lease, the renewal options, and the method of appraisal that defines the repurchase price at the end of lease agreement. The land lease, for example, serves to encumber the facility and to limit its future value in the open market.

Almost any capital project, from new construction to the refunding of outstanding debt, can be financed through leveraged leases. College dormitories, for example, have been successfully financed through TELL arrangements. In considering TELL financing, the managing underwriter should assist the government in developing a feasibility study. This study should include an analysis of the impact of the project's proposed financing terms on the local budget, an estimated rental schedule, and an outline of the legal and financial actions required of the government. Upon completion of this analysis, the managing underwriter, the bond counsel, and representatives of the equity partnership should draft necessary lease, purchase, and financing documents. A firm purchase contract should then be submitted within sixty to ninety days.

Factors to Consider in Using Lease-Purchase Agreements

Before entering into a lease-purchase agreement, a government should consider all of the available financing options, including paying for the asset from current revenue, financing it through a bond issue, or acquiring it through a lease purchase. The government should conduct a present value analysis to determine the cost of each option. In addition, a government should consider using various credit enhancement devices. Bond insurance and letters of credit, for example, decrease the risk associated with lease purchases and can lower the interest rate charged by investors. The costs of the credit enhancement, however, must be compared to the present value of the expected decrease in interest costs.

The project for which lease-purchase financing is being considered should have a clearly defined and essential public purpose—for example, a courthouse, community hospital, or correctional facility. Moreover, the term designated in the lease should not exceed, and preferably should be shorter than, the useful life of the asset.

The use of a lease-purchase agreement to acquire a large asset, such as a building, financed over a ten to thirty-year period, imposes a long-term commitment on a government. Lease purchases do not require voter approval in most states. Therefore, the use of such agreements might evade the normal legal and political approval process associated with long-term commitments that are backed by a jurisdiction's general obligation pledge. This evasion, in turn, might lead to litigation initiated by taxpayer associations or other public groups.

If a lease-purchase agreement has a principal greater than an established threshold and if the payments are financed from general revenues, then the lease-purchase agreement might be counted toward a jurisdiction's statutory debt limit. In addition, rating companies often include lease purchases when assessing the jurisdiction's debt burden. Failure to appropriate funds for a lease purchase will weaken the ability of the jurisdiction to continue to use this type of financing and might adversely affect its overall credit standing. When Bay City, Texas, decided not to continue its lease payments for a golf course, for example, Moody's downgraded the rating of the city's general obligation bonds.

Since property usually will be acquired at the end of the lease, it is advisable to assess the title history, environmental record, and local tax implications of the property before potential legal complications arise. Moreover, contracts can be structured to avoid the possibility that the bankruptcy of a private sector entity serving as lessor or assignor will threaten the flow of lease payments.

Finally, the government should take responsibility for evaluating the documents used to market or re-market the lease purchase. Recently, the re-marketing of vendor lease agreements without adequate disclosure has caused legal problems in several states. The government can protect itself by ensuring that the contract includes a warning that the jurisdiction is not responsible for what dealers disclose or fail to disclose.[10]

Summary and Conclusions

Revenue bonds can play an important role in the long-range planning of strategic facilities. It must be clearly established, however, that the revenues generated by the proposed project are sufficient to (1) cover the cost of operations, maintenance, and debt service; (2) provide a comfortable margin of working capital; and (3) create a reserve fund for emergencies and to cover possible declines in income. In short, revenue bonding must be approached with the principles of sound management and debt administration firmly in mind.

Lease-purchase agreements have been used to finance the acquisition of equipment, such as computers and motor vehicles, for over thirty-five years. More recently, long-term projects, such as the acquisition of real property, have also been financed using lease-purchase agreements. Under this approach, a government might use a nonprofit corporation or a governmental entity as a lessor to finance the acquisition of an asset. This arrangement is commonly used to finance the construction of schools, prisons, and public recreational facilities.

The lessor serves as a channel to the financial markets for the lessee. The government that seeks to acquire the property agrees to make lease payments to the lessor. The lessor, in turn, issues revenue bonds, which are secured by the flow of lease payments.

Tax-exempt leveraged lease (TELL) financing further extends this approach by involving the private sector as the lessor of the facility. An appropriate financing authority issues the revenue bonds and provides loan funds to the private entity to secure the purchase of the publicly leased facility.

The lease-purchase arrangement can be a very favorable financing method for a governmental entity in certain circumstances. It is important, however, that the governmental entity be aware on the "front end" of what is involved in a lease-purchase arrangement so that a fully informed decision can be made as to whether or not to use a lease-purchase arrangement for a particular acquisition. By doing so, a lease-purchase transaction is much more likely to proceed smoothly and with few, if any, surprises.

In the past, the typical municipal bond was a general obligation bond, backed by the full faith and credit of the issuing jurisdiction, sold by competitive bid, underwritten by a bank, and sold to a bank or other traditional financial institution. In today's bond market, however, the typical municipal bond is a revenue bond, sold through negotiation, underwritten by a bond syndicate or municipal bond dealer, and sold to individual investors and bond mutual funds.

Notes

1. Brian Krolicki, Testimony of the National Association of State Treasurers Regarding Public Infrastructure Financing, presented before the Subcommittee on Railroads of the Committee on Transportation and Infrastructure, United States House of Representatives, October 2, 2001.
2. Percy R. Aguila and John E. Peterson, "Leasing Service Contracts," in *Local Government Finance: Concepts and Practice*, eds. John E. Petersen and Dennis Strachota (Chicago: Government Finance Officers Association, 1991), 322.
3. John W. Gillespie Jr., Morgan Stanley & Co. Incorporated, "Tax-Exempt Lease Financing," Paper presented at the First Annual Debt Management Conference, Austin, Texas, (December 5, 1991), 9.
4. John Vogt and Lisa Cole, *Guide to Municipal Leasing* (Chicago: Municipal Finance Officers Association, 1983), 35.
5. Patrice Hill, "State High Court Will Not Review Earlier Ruling on Texas Leases," *The Bond Buyer* (January 24, 1992): 1.
6. Aguila and Peterson, *op. cit.*, 335.
7. Gillespie, *op. cit.*, 7.
8. Vogt and Cole, *op. cit.*, 74-75.
9. Public Securities Association, *A Guide to Certificates of Participation* (New York: Public Securities Association, 1991), 3.
10. Patrice Hill, "States Must Step Up Battle Against Abuses of Vendor Leases," *The Bond Buyer* (September 11, 1992): 1.

Chapter 9

MARKETING AND UNDERWRITING MUNICIPAL BONDS

The marketing of municipal bonds is a complicated process. Local officials must be mindful of the procedures for marketing and underwriting bonds, from the planning of the issue through the actual delivery of the bonds to the winning bidder. Failure to adhere to these procedures can result in unnecessary delays, higher interest costs, and possible legal ramifications. As a practical matter, almost any bond issue that is in proper technical form can be sold at any time. However, whether a particular offering is "successful" at the date of sale depends on the congruence of many factors, including forces in the marketplace that are beyond the control of local officials. Municipal officials often are confronted by uncertainties that they might not fully comprehend. Adherence to accepted marketing procedures, however, can go a long way to reducing these uncertainties to acceptable levels of risk.

Preliminaries to Marketing

Constitutional provisions, general statutes, special legislative acts, and local charters that regulate the authorization and issuance of municipal bonds vary from state to state. Controlling laws are not always conveniently codified. As a consequence, the procedural steps necessary to secure bond authorization often are confusing to local officials and administrators. Expert advice is important to ensure compliance with all applicable legal requirements. Even minor errors might result in annoying delays, expensive litigation, and possible invalidation of the issue or sale.

Bond Ordinances and Referenda

Municipal bonds must be negotiable instruments; that is, they must contain an unconditional promise or order to pay. Bond ordinances or resolutions should be drawn with precision, setting forth, among other things, the nature and limits of the security to be offered. An attorney whose legal opinions satisfy the market where the bonds are to be sold must approve each issue. As a general rule, the city attorney or corporation counsel is not a bond specialist. Therefore, the services must be secured of a bond counsel whose opinion is marketable.

In preparing the opinion, the bond counsel addresses two key legal issues: (1) that the requirements of local laws, state constitution, judicial opinions, and enabling legislation have been met; and (2) if appropriate, that the interest income is exempt from federal and state taxes. The official notice of sale should specify that the legal opinion of the bond counsel will be furnished to the buyer.

Final approval cannot be given until the sale is complete. However, providing preliminary approval before the bidding process begins assures prospective buyers (underwriters) that the legal opinion (called a "transcript of proceedings") can and will be furnished without delay before the bond issue is distributed to investors. The sale is subject to the satisfactory provision of such legal opinion.

Some form of popular referendum is required in most states for the authorization of general obligation bonds. Depending on the prevailing law, a majority vote might be sufficient or a two-thirds vote might be necessary. Revenue bond issues generally do not require approval through public referenda. A few states permit governing bodies to authorize general obligation bonds, within certain limits, without popular vote. Experience has shown, however, that this option should be used sparingly and held in reserve for emergencies. Occasionally, a new issue might represent the unsold portion of a larger issue that has been previously authorized.

Adequate preparation for a public referendum, including broad public notification and appropriate endorsements, is essential to achieving voter approval. In some cases, the referendum might be included on the ballot of a regularly scheduled election. However, a special election often must be held to ensure that the bonds, if approved, can be issued on a timely basis.

Notice of Sale

In most states, local governments are required to sell general obligation bonds through competitive bidding, usually by the submission of sealed bids. The official notice of a competitive sale should be published in *The Daily Bond Buyer*—the newspaper of the municipal bond industry—at least two weeks in advance of the date set for opening bids. It might also be appropriate to include the official notice in regional bond publications. In some states, notices must also be placed in the official state newspaper. In addition to notices of sale, *The Daily Bond Buyer* includes news articles, call notices, a new issue calendar, and other announcements pertinent to the municipal market and financial community.

In the case of a negotiated sale, publication of the official notice serves to alert financial institutions as to the intent of a local jurisdiction to enter into an agreement to have an underwriter participate in setting up the bond issue. In a negotiated sale, the bond issue is not structured until after an underwriter is chosen, allowing for greater flexibility as to the particulars of the issue than is likely in a competitive sale.

The following information should be included in the official notice of sale:

1. Correct legal name of the issuing body, the special law (if any) under which it was organized, and the authority for the sale.
2. Type of bonds to be issued.
3. Amount and purpose of the issue, the maturity schedule, call features (if any), denomination, and registration privileges.
4. Date, time, and place of sale; manner of bidding (sealed or oral); and basis for bidding (e.g., at par, discounts allowed, etc.).

5. Limitations as to interest rate, payment dates of interest, and when and where principal will be paid.
6. Amount of good faith check.
7. Name of approving attorney.
8. Provision made for the payment of principal and interest—from ad valorem taxes, special assessments, or revenue of a particular enterprise.
9. Total tax rate in the governmental unit, rate for each levying body, and constitutional or statutory limits restricting debts or the taxes levied for their payments.

Adequate publicity through the notice of sale gives prospective bidders the opportunity to form their bidding accounts and to secure relevant information regarding the offering. It also eliminates any suspicion of collusion and demonstrates that the jurisdiction is willing to submit its current financial condition to careful inspection.

Split-rate Bids and Supplemental Coupons

If the enabling legislation permits, the best practice is to allow interest rates to be fixed by the underwriters, through either the bidding process or negotiations. When they can determine the interest rates, underwriters can make a bid that best fits the market. If permissible under controlling state regulations, underwriters should be able to bid different rates on various maturities or groups of bonds—known as *split-rate bids*—in order to obtain the most favorable overall net interest cost. Competitive bids are awarded to the underwriters who offer to buy the bond issue at the lowest net interest cost to the issuer. Procedures for determining the net interest cost are discussed in a subsequent section.

Supplemental coupons have been used to attract dealers where state requirements mandate that bonds be sold at par. Supplemental coupons cover the same interest period as one or more regular coupons. When a supplemental coupon is in force, the locality is required to make two interest payments for the period covered by the coupons. Supplemental coupons are usually detached by the underwriter at the time of original delivery from the issuer and might be sold at a discount or held by the dealer until payment date. These coupons often represent the underwriter's profit on the sale of the bond. In recent years, supplemental coupons have fallen out of use in the municipal bond market.

Timing of an Issue

Minor fluctuations are evident in the bond market within the course of every few months, brought on by an excess of supply over demand as well as economic and political trends. By following municipal bond publications and consulting investment bankers, the finance officer can often apply these fluctuations to the advantage of the jurisdiction.

The jurisdiction should avoid setting the date of the sale in the midst of a general rush of new offerings (many large school bond issues, for example, reach the market in late spring or early summer) or immediately following large sales a holiday or on Mondays or Saturdays. It is unwise to enter the market too frequently (thus, the advantage of a bond issue that consolidates several projects). And if dealers have not completed the distribution of a previous issue, a less satisfactory price might be anticipated on a new issue.

The due dates for semiannual interest payments are determined by the date on which the bond is sold. Every local government experiences certain times of the year when its funds are low (for example, just prior to the due date for the payment of property taxes). Therefore, a bond issue should be scheduled to ensure that sufficient funds are available to cover interest and principal payments. The inability to meet these debt service obligations can result in a temporary default, even if payment is delayed by only a few days. Temporary defaults, in turn, can adversely affect the jurisdiction's bond rating.

Bond Prospectus

The publication of all essential information concerning the financial condition of the municipality is a most important factor in the successful marketing of municipal bonds. With the exception of revenue bond issues, however, no elaborate prospectus is necessary. The four-page statistical form, approved by the Investment Bankers Association and the Government Finance Officers Association, usually is adequate. This form provides the information that most investors seek regarding the proposed debt and the provision for payment. It also provides key data as to the adequacy of the community's revenue system and the effectiveness of its administration. Recent financial operations in the municipality, total tax rate and statutory limits restricting debts or the taxes levied for their payments, population according to latest census data, and so forth are also covered.

The bond prospectus should be printed and ready for distribution at the time of the notice of sale. It should be sent, without request, to the investment bankers and other institutions that have previously expressed interested in the jurisdiction's securities. Financial papers that publish the paid notice about the sale will usually carry a news story about the community and, therefore, should also receive copies of the prospectus.

Costs Involved in Marketing Municipal Bonds

The largest buyers of municipal bonds traditionally have been financial institutions that are exacting in their requirements. Failure to comply with their "rules of the game" tends to narrow the market and might be reflected in the interest cost to the local government. Principal and interest should be payable in a large financial center, preferably through a bank located in a city where there is a Federal Reserve Bank. Most large investors prefer to avoid the inconvenience involved in collection of principal and interest payments outside such centers.

The cost of borrowing involves not only the interest payable over the term of the bonds, but also costs incurred in readying bonds for market and their actual delivery to the initial investors. Such costs reflect fees for various legal and financial advisors and the expense of conducting a referendum. A variety of miscellaneous costs include preparation and publication of bond notices and the bond prospectus, obtaining a bond rating, filing fees, court fees, registration or recording fees, certification costs, and costs of delivering the bonds. Some marketing expense might result in a broader sale, culminating in lower interest costs. Other expenses might add little to the marketability of a bond issue.

While no single cost incurred is large, in the aggregate, these marketing costs can amount to a considerable sum. In some instances, total marketing costs amounted to 5% of the value of the bonds. A survey by the Municipal Finance Officers Association found that the average cost for marketing general obligation bonds amounted to $2.00 per $1,000, as compared to $3.85 per $1,000 for revenue bonds and $5.00 per $1,000 for special assessment bonds. As would be expected, the cost per $1,000 declines steadily as the size of the bond issue increases.

Marketing costs usually are reimbursed from the bond proceeds. This practice, however, reduces the amount available for the project or requires an increased borrowing to meet capital costs. In either case, interest costs also attach to that portion of the proceeds used to meet marketing costs.

Ratings for Municipal Bonds

Ratings have assumed considerable significance in determining interest rates and the eligibility of bonds for purchase by certain types of investors. Rating services assign a credit rating to bond issues that assesses the risk of nonpayment of borrowed funds. The better the bond rating, the lower the interest cost that the jurisdiction must pay. For a $1 million bond issued for twenty years at an interest rate of 5%, for example, one rating difference (e.g., AAA versus AA) can amount to about $50,000 in interest costs.

Risk Factors Considered

Municipal bonds are rated only in terms of credit risk and not in terms of their investment merits. Bond ratings appraise two basic risk factors: (1) the risk that depressed economic conditions might impair the ability of the jurisdiction to meet principal and interest payments, and (2) the risk that bond quality will be diluted by an inordinate increase in debt. The first is related to the impact of general economic conditions on a given locality, whereas the second risk is within the control of the issuing jurisdiction.

Rating analysts evaluate a wide range of information concerning economic, debt, financial, and governmental considerations to determine a bond rating. This information is supplied by the jurisdiction and derived independently by the analyst. Rating agencies do not explain completely their reasons for assigning a particular rating, nor do they provide a precise formula for obtaining better ratings.

Analysts evaluate several economic factors, including the area's economic prospects; locational advantages and disadvantages of the jurisdiction; its population, wealth, labor factors; and the diversity of employers. Among the most significant economic variables are the percentage of the local economy that is dominated by the ten largest taxpayers (a measure of the concentration and dependence of the local economy), the rate of unemployment, the tax base per capita, and recent changes in population. Of the various criteria included in the rating analysis, economic factors are the hardest for a locality to improve. Economic development/improvement often is a very long-term proposition for most jurisdictions.

Rating analysts examine various debt factors, including the debt policy, debt structure, debt burden, and debt history of the jurisdiction and its borrowing prospective. The objective is to assess the likelihood that the jurisdiction will be able to meet its financial commitments to the bondholders. Evidence of planning for future debt and having a solid infrastructure is looked upon favorably by the analysts. If public indebtedness becomes too high, analysts are concerned that the jurisdiction might be unable or unwilling to honor its debt commitments. The amount of debt burden is measured against national averages of net debt per capita and the ratio of net debt to the estimated full value of all taxable property within the jurisdiction. Communities with high net debt have cause for concern. On the other hand, low net debt might not necessarily be a positive indicator if such jurisdictions have ignored needed infrastructure improvements by not issuing bonds.

Two important governmental considerations are continuity in management personnel and good fiscal controls. An assessment is made of the local management team as to its professionalism, how long it has been in place, and whether or not managerial and policy-making responsibilities are clearly delineated. The jurisdiction's compliance with the Government Finance Officers Association standards regarding financial reporting and budgeting procedures is determined. Existing or potential overlapping or conflicting intergovernmental relationships are also evaluated.

A number of financial factors are examined. Financial reports and budgets are reviewed to determine existing and future fiscal trends and to assess if revenues meet or exceed expenditures. These data are examined to determine if a sufficient fund balance is available to meet unforeseen contingencies. The diversity of revenue sources is evaluated, and the collection rate for property taxes is identified. The analyst will also seek to determine the jurisdiction's policies regarding interfund transfers, if generally accepted accounting principles (GAAP) are followed, and if pension liabilities are properly funded.

Rating Services

Three nationally recognized rating organizations—Standard and Poor's Corporation, Moody's Investors Service, Inc., and Fitch Investor's Service—rate a wide variety of bonds: tax-supported, revenue or enterprise supported, lease-rental, hospital revenue, mortgage-backed housing, higher education revenue, student loan revenue, and refunded bonds. These rating services use symbols, arranged in order from bonds with the least credit risk to those with the greatest risk (see Table 9-1). The opinions of the rating services might differ on specific bond issues, and some issues are rated only by one service.

Table 9-1 Municipal Bond Ratings

Moody's	Rating		Standard and Poor's
Best quality; carry smallest degree of risk; generally referred to as "gilt-edged." Interest payments protected by large stable margin; principal is secure.	**AAA**	**AAA**	Highest rating assigned to debt obligations indicates ultimate degree of protection as to principal and interest.
High quality by all standards; known as high-grade bonds; margins of protection might not be as large, fluctuations may be of greater amplitude, or other elements make long-term risks appear larger.	**Aa**	**AA**	Also qualify as high-grade obligations; differ from AAA issues only in a small degree.
Possess many favorable investment attributes; considered upper medium-grade obligations. Factors giving security to principal and interest considered adequate, but some elements might suggest susceptibility to impairment sometime in the future.	**A**	**A**	Generally regarded as upper medium-grade; have considerable investment strength, but not entirely free from adverse effects of changes in economic and trade conditions. Interest and principal regarded as safe.
Medium-grade obligations; neither highly protected nor poorly secured. Interest payments and principal security appear adequate for the present, but certain protective elements might be lacking or unreliable over any great length of time.	**Baa**	**BBB**	Regarded as having adequate capacity to pay principal and interest. Adverse economic conditions or changing circumstances more likely to lead to weakened capacity to pay principal and interest.
Contains speculative elements. Protection of interest and principal payments might not be well safeguarded during good and bad times. Uncertainty of position characterizes bonds in this class.	**Ba**	**BB**	Regarded as predominantly speculative with respect to issuer's capacity to pay interest and repay principal according to terms of the obligations.
Generally lacks characteristics of desired investment. Assurance of interest and and principal payments or maintenance of other terms of the contract over any long period may be small.	**B**	**B**	Speculative; quality and protective characteristics outweighed by large uncertainties or major risk exposures to adverse conditions.
Poor standing. Issues may be in default, or elements of danger might be present with respect to principal or interest	**Caa**	**CCC**	High degree of speculation; large uncertainties or major risk exposure.
Obligations are highly speculative. Often in default or have other shortcomings.	**Ca**	**CC**	Highest degree of speculation.
Lowest-rated class of bonds; extremely poor prospects for attaining any real investment standing.	**C**	**C**	Reserved for income bonds on which no interest is being paid.
		D	In default; interest and/or principal payments in arrears.

Service fees for ratings vary in relation to the size of the prospective bond issue, according to the following general schedule:

Issue Size	Amount of Fee
Under $3 million	$ 1,000 - $ 3,000
$3 million to $5 million	$ 2,000 - $ 4,000
$5 million to $20 million	$ 3,000 - $ 6,000
$20 million to $50 million	$ 4,000 - $ 8,000
$50 million to $100 million	$ 6,000 - $12,000
$100 million and over	$10,000 - $25,000

Generally speaking, there is only one rating for all of the general obligation bonds of a particular governmental unit and for all the bonds of a specific revenue project. Some governmental units or revenue projects might have more than one rating, however, because special security has been pledged for some of the bonds.[1] New issues of a governmental unit or revenue project that has previously been rated usually are assigned the same rating as the outstanding bonds unless there have been material changes in the credit situation.

A rating committee reviews the recommendations of the rating analyst and assigns the actual rating. A jurisdiction might appeal the assigned rating by furnishing additional information to the rating service. Jurisdictions can actively pursue better bond ratings by making improvements in one or more of the four areas of evaluation and by proactively selling the community through ongoing contacts with rating services.[3]

A back-and-forth relationship should be established with the rating services. Key staff members should be introduced to the rating analysts, who should be encouraged to ask for information from these staff members as needed. Any written materials, special reports, and newspaper accounts that highlight changes and improvements should be submitted to the rating service. Any major changes in financial policy that might affect the jurisdiction's credit rating should first be discussed with the rating analysts.

Some jurisdictions visit the bond rating services whenever they prepare a new issue. Others make such visits only when seeking a better rating or if a rating downgrade is anticipated. It is important that the team representing the local jurisdiction is well prepared for such meetings and makes a highly professional presentation. A brief introductory statement should highlight the important features in the submitted documents. The rating analysts should be encouraged to ask questions. The "pitch" is less important than the content of the answers. If unsure of an answer, the local team should provide additional information following the meeting. The analysts are particularly interested in information that cannot be obtained from the rating documents that have already been provided.

In addition to evaluating new bond issues, rating analysts maintain surveillance over current ratings. If it is anticipated that a current bond rating might be lowered, a jurisdiction is placed on CreditWatch.

Rating systems have undergone continual improvements, particularly since the advent of high-speed computers. Existing systems are not without deficiencies, however, as summarized in a report of the Joint Economic Committee:[2]

1. Financial institutions place undue dependence on ratings in determining municipal bond investments.
2. Verified information to support ratings often is lacking. This deficiency results from a lack of uniform financial reporting systems among the states, reliance on the issuers to supply their periodic financial data, and inadequate staff to ascertain completeness or biases.
3. The possibility of conflicts of interest exists in situations where bond rating services also function as advisors to investors and as consultants to governmental bodies.

State laws often limit large institutional buyers in the selection of their investments. Therefore, if a jurisdiction is on the list of authorized investments maintained by leading investor states, it is very important that every effort be made to maintain this favored position.

Bond Insurance

Bond insurance guarantees that interest and principal will be paid on the insured bonds, as they become due, and that mandatory sinking fund payments will be made if the issuer of the bonds fails to make these payments for whatever reason. Most municipal bond insurance is sold as part of the new-issue process. The insurance becomes part of the bond description. The buyer of an insured bond owns "insured paper," which trades in its own market as an insured bond, increasing its desirability and its salability.

Bonds can be insured in one of three ways:

1. New bonds can be insured at the time they are underwritten and then sold as insured bonds with the bond insurance contract printed on the bond certificate. Most insured bonds are covered in this way.
2. A municipal bond dealer can buy a block of uninsured bonds (often several million dollars worth) and then buy bond insurance on that block to enhance their selling price. This is called secondary market insurance.
3. A municipal investment trust or municipal mutual fund portfolio can buy an insurance policy for the bonds that are held in the trust/fund. If and when the bonds are sold by the trust/fund, the premium is no longer paid and the bonds are no longer insured.

Insurance premiums are paid by the issuer of the bonds or the investment banks and securities dealers that sell them. There are no direct charges to the investor. However, in exchange for the extra security of guaranteed payment and a triple-A rating, investors usually give up some interest earnings due to the lower coupon rate offered on insured bonds, averaging half a point or $5 per year on a $1,000 bond.

The primary reason that state and local governments insure their bond offerings is to secure the highest ratings possible and, thereby, lower their borrowing costs (see Table 9-2). Insured bonds automatically receive AAA ratings, based on the triple-A claims-paying ability of the insurer. Investors are attracted to

Table 9-2
Value-enhancing Features of Bond Insurance

***Safety*:**	Investors have a backup source of payment to rely on if the primary payer—the issuer—cannot meet its obligations.
***Quality*:**	Insured bonds automatically receive the highest rating available, based on the triple-A claims-paying ability of the insurer.
***Oversight*:**	State insurance departments (particularly those of the states of New York and California) exercise rigorous oversight of the municipal bond insurance industry. Bond insurers are also closely monitored by the major rating agencies, which historically have reaffirmed their triple-A ratings at least once a year.
***Liquidity*:**	Large volumes of triple-A rated, 100%-insured securities are traded every day in the secondary market. Investors who wish to sell their insured bonds before maturity usually find a ready market for such highly rated securities.
***Yield*:**	In most cases, triple-A insured municipals offer higher yields than triple-A uninsured securities.
***Pre-selection*:**	Before an insurer agrees to guarantee a municipal security, its underwriters rigorously analyze the issuer and the specific issue. If a bond is 100% insured by a triple-A-rated municipal bond insurer, investors can be confident that experts have thoroughly researched every aspect of it.
***Surveillance*:**	The performance of every insured issue is monitored to final maturity by the organization that provided the insurance. Surveillance teams make on-site visits to issuers and require a variety of financial reports, which are carefully analyzed for any sign of credit deterioration.

insured bonds because their investments are more secure. In addition, insured bonds have more liquidity and price protection than uninsured bonds. That being the case, why are not all municipal bond issues insured (over half of all new issues in 2002 were insured)?

Bond insurance companies only insure bonds that are of investment-grade quality—that is, those issues that would be rated Baa/BBB or higher by Moody's Investors Service, Standard & Poor's, Fitch Investors Service, or other rating agencies. They work only with bond issuers that have stable, investment-grade credit profiles. Insurers then go through a very thorough risk assessment process. Each bond issue is examined in great detail, including such factors as the issuer's tax base, regional economy, financial condition, existing debt, and expected future borrowing and spending requirements. The goal is to make sure the securities meet the rigorous internal standards of the insurance companies.

One such standard is what is known as *zero-loss underwriting*. This criterion means that the issuer is so strong or is providing such ironclad protections in the bond issue that the insurer believes it will sustain no losses. Zero-loss underwriting contrasts with the actuarial approach used in the general insurance industry, which assumes a certain level of losses will be sustained.

Municipal bond insurance began in the early 1970s when the AMBAC Indemnity Corporation and the Municipal Bond Investors Assurance Corporation (MBIA) began to offer insurance policies to state and local governments to cover their new bond issues. Insurance became important in the mid-1980s, when over 20% of the new issues were insured. By 1995, 43% of the new municipal bond issues were insured.

Eight insurance companies write policies on municipal bonds. Three of these companies provide about 90% of the insurance coverage:

Municipal Bond Investors Assurance	37%
AMBAC Indemnity Corp.	28%
Financial Guaranty Insurance Co.	26%

Companies that insure municipal bonds only insure investment-grade debt securities, and therefore are not exposed to risks from any other lines of business, as are property, casualty, and life insurers. Every bond insurance company has at least one triple-A rating from a nationally recognized rating agency, and every insured bond, in turn, receives a triple-A rating based on the insurer's own capital and claims-paying resources.

Underwriting Municipal Bonds

Local governments seldom deal with the final investor when they issue bonds. Most investors cannot afford to buy whole bond issues, and most local governments do not have the time or resources to market bonds to multiple investors. Large investment syndicates provide the funds to the issuing jurisdictions by underwriting the municipal bonds. Underwriters, in turn, attempt to make a profit by selling bonds to individual investors at a price higher than the purchase price paid by the investment syndicate. The mark-up in price by the underwriters is known as the *spread* and represents compensation for distributing the bonds and for assuming the risk of a change in market value of the bonds. Underwriters do not always achieve a profit. In some cases, the bonds can only be sold at a price lower than the purchase price, and therefore the underwriter takes a loss in the transaction.

Recent Trends in Municipal Bond Underwriting

The underwriting of municipal bonds reached record levels during the late 1980s and early 1990s. During this period, most Wall Street firms undertook major expansion of their municipal departments. According to the Bond Buyer's

Municipal Marketplace, these firms employed over 15,800 municipal bond underwriters in 1992. Many of these municipal departments were staffed with individuals who had an affinity for public policy and the often-grubby realm of courthouse politics.

However, as bond interest rates rose in the mid-1990s, many local officials became reluctant to raise taxes or charge the user fees necessary to back new bonds to finance projects. A crackdown by the Securities and Exchange Commission on inadequate financial disclosures to investors and the scandal of payoffs also took their toll.[4] The discussions during this period of the possibility of a flat tax cast a shadow over the municipal bond market. If enacted, a flat tax would give all bonds the privileged status that municipal bonds enjoy.

Faced with declining profits and growing competition, increased government scrutiny, and the taxpayer rebellion, many Wall Street firms have closed their municipal departments in recent years. Among these firms are CS First Boston; the Donaldson, Lufkin, Jenrette unit of the Equitable Companies; Lazard Freres; and the Chemical Securities unit of the Chemical Banking Corporation. Others have made deep cuts in their municipal departments, including Prudential Securities, Goldman Sachs, Morgan Stanley, Merrill Lynch, Lehman Brothers, and some regional firms.

When the underwriting margins began to decline, the cultural differences with their corporate finance departments made it relatively easy for many firms to close their the municipal departments. As one company spokesman observed: "Being in municipal finance was a way of being in the private sector but feeding a desire to do public service. All the Democrats are in municipal finance."[5]

However, with 13,000 municipalities in need of billions of dollars to finance schools, sewage treatment facilities, parks, roads, and other public improvements, the need will continue for underwriters who understand both financial matters and the labyrinth of government operations. As Robert B. Lamb has noted: "There's a huge need for $2 trillion to $3 trillion worth of new infrastructure and renewal for water systems, sewer systems, and bridges that are decades beyond their useful lives and literally falling down."[6] Furthermore, the trend toward the conversion of public assets to private ventures will also continue to put a premium on investment bankers with knowledge and skills in the operations of government.

Competitive Bidding Versus Negotiated Sales

Underwriters may purchase municipal bonds (a) as the highest bidder at competitive bidding or (b) through a private negotiated purchase. As noted, most states require local governments to sell general obligation bonds through competitive bidding, usually by submission of sealed bids. The sale of revenue bonds might be negotiated, however, because it often is advantageous to the issuer to have the underwriter participate in setting up the issue from the outset. The risks involved for the underwriter in a negotiated sale are much less than for a competitive one. During a negotiated sale, the underwriter will likely have received commitments from a large number of investors prior to the time the bonds are actually issued. With competitive bids, most of the marketing and sales efforts occur after the bidding process has been completed.[7]

In 1974, about 70% of all new bond issues were sold through competitive bidding, with about 29% sold by negotiation. However, with the increased use of revenue bonds, the sale and distribution of municipal bonds has changed significantly. About 80% of all new issues currently are sold by negotiation and only 20% are sold through competitive bids.

In a negotiated sale, an underwriting syndicate is chosen on the basis of such criteria as expertise, financial resources, compatibility, and experience. The bond issue is not structured before an underwriter is chosen. Therefore, the particulars of the issue are more flexible than in a competitive sale. After an underwriter is selected, the process of structuring the bond issue and completing the other origination tasks are then undertaken, primarily by the senior manager of the syndicate in conjunction with the bond issuer. The syndicate will engage in presale marketing and then will negotiate interest rates with the issuer. The issuer often employs a financial advisor not associated with the underwriting firm to represent the issuer's interests in the process.

In a competitive bid sale, all of the tasks necessary to offer bonds for sale are carried out by the issuing jurisdiction, including determining the maturity schedule, preparing the official statement, verifying legal documents, obtaining a bond rating, securing credit enhancement, if advantageous, and timing the sale. These tasks are normally done with the assistance of outside consultants, including a financial advisor and bond counsel. Once the issue is structured, the public sale begins with the publication of an official notice of sale that delineates the proposed purpose, size, maturities, and structure of the anticipated issue, along with instructions for submitting bids.[8]

Underwriters use *The Daily Bond Buyer* as a reference for competitive bidding sales. This publication carries official municipal bond notices and contains information on proposed new issues, invitations for bids, and results of bond sales. It also offers a service used by many dealers to obtain notice of coming municipal bond sales and concise data about the proposed issue, including bidding details and a summary financial statement of the issuer. This service covers all issues of $1 million or more. Smaller issues often are covered by regional publications

Proponents of competitive bidding argue that this type of sale results in lower interest costs, since syndicates have an incentive to offer lower interest rates in order to increase their chances of being awarded the bonds. Competitive bid issues might also result in lower issuance costs. In the mid-1990s, bond issues of $20 million or more sold through competitive bids had an average cost of $5.92 per $1,000 of bonds, whereas negotiated sales had an average underwriter's spread of $6.71 per $1,000 of bonds.

Proponents of negotiated sales also argue that negotiated sales may result in lower interest costs and issuance costs. In a negotiated sale, the syndicate often performs significant premarketing of the bonds. If investors can be found prior to the negotiation of interest rates with the issuer, the syndicate might be less inclined to build a risk factor into the rates. With a negotiated sale, there is also more flexibility with regards to changing the sales date or the structure of the issue in attempting to obtain lower interest rates.

Factors other than costs also might influence the type of sale. Concern for the unbiased award of bids has resulted in increased interest in the use of competitive bid sales either voluntarily or required by law.[9] A competitive bid sale is open to all underwriting firms and is awarded on the basis of lowest cost. Therefore, allegations of preferential treatment can be avoided. Finally, since the bids submitted are final, any financial loss that a syndicate may incur in marketing the bonds is solely the syndicate's responsibility.

Establishing an Investment Syndicate

A syndicate is a temporary alliance of underwriters formed to purchase bonds from the issuer under the guidance of a senior or lead manager who directs the syndicate and coordinates the bond sale. Syndicates vary in size, depending on the amount of the issue and the ease with which the bonds are expected to sell. Syndicates often are made up of both large national underwriters, such as Goldman Sachs or Merrill Lynch, along with smaller underwriters located in the state or region where the bonds are being issued. Syndicates usually consist of firms that specialize in sales to institutional investors, such as pension or mutual funds, as well as firms that sell primarily to individual investors. Most syndicates last about thirty days, although a syndicate might be disbanded sooner if the bonds sell quickly (or if it is unsuccessful in winning the bid).

The syndicate letter or contract lays out the conditions and obligations of membership and specifies the details of the underwriting, the amount of the bonds, bid and offering terms, names of the mangers and members, and similar information. Following Municipal Securities Rulemaking Board regulations, this letter also describes the priority of orders received by the syndicate, usually as follows:

1. Presale Orders: received before the actual bid is submitted.
2. Group Account Orders: Orders filled for the syndicate as a whole, usually at the net offering prices, and credited to each member according to the member's level of participation.
3. Designated Orders: Orders for which specific members receive credit, usually at net prices.
4. Member Takedown Orders: Orders from members for sale to the member's own customers, taken from the account at the full takedown price.

Each member of the syndicate (or joint account) has a share in the account, called participation, and shares in the profits (and losses, if any) of the syndicate according to this participation. Each member is responsible for selling bonds, and when all the bonds are sold, the syndicate profits are then split according to each member's participation. As long as any bonds in the account are still unsold, each member is liable for a proportionate share of the unsold amount. The account is "undivided" in terms of selling and liability.

On occasion, the bonds in the account are distributed at the outset according to the agreed level of participation of each member. Under this arrangement, known as a *divided account*, a syndicate member is required to sell only its obligated percentage of the issue and is not held responsible for other's unsold bonds.[10] Divided accounts most often involve term bonds, since dividing serial bonds would mean that some members of the syndicate might have very few bonds from any maturity with which to work.

Syndicate accounts usually are established to run for thirty days, during which time the offering prices cannot be changed without consent of all or a majority of members. If, at the end of thirty days, the issue has not been sold in its entirety, the account might be renewed and extended by mutual agreement. Or, in an undivided account, the remaining bonds might be divided up among members in accordance with their prorata share, based upon their original participation. Price restrictions binding syndicate members to agreed-upon terms are normally removed after all the bonds are sold or the syndicate is disbanded on a particular issue.

Prior to the announced date for the submission of bids, the members of the syndicate must decide on the price at which the bonds will be offered to the public. The bidding process on a particular issue begins with an opinion from the research staff, usually based on an independent evaluation of the offering. The syndicate members hold several price discussions (usually by phone) during which the spread, prices, yields, reoffering scale, and other information are discussed. Based on these discussions, the account manager will suggest a bid scale and profit margin that he/she believes can be underwritten by the account (see Table 9-3). Members unwilling to make this bid may withdraw from the account and their share of the participation must be distributed among the remaining members.

The syndicate that produced the winning bid on the bond issue outlined in Table 9-3 originally involved 178 firms. Seventy-two of these firms declined to underwrite about $28 million of the $70 million required, because they disliked the price scale, profit spread, or the amount of unsold bond in the market in other accounts. The remaining 106 firms were required to cover the $28 million.

Net Interest Cost and True Interest Cost

The overall goal of the syndicate is to balance two objectives by reaching agreement on a set of yields that is:

1. High enough to attract prospective investors; and
2. Low enough in term of cost to the issuer to win the bid or, in the case of a negotiated bond issue, to meet the financing requirements of the issuer.

Competitive bids are awarded to the syndicate that offers to buy the issue at the lowest interest cost to the issuer. Two different calculation methods are used to measure interest costs to the issuer: net interest cost (NIC) and true interest costs (TIC).

Several calculations must be made on the stated interest rate in order to determine a *net interest cost* (i.e., the bid that the underwriters will make on the bonds) and the production of the bonds at the posted prices (i.e., the anticipated return on the sale of the bonds). The net interest cost is equal to the gross interest cost over the life of the bond issue less any premiums that must be paid,

Table 9-3
Calculation of Production for $70 Million BART Bond Issue

Year Due	Amount Offered ($000)	Coupon Rate (%)	Reoffering Price (Yield) (%) or (100 = PAR)	Reoffering Price per Bond ($)	Production (Col. 2 x Col. 5) ($)
1972	675	6.00	3.60	1,108.90	748,507.50
1973	800	6.00	3.65	1,125.60	900,480.00
1974	925	6.00	3.70	1,140.70	1,055,147.50
1975	1050	6.00	3.75	1,154.30	1,212,015.00
1976	1200	6.00	3.80	1,166.40	1,399,680.00
1977	1325	6.00	3.85	1,177.10	1,559,657.50
1978	1475	6.00	3.90	1,186.40	1,749,940.00
1979	1625	6.00	3.95	1,194.40	1,940,900.00
1980	1775	6.00	3.95	1,206.90	2,142,247.50
1981	1825	4.00	3.95	1,060.39	1,935,202.50
1982	2050	3.95	100	1,000.00	2,050,000.00
1983-86	9475	4.00	100	1,000.00	9,475,000.00
1987-90	11750	4.05	100	1,000.00	11,750,000.00
1991-93	10200	4.10	100	1,000.00	10,200,000.00
1994-96	11400	4.15	100	1,000.00	11,400,000.00
1997-98	8350	4.20	100	1,000.00	8,350,000.00
1999	4000	3.05	4.50	743.40	2,973,600.00
Maximum production at posted prices					$70,842,377.50

For the first eight maturities (1972-79), a 6% coupon rate was established, producing a gradually increasing yield (from 3.60% to 3.95%). The coupon rate for the 1980 maturity was set at 6%, but the yield was held to 3.95%. In 1981, a lower coupon rate was selected (4%), but the yield was still 3.95%. For the next seventeen maturities (1982-98), the yield was held at PAR, while the coupon rate was gradually increased from 3.95% to 4.20%. A coupon rate of 3.05% and a yield of 4.5% was established for the final maturity (1999). This forced the sale of the bonds at a substantial discount. The second lowest bidder use a combination of 6%, 5%, 3.90%, 4%, 4.10% 4.20% and 3% to come within $5,950 of the winning bid.

divided by the total number of "bond years," i.e., the sum of separate calculations for each of the years in which bonds mature.

Consider the following interest costs:

1 year on $100,000 @ 6.0%	$ 6,000
2 years on $100,000 @ 5.5%	$11,000
3 years on $100,000 @ 5.0%	$15,000
Total interest cost	$32,000
Add any discount	$ 1,500
Net interest cost	$33,500
Divided by accumulated bond years	600
NIC as percentage	5.583%

The NIC represents the average annual cost to the issuing jurisdiction to borrow the funds, expressed as a percent per year, without any allowance for the present value of the payments. No bond in the issue actually has a coupon rate of 5.583%, and none has a reoffering yield of 5.583%.

The calculations required to determine the NIC for the BART bond issue are illustrated by the data in Tables 9-4. The number of "bond years" represented by the 675 BART bonds (each with $1,000 face amount) issued in 1967 and maturing in 1972 can be determined by multiplying five (years to maturity) by 675 (bonds). This process is repeated for each of the years of maturity. The total number of bond years for the BART issue is 1,541,000. A total interest cost can be obtained by multiplying the coupon rate (interest rate) times the bond years for each maturity period and summing across all maturity periods. This figure for the BART bonds is $6,389,835. Since only a $8,125 premium was established for the BART bonds, the net interest cost can be calculated as follows:

$$\text{Net Interest Costs} = \frac{\text{Gross Interest Cost less Premium}}{\text{Total Bond Years}}$$

$$\text{NIC} = \frac{\$6{,}389{,}835 - \$8{,}125}{1{,}541{,}000} = 4.4128\%$$

The second method for calculating interest cost is the *true interest cost* (TIC). This method identifies the nominal annual interest rate, which when compounded semiannually, would yield the present value of the bond issue. The future cash flows of the issue are discounted to equal the bid amount for the issue. In financial analysis, this techniques is called the internal rate of return and is widely used in evaluating the desirability of a project. TIC is computed by a mathematical technique called successive approximations. A trial interest cost is selected, and the present value of the future flow of funds is computed. Based on the result, the interest cost is adjusted, and the present value is recomputed. This process is repeated until an answer is obtained that is close enough to the bid amount of the issue.

Computations of true interest costs were rarely undertaken before computers were widely used. In recent years, however, the percent of new issues awarded on the basis of TIC rather than NIC has increased, although both methods con-

Table 9-4
Calculation of Net Interest
Cost for $70 Million BART Bond Issue

Year Due	Amount Offered ($000)	Years to Maturity	Bond Years	Coupon Rate (%)	Total Interest Costs
1972	675	5	3,375	6.00	20,250
1973	800	6	4,800	6.00	28,800
1974	925	7	6,475	6.00	38,850
1975	1,050	8	8,400	6.00	50,400
1976	1,200	9	10,800	6.00	64,800
1977	1,325	10	13,250	6.00	79,500
1978	1,475	11	16,225	6.00	97,350
1979	1,625	12	19,500	6.00	117,000
1980	1,775	13	23,075	6.00	138,450
1981	1,825	14	25,550	4.00	102,200
1982	2,050	15	30,750	3.95	121,463
1983	2,100	16	33,600	4.00	134,400
1984	2,300	17	39,100	4.00	156,400
1985	2,400	18	43,200	4.00	172,800
1986	2,675	19	50,825	4.00	203,300
1987	2,500	20	50,000	4.05	202,500
1988	2,800	21	58,800	4.05	238,140
1989	3,000	22	66,000	4.05	267,300
1990	3,450	23	79,350	4.05	321,368
1991	3,250	24	78,000	4.10	319,800
1992	3,400	25	85,000	4.10	348,500
1993	3,550	26	92,300	4.10	378,430
1994	3,540	27	95,580	4.15	396,657
1995	3,720	28	104,160	4.15	432,264
1996	4,140	29	120,060	4.15	498,249
1997	4,025	30	120,750	4.20	507,150
1998	4,325	31	134,075	4.20	563,115
1999	4,000	32	128,000	3.05	390,400
Totals			1,541,000		6,389,835

tinue to be used. The TIC is considered to be the better measure by some analysts because it provides for the time value of payments by using present value calculations.

Using the data for the three-year bond issue for which the net interest cost was previously determined to be 5.583%, the TIC that most closely yields the present value of the bond issue—$300,000 minus $1,500 or $298,500—is 5.69%, as illustrated by the following calculations:

Year	Total Payment	Present Value Factor @ 5.69%	Present Value of Payment
0.5	$ 8,250	0.97271	$ 8,024.85
1.0	$108,250	0.94616	$ 102,422.18
1.5	$ 5,250	0.92034	$ 4,831.79
2.0	$105,250	0.89523	$ 94,222.96
2.5	$ 2,500	0.87079	$ 2,176.98
3.0	$102,500	0.84703	$ 86,820.58
Totals	$332,000		$ 298,499.34

Production

Underwriters of municipal bonds must be cognizant of the general money market and the desired investment yield of potential buyers over different maturities. Failure to take proper account of these factors will result in a smaller "spread" or gross profit for the underwriters.

The *production* of a given issue can be calculated by first multiplying the reoffering price (yield or par value) by the face amount of each maturity date. This figure is then multiplied by the amount being offered with a given maturity. These calculations are then summed for all maturity periods.

As shown in Table 9-3, the yield for BART bonds maturing in 1972 (i.e., five years after the issue) was 3.60%, times the face amount ($1,000) equals $1,108.90, which was the reoffering price per bond. In other words, an investor would have been expected to pay the underwriter $108.90 over the par value of $1,000 to secure a bond with a five-year maturity period. When multiplied by the amount being offered ($675,000), a production of $748,507.50 results. This amount represents what the underwriters expected to earn on the first segment of the bond issue. The funds provided to BART on these bonds was $675,000, and therefore the "spread" or anticipated gross profit for the underwriters was $748,507.50 minus $675,000 = $73,507.50.

The production of the $2,050,000 bonds issued with a 1982 maturity, on the other hand, was $2,050,000 since these bonds were issued at par. The $4 million issued with a 1999 maturity date were below par, with a reoffering price per bond of $743.30 and a production of only $2,973,500.

Carrying out all of the appropriate calculations on the BART issue results in a maximum production of $70,842,377.50. Since the par amount of the issue plus premium equaled $70,008,125 (i.e., the amount paid by the underwriters to the BART District), the amount available as "spread" or gross profit to the underwriters before expenses was calculated to be $834,252.50.

Tables 9-5 through 9-7 illustrate three bidding options that might be developed for a $9 million bond issue. Each of these options produces a net interest cost of 6%. However, different total debt service costs and "spreads" result from the mix of bonds in the proposed offerings.

The data in Table 9-7 can be used to illustrate the calculation of the net interest cost. The gross interest paid over the life of the bond is $4,318,800. Additional supplemental coupons (a negative premium) in the amount of $1,200 are required. The 6,000 bonds scheduled to mature in the year 15 have a duration of fifteen years and therefore represent 90,000 bond years (6,000 x 15); the bonds scheduled to mature in the year 14 have a duration of fourteen years and therefore represent 84,000 bond years (6,000 x 14), and so forth. The sum of the bond years is 720,000. The gross interest cost plus supplemental coupons equals $4,320,000 divided by 720,000 bond years equals 6.0% as the net interest cost.

The $750,000 in bonds shown in Table 9-5, scheduled to mature in year 4, carry a coupon rate of 6.4%. However, since these bonds are priced at a premium ($1,066.66), the yield to the investor is 6%. The production of these bonds (assuming that all are sold at the reoffering price) is 750 times $1,066.66 or $799,995. The total production anticipated for the bond issue of $9 million is $9,081,233. Therefore, the spread (underwriter's profit) would be $81,233.

The total debt service for the fifteen-year straight serial bond issue with a three-year deferred principal (Table 9-5) is $14,130,000. Table 9-6 shows a fifteen-year annuity serial bond with a three-year deferred principal. The total debt service is $14,501,919, and the spread is only $49,824. Table 9-7 illustrates a fifteen-year straight serial bond with no deferral of principal payments. The total debt service for this option is $13,318,800, and the spread is $199,994. However, additional supplemental coupons are required.

Yield Curves

As the stock market continued to struggle in recent years, many investors turned to bonds and other fixed-income alternatives to achieve predictable income, to protect capital, and to lower overall portfolio volatility. Since bonds have a finite maturity, it is easy to purchase them in maturities that offset long-term anticipated commitments, such as retirement or college expenses. If at all possible, investors should plan to hold long-term bonds until the stated maturity date, rather than buying them if they know that they will need access to cash in the near future. In this way, bondholders will receive the most benefit from their investment, i.e., the stated interest rate and return of their principal.

Expectations of an improving economy, however, usually spell trouble for bonds, since bond prices move in the opposite direction to yields. Increasing yields mean lower bond prices. Therefore, many investors today have become concerned about investing in bonds at current yields.

When interest rates rise, the prices of existing bonds generally fall. Conversely, when rates fall, bond prices generally rise. A ten-year bond, purchased

Table 9-5

Fifteen-Year Straight Serial Bond @ 6% Net Interest Cost
Three-Year Deferred Principal

Year	Amount	Maturity	Rate	Yield	Reoffering Price	Production	Bond Years	Gross Interest	Interest Payment	Principal Payments	Annual Debt Service
1									$544,875	0	$544,875
2									$544,875	0	$544,875
3									$544,875	0	$544,875
4	$750,000	2007	6.40%	6.0000%	1,066.66	799,995.00	30,000	$192,000	$544,875	$750,000	$1,294,875
5	$750,000	2008	6.30%	6.0000%	1,050.00	787,500.00	37,500	$236,250	$496,875	$750,000	$1,246,875
6	$750,000	2009	6.20%	6.0000%	1,033.33	774,997.50	45,000	$279,000	$449,625	$750,000	$1,199,625
7	$750,000	2010	6.10%	6.0000%	1,016.66	762,495.00	52,500	$320,250	$403,125	$750,000	$1,153,125
8	$750,000	2011	6.00%	6.0000%	1,000.00	750,000.00	60,000	$360,000	$357,375	$750,000	$1,107,375
9	$750,000	2012	6.00%	6.0000%	1,000.00	750,000.00	67,500	$405,000	$312,375	$750,000	$1,062,375
10	$750,000	2013	6.00%	6.0000%	1,000.00	750,000.00	75,000	$450,000	$267,375	$750,000	$1,017,375
11	$750,000	2014	6.00%	6.0000%	1,000.00	750,000.00	82,500	$495,000	$222,375	$750,000	$972,375
12	$750,000	2015	6.00%	6.0000%	1,000.00	750,000.00	90,000	$540,000	$177,375	$750,000	$927,375
13	$750,000	2016	5.95%	6.0000%	991.66	743,745.00	97,500	$580,125	$132,375	$750,000	$882,375
14	$750,000	2017	5.85%	6.0000%	975.00	731,250.00	105,000	$614,250	$87,750	$750,000	$837,750
15	$750,000	2018	5.85%	6.0000%	975.00	731,250.00	112,500	$658,125	$43,875	$750,000	$793,875
Totals	$9,000,000					$9,081,233	855,000	$5,130,000	$5,130,000	$9,000,000	$14,130,000
					Spread	$81,233					
						Net Interest Cost		6.0000%			

Table 9-6
Fifteen-Year Annuity Serial Bond @ 6% Net Interest Cost
Three-Year Deferred Principal

Year	Amount	Maturity	Rate	Yield	Reoffering Price	Production	Bond Years	Gross Interest	Interest Payment	Principal Payments	Annual Debt Service
1									$540,000	0	$540,000
2									$540,000	0	$540,000
3									$540,000	0	$540,000
4	$533,493	2007	6.35%	6.0000%	1,058.33	564,611.93	21,340	$135,507	$540,000	$533,493	$1,073,493
5	$565,503	2008	6.25%	6.0000%	1,041.67	589,067.36	28,275	$176,720	$507,990	$565,503	$1,073,493
6	$599,433	2009	6.15%	6.0000%	1,025.00	614,418.86	35,966	$221,191	$474,060	$599,433	$1,073,493
7	$635,399	2010	6.05%	6.0000%	1,008.33	640,691.89	44,478	$269,091	$438,094	$635,399	$1,073,493
8	$673,523	2011	6.00%	6.0000%	1,000.00	673,522.95	53,882	$323,291	$399,970	$673,523	$1,073,493
9	$713,934	2012	6.00%	6.0000%	1,000.00	713,934.33	64,254	$385,525	$359,559	$713,934	$1,073,493
10	$756,770	2013	6.00%	6.0000%	1,000.00	756,770.39	75,677	$454,062	$316,723	$756,770	$1,073,493
11	$802,177	2014	6.00%	6.0000%	1,000.00	802,176.62	88,239	$529,437	$271,317	$802,177	$1,073,493
12	$850,307	2015	6.00%	6.0000%	1,000.00	850,307.21	102,037	$612,221	$223,186	$850,307	$1,073,493
13	$901,326	2016	6.00%	6.0000%	999.67	901,028.21	117,172	$702,800	$172,168	$901,326	$1,073,493
14	$955,405	2017	5.95%	6.0000%	991.67	947,446.66	133,757	$795,853	$118,088	$955,405	$1,073,493
15	$1,012,729	2018	5.90%	6.0000%	983.33	995,847.29	151,909	$896,266	$60,764	$1,012,729	$1,073,493
Totals	$9,000,000					$9,049,824	916,987	$5,501,963	$5,501,919	$9,000,000	$14,501,919
					Spread	$49,824					
						Net Interest Cost		6.0000%			

Table 9-7
Fifteen-Year Straight Serial Bond @ 6% Net Interest Cost

Year	Amount	Maturity	Rate	Yield	Reoffering Price	Production	Bond Years	Gross Interest	Interest Payment	Principal Payments	Annual Debt Service
1	$600,000	2004	6.70%	6.3810%	1,050.00	630,000.00	6,000	$40,200	$553,200	$600,000	$1,153,200
2	$600,000	2005	6.60%	6.2857%	1,050.00	630,000.00	12,000	$79,200	$513,000	$600,000	$1,113,000
3	$600,000	2006	6.50%	6.1905%	1,050.00	630,000.00	18,000	$117,000	$473,400	$600,000	$1,073,400
4	$600,000	2007	6.40%	6.0952%	1,050.00	630,000.00	24,000	$153,600	$434,400	$600,000	$1,034,400
5	$600,000	2008	6.30%	6.0000%	1,050.00	630,000.00	30,000	$189,000	$396,000	$600,000	$996,000
6	$600,000	2009	6.20%	6.0000%	1,033.33	619,998.00	36,000	$223,200	$358,200	$600,000	$958,200
7	$600,000	2010	6.10%	6.0000%	1,016.66	609,996.00	42,000	$256,200	$321,000	$600,000	$921,000
8	$600,000	2011	6.00%	6.0000%	1,000.00	600,000.00	48,000	$288,000	$284,400	$600,000	$884,400
9	$600,000	2012	6.00%	6.0000%	1,000.00	600,000.00	54,000	$324,000	$248,400	$600,000	$848,400
10	$600,000	2013	6.00%	6.0000%	1,000.00	600,000.00	60,000	$360,000	$212,400	$600,000	$812,400
11	$600,000	2014	6.00%	6.0000%	1,000.00	600,000.00	66,000	$396,000	$176,400	$600,000	$776,400
12	$600,000	2015	6.00%	6.0000%	1,000.00	600,000.00	72,000	$432,000	$140,400	$600,000	$740,400
13	$600,000	2016	5.90%	6.0000%	983.33	589,998.00	78,000	$460,200	$104,400	$600,000	$704,400
14	$600,000	2017	5.80%	6.0000%	966.67	580,002.00	84,000	$487,200	$69,000	$600,000	$669,000
15	$600,000	2018	5.70%	6.0000%	950.00	570,000.00	90,000	$513,000	$34,200	$600,000	$634,200
Totals	$9,000,000					$9,119,994	720,000	$4,318,800	$4,318,800	$9,000,000	$13,318,800
					Spread	$119,994					
					Supplemental Coupons			$1,200			
					Net Interest Cost			6.0000%			

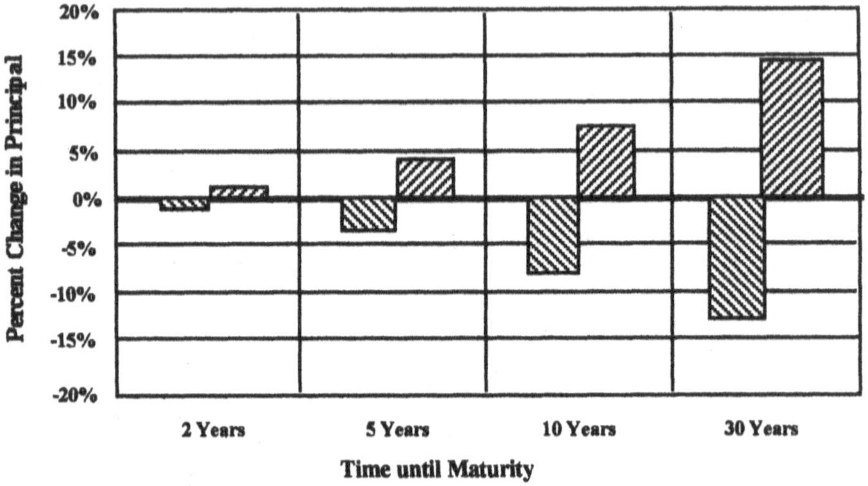

Figure 9-1 Impact on Bond Prices of a 1% Increase or Decrease in Interest Rates

The above chart is for illustrative purposes only and is not indicative of any individual bond's performance. The exact amount of gain or loss will depend on the bond's maturity, the level of current interest rates, and the speed with which interest rates change. Credit quality may also be a factor when dealing with corporate bonds.

for $1,000 and paying 6% interest, will yield $60 annually. Assume that six months later, new bonds are paying 7%. The 6% bond is now worth less, because $1,000 will now buy a bond that yields $70 annually. The price of the 6% bond now falls to where its yield to maturity equals the going interest rate of 7%—somewhere around $931.

This inverse relationship between yield and price increases with time, as illustrated by the hypothetical example in Figure 9-1. How a bond is affected if the yield required by the market is adjusted up or down by one percentage point depends heavily on its maturity. For example, the same 6% coupon bond with five years to maturity would sell off for considerably less than a 6% coupon bond with ten years until maturity. In other words, the longer a bond has to maturity, the more sensitive its price.

Yield curves provide a useful tool that many experts use to observe and predict changes in interest rates. They provide underwriters, traders, and investors a basis by which to compare the returns on bonds of equal quality but with different maturities. A yield curve provides a snapshot of interest rates for a cross-section of bonds with similar credit characteristics but varying maturities. By plotting bond yield as a function of years to maturity and indicating the average rate of return on a bond if held to maturity, the yield curve illustrates what is referred to as the term structure of interest rates.[11] The typical yield curve is positively sloped, indicating that yield is an increasing function of maturity;

that is, the longer the duration of a bond, the higher the expected yield. Yield curves might also be negatively sloped or flat.

A normal or positively sloped curve occurs when short-term rates are relatively low and interest rates increase with maturities. This type of curve usually reflects the assumption that the market is expecting higher rates in the future.

A declining, negatively sloped or "inverted" curve is the special circumstance where short-term rates are actually higher than longer-term rates. This type of curve usually reflects the assumption that short-term rates will be lower in the future.

Finally, the curve can be flat, meaning that rates are the same regardless of the maturity. Obviously, this condition is not likely to persist for very long, as investors will usually shift their investments to shorter maturities since there is no advantage to accepting longer terms.

Another common word used to describe a yield curve is its "steepness," which indicates how fast rates are expected to rise as the time to maturity increases. Since bonds with longer maturities are more volatile, this criterion can help investors find risk and reward values in the curve without exposure to longer-term bonds.

For example, as of December 2002, Treasury bonds with a ten-year maturity carried a 4.22% rate, while Treasury bonds with a thirty-year maturity carried a 5.04% rate. Therefore, nearly 84% of the yield from the thirty-year bond could be achieved in a bond with the same credit characteristics, yet twenty years shorter in maturity. Furthermore, a five-year bond as of December 2002 was yielding 3.30%, which is 78% of the yield of a ten-year bond. In other words, an investment of $10,000 in a five-year bond at 3.30% would yield an annual return of $330 or a five-year return of $1,650. The same investment in a ten-year bond would yield $2,110 over five years. An investment of $10,000 in a thirty-year bond would yield $2,520. The yield on the five-year bond is 78.2% of the yield on the ten-year bond, while the yield on the ten-year bond is 83.7% of the yield on the thirty-year bond.

Why would an investor accept a lesser yield in the short-term if high-yield investments were available? If the expectation is that interest rates are on the rise, then an investor might want to hold open the option of rolling over the investment at the end of five years into a security with a higher yield. On the other hand, if the expectation is that interest rates are likely to decline, the investor might want to lock-in to the higher available rate with the longer maturity. As the steepness of the curve increases or decreases, different points on the curve can be determined that offer relative value without increasing exposure to interest rate risk.

Three theories describe the shape of the yield curve and the predominance of the upward-sloping yield curve.

1. The *expectation hypothesis* states that expectations of future inflation influence the shape of the yield curve. If investors expect inflation to rise in the future, they will require higher interest rates on bonds that extend more years into the future. This requirement accounts for the positive slope of the curve.

2. The *liquidity preference theory* holds that investors are willing to accept lower rates for shorter-term maturities because they perceive them to be less risky than long-term issues (i.e., short-term maturities are "closer to cash"). Borrowers are willing to finance long-term debt at higher rates so they can lock in financing for longer periods, avoiding the risks associated with rolling over debt at unknown future rates to obtain further financing.
3. The *market segmentation theory* suggests that different markets exist for maturities of different lengths. Thus, the positive yield curve would be explained by different equilibriums for each segment of the market. The *preferred habitat theory* is a variation of market segmentation. It holds that investors prefer certain maturities but can be induced to switch if premiums are different.[12]

Unfortunately, none of these theories explains completely the shape of the yield curve or is a reliable predictor of future interest rates. They do contribute useful insights into the market's behavior, however.

Yield curve analysis extends well beyond these theoretical constructs. Professional traders and portfolio managers must understand in considerable detail the complex relationships among price, yield, liquidity, and risk in order to "ride the yield curve," that is, to buy and sell debt securities to obtain the greatest total return on investment.

Submitting Syndicate Bids

Deadlines in municipal bond sales are very strictly observed. On the date of the sale, officials of the issuing jurisdiction usually meet in a body at the stipulated time to receive the competitive bids. The final reoffering scale for a syndicate's bid often is calculated only minutes before the submission deadline, and the bid is phoned to the person who is to deliver it to the issuing jurisdiction. It is customary to require a *good faith check* from each bidder, ranging in amount from 1% to 5% of the par value of the bonds being sold. These checks are held by the issuing jurisdiction until the decision is made on the award. This good faith payment is used to liquidate damages in the rare case when a successful bidder does not take up and pay for the bonds on the prescribed settlement date.

It is customary to receive sealed bids at the vast majority of competitive bond sales. On occasion, a municipality might request auction bids in the hopes of getting a better price due to the on-the-spot competition among the various bidders.

If all bids are on the basis of one coupon rate for the entire issue, the bidder naming the lowest rate receives the award. If the bid entails more than one rate of interest, the award is determined by the lowest average cost (net interest cost). If more than one bidder names the same rate, then whoever bids the highest premium and lowest rate gets the award. Bids on major issues might be quite close among the bidding syndicates. For example, on the $70 million bond issue shown in Table 9-3, the second lowest bidder, using a different combination of coupon rates, came within $5,950 of the winning bid.

For the winning bidder, the next step is to reoffer the bonds, usually at the scale decided upon prior to bidding. Orders are awarded according to the priority stated in the syndicate letter. Since the winning bidder does not actually own the bonds until the issuer has awarded them, all orders are contingent on the actual delivery of the bonds. The *offering date* is the date on which the bonds are sold to the public, and for competitive offerings, this is also the date of the sale. However, if the bonds are to have certificates, they must be printed, arrangements must be made with the Depository Trust Company, and legal work must be completed before the bonds can be delivered. This usually takes about one month—until then the bonds are sold and traded on a *when, as, and if issued* basis. Interest accrues to the seller from the date of sale and up to, but not including, the settlement date.

Investment Banker's Profits

During the week that the BART bonds were first offered, a total of almost $400 million in municipal bonds were listed in The Bond Buyer's Calendar of Sealed Bid Openings, representing sixty-four issues, three-quarters of which had face values of less than $5 million. With this volume of sales in a typical week, the layman often assumes that investment bankers dealing in municipal bonds make tremendous profits. People often are surprised, therefore, by the relative small margin of profit sought by investment bankers.

As a rule, underwriters do not charge a commission when they sell municipal bonds, since they are acting as principals rather than agents. The profit of an investment banker is the *spread*—the difference between the price the underwriter pays the issuer for the bonds and the price the underwriter receives from the resale of those bonds to investors. The amount of the spread depends on a variety of factors, but it is primarily based on the size of the issuance and market conditions at the time of the sale. The spread can be calculated in terms of basis points or "dollars per bond." One percent of the bond issuance equals 100 basis points. In general, the expected profit on a $1,000 bond will vary from around $2.50 to $20 (0.25 to 2.0% of face value). In some cases where the market drops significantly while bonds are being offered, the underwriter might sell the bonds for substantially less than the price paid for them, suffering a loss.

The spread is made up of four separate components:[13]

1. The management fee compensates the underwriters for their efforts in creating and implementing the financing package. The amount of the management fee depends on the complexity of the issuance. The lead underwriter usually splits the management fee with the other lead or comanagers, usually two or three other underwriters, but not with the entire syndicate.
2. The underwriting fee, also known as the risk component of the spread, is designed to compensate the underwriter for the risk incurred by buying the entire issuance before it has received orders from investors for all the bonds. The fee is provided to protect the underwriter in case the market shifts dramatically and interest rates increase before the underwriter has sold all of the bonds.

3. The *takedown* is usually the largest part of the underwriter's spread. It represents the discount at which the members of the syndicate buy or "take down" bonds from the overall underwriting account. The amount of the takedown depends on how difficult the bond issuance is to sell to investors. Easily marketable issues have minimal takedowns, while hard to sell bonds require a larger takedown in order to attract underwriters.
4. The issuer must also reimburse the underwriter for expenses incurred during the development of the financing package and the actual sale of the bonds. These expenses represent the physical costs of running the syndicate, including travel, printing costs, and the underwriter's legal fees.

The takedown is a subset of the overall underwriter's spread. For example, the spread might be 100 basis points, or $10 for each $1,000 of bonds issued. For each $1,000 bond, the underwriter pays $990 to the issuer of the bonds. If the takedown is 50 basis points ($5), each syndicate member buys its bonds at $995 ($1,000 - $5, or the face value minus the takedown), and then offers the bonds to the public at par, or $1,000. The takedown represents the profit to the underwriter who actually sold the bonds. Any net profit over and above the takedown goes into the account and is divided among the various members at the termination of the account according to a predetermined agreement.

The underwriting of municipal bonds reached record levels in the early 1990s. Low interest rates during this period motivated local governments to refinance their bonds just as homeowners were doing with their mortgages. This was a time to borrow for any municipality needing new money. According to the Securities Data Corporation, more than $231 billion worth of municipal bonds were issues in 1992. This record lasted only until 1993, when $289 billion in municipal bonds were issued. The profit on these issues averaged $11 per $1,000. By 1995, however, the level of new issues dropped by more than 45% to $155 billion as interest rates on municipal bonds rose significantly, dampening the drive to refinance. The average profit for an underwriting firm is now around $8 per $1,000.

Outside dealers or underwriters who are not members of the syndicate might have clients who want to purchase bonds from the bond issue. The nonmember will buy the bonds from the syndicate for its customer. The nonmember's profit is known as the *dealer's* or *selling concession* and is taken out of the underwriter's takedown. For example, if the takedown is 50 basis points (or $5), and the selling concession is 25 basis points, the member of the syndicate makes 25 basis points (or $2.50) and the nonmember also makes 25 basis points (or $2.50).

Accrued Interest

Bonds are sold on a "plus accrued interest" basis from the date of the issue or from the last interest payment date if one has passed. The purchaser is only entitled to interest from the time the bond is purchased. The previous owner is entitled to interest up to the time this payment is received. In the case of a municipality selling an issue, the bonds might be dated September 1, and the purchaser might receive delivery and make payment on October 1. The underwriters pay the municipality the accrued interest for the one month after the date of the issue. The underwriters, in turn, collect the accrued interest from the parties to whom they sell the bonds. The investor will receive the full amount of the interest payment on the date it becomes due.

To illustrate this process, assume that a municipality issues $1 million in bonds on July 1, carrying a 6% interest rate paid semiannually. The bonds are delivered to the underwriters on August 1, and the underwriters provide the municipality with $1 million plus the accrued interest on the bonds of $5,000 ($1 million times 6% divided by 12 months). The underwriters have commitments for half of the $1 million issue and receive from the investors $500,000 plus the accrued interest of $2,500. The balance of the issue is sold on September 1. The underwriters receive $500,000 from the investors plus the accrued interest of $5,000 ($500,000 times 6% divided by 12 times 2). On January 1, the investors receive their first semiannual interest payment from the issuer, totaling $30,000. The $5,000 in accrued interest that was received from the underwriters is include in this initial interest payment; therefore, the municipality has to draw an additional $25,000 from its debt service fund. The first set of investors receives $15,000 in interest, but since they had to pay the underwriters $2,500 in accrued interest, they net $12,500. The second set of investors also receives $15,000 in interest, but since they had to pay the underwriters $5,000 in accrued interest, they net $10,000. Note that the underwriters received $7,500 in accrued interest but only paid the municipality $5,000. The difference of $2,500 can be considered the underwriter's compensation for holding $500,000 in bonds during the month of August.

Bond Sale and Delivery

Competitive bids should be made on a basis that permits a comparison of the total cost to the issuing jurisdiction. Officials should insist that all bids comply strictly with the terms of the sale as set forth in the official notice. All competitive bids should be received and opened in public by the governing body at the designated hour, with the bonds awarded to the bidder on the basis of the lowest net interest cost. All of the paperwork that is required to complete the bond transcript should be forwarded to the bond attorneys as soon as possible.

Legal Opinion

A recognized bond attorney must provide a legal opinion that the bonds have been issued in accordance with appropriate statutes and ordinances and represent valid and binding obligations of the issuer. The legal opinion makes the bonds salable. In the past, the legal opinion was issued as a separate document. However, beginning in the 1960s, issuers began to have the opinion printed on the actual bond certificate, thus saving paper and increasing convenience.

The legal opinion also indicates if the bonds are exempt from federal income taxation and if they are also exempt from state taxes. It is also implies that the bond counsel has exercised due diligence, that no errors of commission or omission have been committed in the issuance of the bonds, and that full disclosure has been made to the prospective investors, so far as the lawyers can determine.

The Bond Register

Before the bonds are delivered to the buyer, information required to establish the bond register (sometimes called the bond and interest record) should be recorded. At the time a bond issue is sold, the interest due on each date of maturity should be computed and recorded, as should the payments of principal or payments into a sinking fund. With such records, a complete schedule of debt service requirements can be readily prepared for the current budget and for all outstanding debt obligations.

The bonds should be registered and delivered at the earliest practical date after the sale (no later than thirty days). The winning bidder usually has the option to cancel the obligation if delivery is not made on or before the date specified in the contract. The purchaser should stipulate where the bonds should be delivered.

Termination of a Syndicate Account

When the winning bid has been determined (or a negotiated sale has been agreed upon), the senior manager of the syndicate sends out a letter to the syndicate members describing the reoffering terms, which include the spread, takedown price, and selling concessions. When the bonds are ready to be delivered, all payments are settled. In order to pay the issuer, the senior manager arranges for a loan from either a commercial bank outside of the syndicate or a member of the syndicate that is also a bank.

The secured loan is used to pay the issuer. The bonds are then distributed to the members, who fill their orders and send the payments to the senior manager. Once the manager has received all the payments from the syndicate members, the loan is retired, and the profits are distributed among the members of the syndicate. The last step for the senior manager is to issue a final statement of participants, expenses, and profits.[14]

The syndicate that bid successfully on the BART bonds was composed of 106 underwriters. On the first day following the award of the issue, about $30 million of the $70 million bonds were sold. Another $3.7 million were sold on the second day, leaving $36.9 million in the account for subsequent disposal. The syndicate was terminated after twenty-one days of posting at the original prices, during which time other issues were being sold with relatively higher and more attractive yields. The bonds remaining unsold were distributed to the members of the syndicate in proportion to their share of the underwriting liability. With the syndicate restrictions removed, individual underwriters were free to offer their share of the remaining bonds at below list (and perhaps below cost) prices.

During the first few days of the free market, dealers and brokers engaged in a flurry of transactions to clear the market. Some of the syndicate members took losses, while other dealers (including some members of the former syndicate) stockpiled blocks of bonds at the lower price level. Moreover, various investors seeking a bargain entered the market at this point and were rewarded for having foregone the opportunity to buy on the first day of sale at the posted price level. Within a few months, most of the bonds ended up in institutional or bank portfolios, although BART bonds continued to be offered on the secondary market for many years after the original sale.

Municipal Bond Secondary Market

Like other securities, municipal bonds often are disposed of before they mature. Heirs sell, institutions develop different tax-exempt needs, commercial banks experience cyclical increases or decreases in deposits, syndicates break up and divide the unsold bonds among their members, and so on. Whatever the reasons, bonds return to the market to be offered to the investing public for a second time—hence the term *secondary market*. The volume of transactions in the secondary market, in terms of par value of bonds traded, far exceeds that of the "new issue" market. Daily volume of secondary offerings, as shown in *The Blue List*, together with estimated unadvertised blocks, would suggest a twenty to one annual ratio of secondary to primary market transactions.

The secondary market consists of (1) auction markets and (2) over-the-counter or negotiated trade markets. Municipal bonds are most often traded in over-the-counter markets, in which any individual might establish an account or might arrange for a recognized dealer to act as an agent. Over-the-counter trading markets encompasses generally all types of securities, including United States government bonds, foreign bonds, corporate bonds, railroad stocks, common and preferred stocks, script, rights, warrants, and municipal bonds. Auction markets generally are reserved for securities listed on the national exchanges.

Unlike its corporate counterpart, the secondary market for municipal bonds is not a formal market—there are no regular trading hours and no public listings of sale offerings. The brokering does not occur at a formal institution, such as the New York Stock Exchange. The municipal bond secondary market provides individual and institutional investors a mechanism through which to buy and sell municipal bond holdings prior to the bonds' maturity dates. Thus, investors have an easy and quick way to manage investments and regulate cash flow to suit their specific needs.

Three types of dealers operate in the secondary market:

1. Securities dealers generally comprise a department within a large full-service securities firm that handles the accounts of both individual and institutional investors, as well as other dealers. Securities dealers in large firms might handle specific areas of the municipal bond market (e.g., short-term notes or public utility bonds) and are able to consolidate like orders and strategically buy (or sell) municipal bonds as the market dictates.
2. Dealer banks (trading departments within commercial banks) can trade in general obligation bonds in which they have no direct connection. To en-

sure there is no conflict of interest, dealer banks are prohibited from executing transactions for investors (individual or institutional trusts) whose accounts they supervise.

3. Dealers' brokers trade only with other dealers or brokers and never with individual or institutional investors. Brokers are employed when dealers think they can achieve more efficient trading through a third party. The greatest strengths of brokers are their access to segments of the market, continuous communication with dealers, and their guarantee of anonymity with respect to dealer identity and trading.

Secondary trading is very competitive with spreads ranging from one-fourth of a point ($2.50 per bond) to two points ($20) in the case of obscure issues or odd lots. The average dealer's spread is $10 per $1,000 bond. The most common type of business of a dealers' broker is a *bid-wanted transaction*, where securities dealers or dealer banks ask brokers to place on the market and take bids on bonds that the dealers want to sell to other dealers. Brokers also may handle *bond-wanted transactions*—that is, a broker is contracted to seek a particular bond or bond type desired by a dealer. Brokers might oversee the sale of municipal bonds for a set price to a particular segment of the market, as designated by the selling dealer. Equally important, once a syndicate has been dissolved, an underwriter might contract with a broker to sell the remaining bonds that were not sold by the syndicate.

Having access to up-to-date information is critical to a dealer's ability to trade effectively and efficiently. *The Blue List*, updated daily by Standard and Poor's, is a 100-page compilation of securities, along with their yields, offered for trade by dealers. Dealers who subscribe to the service also can have computer access to this information through the *Blue List Ticker*, which records up-to-the-minute additions and deletions of bond offerings. Municipal dealer *offering sheets* are weekly inventories of bond holdings that individual dealers are offering for sale and include the names of investors, the type of bond, and its yield or sale price. Dealers rely heavily on the *Daily Bond Buyer*, which also provides a wire service—*Munifacts*—that lists daily offerings and bond yields. Wire services, such as the Kenny Wire and the C-Wire, offer over 600 bond dealers up-to-the-minute data on bond sales and purchases.

Two measures are especially watched as indicators of where the bond market is headed. The placement ratio shows the proportion of all bonds (competitive and negotiated) over $1 million that were distributed during the week. The thirty-day visible-supply volume shows all securities scheduled to be offered within a thirty-day calendar period. The *Bond Buyer* publishes three yield indexes on a weekly basis:

- 20-Bond Index reflects the yield on a general obligation bond with a twenty-year maturity. This index is derived from bonds of twenty actual issuers with an average bond rating about halfway between Moody's top four rating categories.
- 11-Bond Index is based on eleven of the twenty issuers in the 20-Bond Index that have an average rating of Aa from Moody's.
- Revenue Bond Index reflects the yield on a thirty-year revenue bond based on bonds from twenty-five issuers covering a variety of purposes.

These indexes help dealers anticipate market trends, spot upcoming demand or supply of specific bonds, as well as know how much risk is involved in trading particular bonds at given yields.

Uniform Practices for Municipal Bond Trading

The Municipal Securities Rulemaking Board (MSRB) is an independent oversight agency established by the Securities Act of 1975. The MSRB regulates the practices of municipal securities dealers, dealer banks, and brokerage firms. As part of its oversight responsibilities, the MSRB instituted rules G-12 and G-15 to codify uniform industry standards for good trading practices.

- Rule G-12 lays out practices regarding dealer transactions, including settlement dates (dates on which payment for bonds and the bonds themselves must be delivered), confirmation of transactions between dealers, reclamation or rejection of bonds already traded by dealers. It also provides rules for finalizing an order that has been confirmed but not completed.
- Rule G-15 requires a verification of a customer's confirmation of transaction. In addition, the MSRB must be supplied with the names and addresses of the customer and dealer, information on whether the transaction was a purchase or a sale, the type of bond traded, its call date and interest rate, the date and time of transaction and settlement, its yield to maturity, and the final price.

In October 1994, the Securities and Exchange Commission (SEC), which oversees the MSRB, released new rules mandating public disclosure in the secondary market. Thousands of cities and public agencies are now required to release an annual financial statement updating information provided in the issuer's official statement. They must also provide information on events that could have an impact on the value of outstanding bonds, such as the loss of a major employer or the closing of a military base. This information is sent to the MSRB and national databanks, which dealers and investors can access. The SEC established these disclosure rules to curtail price gouging by bond dealers, making them more responsible to investors for quoting accurate, up-to-the-minute prices as they resell bonds in the secondary market. When taken together, these rules strive to ensure a fair trading atmosphere for dealers and investors.

Municipal Bond Investors

Most municipal bonds are purchased by four categories of investors: (1) mutual funds, (2) commercial banks, (3) property and casualty insurance companies, and (4) individual investors. The market shares of these investors have shifted over the last few decades due to economic events and changing federal legislation. Commercial banks dominated the market for municipal bond buyers in the 1960s and 1970s. However, banks were superseded in the 1980s and 1990s by individual investors and mutual funds.

Individual Investors

Historically, sales to individual investors have been greatest when interest rates reach their cyclical peak. Thus, the participation of this segment of the bond market has fluctuated widely. Inflation during the 1970s pushed significant portions of the population into higher tax brackets, and the demand for tax-free bonds grew accordingly.[15]

Steep reductions in the 1980s in the marginal tax rates for individual investors in the top bracket reduced the value of tax-exempt securities relative to taxable issues. During the same period, however, mutual funds absorbed an increasingly larger share of the market.[16] While most tax-free debt is held by relatively wealthy, high-income households, a significant share also is held by middle-income households.[17]

The Tax Reform Act of 1986 had a profound impact on the municipal bond market. The elimination of many long-standing loopholes left municipal bonds as the last significant remaining tax shelter. The Act also removed or restricted the tax exemption on many private purpose bonds, the proceeds of which are used primarily to benefit private interests. As a result, the overall supply of tax-free bonds was reduced. Other provisions of the Act, however, made municipal bonds less attractive to banks and insurance companies.[18] By 1994, mutual funds, bank personal trusts, and money market funds held 38.9% of the municipal bonds; individual investors held 35.5%; property and casualty insurance companies held 12%; and commercial banks held only 8.2%.[19] According to the Federal Reserve, individual investors owned $577 billion of the $1.7 trillion invested in municipal bonds in 2002, or 33.94%.

Tax-Exempt Bond Funds

The return on investments in bonds has two components: the income from interest payments and any changes that might occur in the market price of the bonds. As interest rates rise, the market price for existing, lower-yield bonds declines. If the bondholder decides to sell these bonds before they reach maturity, the selling price is likely to be below par. Conversely, if interest rates decline, the same bonds increase in value.

Assume that the current interest rate on a $1,000 bond is 5%, resulting in an annual yield of $50 in interest earnings. If the prevailing interest rate on comparable investments rise to 6%, then the $1,000 bond is only worth about $833— the sum that a buyer would have to invest at 6% to earn $50. On the other hand, if newly issued bonds pay only 4%, the $1,000 bond with a 5% coupon rate is more valuable, since it would take an investment of $1,250 at 4% to earn $50.

In general, the longer a bond's maturity, the greater effect these interest rate changes will have on a bond's price. Short-term bonds are much less affected by interest rate changes. If, for example, interest rates rise by 2%, bonds with a five-year maturity lose about 10% of their value. However, bonds with a fifteen-year maturity lose about 30% of their value.

Bond mutual funds offer investors a way to own a diversified portfolio of bonds. They allow investors to diversify risks across a broad range of issues that are professionally selected and managed. They also provide other conveniences such as having interest payments either reinvested or distributed periodically.

Tax-exempt bond funds were first established in 1961 and have grown rapidly in terms of investment popularity. These mutual funds are maintained by registered investment companies, the assets of which are invested in a diversified portfolio of bonds that are exempt from federal, state, and, in some cases, local income tax. Each fund is a closed-end trust created under the terms of a trust indenture by an investment-banking firm that acts as sponsor. The fund manager invests the assets of the fund according to a stated set of objectives. Selected securities are deposited with a trustee bank (or trust company). In return, certificates, or units, are provided to the sponsor, each certificate representing a fractional, undivided interest in the principal and net income of the trust. These certificates are then distributed to individual investors, either by the sponsors or by a group of investment firms forming an underwriting syndicate.

These funds have the objective of providing tax-free income consistent with preservation of capital and diversification of risk. Private investors, rather than institutional investors, have substantially purchased all fund units. Some funds include in their portfolios only bonds issued within a particular state, thereby gaining exemption from state income taxes as well as federal income taxes.

Shares in the fund are issued and redeemed on demand at a specific net asset value that is determined at the end of each trading day (based on the total market value of the fund's holdings). There is no fixed number of shares. If additional investors want to buy into the fund, additional shares can be issued. Many mutual funds carry no sales load (i.e., they do not charge a commission on the sale).

Most mutual funds hold a mix of bonds of varying maturities and rates to smooth out the ups and downs. These funds might also purchase municipal bonds that represent lease obligations. These investments carry special risks because the issuer of the bonds might not be obligated to appropriate money annually to make payments under the lease. The funds might also invest in inverse floating rate securities, often referred to as "inverse floaters."[20] They also hold complicated derivatives, which are securities based on parts of a bond, such as principal payment or interest. These derivatives have complex rules and often move differently in price from the actual bond. Under normal market conditions, these funds might invest up to 20% of net assets in short-term investments, such as short-term, high-quality municipal bonds or tax-exempt money market funds.

As the prices of bonds in a mutual fund decline, the fund shareholders experience a loss of principal. Unlike individual bonds, which have a defined maturity period and rate of interest, bond funds have neither fixed rates nor a maturity date. The portfolio is always changing, and thus the investor cannot be assured that any loss of principal might subsequently be recovered.

Each fund buys and sells portfolio securities in the normal course of its investment activities. A fund's portfolio turnover rate is the proportion of the fund's investments that is sold and replaced with new securities during the year.

The funds seek to keep portfolio turnover relatively low in order to reduce trading costs and the realization of taxable capital gains. However, funds might make short-term trades to take advantage of market opportunities or to reduce market risk.

Unit investment trusts (UIT) involve a relatively fixed portfolio of investments held until the trust is liquidated at a predetermined date in the future. Investors who want to trade shares of a UIT before it matures can often do so on the secondary market. Unlike a mutual fund, UIT shares in the secondary market might be priced above or below the net asset value of the trust's actual holdings. When buying shares of UITs, an investor typically pays a sales fee, or load, of around 4% or 5%.

As tax-exempt bond mutual funds have increasingly become an investment option for individuals (especially those on fixed incomes) in search of higher yields and security of principal, they have attracted millions of savers away from commercial banks. Tax-free bond funds also were a major beneficiary of cash that fled equity mutual funds seeking a safe haven. While equity funds were experiencing record outflows in 2002, the inflow to tax-free bond funds surged 61% in the first seven months of 2002 to $11.44 billion, far exceeding the $7.08 billion invested during the same period of 2001. Total assets of municipal bond funds increased to $317.4 billion in July 2002.

Officials in the investment industry are concerned about the safety of such investments because many investors might not understand how bond funds operate. Standard & Poor's has introduced new ratings that will attempt to account for changes in interest rates, the value of the dollar, and other factors that might adversely affect the prices of bonds and the mutual funds that buy them. The new rating system is designed to alert investors to the possible volatility of a mutual bond fund. A limited number of bond funds are currently rated by Standard & Poor's in terms of their credit risk—that is, as to whether the bonds in the fund are safe and will produce the expected yields. The new system adds an alphabetical, lower-case rating to cover the market risk of the bond portfolio held by the fund.

Bond Ladder Investing

A bond ladder portfolio is designed to meet the needs of conservative investors who hold their securities to maturity. As opposed to a money market account or bond mutual fund, a bond ladder can offer higher yields, diversification, and liquidity as bonds mature. This strategy often is used by investors seeking the greater income yields of securities with longer maturities without the market risks of a portfolio comprised entirely of long-term bonds. By investing in several securities with staggered maturities, this strategy serves to safely increase yields, soften the impact of interest rate swings, reduce the exposure of principal, and steady equity holdings.

A bond ladder works by spreading investment dollars among bonds and other fixed-income instruments that mature at various times, often between one and thirty years from the time the ladder is built (see Table 9-8). An income

Table 9-8
Sample Bond Ladder

Issuer	Quantity	Coupon	Maturity	Freq.	Price	YTM	Total
Federal National Mortgage Association	$100,000	0.000%	12/28/04	2	$97.705	3.809%	$97,705
Westernbank CD	$50,000	4.450%	5/16/05	1	$100.000	4.450%	$50,000
Arkansas National Bank CD	$50,000	4.700%	1/11/06	12	$100.000	4.700%	$50,026
General Motors Acceptance Corporation	$50,000	4.850%	5/15/06	4	$100.000	4.850%	$50,000
Household Finance Corporation	$50,000	5.250%	5/15/07	2	$100.000	5.250%	$50,000
Federal Home Loan Mortgage*	$100,000	5.000%	11/24/07	2	$100.000	4.938%	$100,000
Caterpiller Financial Services	$100,000	5.250%	5/15/08	4	$100.000	5.250%	$100,000
Total Bonds	**$500,000**	**Average**	**10/7/06**		**Average**	**4.724%**	**$497,731**

* Federal Home Loan bonds called on 8/24/2005 and redeemed at $100.00

portfolio is created in which each group of bonds represents a rung on the investment ladder. In a normal interest-rate environment, shorter maturities will yield less than longer maturities. As each individual bond (rung) matures, the principal becomes available for reinvestment at the then current interest rates. The value of a ladder is the ability to reinvest the principal from the maturing bond into a longer-term bond with a higher yield. As shorter-term investments mature, the principal is invested at the ladder's long end. After a few years, the ladder portfolio might be largely comprised of longer-term securities, typically purchased at higher yields.

The income schedule for the first twelve months and the principal schedule associated with the sample bond ladder in Table 9-9 are as follows:

Income Schedule	
June	$196
July	$196
August	$2,115
September	$196
October	$196
November	$5,927
December	$196
January	$196
February	$2,115
March	$196
April	$196
May	$8,152
Annual	$19,877

Principal Schedule	
2004	$100,000
2005	$ 50,000
2006	$100,000
2007	$ 50,000
2007	$100,000
2008	$100,000
Total	$500,000

Ladder portfolios are very flexible so that they can be structured to meet the unique needs of the individual investor. Ladders typically are built using a variety of fixed-income securities. The ladder might include tax-exempt municipal bonds (especially zero coupon bonds that offer a discounted price and compounded interest), U.S. Treasury and government agency securities, corporate bonds, Ginnie Mae pass-through securities, collateralized mortgage obligations (CMOs), preferred stock or fixed-rate capital securities, and longer-term certificates of deposit.

With a ladder portfolio, principal payments come due every year or so to take advantage of improved interest rates. If interest rates fall, prior ladder holdings have locked up higher yields for longer periods. If interest rates remain the same, the longer-term yields should provide a return greater than if the investment were limited to short-term securities. If interest rates go up, the current market value of the fixed-income portfolio will fall. However, as each rung of the ladder matures, money is available to invest at the higher rates. The net result is a "smoothed" yield with less fluctuation in income because the ladder takes advantage of the effects of dollar cost averaging.

The predictability of income flow that this strategy can offer attracts local governments, foundations, endowments, and other tax-exempt income investors.

Bond ladders often are used by individuals who have received a lump sum, such as from an inheritance, an insurance settlement, the sale of a business, or the maturity of a large bond or CD. Individual investors who might need large amounts of money available on certain future dates to pay for such expenses as a child's education or retirement are also major participants. Ladder portfolios are appropriate for retirement assets, as well as investors who self-direct their retirement accounts, IRAs, Simplified Employee Pension (SEP) plans, Keogh plans, and those who manage retirement fund assets for others.

Investors' Risk

Risk is inherent in all forms of investing. Investing in municipal bonds includes the risk that little or no return might be received on the investment or even that part or the entire investment principal might be lost. Three categories of risk must be considered.

1. Inflation risk: The value of assets or income from investments might be less in the future as inflation decreases the value of money.
2. Interest rate risk: The value of a bond or a fund portfolio might decline because of rising interest rates. Interest rate risk generally is lower for shorter-term investments.
3. Credit risk: An issuer of municipal bonds might not be able to meet its obligations to make interest and principal payments due to changing financial or market conditions.

A fourth category—income risk—might be encountered in connection with mutual fund investments. The income from a fund portfolio might decline because of falling market interest rates. This risk can result when the proceeds from new share sales are invested by the fund, or when bonds mature or are called at market interest rates that are below the current earning rate of the portfolio.

Summary and Conclusions

The mysteries of the process of marketing municipal bonds, insofar as the uninitiated are concerned, are comparable to that of the stock market. Economic forces and new federal regulations have driven some significant changes in the typical municipal bond in recent times. The traditional general obligation bond, sold by competitive bid and underwritten by a bank has been replaced, in large measure, by a revenue bond, sold by negotiation, underwritten by a syndicate, and sold to individual investors and bond mutual funds. Regardless of the format, however, local officials must adhere to accepted principals to reduce the risks and uncertainties with which they must deal in issuing long-term bonds.

Controlling laws are not always conveniently codified. As a result, the procedural steps necessary to secure bond authorization often are confusing to local officials and administrators. Expert legal advice is essential at this stage of the process. Even minor errors might result in extensive delays, expensive litigation, and possible invalidation of the issue or sale.

Three nationally recognized rating organizations rate a wide variety of bonds. These ratings reflect two basic risk factors: (1) that the jurisdiction will be fiscally capable of meeting principal and interest payments, and (2) that existing bonds will not be adversely affected by further increase in debt obligations. State and local governments insure their bond offerings to obtain the highest ratings possible and thereby lower their borrowing costs.

Large investment syndicates underwrite the funds required by local governments to finance capital projects. Their profit is the *spread*—the difference between the price the underwriters pay the issuer for the bonds and the price the underwriters receive from the resale of those bonds to investors.

The secondary bond market provides individual and institutional investors the opportunity to buy and sell municipal bonds prior to their maturity dates. It is estimated that the volume of transactions in the secondary market exceeds that of the new issue market at an annual ratio of twenty to one.

Four categories of investors purchase municipal bonds: (1) mutual funds, (2) commercial banks, (3) property and casualty insurance companies, and (4) individual investors. Many long-standing loopholes were eliminated by the 1986 Tax Reform Act, leaving municipal bonds as the last significant remaining tax shelter for individual investors. Other provisions of the Act made municipal bonds less attractive to banks and insurance companies. Therefore, individual investors and bond mutual funds (which sell shares to individual investors) account for 75% of all bonds currently held.

The power to borrow is one of the most important assets of government. Few local governments have the capability to finance vital capital improvements strictly from annual tax revenues. A sound borrowing policy seeks to conserve rather than exhaust credit. The capacity to borrow must be used with critical regard for its justifiable purposes and with a clear understanding of its safe and reasonable limits. While most states have adopted legislative measures to avoid the financial catastrophe that many local governments faced in the 1930s, the ultimate responsibility still rests with local officials to adopt procedures that will protect their community from "mortgaging its future."

Notes

1. Bond issues secured solely by project revenues often are issued a provisional rating, which remains in effect until the construction is completed and the project has begun to generate revenues.
2. For a further discussion on these points, see Charles Coe, "Obtaining a Better Bond Rating: A Case Study," *Case Studies in Public Budgeting and Financial Management*, edited by Aman Khan and W. Bartley Hildreth (New York: Marcel Dekker, Inc., 2003), 613-628.
3. Joint Economic Committee, *State and Local Public Facility Needs and Financing*, Vol. 2 (Washington, D.C.: U.S. Government Printing Office, December 1966), 11.
4. Lazard Freres, for example, acknowledged that the morass of political scandals was one reason for the company's departure from the municipal bond market.

5. Maynard Toll of CS First Boston, as quoted in *The New York Times* (March 19, 1996), C2.
6. Robert B. Lamb, Stern School of Business, New York University, as quoted in *The New York Times* (March 19, 1996) C2.
7. For a more extensive discussion of the differences between competitive bidding and negotiated sales, see Robert Zipf, *How the Bond Market Works* (New York: New York Institute of Finance, 1997), 99-115.
8. Robert Boyden Lamb, "The Primary Market: Underwriting Municipal Bonds," *The Handbook of Municipal Bonds and Public Finance*, edited by Robert Lamb, James Leighland, and Stephen Rappaport (New York: New York Institute of Finance, 1993), 23.
9. Donald Yacoe, "Crying Cronyism, Lawmaker Seeks Alabama Ban on Negotiated Deals," *The Bond Buyer* (February 7, 1994): 1.
10. John L. Mikesell, *Fiscal Administration: Analysis and Applications for the Public Sector* (Pacific Grove, Calif.: Brooks/Cole Publishing Company, 1991), 421-425.
11. Christina I. Ray, *The Bond Market: Trading and Risk Management* (Homewood, Ill.: Business One Irwin, 1993), 72.
12. Zvi Bodie, Alex Kane, and Alan J. Marcus, *Investments*, 2nd ed. (Boston: Irwin, 1993), 457.
13. Tom McLoughlin, "Choosing an Underwriter for a Negotiated Bond Sale," *Government Finance Review* (June 1990): 28-30.
14. Robert Zipf, *How the Bond Market Works* (New York: New York Institute of Finance Corporation, 1988), 135-146, 154-156.
15. Public Securities Association, *Fundamentals of Municipal Bonds* (New York, 1982), 99-100.
16. Daniel R. Feenberg and James M. Poterba, *Which Households Own Municipal Bonds?: Evidence From Tax Returns* (Cambridge, Mass.: National Bureau of Economic Research, November 1991), 3-10.
17. *Ibid.*, 13.
18. Wilson White, *The Municipal Bond Investor* (Chicago: Probus Publishing Co., 1991), 16; and John Andrew, *Municipal Bonds: The Common Sense Guide to Tax-Free Personal Investing* (New York: The Free Press, 1987), 186-187.
19. Penelope Lemov, "After the Fiscal Quake," *Governing* 8, no. 5, (February 1995): 34.
20. Inverse floaters have variable interest rates that move in the opposite direction from movements in short-term interest rates—rising when prevailing short-term interest rates fall, and vice versa. Prices of inverse floaters can be more volatile than the prices of conventional fixed-rate bonds with comparable maturities.

Chapter 10

PROJECT PLANNING AND OPERATIONS SCHEDULING

Many strategic facility projects continue to be implemented at far less than full efficiency. Important deadlines are missed—often because they were unrealistic in light of an ambitious scope of work. Projects often require substantial time extensions because the anticipated results have not been achieved. All-too-often, items are eliminated from a project schedule in order to meet overall budget and cost constraints. Much of this continued inefficiency can be attributed to a lack of understanding of the techniques of project planning and operations scheduling. When funding has been approved for a specific capital project, it is critical that the appropriate project components be delineated in considerable detail through the development of a project plan and operations schedule. Through effective planning, it should be possible for project managers to organize activities in a more optimal manner. Costs can be more clearly defined and controlled, and time constraints can be utilized more effectively. Firmer assurances can be provided that the work will be completed within schedule deadlines.

Three Fundamental Elements

If a strategic facility project is to be implemented successfully, three diverse and often contradictory elements must be coordinated into a project plan and operations schedule:

1. *Operations*: the things that must be done (tasks, activities, or jobs), each with a sequential relation to other operations and each requiring resources for some time period.
2. *Resources*: the things utilized in a project, often reduced to a common standard of cost, but including personnel, equipment, materials, and time.
3. *Constraints*: conditions imposed by outside factors, such as budgetary limits, completion deadlines, availability of staff resources, inputs from other units, and so forth.

Identifying these three elements in a project plan and operations schedule will permit a strategic facility project to be completed (or maintained) in the best time, at the least cost, and with the smallest degree of risk and uncertainty.

Project Plan

The primary purpose of project planning is to provide mechanisms for continuous control over the operations of a strategic facility project. In this context, a *project plan* can be defined as a coordinated model of the sequence in which all tasks and activities must be performed to complete a given project. *Scheduling* involves the determination of the calendar dates or times when resources will be utilized in accordance with the total resource capacity assigned to the strategic facility project. Resource requirements and availability, task or job sequence, and possible starting and ending times for project activities must be taken into account in order to produce an appropriate schedule.

The successful application of project planning techniques involves two basic requirements. First, it is necessary to formulate a clearly stated work program, including the delineation of project tasks into specific activities, jobs, or work elements, directed toward one or more defined objectives. And second, cost and other resource requirements and constraints must be assigned to each activity in the project. Given this fundamental management information, planning and scheduling techniques have been developed to determine maximum time allotments, as well as costs involved, for each job.

A project plan must be a dynamic tool—it should provide project managers with the capacity to:

- Consider the cost, in dollars and time, of pursuing alternative sequences of activities;
- Establish criteria for the allocation and scheduling of resources;
- Evaluate the accuracy of cost and resource estimates and to assist in refining these estimates;
- Identify and assess the consequences of change with the minimum delay;
- Revise and update the plan with minimum disruption and within an acceptable time period; and
- Assimilate, communicate, and analyze data concerning the progress of the project.

A project plan will have certain practical restraints. Deviations between predicted and actual results, for instance, must be identified quickly so that the necessary action can be taken to correct such situations.

Operations Schedule

An operations schedule must reflect the total resource capacity assigned to the project. It must delineate the availability of resources, the sequence of activities or jobs, the resource requirements, and possible starting times for each activity. The basic requirement in producing an efficient schedule is to level the use of resources, that is, to avoid dramatic shifts—ebbs and flows—in resource requirements (and particularly in staffing requirements). In developing a schedule, the *critical path* (i.e., the longest sequence of activities) is determined not so much by the duration of the various activities as by the segment of resources that can (and should) be assigned out of the total resource capacity available in order to successfully complete each activity.

It might be possible, for example, to clear and develop a neighborhood park site in five weeks using five workers. It also might be possible to clear and develop the same park site in one week with twenty-five workers, or in two and a half days with fifty workers, or in four hours with 250 workers. There is an obvious fallacy in this thinking, however. Efficiency drops off rapidly as jamming grows, that is, as more resources are applied to the project. It might be just as efficient for five workers to take five weeks as it is for ten workers to take two and a half weeks. However, due to the drop in efficiency, it might require fifty workers one week to do the job instead of two and a half days.

The requirement of scheduling, therefore, is to establish the optimal duration for each activity with varying levels of resources to be utilized so that the schedule will remain within the limits of peak efficiency. This approach to scheduling yields a minimum cost for each activity and, presumably, for the total project.

Project planning and operations scheduling techniques are excellent tools of communication because they can show graphically the interrelationships among activities in a project. They also indicate clearly where responsibilities for supervision and management have been assigned. When changes in the plan or schedule are required, the work program should show clearly which activities would be affected by such changes. This focus, by itself, can relieve project supervisors of much unnecessary paperwork that only serves to keep them from their more valuable function—the continuous oversight of project activities.

Performance Requirements and Decision Criteria

The first step in developing a project plan is to identify the performance requirements and decision criteria with which the strategic facility project must comply. Performance requirements or the desired "end product" of a project often are reflected in terms of strategic objectives. For example, an appropriate end product for a construction project often might be defined in terms of general systems specifications. If a research project is to be initiated, a definition of the area to be examined and the subject matter of the final conclusions or recommendations often will suffice. If a physical activity must be performed, such as a move to a new facility, it might be appropriate to describe the conditions to be attained and to identify the measures of accomplishment.

Performance requirements might also define any constraints on how the project is to be carried out—such as imposed schedule deadlines and budgetary limitations (see Table 10-1). Any requirements for doing the work in-house or by subcontract should be stated. Appropriate management philosophies and strategies that are to be applied should be identified. The amount of verification of the project's end-product performance also might be defined.

Decision criteria also might be incorporated into strategic objectives. Such criteria should reflect the relative importance of project performance, development cost, production cost, and ultimate operational costs. These criteria might be expressed in both quantitative and qualitative terms. Eventually, these factors might be translated into more sophisticated decision criteria, such as used in cost-benefit and cost-effectiveness analyses. In this initial stage, however, general decision guidelines will suffice—it is not necessary to be able to forecast every possible contingency.

Once the initial performance requirements have been stated, a sequence of broad tradeoffs must be made. These tradeoffs result in a decision on how much should be spent (cost) for how good an "end-product" (effectiveness). During

Table 10-1
Performance Requirements and Decision Criteria

The staff of the District Health Office has identified the need to establish a prenatal health-care clinic in a section of the county where such health services have not previously been available.

Performance requirements define constraints on how the project is to be carried out:

1. The clinic should be located in appropriate leased space in or near the regional shopping mall in the targeted section of the county.
2. The clinic's programs should be available within four months of the budget authorization.
3. The clinic should be staffed six days a week by professionals augmented by volunteers.
4. The clinic's programs should be offered to optimize access by eligible expectant mothers including those who work.
5. The start-up budget for the first six months (including locating and equipping suitable space) should not exceed $xxx,xxx.

Decision criteria reflect the relative importance of project performance, development cost, production cost, and ultimate operational costs.

this process, it might be discovered that assumptions about one part of the project tend to place unreasonable requirements on some other components. Assumptions might be changed, perhaps several times, in an effort to achieve an optimal design. Certain features of the project might add significantly to the time duration. Activities or even whole tasks might have to be modified in order to conform to schedule deadlines. It might be possible to reduce schedule risks by committing additional funds to the project. It might be possible to improve performance by taking advantage of an emerging technology. These decisions, however, might increase the cost of the project. It might be possible to accomplish some project tasks in parallel, while others will have to be undertaken in sequence. Large enough cost reductions might be possible to offset the additional resource requirements resulting from the overlap.

It might be argued that providing this level of detail will likely provoke disagreement and cause needless management difficulties. On the contrary, that is all the more reasons to take these actions. Any basic disagreement about the goals and objectives of the project should be exposed early and not left to give rise to inevitable misunderstandings and trouble later.

After end products and performance requirements have been identified and appropriate tradeoffs have been made, the required tasks can be organized into some consistent format. The process of further defining tasks, subtasks, and activities can then begin. Schedules and budgets can be prepared. Alternative approaches should be compared with performance requirements and the best ones selected as the basis for decision making.

Finally, there are interactions between the establishment of project objectives, on the one hand, and the planning of the project, on the other. It might be that the desired end product simply cannot be achieved within the specified time frame or for the planned costs. Thus, it might be necessary to relax certain performance requirements to permit a more realistic project plan. Or perhaps the appropriate decision would be to terminate the project immediately, rather than after a large expenditure is made in pursuing unattainable goals.

Task Identification

Operational objectives involve the delineation of more specific tasks that must be effectively carried if the project's strategic and management objectives are to be accomplished. Obviously, if the proper tasks have not been identified at the outset, efforts to plan, schedule, and control them—and to ensure that they comply with established standards—will be in vain.

A *task* can be defined as a set of activities that will lead to the achievement of some desired results in a project. Tasks are the major divisions of the work on a project. It is extremely important to have broad participation in the identification of tasks relevant to a particular project. Task identification is far too important an undertaking to be left to a project planner or even to individual project managers. The active participation of all segments of the project staff is essential in order to increase the probability that all essential tasks will be identified.

Three major approaches can be used in identifying project tasks: (1) a deductive approach, (2) an inductive approach, and (3) a composite approach. Under the deductive approach, tasks are defined more or less intuitively from a description of the expected operations of the project. That is, an attempt is made to develop a picture of the required results of the project activities and to reconstruct the logical sequence back to the required tasks. In this way, the logic between each task and the preceding activities is more clearly identified. This approach sometimes is referred to as backchaining, since the analysis works back through a chain of events, linking the original inputs to the desired project. Experience has shown that this approach tends to identify only the really essential tasks.

The inductive approach works almost in reverse of the deductive method. It begins with a detailed documentation of each task, including the anticipated results of each task. After this examination is finished, the tasks are sorted into logical groups, where the anticipated results of performing each grouping are discussed and recorded.

The composite approach is a combination of the deductive and inductive approaches. An attempt is made to examine the "big picture," while at the same time a group of identified tasks and their anticipated results are also analyzed. Using this approach, the analysts seek to determine how the present tasks should be modified to accommodate the newly stated project. In effect, the "knowns" of existing tasks are modified and rearranged in order to produce the desired results of a new project configuration.

The inductive and composite approaches work best when prior project experience has been recorded and the new project is an attempt to expand and improve upon these efforts. If the activities involved are completely innovative—without prior application—then the deductive approach might be the only route possible for task identification.

An example might help to illustrate these points. A local Public Health Department has established the following strategic objective:

Reduce the incidence and prevalence of disease and/or conditions declared to be dangerous to the general public by providing surveillance and epidemiological services.

A management objective that supports this strategic objective would be:

Increase public awareness of the need for early detection of cervical cancer through public health outreach workers and educational materials.

A related management objective, which includes measurable performance criteria, would be:

Provide during the current fiscal year approximately 140,000 pap smears for women who are not currently receiving this service.

Operational objectives would include:

Establish five pap test clinics in neighborhood health centers and assign personnel to staff these clinics in the evening hours.

Work in cooperation with the county health department and specified health-care providers to disseminate information about the need for early detection and the availability of these clinics.

A number of specific tasks must be undertaken to achieve these objectives, including:

Determine which neighborhood health centers can best be used to reach the target population;

Determine the media format best suited to publicize this project;

Establish the staffing requirements and personnel schedules for the pap test clinics; and

Assign follow-up responsibility for evaluating the effectiveness of the project.

An analysis of the feasibility of implementing this project might identify some potential obstacles:

- The Health Department has no legal authority to obtain the cooperation needed from other health-care providers.
- Some resistance might arise from departmental personnel being assigned to staff clinics at night.
- Additional clinics will require additional staff, which has not been budgeted for the current fiscal year.
- Not all public health outreach workers have the skills necessary to perform pap smears.
- Legal implications of the project and referral requirements must be determined.

Implementation strategies for this project must describe those activities that would respond to both sets of necessary actions—the management and operational objectives and the potential obstacles.

Brainstorming, Opportunity Analysis, and the Delphi Technique

Organized brainstorming sessions often can be useful in identifying tasks and activities appropriate to a given project (see Table 10-2). Such sessions should be fairly unstructured, freewheeling, and unconstrained. All ideas should be recorded no matter how "far-out" they might seem at first. All project staff should be involved in these sessions.

It might be desirable for the project manager to maintain a relatively low profile in these sessions. A member of the project team can be appointed to serve as the session leader, so that the opinions of the manager will not overly bias the discussion or lead to premature closure. In this way, the manager can adopt the "observer's role" and not unduly influence the flow of ideas by his or her responses. This approach also tends to increase the involvement of those project personnel who are selected to serve in the facilitator's role. Efforts to refine, combine, and assign priorities to the ideas generated in the brainstorming sessions should follow only after the project has been thoroughly discussed and all participants have had an opportunity to express themselves.

Along similar lines, an *opportunity analysis* might be conducted to raise the enthusiasm and morale of those involved. Periodic sessions are held to discuss the current status of the project and to explore opportunities that might be presented. Many of the ideas generated in such sessions might not be relevant to the more pressing requirements of the project. However, an effective project manager cannot afford to overlook any possibilities in a preoccupation with status quo procedures. Such an exercise should help develop more positive attitudes among the staff.

Ideas about project activities also can be elicited and refined through the use of the *Delphi technique*. The relatively free exchange of brainstorming is replaced by a more formal exchange of information under the control of a steering group or exercise manager. This technique involves an iterative series of interrogations (usually through the use of questionnaires or structured interviews) of a panel of knowledgeable individuals. Responses are not matched with respondents, and the participants often are not revealed to one another until the end of the exercise. In this way, the psychological drawbacks of face-to-face confrontations are avoided as participants review one another's opinions.

After each round, the information generated in the previous rounds is fed back to the participants so they might use it to revise their earlier responses (and often, to modify their attitudes concerning the project). Irrelevant or redundant materials might be eliminated to assist in sharpening the focus in subsequent iterations. Participant opinions tend to converge with feedback, although after several iterations, a spread of opinions is still a normal outcome.

Rather than forcing unanimity, a statistical index is used to represent the group response. The assumption is that through this approach the pressure of conformity can be reduced, and the opinion of every participant will play a role in the final determination of categorical responses.

The preceding discussion implies a linear progression from defining end products to examining performance requirements to identifying the specific

Table 10-2
Brainstorming the Establishment of a Prenatal Health-Care Clinic

The Jefferson County Health Department has undertaken to establish a prenatal health-care clinic in a section of the county where such health services have not previously been available. To accomplish the objectives of this project, four basic tasks must be initiated: (1) adequate space must be obtained and equipped for the clinic; (2) a clinic staff must be hired, trained, and certified; (3) programs of the clinic must be publicized; and (4) eligible applicants must be screened and enrolled. These major tasks, in turn, can be divided into a number of subtasks or activities in order to provide a basis for establishing a network analysis. The following activities were identified in a brainstorming session by the administrative staff of the County Health Department:

Certify professional and volunteer staff members.
Negotiate a rental contract for clinic space.
Orient staff to agency procedures.
Train staff in clinic operations.
Open clinic to eligible applicants
Secure medical supplies, drugs, and informational materials.
Order office equipment for the clinic.
Secure office supplies and materials.
Assign/hire clinic staff.
Locate appropriate space for the clinic.
Equip office and clinic space (including physical modifications to rented space).
Publicize the availability of the clinic and its programs.
Screen initial applicants for eligibility and complete their enrollment in the program.

These activities are not listed in any particular order. Often in such brainstorming sessions, ideas will flow in a somewhat unstructured fashion. This approach should be encouraged to ensure that all ideas get out on the table

activities of the project. The logic of such a process is sound. However, seldom is it possible to follow this process in a straightforward manner. Many loops are made during project planning. Some are relatively small, but others might require major changes in the whole concept of the project.

An active set of decision loops—even loops within loops—produce increasingly better project plans. It is important, however, to bring the planning process to a conclusion so that implementation can begin—before funds are wasted on superfluous refinements and unnecessarily detailed restrictions are placed on doing the job itself. Project planning should provide a basis for project direction and a blueprint for project implementation. Typical products of this process include:

- Project specification
- Identification of project tasks and activities
- Functional project plans related to organizational responsibilities
- Work breakdown schedules
- Activity networks
- Operations schedules
- Cost estimates and budgets

Work Breakdown Schedule

As has been noted, an initial step in formulating a project plan is to establish the major objectives to be accomplished and each of the supporting objectives for the entire project. These objectives must be linked together so that the project manager can see the project in its true perspective—so that the relationships are clear between and among all of the procedural steps. A *work breakdown schedule* (WBS) is one important technique for developing a preliminary outline or schematic as to the way in which supporting objectives mesh together to ensure the attainment of the major objectives. Work breakdown schedules have been used successfully in the private sector for a number of years. Many of us learned the fundamentals of this technique, albeit under a different name, when we were struggling with English composition in junior high school.

Divide and Conquer

In simple projects, the major objectives and the supporting objectives might be so obvious that complicated listings or other arrays of information are not required. In more complex projects, hundreds of individual activities and events might be required and their linkages might not be easily recognized and related. In such projects, the work breakdown schedule aids in the identification of objectives, allowing the manager to examine the groves of trees within the forest if not the individual trees.

The basic idea of a work breakdown schedule is to divide the total project into major tasks, then to subdivided these tasks into subtasks, the subtasks into activities, and so on. The work might be subdivided through as many stages or levels as necessary to provide final work units of the desired size. At the lowest level, the work units should be small enough to permit adequate visibility and control without creating an unwieldy administrative burden.

It is not possible to state precisely just how detailed the work breakdown schedule should be or exactly how many levels are needed for any given project. It should be detailed enough to allow the eventual formulation of an operations schedule that will accurately reflect the interrelationships among all the events and activities which make up the entire project. Each part of the WBS should be subdivided to the number of levels useful for managing the project. Excessive zeal in pushing the WBS into too much subdivision, however, might well result in an unproductive management structure. It is not necessary to extend the WBS to the same number of levels for all tasks. Insistence on a uniform number of subdivisions might yield final units that are too small in some cases and too large in others. Tasks should be subdivided into smaller units according to their interrelatedness. Routine, repetitive work need not be excessively subdivided.

Since a good WBS is designed to serve many project purposes, it is not necessary to manage all project activities at the same level of detail. The structure of the WBS should be flexible enough that it can be expanded over time—both in depth and in scope. The WBS need not be detailed initially to the desired depth in all areas. In fact, an early version of the WBS—containing only two or three levels of task subdivision—might provide a sufficiently sound basis for project planning. As the time approaches for initiating certain parts of the project, tasks can be further subdivided into additional levels as might be appropriate for cost and schedule control. Thus, managers with different responsibilities can look at large or small segments of the project presented in varying degrees of detail.

The initial division of work should not be made strictly along organizational lines—this nullifies much of the usefulness of the WBS. Any schedule below the first level will only reflect what the separate organizational units require and will not reflect the dependencies or obligations among these units. Dividing tasks according to organizational responsibilities, therefore, should be deferred to a low level within the WBS.

A work breakdown schedule can be used for a variety of purposes in addition to describing the tasks necessary to realize the management and operational objectives of a project. A WBS can be used as a common framework for budgeting and control of project costs, preparing unit cost work statements, issuing work authorizations, scheduling work, reporting and monitoring the status of work activities, and tracking technical performance. In essence, a WBS can provide project managers with an important tool for the integration of planning and control functions at various levels of responsibility and authority within an organization. It also serves as an important mechanism for the communication of project management information.

The WBS Format

One of the characteristics of a good manager is consistent, orderly, but flexible thinking. Therefore, a WBS should be structured in a consistent manner, according to some orderly identification scheme that will also provide the flexibility for expansion, if necessary, during the time required to complete the project. Such a structural approach is provided through the so-called indented decimal system (see Table 10-3).

The straightforward application of this system is relatively simple and provides a readily understood mnemonic. The decimal format makes it easy to build the WBS into an information system and to develop cost accounting procedures that are useful to the management of the project. For example, account-

Table 10-3
A Work Breakdown Schedule
for Prenatal Health-care Clinic

1.0 Secure and equip space for the clinic
  1.1 Locate appropriate space for the clinic
  1.2 Negotiate rental contract on clinic space
  1.3 Equip office and clinic space
    1.3.1 Make physical modifications to rented space, as necessary to accommodate clinic layout
    1.3.2 Order office equipment for the clinic
    1.3.3 Order medical supplies, drugs, and other materials
    1.3.4 Order office supplies and materials
  1.4 Certify clinic staff
2.0 Hire/assign clinic staff
  2.1 Orient staff to agency procedures
  2.2 Train staff in clinic operations
  2.3 Certify professional and volunteer staff members
3.0 Publicize programs and screen applicants
  3.1 Develop informational materials on clinic programs
  3.2 Publicize the availability of the clinic and its programs
  3.3 Screen initial applicants for eligibility and complete their enrollment in the program

ing codes can easily be expanded to include the numerics of a project's work breakdown schedule so that costs can be monitored at various levels of activity.

The first subdivision (1.0, 2.0, 3.0, and so on) represents the major tasks of the project associated with the major management objectives. The second level (1.1, 1.2, 2.1, 2.2, etc.) represents the further breakdown of major tasks into subtasks. The third level (1.1.1, 1.1.2, 1.1.3, etc.) begins to identify specific activity clusters or job assignments that are required to successfully carry out the subtasks.

The work specified in each division is logically the sum of all the work described in the elements contained in that division or its subdivisions. Subtasks and activities are the logical divisions of larger tasks and should be distinct from each other. For this reason, each entry in the WBS should have its own, unique descriptive title that provides the project manager and others with a brief identification of that work unit so that it is distinguishable from other work units. These descriptive labels need not be long and complicated. In no case, however, should the title of one level repeat words used in the prior level. The numerical designation provides the traceability to larger groupings of work units at higher levels. The principal idea is to give the work units usable, understandable names.

It should be evident that no task should be divided into a single subtask, and no subtask should be subdivided into a single activity. Just as Ms. Finch, our eighth grade English teacher, used to drill into our heads, if there is a 1.1.1, there must be a 1.1.2. This admonition seems obvious, and yet, failure to adhere to this basic rule accounts for many shortcomings in the application of the WBS approach. It is also important to maintain the integrity of the task hierarchy—to guard against the misplacement of activities under an inappropriate subtask or to repeat the same activity under more than one subtask.

A graphic display similar in layout to that of a decision tree or an organization chart (see Figure 10-1) is also a highly effective way to represent a work breakdown schedule. Major objectives and associated tasks are indicated at the top of the chart, with the second level containing supporting objectives and subtasks, the third level indicating some of the more detailed work required to complete these second-level supporting objectives, and so forth. Such a schematic diagram can be displayed on a wall to provide staff members with a total view of the project and the interrelatedness of various project activities. Typically, each box on the chart contains a task identifier and the name of the task or activity.

With the addition of narrative descriptions of each of the major tasks and subtasks, a WBS can serve as a more detailed project plan. Individuals with various functional responsibilities in the organization should be able to refer to the WBS as a common source of information for the fulfillment of their planning and control responsibilities. Since there is no need to provide the same level of subtask division for each task, flexibility of the schedule can be maintained. This flexibility is especially important in the early developmental stages of a project. In fact, the WBS can be sent out to various personnel with the work only divided into major tasks. As the planning of the project is further refined, the major tasks can be subdivided. By issuing a first draft of a WBS, the project manager also allows for the fuller participation of affected personnel. Such a process might result in a better WBS and a more successful project. At a minimum, however, such a process allows relevant personnel to participate in the development of the operations schedule and the monitoring and control devices that will be applied to the project. By providing for such participation, greater cooperation and understanding of the project might be anticipated, as well as a greater potential for realizing a successful project. The characteristics that should be kept in mind in developing a work breakdown schedule is summarized in Table 10-4.

Milestone Charts and Arrow Diagrams

Contemporary techniques for project planning and operations scheduling can be traced back to the work of pioneers in the field of scientific management, such as Frederick Taylor and Henry Laurence Gantt. Taylor's time and motion studies are familiar to students of industrial engineering and business administration. Gantt Charts form the basis for many current production scheduling systems. The relative simplicity of the Gantt Chart is one reason why this technique continues to receive widespread application. The so-called time-line diagram is one of the more common forms of Gantt Charts used today.

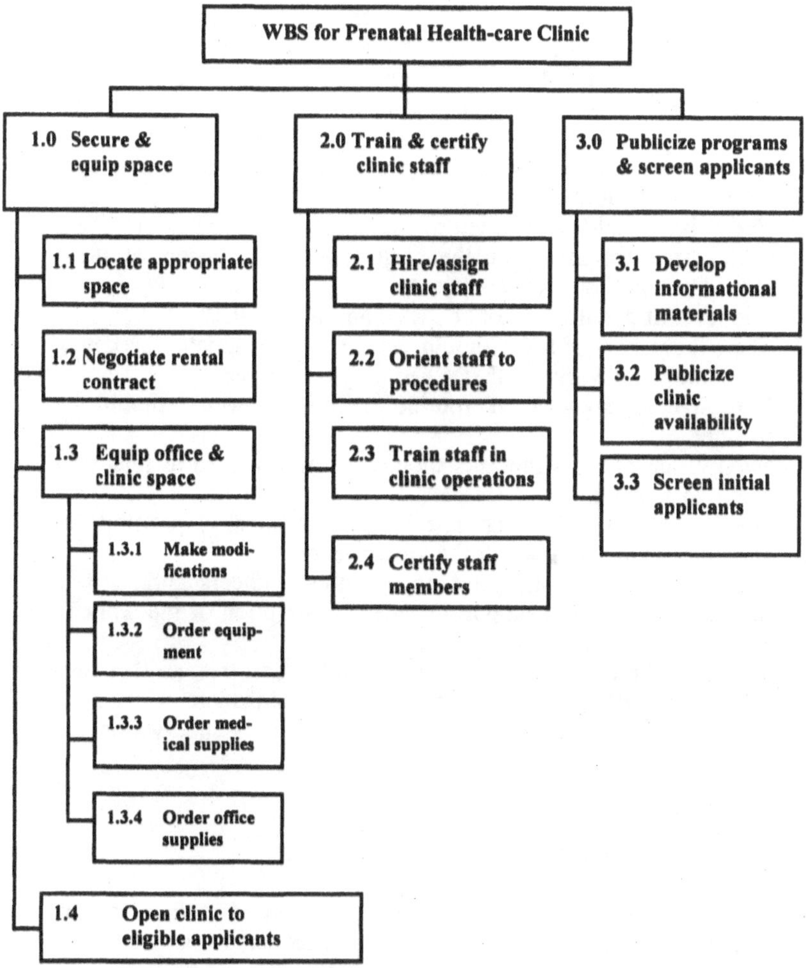

Figure 10-1 Graphic Display of Work Breakdown Schedule

Table 10-4
Work Breakdown Schedule Summary

- The WBS should be structured in a consistent, orderly, and hierarchical manner.
- The work specified in each WBS element is the sum of all the work specified in the elements immediately below it.
- When a work element (task or subtask) is subdivided, all the work in that element is assigned to one of the immediately subordinate units.
- No work should be described in more than one element at a specific level of subdivision.
- The WBS should be detailed to the extent necessary to provide a useful basis for managing the project; the subdivision of these should be based on interrelatedness.
- The level of detail need not be the same for all tasks.
- The subdivision of tasks should permit, if appropriate, the development of a network or other scheduling techniques.
- Extensive subdivision of routine, repetitious work should be avoided.
- Subdivision of tasks/subtasks should not be extended to relatively small cost efforts.
- Breaking down tasks according to organizational responsibilities should be avoided except at the lowest levels.
- To maintain clarity and promote a common understanding, it is desirable to provide a supporting verbal description of the work in each WBS element.
- These descriptions should be concise and jargon-free, so that they are understandable within and outside the organization.
- Redundancy should be eliminated in the various subdivision descriptions.

Determining Milestones

Milestones are key elements or points in time that can be used to measure the progress of a project. A *milestone chart* provides a sequential list of the various tasks to be accomplished in a project (tasks, in turn, can be broken down into specific activities if this level of detailed is warranted). This approach also contributes to an increased awareness of the interdependencies between tasks. The list of tasks and milestones are displayed adjacent to a time scale. Symbols on the time scale identify the dates (or times) that each milestone is scheduled to be initiated, when it is completed, if slippage has occurred, and so forth. These data can be accumulated in machine-readable form coded for various sorts: by organizational units, by project and subproject, and by performance status.

The duration of each task is indicated by an elongated U-shaped symbol. To show how the work is actually progressing, a line or bar can be drawn within

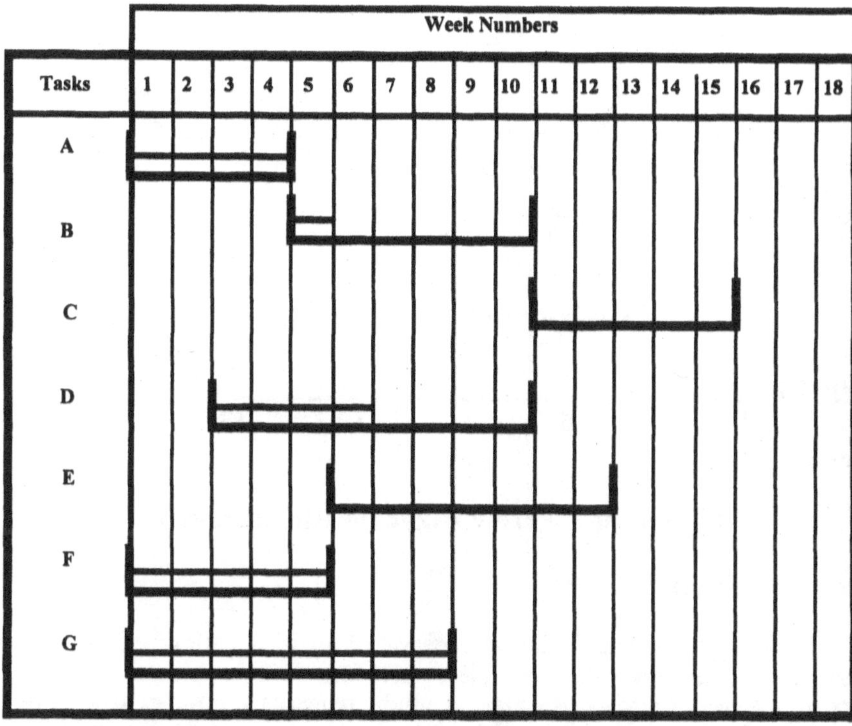

Figure 10-2 Milestone Chart

the uprights of this symbol (see Figure 10-2). The length of this line represents the amount of work actually completed to date. Bars to the left of any observation point represent underaccomplishment, while those to the right represent overaccomplishment. Reasons for any delays can be noted on the chart by the use of codes or symbols.

The milestone approach has several limitations. Relationships among tasks (milestones) still are not fully established. While listed in chronological sequence, milestones are not necessarily related in a logical sequence and not all of the important interrelationships can be displayed. Further, the milestone chart does not allow for measuring the effect of changes and slippages; it merely improves the reporting of them.

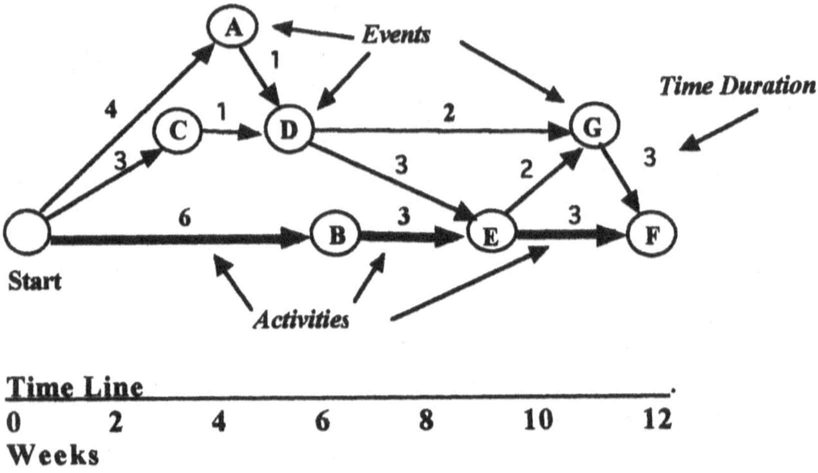

Figure 10-3 Arrow Diagram Illustration

Arrow Diagrams

An arrow diagram provides the initial portrayal of a critical path network. In an arrow diagram, the elements of a project—*activities*—are represented on a network by a series of arrows. An activity might represent a process, task, procurement cycle, or waiting time and might simply represent a connection or *interdependency* between two events on the network. An *event* is a specific, definable accomplishment in a project plan, recognizable at a particular point in time. An activity cannot be started until the event preceding it has occurred. Events do not consume time or resources and are normally represented in the network by circles, squares, or rectangles (called *nodes*).

If an activity is denoted as a direct link between two events (nodes) in a network, an arrow (symbolizing the activity) indicates the direction of dependency and time flow from one node to another. A dependency relationship is assumed to mean that, before the dependent activity can be initiated, the other related activity must be completed.

Since the nodes in the arrow diagrams represent the completion of an activity (i.e., an event), the term "Start" often is used to anchor the initiation of the network (see Figure 10-3). Each arrow represents a linkage between events; more than one arrow can designate the same activity. Two arrows that terminate at the same node, for example, represent the same activity. This approach has certain advantages in determining time durations and in delimiting the critical path, as will be subsequently illustrated.

An arrow diagram is composed of a series of sequential relationships or *paths*. Each path should be completed in the indicated sequence in order for the various activities to be carried out in proper relation one to another and for the overall project to be successfully implemented. Once the various connections have been drawn, a critical route can be determined and progress can be more easily measured against key checkpoints or milestones.

Associated with each arrow (activity) in the network is a time estimate called its *duration*—the amount of time required to complete the activity represented by the arrow. The next step, therefore, is to assign time estimates to each of the paths or arrows. Each arrow (activity) leading to a given node (event or activity completion) is assigned the time duration for the designated activity. In this way, all of the possible paths to that node can be easily traced.

Network Analysis and the Critical Path Method

The techniques of network analysis provide a useful and straightforward approach by which to map the various steps required to implement a project. Network analysis provides a basis for determining the order in which activities should be undertaken—either their sequence or priority—and the critical linkages among activities. Even the most detailed and apparently complex networks are merely composites of a number of relatively simple networks. By understanding the basic techniques of network analysis, the project manager should be able to convey specific assignments to those responsible for carrying out the various activities of the project.

Origins of Network Analysis

Industrial managers have used network analysis techniques in production planning since the early 1900s. Process flow charts and programming techniques similar to the network analysis methods that form the basis for the Program Evaluation and Review Technique (PERT) were developed by industrial engineers prior to World War II. Similarly, business program analysts for many years have used a work programming approach that parallels the network algorithms used in both PERT and the Critical Path Method (CPM).

An investigation was initiated in 1956 at E.I. DuPont de Nemours to determine the extent to which the emerging capacity of high-speed computers might be applied to improve the planning, scheduling, and progress reporting of the company's engineering projects. Late in 1957, Morgan R. Walker, a DuPont engineer, and James E. Kelley Jr., a Remington-Rand computer specialist, ran a pilot test on a unique arrow diagram, which subsequently came to be known as the Critical Path Method.

Concurrently, the U.S. Navy Special Projects Office, Bureau of Ordinance, established a research team to work on a similar strategy. The assignment of the SPO team—a project called PERT (Program Evaluation Research Task)—was aimed at formulating techniques for the efficient management of huge, complicated weapon systems development projects. What emerged was an approach to solve some of the fast multiplying problems of large-scale projects in which complex logistics, technical innovation, and concurrent activities must be integrated. PERT is credited (along with a dedicated management) with making it possible for the Navy to produce an operational ballistic missile-firing nuclear submarine years ahead of schedule. PERT was subsequently adapted as the Program Evaluation and Review Technique and extended to hundreds of management situations, setting a pattern for project planning and control systems of the future.

Similarities Between CPM and PERT

PERT is the more sophisticated of the two approaches, being designed to deal with large-scale projects that are characterized by: (1) unclear objectives, (2) multiple and/or overlapping management responsibilities, (3) relatively high levels of uncertainty as to time requirements and costs, (4) complex problems of logistics, and (5) problems of sufficient complexity to justify the use of high-speed computers to track the project in some detail. The Critical Path Method, on the other hand, has been described as a "back-of-an-envelope" or "in-the-field" approach, with much less dependence on data processing and computer programming experience. CPM techniques are particularly applicable to well-defined projects under the direction of a single management, with relatively clear objectives and limited levels of uncertainty.

As both of these methods have been revised and improved, attractive features of one approach have been incorporated into the other. The arrow diagram or network is common to both methods. It is necessary to identify a "critical path" in the development of a PERT network, and the "three time estimates" used in PERT for dealing with uncertainty can also be applied in CPM. In current applications, differences are found in the diagram formats rather than in the underlying conceptual framework.

CPM focuses on the "doing," while PERT focuses on what is "done." The Critical Path Method is *job-* or *activity*-oriented. Jobs or activities are linked together in a sequence of dependence to form an arrow diagram. PERT is an *event*-oriented network. An event might be defined as the completion of an activity or task (i.e., a milestone). The same nine-activity project is illustrated as a PERT diagram and as a CPM diagram in Figure 10-4.

The Critical Path Method has proven useful in guiding elemental as well as more complex public projects. CPM is relatively easy to understand and apply. While software has been developed to permit the formulation of a CPM analysis on personal computers, the techniques are also amenable to sketching on a note pad. Further, CPM can be used as a convenient tool to communicate project assignments—it provides a quick reference for relationships among dependent activities. For these reasons, the techniques of the Critical Path Method will serve as the primary focus in the balance of this discussion.

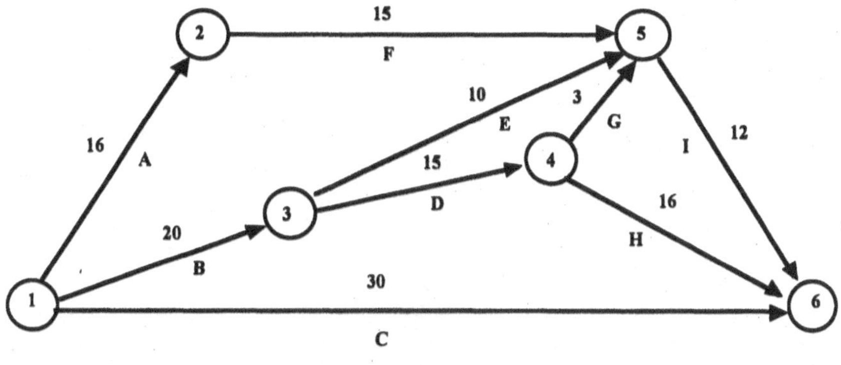

Figure 10-4a PERT Diagram for Nine-activity Project

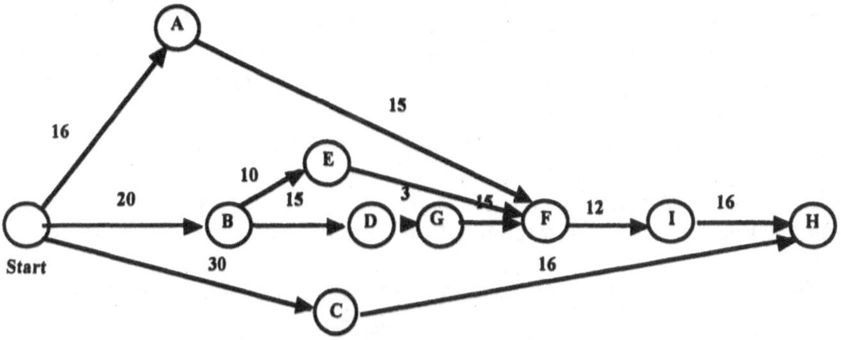

Figure 10-4b CPM Diagram for Nine-activity Project

Application of CPM

Under the Critical Path Method, management functions are divided into two distinct phases: (1) planning—deciding *what* should be done; and (2) scheduling—determining *when* activities should be initiated. With this separation, it is possible to determine which activities actually control significant completion times. Thus, project supervision can be based on the notion of management by exception. Attention can be directed to those activities most critical to the achievement of management and operational objectives. CPM facilitates the selection of a best route to be followed to reach these objectives. Potential obstacles and delays that might be encountered along the way also are more clearly identified.

Calculations on the Network

A key step in the CPM process is to assign time estimates to the arrows that form the various paths within the network diagram. A time estimate or *duration* is the amount of time required to complete the particular activity represented by a given arrow. Multiple arrows terminating at the same node (event) should be assigned the same duration.

The efforts of the Jefferson County Health Department to establish a prenatal health-care clinic in a section of the county where such health services have not previously been available can be used to further illustrate these CPM procedures. The initial perceptions as to the linkages among the fourteen activities previously identified in the work breakdown schedule are shown in Table 10-5. For each activity, the linkages to other activities are shown in Table 10-6, along with an identification of the activities that must precede a particular activity and those activities that follow from the designated activity. Note that activities 1.1 and 2.1 have no preceding activities and therefore are the initial activities of the project. Activity 1.4 shows no activities following its completion and therefore is the last activity of the project. The arrow diagram for this project is shown in Figure 10-5.

The estimated time duration for each of the fourteen activities has been loaded on to the arrows in the network in Figure 10-6. Each arrow leading to a given node (event or activity completion) is assigned the time duration for the designated activity. In this way, all of the possible paths to that node can be easily traced.

Beginning at "Start," the time duration for each path should be summed to determine:

1. The earliest possible time that an activity that terminates at a give node can be completed—known as the *earliest possible occurrence* or EPO.
2. How long it will take to complete the entire project (*project duration*).
3. Which activities establish and control the project duration (the *critical path*).
4. How much leeway (*float*) exists for those activities that do not control the project duration.

In Figure 10-6, for example, the path from Start to 2.1 (hire/assign clinic staff) to 2.2 (orient staff to agency procedures) to 2.4 (certify staff members) is estimated to take eight weeks. The path from Start to 2.1 to 2.3 (train staff in clinic operations) to 2.4 would take eleven weeks. Therefore, the EPO for the completion of activity 2.4 is eleven weeks. Other activities dependent on the completion of this activity (for example, screening applicants for eligibility) cannot begin until eleven weeks into the project.

The EPO of the final activity node has added significance—it is the earliest possible completion time for the entire project. Activity 1.4 (open clinic to eligible applicants) cannot begin until fifteen weeks into the project and has a duration of one week. Therefore, the *project duration* for the establishment of the prenatal health-care clinic is sixteen weeks.

Table 10-5
Linkages and Predecessor-Successor Relationships

The following statements might be assumed to reflect the initial perceptions as to the linkages among the fourteen activities that comprise the management plan for the establishment of the prenatal health-care clinic:

1. Locating the clinic space (1.1) and hiring and/or assigning staff to work in the clinic (2.1) are the initial subtasks of the project and can be performed concurrently.
2. Ordering office equipment (1.3.2) must follow after the rental contract for the clinic space have been negotiated (1.2).
3. Developing the appropriate layout of the space (1.3.1) is dependent, in part, on the receipt of office equipment (1.3.2) and securing office supplies and materials (1.3.4).
4. Staff members cannot be certified (2.4) until they have been hired and/or assigned (2.1), oriented (2.2), and trained (2.3).
5. The orientation (2.2) and training (2.3) of the staff can be carried out concurrently.
6. Publicity on the clinic programs (3.2) must precede the screening and enrollment of eligible applicants (3.3).
7. Program publicity cannot begin until space has been secured (1.2) and program information has been developed (3.1).
8. The new clinic can be opened only after all other activities have been completed.

Table 10-6
Linkages and Predecessor-Successor Relationships for the Establishment of a Prenatal Health-care Clinic

Activity	Linked to:	Preceded by:	Followed by:
1.1	(1.2), (1.3.4)	None	(1.2), (1.3.4)
1.2	(1.1), (1.3.2), (3.1)	(1.1)	(1.3.2), (3.1)
1.3.1	(1.4), (1.3.2), (1.3.4)	(1.3.2),(1.3.4)	(1.4)
1.3.2	(1.2), (1.3.1)	(1.2)	(1.3.1)
1.3.3	(1.3.4), (1.4)	(1.3.4)	(1.4)
1.3.4	(1.1), (1.3.1), (1.3.3)	(1.1)	(1.3.1), (1.3.3)
1.4	(1.2.1), (1.3.3), (3.3)	(1.3.1),(1.3.3), (3.3)	None
2.1	(2.2), (2.3)	None	(2.2), (2.3)
2.2	(2.1), (2.4)	(2.1)	(2.4)
2.3	(2.1), (2.4)	(2.1)	(2.4)
2.4	(2.2), (2.3), (3.3)	(2.2), (2.3)	(3.3)
3.1	(1.2), (3.2)	(1.2)	(3.2)
3.2	(3.1), (3.3)	(3.1)	(3.3)
3.3	(1.4), (2.4), (3.2)	(2.4), (3.2)	(1.4)

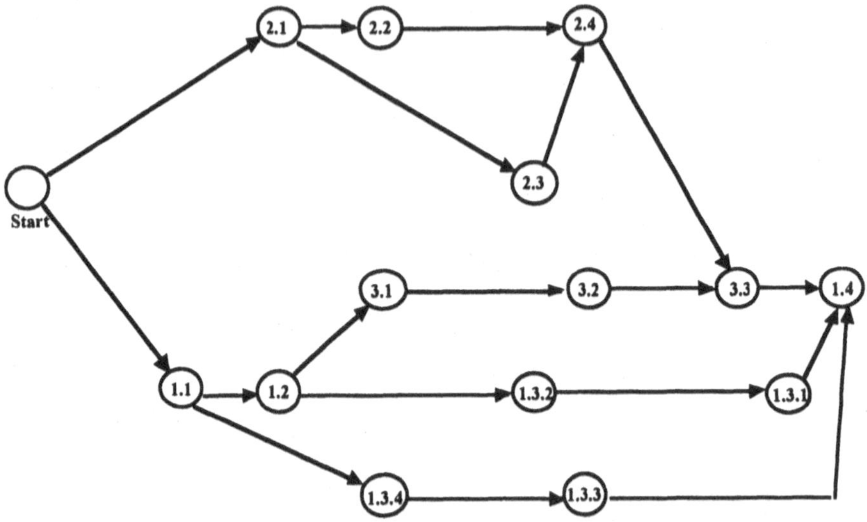

Figure 10-5 Arrow Diagram for Prenatal Health-care Clinic

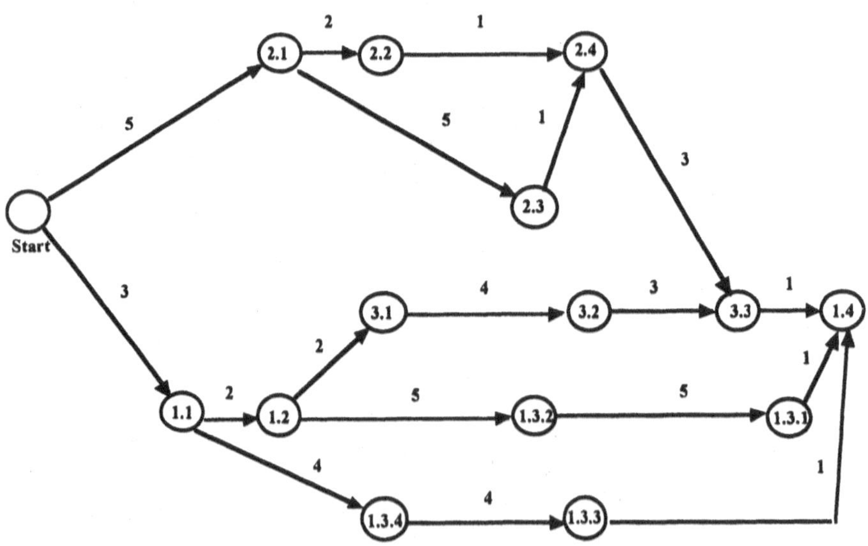

Figure 10-6 Arrow Diagram with Duration Estimates

Operational Leeway: Float

The *float* of a given activity is the amount of time that the activity can be delayed or the duration of that activity extended without affecting the earliest possible occurrence (EPO) of any other activity. To determine this operational leeway, calculations must be made by taking the EPO of the final activity node and subtracting the time durations back to the nodes that lead to this final activity. This process is repeated for each node, in turn, back to Start. These calculations determine the *latest possible occurrence* or LPO, that is, the latest time that all of the activities terminating at a given node can finish without causing the project to exceed the originally determined duration.

Whereas the EPO is the longest path from Start to a given node, the LPO is the shortest path from the termination of the project back to a given node. The difference between the EPO and LPO represents the float for that activity.

The Critical Path

It should be clear that no activity with a positive float can control the duration of the entire project. The durations of these activities can be extended by an amount equal to their float without affecting the EPO of any other activity. This means that the EPO of the last activity node will not be affected and, hence, that the project duration will not be altered. This characteristic of float limits the search for "critical" activities to those that have zero float.

Not all activities with zero float control the project duration, however. The controlling activities are those that have zero float and form a continuous path, starting at the first activity and ending at the last one. In Figure 10-7, this path is made up of the links between 1.1, 1.2, 3.1, 3.2, 3.3, and 1.4. If any of these activities are delayed, the project completion time will increase by the amount of that delay. This sequence of activities defines the *critical path.*

To outline another example of a critical path, assume that the Rurbana Sewer and Water Utility Commission has approved the construction of a new water storage tank and pumping station to serve the needs of an expanding residential neighborhood. The pumping station will include facilities for treatment and testing of the water supply. A gas driven generator will also be installed to provide emergency power to the pumps in the event of a power failure in the main electricity supply. The descriptions, linkages, and estimated durations of the various activities identified for this project are given in Table 10-7.

The arrow diagram that delineates the sequential relationships among these activities is shown in Figure 10-8. The critical path for this project is defined by the sequence of activities A, C, D, F, K, O, L, P, Q, and R. The earliest possible completion of the activities on the critical path (and therefore the proposed project) is 160 days. Any delays encountered on this critical path will result in a delay in the completion of the project.

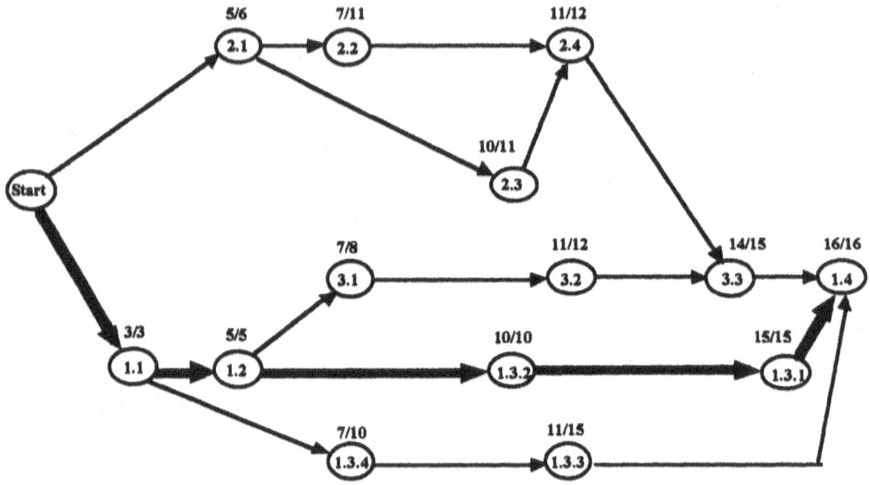

Figure 10-7 Arrow Diagram Showing EPO/LPO for Each Activity Node

Summary of CPM Procedures

The steps involved in applying the Critical Path Method can be summarized as follows:

1. Define the activities or tasks that make up the project.
2. Define the linkages and performance sequence for each activity.
3. Draw an arrow diagram or network that defines the sequence of performing the various activities.
4. Estimate the duration of each activity.
5. Calculate the EPO and LPO for each activity node (event).
6. Determine the float for each activity (the LPO minus the EPO).
7. Locate the critical path, i.e., those activities with zero float that form a continuous sequence from the beginning to the end of the arrow diagram.

Table 10-7
Linkages and Predecessor Relationships for the Construction of Water Storage Tank and Pumping Station

Activity	Description	Linked to	Preceded by	Duration
A	Clear site	B, C	(None)	10
B	Trench for utilities	A, D	A	5
C	Prepare site for construction	A, D, E	A	15
D	Lay foundation for pump station & generator	B, C, F, G	B, C	15
E	Erect tower for water storage tank	C, H	C	20
F	Construct pump station building	D, N, K	D	35
G	Install emergency generator	D, H	D	10
H	Install water storage tank	E, G, J, K	E, G	20
I	Install pump	N, P	N	10
J	Connect water tower to pump station	H, L	H	10
K	Install electric service	F, H, O	F, H	20
L	Install water treatment equipment	J, M, O, P	J, O	20
M	Install testing equipment	L, R	L	15
N	Rough in plumbing in pump station	F, I	F	10
O	Connect generator to pump station	K, L	K	10
P	Complete finish work on building	I, L, Q	I, L	15
Q	Paint building	P, R	P	10
R	Inspection and testing	Q, M	Q, M	10

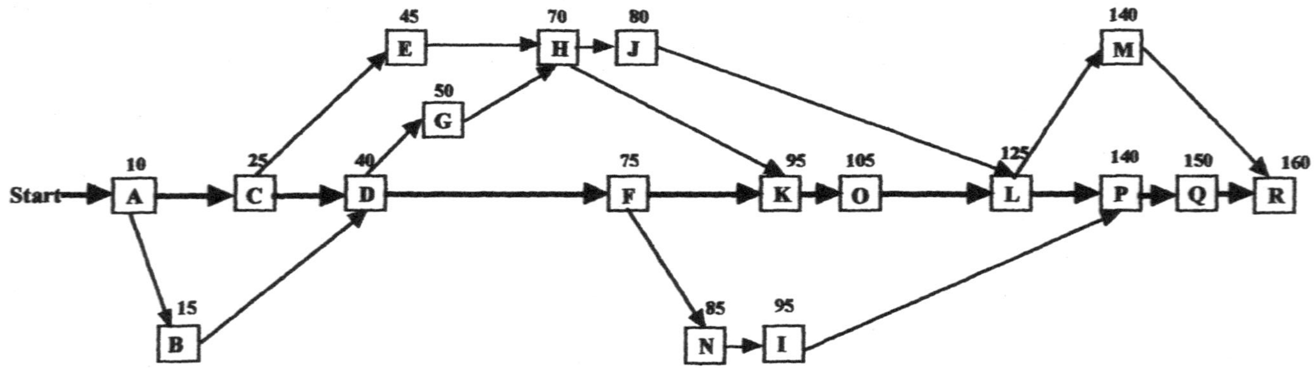

Figure 10-8 Arrow Diagram for Water Storage Tank Project

Once the actual project is implemented, the critical path can be continuously monitored so that potential delays can be identified before they occur. Such delays can be avoided by shifting personnel, materials, or other resource inputs to the critical path from those paths that have "float." Thus, the identification of the critical path also provides the project manager with a dynamic control mechanism.

In addition, the CPM network offers a convenient form of shorthand to express a complex set of relations and a medium of communication and prediction. It facilitates the subdivision of work so that each person involved can proceed with the more detailed planning of his or her part of the project.

The CPM approach provides a basis for an analysis of the costs involved when efforts are launched to utilize float time in order to reduce overall project costs. Or, in those instances where a project deadline is imposed and therefore the critical path may be reduced, CPM can assist in the determination of the cost of crash scheduling. In general, the CPM approach determines: (1) the sequential ordering of activities, (2) the maximum time required to complete the project, (3) the costs involved, and (4) the ramifications in time and costs for altering the critical path.

Crash Scheduling

A project manager might be tempted to use all available staff resources to complete the critical activities as they occur in the project plan. Depending on the nature of the project, however, such crash scheduling might merely result in a shift of the critical path to other activities having minimal float. It also might produce a "staffing overload," whereby too many resources are assigned over too short a period of time. The result might be increased inefficiency, as staff members literally get in each other's way. Crash scheduling at the outset of a project might use up a management option that could become important later on once the project is under way. The ability to "crash" on a critical path activity when it falls behind schedule (that is, to reassign staff resources in an effort to get the critical activity back on schedule) is an important aspect of dynamic project management.

The general procedures for crashing scheduling are as follows:

1. Determine the minimum project time and associated critical path (a) if all activities are completed in normal time, and (b) if all activities are crashed. The minimum project time when all activities are crashed determines the stopping point for the crash schedule analysis.
2. Identify and crash the activity on the critical path with the minimum crash per unit of time. If there is more than one critical path, crash the activity on each path with the minimum crash per unit of time.
3. Revise the network, adjusting for the time and cost assigned to the crashed activity(s).
4. Determine the critical paths, using normal activity times for noncrashed activities and crash schedule times for crashed activities. If the project time equals the crash schedule time computed in step 1, stop; otherwise, return to step 2.

The use of three time estimates, as described below, can provide the basis for determining the crash-time for a given activity—usually the most optimistic time estimate or *a*. The normal-time estimate can be either the most likely time, *m*, or the computed expected time, *te*.

The procedures for crash scheduling can be illustrated by the following example. The normal and crash times and normal and crash costs for a project with seven subtasks are given in Table 10-8. The project network is shown in Figure 10-9; activities A, C, and G form the critical path. Assuming normal times for the subtasks, the project duration is forty-four weeks at a total cost of $64,000. If all activities are crash scheduled, the project time is twenty-eight weeks at a total cost of $105,000. The crash-time cost per unit of time can be estimated by the following formula:

$$\frac{\text{Crash Cost - Normal Cost}}{\text{Normal Time - Crash Time}}$$

Activity C on the critical path has the minimum crash cost per week (i.e., $20,000 minus $16,000 divided by 4 = $1,000). Crash scheduling this activity reduces the project duration by four weeks but adds $4,000 to the total project cost. Activity G has a crash cost of $1,250 per week; crash scheduling this activity reduces the project duration by another four weeks and adds $6,000 to the total project cost. Activity A also has a crash cost of $1,250 per week, and crash scheduling this activity would reduce the project duration by eight weeks to twenty-eight weeks and add $10,000 to the total project cost. However, crash scheduling this activity shifts the critical path to activities A, B, D, and G, which now have a project duration of thirty-two weeks. The final adjustment that can be made is to crash schedule activity B, which would bring the project duration back to the targeted twenty-eight weeks at a total project cost of $93,000, or $12,000 less than if all of the activities are crashed.

With this information in hand, it must be decided if shortening the project duration from forty-four weeks to twenty-eight weeks is worth an additional $29,000. Perhaps a compromise would be to accept the thirty-two week duration (at an additional cost of $19,000 or a total cost of $83,000) by shifting the critical path to activities A, B, D, and G.

Estimating Time Durations: The Problem of Uncertainty

It often is difficult to predict the exact time duration of any given task or activity in a project. In such cases, it might be appropriate to provide a time estimate that reflects the *most likely value* of an unknown distribution function. If the variance of this distribution is relatively small, the most likely time duration might provide a reasonably close approximation of the actual time required to complete the activity. If the variance is large, however, the duration is said to be *uncertain*.

Table 10-8
Normal and Crashed Times and Normal and Crashed Costs for a Project with Seven Subtasks

Activity	Time (in weeks) Normal	Time (in weeks) Crashed	Costs Normal	Costs Crashed	Crash Cost per Week
A*	14	6	14,000	24,000	1,250
B	12	8	10,000	20,000	2,500
C*	18	14	16,000	20,000	1,000
D	6	4	8,000	12,000	2,000
E	4	2	4,000	9,000	2,500
F	8	6	4,000	7,000	1,500
G*	12	8	8,000	13,000	1,250
Total			64,000	105,000	

*Activities on the critical path.

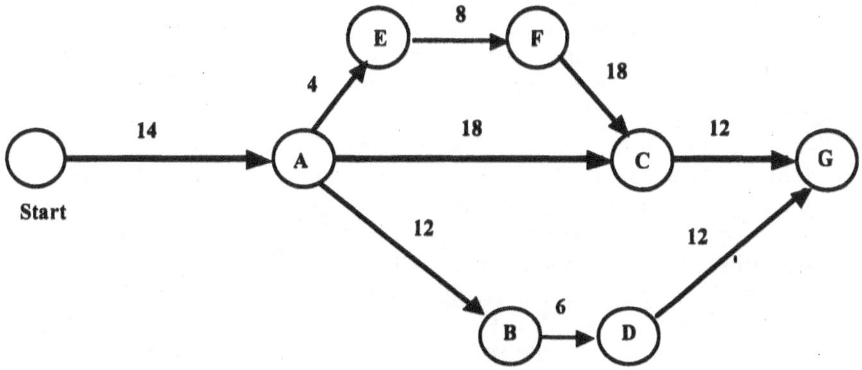

Figure 10-9 Arrow Diagram for Project with Seven Subtasks

Beta Distribution

It is frequently argued that public projects all-too-often manifest such uncertainty as to severely limit the application of the rigor of network analysis techniques. This argument is fallacious, however, since these techniques were first developed and applied in industry and in the military because of uncertainty in time estimates.

The approach adopted by the original PERT team led to the development of the so-called beta distribution formula:

expected time = 1/6 $(a + 4b + c)$,
where: a = the most optimistic time estimate
b = the most likely time estimate
c = the most pessimistic time estimate

The beta distribution or expected time formula is based on the assumption that the duration of any activity or project is unimodal (that is, only one mode exists—*b*). It further is assumed that the variance of the distribution is the square of the standard deviation which, in turn, can be estimated as roughly one-sixth of the range (i.e., the difference between the most optimistic and the most pessimistic time estimate).

The application of the beta distribution formula is relatively simple. When some doubt exists as to the appropriate time duration to be assigned to any activity, the project manager should ask those who will be responsible for carrying out the activity: "If everything goes right with this job, what is the shortest time you will require to complete this activity?" Then the manager should ask: "If everything goes wrong—if the absolute worst happens—what is the longest time period required to complete this activity?" Finally, assuming the range established by the answers to the first two questions, the manager should ask: "What is the most likely time required to complete this activity?"

To gain a clear understanding of how the beta distribution formula can be applied under conditions of uncertainty, consider the following examples:

Example 1: Assume that the most optimistic time for the completion of some activity is fifteen days; the most likely time in the judgment of the staff is twenty-five days; and the most pessimistic time is thirty-five days. Applying the formula, the estimated time for completion would be:

$$1/6\ (15 + 4 \times 25 + 35) = 25$$

Thus, the most likely time and the computed time estimate are the same, which follows from the fact that the distribution of variance approximates a normal curve. The standard deviation in this example is 3.33 days (i.e., the most pessimistic time minus the most optimistic time, divided by six).

Example 2: Assume that the most optimistic and most likely time estmates remain the same (fifteen and twenty-five days respectively), but that the most pessimistic time estimate is extended to forty-seven days due to the uncertainty surrounding the completion of various activities. These conditions result in a distribution that is skewed to the left. Therefore, the computed time estimate lies to the right of the most likely time (i.e., the expected time is greater than the most likely time). Applying the beta distribution formula, expected time equals twenty-seven days (i.e., 15 + 4 x 25 + 47, divided by 6), and the standard deviation in this example is five days.

Example 3: In the final example, the most likely and pessimistic time estimates are the same as in the first example (twenty-five and thirty-five days respectively), while the most optimistic time estimate is reduced to nine days. These estimates result in a distribution that is skewed to the right, with the expected time at twenty-four days being smaller than the most likely time. The standard deviation in this example is 4.33 days (i.e., 35 minus 9, divided by 6).

Relationship Between Expected Time and Variance

As might be seen from these three examples, expected time and variance—although statistically related—act somewhat independently in real-world situations. Expected time corresponds to "average" in common language—there is a 50% probability that the estimated time will be exceeded by the actual duration. Variance, on the other hand, is a measure of uncertainty. If the variance is large, there is greater uncertainty as to the time in which the activity will be completed. If the variance is small, it follows that the uncertainty will be small. Thus, although the estimated time in the third example is less than in the first (twenty-four days as compared to twenty-five days), the third example evidences greater uncertainty, as illustrated by the larger variance (i.e., the square of the standard deviation or 18.75 days).

The concept of variance can be used to evaluate the probability (or risk) of meeting a specific time schedule. An F value can be determined by subtracting the earliest possible occurrence for any given activity from some imposed schedule completion time (S) and dividing the result by the standard deviation for that activity. By consulting a table of values for the normal curve, this F value can then be interpreted in terms of the probability of meeting the imposed schedule.

To illustrate these procedures, assume that three time estimates are obtained for each activity in the water storage tank project previously outlined in Table 10-7. These three time estimates are shown in Table 10-9. The values of the *te* and the variance must be computed for each activity. Using the *te* values, the EPO and LPO can be determined for each activity in the network, and a new critical path can be identified for the project, as shown in Figure 10-10. The greater uncertainty regarding the estimated time requirements of activities G and

Table 10-9
Estimated Time Durations

Activity	Optimistic	Most Likely	Pessimistic	te	SD	SD2
A*	**5**	**10**	**20**	**10.83**	**2.5000**	**6.250**
B	3	5	10	5.50	1.1667	1.361
C*	**6**	**15**	**32**	**16.33**	**4.3333**	**18.778**
D*	**5**	**15**	**24**	**14.83**	**3.1667**	**10.028**
E	10	20	28	19.67	3.0000	9.000
F	15	35	45	33.33	5.0000	25.000
G*	**5**	**10**	**30**	**12.50**	**4.1667**	**17.361**
H*	**10**	**20**	**40**	**21.67**	**5.0000**	**25.000**
I	5	10	15	10.00	1.6667	2.778
J	5	10	20	10.83	2.5000	6.250
K*	**5**	**20**	**33**	**19.67**	**4.6667**	**21.778**
L*	**4**	**20**	**28**	**18.67**	**4.0000**	**16.000**
M	5	15	25	15.00	3.3333	11.111
N	5	10	20	10.83	2.5000	6.250
O*	**5**	**10**	**20**	**10.83**	**2.5000**	**6.250**
P*	**5**	**15**	**35**	**16.67**	**5.0000**	**25.000**
Q*	**4**	**10**	**22**	**11.00**	**3.0000**	**9.000**
R*	10	10	10	10.00	0.0000	0.000
Duration	64	155	294	163.00		155.444
Standard Deviation =		(294 – 64)/6	= 38.33			12.468

*Activities on the critical path.

H results in a shift of these activities on to the critical path replacing activity F. The new project duration is extended to 163 days.

Given the adjusted critical path, what is the probability of completing the project within 150 days or less? The calculations to determine the F value are as follows:

$$F = \frac{\text{Imposed Schedule Deadline minus Expected Duration}}{\text{Standard Deviation of Expected Duration}}$$

$$F = \frac{150-163}{38.33} = -\ 0.3391$$

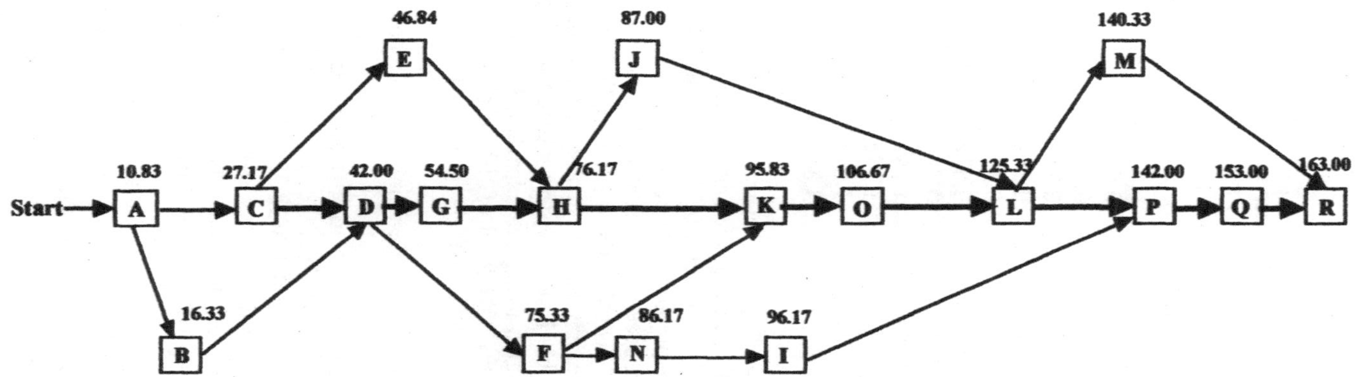

Figure 10-10 Adjusted Arrow Diagram for Water Storage Tank Project

Table 10-10
F Values for Various Levels of Risk/Probability of Success

Probability of Success	F Value	Negative F Value
50%	0.00000	50%
55%	0.12085	45%
60%	0.25163	40%
65%	0.38217	35%
70%	0.52253	30%
75%	0.67277	25%
80%	0.84294	20%
85%	1.04282	15%
90%	1.28256	10%
95%	1.64173	5%
100%	3.87000	0%

From a table of values for the standard normal distribution function, it can be determined that the value for -0.3391 is 0.3665. In other words, there is only a 37% chance of the project being completed in 150 days. The F values for various probabilities of success are provided in Table 10-10.

This method of assessing risk can be applied in reverse to determine an appropriate duration for any activity in a project (or for the total project duration), given some acceptable level of risk (as determined by the project manager or decision maker). Again using the expected duration in the water storage tank project, assume that a 20% level of risk is chosen. What time duration should be allowed for the completion of the project? The appropriate formula is as follows:

Imposed Schedule Deadline = F(Standard Deviation of te) + te

The F value for a 20% level of risk (that is, an 80% probability of success) is approximately 0.843. Therefore, the project duration to achieve this projected level of success would be 0.843(38.33) plus 163, or approximately 195 days. To raise the probability of success to a 90% level (10% level of risk) would require approximately 17 additional days (or a total of 212 days), whereas to approach a success level of 100% would require nearly 148 days beyond the 163 day duration.

It might be possible to reduce the level of risk (increase the probability of success) from the 50% level (assumed by the beta distribution) by adding a relatively small amount of time to the estimated project duration. However, the increments of time required become increasingly larger above the 90% level of success, often beyond any realistic expectations. Changes in the standard deviation of the expected duration will have a significant impact on the additional time required to increase the probability of success. Reducing the standard deviation (reducing the uncertainty) will reduce the additional time duration required for any chosen level of success.

In most situations, the three time estimates approach of the beta distribution gives a more pessimistic outlook than would be obtained by using only the most likely duration. Staff members have a tendency to "hedge their bets" when asked to provide three time estimates, i.e., to be more conservative. In many projects, the manager should use the best time estimate possible and then control the project in a dynamic fashion. In short, regardless of how the estimate of time is obtained, a major responsibility of management is to control the project once implementation is begun.

Leveling Resources

A basic requirement in preparing an operations schedule is to level the use of resources. This leveling is accomplished by using the total float times to select the best starting time for each activity. Thus, in developing a schedule, the critical path is determined not so much by the duration of the various activities, but by the segment of resources (personnel, equipment, funds, etc.) that can be assigned out of the total resource capacity in order to complete each activity.

Assume, for example, that a staff of fifteen persons is available to work on a given project. Obviously, not all of the staff members have the same skill levels, and therefore the first scheduling challenge is to assign the appropriate personnel to the various tasks and activities within the scope of the project. However, it is also important to avoid periods when various staff members might be idle, waiting for others to complete their assignments. An optimal staffing approach would be to gradually increase the number of persons assigned to the project until a maximum loading is achieved and then to gradually decrease the numbers until the project is completed.

This situation illustrates the essence of the resource allocation problem. A plan shows the proper sequence and optimum utilization of resources for minimum durations. However, in order to arrive at a schedule (so that the work required to complete the project can be carried out most effectively), it is necessary to allocate the available resource capacity according to the priorities indicated by the plan to remain within the limits of peak efficiency.

If the project is to be kept on schedule and deadlines are to be met, some guidelines are required to assist the project manager in the task of assigning these limited resources. A relatively simple approach can provide these guidelines:

1. Allocate resources serially in time; that is, for the first time period, schedule all jobs possible given staff (or other limited resources), then do the same for the second time period, and so on.
2. When several jobs compete for the same resources, give preference to the jobs with the least float or slack time.
3. Reschedule noncritical jobs (those not on the critical path), if possible, in order to free resources for scheduling critical jobs.

By making these minor adjustments in scheduling—utilizing the float or slack time of various tasks to make "early starts"—it often is possible to maintain the project on schedule, within bounds of the limited staff resources, and, at the same time, to achieve a more even distribution of staff commitments. Under conditions of limited resources, it might be necessary to extend the time period of the project in order to maintain the constraints. By utilizing the basic programming approach, however, the necessary time extensions to achieve an optimal schedule can be minimized.

Computer Applications

Mainframe (and later minicomputer) programs have been written to handle project planning tasks formerly relegated to hand-drawn milestone, PERT, and CPM charts. Large mainframe systems, such as Atemis, Phoenix PMS, Project Manager, Vision, SAS/O.R., and Telleplan, support virtually every function, method, analytic technique, and reporting style that a manager could want in such software. Large systems also offer access to large databases, provide built-in multiuser capabilities, and facilitate an evaluation of the scope and progress of a project in considerable detail by drawing on broad organizational data resources. These mainframe programs are relatively expensive, however, costing $15,000 to $200,000.

The first project planning software for desktop use was released in 1983 and was written for the IBM PC. Since project planning is a highly visual process, based on the use of charts, diagrams, and tables to track and analyze project data, the Macintosh should be a natural engine for such systems. Initial software developed for the Macintosh in 1988 includes *MacProject* and *Micro Planner*. More recently, many new project planning software packages have been introduced. Over twenty-five desktop programs are currently available, ranging in price from $99 to $1,995.

MacProject II, the most popular Macintosh project-management software, provides most of the basic tools that project planners need. It support the Critical Path Method and PERT networks, draws Gantt charts, keeps track of hundreds of separate project-resource categories, and has single and multiple project calendars, detailed project budgets, and similar technical desiderata. *MacProject II* can consolidate projects and work with subproject and supraproject hierarchies—permitting many related projects to be interconnected. It can perform resource-constraint analyses and accomplish many other technical tasks required in project planning. The manuals and menus for *MacProject II* are reasonably easy to apply once some effort has been devoted to understanding how projects should be managed using automated methods.

MacProject Pro, the successor to *MacProject II*, offers many new features with no particular drawbacks in terms of speed or hardware requirements compared to earlier versions. A powerful project outliner allows users to juggle connected tasks lists and to brainstorm on-screen in the PERT chart. The software facilitates the tracking of activities and related components on a network and the exchange of data with other packages. *MacProject Pro* handles files from *Excel* and many other spreadsheets and databases. It is possible to use *MacProject Pro* on large projects—there is no software limit on number of tasks, and users can link cross-dependent projects and resources. A good suite of outputs—reports and graphics—also is available.

Microsoft Project 2002 includes a Project Guide, which helps users navigate through the project management process while allowing them to learn, discover, and explore the available features of the software. The Project Guide provides instructions and controls for completing a variety of project management tasks, including setting the collaboration options of a new project and simplifying the establishment of the project calendar, base calendars, resource calendars, and other calendar-related options. By following these instructions, users can quickly accomplish tasks, such as defining project dimensions, entering tasks, and assigning resources.

Microsoft Project 2002 also includes a Resource Availability Graph to provide project and functional managers with a flexible, graphical tool for understanding when and why resources might be overallocated. Using the Resource Availability Graph, users can view the time-phased work, availability, and remaining availability of one or more resources, grouped by project. The Resource Availability Graph uses the following elements:

- *Charts* to display a graphical representation of the selected time-phased data for the selected resources.
- *Tables* to display a tabular representation of the selected time-phased data for the selected resources.
- *Legends* to describe the resources, time-phased data, and duration.

KeyPlan is a software package designed for users who are not already familiar with the project planning process. *KeyPlan* uses an outline format similar to a work breakdown schedule, the entries to which later become parts of the project plan. Project planning begins with a brainstorming session wherein project tasks, milestones, and subplans are identified within the outliner window. These elements eventually are converted into a network diagram (PERT) that shows the order of task precedence. Summary information for the network is provided in a task information window at the bottom of the screen. The program also calculates and displays the project's critical path (or paths). Procedures for editing network diagrams make good use of the graphic interface to create or remove tasks, modify project schedules, and create dependencies. The user can annotate Gantt charts, network diagrams, or resource histograms with text or other graphics. Project dependencies that might eventually crash into each other are tracked, and such potential conflicts are flagged immediately, making this software a dynamic tool for project management.

SmartDraw is a software package that facilitates the creation of project management charts in minutes. It is easy to use and includes an extensive collection of symbols and templates to create Gantt charts, PERT charts, timelines, workflow diagrams, project plans, and schedules. Drag-and-drop graphics available from the built-in libraries makes drawing easy. *SmartDraw* automatically aligns and arranges everything to look very professional.

FastTrack Schedule and *Great Gantt!* are more limited software packages that concentrate primarily on the production of high-quality milestone and Gantt charts. These software packages do not have the capacity for CPM project management, although Great Gantt! can read MacProject files directly, creating Gantt charts from networks. Lacking CPM or PERT capabilities means that these products cannot handle complicated task interdependencies, resource conflicts and constraints, or any of the other problems that prompted the development of these network analysis techniques.

FastTrack provides several methods for tracking the project schedule, including the capability to define multiple bars per activity. The project manager has the ability to track the original project schedule, the revised schedule, and the actual schedule in one line. A project manager might also use this feature to track multiple people working on the same task. Another innovative feature is the summary line, which offers the ability to rollup a summary of activities, costs, or anything else tracked in a data column and presents it at the bottom of the screen in synch with the project timeline.

With the recent introduction and enhancement of these desktop software packages, most public agencies that have any computing capabilities can get into the business of project planning without having to rely on complicated mainframe applications. While the microcomputer has replaced the "back of the envelope" approach to project management, it has also significantly enhanced the range of analyses that can be carried out to ensure that project objectives will be achieved as efficiently and effectively as possible.

Dynamic Response Cycle

Project management is best served by a real-time control system—one that makes it possible to respond to situations according to their degree of urgency. Failure to proceed beyond determining the critical path has prevented many users from realizing the full benefits of CPM and PERT. Once the plan and schedule are determined, the project must be monitored against actual performance, and management control must be exercised at all levels of supervision. Deviations from the predicted schedule should be used to revise the project plan, adjust the allocation of resources, and recalculate the overall schedule for the balance of the project. However, managers do not need to be informed if no action is required or if the program is self-correcting. This is *management by exception* as it should operate.

Two major fallacies associated with the application of these project planning and scheduling techniques are (1) assuming that these methods will do everything, and (2) assuming that they can be of no help at all. These techniques are criticized, at times, as not being all that useful because they cannot prevent such problems as missed deadlines established for projects or cost overruns, nor can they avert delays due to bad weather or other natural causes. The fact of the matter is that no method will ever eliminate or prevent these problems of project management. The idea is to attack such problems methodically—this is the essence of good project management.

To say that effective use cannot be made of these methods is to ignore the many occasions on which they have been of significant assistance in projects, both large and small. Any method that provides a better answer to the problems of management should be used. The real issue seems to be not whether the method itself can be useful, but whether people will adopt it and apply it.

Management has been defined as the judicious allocation of resources to accomplish agreed-upon objectives according to a plan and schedule. Effective management also requires the ability to forestall the development of unfavorable situations by reacting quickly to deviations between predicted and actual results. Of necessity, management involves a balance between subjective ability and objective (or scientific) methods.

The complexities of government and increased demands for more effective utilization of limited public resources give rise to the need for a new breed of public management personnel. This new breed cannot afford to operate on its wits alone, as public managers often were able to do in the past. Like it or not, today's public managers must be willing to understand and use all the management techniques at their disposal. A new project cannot be launched, a new strategic facility built, or any public project successfully initiated and operated unless there is a *plan* and a *schedule* of work—one which permits public managers to exercise *dynamic control* throughout the project.

Chapter 11

INVESTMENT STRATEGIES

Local governments accumulate cash balances for various reasons. Bonds for capital improvements are usually issued before a project begins, whereas the disbursement of these funds occurs only as the bills are paid throughout the construction period. Intergovernmental transfers often are made in lump sums as a result of statutory regulations or administrative practices governing such payments. A large inflow of revenue occurs just prior to the penalty dates on the tax calendar. For these and other reasons, jurisdictions often are able to meet current obligations and, at the same time, have some uncommitted cash left over to invest in interest-yielding securities. The investment of such funds that otherwise would be temporarily unproductive offers a source of additional revenue without increasing taxes.

Investment Strategies in Debt Administration

The investment and liquidation of funds play an important role in debt administration. The funds to meet debt service requirements often come from several sources, including short-term investments, and must be brought together on a timely basis to meet these obligations. Principal payments on certain types of bonds are not made until the debt matures. Therefore, the resources required to service the debt should be invested in a sinking fund, which accumulates a fund balance including interest sufficient to meet the eventual debt payment. The overlap in these financial management responsibilities suggests that they be examined together—first looking at the strategies and procedures for managing investments and then applying these procedures to the administration of debt.

Public Investment Criteria

The first step in developing an investment strategy is to determine the funds that are available for investment and the duration of their availability. Cash flow projections should be made to reflect the impact of various economic conditions on the overall availability of funds. High interest rates and an intervening credit crunch, for example, might cause suppliers to shorten their credit terms and to press for more prompt payment of invoices. Conversely, cheap credit and lower interest rates might ease supplier terms. Information on these broader conditions should enable the financial manager to arrive at reasonable predictions as to how much money will be available to invest and for how long.

It has been said that the ideal investment is one that yields a high return at no risk, offers promise of substantial growth, and is instantly convertible into cash if money is needed for other purposes. This ideal specimen, of course, does not exist in reality. Each form of investment has its own special virtues and shortcomings. In general, securities with little risk, high liquidity, and short maturities also have low yields. For an investment to provide a high yield, one or more of the other relevant criteria must be compromised.

Principal criteria to be considered in selecting specific securities in which to invest public funds are (1) safety/risk, (2) price stability, (3) liquidity/marketability, (4) maturity, and (5) yield. Public officials generally adhere to a set of investment principles that accord the highest priority to safety, followed by liquidity and yield.

The risk characteristics of securities must be understood before decisions are made about which specific instruments to purchase. In many states, the investments of local governments are restricted to securities that are *collateralized* or backed by the United States government. Even these investments—for example, long-term government bonds—"fluctuate in value and thus present some risk if they must be sold prior to maturity in an unfavorable market."[1]

Public officials are very much aware that government funds must be employed to achieve expressed objectives. Local finance officers might find their positions in jeopardy if a portion of these public funds is lost as a consequence of risky investment practices. As a consequence, local governments tend to invest in low-risk securities with relatively low rates of return. Some localities, however, are large enough and financially strong enough to take limited risks without serious damage. If the risk is only slightly higher, an investment in a higher-yielding security might be appropriate.

In addition to serving as income-producing assets, short-term investments constitute cash reserves. In the event of an unexpected cash shortage, the first reaction often is to convert some financial assets into cash. The desire to avoid financial loss under such circumstances explains the concern of public officials for the price stability of short-term investments.

Generally speaking, U.S. Treasury bills (T-bills) are the most stable of all money market instruments, principally because they are backed by the full faith and credit of the federal government. In addition, T-bills are usually issued on a short-term basis, maturing before new market conditions alter the assumptions on which the investment strategy was based. Other investment instruments characterized by price stability are federal agency issues and certificates of deposit.

The concept of *liquidity* involves managing investments so that cash will be available when needed. The basic question is: "Can a security be sold quickly and easily when the need arises?" *Marketability* varies among money market instruments, depending not only on the price stability of the instrument but, more importantly, on the extent of the secondary trading markets available to it. Treasury bills, for example, are practically riskless and are actively traded. As Harrell and Cole observe, "the sheer volume of Treasury bill issues and their tradeability in the secondary market establish the bills as the nearest equivalent to pure cash in the market."[2] Federal agency issues and certificates of deposit also have excellent liquidity.

The *maturities* of the various securities and their impact on the portfolio mix must be understood before a financial manager decides to invest in them. Sale or redemption of a security prior to the agreed upon maturity date usually results in the loss of accrued interest. This predicament can be avoided by buying a mix of securities with scattered maturity dates. In this way, at any time that cash is needed, some asset is likely to be near maturity, and therefore losses from premature sales can be avoided.

The liquidity problem can be addressed by selecting investments that mature at times when the locality is likely to need cash. Part of an investment portfolio might be earmarked for capital projects and part for anticipated operating expenses. In managing the portfolio, the maturity dates of holdings should be synchronized with the dates when funds will be needed to meet these obligations. It is relatively easy to align these dates, because securities usually are classified according to their maturity periods, such as thirty days, ninety days, one year, or five years.

Yield

Yield is the ultimate measure of successful financial management in a market economy. Yield is defined as the actual rate of return of a security's cash flows. It is the equivalent rate of return that equates the *invoice price* of a security (that is, principal plus accrued interest) with the present value of its coupon and principal payments. For example, the yield for a bond with a 4% coupon rate and an invoice price of $1,021.27 that matures five years after it is issued is 3.5%. In other words, an investor would have to pay $21.27 over par value ($1,000) to cover any premium and accrued interest. Over the five-year period to maturity, the investor would earn $200 in interest (4% per year for five years), and at maturity would receive $1,000 in principal. The net return on the investment is $178.73 ($200 minus $21.27), which is the equivalent of a 3.5% return over five years on the invoice price of $1,021.27.

The yield on an investment is conditioned by several exogenous factors, including interest rates, minimum investment requirements, and the maturity dates of investments. In general, the longer the maturity of an investment, the higher the yield. Any premiums and accrued interest that the investor must pay are spread over a longer period, thereby resulting in a higher yield. In the previous example, if the maturity of the investment were ten years instead of five years, the yield would be 3.71%. (The annual return on the investment is $40 times 10 = $400 minus $21.27 = $378.73 for an annual yield on $1,021.27 of 3.71%.) The yields on several different levels of investment with different maturities are shown in Table 11-1. To maximize the yield, it is important to design an investment schedule whereby each security will mature as close as possible to the time that the funds invested will be needed to cover operational or capital needs.

In spite of the constraints imposed by safety and liquidity, local governments are becoming increasingly interested in yield. As a first step, many financial executives have increased their efforts to monitor account balances to ensure that excess cash is invested immediately. In addition, some localities are moving away from state and local government obligations, which characteristically have low yields, in favor of higher-yield, high-grade corporate securities. At the same time, however, many local officials still rank yield as the least important of all the criteria in selecting an investment instrument.

Table 11-1
Yield on Securities with Various Invoice Prices

Invoice Price	Premium or Discount	Coupon Rate	Maturity	Annual Interest	Total Interest	Total Return	Net Return	Yield
$1,021.27	$21.27	4%	5	$40	$200	$1,178.73	$178.73	3.50%
$1,000.00	$0.00	4%	5	$40	$200	$1,200.00	$200.00	4.00%
$980.00	-$20.00	4%	5	$40	$200	$1,220.00	$220.00	4.49%
$990.00	-$10.00	4%	5	$40	$200	$1,210.00	$210.00	4.24%
$995.00	-$5.00	4%	5	$40	$200	$1,205.00	$205.00	4.12%
$1,100.00	$100.00	4%	5	$40	$200	$1,100.00	$100.00	1.82%
$1,025.00	$25.00	4%	5	$40	$200	$1,175.00	$175.00	3.41%
$1,020.00	$20.00	4%	5	$40	$200	$1,180.00	$180.00	3.53%
$980.00	-$20.00	5%	10	$50	$500	$1,520.00	$520.00	5.31%
$990.00	-$10.00	5%	10	$50	$500	$1,510.00	$510.00	5.15%
$995.00	-$5.00	5%	10	$50	$500	$1,505.00	$505.00	5.08%
$1,100.00	$100.00	5%	10	$50	$500	$1,400.00	$400.00	3.64%
$1,025.00	$25.00	5%	10	$50	$500	$1,475.00	$475.00	4.63%
$1,020.00	$20.00	5%	10	$50	$500	$1,480.00	$480.00	4.71%
$980.00	-$20.00	5.5%	15	$55	$825	$1,845.00	$845.00	5.75%
$990.00	-$10.00	5.5%	15	$55	$825	$1,835.00	$835.00	5.62%
$995.00	-$5.00	5.5%	15	$55	$825	$1,830.00	$830.00	5.56%
$1,100.00	$100.00	5.5%	15	$55	$825	$1,725.00	$725.00	4.39%
$1,025.00	$25.00	5.5%	15	$55	$825	$1,800.00	$800.00	5.20%
$1,020.00	$20.00	5.5%	15	$55	$825	$1,805.00	$805.00	5.26%

Types of Securities

Local governments and other public organizations often hold short-term securities that can be readily converted into cash either through the market or through maturity. The most attractive instruments that meet these criteria are federal securities, which are practically riskless, since they are backed by the full faith and credit of the federal government. Other securities carry varying degrees of risk and, therefore, must offer higher interest to make them attractive. Understanding the unique features of each type of the security available to local governments is critical to the formulation of prudent investment strategies. Short-term securities in which local governments most often invest are arrayed in Table 11-2 against the characteristics described above. The majority of states allow municipalities to use a variety of investment instruments, including U.S. Treasury bills, commercial bank certificates of deposit (CDs), savings and loan deposits, federal agency securities, and repurchase agreements. However, the majority of states also prohibit local governments from investing in banker's acceptances and commercial paper (which generally earn higher rates of return than the approved securities).

Table 11-2
Short-Term Securities Available to Local Governments

Investment Instruments	Issuer of Obligations	Denominations	Maturities	Marketability	Yield Basis	Comments/Restrictions
Treasury Bills	United States government	$10,000 to $1 million	3, 6, 9 & 12 months	Excellent secondary market	Discounted on 365-day basis Also offered as tax anticipation bills through special autions	Popular investment Can be purchased in secondary market for varying maturities
U.S. Agency Securities	Various federal agencies	$1,000 to $25,000	30 days 270 days 1 year	Good secondary market	Discounted on a 360-day basis	Not a legal obligation of or guaranteed by the federal government
Negotiable Certificates of Deposit	Commercial banks	$500,000 to $1 million	Unlimited 30-day minimum	Active secondary market	Interest maturity on 360-day basis	Backed by credit of issuing bank
Non-negotiable Certificates of Deposit	Commercial banks & savings and loan associations	$1,000 minimum (usually $100,000)	30-day minimum	Limited secondary market	Interest maturity on 365-day basis	Lower interest rates for amounts under $100,000 90-day interest penalty for early withdrawl
Repurchase Agreements	Commercial banks	$100,000 minimum	Overnight minimum 1 to 21 days common	No secondary market	Established as part of purchase Yield generally close to prevailing federal rates	Open: can liquidate at any time Fixed: maturity set for specific period
Bankers Acceptances	Commercial banks	$25,000 to $1 million	Up to 6 months	Good secondary market	Discounted on 360-day basis	Backed by credit of issuing bank with specific collateral
Commercial Paper	Promissory notes of finance companies	$100,000 to $5 million	5 to 270 days	No secondary market	Either discounted or interest-bearing on a 360-day basis	Dealers often will negotiate agreements to buy back the security at a lower rate prior to maturity

U.S. Treasury Securities

U.S. Treasury bills (T-bills) are the most important money market instrument available for local government investment. They represent an obligation of the United States government to pay a fixed sum of money after a specified period of time from date of issue. T-bills are negotiable, noninterest-bearing securities that have virtually no default risk and are the most liquid of money market instruments. The Treasury auctions three-month (thirteen weeks) and six-month bills (twenty-six weeks) on a weekly basis (Mondays) and one-year bills each month.

T-bills are issued at a discount and then mature at par value. The amount of the discount varies at the time of issuance. The difference between the selling price and the face value represents the yield or return on investment. The minimum denomination is $10,000, with additional amounts available in increments of $5,000. The price of Treasury and other federal agency securities are quoted per $100 of value. For example, if the price per $100 were 99.052, then the price of a security with a par value of $10,000 would be $9,905.20. The investor would receive $10,000 at maturity. If the security is a 182-day T-bill, the yield would be 1.919% ($10,000 - $9,905.20 = $94.80 x 365/182 = 190.12 divided by $9,905.20 = 1.919%).

Underlying the pricing system for investment securities is a system of "basis points." There are 100 basis points in each percentage point, so a basis point is one-hundredth of a percent. For example, if a thirteen-week T-bill's discount drops from a 1.67 to a 1.60 discount yield, the yield has declined seven basis points. The dollar value of the decline is $1.75 per $10,000 par amount of the T-bills (.0007 x 13/52 x $10,000).

T-bills are sold either by competitive bid or by noncompetitive tender. A noncompetitive tender simply states the number of T-bills the buyer desires, which will be awarded at the average price of the competitive bids accepted. The Treasury determines the number of bills it wishes to sell before the bidding begins, and the noncompetitive tenders are allocated first, with the remaining bills awarded to the competitive bidders, highest price (lowest discount yield) bids first.

Assume, for example, that the Treasury announces the sale of $50 million of one-year T-bills. Noncompetitive buyers offer to purchase 3,000 bills (or $30 million of the $50 million to be issued). The competitive bids on the remaining 2,000 bills range from a high of $9,775 to a low of $9,650, with an average of $9,700. The noncompetitive buyers would pay the average bid price and receive a yield of 3.093% (i.e., $10,000 minus $9,700 = $300 divided by $9,700 = 3.093%). The yield on the bonds purchased at $9,650 would be 3.627%, while the yield on the bonds purchased at $9,775 would be 2.302%.

The buyer of a T-bill does not receive a certificate. Ownership is recorded on the computer at the buyer's clearing bank and, in turn, on the computers of the Federal Reserve System. This book-entry procedure permits the daily trading of billions of dollars of T-bills without the shifting of countless pieces of paper to record the transactions. Each owner gets periodic statements from the bank, acting as custodian, regarding the T-bills owned.

Treasury securities can be purchased through a broker (at a cost of $50 to $60 per transaction) or with no commission cost through a program called Treasury Direct. The Treasury Direct program is designed for the investor who intends to hold the securities until they mature and requires that the interest and principal payments from Treasury securities be deposited directly into a checking or savings account. Therefore, investors who want to actively trade Treasury securities must buy them through a broker.

T-bills have virtually no default risk and are the most liquid of money market instruments. An attractive feature of T-bills is the ready market for resale. T-bills are traded at a "discount yield," which determines the size of the discount and the price of the bill. If the holder has a sudden need for funds, T-bills can be sold quickly for relatively predictable prices on the so-called secondary market. This characteristic has earned T-bills the label of "near money."

U.S. Treasury notes are intermediate term obligations, issued in two-year, three-year, five-year, and ten-year maturities. *Treasury bonds* are long-term obligations, issued in maturities from ten to thirty years.[3] Treasury notes and bonds are interest-bearing, negotiable securities, with coupon interest paid semiannually. When originally issued, notes with two- or three-year maturities are available in $1,000 increments, with a minimum purchase of $5,000. Treasury bonds, notes, and bills are backed by the full faith and credit of the federal government and are prime obligations with an implied AAA rating.

The Treasury sells two kinds of notes and bonds, fixed-principal and inflation-indexed. Both pay interest twice a year, but the principal value of inflation-indexed securities is adjusted to reflect inflation as measured by the Bureau of Labor Statistics' Consumer Price Index for All Urban Consumers (CPI-U). With inflation-indexed notes and bonds, semiannual interest payments are calculated on the basis of the principal value of the security adjusted for inflation. At maturity, the security is redeemed at its inflation-adjusted principal amount or its par value (the amount paid to buy the security), whichever is greater. Treasury Inflation-Indexed Securities, sometimes referred to as Treasury Inflation-Protected Securities (TIPS), pay a fixed rate of interest applied to the inflation-adjusted principal. Specifically, each semiannual interest payment is calculated by multiplying the inflation-indexed principal (regardless of whether it is greater or less than the par value) by one-half the interest rate that was determined at auction.

The Treasury issues notes in regular cycles, like T-bills, but much less frequently (monthly for two- and five-year notes, quarterly for ten-year notes). Both competitive bids and noncompetitive tenders might be made for notes. All notes are noncallable by the Treasury. T-bonds, when issued, are auctioned semiannually (usually in February and August) through a process similar to that used for notes. Some T-bonds have a call feature; the Treasury might call them at par five years before the maturity date.

In normal financial markets, the yield on long-term bonds is greater than on short-term instruments such as T-bills and money market funds. In today's market, however, the gap between short-term and long-term rates is not great. In October 1998, for example, the yield earned on ten-year Treasury notes dropped to 4.16%. According to the Federal Reserve Board, the last time the yield was that low was in December 1964. Interest rates fall because the money available to lend is greater than the demand for money to be borrowed. Interest rates also tend to follow inflation, and the current rate of inflation in the United States is relatively low.

Zero Coupon Treasury Securities

Zero coupon Treasury securities represent ownership of interest or principal payments on United States notes or bonds. Instead of periodic interest payments, these securities are purchased at a discount of 20% to 90% off the $1,000 face value. Owners of zero coupon treasuries receive no payment of interest until maturity. These securities are available in a wide range of maturities spanning one to thirty years. The major security dealers maintain an active secondary trading market. A United States Savings Bond is the best known zero coupon security.

The most popular type of zero coupon Treasury securities are STRIPS (Separate Trading of Registered Interest and Principal Securities), introduced in 1986 to meet the needs of investors for ready access to the zero coupon securities. The Department of the Treasury does not issue STRIPS. Instead, the Treasury declares that certain issues of Treasury notes and bonds are eligible to be split into separate interest and principal payments, with each payment trading as a separate security. This splitting up, or "stripping," of the issue is done by government bond dealers and others, and not by the Department of the Treasury.

For example, a ten-year Treasury note consists of twenty interest payments —one every six months for ten years—and a principal payment payable at maturity. When this security is "stripped," each of the twenty interest payments and the principal payment become separate securities and can be held and transferred separately. STRIPS can only be bought and sold through a financial institution, broker, or dealer. STRIPS are registered in the name of the holder and are held in book-entry form through the wire system of the Federal Reserve, facilitating the trading and liquidation of these securities by the holders. If sold before maturity, the market price will depend on the prevailing levels of interest rates.

Interest earnings from zero coupon securities are automatically reinvested at the same yield basis at which the investor originally bought the bond. This guaranteed compounding feature is attractive enough that investors are willing to pay higher prices (and receive lower yields) for zero coupon securities than for regular coupon bonds.

STRIPS are popular with investors who want to receive a known payment at a specific future date. For example, some State lotteries invest the present value of large lottery prizes in STRIPS to be sure that funds are available when needed to meet annual payment obligations that result from the prizes. Pension funds invest in STRIPS to match the payment flows of their assets with those of their liabilities to make benefit payments. STRIPS are also popular investments for individual retirement accounts, 401(k)-type savings plans, and other income tax-advantaged accounts that permit earnings to accumulate without incurring immediate income tax consequence

Older zero coupon securities derived from Treasury bonds were issued by private companies. However, none have been issued since the mid-1980s, due to the STRIPS program. CATS (Certificates of Accrual on Treasury Securities), created by Salomon Brothers, were the most widely traded "physical" zero coupon Treasury security, with over $45 billion (face value) of CATS issued between 1982 and 1986. Treasury Investment Growth Receipts (TIGRS), introduced by Merrill Lynch, were frequently purchased to provide a college education fund with a minimal initial investment. As a gift, TIGRS offered a tax-advantage to both parents and to a child (with a custodial account). Lehman Brothers created LIONS (Lehman Investment Opportunity Notes) to compete with the other zero coupon bonds in the feline menagerie.

Federal Agency Securities

Federal agency securities are excellent investment instruments for state and local governments, often characterized as close substitutes for Treasury bills. These securities are issued by government-sponsored, privately owned agencies that have been established to implement various federal policies. These agencies include the Federal Farm Credit Bank System, Farm Credit Financial Assistance Corporation, Federal Home Loan Bank System, National Mortgage Association (Fannie Mae), Student Loan Marketing Association (Sallie Mae), and Federal Home Loan Mortgage Corporation (Freddie Mac). The Financing Corporation and the Resolution Trust Company were set up by Congress in the late 1980s to deal with problems caused by the failure of savings and loan institutions with resulting difficulties for the Federal Savings and Loan Insurance Corporation.

Federal agency securities pay interest rates about 1.5 percentage points higher than Treasury bonds. Most agencies have minimum denominations of $10,000 with additional increments of $5,000.

Agency securities are traded in an over-the-counter market, similar to U.S. Treasury obligations, and usually by the same dealers. However, the spreads are somewhat wider, and therefore it is more costly to trade in this market than in the Treasury market. Investors can choose from discounted notes, interest-bearing notes and bonds, and floating-rate notes. Although the full faith and credit of the federal government does not back these securities, each agency guarantees its own issued securities. Thus, the risk factor is considered to be very low. These agency securities have less liquidity, however, because the market for agency paper is smaller than for T-bills and T-bonds. While agency securities trade at a yield premium over T-bills, interest earnings are subject to federal income tax, and some agency securities are subject to state and local taxes.

Bank Investments

The popularity of *certificates of deposit* (CDs) has increased dramatically among governmental subdivisions in the past several years. A certificate of deposit is a receipt for funds that have been deposited in a commercial bank for an agreed-upon period of time. The owner of the CD receives both principal and interest on the maturity date. CDs might be purchased for various amounts, but those under $100,000 usually carry significantly lower interest rates. CDs are sold according to specified maturity periods, typically ranging from 14 to 180 days. Some banks, however, offer CDs with maturity periods of up to five years.[4]

There are two types of CDs: (1) negotiable, which the original investor can sell to another party on the secondary market; and (2) non-negotiable, which must be retained by the original investor until maturity. The ability to sell prior to maturity if funds are needed gives CDs the liquidity necessary to make them competitive in the money market and therefore makes them attractive to investors. Emergency liquidation of a CD prior to maturity can result in a loss of interest, however. Although a CD might have been purchased for only thirty or sixty days, in some cases a bank might require a penalty of ninety days' interest for early withdrawal.

A *repurchase agreement* is a contract between two parties whereby one party (e.g., a bank, perhaps acting as an agent for another party) sells an instrument (such as a T-bill) to another party (e.g., a municipality) and agrees to buy it back at a later date (often the next day) at a specified higher price. Repurchase agreements are frequently entered into for very short periods of time, usually from one to twenty-one days. They often represent investment transaction where the original holder of the instrument requires capital to cover short-term obligations. While a repurchase agreement has legal characteristics of both a sale and a secured transaction, in economic terms, the buyer is lending money to the seller on a short-term basis. The securities purchased by the bank or agent serve as collateral for the loan. And the loan, in effect, is repaid when the seller repurchases the securities.

The minimum amount is usually $100,000, with increments of $5,000 above the minimum. Lower minimums can sometimes be negotiated, however. Two types of repurchase agreements are available. With a fixed agreement, a specific interest rate and maturity period for the amount invested are established at the outset, and a penalty might be levied if the agreement is liquidated prior to maturity. An open agreement means that the agreement might be liquidated at any time, with the interest rate—which might be slightly lower than for a fixed agreement—dependent on the duration of the transaction. A fixed repurchase agreement might be set for $100,000, with a 12.5% annual interest rate for six days. The return on investment if held for six days would be $205.48. If the agreement is liquidated prior to maturity, the bank has the option of levying a penalty.

Repurchase agreements are the most flexible investment instruments available because they allow a locality to negotiate both yield and maturity. Little risk is involved in such agreements because the principal is guaranteed and the return is fixed. However, no secondary market exists for repurchase agreements. They can be used most effectively to invest unexpected windfall revenues on a very short-term basis while alternative investments are being considered.

Banker's acceptances are time drafts or letters of credit negotiated by commercial banks to finance the export, import, shipment, storage of goods, or other foreign trade transactions.[5] These notes do not bear interest, but are sold at a discount. The bank guarantees to honor the full face value of the draft of a private company on the due date (typically sixty to ninety days after issue) by stamping "accepted" on the draft. In making such a guarantee, a well-known bank can significantly enhance the marketability of obligations of less well-known companies. Both the issuer and the accepting bank guarantee the draft.

An export-import company, for example, might require $100,000 as a down payment on a foreign shipment of goods. The company might arrange for an American bank to issue, in the name of the exporter, an irrevocable letter of credit, which specifies the details of the shipment. The exporter can then draw a draft on the American bank and present it to an overseas bank for immediate payment. The draft is returned to the bank that issued the letter of credit, which stamps it "accepted," thereby incurring the liability to pay the draft when it matures. The export-import company is obligated to deposit the $100,000 plus a specified interest in time to honor the acceptance at maturity. Alternatively, the bank might accept a time draft from the company for $101,500, repayable in twenty-one days. An investor provides the $100,000, and, at the end of the twenty-one days, the account of the export-import company is charged $101,500, the investor is paid $101,200, and the bank retains $300 as its "placement fee." The $1,200 return on $100,000 is the equivalent of a 20.5% annual return on investment.

Banker's acceptances are sold in denominations ranging from $25,000 to $1 million. Major investors include the accepting banks, foreign central banks, money market funds, corporations, and other domestic and foreign institutional investors. The risk of default is very low, and dealers in the secondary market create sufficient liquidity for these instruments to continually attract investors. There are no known cases of principal loss to investors in the more than seventy years that banker's acceptances have been used in the United States.

Money market funds might be considered as an alternative to a savings account. The administrator of the money market fund pools the funds of hundreds or even thousands of investors to give each investor interest rates that otherwise might not be possible. Investments made in amounts of $250,000 and up generally command higher interest rates than do lesser amounts.

Money market accounts often are set up to serve as a combination savings and checking account. Checks can be written on deposited funds. Money market funds are completely liquid, since they might be withdrawn at any time without penalty. Many banks offer a number of "perks" along with money market accounts. Tax-free accounts might also be available for municipal funds.

All of the securities described above are excellent, safe investment alternatives for local jurisdictions. The specific yield-liquidity-safety configurations of each should be considered when making investment decisions. A locality usually purchases a mix of investments with varying yield-liquidity-safety arrangements, depending on which considerations public officials wish to emphasize in the overall investment program.

Commercial Paper

Commercial paper is an unsecured promissory note issued for a specific amount with maturities ranging from 3 to 270 days. Most issues have an average maturity of 30 to 45 days. Corporations with short-term capital needs often issue commercial paper. Finance companies, bank holding companies, municipal authorities, and more recently, foreign corporations and sovereigns also issue commercial paper. Automobile finance companies, such as General Motors Acceptance Corporation, are among the largest issuers. Commercial paper typically is sold in large denominations (in multiples of $100,000) as a discounted security. Issues are purchased for an amount below their face value and then are paid back at full face value upon maturity. The difference between the face value and the purchase price represents the yield earned on the investment.

The rates offered on commercial paper depend on several factors: the credit rating of the issuer, the paper's maturity, the total amount of money sought by the issuer, and the general level of interest rates. Almost all commercial paper is rated by one of the major rating agencies to provide an indication of the credit risk involved with each issue. Commercial paper offers higher yields than T-bills or other short-term investment options of similar maturities to compensate investors for the higher risk. No secondary trading market exists for commercial paper, and consequently, liquidity is generally low—investors usually must hold the paper until maturity.

At maturity, the commercial paper can be paid off or rolled over into a new commercial paper issue at the prevailing market interest rate. A remarketing agent is responsible for finding new investors if existing investors decide not to reinvest in the commercial paper. A bank letter of credit or some other type of liquidity provision typically backs commercial paper. If new investors cannot be found and if the issuer is unable to provide the funds to pay-off the existing investors, then the issuer might draw on the letter of credit in order to obtain the necessary funds. As a result of the higher default risks, many states have restrictions against investment by local governments in commercial paper.

The relative ease of issuance of commercial paper results in greater flexibility and the ability to match the amount and timing of funds with the issuer's needs. However, rising interest rates might negate the advantage of short-term paper. The use of commercial paper might be precluded by disruptions in the capital market. The costs of remarketing and obtaining a bank letter of credit or another type of liquidity provision offset some of the interest rate savings normally associated with commercial paper.

Local governments often use commercial paper to meet short-term cash management needs, to finance equipment, to provide interim construction financing for capital projects, and to provide loans to business entities. Issuing short-term paper at tax-exempt interest rates allows for the possibility of positive arbitrage.

Stocks

Historically, the stock market has proven to be an excellent long-term investment option. However, short-term performance is virtually impossible to predict. Stocks are affected by two types of risk—nonmarket risk and market risk. *Nonmarket risk*, also called specific risk, arises from the likelihood that events specific to a company or its industry will adversely affect the price of a stock. The risk that nonmarket factors will adversely affect the overall value of a stock portfolio can be reduced through diversification—owning several different stocks in different industries, the prices of which have shown little correlation to each other. *Market risk* is associated with the overall movements of the stock market. Market risk cannot be totally eliminated no matter how many different stocks might be included in a given portfolio. It is possible, however, to measure market risk by applying two analytical tools—beta and standard deviation.

Beta is a statistical measure of how movements in the stock market have historically impacted the price of a stock. A pattern can be developed to gauge the exposure of a particular stock to stock market risk by comparing the movements of that stock to the movements of the Standard & Poor's (S&P) 500.[6] A stock with a beta greater than one should rise or fall to a greater extent than movements in the S&P 500. A stock with a beta less than one should rise or fall to a lesser extent than the S&P 500. Beta measures movements on average, and therefore an exact correlation cannot be expected with each market movement.

Standard deviation measures the volatility of a stock's price regardless of the cause. It basically gauges how much the short-term returns of a stock have moved around its long-term average return. The most common way to calculate standard deviation is from an average monthly return over a three-, five-, or ten-year period, which is then annualized. Generally, the higher the standard deviation, the more volatile the stock. Standard deviation does not distinguish between positive and negative volatility. Therefore, a stock's range of returns should be reviewed over a period of years to determine whether it has a tendency to return more or less than its average return.

Diversification

An article in the October 8, 2002, issue of *The Wall Street Journal* presented some interesting statistics regarding the relative performance of stocks versus bonds over the past fifteen years. The total return for the Standard & Poor's 500 stock index from the end of the third quarter of 1987 through September 2002 was 264%, compared with 382% for long-term Treasury bonds over the same period. On an annualized basis, bonds compiled an annual return of 11%, while stocks appreciated by 9% per year.

Too often bonds are discussed as an alternative to stocks, rather than as a staple of any diversified investment portfolio. If there was a lesson to be learned from the recent collapse of the stock market, it is that the fundamental rules of investing should never have been ignored. A properly constructed investment portfolio should have an allocation of stocks and bonds—stocks for growth, complemented by bonds, which provide balance and cash flow.

The longest bull market in history gave rise to a generation of financial advisors who had never experienced the devastating effects of a bear market. This new breed came to believe that diversification was accomplished by spreading investment dollars throughout a variety of stock sectors. Their thinking was that the more conservative blue chip stocks would provide shelter from a down market when the more aggressive growth stocks in their portfolio started to falter.

As stocks begin to rise again, hopefully these advisors will have learned the lessons of the recent past. A good start would be for the financial media to end its preoccupation with stocks versus bonds comparisons. The investing public would be better served by illustrating how these two investments complement each other in a well-designed portfolio.

Convertible Securities, Index Funds, and Mutual Funds

Direct purchase of stocks is generally not recommended for short-term investments of public funds. Some states prohibit the investment of public funds in the stock market. If a fund manager feels inclined to invest in stocks, he or she should do so through convertible securities or a mutual fund or index fund with a proven track record.

Convertible securities offer the pay out of bonds with the potential appreciation of stocks. The security is issued as a bond with a $1,000 par value and a fixed maturity rate and pays a coupon typically on a semiannual basis. Investors are given the option of converting the bond into a predetermined amount of common stock before the bond matures or is called. If this option is exercised, the strike or conversion price is determined by dividing the par value by a conversion ratio. Convertible securities provide favorable leverage by generally allowing the investor to participate more in the rise of the common stock than in the fall. Therefore, convertible securities provide a hedge against inflation, while providing a fixed income and maintaining value even if prices falter.

Companies issue convertible securities as a means of raising capital at lower interest rates than associated with straight debt securities. The yield on a convertible security typically is one to two percentage points less than a comparable bond. In exchange, investors receive a steady income stream provided by the bond coupon or dividend, while maintaining the right to trade the fixed income for the underlying common stock at the holder's option.

Index funds were originally introduced as an investment strategy for institutional pension funds. In 1976, Vanguard offered an index fund to individual investors. The goal of an index fund is to match the performance of some benchmark that it is tracking, such as the Standard & Poor's 500, Dow 30, or Wilshire 5000. The concept of an index is based on the Efficient Market Theory, which asserts that stocks and bond markets are efficiently priced at any given time and that an average investor could not beat the stock market on the whole. In fact, over long periods of time, only a small percentage of actively managed funds have beaten the market. So if you can't beat 'em, join 'em.

A pure index fund invests in every stock in the benchmark index it is tracking. A quasi-index fund tries to outperform the benchmark by using options or futures. Several mutual fund companies carry index funds—Vanguard, Dreyfus, Fidelity, and Bull & Bear, to name a few. Index funds have lower portfolio turnover and minimal research requirements and therefore have lower costs than actively managed funds. Although index funds offer more predictable results, they are fully vested at all times, and if the market declines, so will the fund.

Exchange-traded funds (ETFs) are like index mutual funds except that they are bought and sold through brokers and trade like a stock. Some of the earliest

ETFs mimicked the Dow, NASDAQ, and S&P 500. The Standard & Poor's Depository Receipt or SPDR (or "spider") is one of the more prominent of these exchange-traded index investments. As ETFs have become popular, indexes have been established for smaller components of the entire stock market—ETFs that invest only in small company stocks, in one sector such as technology or biotechnology, or in foreign stocks.

SPDRs can be expected to move up or down in value with the S&P 500 Index. Dividends are paid quarterly, based on the accumulated stock dividends held in the trust, less any expenses of the trust. SPDRs can be bought or sold anytime during the trading day, and they can be shorted.[7] When entering a short trade for a stock, the trade just before the short trade must be at a higher price than the previous trade—called an "uptick." In other words, the price of the stock must be rising. The initiator of a short sale is betting that the price of the stock will drop following the uptick. The uptick rule does not apply to SPDRs, however.

Investing overseas is more difficult than investing domestically. Accounting and reporting rules differ from those in the United States, and it is not an easy task to paint an accurate picture of a country or an individual company. Therefore, when investing overseas, it often makes sense to use professionally managed investments. The *World Equity Benchmark Series* (WEBS) are similar to SPDRs. WEBS trade on the American Stock Exchange and track the Morgan Stanley Capital International (MSCI) country indexes. WEBS are available for the following countries: Australia, Austria, Belgium, Canada, France, Germany, Hong Kong, Italy, Japan, Malaysia Free, Mexico, Netherlands, Singapore, Spain, Sweden, Switzerland, and the United Kingdom.

According to Morningstar, Inc., which follows the mutual fund industry, there were 6,742 *mutual funds* in 2000, the year that the stock market peaked. The number of funds had increased by 46% in the six years in which the bull market prevailed. However, when the stock market bubble burst in 2000, investors began to lose interest in a number of these funds and some fund management companies merged, sold, or simply shut down many of their funds. Technology-oriented funds were especially hard hit. By mid-2003, the number of funds had declined by nearly 11% from the 2000 peak. However, these funds still hold about $7 trillion in assets for approximately half of all households in the United States.

Mutual funds impose fees in different ways to cover the costs associated with their operations. The ways in which these fees are charged can impact the return on investment. Funds that involve so-called Class A shares typically impose a front-end sales charge deducted from the initial investment. Most funds offer "breakpoint" discounts for large investments in A shares, so as the size of the investment increases, the sales charge might decrease. Many mutual funds allow investors to aggregate holdings in related accounts to reach a breakpoint.

Class B shares typically do not have a front-end sales load but might impose higher annual operating expenses than A shares. The operating expenses include the management fee, which covers the cost of the fund's managers, traders, and research analysts; administrative costs, which include producing and mailing account statements and annual reports; and, for some funds, a 12b-1 fee, which covers distribution and marketing expenses. B shares also might impose a contingent deferred sales charge or CDSC, which the investor must pay if the shares are sold within a certain number of years. Given the CDSC and lack of breakpoints, investors often find B shares to be most appropriate when investing modest amounts for longer periods.

Class C shares typically do not charge a front-end load and generally impose lower CDSC than B shares, such as a 1% for one year. Sales charges are applied to C shares on an annual basis based on the fund's expense ratio. Investors who want flexibility and who have a shorter investment time horizon might find that C shares best meet their individual needs.

Investors can also buy mutual funds through fee-based accounts. Instead of paying a sales charge or commission on each transaction, the investor is charged an annual fee, billed quarterly in advance, based on a percentage of the account's value. These accounts offer funds as either no-load shares or A shares where the sales charge is waived.

Derivatives

Derivative securities have received considerable coverage in the media in recent years, stemming from the decision of some local governments to seek bankruptcy court protection largely as a result of the these investments. Derivative securities derive their value from some form of investment, such as Treasury bonds, corporate stocks and bonds, foreign currencies, or commodity contracts. In essence, they are bets that future interest rates will move in a particular direction. Derivatives were originally created to act as a safety device against dramatic changes in interest rates. They can be used for hedging—attempting to reduce risk by offsetting one investment position with another. When used in this manner, derivatives are relatively safe. However, investment bankers have concocted a broad range of derivatives, often customized to suit the needs of their clients. The risk can become great when derivatives are used as a speculative investment vehicle

The simplest type of derivatives is *futures*—contracts that set a price today but specify acceptance or delivery at some time in the future. A sausage maker might buy hog futures to protect against price increases, whereas a hog farmer might sell such futures to ensure against losses if the price goes down. Speculators might either buy or sell futures in the hope that a change in price will allow them to make money by reversing the transaction tomorrow.

Since every order to sell must be matched by an order to buy, derivative markets as a whole balance out to zero—as opposed to the stock market, where companies might issue shares regardless of whether there are buyers. The price of futures is constrained by the current cost of the underlying commodity. Otherwise, if the price of gold futures, say, increased above a certain point, speculators could profit by buying gold today and holding it for sale on the delivery date.

Options are another form of derivatives. Options grant the investor the right to buy or sell a stock (or other types of securities) at a fixed price for some period. Options are bets on the stock's future price, and the cost of the option is the ante for getting into the game.

Derivatives are designed to help corporations guard against sudden shifts in global financial markets—a plunging yen, a jolt in French bonds, a rapid rise in Hong Kong stocks, and so forth. One of the more popular derivatives is known as an "interest rate swap" that allows a company to exchange a fixed interest rate for a floating rate payment. Company A wants to benefit from falling interest rates; company B would like to protect itself against a possible rise in interest rates. Company A "lends" B $100 million at a fixed rate (say 8%), and B "lends" A $100 million at a variable rate. In some cases, such arrangements can greatly reduce the financing costs to the company. Each month, the accounts are balanced. If the variable rate is greater than 8%, A pays B the difference; if it is less, B pays A. Although the loan principal is recorded on the books of each company, it is an accounting fiction.

In the derivatives market, these swaps take on a value of their own. By looking at today's interest rate, investment analysts can figure out how much income a swap will generate and for whom. The swap can then be sold for an appropriate price. Derivatives often are designed to benefit from a falling interest rate. As the rate falls, the securities derive an additional value, and it is this "margin" that is sold to other investors. To add another layer of complexity, companies might exchange the payments from debts denominated in different currencies. For example, the income from U.S. Treasury bills might be exchanged for dividends generated by a portfolio of Japanese stocks. Each combination allows the participants to trade a different set of potential risks and benefits.

Derivatives offer higher yields than the average market rate, which makes them attractive at times when short-term interest rates are low. Derivative securities were the hottest area of investment in the early 1990s, growing to over $12 trillion in contracts by the end of 1992. But like many rapidly rising investment schemes, the fall can be even more rapid. And when the Federal Reserve began to raise interest rates in 1994 in an effort to cool the economy, many derivatives loss value dramatically. For unsuspecting municipal governments and other public organizations, the consequences were devastating.

A survey by the General Accounting Office in early 1994 indicated that among 3,737 state and local government agencies, 288 reported using derivatives to some extent. In October 1994, the House Banking Committee staff compiled a list of nineteen government or public funds that had suffered substantial losses due to derivatives. Investors who had borrowed money to buy derivatives faced particularly harsh losses. The Florida Treasurer's Office reported a $175 million loss in its portfolio, partly due to derivatives. The Eastern Shoshone Tribe in rural Wyoming invested nearly $5 million in mortgage derivatives in 1993 at the encouragement of a brokerage firm in Houston, Texas. As the values dropped substantially, the 3,000 members of the tribe (70% of the members were unemployed at the time) were left with little to show for their investment.

In December 1994, it was announced that Orange County, California, had suffered a loss of $1.6 billion in its investment pool. This loss was the largest ever recorded by a local government investment pool and led to the county filing for bankruptcy protection.

The loss was the result of unsupervised investment activity of the county treasurer, Robert Citron, who was entrusted with a $7.5 billion portfolio belonging to county schools, cities, special districts, and the county itself. Citron was able to increase returns on the pool by investing in derivative securities and leveraging the portfolio to the hilt. The pool was in such demand due to its track record that Citron had to turn down investments by agencies outside Orange County. About 185 cities, schools districts, and other government agencies in southern California had money invested in the Orange County investment pool. Some local school districts and cities even issued short-term taxable notes to reinvest in the pool (thereby increasing their leverage even further).

A 1992 audited report, conducted by Steve Lewis, the State Auditor-Controller, had warned that county money had been placed into high-risk investments, including some that violated state rating requirements. The report further pointed out that these investments were being made without consultation with the county investment committee. John Moorlach, who ran for County Treasurer in 1994, warned that the pool was too risky. Unfortunately, he was widely ignored and Citron was reelected.

Citron was betting that interest rates would fall or stay low. The $7.5 billion of investor equity was leveraged into a $20.5 billion portfolio. Through reverse repurchase agreements, Citron pledged the county's securities as collateral and reinvested the cash in new securities, mostly five-year notes issued by government-sponsored agencies.

The strategy worked fine as long as interest rates went down. In February 1994, however, the Federal Reserve Bank started a series of six consecutive interest rate increases that caused severe losses to the county's investment pool. Initially, announced as a "paper" loss, the county declared bankruptcy shortly thereafter and decided to liquidate the portfolio, thereby realizing the paper loss. After filing for bankruptcy, the county missed payment on a $100 million debt, which was part of the county's pension fund. Moody's Investors Service promptly downgraded the affected bonds to "junk" status, making them worth far less and calling into question the worth of other Orange County bonds.

Robert Citron resigned as county treasurer just before the county filed for bankruptcy. The County Board of Supervisors appointed Thomas W. Hayes, former California State Treasurer, to restructure the county's $20 billion investment fund and retained Salomon Brothers for investment advice. Shortly after filing for bankruptcy protection, the semiannual property taxes were due, amounting to about $1 billion. The supervisors announced that these funds would be invested in low-risk, short-term securities, separate from the troubled investment pool.[8]

The core problem of derivatives stems from the fact that some investment firms sold extremely complex securities and, in some cases, did not adequately informed the customers of the risks. Local governments and other public organizations—not well-versed in the vagaries of the investment marketplace—only saw the opportunity for high yields on short-term investments at a time when other options were hovering around 3%.

The National Association of Securities Dealers has issued a set of rules to govern the sales of government securities, which includes "structured notes," a type of derivative backed by government bonds. The Federal Reserve Board has ordered investment banks dealing in derivatives to provide customers with a more complete explanation of the pitfalls of certain risky derivatives.

Municipal Derivatives

Municipal derivatives were originally developed for and sold to municipal bond mutual funds. Few, if any, municipal derivatives have been sold to individual investors, but that could change at any time, since sales to individuals have been proposed at major municipal bond firms. Municipal derivatives are created by dividing a fixed-rate bond into two parts, called a "floater" and an "inverse floater." While the interest and principal payments of the issuer remain unchanged, the division of interest payments between the floater and the inverse floater might vary during the life of the bond. The rate paid on the floater is a variable rate, determined by one of the methods used to set rates on variable rate bonds. A common method is to have a periodic auction of the floaters (often every thirty-five days to compete in the short-term investment market). The rate paid on the inverse floater is the difference between the fixed rate paid on the original bond and the amount paid on the floater.

To illustrate this process, assume an underwriter takes $200,000 (face value) in bonds with a 6% coupon rate, maturing in twenty years and splits this amount into two parts: $100,000 face amount of floaters and $100,000 face amount of inverse floaters. Further assume that the initial rate set on the floaters (by auction) was 5.5%. The holders of the $100,000 face amount of floaters receives $5,500, while the holders of the $100,000 face amount for inverse floaters receive $6,500 (i.e., the difference between the $12,000 in interest earned at the fixed rate of 6% and the amount allocated to the floaters). If short-term interest rates increase, the interest paid on the floaters will increase, and the interest paid on the inverse floaters will decrease. Not only will the income from the inverse floaters decline, but the price will also decline, along with bond prices generally. Therefore, those who invest in floaters are betting that interest rates will rise, while those who invest in inverse floaters are betting that interest rates will fall.

Arbitrage

Proceeds from a bond issue are usually invested in short-term securities until either they are required for payment toward the acquisition or construction of the capital improvement or, in the case of a refunding issue, used to call the original bonds. *Arbitrage earnings* can be generated from these short-term investments. In the municipal bond market, arbitrage is the difference between the interest paid on an issuer's tax-exempt bonds and the interest earned by investing the bond proceeds in taxable securities. For example, a municipality issues $10 million in bonds with a 4.5% coupon rate and, for the first three months, invests the $10 million in short-term securities earning 5% interest. The difference between the $125,000 earned during this three-month period and the $112,500 in interest payment due represents arbitrage. *Negative arbitrage* results when interest rates on the investments are below the interest rates on the bonds

During the 1980s, the federal government became concerned that local governments were abusing their borrowing power by issuing municipal bonds unnecessarily in order to try to earn arbitrage. The 1986 Tax Reform Act established a variety of restrictions and regulations designed to prevent such abuse. Federal arbitrage rules state that the yield on the investment of tax-exempt bond proceeds can only be 1/8 of 1% higher than the interest rate on the bond issue. Otherwise, arbitrage restrictions apply. For example, if the yield on the refunding bond is 5%, the issuer is limited to a 5.125% return on the investment of the bond proceeds. The issuer can purchase special low-yield U.S. Treasury securities, called the state and local government series, to meet this requirement if the normal market instruments are paying more.

There are exceptions to the yield restriction, however. Arbitrage might be earned for certain temporary periods if the bond proceeds are used for certain kinds of projects and spent within specified periods of time. At the end of the permitted temporary period, the issuer must restrict the yield on the remaining proceeds.

If the issuer does earn prohibited arbitrage that had not been foreseen, any earnings in excess of the bond yield must be returned to the U.S. Treasury in a process called "rebating." Failure to adhere to federal arbitrage provisions, in certain circumstances, can cause the municipal bonds to lose their tax-exempt status retroactive to the date of issue. The Internal Revenue Service can also assess a monetary penalty.

Another regulation limits advance refundings to one time for each original bond issue. This limit prevents governments from repeatedly refunding the same issue each time interest rates drop in an attempt to realize even greater arbitrage earnings. Therefore, issuers must carefully choose the timing of an advanced refunding. Private activity bonds cannot be advance refunded at all. This restriction prevents the federal subsidization of private activities through tax-exempt arbitrage earnings.

State Investment Pools

A number of states have established investment pools to facilitate the amalgamation of local government funds to achieve a wider market for short-term investments and the yield advantages of larger investment blocks. These pools should be particularly attractive to smaller local governments seeking greater returns on their investments through the professional management that such fund consolidation can achieve. The success of these investment pools, in large measure, depends on the financial skills and prudence of those who manage them. The $1.7 billion loss experienced by the Orange County investment pool in 1994 illustrates the potential problems with such pools when higher risk investments and overextended borrowing practices are pursued. To bolster confidence, some states have sought ratings for their investment pools, have adopted guidelines for the regulated money market regarding the average maturity of holdings, and, in some cases, have contracted with private financial advisors to manage these pooled investment funds.

An Investment Matrix

An investment matrix for local government is presented in Table 11-3. *Characteristics* refer to broad sets of circumstances that reflect the economic and fiscal environment of a given jurisdiction. *Emphasis* suggests the investment elements to which financial managers might attach the greatest importance, given the stated characteristics. *Investment options* identify the types of investments that best "fit" the characteristics and emphasis used to describe a particular jurisdiction.

Yield-Liquidity-Safety Mix

It is important that the yield-liquidity-safety mix be considered in every investment decision. The emphasis placed on any particular element is a function of the fiscal and economic circumstances confronting the locality. However, as suggested earlier, many public officials tend to overemphasize safety and, as a result, invest in securities with relatively low rates of return.

When the resources of a jurisdiction are limited, yield cannot serve as the primary objective because high-yield securities usually have correspondingly higher risks associated with them. A resource-limited community must be more concerned with the safety of its investments and its ability to convert these investments to cash on short notice. A small, rural jurisdiction, with relatively limited resources

> cannot afford the luxury of losing any part of its principal investment. As a result of its concern for security, its investment options are limited to securities with rapid convertibility to cash so that the ability of the jurisdiction to undertake major capital expenditures is not handicapped by funds being tied up in non-maturing financial assets.[9]

The investment options available under such circumstances are determined by the safety-liquidity considerations. The investments of such localities, of necessity, are concentrated in low-risk, low-yield securities, such as T-bills, federal agency securities, and participation in state investment pools. As a tradeoff for the safety of its investments, the locality is forced to accept a level of yield that is not optimal. At the same time, it retains the leverage to convert its investments easily to cash if the need arises. Smaller jurisdictions, unable to afford an investment manager because of the relatively small amounts to be in

Table 11-3
Investment Matrix for Local Government

Characteristics	Emphasis Yield	Liquidity	Safety	Investment Options
Limited resources; low tax base; minimal cash balance		X	X	Investment of cash balances at guaranteed rates through local banks and other depository institutions Treasury bills and notes Federal agency securities State investment pools
High income; high tax base; large cash balances; expanding economy	X			Certificates of deposit Commercial paper Repurchase agreements Index funds and convertible securities State investment pools
Minimum training in financial management	X		X	Contracts with banks to invest excess balances Treasury bills and notes State investment pools
Elected treasurer			X	Certificates of deposit Treasury bills and notes Federal agency securities State investment pools
Cash investment manager	X	X	X	Certificates of deposit Treasury bills and notes Federal agency securities State investment pools Index funds and convertible securities
High rate of tax delinqeuncy		X	X	Treasury bills and notes State investment pools
Low rate of tax delinqeuncy	X		X	Certificates of deposit Treasury bills and notes Federal agency securities State investment pools
Upward trend in interest rates	X	X		Certificates of deposit (purchased on a short-term basis) Treasury bills Index funds and convertible securities
Downward trend in interest rates			X	Certificates of deposit (locked in at prevailing rates of interest) Commercial paper
Capital expenditure needs		X	X	Treasury bills Certificates of deposit Repurchase agreements

vested, might authorize their banks to automatically invest any surplus funds in money market funds, certificates of deposit, or other short-term securities.

Jurisdictions with appreciably larger annual budgets, larger population bases, and professional management staffs whose primary responsibility is handling these investments are likely to be more aggressive in their investment strategies. While their strategies pay adequate attention to safety and liquidity, the yield of investments is pursued with greater intensity, often resulting in rates of return two to four percentage points higher than smaller jurisdictions.

Investment models adopted by such jurisdictions are designed to predict the movement of interest rates over time. Fund managers are able to ride the interest rate curve with investments. These jurisdictions are not threatened by cash flow problems but have a steady inflow of revenue through taxes, fees, and transfers. As a consequence, financial assets can be structured to emphasize higher-yield, long-term securities.

The Fund Manager

Individuals assigned the responsibility for managing the cash reserves of public entities often are entrusted with significant discretionary authority. From that perspective, a fund manager has more potential to do harm than does the chief executive officer. A fund manager might single-handedly lead a government to financial ruin if bad investments are made. For that reason, public officials must exercise considerable caution when selecting a fund manager. Ideally, the fund manager should possess both formal education and related experience in investment banking, financial counseling, or related fields. A strong track record is a must. Equally important are positive character traits and a demonstrated practice of using good common sense.

The fundamental objective of short-term investments should be to maximize yield and minimize risk. In formulating an investment strategy, the fund manager should investigate the investment instruments available in the market, determine their relative yields for the maturities required, and evaluate the difference in risk associated with them. On the basis of this evaluation, a strategy should be developed that reflects the overall objectives of the community. This strategy should be submitted to a finance committee for formal review and approval. In this way, the fund manager can attain broader counsel on the implementation of an appropriate investment policy, gain insight, and decrease personal liability.

Over the past several years, the standards of discretion for fund managers have changed, in some cases considerably so. Several states have adopted legislation regulating the amount of discretionary authority that can be granted to fund managers. The gist of these laws is that fund managers are expected to handle public funds in a responsible, generally conservative manner so as to minimize the likelihood of loss of principal. A fund manager should exercise extreme caution when considering investments where even a remote possibility of loss of principal exists.

On the other hand, a fund manager might be held accountable if the funds are invested in such a conservative manner that the earning potential of the funds is not maximized. The mix of investments entered into by the manager must be appropriate to the financial condition of the entity represented and must take into consideration the status of the state and national economy.

Constraints on Public Investments

The inadequacy of resources is a major constraint on the maximization of investment returns. A locality cannot invest in the money market unless it can raise enough revenue to satisfy current obligations and accumulate a surplus. Whereas some local governments are relatively affluent and have large tax bases, others often are hard-pressed to maintain and deliver needed services to their citizens. Thus, central to the issue of optimal return on investment is the question of resources: (1) the availability of surpluses to invest, and (2) the technical expertise necessary to manage a portfolio of investments.

Investment activities of local governments are regulated by state statutes that are presumed to reflect public policy. Some of these regulations restrict the investment opportunities available to localities, thereby depriving the public of the benefits of efficient investment of public funds. Such regulations were once necessary to control the imprudence of some local officials in the management of public funds. More recent developments have tended to render typical state investment laws obsolete.

> First, the money markets themselves have become increasingly sophisticated and competitive, with a myriad of financial institutions seeking investment capital through new securities and instruments. Thus, the options available to investment officers have increased dramatically.[10]

Securities are now available with varying levels of risk, investment return, and maturities. Whatever the financial objectives of a locality, a range of appropriate investment strategy is available.

> Secondly, the sophistication of state and local government investment officials has grown in the past decade. . . . With increasing specialization and professionalism common throughout the state and local government sector, these public money managers increasingly rival their private sector counterparts in their understanding of investment securities and relative risks and rewards.[11]

Some local jurisdictions have self-imposed additional restrictions and limitations on their investment policies. Localities have tried to mitigate risk by setting up a variety of investment criteria designed to diversify investment holdings and to avoid investments in weak financial institutions. The objective is to identify appropriate eligibility standards, investment limits, and safekeeping requirements. The overriding goal remains to minimize risk and maximize investment income.

The requirement that banks pledge securities as collateral to secure public deposits and investments imposes excessive costs on the financial institution—costs that are usually passed on to the public entity in the form of reduced rates of return. Experts argue that in the event of widespread failures in the banking system, many of the securities used for collateral pledges could prove equally worthless. The positive benefits associated with collateralization become most obvious, however, when a public organization deals with a single financial institution and the institution defaults because of poor management or some other microeconomic factors. A case in point is the 1982 collapse of Penn Square Bank, in which collateralization provisions protected the assets of the state and its political subdivisions. Collateralization is akin to an insurance policy aimed at protecting the safety of public deposits.

The failure in the 1980s of several investment companies specializing in government securities, combined with the more recent near bankruptcies of several local governments resulting from highly speculative investments, has lead to a renewed emphasis on the safety of local government investments. In the 1980s, investment companies bought securities from savings and loan associations seeking to raise cash temporarily. These securities were then sold as repurchase agreements to local governments with idle cash to invest. The local governments that lost money in these incidents neglected a cardinal rule of investment: get possession of the securities. They allowed the dealers to retain control of the securities, and some of these dealers, in turn, pledged the same securities to other investors. State laws guiding public investments generally require localities to take physical possession of investment securities as well as collateral.

The structure of many local governments is not consistent with the maximization of returns from short-term investments. Some local officials do not see the utility of "gambling" with the taxpayers' money and prefer to leave surplus funds secured on deposit with banks. To the extent that these funds are not invested, returns cannot be optimized. In addition, several procedural requirements often are in force in local government, including:

- Requirements that fund managers obtain prior approval before an investment security is bought or sold.
- Requirements that written quotations be obtained for all investment purchases.
- Prohibitions on the use of wire transfers for investment transactions.
- Restrictions that narrow the range of potential money market instruments.

Legal constraints influence the formation of banking relations, the level of bank compensating balances, and the safety-liquidity requirements of the securities in which a local government might invest. Local governments often cannot achieve optimal returns on their investments because they are not at liberty to use their discretion in investing in securities that meet their individual needs.

Political constraints are evident in several forms, including prohibitions against the use of nonlocal banks or investing outside the local area and the practice of sharing deposits among all banks in the community. The primary argument in support of these prohibitions is the notion of "keeping the money at home." As long as investments are limited to local options, however, local governments might be foregoing higher interest rates available in other markets.

Exogenous Factors

Exogenous factors might be more important in determining investment yields than the characteristics of the investment instruments themselves or the ability of the local government to accumulate resources for investment. Maturity dates are an important determinant in choosing investments. For this reason, it is important to design an investment pattern whereby each security will mature close to the time when the money invested will be needed to cover operational needs.

Through its forecasts, a locality might determine that a given sum of money will be available for a ninety-day period. This amount might be invested in, say, a three-month T-bill. Another sum, available for only thirty days, might be invested in a certificate of deposit. In some cases, funds might be available for only a day or a week at a time. These funds might be invested in repurchase agreements or other securities that can be held for indeterminate periods.

Suppose, for example, an investment officer determines that about $500,000 will be available for investment from May 1 to June 10. After taking bids from several banks and brokers, a list of maturity dates and yields is developed as follows:

Issue	Maturity Date	Yield
T-Bills	June 11	3.185
Certificate of Deposit	June 8	2.850
Banker's Acceptances	June 13	3.563
Repurchase Agreement	June 15	3.900

Although the banker's acceptances and repurchase agreements offer the highest yields, their maturity dates occur after June 10, when the principal must be available for other uses. The CD has the lowest yield, but it might be considered the best alternative because it matures prior to the June 10 date. The T-bills mature on June 11 and might be the best choice, depending on the possibility of a one-day leeway in the need for these invested funds. Although the amount available for investment is substantial, the primary consideration might be the maturity date of the investment, despite a smaller yield than might be considered optimal.

Wide fluctuations in interest rates have occurred over the past several years. It is important for a portfolio manager to understand how these fluctuations can affect investment decisions. The manager should endeavor to predict the interest rate cycle and use those predictions in managing the jurisdiction's investments.

It might be determined, for example, that $125,000 is available for investment during a 180-day period, after which the principal and interest will be applied to finance a capital project. After taking bids from several investment firms and banks, the manager decides to invest the funds at 3.15%. No consideration is given to the possibility that interest rates could be rising, and investment is "locked in" at 3.15%. The expected yield on this investment is $125,000 x 0.0315 x 180/360 = $1,968.75.

Instead of locking in the investment for the full 180 days, the manager could have decided to purchase a short-term CD and to reevaluate the movement of interest rates at its maturity. The rate bid for a thirty-day CD is 3.075%; therefore, the expected yield for the thirty days is $390.63. At the end of thirty days, bids are again sought and the following quotations received:

14 to 30 days	3.45%
31 to 60 days	3.88%
61 to 90 days	3.95%

A new CD might be purchased for another sixty days at 3.88%, with the expectation of a further evaluation of the interest rate situation at the end of that time. The expected yield for this sixty-day period on $125,390.63 (i.e., $125,000 + $390.63 interest) is $810.86. Assume that at the end of the sixty-day period, the interest rates have peaked. At that time, the cash manager decides to "lock into" the current rate of 3.75% for the remaining ninety days. The expected interest yield on the $126,201.49 ($125,390.63 + $810.86) is $1,183.14. Thus, under this managed approach, the total interest earned would be $390.63 + $810.86 + $1,183.14 = $2,384.63. This yield is $415.88 more than under the initial approach. This second approach also creates a measure of liquidity to respond to unexpected cash flow problems.

Summary and Conclusions

Safety of principal is an important component of any investment strategy. Concerns about safety, which had diminished over the previous decade, have again been raised as a result of several recent governmental investment disasters. The renewed level of awareness concerning investment safety has led to the enactment of new legislation in several states. Existing laws (1) limit banks with which local governments can do business, (2) specify the amounts that can be left on deposit in each bank, and (3) require collateral for uninsured funds. Additional requirements that mandate fund oversight and specify requirements regarding appropriate investment instruments are likely.

In addition, public funds on deposit in commercial banks and savings and loans associations are protected under the Federal Deposit Insurance Corporation and the Federal Savings and Loan Insurance Corporation. Under these circumstances, safety cannot be used as the only measure of an investment strategy. Nonetheless, investment options open to local governments have been proscribed by state laws and by self-imposed local statutes. Local financial managers must operate within these parameters or be in violation of the law.

Liquidity is an important investment consideration, especially when a need for funds occurs unexpectedly. Careful planning and structuring of the portfolio mix, however, will ensure that liquidity is built into the investment strategy. Since various securities mature in 30, 90, 180, or 270 days, one year or even longer, a locality can structure its assets in such a way that securities will mature at the time the funds are needed for other commitments.

Yield or return on investment is the paramount criterion for measuring the success or failure of an investment strategy. Confronted with continuing demands to provide improved and expanded services, many local governments face: (1) the need to expand revenues if these demands are to be met, (2) already heavily burdened taxpayers, and (3) narrow restrictions on their ability to borrow to finance public expenditures. Under these circumstances, local governments can be expected to respond enthusiastically to any source of additional revenue that does not involve increased taxation or additional debt. The financial asset portfolio is such a source, and the net return on investments can be an especially important source of revenue.

The role of the fund manager in the foreseeable future is likely to become more complicated, with stronger regulatory oversight. Large investments will more likely require approval of finance committees and/or concurrence of investment experts. The role will require more consensus building, self-education, and legal understanding. The primary benefits of an investment strategy, however, will continue to be measured in terms of the increased interest earned through the investment of temporarily idle cash.

Notes

1. Municipal Finance Officers Association, *A Treasury Management Handbook for Small Cities and Other Governmental Units* (Chicago: Municipal Finance Officers Association, 1979), 41.
2. Rhett D. Harrell and Lisa A. Cole, *Banking Relations: A Guide for Local Government* (Chicago: Municipal Finance Officers Association, 1982), 27.
3. The Treasury Department has not offered a Treasury bond since its decision in October 2001 to suspend issuance of the thirty-year bond. For current yields of Treasury bills, notes, and bonds, see www.publicdebt.treas.gov/sec/sec.htm.
4. See www.money-rates.com/cdrates1.htm for current interest rates and maturity periods for certificates of deposit.
5. Frank Pataucci and Michael Lichtenstein, *Improving Cash Management in Local Government: A Comprehensive Approach* (Chicago: Municipal Finance Officers Association, 1977), 59.
6. The Standard & Poor's 500 is an unmanaged index generally considered representative of the U.S. stock market and has a beta of 1. A specific stock with a beta of 1 means that, on average, it will move parallel to the S&P 500—the stock should rise 10% when the S&P 500 rises 10% and should decline 10% when the S&P declines 10%.
7. Selling stock short simply means that a stock is sold with the hope that it will go down in value. If it does, the stock is bought back at a lower price. The difference between the price at which the stock was sold and the price at which it was bought back represents the investor's profit. The investor does not own the stock at the time of the sale, but must buy the stock in order to complete the transaction.
8. For further details on this financial fiasco, see Philippe Jorion and Robert Roper, *Big Bets Gone Bad: Derivatives and Bankruptcy in Orange County* (New York: Harcourt Brace, 1995).
9. Chukwuemeka O'Cyprian Nwagwu, *Cash Management in Local Governments* (Blacksburg, Va.: Center for Public Administration and Policy, 1985), 203.
10. Committee on Cash Management, *Model Investment Legislation for State and Local Governments* (Chicago: Government Finance Officers Association, 1984).
11. *Ibid.*, 6

Chapter 12

DEBT ADMINISTRATION

Debt administration was a relatively routine task when long-term debt was a relatively small part of the overall financial commitments of local governments. The basic requirement was to ensure that sufficient funds were set aside each year from general revenue sources to cover the jurisdiction's debt service obligations or, in the case of term bonds, to build an adequate sinking fund and to cover annual interest charges. However, new and diverse bond offerings, coupled with a significant increase in long-term borrowing, have resulted in increased responsibilities for the administration of public debt.

Tracking and Reporting Public Debt

Accurate and complete reporting of public debt obligations develops confidence on the part of investors and the general public as to the financial management of a local government or public organization. The relatively small investment of time and expense in preparing such reports often is repaid many times over through lower interest rates.

Capital Project Funds

Capital project funds account for the resources required to construct or purchase specific strategic facilities. These resources come from the issuance of bonds or other long-term obligations, from intergovernmental grants, or as transfers from other public funds. A capital project fund is terminated when the capital project is completed. The accounting results are transferred to a *debt service fund*, which is used to track the payment of interest and principal of the long-term debt on each strategic facility.

Bonds frequently are not sold on the date of issue. Assume, for example, that bonds with an issue date of July 1, 2004, were not sold until September 1, 2004. The purchaser of these bonds receives semiannual interest payments from the date of issue (that is, on January 1, 2005, on July 1, 2005, and every six months thereafter) and not from the date of purchase. Therefore, when the bonds are sold, the *accrued interest* is added to the purchase price—the buyer must pay the seller the equivalent of interest for the period from the issue date (or last coupon date) up to, but not including, the date of purchase. This accrued interest, in turn, will be included in the interest payment received by the buyer on January 1, 2005. By convention, interest on municipal bonds is calculated on a 360-day year basis.

Accrued interest from the sale of bonds cannot be used in the capital project fund to pay for construction. It must be transferred to the debt service fund to be used as a partial offset to the amount needed for the first interest payment.

Therefore, only funds sufficient to pay the interest from the purchase date to the interest payment date will have to be transferred from the general fund to the debt service fund.

Some states do not permit bonds to be issued at a discount (below face value). This prohibition might force the issuing authority to pay a higher interest rate on the bonds to ensure their sale. When a discount is allowed, the full face value of the bonds is still required to complete the authorized project, and the difference might have to be made up from the general fund or the debt service fund. When bonds are sold at a premium, the difference between the purchase price and the face value is transferred to the debt service fund and used with other resources to pay off the bonds.

The capital project fund often receives proceeds from the sale of bonds or transfers of moneys from other sources (such as state or federal grants) before these resources are needed to acquire the capital asset or to cover construction costs. These resources should be invested to produce additional revenue. This investment revenue, in turn, is transferred to the debt service fund for payment of the principal or interest of the debt.

Administration of a capital project fund can be best understood by tracing a typical set of transactions. Assume that the City of Rurbana proposes to construct an addition to its existing administration building at an estimated cost of $2,000,000. Matching grants of $500,000 from the state and $500,000 from the federal government are available for this project. The Rurbana taxpayers have approved a bond issue referendum for $1,000,000 to meet the local share of the project's financing.

Regardless of the method by which moneys are transferred from one governmental unit to another, the results are the same: the capital project fund receives revenue from the granting agencies. Assume that the grants are received at the outset of the project and are invested in short-term, sixty-day certificates of deposits at 3% rate of interest. The resulting earnings of $5,000 ($1,000,000 x 0.03 x 60/360) should be deposited in the debt service fund.

Land adjacent to the existing administration building is purchased on which the addition will be constructed. Two landowners agree to purchase prices, totaling $100,000. A third landowner cannot obtain his desired price; his land is secured through eminent domain, with a court-ordered settlement of $40,000.

In governmental fund accounting, capital assets are recorded as expenditures in the capital project fund and as fixed assets in the general fixed assets account group. The land sales and the judgment are paid on a proportional basis from three sources: the state grant (1/4), the federal grant (1/4) and the proceeds of the bond sale (1/2). Grant funds are thus reduced to $930,000. This amount plus previously earned interest is invested in a thirty-day CD at 2.5%. The resulting earnings of $1,947.92 [($930,000 + $5,000) x 0.025 x 30/360] are deposited in the debt service fund.

The bonds, dated July 1, 2004, are issued as twenty-year general obligation bonds with an interest rate of 5%, payable semiannually on December 31 and June 30. For illustrative purposes, it will be assumed that the issue is for term bonds, wherein interest on the full amount of principal is payable over the twenty-year period to maturity.

The bonds are sold on September 30, 2004, at a premium of 2%, or $20,000, plus accrued interest of $12,500 ($1,000,000 x 0.05 x 3/12). The accrued interest and premium on the sale of the bonds are transferred to the debt service fund. From the sale of the bonds, $70,000 is paid toward land acquisition, and the balance of $930,000 is combined with the balance of the grant funds ($930,000 + $5,000 + $1,947.92), for a total of $1,866,947.92. This amount is invested in a ninety-day CD at 3.25%, yielding $15,168.95 on December 29, 2004.

On October 1, 2004, a construction contract is let for the addition to the administration building, which is designed to be built for $1,700,000. A contingency allowance of $85,000 is provided to accommodate any necessary plan changes. The contract calls for completion of the building by November 1, 2005. The Public Works Department will make the necessary land improvements and landscape the grounds at the completion of the construction phase. The estimated cost of $75,000 is encumbered at the outset of the project.

The Sunshine Construction Company is to receive quarterly payments on the basis of percentage of completion of the project and approval by the construction supervisor. During the first year, the following payments are approved, based on invoices submitted by the company:

December 31, 2004	$400,000
March 31, 2005	$250,000
June 30, 2005	$250,000

Individual entries are made to record each of these amounts when the invoices are received and approved. The balance of the grant funds and bond proceeds continues to be available for short-term investment in certificates of deposit or other securities.

Only $650,000 of the accounts payable is actually paid during the fiscal year (the June 30, 2005, payment is made early in the next fiscal year). Closing entries as of June 30, 2005, to close out the revenue, proceeds, and expenditure accounts are as follows:

	Debit	Credit
Proceeds from bonds	$1,020,000	
Revenue	1,000,000	
Expenditures		$ 790,000
Accounts payable		250,000
Operating transfer to debt service fund		20,000
Reserve for encumbrances		860,000
Fund balance		100,000

The capital project fund has $960,000 available at the start of the second fiscal year (July 1, 2005). Interest that has accumulated in the debt service fund to this point amounts to $43,490.26. Thus, $1,003,490.26 is still available for short-term investment.

On July 10, 2005, a contract change is approved that increases the construction contract to $1,750,000. The third quarterly payment of $250,000 is also made on that date. On September 30, 2005, another payment is approved for $500,000.

The project is not completed until December 1, 2005, because of the addition to the contract. At that time, an invoice is received for the balance of the contract. The retained percentage on this project (pending final approval) is 5% of the contract price, or $87,500. Therefore, the December payment to Sunshine Construction is $262,500 ($350,000 - $87,500).

The Public Works Department completes its work at a cost of only $60,000, releasing $15,000 of the $75,000 encumbrance back to the fund balance. By February 28, 2006, the contractors make the corrections to the project needed for final approval, and the retained percentage ($87,500) is paid. The fund balance account is then closed, and the balance of cash on hand—the $15,000 unused encumbrance plus $35,000 unused contingency allowance—is transferred to the debt service fund as a residual equity transfer. (See Table 12-1 for a summary of the interest earned on short-term investments.)

Debt Service Funds

Debt service funds are used to account for (1) the accumulation of resources from which the principal and interest on long-term debt is paid, and (2) the investment and expenditure of those resources. Whenever possible, several debt issues should be accounted for in a single fund, since the fewer the number of funds, the less complicated the accounting for long-term debt. One fund needs only one set of financial statements; many funds need many sets of financial statements.

The money required for the repayment of debt, as well as the interest on the bonds, might come from several sources. If the locality or authority earmarks a special source for the repayment of bonds, a special revenue fund might be set up to collect the money and transfer it to the debt service fund. Often revenue is collected from various sources in the general fund and then transferred to the debt service fund. Many bond indentures require that the money needed for servicing the bonds have first claim on the general revenue of the governmental unit.

Since the resources needed to service the principal and interest on serial bonds is received and expended each year, there is no accumulation of resources on which interest can be earned. The resources needed to service the principal on term bonds, zero coupon bonds, and compound interest bonds, however, are not needed until the debt matures and, therefore, can be invested. Thus, the assets and the fund balance increase annually, providing a *sinking fund* that eventually will be used for payment of the debt.

A sinking fund spreads the repayment costs over the life of the bond issue, thereby avoiding large, irregular demands on the annual budget. The amount that should be earmarked each year for the sinking fund is determined by (1) the dollar value of the bonds to be retired, (2) the number of payments to be made into the account, and (3) the anticipated rate of earnings on the invested funds. Sinking fund requirements should be recomputed each year. Should a surplus in excess of actuarial requirements develop, it might be possible to lower future requirements. It is sound debt management practice, however, to absorb any significant surplus gradually over several fiscal periods rather than making a large reduction in payments in a single year. Should a deficit arise, adjustments should be made as soon as possible by increasing the level of payments into the sinking fund. New investment opportunities should also be sought to produce a greater return.

The same example used to explain the administration of a capital project fund can also be used to illustrate the operations of a debt service fund. Term bonds with a face value of $1,000,000 were issued at 5% for twenty years. Semiannual interest payments on these bonds are $25,000 ($1,000,000 x 0.05 x 1/2). These semiannual payments are transferred from the appropriate source (e.g., general fund) just prior to the date on which the interest payments are due. Since the bonds were sold three months after the date of issues, only $12,500 is needed for the first interest payment. The other $12,500 comes from the accrued interest received upon sale of the bonds.

A fiscal agent often makes interest payments to bondholders on behalf of the locality. In that case, the handling charges made by such agents (usually 1% or less) must also be included in the annual transfers to the debt service fund for interest payments.

The estimated amount needed to build up the sinking fund can be developed from an annuity table or by applying the annuity formula. For example, if the fund can earn 4.5% each year on its investments, consulting an annuity table will show that one dollar invested annually for twenty years at 4.5% will return $31.37. Thus, it would take $31,877.59 added to the sinking fund each year, invested at 4.5%, to equal $1,000,000 at the end of twenty years ($1,000,000 divided by $31.37 = $31,877.59). No long-term investments are purchased in the first year because the payment to the sinking fund is generally not received until the end of the year. During the second and all succeeding years, however, the transfers as well as any earnings made in prior years will be invested.

The interest earned from short-term investments during the construction period is summarized in Table 12-1. The $50,000 fund balance, transferred to the debt service fund when the capital project fund is closed, is added to the $56,194.45 in earned interest for a total of $106,194.45. These funds, invested on March 1 at 4.5%, earn $1,592.92 through June 30. The year-end balance of $20,900 from the first year of the sinking fund (see Table 12-1) earns $940.50 during the second year. Thus, at the end of the second year, the sinking fund has a substantial balance of $129,627.87. This fund balance invested at 4.5% for an additional eighteen years would total $286,280 when the bonds reach maturity [$(1.045)^{18}$ x $129,627.87 = $286,280]. Therefore, the balance that must be accrued in the sinking fund is reduced to $713,720 (i.e., $1,000,000 minus $286,280). Annual payments of $26,576.70, invested at 4.5% over the eighteen-year period, will yield the sum required in the sinking fund to cover the balance of the principal payment ([0.045 ÷ $(1.045)^{18}$ – 1] x $713,720 = $26,576.70). The payment schedule for the sinking fund is detailed in Table 12-2. Thus, the total payment to the sinking fund over eighteen years required to fund the $1 million term bond is $478,380.60 (i.e., $26,576.70 x 18). An additional $126,194.45 represents the transfers in the first two years of the sinking fund. The interest earned on the sinking fund transfers totals $395,424.85.

Table 12-1
Interest Earnings on Short-Term Investments

Investment Period	Funds Available	Rate	Interest Earned	Drawdown
7/03-8/31	1,000,000.00	3.00%	5,000.00	70,000
9/01-9/30	935,000.00	2.50%	1,947.92	70,000
10/01-12/29	1,866,947.92	3.25%	15,168.95	400,000
12/30-3/31	1,482,116.87	3.25%	12,042.20	250,000
4/01-6/30	1,244,159.07	3.00%	9,331.19	250,000
7/01-9/30	1,003,490.26	3.50%	8,780.54	500,000
10/01-11/30	512,270.80	2.75%	2,347.91	262,500
12/01-2/28	252,118.71	2.50%	1,575.74	147,500
Totals			$56,194.45	$1,950,000.00
Funds Balance	$106,194.45			

Table 12-2
Sinking Fund Requirements on Twenty-Year Term Bonds

Year	Estimated Transfer for Bond Payments	Estimated Fund Earnings @4.5%	Estimated Yearly Fund Balance Increase	Estimated Year-End Fund Balance
1	20,000.00	900.00	20,900.00	20,900.00
2	106,194.45	2,533.42	108,727.87	129,627.87
3	26,576.70	5,833.25	32,409.96	162,037.82
4	26,576.70	7,291.70	33,868.40	195,906.23
5	26,576.70	8,815.78	35,392.48	231,298.71
6	26,576.70	10,408.44	36,985.14	268,283.85
7	26,576.70	12,072.77	38,649.47	306,933.32
8	26,576.70	13,812.00	40,388.70	347,322.02
9	26,576.70	15,629.49	42,206.19	389,528.21
10	26,576.70	17,528.77	44,105.47	433,633.68
11	26,576.70	19,513.52	46,090.22	479,723.90
12	26,576.70	21,587.58	48,164.28	527,888.17
13	26,576.70	23,754.97	50,331.67	578,219.84
14	26,576.70	26,019.89	52,596.59	630,816.43
15	26,576.70	28,386.74	54,963.44	685,779.87
16	26,576.70	30,860.09	57,436.79	743,216.67
17	26,576.70	33,444.75	60,021.45	803,238.12
18	26,576.70	36,145.72	62,722.42	865,960.53
19	26,576.70	38,968.22	65,544.92	931,505.46
20	26,576.80	41,917.75	68,494.55	1,000,000.00
Totals	$604,575.15	$395,424.85	$1,000,000.00	

Long-Term Debt Control

Accurate debt records are vital to short-term and long-term financial operations. Such records include auditable ledgers as to the identity, purpose, and amount of debt commitments associated with capital projects and the debt service payments made. From these records, it should be possible to determine quickly and accurately the principal and interest requirements on the total debt over the full maturity of all issues. Such computations are needed to determine the fiscal capacity to meet the requirements for future capital improvements and to plan the retirement schedule for any new borrowing.

Long-term debt can best be controlled through a subsidiary ledger, such as a bond and interest register (see Table 12-3). By collecting in one place all pertinent information regarding individual bond issues, this ledger allows management to trace the complete history of each issue. It also assists in establishing a schedule of debt service requirements and in posting transactions to the general ledger, bonded debt ledger, and interest payable ledger.

A subsidiary bonded debt ledger should include a sheet for each bond issue, showing the project title and purpose, amount of bond originally outstanding, date of bonds, interest rates, amount retired to date, and balance outstanding. A separate sheet is maintained on each bond issue in an interest payable ledger. Interest payments, as they come due, are entered in the "credit" and "balance" columns. As payments are made, the amount is entered in the "debit" column, and the balance payable is reduced by a corresponding sum. An overall schedule of debt service requirements can be readily computed from these records. And a maturity and interest calendar for all debt can be compiled to monitor revenue needs for debt service on a month-to-month basis. The calendar must be adjusted and updated as new bond issues are marketed.

The *general fixed assets account group* provides a record of all fixed assets purchased, constructed, or obtained by contract. Fixed assets obtained by gift should be recorded at the fair market value when donated. Assets obtained through foreclosure should be recorded at the appraised value of property or the total taxes or assessments plus costs, whichever is lower. Cash or liability transactions involved in the buying or selling of the asset are not recorded in the general fixed asset account group, however. Although not maintained for external reporting purposes, depreciation should be recorded in supplemental records for internal costing purposes.

When an asset is sold, destroyed, or otherwise rendered valueless, it is removed from the account group by debiting the general fixed assets account for the original amount recorded and crediting the particular fixed asset. Improvements to a fixed asset—adding to its value—require an entry comparable to the original entry, but only for the amount of the improvement. General repairs—needed to keep the fixed asset in the same operating condition—are not considered improvements and should not be added to the value of the fixed assets in the account group.

The *long-term debt account group* is used to maintain records of long-term liabilities, such as serial bonds, long-term notes, and long-term commitments arising from lease or purchase agreements. Separate records of long-term debt are

Table 12-3
City of Rurbana: Board of Education
Bond and Interest Register

Title: Woodrow Wilson Elementary School
Authorized by: Referendum 03457 (3/15/03)

Sold to: Prince Waterdown & Associates
Price: $2,920,700
Bonds dated: 7/1/03

Amount of Issue: $2,920,700
Purpose: Expansion of elementary school capacity
Coupon rate: 5.6%
Payable: Semiannually
Payable at: Capital City Trust
Bonds payable at: Capital City Trust

Date of Maturity				Interest Due		Principal Due		Principal &
Month	Day	Year	Coupon Nos.	Bond Nos.	Amount	Bond Nos.	Amount	Interest Due
Jan.	1	2004	10001-12920	0001-2920	81,780	0001-2920		81,780
July	1	2004	20001-22920	0001-2920	81,780	0001-2920	129,354	211,134
Jan.	1	2005	30129-32920	0129-2920	78,158	0129-2920		78,158
July	1	2005	40129-42920	0129-2920	78,158	0129-2920	136,598	214,756
Jan.	1	2006	50265-52920	0265-2920	74,333	0265-2920		74,333
July	1	2006	60265-62920	0265-2920	74,333	0265-2920	144,247	218,580
Jan.	1	2007	70409-72920	0409-2920	70,294	0409-2920		70,294
July	1	2007	80409-82920	0409-2920	70,294	0409-2920	152,325	222,619
Jan.	1	2008	90561-92920	0561-2920	66,029	0561-2920		66,029
July	1	2008	100561-102920	0561-2920	66,029	0561-2920	160,856	226,884
Jan.	1	2009	110722-112920	0722-2920	61,525	0722-2920		61,525
July	1	2009	120772-122920	0772-2920	61,525	0772-2920	169,863	231,388
Jan.	1	2010	130892-132920	0892-2920	56,769	0892-2920		56,769
July	1	2010	140892-142920	0892-2920	56,769	0892-2920	179,376	236,145
Jan.	1	2011	151071-152920	1071-2920	51,746	1071-2920		51,746
July	1	2011	161071-162920	1071-2920	51,746	1071-2920	189,421	241,167
Jan.	1	2012	171260-172920	1260-2920	46,442	1260-2920		46,442
July	1	2012	181260-182920	1260-2920	46,442	1260-2920	200,028	246,471
Jan.	1	2013	191460-192920	1460-2920	40,842	1460-2920		40,842
July	1	2013	201460-202920	1460-2920	40,842	1460-2920	211,230	252,072
Jan.	1	2014	212672-212920	2672-2920	34,927	2672-2920		34,927
July	1	2014	222672-222920	2672-2920	34,927	2672-2920	223,059	257,986
Jan.	1	2015	231894-232920	1894-2920	28,682	1894-2920		28,682
July	1	2015	241894-242920	1894-2920	28,682	1894-2920	235,550	264,232
Jan.	1	2016	252130-252920	2130-2920	22,086	2130-2920		22,086
July	1	2016	262130-262920	2130-2920	22,086	2130-2920	248,741	270,827
Jan.	1	2017	272379-272920	2379-2920	15,121	2379-2920		15,121
July	1	2017	282379-282920	2379-2920	15,121	2379-2920	262,671	277,792
Jan.	1	2018	292642-292920	2642-2920	7,767	2642-2920		7,767
July	1	2018	302642-302920	2642-2920	7,767	2642-2920	277,380	285,147
Totals					$1,473,000		$2,920,700	$4,393,700

maintained for special assessment funds, proprietary funds, and profit-type fiduciary funds.

Over the years, transfers from the general fund and interest on investments build up a sinking fund to an amount equal to that needed to pay off the bonds. The data in Table 12-2 illustrate the final year transactions. At the beginning of the year 20, the fund balance should equal $931,505.46. A final transfer from the general fund of $26,576.80 would be made to bring the total available for investment to $958,082.26. This amount will earn $41,917.75 (at 4.5%) to bring the total in the sinking fund to $1,000,000. Upon recording the matured bonds payable in the debt service fund, the equivalent amount in the general long-term debt account group would be closed out.

Financial Reporting

Annual financial reports concerning public debt are of major interest to bondholders, public officials, and the public in general. These reports are also important to the basic credit rating of the governmental unit. If adequate debt records are maintained throughout the year, the preparation of such annual reports can be a relatively simple procedure. As financial analysts often point out, however, such reports are a major point of weakness in the management of government resources.

Annual financial reports concerning debt should cover several basic categories of information:

1. All outstanding debt should be listed by type of issue (general obligation, special assessment, or revenue bonds). The following information should be provided for each bond issue: date of issue, original amount, date of maturity, coupon (interest) rate, total interest, amount of principal and interest presently outstanding, and the amount carried in sinking funds, if any. This information can be taken directly from the *bond and interest register*.
2. For each broad classification of debt, information should be presented as to the annual schedule of debt service, including interest, amortization requirements, and total debt service requirements. This statement should also include data as to the level of unfunded debt, that is, *short-term borrowing* that constitutes an obligation payable out of current revenues.
3. *Overlapping debt* should be clearly identified—that portion of the debt of the school district, county, township, or special districts payable from taxes levied by the reporting jurisdiction.
4. A computation should be made of the jurisdiction's *legal borrowing status*.
5. If term bonds, zero coupon bonds, or compound interest bonds are outstanding, a *sinking fund balance sheet* should be included in the financial report to record the relation of sinking funds to actuarial requirements and a listing of current holdings.
6. Debt arising from the issuance of revenue bonds in proprietary funds must also be shown, including complete information on the facilities that support such debt.

The report should include, as appropriate, the name of the corporate trustee, consulting engineers, and attorneys approving the legality of the issue.

Revenue bond ordinances might require an annual report by an independent certified public accountant, including a current balance sheet and a statement of any contingent liabilities not shown on the balance sheet. Particular types of revenue bonds (e.g., for water or sewer utilities) often require supplemental information, such as average daily supply and consumption, storage capacity, number of customers, consumption per customer, method of billing, legal provisions, and so forth. Special assessment bonds guaranteed by the jurisdiction should also be shown in the schedule of debt.

GASB Financial Reporting Model

The Governmental Accounting Standards Board (GASB) has developed a new model for preparing the financial statements of state and local government (see Table 12-4). These new guidelines change the format for communicating financial information to legislative oversight bodies, creditors, citizens, the media, organizations that rate municipal bonds, and anyone else interested in how a government is doing financially. Annual financial statements must show information about the full cost of providing government services and must include information about a government's infrastructure—its buildings, bridges, and roads. The GASB guidelines also require an analysis, in narrative form, of the jurisdiction's financial activities during the fiscal year. Important new data are added to the current fund accounting approach, and financial information is provided from a total government perspective. These changes are important to potential lenders and taxpayers because of the need to capitalize and depreciate general capital assets.

The annual financial report begins with an analysis of the government's overall financial position and the results of the previous year's operations. This section of the report—known as *management's discussion and analysis* (MD&A)—is designed to assist in assessing whether the government's finances have improved or deteriorated. It includes a comparison of the current year to the prior year, based on financial information about assets, liabilities, revenues, and expenses. In addition, the analysis should explain significant variations in fund-based financial results and budgetary information and should describe capital asset and long-term debt activity during the year.

Financial reporting on *infrastructure assets* (long-term capital assets such as roads and bridges) has been a contentious issue. Some authorities maintain that the value of the information does not justify the cost, complexity, and effort involved in collecting it. After extensive discussions, the GASB concluded that infrastructure reporting is vital to demonstrating accountability for all government assets and the cost of services. However, implementation of infrastructure-asset reporting has been delayed and, for now, estimated costs will be allowed for infrastructure assets acquired before the effective dates of the model. The GASB model does require prospective reporting of major general infrastructure assets acquired after the model is implemented.

Table 12-4
Important Features of Government-wide Financial Statements

Capital assets, including infrastructure, are to be reported in the government-wide statement of net assets. *Depreciation expenses*—the cost of using capital assets—are to be reported in the statement of activities.

- *Infrastructure assets* are not required to be depreciated if (1) an asset management system is used that has certain characteristics and (2) the government can document that assets are being preserved approximately at (or above) a condition level established and disclosed by the government. Disclosures about infrastructure assets are made in required supplementary information, including the physical condition of the assets and amounts spent to maintain and preserve them over time.
- *Net assets* are to be identified in three categories: (1) invested in capital assets, net of related debt; (2) restricted; and (3) unrestricted. Restricted net assets are those assets for which the use is constrained by law (for instance, by constitutional provisions or enabling legislation) or externally (such as by creditors or the laws of other governments).

Statement of activities is to be presented in at least the same level of detail provided in the governmental fund statements—generally, expenses and program revenues by function (for example, public safety). Governments are encouraged to provide more detailed information where relevant (for example, fire protection).

- *Program expenses* should include all direct expenses.
- *Overhead and other indirect expenses*, if allocated to individual programs, should be shown in a separate column.

Special and extraordinary items are to be reported separately from other revenues and expenses to permit users to determine if the government's conventional, recurring revenues and expenses are balanced.

- *Special items* are significant transactions or other events within the control of management that are either unusual or infrequent in occurrence, such as the proceeds from a sale of parkland.
- *Extraordinary items* are beyond government's control and are both unusual and infrequent, such as the cost of cleaning up a natural disaster.

The GASB model provides practical guidance on establishing estimated costs and reporting general infrastructure assets. If historical cost data are not available, governments are expected to report estimated historical cost for major general infrastructure assets acquired in fiscal years ending after June 30, 1980. GASB has provided ways to estimate historical cost and to calculate accumulated depreciation and depreciation at transition.

Governments that elect to use the *modified approach* to reporting infrastructure will be required to disclose the assessed physical condition of infrastructure assets (such assessments to be performed at least every three years) and describe the criteria used to measure and report asset condition. The condition level at which the government intends to maintain the assets also must be identified. And a comparison must be provided of the estimated annual dollar amount required to maintain and preserve the assets at the condition level established by the government with the actual expenses for at least the last five years.

Governments will need capital-asset records that support the opening balances at transition of capital assets and accumulated depreciation. These records should enable the calculation of depreciation for government-wide reporting of general capital assets. Retroactive reporting of general government infrastructure assets is not required until four years after the GASB model is implemented. However, governments need to understand that any debt related to such infrastructure must be included in the government-wide statement of net assets upon implementation. Governments that do not report the depreciated value of infrastructure assets will report fewer net assets, with some governments conceivably reporting more liabilities than assets.

Under the provisions of the GASB model, *full accrual accounting* procedures should be used to prepare financial statements for all activities of government—not just those for which costs are covered by charging a fee for services, as was previously required. This approach includes both current assets and liabilities (such as cash and accounts payable, respectively) and capital assets and long-term liabilities (such as buildings and infrastructure, including bridges and roads, and general obligation debt). Accrual accounting also reports all of the revenues and costs of providing services each year, not just those received or paid in the current year or soon thereafter.

The required government-wide statements should help determine the extent to which the government has invested in capital assets, including infrastructure. In addition to the annual report, an interim report covering much of the same information should be prepared midway in each fiscal year for distribution to those interested in the financial status of the jurisdiction. In short, the new financial statements should give government officials the means to more clearly demonstrate their stewardship in the long term in addition to the short-term fund or budgetary focus.

Distribution of Revenues and Issuance of Additional Bonds

Income derived from the operation of a self-supporting project, in most cases, are deposited in a *reserve fund*. Moneys in the reserve fund are then distributed monthly by the trustee or other handler of funds in the order established by the bond resolution or trust indenture (see Table 12-5). Moneys remaining in the reserve fund after the required distributions have been made might be placed in a *surplus fund*, to be divided among various categories such as:

- Redemption account to retire bonds in advance of maturity.
- Payment in lieu of taxes—when an authority purchases an operation that had been a private corporate unit, payments might be made in lieu of taxes either by legislative requirement or to create good will.
- Other lawful payments, including improvements and extensions to the facility or support of other bond interest.

Table 12-5
Distribution of Revenues from Self-Supporting Projects

1. *Operations and maintenance* (O&M) have first claim on the reserve fund. Without proper O&M funds, a facility might experience severe loss of income. Revenue bonds are commonly payable from net revenues—that is, gross receipts less operating and maintenance costs.
2. *Bond service account* should receive monthly payments sufficient to cover the next semiannual interest payment as well as the next principal payment on serial bonds.
3. A *sinking fund* is sometimes required in the case of term bonds, zero coupon bonds, and compound interest bonds, in lieu of principal payments on serial bonds.
4. *Debt service reserve fund* is gradually built up to equal a full year's maximum principal and interest in the case of serial bonds, or two year's interest in the case of term bonds.
5. A *renewal and replacement fund* (sometimes called a *replacement reserve*) is established to replace equipment and provide necessary repairs beyond normal maintenance. Funds are paid into this account in amounts recommended by the consulting engineer and might be cumulative.
6. A *reserve maintenance fund* might be established to meet unusual or extraordinary maintenance charges that have not been budgeted. Some jurisdictions combine the reserve maintenance fund with the renewal and replacement fund.
7. *Working capital fund*, to cover unforeseen contingencies, should be equivalent to about one-tenth of the annual gross revenues.

When a strategic facility is being constructed, it is not always possible to foresee just what the future will hold. It might be necessary to increase the size of the facility or to make other improvements that will require additional financing. Sufficient leeway should be provided in the bond indenture or resolution to permit the issuance of additional bonds.

Two basic types of trust indentures are:

- Closed-end indentures, which do not permit the issuance of parity bonds except as necessary to complete the project if initial financing proves insufficient; and
- Open-end indentures, which permit the issuance of additional bonds but provide a formula that prescribes the conditions to be met.

In the first case, additional bonds must be junior in lien to the then outstanding bonds—that is, have a secondary claim on available revenue. If bonds of equal rank are permitted, safeguards must be established to prevent the undue dilution of the security of the original bonds.

Debt Service Retirement

Prompt payment of all principal and interest requirements is the most direct evidence of sound debt administration. The way in which a jurisdiction administers its debt service is one of the most important factors in determining its credit standing for future borrowing. Even temporary defaults might adversely affect a municipality's ability to borrow at optimal interest rates. Well-defined administrative procedures—including advanced planning regarding the payment calendar and sound management of sinking funds and capital reserves—are essential to ensure regularity in the payment of interest and redemption of principal.

Payment Calendar

The first step is to establish an information system regarding interest and redemption requirements over the life of the bond issues. For this purpose, the bond and interest register and the ledgers for bonded debt and interest form a ready basis for the development of a *payment calendar*. Whenever a new bond issue is marketed, a schedule should be prepared showing the amount due on each principal and interest date. This schedule should be incorporated into a consolidated payment calendar to show the timing of total cash requirements. If sinking funds or other debt service funds are involved, these obligations must also be taken into account in the annual budget process.

The allotment of funds for principal and interest payments must be timed to provide cash when it is needed. Budget officials must plan ahead to ensure that any early payments required in the following fiscal year can be met. Provision must be made in the tax collection system to generate adequate funds in the early part of the new fiscal year. Alternatively, a sufficient fund balance must be carried over from the previous fiscal year.

Payment of all principal and interest requirements should be made through a single agency, for example, the City Treasurer's office or some other designated fiscal agent. In many cities, such payments also require authorization by the Director of Finance or the Controller. It is usually a good administrative practice to appoint a bank or trust company in the financial center in which a municipality's bonds are marketed to serve as its paying agent. Funds are deposited with the paying agent in advance of interest and principal due dates, and the agent oversees the payment of coupons and matured bonds as they are submitted. Investors prefer this arrangement. It saves the municipality considerable routine work, and the paying agent is equipped to handle this function at a relatively low cost.

Sinking Funds

A major problem in the use of sinking funds (and one contributing to severe restrictions in many states regarding this method of financing) stems from the technical difficulties of managing the trust accounts. Local governments are restricted by law in many states as to the types of sinking fund investments that can be made. Investments are usually limited to federal, state, and municipal bonds. Within these categories, investments should be limited to high-grade issues and should exclude revenue bonds on projects with unproven earning power. Bonds with equal security might vary in terms of their yield, and the relationship of maturity to yield tends to vary with changes in market conditions. Analysis of the bond market, therefore, is essential to secure the maximum earnings for sinking funds compatible with the safety of investment.

While some controversy surrounds the practice, there are certain advantages for a municipality to invest sinking funds in its own securities. This approach avoids the complex analysis required when selecting bonds of other jurisdictions. It simplifies the administration of the sinking fund and lowers costs. And it affords a ready market for a municipality's borrowing that might be particularly important when the general market is uncertain.

The principal argument against this practice is that the sinking fund might become a dumping ground for excessive amounts of tax notes issued to offset inadequate administration. Under such conditions, the security for payment is little more than a collection of IOUs. With proper safeguards, however, this investment practice remains a viable alternative to other forms of sinking fund investments.

When a municipality invests in its own bonds, it does not increase its net debt any more than if it sold these bonds to outside investors. And when it buys in its outstanding bonds, it decreases its net debt just as much as if it invested in other municipals. In either case, the taxpaying capacity in relation to net debt is not affected.

In addition to security, sinking fund investments must have liquidity—the maturities of the various investments must be so timed that funds will be readily available to retire the principal of term bonds, zero coupon bonds, or compound interest bonds when it comes due. Without careful investment planning, it might be necessary to sell the holdings of the sinking fund in the open market, with the possibility of taking a loss. Investing in several different types and sizes of offerings often can ensure greater flexibility.

To the extent permitted by state law, sinking funds should be consolidated to simplify transactions, to save time in putting the funds to work, and to secure a better investment position. Separate fund accounts should be maintained, however, for administrative purposes in calculating annual contributions. Whenever possible, sinking fund investments should be registered. An independent audit of the sinking fund should be made annually in addition to regular auditing by the controller of all sinking fund transactions.

It should be evident from this discussion that the management of a sinking fund is a complex task that should not be undertaken without adequately trained personnel and proper safeguards to protect the integrity of the funds. As has been noted, a number of states have legislated against term bonds secured by sinking funds insofar as general obligation borrowing is concerned. However, such funds remain as a viable means of financing many revenue-producing projects, whereby annual contributions to the fund are generated by the self-supporting facilities. In such cases, adherence to the guidelines outlined above is especially important since such debts often are outside the protection of the full faith, credit, and taxing power of the jurisdiction.

Recording and Canceling Coupons and Bonds

The final step in servicing a municipal debt involves the recording and canceling of coupons and bonds that have been paid. Following each scheduled payment, coupons scheduled for payment and bonds that have reached maturity must be checked to determine if any have not been redeemed. Some will always be slow to come in, and occasionally, some might be missing permanently. Records of canceled coupons and redeemed bonds must be maintained for several years after the final maturity date.

Many commercial banks and trust companies that serve as paying agents for municipal bonds include all phases of recording and cancellation as part of their services. These banks and trust companies provide the municipality with a certified list of the canceled coupons and redeemed bonds. Municipalities might mandate that the disposition of these documents take place in the presence of the Director of Finance or the Controller and at least one other municipal official. The "mortgage burning" ceremony is one that still has considerable significance for many small communities.

Refunding and Conversion

Issuing new bonds to retire outstanding debt is called *refunding*. Refunding bonds can result in savings if the interest rate on the new bonds is lower than the interest rate on the existing bonds. Refunding bonds can be used to remove restrictive bond covenants that apply to existing bonds. Local governments also can use refunding bonds to restructure its debt service obligations.

Refunding Callable Bonds

The most common reason for refunding is to achieve lower interest rates. When outstanding bonds bear interest rates substantially higher than those currently obtainable in the bond market, it might be appropriate to determine whether a refunding can be carried out to the advantage of the issuing government—either refunding the full amount of the outstanding debt or some portions thereof. This process is sometimes referred to as a "high-to-low refunding" because of the conversion of long-term debt from a higher interest rates to lower interest rate bonds.

Refunding is generally developed through the exercise of the call provision that was included into the original bond issue. Bonds might be made callable at any time after the date of issue. In practice, however, the call normally is exercised with appropriate notice only on interest payment dates. A bond issue might be made part callable and part noncallable. Bonds can be made callable at par or at a premium.

Callable bonds afford greater flexibility in the jurisdiction's debt structure. If the initial retirement schedule proves to be too rapid, or a period of declining revenues is encountered, bonds can be recalled and refunded at more favorable terms. During periods of high interest rates, the call feature permits bonds to be issued and then refunded at lower rates at some time during their term if the market changes or the jurisdiction's credit rating improves. The callable feature permits the retirement of revenue bonds to be accelerated if the revenue capacity of a project expands.

Bonds issued within ninety days of the call date of the outstanding bonds are called "current refunding bonds." Relatively few limits are placed on current refundings. Bonds that are issued more than ninety days in advance of the call date are called "advance refunding bonds." The timing of an advanced refunding must be carefully chosen, since there are numerous federal regulations regarding the use of advance refunding bonds.

Advanced Refunding

In the early 1960s, some jurisdictions engaged in the practice of refunding bonds to take advantage of falling interest rates. Some jurisdictions had three sets of bonds outstanding on the same project—the original bonds, an initial set of refunding bonds, and a secondary set of advanced refunding bonds issued to refund a portion of the first set of refunding bonds. The effect was to have three sets of tax-exempt interest being paid on the same basic improvement. However, the revenues generated from the refunding bonds usually were invested in securities that had higher interest returns (arbitrage) than were required to service the outstanding bonds.

In August 1966, the U.S. Treasury ruled that the interest on such refunding bonds would not be considered tax-exempt:

1. Where all or a substantial part of the proceeds of the issue (other than normal contingency reserves such as debt service reserves) is only to be invested in taxable obligations that are, in turn, to be held as security for the retirement of the obligations of the governmental unit.
2. Where the proceeds of the issue are to be used to refund outstanding obligations that are first callable more than five years in the future and, in the interim, are to be invested in taxable obligations held as security for the satisfaction of either the current issue or the issue to be refunded.

The 1986 Tax Reform Act further limited local governments to one advance refunding for each original bond issue. This limit prevents governments from repeatedly refunding the same issue each time interest rates drop in an attempt to realize even greater arbitrage earnings. Private activity bonds cannot be advance refunded at all. This restriction prevents the federal subsidization of private activities through tax-exempt arbitrage earnings.

Refunding to Adjust Contract Terms

Revenue bond issues often involve complex and lengthy indentures. It might become necessary to issue additional debt at some time prior to the maturity of the outstanding bonds. However, the terms of the existing contract might unduly restrict the issuance of new bonds. The restrictions might have been appropriate to carry out the original financing. However, under current conditions, they might impede the accomplishment of the present objectives. Therefore, the issuing authority might find it desirable to arrange for the refunding of the outstanding debt in order to eliminate or modify the restrictive covenants.

Refunding to eliminate restrictive covenants frequently results in substantial additional costs. This fact underlines the importance of holding the restrictive elements in each bond indenture to a minimum, consistent with the original intent of the bond issue.

Refunding to Consolidate Debt

It might be possible to use refunding to consolidate a jurisdiction's outstanding debt (or some portion thereof). To illustrate this approach, assume that a major expansion must be made to a city's sewage treatment facilities to be in compliance with revised state and federal standards regarding effluent discharges. The Sewer and Water Commission and City Council agree that an adjustment should be made in the sewer service charges sufficient to meet the debt service requirements.

In Table 12-6, it is assumed that the annual yield from the authorized increase in sewer service charges will be $1 million, with an estimated increase in this yield at a compound rate of 2% per annum. The city still has $6 million in bonds outstanding from a previous issue for the sewer treatment system, bearing a 5% interest rate and maturing serially in annual amounts of $500,000. The new sewage treatment facilities will cost $8 million, with the proposed bonds to be issued for thirty years with a uniform coupon rate of 5%.

It would not be possible to finance additional bonds under these conditions because the debt service in the first year would be $800,000 on the old bonds and $520,000 on the new bonds. Thus the total debt service would exceed the total revenues of $1,000,000 available for the first year.

The refunding of the outstanding bonds along with the issue of new bonds might be a viable approach. The total funding required to achieve this consolidation is $14,200,000, including the refunding costs of $200,000. One plan for accomplishing the consolidation is shown in Table 12-6. In year 1, the 5% interest rate is applied to the outstanding principal of $14.2 million, resulting in an interest payment of $710,000. This interest payment would leave $290,000 from the $1 million in annual revenues dedicated to debt service to be applied to reduce the outstanding principal. In year 2, the 5% interest rate is applied to the outstanding principal of $13.91 million, resulting in an interest payment of $695,500, leaving $324,500 from the $1.02 million in projected annual revenue to be applied to reduce the outstanding principal. As the annual revenue increases (at 2% per year), the funds available to reduce the outstanding principal increase. Therefore, the decrease in the annual interest payments is accelerated.

Table 12-6
Consolidation of Existing and Proposed Debt Through Refunding

Year	*Estimated Annual Revenue* <u>*2%/Annum*</u>	*Debt Service Requirement on Existing $6 million* <u>*Debt*</u>	*Debt Service Requirement on New $8 million* <u>*Debt*</u>	*Debt Service on $14 Million at 5% Combined New Debt ($8 Million) and Refunding ($6 Million)* <u>*with $200,000 Refunding Costs*</u>			
				<u>*Principal*</u>	<u>*Interest*</u>	*Total Debt* <u>*Service*</u>	*Outstanding* <u>*Principal*</u>
							$14,200,000
1	$1,000,000	$800,000	$520,000	$290,000	$710,000	$1,000,000	$13,910,000
2	$1,020,000	$775,000	$520,000	$324,500	$695,500	$1,020,000	$13,585,500
3	$1,040,400	$750,000	$520,000	$361,125	$679,275	$1,040,400	$13,224,375
4	$1,061,208	$725,000	$520,000	$399,989	$661,219	$1,061,208	$12,824,386
5	$1,082,432	$700,000	$520,000	$441,213	$641,219	$1,082,432	$12,383,173
6	$1,104,081	$675,000	$520,000	$484,922	$619,159	$1,104,081	$11,898,251
7	$1,126,162	$650,000	$520,000	$531,250	$594,913	$1,126,162	$11,367,001
8	$1,148,686	$625,000	$520,000	$580,336	$568,350	$1,148,686	$10,786,665
9	$1,171,659	$600,000	$520,000	$632,326	$539,333	$1,171,659	$10,154,339
10	$1,195,093	$575,000	$520,000	$687,376	$507,717	$1,195,093	$9,466,963
11	$1,218,994	$550,000	$520,000	$745,646	$473,348	$1,218,994	$8,721,317
12	$1,243,374	$525,000	$520,000	$807,308	$436,066	$1,243,374	$7,914,009
13	$1,268,242		$520,000	$872,541	$395,700	$1,268,242	$7,041,467
14	$1,293,607		$520,000	$941,533	$352,073	$1,293,607	$6,099,934
15	$1,319,479		$520,000	$1,014,482	$304,997	$1,319,479	$5,085,452
16	$1,345,868		$520,000	$1,091,596	$254,273	$1,345,868	$3,993,856
17	$1,372,786		$520,000	$1,173,093	$199,693	$1,372,786	$2,820,763
18	$1,400,241		$520,000	$1,259,203	$141,038	$1,400,241	$1,561,560
19	$1,428,246		$520,000	$1,350,168	$78,078	$1,428,246	$211,392
20	$1,456,811		$520,000	$211,392	$10,570	$221,962	$0
21	$1,485,947		$520,000				
22	$1,515,666		$520,000				
23	$1,545,980		$520,000				
24	$1,576,899		$520,000				
25	$1,608,437		$520,000				
26	$1,640,606		$520,000				
27	$1,673,418		$520,000				
28	$1,706,886		$520,000				
29	$1,741,024		$520,000				
30	$1,775,845		$520,000				
	$40,568,079	$7,950,000	$15,600,000	$14,200,000	$8,862,520	$23,062,520	

Sale of Refunding Bonds

Refunding bonds might be sold for cash and the outstanding bonds redeemed in cash, or the refunding bonds might be exchanged with the holders of the outstanding bonds. In the case of financial difficulties, such as default, a refunding plan, as part of the reorganization of debt, might be mandated and supervised by the courts.

Five elements need to be considered in connection with the sale of refunding bonds: (1) the timing of the sale, (2) the maturity schedule of the refunding bonds, (3) the time of settlement on the new bonds, (4) the refunding costs, and (5) the redemption provisions for the refunding bonds. The security that is pledged in support of the refunding bonds should be the same as the original issue. Maturities might have to be rearranged to accommodate higher coupon rates on early maturities. Or a rate limitation might have to be placed on those maturities to bring the debt service within the bounds determined in the planning of the issue. It might be appropriate to accelerate the maturity schedule on the refunding bonds to increase the interest savings at some future date. Such acceleration might be desirable if the issuing jurisdiction can afford to pay the refunding costs from current funds and is willing to forego the realization of the savings for a number of years.

Settlement on the refunding bonds should be a few days in advance of the due date on the called bonds in order that the issuing jurisdiction might be assured of having the cash in hand to meet the requirements for paying off the called bonds. Assuming no debt limit problems, the jurisdiction might prefer to complete settlement on the refunding bonds prior to the issuance of the call of the outstanding bond. This procedure is particularly appropriate in cases where the likelihood of litigation might delay the delivery and settlement of the refunding bonds beyond the date for the redemption of the old bonds. While prior settlement involves the payment of overlapping bond interest, the net amount of such duplication can be reduced through the short-term investment of the revenue from the new issue.

If state laws permit, it might be appropriate to increase the amount of the refunding issue by the amount of the refunding costs. While this approach reduces the net savings in current dollars, it should have little effect on the overall savings realized in terms of present worth dollars.

Including a call option in the refunding bonds will increase interest costs and thereby decrease the amount of interest savings that can be attained. On the other hand, a call option on bonds that will mature in several years (e.g., at least five) might be justified if the refunding is in a market of medium to high interest rates.

Cost Considerations

Bond issuers generally target a level of present value savings as a guideline for determining when to issue refunding bonds. Such savings usually are measured as a percentage of the refunded bond issue—for example, 4% or 5% is a common target. In other words, the savings achieved through the refunding bonds should represent 4% to 5% of the cost of the bond issue, expressed in present value terms.

The amount of money saved from refunding depends on several factors, including:

- Difference between the prior and new bond interest rates
- Maturity date of the prior bonds
- Call date on the prior bonds
- Yield on escrow investments
- Call premium on prior bonds
- Costs involve in issuance of the refunding bonds

The earlier a bond issue is refunded, the greater the issuer's savings. Once the first call date on a bond issue has passed, an increasingly lower current interest rate is required on the refunding bonds to achieve a target level of savings. Smaller issues or specific maturities of an issue might not be worth refunding, even if the target in terms of percent savings is achieved. The absolute dollar savings might not be sufficient to justify the time, expense, and effort of executing a refunding issue.

Since most investors insist on a premium for callable bonds, the resultant net savings must be carefully considered. The steps required include a determination of:

1. The probable interest rate that could be achieved on the refunding bonds if offered in the prevailing market.
2. The gross amount of interest to be saved in terms of the current dollars payable in the years in which the savings will occur, and the present worth of dollars to be saved at future dates.
3. The cost of refunding—the call premiums payable and the costs incident to the issuance of refunding bonds.

Refunding bonds have the same types of issuance costs as a new issue. In essence, the government repeats these costs during the life of the debt. Failure to reduce all factors to a net present worth can result in a refunding that is apparently favorable but which, in fact, is disadvantageous to the issuing jurisdiction.[1]

After the sale of the refunding bonds, the proceeds are held in an escrow account until the prior bonds are called. New bonds are issued in an amount sufficient to cover the principal, interest, and call premium of the prior bond issue. If the proceeds are invested in secure investment vehicles, the original bonds are considered "defeased" and are no longer considered a liability of the issuer.

Secure investments include U.S. Treasury notes or other obligations guaranteed by the federal government. Additionally, the rating on the original bonds is upgraded to AAA, since there is a guaranteed source of repayment. The escrow fund is used to meet debt service obligations of the original bond issue until the call date, at which time the remainder of the escrow fund is used to redeem the outstanding bonds.

Refunding issues do not have to go through the same legislative and/or constitutional approval process as the original bonds since the original bond issue was already approved. Refunding issues are typically sold through a negotiated sale because of their complexity.

Refunding Mature Bonds

The practice of refunding mature or maturing bonds should be avoided if at all possible and, if necessary, should be undertaken with great discretion.[2] Conditions might arise, however, that require refunding to eliminate irregularities in the existing debt schedule. Such irregularities result from overly optimistic retirement schedules or from sudden shifts in economic conditions beyond the control of the local jurisdiction that lead to changes in the municipality's revenue system. Refunding might also be preferable to emergency borrowing, particularly when a good credit relationship has been established in connection with outstanding debt.

Refunded bonds should be scheduled into the debt retirement program as soon as possible within the jurisdiction's financial capacity. A retirement period that is excessively long might seriously limit future borrowing. On the other hand, the retirement period of the refunding bonds should be of sufficient duration to avoid the need for further refunding.

Forced Refunding

During a period of reduced economic activity, a local government might use refunding to restructure its debt service requirements in order to defer or stretch out debt obligations until the financial situation improves. At times, a municipality might find it absolutely necessary to refund outstanding debts to avoid default on bonds or serious disruption of its financial operations. Unfortunately, such forced refunding often encounters unfavorable market conditions, since the economic factors that give rise to the need for refunding might be widespread. This situation confronted many local governments during the depression years of the 1930s. Under such circumstances, a municipality—unable to sell refunding bonds to new investors—might be forced to negotiate with existing bondholders for the exchange of their holdings for new maturities. Since bonds might be widely held and bondholders difficult to locate, this undertaking can be most cumbersome, particularly if the issue has turned over in the secondary trading market.

Forced refunding should never be unduly postponed. It is a matter of good financial administration to anticipate such emergencies and to take the necessary steps with sufficient lead-time to resolve the problem in an orderly and businesslike manner. A frank and open presentation of the municipality's financial problems is necessary to secure understanding and cooperation from major bondholders.

Defaults

No matter how satisfactorily resolved, the default of a debt obligation is likely to result in a decline in the jurisdiction's credit standing, producing skepticism among lenders and, in turn, causing major difficulties in negotiating favorable interest rates on future bond issues. Even temporary defaults, if allowed to extend beyond the normal ninety-day grace period, might result in the removal of a city from the listing of securities approved for fiduciary investments.

Defaults During the Depression

By far the largest number and most severe defaults took place during the depression era from 1929 through 1938. The total debt of all governmental units with recorded defaults during this period was approximately $5.5 billion, or approximately 30% of the average net municipal debt outstanding at the time. The most prominent default of this period was that of the City of New York, with total indebtedness of slightly over $2.5 million. Lasting only a few days, the New York City default involved some general obligation notes issued in anticipation of delinquent tax collections. The $5.5 billion figure included approximately $160 million in default by the state of Arkansas, $190 million in default by local governmental units with less than 5,000 population, and $400 million in default by special purpose and special assessment districts.

Prior to the depression, municipal debt had increased at a very significant rate, in large measure due to speculative overdevelopment of real estate in the 1920s and the lack of realistic debt limits. In some cases, the officers of real estate companies became municipal officials and promoted bond issues to enhance their real estate holdings. Special assessment or local improvement districts often were created to finance the improvement of undeveloped and speculative areas. The issuance of debt in the name of overlapping units made debt limits ineffective.

The capacity of local government to pay these debts did not increase nearly as rapidly as the debts themselves. Encouraged by the availability of capital at fairly low interest rates in the late 1920s, many municipalities with unbalanced budgets were able to borrow enough to cover their operating deficits. This borrowing added to the already large fixed charges of many communities. In 1932 and 1933, however, municipal borrowing was greatly curtailed as a consequence of rapidly rising interest rates, bank failures, and the loss of public confidence in municipal bonds.

Municipal revenues rapidly declined as wealth, income, and assessed values plunged downward in the early years of the Depression. The decrease in local tax revenues, for which there were no adequate substitutes, was not accompanied by commensurate declines in expenditures. Many governments were faced with rising debt service charges, the result of unwieldy debt structures. They were also confronted with increased demands for unemployment relief payments. Therefore, many local governments with deficit budgets were forced to default.

The defaults of the Depression led to the enactment of the Federal Municipal Bankruptcy Act. Under this act, any local government that has defaulted on its debt because of its inability to meet its commitments can apply for relief to the applicable Federal District Court which can approve a plan for the reorganization of the debt of the issuer. After the Second World War, several large bond issues to finance toll roads ran into difficulties in terms of covering debt service payments from net earnings. Such entities as the West Virginia Turnpike and the Calumet Skyway were eligible for reorganization under the Federal Municipal Bankruptcy Act. However, they did not resort to this course of action, relying on more conventional refunding procedures instead.

Types of Defaults

Minor or temporary defaults involve failure to meet the maturity payment of a single security or temporary postponement of interest payments. Such minor defaults might be the result of unanticipated declines in revenue collections, the shutting off of normal lines of bank credit, and/or a temporary inability to market refunding bonds. They usually can be corrected without disturbing the jurisdiction's general debt structure or further interrupting debt service. Adjustment strategies include: (a) payment during the grace period from belated tax receipts; (b) short-term bank loans; (c) small issues of refunding bonds; or (d) security exchanges. This latter strategy is particularly effective for relatively recent bond issues. Bondholders are contacted and negotiations are conducted to effect an exchange of outstanding bonds for new securities that more closely fit the jurisdiction's long-term ability to pay.

A second, more serious class of defaults involves local governments that have encountered such financial problems as peak debt service in periods of low-paying capacity, serious breakdowns in the local economic base, and/or abnormally high tax delinquency. Under such circumstances, the municipality might experience difficulties in meeting current expenses as well as long-term obligations. Adjustments usually are made by refunding or partially refunding a few years' obligations in order to free up some financial resources to meet current operating costs. It might be possible to accomplish this adjustment without a major disturbance to the general debt structure and without any scaling of debt. Once current obligations are returned to a more balanced basis, attention can be redirected toward long-term obligations that might require further readjustments to reflect sound principles of debt administration.

The third class of debt involves situations in which the jurisdiction is confronted by abnormally high debt, severely curtailed revenues, and significant accumulation of operating deficits, with little or no prospect for correction except through a comprehensive refunding plan. Such a plan usually involves a complete reconstruction of the entire debt retirement schedule and a scaling down of interest and even principal payments.

Scaling of debt involves the actual reduction in the jurisdiction's commitments and becomes necessary when the total obligation is clearly beyond the local government's capacity to pay. Investors naturally are reluctant to forego any portion of their contractual rights, and particularly so with regards to principal. Unless the situation is hopeless, they tend to prefer extensive postponements, with the expectation that subsequent growth and development in the locality will eventually restore the protection of their investment. Thus, when necessary, scaling can be more readily accomplished through a reduction in interest rates.

Steps in Readjustment

Insofar as possible, the jurisdiction should take the initiative in readjustment and in planning and implementing the refunding plan. Serious defaults require time for careful deliberation before commitments are made. By exercising the initiative, the jurisdiction might gain the necessary cooperation from investors to successfully resolve the pending financial crisis. Attempting to cover up the financial problems merely exacerbates the uncertainty, increases expenses, and ultimately might result in the local government being placed in receivership. At this point, local officials no longer can control the readjustment process.

When it is evident that readjustment is unavoidable, an official statement should be issued to the jurisdiction's creditors. This statement should give notice of jurisdiction's inability to meet its obligations, identify the causes and probable duration, and outline the steps contemplated to correct the situation as expeditiously as possible. Financial records should be opened to bondholders, and a summary analysis should be distributed, outlining the jurisdiction's financial status and capacity to pay. This analysis should be followed by frequent reports of financial and economic conditions and trends. Only by such means can the local government retain the initiative and assure the most constructive negotiations with its creditors.

A complete investigation of all relevant factors—financial, administrative, and economic—is a prerequisite to the planning of corrective action. Reliable experts should be consulted and a competent fiscal adviser retained. The relationship between outstanding obligations and normal capacity to pay must be ascertained, and operating costs should be examined to determine if they provide any basis for adjustments. The jurisdiction must evaluate its financial status and relation to resources and liabilities, both immediate and future. In short, the jurisdiction should approach its creditors with full knowledge of where it stands and of the reasonable expectations regarding the capacity to recover from its financial difficulties.

To be successful, the refunding plan must provide (1) mechanisms to release current accounts from accumulated deficiencies, and (2) financing procedures that will assure the maintenance of balanced operations. While a brief hiatus from full debt service obligations might be necessary, such postponement is valid only if it is used as a means of systematically adjusting current accounts. Such refunding as is necessary should postpone the retirement of as little debt service as possible. Restructuring the debt obligations should not trade a difficult immediate situation for an impossible future one. Callable bonds should be used to the extent possible to permit the re-refunding at lower interest rates if justified by market conditions. The use of callable bonds also facilitates accelerating the retirement process when conditions improve.

Adjustment of serious defaults, at best, involves a process of compromise, in which there is little opportunity for impartial settlement. Furthermore, refunding arrangements might contain the potentialities for recurring financial difficulties for several decades in the future. The experiences of many communities in the 1930s offer ample support for the necessity of sound debt policies.

Summary and Conclusions

Debt administration is one of the most significant responsibilities of local government officials. Furthermore, the role of debt administration in municipalities and other public organizations has changed dramatically over recent years. This role has evolved from that of a coordinator of the timing and marketing of bond issues to one of key decision maker and negotiator in the bond issue process. The role is further expanding to include information management. Local jurisdictions that issue debt have increasing responsibilities to furnish accurate and timely information to their investors and to the capital market in general

Debt administration requires the establishment of systematic procedures for maintaining records, for annual financial reporting, and for the accountability of funds. Such procedures are essential to develop confidence on the part of investors and the general public as to the overall management of a jurisdiction's financial affairs.

An important part of debt administration is the recognition of the appropriate use and pitfalls of short-term borrowing. A careful examination and, if necessary, adjustment of the tax collection system might obviate the need for short-term borrowing except for emergency purposes. The use of bond anticipation borrowing, however, might provide a fiscally sound strategy if applied with discretion.

The most direct evidence of sound debt administration is the prompt payment of all debt service charges. To achieve this objective, it is necessary to track the interest and redemption requirements over the life of all outstanding issues. Significant attention must be paid to the information systems used by governments to collect, report, review, and store this information.[3]

From an information perspective, debt administration goes beyond the new legal requirements established by the Governmental Accounting Standards Board (GASB). Satisfying broader regulatory and financial reporting requirements becomes an important benefit of the process. One of the key objectives is to deliver information to the purchasers of securities in the secondary market. A large repository of information focused on the results of bond sales is required when the objective is to develop performance evaluation techniques.

A critical part of the debt administrator's responsibilities involves the careful management of sinking funds and other debt service funds. Recording and cancellation of coupons and retired bonds must be undertaken in an orderly manner to ensure the proper closing out of debt obligations.

Finally, refunding procedures and safeguards against defaults should be clearly understood by local officials. Most states have adopted legislative measures to circumvent the financial catastrophe faced by many local governments in the 1930s. The ultimate responsibility, however, still rests with local officials to adopt debt administrative procedures that will protect their community from "mortgaging its future."

Notes

1. Lennox L. Moak, *Administration of Local Government Debt* (Chicago, Ill.: Municipal Finance Officers Association, 1970), 400-416.
2. Refunding merely to effect a temporary tax reduction has no justification. The motivation is usually political. In some flagrant cases, bonds have been refunded just prior to elections to "improve" the record of incumbent office holders even though existing debt commitments could be readily met under the established schedule. Such practices result in unstable fluctuations in the tax levy, rising debt trends, and serious disruptions of the jurisdiction's debt structure.
3. *DBC Debt Manager* is a database management system that tracks critical information on outstanding debt from issuance through maturity. *DBC Debt Manager* combines the bond math library of *DBC Finance*, a leading software package focusing on municipal finance, with an industry-standard database management platform. For further information on *DBC Debt Manager*, see dbcinc.com.

Appendix

STRATEGIC FACILITIES PLANNING GLOSSARY

Accretion of a discount: Accounting process by which the book value of a security purchased at a discount is increased during the period that the security is held. Accretion reflects the increase in the security's holding value as it approaches the redemption date.

Accrued interest: Interest earned on a security that has not yet been paid to the investor. Usually calculated on the basis of a 360-day year (assuming that each month has thirty days). Alternative methods for counting days are used for certain types of securities (e.g., some municipal notes and some bonds that bear interest at a variable rate).

Ad valorem tax: Direct tax calculated "according to value" of property, based on an assigned valuation (market or assessed) of real property. A lien on the property that is enforceable by seizure and sale of the property in virtually all jurisdictions. In certain cases, this tax is based on a valuation of tangible or intangible personal property.

Advance refunding: Outstanding securities are refinanced prior to the date on which they become due or are callable by the proceeds of a new issue of securities. For a period of time, both sets of securities are outstanding. Generally, the proceeds of the new issue are invested in government securities, which are placed in escrow. The interest and principal repayments on these short-term securities are then used to repay the old issue, usually on the first call date.

A fortiori analysis: A method of deliberately "stacking the deck" in favor of one alternative to determine how it might stand up in comparison to other approaches.

Age-cohort survival model: Analyzes the population by narrow age categories (cohorts) according to vital statistics on births, deaths, and net migration patterns (inflows or outflows of population).

Amortization of a premium: Accounting process by which the book value of a security purchased at a premium is decreased during the period that the security is held. Reflects the decrease in the security's holding value as it approaches the redemption date.

Amortization of debt: Process of paying the principal amount of an issue of securities by periodic payments either directly to security holders or to a sinking fund for the benefit of security holders.

Amortization schedule: Table showing the gradual repayment of an amount of indebtedness, such as a mortgage or bond, over a period of time. Often set up to show interest payments in addition to principal repayments.

Annual assessment: The values for all real property are updated each year.

Arbitrage: Difference in the interest paid on an issuer's tax-exempt bonds and the interest earned by investing the bond proceeds in taxable securities. Arbitrage is governed by Internal Revenue Service regulations (1.103-13 through 1.103-15). If the IRS finds that bonds are in violation of these regulations, the interest becomes taxable for federal income tax purposes

Arrow diagram: Initial portrayal of a critical path network. Elements of a project—activities—are represented by a series of arrows. Specific, definable accomplishments in a project plan, recognizable at a particular point in time, are identified as events.

As agent trade: Securities transaction executed by a dealer on behalf of and under the instruction of another party. The dealer does not act in a principal capacity, must be willing to disclose the identity of the other side of the transaction in order to function as a customer's agent, and may be compensated by a commission or fee rather than by a mark-up.

Assessed valuation: Appraised worth of property, as set by a taxing authority for purposes of ad valorem taxation. Assessment methods vary from state to state, with the method generally specified by state law. In some states, the assessed valuation is equal to the full or market value of the property. In other jurisdictions, the assessed valuation is equal to a percentage of the full or market value.

Assignment: Form imprinted on a registered security certificate which, when completed and signed by the registered owner, authorizes the transfer of the security into the name of a new owner (designated on the form as the "assignee").

Associated costs: Any costs involved in utilizing project services in the process of converting them into a form suitable for use or sale at the stage benefits are evaluated.

Auction market: Market for securities in which trading in a particular security is conducted at a specific location with all qualified persons at that post able to bid or offer securities against orders via outcry. Very few municipal securities are traded in an auction market system.

Authority: Unit or agency established to perform specialized government functions, usually financed by service charges, fees, or tolls, although it may also have taxing powers. In many cases, authorities have the power to issue debt secured by the lease rental payments made by a governmental unit using the facilities constructed with bond proceeds. An authority may function independently of other governmental units, or it may depend upon other units for its creation, funding, and administrative oversight.

Authorizing resolution or ordinance: Document adopted by the issuer that implements its power to issue municipal securities. Legal grant of such authority may be found in the enabling provisions of the constitution, statutes, charters, and ordinances applicable to the issuer. Adoption of an authorizing resolution or ordinance by the issuer's governing body is a condition precedent to the issuance of the proposed securities.

Average life or average maturity: Number of years to the point at which half of an issue will have been redeemed; reflects the rapidity with which the principal of an issue is expected to be paid.

Award: Acceptance by the issuer of a bid by an underwriter to purchase a new issue of municipal securities. The date of the award is generally considered the "sale date" of an issue.

Balloon maturity payment: Redemption of a maturity within a serial issue of securities (usually a later maturity) that involves a disproportionately large percentage of the principal amount of the original issue.

Banker's acceptance: Draft or bill of exchange that represents moneys due at a future date, the payment of which has been guaranteed by the "accepting" bank. Most commonly generated in import or export transactions.

Basis point: One one-hundredth of 1 percent. Yield differences among fixed-income securities are stated in basis points.

Basis price: Price of a security expressed in terms of the yield to be realized by the purchaser.

Bearer security: Security that has no identification as to its owner and presumed to be owned by the bearer or the person who holds it. Bearer securities are freely negotiable, since ownership can be quickly transferred from seller to buyer by delivery of the instrument. However, coupons must be clipped and presented to the trustee in order to receive interest. It has not been legal in the United States to issue bearer bonds in the municipal or corporate markets since 1983.

Benefit assessments: Annual fees levied to benefit specific public services and facilities such as road maintenance, street lighting and landscaping.

Benefit/cost ratio: Present value of benefits divided by the present value of costs (or average annual benefits over average annual costs).

Beta distribution formula: Assumes that the variance in the distribution of estimated times is the square of the standard deviation, which can be estimated as roughly one-sixth of the range (i.e., the difference between the most optimistic and the most pessimistic time estimate).

Bid: Proposal to purchase securities at a specified price. With respect to a new issue of municipal securities, the bid specifies the interest rate for each maturity and the purchase price. The purchase price is usually stated in terms of par, par plus a premium, or par minus a discount.

Bidding limitations: Restrictions (if any) stated by the issuer in the notice of sale on the terms of bids submitted by prospective underwriters. Might include indications of the maximum range of permissible interest rates, number of different interest rates permitted, whether a particular interest rate structure is required (or prohibited), and whether a discount bid is allowable.

Bidding syndicate: Two or more underwriters that act together to submit a proposal to underwrite a new issue of municipal securities.

Bid form: Document to be completed by underwriters interested in submitting a bid on a new issue of municipal securities to be sold at a competitive sale. Generally included in the notice of sale.

Bid-wanted transaction: Securities dealers or dealer banks ask brokers to place on the market and take bids on bonds that the dealers want to sell to other dealers.

Blue List: Daily publication (*The Blue List of Current Municipal Offerings*) listing municipal bonds and notes being offered by dealers in the inter-dealer market. The par value, issuer, interest rate, maturity date, price or yield, and offering dealer are indicated for each security offered.

Bond: A security (usually with more than one year to final maturity date) with interest paid (usually semiannually) either directly to the owner or by coupons attached to the bonds. Bonds may be classified according to maturity structure (serial vs. term), source of payment (general obligation vs. revenue), method of transfer (bearer vs. registered), issuer (state vs. municipality vs. special district), or price (discount vs. premium).

Bond and interest register: Information maintained for each bond issue by the issuer or its agent. May include the date of issue, original principal amount issued, paying agent, certificate numbers, coupon numbers (if any), maturity schedule for life of the issue, amounts and dates of principal and interest payments made, and outstanding balances of principal and interest

Bond anticipation notes (BANs): Notes issued in anticipation of an issue of bonds and repaid when the bonds are sold.

Bond bidding scale: Display of the maturies, coupon rates, reoffering yields or prices, and other information on a new issue of municipal bonds.

Bond Buyer, The: Daily trade paper of the municipal securities industry. Contains advertisements for offerings of new issues of municipal securities, notices of bond redemptions, statistical analyses of market activity, results of previous bond sales, and articles relating to financial markets and public finance.

Bond buyer indexes: Indicators published on a periodic basis by *The Bond Buyer* showing the price levels for various groups of municipal securities. Three of the indexes represent weekly averages of the yields that would be offered to investors if an issuer were to bring certain types of securities to market at par on a given day.

Bond contract: Agreement that obligates the issuer to perform by virtue of issuing its bonds. The terms of the agreement may be determined by reference to specified documents associated with the bond issue. Typically, the bond resolution or ordinance, trust indenture, and security agreements constitute parts of the contract, as do those laws in force at the time of issuance. The documents that form the bond contract vary according to the terms of each issue.

Bond counsel: An attorney (or firm of attorneys) retained by the issuer to give a legal opinion that the issuer is authorized to issue proposed securities. The opinion also indicates that the issuer has met all legal requirements necessary for issuance and that interest on the proposed securities will be exempt from federal income taxation and, where applicable, from state and local taxation.

Bonded debt: Portion of an issuer's total indebtedness represented by outstanding bonds.

Bond election or bond referendum: Process whereby the voters are given the opportunity to approve or disapprove a proposed issue of municipal securities. Requirements for voter approval may be imposed by constitution, statute, or local ordinance. A referendum is most commonly required in connection with general obligation bonds.

Bond equivalent yield or coupon equivalent yield: Return on a discounted security, figured on a basis that permits comparison with interest-bearing securities. On short-term (under six months) discounted securities, the bond equivalent yield is an annualized rate of return. On longer term discounted securities, the bond equivalent yield is determined by a computation that adjusts for the absence of periodic payments over the life of the security.

Bond fiscal year: Twelve-month accounting period, established under some contracts, used in connection with an issue of municipal bonds. Principal and interest payments are scheduled in accordance with the bond fiscal year, which may not necessarily coincide with the issuing agency's own fiscal year. The bond fiscal year may be established in order to take full advantage of the scheduled cash flow of projected pledged revenues.

Bond funds: Registered investment companies, the assets of which are invested in diversified portfolios of bonds.

Bondholder: Owner of a municipal bond. The owner of a registered bond is the person whose name is recorded on the bond register. The owner of a bearer bond is the person having possession of it.

Bond insurance: Guarantee that interest and principal will be paid as they become due and that mandatory sinking fund payments will be made if the issuer of the bonds fails to make these payments for whatever reason.

Bond proceeds: Money paid to the issuer of municipal securities by the purchaser or underwriter. Used to finance the project or purpose for which the securities were issued and to pay certain costs of issuance as may be provided in the bond contract.

Bond purchase agreement: Contract between the underwriter and the issuer setting forth the final terms, prices, and conditions upon which the underwriter purchases a new issue of municipal securities.

Bond register: Record maintained by a transfer agent or registrar on behalf of the issuer that lists the names and addresses of the owners of registered bonds.

Bond resolution or ordinance: Document that authorizes the issuance and sale of municipal securities. The authorizing resolution or ordinance approves the issuance of the securities. The sale is usually authorized in a separate document known as the "sale" or "award" resolution. All such resolutions, taken together, constitute the bond resolution, which describes the nature of the obligation and the issuer's duties to the bondholders. State law or local ordinances may prescribe whether a bond issue may be authorized by resolution, or whether the more formal procedure of adopting a bond ordinance is required.

Bond service account: Amount that is sufficient to pay the next semiannual interest payment, as well as the principal of the next bonds that are maturing. In the case of term bonds, a mandatory sinking fund is usually required in lieu of principal payments on serial bonds.

Bond transcripts: All legal documents, including minutes of appropriate meetings of the issuer, associated with the offering of a new issue of municipal securities. Bond counsel's opinion is given after a review of the transcript and becomes a part thereof.

Bond-wanted transactions: A broker is contracted to seek a particular bond or bond type desired by a dealer.

Bond year: $1,000 of debt outstanding for one year. The number of "bond years" in an issue is equal to the product of the number of bonds (one bond equals $1,000 regardless of actual certificate denomination) and the number of years from the dated date (or other stated date) to the stated maturity. The total number of bond years is used in calculating the average life of an issue and its net interest cost.

Book-entry: Method of recording and transferring ownership of securities electronically, eliminating the need for physical certificates.

Book value: Value at which a security is carried on the inventory lists or other financial records of an investor. May be the original cost of acquisition of the security or original cost adjusted by amortization of a premium or accretion of a discount. The book value may differ significantly from the security's current value in the market.

Broker or municipal securities broker: Person or firm that acts as an intermediary by purchasing and selling securities for others rather than for its own account. For purposes of the Securities Exchange Act of 1934, the term does not include a dealer bank.

Broker/dealer: General term for a securities firm that is engaged in both buying and selling securities on behalf of customers and also buying and selling on behalf of its own account.

Broker's broker: Broker that deals exclusively with other municipal securities brokers and dealers and not with public investors. Services of a broker's broker are available, generally at a standard fee established by each broker's broker, only to certain municipal securities professionals that are selected by the broker's broker.

Budget: Plan of financial operation embodying an estimate of proposed expenditures for a given period and the proposed means of financing them. Used without any modifier, the term usually indicates a financial plan for a single fiscal year.

Callable bonds: Bonds that the issuer is permitted or required to redeem before the stated maturity date at a specified price, usually at or above par, by giving notice of redemption in a manner specified in the bond contract.

Call premium: Dollar amount paid by the issuer as a "penalty" for the exercise of a call provision, usually stated as a percent of the principal amount called.

Call price: Price established in the bond contract at which securities will be redeemed, if called. Generally at or above par (although it may be at or above the "compound accreted value" on certain types of securities) and stated as a percentage of the principal amount called.

Cap: Top interest rate that can be paid on a floating-rate security.

Capital appreciation bonds: Bonds for which the interest component is held by the issuer and compounded at a stated rate so that at the bonds' maturity, the investor receives a lump sum payment, consisting of both the principal and the compounded interest. Also known as compound interest bonds, accumulators, or municipal multiplier bonds.

Capital budget: Identifies the capital expenditures to be incurred to meet long-term needs for public improvements (strategic facilities) and the means of financing these commitments for the current fiscal period.

Capital improvements program (CIP): Documents improvement priorities over a longer time period (usually five to six years).

Capital project fund: Accounts for the resources required to construct or purchase specific strategic facilities. These resources come from the issuance of bonds or other long-term obligations, from intergovernmental grants, or as transfers from other public funds.

Cash proffer system: Fee paid by developers in conjunction with rezoning requests in jurisdictions where the demand for facilities and services from residential growth has outpaced tax revenues.

Certificate: Physical document representing a security, typically setting forth certain information concerning the issuer of the securities and details of the specific issue. The American National Standards Institute publishes guidelines for the format of registered municipal securities certificates.

Certificate of deposit (CD): Negotiable instrument representing a large time deposit at a commercial bank. Most CDs are interest bearing (typically paying interest at maturity), but some discounted CDs are issued.

Certificate of indebtedness: A floating rate bond with short demand features.

Certificate of participation (COP): Municipal security that is funded from revenues for the lease of equipment or other property.

Clearing agent: Firm or bank that handles the clearance and settlement of securities transactions on behalf of its clients. The term generally is not used to refer to one of the registered clearing agencies.

Closed lien or closed-end indenture: General characterization of the security provisions on a revenue bond where the issuer is precluded from issuing any additional bonds that have an equal claim on the pledged revenues.

Closing: Meeting of concerned parties on the date of delivery of a new issue of municipal securities for the issuer to make delivery of the signed securities (or other evidences of indebtedness) and the requisite legal documents in exchange for the purchase price.

Collar: Upper and lower limits (cap and floor, respectively) on the interest rate of a floating-rate security.

Collateralized mortgage obligation (CMO): Bond backed by a pool of mortgage loans or mortgage pass-through securities.

Commercial paper (tax-exempt): Short-term, unsecured promissory notes issued in either registered or bearer form, and usually backed by a line of credit with a bank.

Commission: Form of remuneration received by a broker, dealer, or dealer bank purchasing or selling securities when acting as agent for a customer. Typically a charge to the customer of a set fee per security, although many dealers accept the concession as the sole form of remuneration on this type of trade.

Competitive bid: Method of submitting proposals for the purchase of a new bond issue by which the securities are awarded to the underwriting syndicate presenting the best bid according to stipulated criteria set forth in the notice of sale.

Compound interest bond: Long-term security in which the semiannual "interest" on the security is reinvested at a stated rate, with the investor receiving all investment return (i.e., compounded interest payments) at maturity.

Concession or dealer's allowance: Amount of reduction from the public offering price that a syndicate grants to a dealer who is not a member of the syndicate, expressed as a percentage of par value. In the secondary market, bonds are usually offered to other dealers "less a concession." The price is expressed in terms of a net offering price (in basis or dollar price terms) minus a differential (in points or dollars per security) granted between professionals. This differential is called the "concession."

Condition level: Level at which a government intends to maintain its capital assets. Under the requirements of the Government Accounting Standards Board, the estimated annual dollar amount required to maintain and preserve existing capital assets at the established condition level must be compared with the actual expenses for at least the previous five years.

Conduit financing: Issuance of securities by a governmental unit to finance a project to be used primarily by a third party, usually a corporation engaged in private enterprise. Security for this type of issue is the credit of the private user rather than the governmental issuer. A common type of conduit financing involves industrial development bonds.

Constraints: Limits within which a solution to a problem must be sought. Conditions imposed by outside factors such as budgetary limits, completion deadlines, availability of staff resources, and inputs from other units.

Construction loan notes (CLNs): Notes issued to fund construction of housing projects. Permanent financing from which the CLNs are repaid is provided by bond proceeds or some prearranged commitment.

Consulting engineer: Expert who assists in the preparation of feasibility studies for proposed construction projects. These studies forecast construction costs and may include a rate analysis to provide substantiation that debt service can be met from pledged revenues.

Contingency analysis: Permits the construction of alternative future scenarios and an examination of the effects of each scenario for maintenance or replacement options.

Convertible securities: Offer the pay out of bonds with the potential appreciation of stocks. Investors are given the option of converting a bond into a predetermined amount of common stock before the bond matures or is called.

Coupon: Detachable part of a bond that evidences interest due. The coupon specifies the date, place, and dollar amount of interest payable. Historically, coupons were redeemed (usually semiannually) by detaching them from bonds and presenting them to the issuer's paying agent for payment or to a bank for collection. Bearer bonds are no longer issued in the United States and, hence, physical coupons are increasingly scarce. However, dealers and investors still refer to the stated interest rate on a registered or book-entry bond as the "coupon."

Coupon bond: Bearer bond, or a bond registered as to principal only, carrying coupons as evidence of future interest payments. Prior to June 30, 1983, most municipal bonds were issued in coupon form. However, after that date, all long-term municipal bonds must be issued in registered form.

Coupon rate: Annual rate of interest payable on a coupon security expressed as a percentage of the principal amount.

Covenants: Issuer's enforceable promise to perform or refrain from performing certain actions, generally stated in the bond contract.

Critical path method (CPM): Approach to the planning and scheduling of the activities of a capital improvements project in which attention is directed to those activities most critical to the achievement of management and operational objectives. CPM facilitates the selection of a "best route" to be followed to reach these objectives and identifies potential obstacles and delays that might be encountered along the way.

Current yield: Ratio of the annual dollar amount of interest paid on a security to the purchase price or market price of the security, stated as a percentage. For example, a $1,000 bond purchased at par with an 8% coupon pays $80 per year, or a current yield of 8%. The same bond, if purchased at a discount price of $800, would have a current yield of 10%.

CUSIP number: Unique nine-digit numbers assigned to each series of securities. The Committee on Uniform Security Identification Procedures was established under the auspices of the American Bankers Association to develop this uniform method of identifying securities.

Dated date: Date of a bond issue, printed on each security, from which interest on the issue usually starts to accrue, even though the issue may actually be delivered at some later date.

Dealer: Person or organization that engages in the business of underwriting, trading, and selling securities.

Debt limit: Maximum amount of debt that an issuer of municipal securities is permitted to incur under constitutional, statutory, or charter provisions. Usually expressed as a percentage of assessed valuation of taxable property.

Debt ratios: Comparative statistics showing the relationship between a jurisdiction's outstanding debt and such factors as its tax base, income, or population. Such ratios are often used in the process of determining credit quality of an issue, primarily on general obligation bonds. Some of the more commonly used ratios are (a) net overall debt to assessed valuation, (b) net overall debt to estimated full valuation, and (c) net overall debt per capita.

Debt service: Amount of money necessary to pay interest on an outstanding debt, the principal of maturing serial bonds, and the required contributions to a sinking fund for term bonds. Debt service on bonds may be calculated on a calendar year, fiscal year, or bond fiscal year basis.

Debt service fund: Fund used to track the payment of interest and principal of the long-term debt on each capital project.

Debt service reserve fund: Fund maintained as a back up to meet the debt service requirements of revenue bonds. In the case of serial bonds, this fund is gradually built up to equal one-year's maximum principal and interest requirements. In the case of term bonds, the requirement usually is two years' interest.

Debt service schedule: Table listing the periodic payments necessary to meet debt service requirements over the period of time that the securities are to be outstanding.

Default: Breach of some covenant, promise, or duty imposed by the bond contract. The most serious default occurs when the issuer fails to pay principal, interest, or both, when due. Other "technical" defaults result when specifically defined events of default occur, such as failure to perform covenants included in the bond contract.

Defeasance: Provision for the payment of a bond issue from sources other than the issuer.

Delivery date: Date on which securities are delivered in exchange for the payment of the purchase price. In the case of new issues, the delivery date, not the stamped date, is considered the date of issuance.

Delphi technique: A formal exchange of information under the control of a steering group or exercise manager, involving an iterative series of interrogations of a panel of knowledgeable individuals.

Demand bond or note: Long-term-maturity security that is subject to a frequently available put option or tender option feature. The holder may put the security back to the issuer or its agent at a predetermined price (generally par) after giving specified notice. Many of these securities are floating or variable rate securities, with the put option exercisable on dates on which the floating rate changes.

Denomination: Par value amount represented by a particular securities certificate. Bearer bonds are typically issued in denominations of $1,000 or $5,000 par value per certificate. Registered bonds are typically issued in variable denominations, multiples of $1,000 up to $100,000 or more per certificate.

Depository: Clearing agency registered with the Securities and Exchange Commission that provides immobilization, safekeeping, and book-entry settlement services to its participants.

Depreciation curves: Show the rate of deterioration as a function of such factors as age, original construction material, climate, intensity of use, and the like.

Derivative: Any type of transaction whose value depends, at least in part, upon the value of a related asset or liability. Their value is derived from some form of investment, such as Treasury bonds, corporate stocks and bonds, foreign currencies, or commodity contracts. The simplest form of derivatives are futures—contracts that set a price today but specify acceptance or delivery at some time in the future.

Detachable warrant bonds: Holders of this type of bonds are given the right, at some future date, to purchase more of the same securities to which the warrant is attached, at the same price and rate of return as the original bond.

Direct costs: Costs incurred for a specific purpose that are uniquely associated with that purpose.

Direct net debt: Gross debt of a jurisdiction, less all revenue bonds, other self-supporting debt, and cash flow notes.

Discount: Amount by which the purchase price of a security is less than the principal amount or par value.

Discounted security: Security that is sold on the basis of a bank rate of discount. The investment return is realized solely from the accretion of this discounted amount to the security's maturity value. The most common type of discounted security is the U.S. Treasury bill. Some municipal notes are issued on a discounted basis.

Discount note: Short-term obligations issued at discount from face value, with maturities ranging from overnight to 360 days. These notes have no periodic interest payments; the investor receives the face value of the note at maturity.

Discount rate: Rate the Federal Reserve charges on loans to member banks.

Divided account: Bonds are distributed according to the agreed level of participation of each member of a syndicate. Syndicate members are required to sell only their obligated percentage of the issue and are not held responsible for unsold bonds of other members.

Dollar price: Quoted price of a security, expressed in terms of dollars per $100 par value. The dollar price may be the transaction price, or it may be derived from the yield price (basis price) of the transaction.

Double-barreled bonds: Bonds secured by both a defined source of revenue (other than property taxes) plus the full faith and credit of an issuer that has taxing powers.

Double exemption: Securities that are exempt from state as well as federal income taxes.

Downgrade: Lowering of a bond rating by a rating service.

Drawdown schedule: Estimated schedule of payments on a construction project, which shows the periodic payments, or "draws," to which the contractor is entitled at progressive stages of completion.

Due diligence: Process of thorough investigation of a bond issue, usually by underwriter's counsel. Such inquiry is made to assure that all material facts are fully disclosed to potential investors and that there have been no material omissions or misstatements of fact.

Duration: Measure of the timing of the cash flows (i.e., the interest payments and the principal repayment) to be received from a given fixed income security. The duration of the security is equal to the sum of the present values of each of the cash flows weighted by the time to receipt of each cash flow divided by the total of the present values of the cash flows.

Effective interest cost: Rate at which the total debt service payable on a new issue of bonds would be discounted to provide a present value equal to the amount bid on the new issue.

Effective interest rate: Actual rate of interest earned by the investor on securities, which takes into account the amortization of any premium or the accretion of any discount over the period of the investment.

Embedded option: Provision giving either the bond issuer or the bondholder an option to take some action against the other party. The most common embedded option is a call option, giving the issuer the right to call, or retire, the debt before the scheduled maturity date.

Enterprise activity: Revenue-generating project or business that provides funds necessary to pay debt service on securities issued to finance the facility. Debts of such projects are self-liquidating when the projects earn sufficient moneys to cover all debt service and other requirements imposed under the bond contract.

Equivalent uniform annual net return (EUANR): Combines all costs and all expenses into one single annual sum that is equivalent to all disbursements uniformly distributed over the analysis period.

Event: Specific, definable accomplishment in a project plan, recognizable at a particular point in time. A project activity cannot be initiated until the event preceding it has occurred.

Excise tax: Indirect tax levied upon the manufacture, sale, or consumption of commodities or upon the license to pursue certain occupations or upon corporate privileges within a taxing jurisdiction. Examples of such taxes include sales and use taxes and taxes on alcohol and cigarettes.

Expectation hypothesis: The shape of the yield curve will be influenced by future inflation.

Externalities: Side effects or unintended consequences that might be beneficial or detrimental to a strategic project.

Extraordinary redemption: Redemption of outstanding bonds under an unusual circumstance such as destruction of the financed facility.

Face amount: Par value (principal or maturity value) of a security appearing on the face of the instrument.

Farmers Home Administration: Agency of the federal Department of Agriculture empowered to make loans to farm owners or tenants primarily to finance the acquisition and improvement of farm properties. FmHA also makes loans to qualified municipal issuers for certain community facilities. The agency funds its loans through the issuance of Certificates of Beneficial Ownership (CBOs), most of which are purchased by the Federal Financing Bank.

Feasibility study: Report detailing the economic practicality and the need for a proposed capital improvement. May include estimates of revenues that will be generated and details of the physical, operating, economic, or engineering aspects of the proposed project.

Federal Home Loan Mortgage Corporation: Federally created corporation established to facilitate the financing of single-family residential housing by creating and maintaining an active secondary market for conventional home mortgages. The Corporation finances its mortgage purchases through the issuance of two types of securities. Guaranteed mortgage certificates (GMCs) represent undivided interests in mortgages underwritten by the Corporation, which pay interest semi-annually and return principal amounts annually.

Mortgage participation certificates (PCs) are pass-through instruments, guaranteed by the Corporation, under which a pro-rata share of principal and interest collections are paid monthly to each holder.

Federal National Mortgage Association: Government-sponsored private corporation authorized to purchase and sell mortgages and to otherwise facilitate the orderly operation of a secondary market for home mortgages. The purchase of mortgages by FNMA is financed by the sale of its corporate debentures and notes. Sellers of mortgages may be required to purchase FNMA stock in connection with some transactions.

Financial advisor: Consultant who advises the jurisdiction on matters pertinent to a bond issue, such as structure, timing, marketing, fairness of pricing, terms, and bond ratings. May also be employed to provide advice on subjects unrelated to a new issue of municipal securities, such as advising on cash flow and investment matters. Financial advisors are sometimes referred to as "fiscal consultants" or "fiscal agents."

Financial reports: Records must be kept and provided for audit annually by independent certified public accountants.

Firm price: Designation that a quotation (a bid or an offering price) will not be changed for a specified period of time and will be the price of any transaction executed with the party to whom the quotation is given during that period.

Fiscal year: Twelve-month period at the end of which financial position and results of operations are determined. Financial reporting, budgeting, and accounting periods are determined on the basis of the applicable fiscal year.

Fitch Investors Service: Independent service company based in New York City that provides ratings for municipal securities and other financial information to investors.

Fixed costs: Costs that are the same regardless of a project's size or duration.

Flexible interest bond: Interest rate changes at intervals according to an index, formula, or other standard of measurement as stated in the bond contract. One common method is to calculate the interest rate as a percentage of the rate paid on selected issues of Treasury securities on specified dates.

Float: Amount of time that an activity can be delayed or the duration of that activity extended without affecting the earliest possible occurrence (EPO) of any other activity.

Floor: Lower limit for the interest rate on a floating-rate bond.

Flow of funds: Order and priority of handling, depositing, and disbursing pledged revenues, as set forth in the bond contract. Generally, the revenues are deposited, as received, into a general collection account or revenue fund for disbursement into the other accounts established by the bond contract.

Full disclosure: Principle that accurate and complete information, material to a securities transaction, must be made available to purchasers or prospective purchasers. Material facts may include descriptions of the issuer and the true obligor in a conduit financing, as well as the structure of a bond issue and the security therefore. Full disclosure enables the investor to evaluate the credit quality of an issue.

Fully registered: Security that has been registered as to both principal and interest. Such securities are payable only to the owner, or to order of the owner, whose name is noted on records of the issuer or its agent.

Funded interest: Portion of the proceeds of a bond issue that is set aside to pay interest on the securities for a specified period of time. Interest is commonly capitalized for the construction period of a revenue-producing project

Fungibility: Inherent characteristic of existing in many separate units, each of which is the same as, and can be used in place of, any other unit. Municipal securities are considered generally to lack fungibility. Given the large number of issues and the relatively small principal amount outstanding on most issues, persons seeking to replace securities of a specific issue (e.g., in order to make delivery on a transaction) often find it difficult to locate identical securities elsewhere in the market.

Futures: Contracts that set a price today but specify acceptance or delivery at some time in the future; a form of derivatives.

General fixed assets account group: Records at cost all fixed assets purchased, constructed, or obtained by contract.

General obligation (GO) bonds: Bonds that are secured by the full faith and credit of an issuer with taxing power. GO bonds typically are secured by a pledge of the issuer's ad valorem taxing power. Such bonds constitute debts of the issuer and normally require approval by election prior to issuance. In the event of default, the holders of general obligation bonds have the right to compel a tax levy or legislative appropriation, by mandamus or injunction, in order to satisfy the issuer's obligation on the defaulted bonds.

Good faith deposit: Sum of money provided by an underwriter or underwriting syndicate to an issuer of municipal securities sold on a competitive bid basis as an assurance of performance on its bid. Usually in an amount from 1% to 5% of the par value of the issue, and generally is provided in the form of a certified or cashier's check, which is returned to the bidder if his or her bid is not accepted.

Governmental Accounting Standards Board (GASB): Standard-setting body that prescribes accounting practices for governmental units in maintaining their financial records and releasing financial data to the public. GASB is associated with the Financial Accounting Foundation and comparable to the Financial Accounting Standards Board.

Government Finance Officers Association: Organization of state and local government finance officers formed to improve professional standards of government fiscal and debt administration. Formerly named the Municipal Finance Officers Association (MFOA).

Government National Mortgage Association (GNMA): Agency of the federal Department of Housing and Urban Development empowered to provide special assistance in financing home mortgages. GNMA is responsible for managing and liquidating federally owned mortgage portfolios. Two types of securities are issued, pledging the full faith and credit of the United States Government: (1) mortgage-backed bonds, and (2) pass-through securities by which principal and interest payments on mortgages in specified pools are passed on to the holders of such certificates.

Grant anticipation notes (GANs): Notes issued on the expectation of receiving grant moneys, usually from the federal government, payable from the grant funds, when received.

Hedge: Investments made with the intention of minimizing the impact of adverse movements in interest rates or securities prices.

High-yield bond: Bonds rated Ba or BB or below, issued by lower-rated corporations, sovereign countries, and other entities and offering a higher yield than more creditworthy securities. Sometimes known as junk bonds.

Housing revenue bonds: Bonds secured by revenues derived from rentals from house mortgages or financed housing projects. Multi-family housing revenue bonds are issued to finance construction of multi-family housing projects, typically for the elderly or for moderate- and low-income families. Single-family mortgage revenue bonds are issued to finance mortgages on single-family homes, either directly by purchasing newly originated or existing mortgage loans or indirectly by allowing lenders to purchase mortgage loans using bond proceeds.

Indenture: Statement of the contract between the issuer of bonds and the buyer of the bonds.

Index funds: Seek to match the performance of some benchmark that they are tracking, such as the Standard & Poor's 500, Dow 30, or Wilshire 5000.

Indirect costs: Any costs associated with more than one activity or program that cannot be traced directly to any of the individual activities. In the public sector, the terms indirect cost and overhead are often used interchangeably.

Industrial development bonds: Securities issued by a state, local government, or development agency to finance the construction or purchase of industrial, commercial, or manufacturing facilities to be leased to or purchased by a private user. Backed by the credit of the private user and generally not considered liabilities of the governmental issuer (although in some jurisdictions an issuer with taxing power may also back them).

Inflation protection bonds: Bonds, the principal amount of which is adjusted for inflation—as measured by the Consumer Price Index—while the interest rate remains fixed. Adjustment for inflation is subject to capital gains at maturity.

Inheritable asset: Previous investments that can be used to the particular advantage of one alternative over another.

Insider trading: Act of purchasing or selling securities (or derivative instruments based on those securities) based on information known to the purchasing or selling parties in their capacity as insiders (e.g., as employees of the issuer of the securities) or as a result of information illicitly provided by an insider. Such trading is in violation of SEC Rule 10b-5.

Institutional sales: Sales of securities to banks, financial institutions, bond funds, insurance companies, or other business organizations that possess or control considerable assets for large-scale investing.

Insured paper: Municipal bonds that are insured, which trade in their own market, increasing their desirability and salability. Most municipal bond insurance is sold as part of the new-issue process, with the insurance becoming part of the bond description.

Interest: Amount paid by a borrower as compensation for the use of borrowed money. Generally an annual percentage of the principal amount.

Interest rate: Annual rate, expressed as a percentage of principal, payable for use of borrowed money.

Intermediate range: Designation given to the maturities of a serial issue between the short-term maturities and the long-term maturities. Typically intermediate range maturities are from six to fifteen years from issuance.

Inverse floater: Interest payments for these securities fluctuate in an opposite direction from market interest rates.

Invested sinking fund: Sinking fund that requires the periodic deposits of money be invested to maturity and used to redeem term bonds. These funds usually are invested in U.S. Treasury obligations.

Investment costs: Expenses incurred to obtain future benefits; might be classified as sunk costs or actual project outlays, depending on their timing.

Investment grade: Broad credit designation given bonds that have a high probability of being paid and minor, if any, speculative features. Bonds rated BBB or higher by Standard and Poor's Corporation or Baa or higher by Moody's Investors Service, Inc., are deemed to be "investment grade." Banking law requires that certain types of securities acquired by bank portfolios must be both marketable and "investment grade."

Invoice price: Quoted price of a bond plus any accrued interest that the buyer must pay to the seller.

Issue date: Date of a bond issue from which the bondholder is entitled to receive interest, even though the bonds may actually be delivered at some other date.

Issue of bonds or securities: Bonds or securities sold in one or more series that are authorized under the same resolution or indenture and have the same issue date.

Issuer: Entity (state, political subdivision, agency, or authority) that borrows money through the sale of bonds or notes and is obligated to pay principal and interest on a debt security.

Joint account: Account that is formed by two or more municipal securities dealers for the purpose of purchasing and distributing an agreed-upon block or blocks of securities.

Jumbo certificate: Certificate for a registered security that is in an unusually large denomination. Persons who hold large amounts of securities (e.g., securities depositories, large institutional investors) often keep most of their holdings in jumbo certificate form.

Junior lien bonds: Bonds that have a subordinate claim against pledged revenues.

Junk bond: Debt obligation with a rating of Ba or BB or lower, generally paying interest above the return on more highly rated bonds. Sometimes known as high-yield bonds.

Latest possible occurrence (LPO): Latest time that all of the activities terminating at a given node can finish without causing a project to exceed the originally determined duration.

Lease rental bonds: Bonds from an issue that is secured by lease payments made by the party leasing the facilities financed by the issue. Typically, these bonds are used to finance construction of facilities (e.g., schools or office buildings) used by a state or municipality, which leases the facilities from a financing authority.

Legal opinion: Written conclusions of bond counsel that the issuance of municipal securities and the proceedings taken in connection therewith comply with applicable laws, and that interest on the securities will be exempt from federal income taxation and, where applicable, from state and local taxation.

Letter of credit: Commitment, usually made by a commercial bank, to honor demands for payment of a debt upon compliance with conditions and/or the occurrence of certain events specified under the terms of the commitment. Bank letters of credit are sometimes used as additional sources of security for issues of municipal notes, commercial paper, or bonds. The bank issues the letter of credit committing to pay principal and interest on the securities in the event that the issuer is unable to do so. A letter of credit may also be used to provide liquidity for the retirement of commercial paper or put bonds.

Level debt service: Maturity schedule in which the combined annual amount of principal and interest payments remains relatively constant over the life of the issue.

Leveraged lease: Lease agreement wherein the lessor finances the purchase of the asset being leased by borrowing funds from a lending institution. The lessor pays the lending institution back from the lease payments received from the lessee. Under the loan agreement, the debtor has rights to the asset and the lease payments if the lessor defaults.

Limited tax bonds: General obligation bonds secured by the pledge of a specified tax (usually the property tax) or category of taxes which is limited as to rate or amount.

Liquidity: Quality of being readily convertible into cash without substantial transaction costs. Any discrepancy between the investment's acquisition cost and its current market value will affect the liquidity of a particular investment. Liquidity is a function of both maturity and marketability. A "liquid" municipal security is generally both short-term and highly marketable.

Liquidity preference theory: Investors are willing to accept lower rates for shorter-term maturities because they perceive them to be less risky than long-term issues. Borrowers are willing to finance long-term debt at higher rates so they can lock in financing for longer periods, avoiding the risks associated with rolling over debt at unknown future rates to obtain further financing.

Load: Commission charged in the sale of mutual fund or municipal investment trust shares.

Long-term debt account group: Maintains records of long-term liabilities, such as serial bonds, long-term notes, and long-term commitments arising from lease or purchase agreements.

Lower floater: Term for a security with a variable or floating interest rate that also has a put option feature, permitting the holder to put the securities back to an agent of the issuer on demand or on short notice. The put option feature has the practical effect of making the securities short-term. The variable interest rate on the securities, therefore, tends to fluctuate in the "lower" range of interest rates appropriate for short-term securities.

Maintenance and insurance covenant: Properties funded through revenue bonds must be kept in good working condition at all times. Insurance must be carried on the facility corresponding in amount and in kind to the coverage normally carried under a similar private enterprise.

Management objectives: Describe specific program actions in terms of how and where specific resources (project budgets) will be used. Management objectives identify the commitments required to translate a strategic objective into specific activities.

Management's discussion and analysis: Requirement of the Governmental Accounting Standards Board (GASB) designed to assist in assessing whether the government's finances have improved or deteriorated. Includes a comparison of the current year to the prior year, based on financial information about assets, liabilities, revenues, and expenses

Manager: Member (or members) of an underwriting syndicate charged with primary responsibility for conducting the affairs of the syndicate. Largest underwriting commitment is generally taken by the manager.

Mark-down: Remuneration received by a dealer or dealer bank selling securities on behalf of a customer to a third party. Consists of the differential between the price of the sale to the third party and the (lower) price paid to the customer by the dealer. Mark-down also refers to the difference between the cost at which securities were acquired and their current offering price, in cases in which the market value of the securities has declined since their acquisition.

Marketability: Ease or difficulty with which securities can be sold in the market. Depends upon many factors, including the security's interest rate, provisions, maturity, and credit quality. In the case of a new issue, marketability also depends on the size of the issue, the timing of its issuance, and the volume of comparable issues being sold.

Market risk: Associated with the overall movements of the stock market, measured by applying two analytical tools—beta and standard deviation.

Market segmentation theory: Different markets exist for maturities of different lengths. The *preferred habitat theory*, a variation of market segmentation, holds that investors prefer certain maturities, but can be induced to switch if premiums are different.

Mark-up: Form of remuneration received by a dealer or dealer bank when selling securities as principal to a customer. Any remuneration in addition to the concession received by the dealer as a result of increasing the offering price on the securities. Mark-up also refers to the difference between the cost at which securities were acquired and their current offering price, in cases in which the market value of the securities has risen since their acquisition.

Mass cyclical assessment: All properties in a taxing jurisdiction are assessed in a particular year and the determined values do not change until the next scheduled assessment, except for new construction, demolition, or change in use.

Maturity: Date upon which the principal of a security becomes due and payable to the security holder.

Maturity value: Amount (other than a periodic interest payment) that will be received at the time a security is redeemed at its maturity. On most securities, the maturity value equals the par value. On zero coupon, compound interest, and multiplier bonds, however, the maturity value will equal the principal amount of the security at issuance plus the accumulated investment return on the security.

Measures of effectiveness: A basic scoring technique for determining the increments of output achieved relative to the investment of additional increments of cost, often expressed in relative terms

Milestone chart: Sequential list of the various tasks to be accomplished in a project. Tasks and milestones are displayed adjacent to a time scale. Symbols on the time scale identify the dates (or times) that each milestone is scheduled, when it is completed, if slippage has occurred, and so forth.

Milestones: Key elements or points in time that can be used to measure the progress of a project.

Millage: Rate used in calculating taxes based upon the value of property, expressed in mills per dollar of property value. A mill is one-tenth (0.1) of one cent or .001 of one dollar. Rates of taxation based on assessed valuation often are expressed in mills.

Money market funds: Open-ended mutual funds that invest in short term, high-quality securities.

Money market instruments: Short term and highly liquid obligations that are commonly traded in the money market. The following securities are commonly traded in the money market: certain U.S. government securities, bankers' acceptances, certificates of deposit, Eurodollar deposit, and repurchase agreements.

Moral obligation bonds: Revenue bonds that, in addition to their primary source of security, possess a structure whereby a state pledges to make up shortfalls in a debt service reserve fund, subject to legislative appropriation. Legislative authorization typically grants the state legislature the authority to apportion money to support the debt service payments on such securities, but does not legally oblige the legislature to do so.

Mortgage pass-through: Securities representing a direct interest in a pool of mortgage loans. The pass-through issuer or servicer collects payments on the loans in the pool and "passes through" the principal and interest to the security holders on a pro rata basis.

Multiplier bonds: Long-term municipal securities on which the investment return accretes at a stated compounded rate to maturity, at which time the investor receives a lump-sum payment comprised of the initial principal amount plus the total investment return.

Municipal Securities Rulemaking Board (MSRB): Independent self-regulatory organization, established by the Securities Acts Amendments of 1975, charged with primary rulemaking authority over dealers, dealer banks, and brokers in municipal securities. Its fifteen members represent three categories—securities firms, bank dealers, and the public—each category having equal representation on the Board.

Munifacts: Private wire communication system originating in the New York editorial offices of *The Bond Buyer*. Munifacts transmits current bond market information to the offices of its subscribers.

Mutual funds: Pooled cash of many investors are invested to meet the fund's stated investment objective. Mutual funds stand ready to sell and redeem investors' shares at any time at the fund's current net asset value, which equals total fund assets divided by shares outstanding. Also known as an open-end investment company to differentiate it from a closed-end investment company.

Negotiated sale: Sale of a new issue of municipal securities through an exclusive agreement with an underwriter or underwriting syndicate selected by the issuer. Distinguished from a competitive sale, which requires public bidding by the underwriters. Primary points of negotiation for an issuer are the interest rate and purchase price on the issue. The sale of a new issue of securities in this manner is also known as a negotiated underwriting.

Net benefits: Difference between the present value of benefits and the present value of costs.

Net capital rule: SEC regulation that requires broker/dealers to maintain "net capital" equal to or greater than a specified percentage of certain liabilities incurred by the dealer or a specified percentage of the aggregate of transactional moneys owed to the dealer by customers. Net capital is the net worth adjusted by certain deductions for illiquid assets and reserves against possible market losses on securities positions. Broker/dealers are required to suspend or terminate their securities activities if they are unable to meet this test.

Net interest cost (NIC): Method of computing the cost of borrowing on a new bond issue and awarding the bonds on competitive new issue. Total amount of interest paid over the life of the issue (plus any discount or minus any premium paid for the issue) is divided by the accumulated bonds years for the issue.

Net present value: The algebraic difference in the present worth of both outward cash flows and inward flows of income or benefits.

Net price: Price at which a security is offered to the general public. Transactions between municipal securities professionals generally are based on the net price less a concession or dealer's allowance.

Net revenues: Amount of money available after subtracting from gross revenues such costs and expenses as may be provided for in the bond contract. Costs and expenses of operations and maintenance are most often deducted.

Network analysis: Provides a basis for determining the order in which activities should be undertaken—either their sequence or priority—and the critical linkages among activities. Often used to "map" the various steps required in the implementation of a capital improvements project.

New housing authority bonds: Bonds issued by local housing authorities to finance public housing. Bonds are secured in the first instance by revenues from the financed project, with a guarantee by the Department of Housing and Urban Development available to cover any deficiency. Also called "public housing authority bonds" or "PHA bonds."

Nominal interest rate: Annual rate of interest payable on a security expressed as a percentage of the principal amount. Does not take into account any discount (or premium) in the purchase price of the security.

Nominal quotation: Indication of the approximate market value of a security, provided for informational purposes only. Does not represent an actual bid for or offer of securities. May also be referred to as an "indication."

Non-appropriation clause: A lease-purchase agreement is terminated if the lessee government fails to make the specified lease payments.

Non-callable bonds: Bonds that cannot be called either for redemption by or at the option of the issuer before their specified maturity date.

Nondiscrimination covenant: Guarantees that neither preferential treatment nor discrimination shall be applied to any groups in the matter of payment of rates for services.

Non-litigation certificate: Document executed prior to delivery of a new bond issue certifying that there is no litigation known to the issuer to be currently pending, threatened, or contemplated that would affect in any materially adverse manner the validity or security of the bonds issued; the issuance, execution, or delivery of the bonds issued; the existence or boundaries of the issuing entity (on general obligation bonds); or the validity or legality of provisions authorizing the payment of principal and interest on the bonds.

Nonmarket risk: Arises from the likelihood that events specific to a company or its industry will adversely affect the price of a stock; also called specific risk.

Notes: Short-term promises to repay a specified principal amount on a date certain, together with interest at a stated rate, payable from a defined source of anticipated revenue, such as taxes, federal and state aid payments, and bond proceeds. Usually mature in one year or less, although notes of longer maturities are also issued.

Notice for tenders: Invitation by the issuer of bonds that is made to bondholders to sell bonds back either at a predetermined price or at a price that the bondholder will accept. The notice usually allows the issuer to reject tender offers in whole or in part.

Notice of redemption: Publication announcing the issuer's intention to call outstanding bonds prior to the stated maturity dates.

Notice of sale: Publication by an issuer describing the terms of sale of an anticipated new offering of municipal securities. Notice generally contains the date, time, and place of sale, amount of issue, type of security, amount of good faith deposit, basis of award, name of bond counsel, maturity schedule, method of delivery, time and place of delivery, and bid form.

Objective function: Involves the identification and quantification, in dollar terms to the extent possible, of the benefits and costs associated with each alternative course of action.

Odd coupon: Interest payment for a period other than the standard six months. Payment for a period of less than six months is a "short" coupon; payment for a period of more than six months is a "long" coupon. Usually only the first interest payment on an issue would be an odd coupon, but some issues have an odd last coupon.

Odd lot: Principal amount of securities that is smaller than that which is considered a normal trading unit. Dealers typically bid lower for an odd lot than for a larger block.

Offer: Proposal to sell securities at a stated price or yield.

Offering circular: Document generally prepared by the underwriters about an issue of securities expected to be offered in the primary market. Basic information is disclosed to investors regarding the securities to be offered and is used as an advertisement for the sale of the securities.

Offering date: Date on which bonds are sold to the public, and for competitive offerings, this is also the date of the sale.

Offering price: Price or yield at which dealers or members of an underwriting syndicate will offer securities to investors.

Offering sheets: Weekly inventories of bond holdings that individual dealers are offering for sale. They include the names of investors, the type of bond, and its yield or sale price.

Official statement: Document published by the issuer that generally discloses material information on a new issue of municipal securities, including the purposes of the issue, how the securities will be repaid, and the financial, economic, and social characteristics of the issuing government. Investors may use this information to evaluate the credit quality of the securities.

Open lien or open-end indenture: General characterization of the security provisions on a revenue bond that permit additional securities to be issued which have an equal claim on the pledged revenues under certain circumstances (typically upon satisfaction of an "additional bonds test").

Operational objectives: Most often associated with the implementation and control of specific tasks and the assignment of specific resources to achieve strategic and management objectives.

Operations: Things that must be done (tasks, activities, or jobs), each with a sequential relation to other operations and each requiring resources for some time period.

Operations and maintenance fund: Fund established by the bond contract of a revenue bond issue into which moneys to be used for the purpose of meeting the costs of operating and maintaining the financed project are deposited. Under a typical revenue pledge, this fund is the first (under a net revenue pledge) or the second (under a gross revenue pledge) to be funded out of the revenue fund.

Opportunity analysis: Periodic sessions held to discuss the current status of a capital improvements project and to explore opportunities that might be presented. These sessions are intended to raise the enthusiasm and morale of those involved.

Options: Grant investors the right to buy or sell a stock (or other types of securities) at a fixed price for some period.

Original issue discount: Amount by which the par value of a security exceeds its public offering price at the time it was originally offered to an investor. The discount is amortized over the life of the security and generally treated as tax-exempt interest. If the security is sold before maturity, any profit realized on such sale is figured for tax purposes on the adjusted cost basis.

Overall net debt: The sum of direct net debt and a jurisdiction's proportionate share of the debt of other overlapping government units (for example, the county, school district, and special purpose district).

Over-the-counter market (OTC): Market for securities that are traded other than on a national securities exchange. The over-the-counter market is characterized most particularly by a system of dealer market-making rather than the auction market system common on the securities exchanges. Municipal securities are traded almost exclusively in the OTC market.

Par: 100% of the face value of a security.

Parity bonds: Two or more issues of bonds that have the same priority of claim or lien against pledged revenues.

Par option: Redemption provision that permits the issuer to call securities at par.

Par value: Amount of principal that must be paid at maturity. Also referred to as the face amount of a security.

Paying agent: Entity responsible for transmitting payments of interest and principal from an issuer of municipal securities to the security holders; usually a bank or trust company, but it may be the treasurer or some other officer of the issuer as well. The paying agent may also provide other services for the issuer, such as reconciliation of the securities and coupons paid, destruction of paid securities and coupons, and similar services.

Payment date: Date on which interest, or principal and interest, is payable on a municipal security. Interest payment dates usually occur semiannually for bonds.

Per capita debt: Amount of outstanding debt divided by the population residing in the issuing municipality. Often used as an indication of the issuer's credit position since it can be used to compare the proportion of debt borne per resident with that borne by the residents of other municipalities.

Planning gap: The discrepancy between desirable goals and objectives and expected performance.

Point: One percent of par value. Municipal dollar prices are quoted in terms of a percentage of $1,000; therefore, a point is worth $10 regardless of the actual denomination of a security. A security discounted 2 1/2 points, or $25, is quoted at "97 1/2" (97 1/2 percent of its value), or $975 per $1,000.

Population estimates: Refer to the size of the current population in a given area, calculated in lieu of an actual census count and used to update population data gathered during the last census.

Population forecasts: Involve the application of expected population trends to a base population. A population forecast is the set of projections deemed most likely to occur.

Population projections: Refer to the size of the population at some point in the future, indicating what changes might occur, given assumptions inherent in the projection method and data.

Position trading: Type of trading activity in which a dealer purchases securities and holds them ("positions" them) in its trading inventory, based on the expectation that the value of the securities will rise due to a decline in interest rates or credit considerations about the security itself.

Premium: Amount by which the price paid for a security exceeds the security's par value.

Premium call: Redemption provision that permits the issuer to call securities at a price above par (or, in the case of certain original issue discount or multiplier securities, above the compound accreted value).

Premium call price: Price in excess of par value that the issuer agrees to pay upon redemption of its outstanding bonds prior to the stated maturity date. Amount of premium to be paid, expressed as a percentage of par, often declines as the possible redemption date approaches the maturity date.

Prepayment: Unscheduled partial or complete payment of the principal amount outstanding on a mortgage or other debt before it is due.

Prepayment risk: Risk that falling interest rates will lead to heavy prepayments of mortgage or other loans, forcing the investor to reinvest at lower prevailing rates.

Presale order: Order given to the syndicate manager prior to the purchase of securities from the issuer, which indicates a prospective investor's intention to purchase the securities at a predetermined price level. Presale orders are normally afforded top priority in allocation of securities from the syndicate.

Present value: Value at the current time of a cash payment that is expected to be received in the future, allowing for the fact that an amount received today could be invested to earn interest for the period to the future date.

Primary market: Market for new issues of municipal securities.

Principal: Face amount or par value of a security payable on the maturity date.

Prior issue: Outstanding issue of municipal bonds. The term is usually used in the context of refunding to denote the obligations being refinanced, sometimes called "refunded bonds." Also used with respect to previous bond issues that normally possess a first or senior lien on pledged revenues.

Private activity bonds: Municipal bonds, used either entirely or partially for private purposes, which must meet the test of qualification outlined within federal tax law in order to obtain tax-exempt status.

Production: Total amount of proceeds that would be received by an underwriting syndicate if all securities held by the syndicate were sold at the prices listed in the reoffering scale.

Program Evaluation and Review Technique (PERT): Network analysis approach designed to deal with large-scale projects characterized by (1) unclear objectives, (2) multiple or overlapping management responsibilities, (3) relatively high levels of uncertainty as to time and cost requirements, and (4) complex problems of logistics.

Project notes: Notes issued under a program of the Department of Housing and Urban Development to fund local housing or urban renewal projects, secured by revenues from those projects and are guaranteed by the federal government.

Project plan: Coordinated model of the sequence in which all tasks and activities must be performed to complete a given capital improvements project.

Property taxes: A group of taxes levied on the value of different kinds of property determined by the individual states to be subject to taxation. Usually levied on an *ad valorem* basis—that is, according or in proportion to the value of the property subject to taxation.

Prorate share: Percentage of the total liability of an undivided underwriting account for which a particular account member bears liability. This share is equal to the original percentage participation accepted by the member. Used to determine the member's portion of syndicate profits or losses.

Protective covenants: Agreements in the bond contract that impose duties upon the issuer in order to protect the interests of the bondholders. Typical protective covenants relate to such items as maintenance of rates adequate to cover debt service, segregation of funds, proper project maintenance, insurance, maintenance of specified books and records, and tests for the issuance of additional parity bonds.

Provisional rating: Typically assigned when the debt service is secured solely by revenues to be derived from a project the construction of which is financed by the bond issue. Indicates the anticipated credit quality of an issue after the construction or interim period is concluded. A provisional rating does not represent a judgment of what might happen if problems are experienced during the construction or interim period. Investors must exercise their own judgment with respect to such potential risk. The rating remains provisional until the construction is completed and the project has begun to generate the revenues.

Put bonds or tender option bonds: Obligations that grant the bondholder the right to require the issuer or the issuer's agent to purchase the bonds, usually at par, at a certain time or times prior to maturity or upon the occurrence of specified events or conditions.

Qualified bid: Bid in the secondary market entered to purchase bonds subject to conditions set forth by either party to the transaction. For example, the purchaser might stipulate that an acceptable legal opinion must be available on the security, or that the bid is only valid if the seller can guarantee delivery by a certain date.

Qualified legal opinion: Conditional affirmation of the legality of securities, before or after they are sold. An unqualified or "clean" legal opinion, on the other hand, is an unconditional affirmation of the legality of securities.

Rate covenant: The jurisdiction issuing revenue bonds pledges to fix rates that are sufficient to meet operation and maintenance charges, as well as annual debt service requirements, and to provide for certain reserves.

Rating agencies: Organizations that provide ratings of the credit quality of securities issuers. The term is most often used to refer to the two nationally recognized agencies, Moody's Investors Service, Inc. and Standard & Poor's Corporation.

Ratings: Evaluations of the credit quality of notes and bonds usually made by independent rating services. Intended to measure the probability of the timely repayment of principal and interest on municipal securities. Ratings are initially made before issuance and are periodically reviewed and may be amended to reflect changes in the issuer's credit position.

Real estate mortgage investment conduit (REMIC): Most collateralized mortgage obligations (CMOs) are now issued in REMIC form because of changes in the 1986 Tax Reform Act. REMICs create certain tax advantages for the issuer. The terms REMIC and CMO are now used interchangeably.

Realized compound yield: Measure reflecting the return to be received from reinvestment of the periodic interest payments received at an assumed reinvestment rate (or rates). This yield is in addition to the direct return on a fixed income security that pays period interest.

Record date: Fixed date prior to the interest payment date on an issue of registered securities. Interest payments will be sent to the persons who are listed as the registered owners of the security on the record date.

Recurring costs: Operating and maintenance costs that vary with both the size and duration of the project, including salaries and wages, employee benefits, maintenance and repair of equipment, miscellaneous materials and supplies, transfer payments, insurance, and direct overhead costs.

Redemption: Transaction in which the issuer returns the principal amount represented by an outstanding security (plus, in certain cases, an additional amount). Redemption can be made under several different circumstances: at maturity of the security, as a result of the issuer's call of the securities, or as a result of the security holder's election to exercise a put or tender option privilege.

Redemption provisions or call features: Terms of the bond contract requiring the issuer to redeem or "call" all or a portion of an outstanding issue of bonds prior to their stated dates of maturity at a specified price, usually at or above par.

Referendum: Public approval (vote) required in most states for the authorization of general obligation bonds. Depending on the prevailing law, a majority vote may be sufficient or a two-thirds vote may be necessary.

Refunded bonds: Bonds that have been redeemed by a new issue of bonds.

Refunding: Procedure whereby an issuer refinances an outstanding bond issue by issuing new bonds. Two major reasons for refunding are to reduce the issuer's interest costs or to remove a burdensome or restrictive covenant imposed by the terms of the bonds being refinanced.

Registered bonds: Bonds the owners of which are designated on records maintained for this purpose by a registrar. The ownership of these bonds cannot be transferred without the registrar recording the transfer on these records. The principal and interest on "fully registered" bonds is paid directly by check (or other funds transfer) to the registered owner.

Registrar: Person or entity responsible for maintaining records on behalf of the issuer for the purpose of noting the owners of registered bonds.

Reinvestment risk: Risk that a purchaser of a fixed income security incurs that interest rates will be lower when the purchaser seeks to reinvest income received from the security.

Renewal and replacement fund: Fund established by the bond contract of a revenue bond issue into which moneys are deposited to cover anticipated expenses for major repairs of the project or its equipment or for replacement of equipment.

Reoffering scale: Prices and/or yields, listed by maturity, at which securities are offered to the public by the underwriters.

Repurchase agreement: Agreement consisting of two simultaneous transactions whereby one party purchases securities from a second party and the second party agrees to repurchase the securities on a certain future date at a price that produces an agreed-upon rate of return.

Research and development costs: "Front-end" costs that might or might not figure into the actual expenses of a given capital project. If incurred explicitly in support of a given strategic facility, such cost should be included as a project expense.

Reserve fund: Basic fund into which all receipts and income derived from the operation of a self-supporting project are deposited. The trustee or other handler of funds then distributes moneys in the reserve fund on a monthly basis. Sometimes referred to as a capital reserve.

Reserve maintenance fund: Fund established by the bond contract of a revenue bond issue into which moneys set aside for extraordinary maintenance or repair expenses are deposited. The fund is intended to protect the bondholders by ensuring against interruptions of project's operation due to unavailability of moneys to pay for repairs of unexpected damage or breakdown.

Resources: Things utilized in a project, often reduced to a common standard of cost, but including personnel, equipment, materials, and time.

Revenue anticipation notes (RANs): Notes issued in expectation of receiving some revenues in the relatively near future, which will be used to pay off the notes.

Revenue bonds: Bonds that are payable from a specific source of revenue and to which the full faith and credit of an issuer with taxing power is not pledged. Bondholders cannot compel taxation or legislative appropriation of funds not pledged for payment of debt service. Generally, no voter approval is required prior to issuance of such obligations.

Revenue fund: Fund established by the bond contract of a revenue bond issue into which all gross revenues from the financed project are initially placed and from which the moneys for all other funds are drawn.

Scaling of debt: Reduction of interest and principal payment commitments when total debt obligations are clearly beyond the jurisdiction's capacity to pay.

Scheduling: Determination of the calendar dates or times when resources will be utilized in accordance with the total resource capacity assigned to the capital improvements project.

Secondary market: Market for securities previously offered and sold.

Securities and Exchange Commission (SEC): Federal agency responsible for supervising and regulating the securities industry. Generally, municipal securities are exempt from the SEC's registration and reporting requirements. Brokers and dealers in municipal securities, however, are subject to SEC regulation and oversight. The SEC also has responsibility for the approval of MSRB rules and, pursuant to SEC Rule 10b-5, has jurisdiction over fraud in the sale of municipal securities.

Security: Instrument evidencing debt of or equity in a common enterprise in which a person invests with the expectation of financial gain. Term includes notes, stocks, bonds, debentures, or other forms of negotiable and nonnegotiable instruments of indebtedness or ownership.

Security for the bonds: Specific revenue sources or assets of an issuer that are pledged for payment of debt service on a series of bonds, as well as the covenants or other legal provisions protecting the bondholders.

Self-supporting or self-liquidating debt: Debt that is to be repaid from proceeds exclusively generated by the enterprise activity for which the debt was issued.

Selling group: Group of municipal securities brokers and dealers that assists in the distribution of a new issue of securities. Selling group members are able to acquire new issue securities from the underwriting syndicate at syndicate terms (i.e., less the total takedown) but do not participate in residual syndicate profits nor share any liability for any unsold balance.

Sensitivity analysis: Assesses the relative magnitude of changes in costs and output indicators if key elements in the analysis have different values than those considered most likely.

Serial bonds: Bonds of an issue in which some bonds mature in successive years without interruption.

Serial issue: Issue of bonds having maturities scheduled over several years, thereby allowing the issuer to amortize principal over a period of years. Maturity schedules for serial bonds often provide for level debt service or level principal payments.

Settlement: Delivery of and payment for a security. In the case of a new bond issue, settlement usually occurs within thirty days after the securities are awarded, which allows for the completion of certain legal matters and, in some cases, printing of the securities. In the case of the purchase of a security in the secondary market, settlement occurs upon delivery of and payment for the security, usually five business days after purchase.

Sinking fund: Fund established by the bond contract into which periodic deposits are made by the issuer to assure the timely availability of sufficient moneys for the payment of debt service requirements. Amounts of revenues to be deposited into the sinking fund and payments therefrom are determined by the terms of the bond contract.

SLGS: An acronym (pronounced "slugs") for State and Local Government Series. SLGS are special federal securities sold by the U.S. Treasury to states, municipalities, and other local government bodies through individual subscription agreements. The interest rates and maturities of SLGS are arranged to comply with arbitrage restrictions imposed under Section 103 of the Internal Revenue Code. SLGS are most commonly used for deposit in escrow in connection with the issuance of refunding bonds.

Social costs: Subsidies that would have to be paid to compensate persons adversely affected by a project or program for their suffering or "disbenefits."

Special assessment: Charge imposed against a property that receives a special benefit by virtue of some public improvement, separate and apart from the general benefit accruing to the public at large.

Special assessment bonds: Obligations payable from revenues collected through special assessments.

Special districts: Single-purpose or limited-purpose units of government formed under state enabling legislation to meet certain local needs not satisfied by existing general purpose governments in a given geographical area. In some states, special districts (such as school districts) may be granted taxing powers.

Special obligation bonds: That portion of a full cash refunding bond issue which is secured by the interest earnings on federal securities purchased with the proceeds of the refunding bonds.

Special tax bonds: Bonds secured by one or more designated taxes other than ad valorem taxes. For example, bonds for a particular purpose might be supported by sales, cigarette, fuel, or business license taxes. The designated tax does not have to be directly related to the project purpose. Such bonds are not considered "self-supporting" debt.

Split-rate bids: Different coupon rates are bid by underwriters on various maturities or groups of bonds in order to obtain the most favorable overall net interest cost.

Split ratings: Assignment of materially different ratings on an issue of municipal securities by the nationally recognized rating services.

Spread: Differential between the price paid to the issuer for the new issue and the prices at which the securities are initially offered to the investing public. Usually expressed in points or fractions thereof.

Stepped coupon or step rate bonds: Serial issue of bonds on which the interest rate periodically changes (generally by increasing) over the life of the issue for all bonds that remain outstanding. The use of this financing technique may result in interest cost savings by structuring the issue with a high percentage of the principal maturing in the early years.

Strategic facilities: Relatively large-size, fixed-capital assets, having a relatively long life, funded by expenditures of a nonrecurring nature, and designed to provide new or expanded government capacity for the delivery of public services.

Strategic objectives: Define the expected change in conditions, welfare, or behavior as a consequence of the initiation of some project, program, or activity. Strategic objectives specify what the organization proposes to do and *why* it proposes to do so.

Strip call: Redemption of municipal bonds by calling a portion of each outstanding maturity or selected maturities, as provided in the bond contract. A strip call may be proportional by redeeming in each maturity the proportion that the maturity bears to the total amount of principal outstanding. Or it may be a level debt service reduction, whereby an amount is redeemed in each maturity so that annual debt service payments remain constant.

STRIPS (Separately Traded Interest and Principal Securities): Zero coupon Treasury securities created by splitting regular bonds into separate interest and principal payments and selling these separately.

Structuring an issue: The process of formulating an issue within the issuer's legal and financial constraints so that the security is marketable. The issuer must determine the maturities, the method of repayment, redemption provisions, application of proceeds, security provisions, and covenants.

Suitability: Appropriateness of a particular security as an investment for a particular investor, taking into account the investor's financial capabilities and sophistication, tax status, investment objectives, and other relevant considerations.

Sunk costs: Costs that benefit more than one project or program and should not be included in the direct cost estimate for a specific project or program.

Super sinker: Term maturity that will be the first to be called from a sinking fund into which all proceeds from prepayments of mortgages financed by the issue are deposited. Super sinkers are usually from single-family mortgage revenue issues with several term maturities. The super sinker maturity is considered attractive to investors because it offers long-term interest rates on what is effectively a short-term security.

Supplemental coupons: Additional interest coupons attached to a new issue security that reflect an issuer's commitment to pay additional interest, above the stated interest rate on the issue, for a short period of time following issuance of the securities. Supplemental coupons are detached and either sold on a discounted basis or held by the underwriters until redemption at their stated maturity.

Surplus fund: Fund established by the bond contract of a revenue bond issue into which moneys are deposited that remain after operations and maintenance, sinking fund, debt service reserve, and other mandated distributions have been satisfied. Moneys in this fund may be used for any lawful purposes of the enterprise.

Swap: Sale of a security and the simultaneous purchase of another security for purposes of enhancing the investor's holdings. May be used to achieve desired tax results, to gain income or principal, or to alter various features of a bond portfolio, including call protection, diversification or consolidation, and marketability of holdings.

Syndicate: Group of underwriters formed to purchase a new issue of municipal securities from the issuer and offer it for resale to the general public. Organized for the purposes of sharing the risks of underwriting the issue, obtaining sufficient capital to purchase an issue, and for broader distribution of the issue to the investing public. One of the underwriting firms will be designated as the syndicate manager or lead manager to administer the operations of the syndicate.

Takedown: Income derived from the sale of the securities, normally the largest component of the spread, similar to a commission. Bonds sold by a member of the syndicate are entitled to the full takedown (also called the "total takedown"). Bonds sold by a dealer who is not a member of the syndicate receive only that portion of the takedown known as the concession or dealer's allowance, with the balance (often termed the "additional takedown") retained by the syndicate.

Task: Set of activities that will lead to the achievement of some desired results in a capital improvements project. Tasks are the major divisions of the work on a project.

Tax anticipation notes (TANs): Notes issued in anticipation of future tax receipts, such as receipts of ad valorem taxes which are due and payable at a set time of the year.

Taxes: Compulsory charges levied by a governmental unit for the purpose of raising revenue. Tax revenues are used to pay for services or improvements provided for the general public benefit.

Tax rate: Amount of tax stated in terms of a unit of the tax base; for example, ten mills per dollar of assessed valuation of taxable property.

Tax rate limit: Maximum rate or millage of tax that a local government may levy. This limit may apply to taxes raised for a particular purpose or for all purposes, to a single government or class of governments, or to all governments operating in a particular area.

Tax roll: Official list showing the amount of taxes levied against each taxpayer or parcel of property, prepared and authenticated in proper form to warrant the collecting officers to proceed with administering the tax.

TELL financing: Approach to generating capital funds by selling public facilities to private investors and then leasing back the facility at subsidized rates, thus "leveraging" the private investment. The sale is financed through tax-exempt revenue bonds.

Tender offer: Proposal by the bondholder to sell his bond to the issuer or the issuer's representative for a stated price.

Tender option bonds: Bonds that offer the investor the option of submitting the bonds for redemption before maturity. Also know as put bonds.

Term bonds: Municipal bonds that mature on the same date and must be redeemed by a lump sum principal payment. The issuer usually agrees to make periodic payments into a sinking fund for mandatory redemption of term bonds before maturity or for payment at maturity.

Transcript of proceedings: Legal opinion that the proposed bond issue is in compliance with the requirements of local laws, state constitution, judicial opinions, and enabling legislation and, if appropriate, that the interest income is exempt from federal and state income taxes.

Transfer: Process of effecting a change in the ownership of a registered security by updating the list of registered holders of an issue and issuing a new securities certificate (or, in some cases, reissuing the old certificate) with the new registered owner's name imprinted on it.

Transfer agent: Party appointed by an issuer to maintain records of securities owners, to cancel and issue certificates, and to address issues arising from lost, destroyed, or stolen certificates.

Treasury securities: Debt obligations of the United States Government sold by the Treasury Department in the form of bills, notes, and bonds

True interest cost: Method of computing the borrowing cost to the issuer. True interest cost is defined as the rate, compounded semiannually, necessary to discount the amounts payable on the respective principal and interest payment dates to the purchase price received for the new issue securities. These computations produce a figure slightly different from the net interest cost method since the time value of money is considered. Also known as Canadian Interest Cost.

True market value: The price at which a willing buyer and a willing seller reach agreement on the sale of a property.

Trust indenture: Contract between the issuer of municipal securities and a trustee for the benefit of the bondholders. The trustee administers the funds or property specified in the indenture in a fiduciary capacity on behalf of the bondholders. The trust indenture is generally a part of the bond contract. It establishes the rights, duties, responsibilities, and remedies of the issuer and trustee and determines the exact nature of the security for the bonds. The trustee is generally empowered to enforce the bond contract on behalf of the bondholders.

Underwriting: Process of purchasing all or any part of a new issue of municipal securities from the issuer and offering such securities for sale to investors.

Underwriter: Dealer who bids for or buys new issues of bonds and sets the reoffering prices for these issues. The securities may be acquired either by negotiation with the issuer or by award on the basis of competitive bidding.

Unit investment trust: Investment fund created with a fixed portfolio of tax-exempt investments that are sold in fractional, undivided interests. As investments are paid off, investors are provided with a steady, periodic flow of income.

Unit investment trust (municipal): Fixed portfolio of bonds sold in fractional, undivided interests.

Unlimited tax bond: General obligation bond secured by a pledge of taxes that are not limited in rate or amount.

Upgrading: Raising of a rating by a rating service due to the improved credit quality of the issue or issuer. The term also refers to the replacing of a security in an investment portfolio with one of a higher quality.

Variable costs: Costs that might change significantly as the scope of the project is increased. Some uncertainty might exist regarding these costs, particularly if the project has a relatively long duration

Variable rate bonds: Bonds with interest rates that fluctuate according to the market and which the owner can redeem at predetermined, set intervals. Also know as variable rate demand obligations (VDROs).

Warrants: Securities, generally sold attached to other securities of the same issuer, which give the owner the right to purchase additional securities of the same issuer, described on the warrant, within a stated period of time at a stated price. The warrant generally is detachable and tradable separate from the security with which it was originally sold.

When, as, and if issued: Phrase used to describe the time period in the life of an issue of securities from the original date of the sale by the issuer to the delivery of the securities to, and payment by, the underwriter. Sales made during the "when, as, and if issued" period are subject to receipt of the securities from the issuer by the underwriter in good form.

Work breakdown schedule (WBS): Technique for developing a preliminary outline or "schematic" as to the way in which supporting objectives mesh together to ensure the attainment of the major objectives of a capital improvements project.

Working capital fund: Fund equivalent to about one-tenth of a year's gross revenues of a self-supporting facility, established to cover unforeseen contingencies.

Yield: Annual percentage rate of return earned on a security. Yield is a function of a security's purchase price and coupon interest rate.

Yield curve: Graph that plots market yields on securities of equivalent quality but different maturities at a given point in time. The vertical axis represents the yields, while the horizontal axis depicts time to maturity. The term structure of interest rates, as reflected by the yield curve, will vary according to market conditions, resulting in a variety of yield curve configurations.

Yield to call: Yield on a security calculated by assuming that interest payments will be paid until the call date, when the security will be redeemed at the call price.

Yield to maturity: Yield concept designed to give the investor the average annual yield on a security. Based on the assumption that the security is held to maturity and that all interest received over the life of the security can be reinvested at the yield to maturity.

Zero coupon bonds: Bonds where no periodic interest payments are made. Investors receive one payment at redemption (call or maturity). The maturity value an investor receives is equal to the principal invested plus interest earned compounded semiannually at the original interest rate to maturity.

Zero-loss underwriting: Criterion applied in insuring municipal bonds, which means that the issuer is so strong or is providing such ironclad protections that the insurer believes the bond issue will sustain no losses. Zero-loss underwriting contrasts with the actuarial approach used in the general insurance industry, which assumes a certain level of losses will be sustained.

Index

About the author. . .

ALAN WALTER STEISS is an Adjunct Professor, School of Public and International Affairs, Virginia Polytechnic Institute and State University, and a Consultant, Strategic Planning and Information Management Systems, Blacksburg, Virginia. Dr. Steiss has served as a faculty member and research administrator at the University of Michigan and at Virginia Polytechnic Institute and State University, and as a consultant to various state and local government agencies. He received the B.A. degree (1959) from Bucknell University, Lewisburg, Pennsylvania, and the Master of Urban and Regional Planning (1966) and Ph.D. (1969) degrees from the University of Wisconsin-Madison. He is the author of numerous books and professional papers, including *Strategic Management for Public and Nonprofit Organizations* and *Financial Planning and Management in Public Organizations*. His book, *Local Government Finance: Capital Facilities Planning and Debt Administration*, published by Lexington Books in 1975, was the first comprehensive work on the subject. This current book is a significant update of that earlier work.

www.ingramcontent.com/pod-product-compliance
Lightning Source LLC
LaVergne TN
LVHW090259210926
848480LV00001B/71